LOUD & CLEAR

The Expressions of a Man on Death Row

By Clinton Lee Young

This book is dedicated to my son.

This rollercoaster that has been my life,

it all took me to the place

where he was brought into this world.

Foreword

In April 2003, at just nineteen years old, Clinton Young was convicted of capital murder and sentenced to death in Midland County, Texas. For the next eighteen and a half years, Clinton spent at least twenty-three hours a day in a solitary confinement cell, awaiting execution. Deprived of human contact, he found a lifeline to the outside world by writing blogs that chronicled his life on the most notorious death row in the United States. These blogs, shared by a group of friends on a dedicated website, were read by people across the globe. They became more than just a way for Clinton to stay sane—they forged connections with supporters he would never have met otherwise. Those supporters later proved to be essential to secure Clinton's release.

Clinton's writings offer an unprecedented window into life behind bars: stories of lockdowns, conversations with fellow inmates, uses of force, witnessing hundreds of men taken to their executions, and even his own scheduled death. With a sharp intellect, unique sense of humor, provoking thoughts, and raw vulnerability, Clinton captured the day-to-day struggles, fears, and reflections of a man confined in an eight-by-twelve-foot cell. His blogs go far beyond the prison walls—they're a testament to the resilience of the human spirit, the will to live, and the strength it takes to hold on to hope when all seems lost.

This book is more than a diary of life on death row; it is a stark reminder of what truly matters in life. As we focus on money, status, and ambition, Clinton's story reminds us to cherish one of the most overlooked blessings: the freedom to live life with those we love. This book is a chronicle of a nineteen-year-old boy maturing into a thirty-eight-year-old man under the most harrowing circumstances imaginable. Yet prison does not define Clinton. He is much more than the walls that confined him for nearly two decades.

In September 2021, after eighteen years on death row, Clinton's conviction and sentence were overturned due to egregious prosecutorial misconduct. He was released on bond in January 2022, finally free to pursue the dreams he had written about during his years in solitary confinement. Despite receiving no help from the State, Clinton rebuilt his life with incredible strength and determination: working in the oil fields, acquiring a home, starting a family, adopting a dog, and becoming a vocal advocate for criminal justice and prison reform.

Realizing the blessing of regaining his freedom, Clinton made it his mission to fight for those he left behind. He gave a speech before the Texas House of Representatives, lectured law school students, appeared on radio and television shows like *The Prison Show* and *Execution Watch*, started his own podcast, and even helped wrongfully convicted inmates get legal counsel. Against all odds, Clinton proved to be a successful and contributing member of the same society that had once condemned him twenty years earlier.

But in October 2024, Clinton's story took another devastating turn. Unwilling to value Clinton's change and positive contributions to society, the State retried him for capital murder under Texas' infamous Law of Parties. Convicted once again, he was sentenced to life in prison. The last blog in this book is the first he wrote after his return to the Texas Department of Criminal Justice in October 2024.

Imagine this: spending nearly twenty years in solitary confinement, being released into a world you've dreamed of for decades, and then having it all ripped away just as you begin to rebuild your life. To taste freedom only to have it taken away is a kind of torture that few can imagine.

In the end, Clinton's story is not just about the injustice he endured but the resilience and unimaginable strength of the human mind—a reminder that even in the darkest corners of life, hope can survive, and strength can prevail.

Merel Pontier

Legal Director,
Clinton Young Foundation

Introduction

Reading over these blogs stirred up a range of emotions, as well as a couple of cringe-worthy moments. Entering prison at such a young age, I was forced to find myself and basically grow up in a cell. It is difficult to properly evolve in all ways while in prison. Mainly do to the nature of how prisons are managed. It is made even more difficult in solitary confinement, which is counterproductive to good mental health. Writing became an escape for me. A way to focus my energy. I don't think it would be shocking for people to learn that upon my entering death row at nineteen years old, I was a bit angry over my confinement. My emotions were not always channeled in the best way. At the time it felt best. In hindsight I wasted a great deal of time being angry.

One of the side effects of long-term segregation, it is the intensity of emotions. Rage is a key side-effect of the security housing unit syndrome. Which is a fancy title for solitary caused declines that a person goes through. I have seen many people break mentally during my eighteen and a half years on death row. When people ask me how I managed to stay sane, the only answer that I can give is I fought. I didn't have time to go crazy, I was too busy fighting to live. These blogs detail that journey. Sadly, there are blogs missing from a couple of years, as well as a few here and there. This is due to someone who was supposed to help me. She, in a fit of jealousy, had deleted many of them. This is also why I had complications with websites.

I tell you what, sitting in a cell fighting for life, while having to depend on other people, then have them undo work that was done. Yeah, it is a special kind of hell to go through.

While a few caused some setbacks, many more have helped me advance over the years. There has truly been some wonderful people from all over the world who have crossed my path. A reporter asked me upon my release, if after all that has happened, have I lost faith in humanity? My response was 'no.' If anything, my faith in humanity has become greater. As so many people showed me love and support. There are far more good people in this world than bad. The bad tend to get all the attention. That and they are often allowed to cause more harm, because good people fail to speak up.

I hope that after reading this book, you will subscribe to my Patreon account. The QR code to help quickly locate it, is in the back of this book.

There are radio stations and websites listed throughout this book. Many are outdated. Clintonyoungfoundation.com is still active. It has grown to much more than just my case. A small group of people dedicated to the big fight. If you can support it, please do. As well as share links to it. Education is the key to ending injustice. Saveaninnocentlife.com was my personal website. We are deciding how to best go forward with it. It contained my writings of various sorts. Something I had in place before the CYF non-profit was established. These are the only two websites that are active and legit. The Clinton Young Foundation can be found on all social media platforms. Please follow them on Facebook, Instagram, TikTok, etc.

These blogs, as they cover years of life, they also capture moments in history. My mother and I have a far greater relationship now as both of our emotional resolve has strengthened. Allowing us to communicate more effectively. The wife I write about is now the ex-wife. Both of us were too young and trying to bring some form of happiness and stability to a chaotic and soul-crushing situation. Trying to have something "normal" for me was an ability to mentally escape the confines of death row. That relationship ended almost as fast as it started. Due to my experience and seeing what others went through, I gave up on prison relationships. More so while on death row, just too much pain. I would eventually get married again to a wonderful woman. This time after knowing each other for a long time while I was free. From this union came my greatest gift.

I was blessed to have a son. A beautiful boy with a personality that lights up every room. I did not know it was possible to love so deeply, until he came into this world. It is bittersweet as now I am back fighting a wrongful conviction. I have him, but cannot be there for him. Something that causes a great deal of pain for me.

I had this book put together and will write another one about my life. The proceeds from my personal books will go towards my son. To save and invest for his future. That he not know struggle as I have and his relatives before me. It is one of the few ways I can be a dad and just overall be a man, that helps to take care of my son.

Thank you for helping me be a better dad,

Clinton

Table of Contents

Foreword ii

Introduction iv

Uncensored, May 22, 2005 1

Uncensored, May 26, 2005 6

Uncensored, May 28 to June 2, 2005 14

Uncensored, June 10 to June 12, 2005 17

Uncensored, June 19, 2005 23

Uncensored, June 27, 2005 29

Uncensored, July 15 to July 16, 2005 33

Uncensored, August 02, 2005 38

Uncensored, August 18, 2005 44

Uncensored, August 20 to August 26, 2005 47

Uncensored, August 27, 2005 52

Uncensored, December 02, 2005 57

Loud & Clear, May 18, 2006 62

Loud & Clear, June 10 2006 65

Loud & Clear, June 28 2006 68

Loud & Clear, July 13, 2006 71

Loud & Clear, August 14, 2006 73

Loud & Clear, October 2, 2006 77

Loud & Clear, October 8, 2006 82

Loud & Clear, October 19, 2006 87

Loud & Clear, November 13, 2006 91

Loud & Clear, November 20, 2006 95

Loud & Clear, January 1, 2007 101

Loud & Clear, November 11, 2008 105

Loud & Clear, January 26, 2009 108

Loud & Clear, February 11, 2009 111

Loud & Clear, March 5, 2009 115

Loud & Clear, March 9, 2009 116

Loud & Clear, April 1, 2009 119

Loud & Clear, May 27, 2009 122

Loud & Clear, July 29, 2009 129

Loud & Clear, August 26, 2009 132

Loud & Clear, September 8, 2009 133

Loud & Clear, September 14, 2009 138

Loud & Clear, September 23, 2009 143

Loud & Clear, November 16, 2009 145

Loud & Clear November 29, 2009 147

Loud & Clear, 12 August, 2010 149

Loud & Clear, August 24, 2010 150

Loud & Clear, September 9, 2010 153

Loud & Clear, September 21, 2010 158

Loud & Clear, September 29, 2010 160

Loud & Clear, September 30, 2010 162

Loud & Clear, October 18, 2010 164

Loud & Clear, November 7, 2010 168

Loud & Clear, March 11, 2011 170

Loud & Clear, July 20, 2013 175

Loud & Clear, January 17, 2014 179

Loud & Clear, January 26, 2014 184

Loud & Clear: February 20, 2014 186

Loud & Clear – Insane Opinion 192

Loud & Clear, Never ending confusion 198

Loud & Clear, May 2, 2014 201
Loud & Clear, May 29, 2014 205
Loud & Clear: Major Disruption 208
Loud & Clear: Why the Death Penalty 209
Loud & Clear: A Dutch Tragedy 215
Loud & Clear: Bird Shit and Toilet Water 217
Loud & Clear: November 18, 2014 221
Loud & Clear: January 26, 2015 222
Loud & Clear: A new year 225
Loud & Clear, March 1, 2015 227
Loud & Clear, March 5, 2015 232
Loud & Clear, March 10, 2015 240
Loud & Clear: March 30, 2015 245
Loud & Clear, April 7, 2015 249
Loud & Clear, April 24, 2015 254
Loud & Clear, June 7, 2015 259
Loud & Clear, June 9, 2015 264
Loud & Clear, August 2, 2015 268
Loud & Clear, August 16, 2015 271
Loud & Clear, August 18, 2015 274
Loud & Clear, March 16, 2016 279
Loud & Clear, March 23, 2016 281
Loud & Clear, May 16, 2016 283
Loud & Clear, June 6, 2016 287
Loud & Clear, August 23, 2016 289
Loud & Clear, September 26, 2016 290
Loud & Clear, January 2017 292
Loud & Clear, March 1, 2017 295

Loud & Clear, March 1, 2017 298
Loud & Clear, March 23rd, 2017 300
Loud & Clear, April 20, 2017 302
Loud & Clear Topic: follow up. 306
Loud & Clear, May 1, 2017 309
Loud & Clear, May 2, 2017 311
Loud & Clear, May 4, 2017 313
Loud & Clear: May 16, 2017 316
Loud & Clear, May 18, 2017 321
Loud & Clear, May 22, 2017 322
Loud & Clear, June 17, 2017 325
Loud & Clear, July 15, 2017 330
Loud & Clear, August 20, 2017 333
Loud & Clear, August 15, 2017 337
Loud & Clear, September 14, 2017 340
Loud & Clear, September 17, 2017 343
Loud & Clear, October 8, 2017 346
Loud & Clear, October 14, 2017 350
Loud & Clear, October 21, 2017 354
Loud & Clear, November 5, 2017 359
Loud & Clear, November 12, 2017 363
Loud & Clear, November 19, 2017 366
Loud & Clear, November 28, 2017 369
Loud & Clear, December 2017 371
Loud & Clear, February 1, 2018 374
Loud & Clear, February 4, 2018 379
Loud & Clear, February 10, 2018 381
Loud & Clear, February 23, 2018 386

Loud & Clear, March 2018 389

Loud & Clear, March 4, 2018 391

Loud & Clear, May 20, 2018 393

Loud & Clear, June 28, 2018 396

Loud & Clear: September 27, 2018 399

Loud & Clear: October 8, 2018 401

Loud & Clear: January 8, 2019 405

Loud & Clear, February 24, 2019 407

Loud & Clear, July 7, 2019 410

Loud & Clear, August 11, 2019 412

Loud & Clear, Aug 18, 2019 413

Loud & Clear, August 20, 2019 414

Loud & Clear, August 27, 2019 417

Loud & Clear, September 19, 2019 419

Loud & Clear, September 29, 2019 421

Loud & Clear, November 10, 2019 424

Loud & Clear, December 1, 2019 427

Loud & Clear, December 30, 2019 430

Loud & Clear, February 2, 2020 431

Loud & Clear, March 16, 2020 434

Loud & Clear, April 12, 2020 437

Loud & Clear, April 19, 2020 440

Loud & Clear, May 6, 2020 443

Loud & Clear, May 18, 2020 444

Loud & Clear, May 28, 2020 446

Loud & Clear, June 1, 2020 447

Loud & Clear, June 7, 2020 450

Loud & Clear, June 28, 2020 454

Loud & Clear, September 7, 2020 459

Loud & Clear, September 10, 2020 461

Loud & Clear, September 16, 2020 465

Loud & Clear, September 24, 2020 466

Loud & Clear, September 12 – 475

October 4, 2020 475

Loud & Clear, October 11, 2020 481

Loud & Clear, November 5, 2020 483

Loud & Clear, January 12, 2021 484

Loud & Clear, January 27, 2021 485

Loud & clear, February 11, 2021 489

Loud & Clear, February 8, 2021 492

Loud & Clear, March 7, 2021 497

Loud & Clear, May 2, 2021 500

Loud & Clear, May 3, 2021 502

Loud & Clear, May 31, 2021 504

Loud & Clear, June 27, 2021 507

Loud & Clear, June 30, 2021 509

Loud & Clear, August 16, 2021 511

Loud & Clear, September 19, 2021 513

Loud & Clear, September 27, 2021 516

Loud & Clear, November 25, 2021 517

Loud & Clear, November 18, 2024 518

Afterword 520

Uncensored, May 22, 2005

Greetings to all!

Today is the 22nd of May. It is currently 1:06 a.m. I have been meaning to sit down and write this all weekend. Richard was executed on the 19th of May. I saw him at visitation a couple of days before his date. I spoke to him a little bit. You know, as I sit here writing this, I can't think of anything to write. I mean, it really is as if he is still here. The prison keeps us so isolated and doesn't inform us if someone has a date or if they die or not. We have to find out from the free world. There have been times I have been talking to people, and they ask me where a certain person is housed. I tell them, "Man, they killed that dude like three months ago." The reply was, "No shit? Damn, I didn't even know."

It is done very clean and quiet. Plus, Texas kills so many that it isn't that big of a deal to the public really, as far as the media goes. The "familiarity breeds comfort." I have noticed that when they go to kill a guy in New England, it makes the front page of USA Today. Though if it isn't a high-profile case in Texas, it doesn't even make the state-by-state section! I've seen Richard's mother walking around at visitation. I wondered what was going through her mind. I also wondered how my mother would handle my execution. My heart goes out to Richard's family.

I did not know him that well. When I first moved next to him on F-Pod Level 3, I did not talk to him for the first couple of hours, as I was burning up from the pepper spray. He asked me if I wanted to write an article for Uncensored about the Use of Force. That is what kicked off our conversation. We went to outside recreation together. We were in separate cages as Death Row inmates can't have contact with each other through the bars. We talked about hometowns, families, cars, women, our cases, the difference from when he was growing up compared to when I was growing up, and how to resist the oppression tactics of the Texas Department of Criminal Justice. Through conversation, we realized we had a lot in common.

Then two weeks later, he received his date to die. We had talked a lot in those two weeks. I told the guy in the cell next to me, "That is it. I am not talking to no one else. Every time I start to get cool with someone, they end up with a date." Truthfully, it happens so much that it has become a part of life down here. Speak of the devil. The guy in the cell next to me just asked me if they killed Wolfe. I told him, "Yeah, on the 18th they did." His reply was, "Damn, I didn't even know he had a date." He had seen an article about it in the paper.

It seems to only be getting worse. An article was put out on March 17, 2005, about a wider Death Penalty Lawyer Pool. It stated that former prosecutors with no experience as defense lawyers could qualify to represent death penalty cases! That is like having the person that shot you give you CPR! They became prosecutors because they want to punish. Friedrich Nietzsche stated, "Distrust all in whom the impulse to punish is powerful!" The House Criminal Jurisprudence Committee Chairman Terry Keel, R-Austin, actually stated that House Bill 265, which would allow prosecutors to defend capital cases, would actually make Texas standards "the best in the nation in terms of qualifications." Now the last four words are the ones to pay attention to: "in terms of qualifications!" Yeah, they will be qualified, but that is about it! Qualified to help Texas kill us faster!

There is a guy here—I won't mention his name as I do not have his permission to do so—but the prosecutor in his case was busted for using methamphetamines while in public office! He was shooting up between court breaks!!! "I inject, Your Honor! I mean, object." :)

In other news, some attention has been shined on a possible wrongful execution. Cameron Willingham, who was executed February 17, 2004, for his alleged role in a fire that resulted in the death of his three kids. It seems that due to new forensic evidence, the fire was accidental. The same evidence helped free Ernest Willis after 17 years on death row. Though Mr. Willis got off after Cameron got executed. I guess the state figured that they got to get one before they give one.

Well, back to Richard. To all those who tried to help him: don't give up. He would want you all to keep fighting. There is strength in numbers. I will be placing articles now, as much as possible. My case is still in the State Courts. Nothing has been ruled on yet. Though I still have a lot to write about, as I will be posting information about my case, death row, etc. Pretty much the same as Richard did. Though I will also drift to other issues as well.

The next article I write will be about the family of the victims in the case that resulted in me coming to death row, as well as the emotional impact it had on myself from seeing them and knowing that they think that I was the one responsible for their loved one's death. I was not the shooter in this case and can actually prove this fact. I will also be posting polygraph test results which showed the co-defendant lied as well as other statements from people who overheard the co-defendant brag about getting away with murder. I am going to go ahead and bring this to an end. Use the pain to fuel the fire that burns within.

I leave as I came. Stand Tall, Fade All, Never Fall.

Clinton Young

#999447

Polunsky Unit

Death Row

3872 F.M. 350 S.

Livingston, TX 77351

By Robert Shields, #999166

"Richard asked me to track the events of May 19th, so here they are:

May 19th – 8th Murder Day of 2005

8:05 a.m. – Rich Cartwright leaves to go visit his loved ones for the very last time, looking remarkably calm.

8:20 a.m. – Just heard on the news that Bryan Wolfe was indeed murdered by the State of Texas last night.

11:57 a.m. – It seems like insanity to be doing this, but I climb up into my window to do what I can to get a last glimpse of a man I have considered a friend since we were on the work program way back in '98.

12:01 p.m. – Death chariot arrives!

I am a bit surprised to see no wardens and only five grim reapers in grey gather around. No sign of the handshaking contest either! What's really going on here?

12:03 p.m. – Property Officer Hill brings out Rich's property and clothes. I guess I missed the funeral procession of Rich leading the grey suits' army from the visitation building. He must already be in 12 Building, getting shackled up for a safe trip to Huntsville.

12:05 p.m. – Ms. Hill comes out shaking her head with Chi-town's cross dangling in her hand. He must have been wearing it at visitation, which I am sure they are not happy about, considering he was strip-searched before he went out there.

12:08 p.m. – Richard comes out standing tall with his (bald) head held high, but not looking so happy. As he steps up into the van, he looks over at us in our little windows and wags his tongue at us. Basically, he is telling us no matter what, he's not gonna let them break him, and neither should we.

12:10 p.m. – The grey-suited grim reapers climb into their death wagon and drive off without putting on their seatbelts. BAD! Remember to click it or ticket! I know Richard wanted to wear his seatbelt after seeing Mr. Bible hobble around in here from the injuries he sustained while not seatbelted in when they crashed a TDCJ van he was being transported in.

The future is uncertain, but 6 p.m. will come way too soon for all of us. I sure hope Richard can receive that miracle. We'll just have to wait and see.

Well, I just heard the news and don't know what to say. Even with my pessimistic attitude, I expected it, but just the same, hearing it hit me hard. Rest in peace, Richard Michael. You will be missed.

My sincere condolences go out to all of you who have been there for Rich—his family, friends, and loved ones. I know that all of your love, prayers, and support helped him make it through. He talked more about all of you and God than he did about his situation. Stay strong and keep your heads up so he can see the smiles on your faces. Whenever he is not busy doing the chicken dance, I'm sure he'll look down on y'all.

I do not think most of you realize what you have been reading these past few months. I highly doubt you will ever see something like this anywhere. Not many men in prison would have the balls to open themselves up so completely, baring their soul, giving everyone a chance to judge him and everything he loves. On top of all that, he has opened himself up so that you can see his deepest thoughts.

A lot of dudes have called him crazy or things like that because the whole prison lifestyle has hardened them to the point that they cannot even understand where he is coming from. I cannot imagine what it takes to show the world the mental and emotional turmoil that he is going through. I have seen how hard these last few days have been for him. I know how much all of your support has meant to him, helping him get through this trying time. It's hard enough to deal with this situation without putting yourself out there like that, opening yourself up to all kinds of criticism from inside and outside of these walls.

I truly don't know how he does it. Everyone rides this roller coaster we call life, but I am really struggling with it right now. Sitting here on this bunk, trying to sort through the thoughts and emotions that run confusingly through my mind.

This is not the first time that I have sat helpless in this cell while a friend, someone who I have talked with, ate with, argued with, and laughed with, was led off to be murdered by the State of Texas. You would think it gets easier, but it does not.

Rest in Peace, Rich.

Here is a poem of mine that Richard wanted me to share with you:

This is no kind of life

Every breath I take

Is a step towards an

Untimely death

The screams that well

Up inside of me are

Just enough to fuck

Me up again and again

I have got to get out

There is so much I want

To accomplish before

I reach my end

Waiting for that

Chemical Cocktail

So far away but

I am coming back again

I feel the needle

Pierce my arm

Pain made to order

I've got to accept fate

Execution halts my breath

Helter-skelter spiral death

Bloodbath in paradise

Forever sleeping…

Uncensored, May 26, 2005

Greetings to all!

I got a letter from Suzanne. I could feel her pain through her words. There is so much I wish I could write or say about Richard. I just do not know what to say. I feel like I need to write something, but I can't find the words.

I read an article about his execution. Reading about it brought his murder to reality. I mean, I knew he was executed, but it didn't fully sink in. We are so isolated that when someone is executed, it is as if it never happened—until it is read about in the newspaper. I am a Level 2, so I couldn't listen to the radio news about his execution. I had to find out at first from the officers.

One thing about Richard's writing is his ability to be humble. Not many can do that. I am used to locking everything in—well, to a degree. Richard's family, Suzanne, and many others who got to know Richard, "the man behind the mask" (the mask being the stereotypes of Death Row), are going through a lot of pain right now.

It was once said that a man's dying is more the survivors' affair than his own. His pain is over now. We must cope with ours.

In the newspaper article about Richard's death, they quoted the victim's family saying, "At least we know he's not going to hurt anyone else." The victim's family in the offense that got me sent to Death Row said the same thing. My question is: what about the co-defendants who did not come to Death Row because they helped the prosecutors? The article stated that one of the guys who was supposedly with Richard had cut the victim's throat. This co-defendant isn't on Death Row! He got fifty years! So he is walking around in general population and could be released in about fifteen years. Who is to say that he won't hurt anyone else?

A co-defendant in the case against me admitted to shooting the victim. He was facing Capital Murder, though as a reward for his testimony against me, he only got 15 years! He can go home in three more years. He didn't even get the 15 years for murder. So he actually got away with murder. He got away the first time—why not do it again!

The only reason the prosecutors went after me is because of my past. Out of all of the people involved, I had the worst past. Nothing truly bad. Some things look bad because of the way they are labeled. I actually had ten times the amount of people testify that I was a good person than the prosecutors had to say I was a bad person. This is why they had to get people to lie! Out of all my life, they could only find three people to say I was dangerous.

One was a teacher who used to call me stupid in front of the whole class because I had trouble spelling—in first grade! Second was a caseworker from T.Y.C. (Texas Youth Commission) who stated I assaulted him when he went to break up a fight. Now he would be a good prosecution witness, but I beat the charge! Other inmates and officers who saw the entire fight stated that I did not hit him, so the supervisor of the T.Y.C. facility dismissed the charge.

Number three was another T.Y.C. worker who stated I hit her while she was breaking up a fight. She stated this at trial. However, in her report of the incident when it occurred, she made no mention of being assaulted. My lawyers couldn't locate the report, so she was able to lie. However, I am now in possession of this report and can show she is a liar. She really didn't like me, as I did not adhere to authority and rules very well while at T.Y.C.

Then there were the psych doctors. A neurologist testified for the prosecution that A.D.H.D. (which I have had all my life) was not a legitimate condition. Some doctors agree, though you wanna know the #1 problem with this doctor saying he didn't believe in it? His phone number to his office is 1-800-###-2343, which translates to 1-800-$$$-ADHD! He treated and prescribed medicine for A.D.H.D., which he stated on the stand in my trial was not a legitimate condition.

So I can say that every witness brought forth by the prosecution to testify is a liar and/or has reasons to lie.

My ex testified that I used to hit her. When she stated that on the stand, I told my lawyer, "Man, I swear I never hit that girl." She has since written a statement for the court that the prosecutors had her lie! She is one of the four people who wrote statements saying that she was instructed to lie and not to talk to my defense lawyers.

One of the main things I tried to show in my trial, other than that I was innocent of murder, was to show the victim's family that I was not the one who killed their loved one. The prosecutors admitted into evidence a picture of the victim, Samuel Petry, and his granddaughter. I only really cried twice during my trial: once when my baby sister testified for me, and once when they showed that picture. I told my lawyer, "I didn't kill that man." His reply was, "I know, but we have to make those 12 people realize that." I guess we didn't succeed!

Now people might wonder, "Well, why did they convict you?" Just as everyone thinks that everyone on Death Row in Texas has killed someone. This is not true. Texas has a law called the "Law of Parties," meaning a person can be found guilty if they are a party to the offense. It is a "Ride with an outlaw, die with an outlaw" law. However, to give the death penalty, the prosecutor has to prove that the defendant anticipated that a human life would be taken and/or intended for a human life to be taken.

The co-defendants in the case that got me placed on Death Row testified that I was the shooter. However, the evidence suggests otherwise. Plus, the co-defendant in both murders bragged about getting away with murder and failed a polygraph test. There is not one fingerprint from me in the whole case. My entire trial was a puppet show.

Samuel Petry's wife and two sons sat through the whole trial. At first, I was embarrassed that they actually thought I was the shooter. Then I got angry. My thinking was, "How the hell can they say I did it and think I did it when they weren't even there?" I knew that the prosecutor pumped their heads up with propaganda. I had hoped that by the end of the trial, they would realize that the prosecutors were full of it. Though right at the very end, when Mrs. Petry testified about how she was impacted as a victim, she stated that she wanted me to get the death penalty so that I could not hurt anyone ever again.

Yet, Mark Ray, who admitted to shooting the victim, only got 15 years, and David Page, who bragged about getting away with murder, only got 30 years. Not one of them received time for murder!

I did not testify in my trial. I wanted to, but my lawyer begged me not to. A paralegal whom I grew close to, who worked on my case, also begged me not to. They were worried that the prosecutors would twist my words and/or make me mad, casting me in a negative light for the jury. I now regret not speaking for myself. If I get a new trial, I will testify on my own behalf.

When I received the death sentence, the victim's wife yelled out, "Thank God," and my mother yelled out, "No!" and collapsed. The first thought that ran through my mind was, "Why is she thanking God for these people telling me that they are going to kill me?" Truthfully, though, people always use religion for their own personal agenda. It was once stated, "Man will wrangle for religion, write for it, fight for it, die for it; anything but live for it."

I wish I could talk to Mrs. Petry for a few hours. Though, I don't think that it would help anything. She has a lot of anger and unwanted feelings that need to be focused on someone, and I am the easiest target. If it helps her to cope, then it is okay.

I want to go back within the walls of this death camp for a second. From the cell that I am in, I can see the outside recreation yard and half of the control picket. The pods are shaped in octagons with a wall in the middle. A guy was on the rec yard who has had a heart attack and heart surgery before.

I was talking to the guy in the dayroom (my cell is on 2 Row). I looked at the outside rec yard (it can be seen through big glass windows, so the control picket can see the whole yard). I noticed that the guy was grabbing his chest and bending over. I told the guy in the dayroom, "Hey, look out, dude. Get the picket officer's attention. Ole cat on the rec yard looks like he is having a heart attack again." So after about two minutes of yelling, she finally looked outside and then told an officer to go check on him. By then, he was lying on the ground!

A sergeant came and had the officers call medical. Fifteen minutes from when I first saw him grasping his chest, medical finally showed up! They were walking and taking their sweet time. Now the officers did keep an eye on the guy and talked to him, so if he would have died, the only ones to be blamed would be medical. They work for U.T.M.B. (University of Texas Medical Branch out of Galveston, TX). The TDCJ officers did follow procedure, so I can't blame them. It did amaze me how slow the medical staff was walking!

I do not know the guy's condition. It has been about five and a half hours since he left. He hasn't come back yet, though I hear he is alive and will be okay. No thanks to medical!

On another note, the quality of food has increased now that a new administration has been put in place over the Polunsky Unit Death Camp! There for a while, the food actually stunk! I mean, to the point that it would make me gag if I tried to eat it! We still are not getting steak, but prison food has gotten a lot better.

Captain Wickersham is now gone. For the most part, things have calmed down now that he is gone, as well as Warden Jones, who was a complete idiot. I was on F-Pod Level 3 and was talking to him one day. Halfway through the conversation, I told him, "You really are more stupid than you look, huh?" His reply was, "What is that supposed to mean?"

I told him, "You got to be stupid if you think that I will fall for a case about that BS you are talking." (He was tossing around mild threats.) He then walked away.

I look at it like this: I am here to die. I fully expect to die. This environment is so oppressive that death looks a lot better than living in this hellhole. There is nothing these people can do to me, short of killing me, that will really affect me.

I have spent most of my time here on Level 2 and 3. This is something that a person would have to experience to even halfway understand. I don't think anyone can fully understand this place, why they do what they do, and why the courts are so bloodthirsty.

Anyway, I am glad that someone finally made the intelligent choice of removing Captain Wickersham and Warden Jones. Well, I have covered enough ground for today. I am going to go ahead and wrap this up.

I leave as I came.

Clinton Young

#999447

Polunsky Unit

3872 F.M. 350 S.

Livingston, TX 77351

I just received Richard's final Uncensored articles as well as a letter from Suzanne that talked about hateful emails made by Grey Suits who work here at TDCJ. It seems that the swine want to put their two cents in! Not all Grey Suits are swine! An officer is someone who is professional, comes to work, does his time, and goes home to his family. He is just working to support his family. I respect that! A swine is the Grey Suits who feel they are a spoke in the murder machine wheel. They take this shit personally and send hateful emails and other cowardly B/S! They want to talk shit about Richard and the way he was in here, as well as his associates, which include myself.

Richard was a MAN! He stood for what he believed in. He refused to submit. I have noticed a certain "change" in the behavior of certain Grey Suits since I started posting articles (the TDCJ officers wear grey). The thing about me, though, is I like a challenge and I like controversy! I am here to die! I do not want a life sentence. So that means that nothing I do here will have any impact on me in any shape, form, or fashion! I am only fighting my conviction! Though due to the Law of Parties, I do not hold much hope in that. I do have a chance, as I can prove I didn't shoot anyone, and I can prove I did not get a fair trial! But I will continue to live as if I am going to die.

Suzanne is just doing what she believes in! So why send her hateful emails? Come up to my door and tell me what you think! Tell those whom I associate with what you think. We always tell y'all, correct? "Of mice and men!" People have a fight-or-flight response when faced with certain situations. I can't run too fast!

I will say this one time to the swine playing little games with those trying to help me and other DR convicts: If you want to play, we can play. Though next time, it will not just be one or two people going off! Bonds have been tied, and words given. So, if you wish to retaliate against me for writing these articles or harass Suzanne for posting them, then go ahead and get yours. I will get mine.

I've got to live in this piece of shit fucking hellhole for some shit I didn't do and didn't even know was going to happen! I had to listen to my mother's screams and see her being restrained by my stepfather and lawyer's secretary when I got the death penalty. I had to walk by her when I was being escorted out of the courtroom and see her reaching out for me, crying and screaming, "No, not my baby," and seeing the look of defeat on the strongest person I know's face! I have to see the tears on her face when she goes to leave after a visit. That is the pain that fuels my rage. I just have to find a direction to point it in. Ya dig?

So to the swine who want to play games: When you talk to your wife and/or children and they ask you, "Daddy, what did you do today?" or "Honey, how was work?" I want you to be honest and say, "Well, I went to work and played little childish games with a bunch of guys who are waiting to die in a state that has said they don't care about innocence and keeps killing more and more, thus taking away all of these guys' hope, all because I get to wear a uniform and get paid roughly $30,000 a year if I am lucky!"

That doesn't make much sense, does it? No, it doesn't. I am focusing my rage through my writings. Let it be done in peace. You live your life, let me live what is left of mine. I am tired of seeing people I have grown close to get slaughtered by the state!

The only reason I keep fighting is for my wife, friends, baby sister, and my mother. That is it. My whole life has been nothing but pain, damn near! I just seemed to have gotten a raw deal! If I did not have them, I would not give a shit one way or another. Death is nothing but the next great adventure!

I treat people with respect, and I ask the same in return. I am mostly just really angry at this point, but I have made my mind up about a few things. Reading what Richard's family wrote kind of pushed me over the edge, and right after reading that, I read about stupid swine who work here. It helped me make my mind up about a few things! Richard asked me to be honest, so I am. My anger comes from the heart. Every day, I wake up and ask myself, "Why am I even trying? Why be passive?"

Then people treat me like a caged animal—why not act like one? I am here to die. These people are trying to murder me! What would you do if someone was trying to kill you? Would you resist or submit? I used to think, "Well, the guards aren't the ones actually doing it." But if they feel they are and act as if they are, then are they not just as guilty as the rest who are trying to kill me? Yes, they are!

Plus, to top it off, I have a Quarter Million Dollar Court-Ordered hold on my account! So, I can't even go to commissary! So I really do not have any reason to be good and/or follow these stupid oppressive rules! I have already told my wife, "I will chill for as long as they allow me to." I love the girl to death! She told me she would stay by me through thick and thin.

I am getting too aggravated. I gotta open some books and step away from this hell I call home. I am gone.

Clinton Young

Polunsky Unit Death Camp

From Suzanne:

June 1, 2005, was the last day I received said emails. Therefore, as promised, I took my comment off Rich's last Uncensored. Thanks.

This is from Margherita to Irene, in which we have permission to share:

Verona, Italy – 1st June 2005

Dearest Irene,

Two weeks have passed since those terrible days, and only one week since I'm back home in Italy. Just today I started my job. But my life has changed forever.

The day before my flight, I found on L. of H. mailing list the last "Uncensored" from Richard Cartwright. I printed it, and I want you to know that it was my reading during the whole flight! And while I was reading, my pains came up to the surface.

In fact, I'd experienced so many pains and sorrows inside my heart and soul but wasn't completely aware of them due to that cold and cruel death's ritual. Now I am okay, as I am able to feel and to welcome all this sorrow. I want to sip it till the last drop.

I lost my soulmate. Bryan died two weeks ago, in that inhuman way, over the Cross in the death chamber. In those terrible moments, as Richard wrote, I found Irene's arms to welcome me, and I felt like I was in my mother's embrace. Thank you, Irene. I will be grateful to you for motherly comfort.

We shared many hours in the visiting room, and I felt all your love and support to me and Bryan's family as if you were my own mum. I found you waiting for me outside the Wall that evening. Regardless of your deepest pain, you found the strength to console mine.

Thanks to Layne and Diane too and all Richard's friends I met in those days. Thanks to Irene Wilcox, who was really so kind to me not only in those days but in all my prior visits. I will be eternally grateful to Richard for his writings because I had the opportunity to know Bryan's last moments, even on the other side of the visiting room.

I hope all this will end one day. Maybe we all are too tired at this moment to fight, but we must do it! I will keep praying for you all and for all the people still on death row.

I wish to thank all my Texan friends for your love and such strong support—old friends and new ones. They are so numerous! You all are deeply inside my heart forever!

Love,

Margherita

Bryan Wolfe's girlfriend

Uncensored, May 28 to June 2, 2005

Greetings To All!

The last Uncensored article I wrote was pretty much all over the place. I did get a little aggravated when I found out TDCJ guards were sending hateful e-mails to Suzanne in relation to Richard. The main thing that pissed me off was that it showed the guards were taking their job home with them, which shows that they believe they are helping Texas kill us! So that makes it personal.

A while back, I was coming back from a visit. The female guard who was escorting me asked, "Why do y'all hate us?" I told her, "First off, not all inmates hate you all. Some think they are officers too!" She laughed at the truthfulness of my statement. I said, "Though seriously, it is like this. We are here to die. When it comes time to go to the Walls Unit to be slaughtered, and the rank tells you to help load me up in the van, you're gonna help."

Her reply was, "First off, they don't ever ask me to help with that, and if they did, I would not do it. I just work here." I told her, "I hear ya!"

Truthfully, it basically comes down to this: the officers are going to back and support each other. Their motto, which is on most officers' hats, is "We take care of our own." So convicts should look out for each other and support each other. Though sadly, this doesn't always happen.

If an officer gets assaulted, there have been times when other officers have retaliated by assaulting the offender. Though not always, it is rare that the officers retaliate like that. A lot of people don't understand the life behind these walls. In prison, it is an "only the strong survive" environment. Even some officers adhere to this ideology.

Just as a lot of people don't understand why myself, Richard, and a few others let the good squad pepper-spray us and run in on us. I mean, they do have a shield and riot protection gear on—helmets and pads! So it isn't like the officers can get hurt that much. It is a show of resistance and that we will not accept the pointless oppression.

One guy here asked me, "Man, why do you do that crazy shit?" This was after I got gassed four times with a total of 20 ounces of pepper spray. My reply was, "Well, I can't skydive or bungee jump!" All joking aside, it is a rush!

There is a very large chance of the convict getting hurt. There is a metal desk, a metal bunk, plus the toilet. On top of that, you get an average of five 200-pound men running in on the person. So, a thousand pounds smashing a person up against a metal desk can result in a serious injury! It does send the message that we are not afraid to go to an extreme to stand up for something and that we aren't afraid to resist.

Hell, my biological father used to beat the hell out of me with 2x4 boards. So I damn sure am not afraid of getting punched on or gassed. I treat others as they treat me.

There are a lot of stupid rules here. One of them is that our face is supposed to be clean-shaven. My thinking is, I am here to die—why the hell are they worried about me shaving?! They say it's for security reasons! Ha! The real reason is they want to maintain absolute control.

Other prisons and Death Rows across the nation let the convicts grow their hair and beards. Some Death Rows allow convicts to have contact visits with their loved ones. Texas has the only Death Row in the United States that does not have TVs. We can have a radio. We used to have a lot of problems with the reception. However, Major Nelson had them come in and fix the coax cable and all that good stuff.

I spend a majority of my time on Level 2 and 3, so I hardly ever have a radio. Only Level 1s can have a radio. So I naturally did not care too much about the reception. I mainly just mentioned it to thank Major Nelson for getting the antenna fixed for those who do care about listening to the radio. If I am going to knock them when they do wrong, then I am going to give them their praise when they do right!

I want to get off the subject of prison life and write about a few other things that are interesting to me so that the readers can get to know me a little better.

I get National Geographic and The Smithsonian magazines. The June issue for both had King Tut, the ancient Pharaoh of Egypt, on the cover. The story is about them taking King Tut's body and doing a CT scan of his whole body. They then constructed a model of what he looked like by using data from the CT scan.

The readers can go to (http://www7.nationalgeographic.com/ngm/0506/feature1/index.html) and view King Tut's tomb and the model that was created of him. I do not know about you all, but I think that is pretty neat, myself. I mean, you are looking at the face of a man who lived 3,300 years ago! That is awesome. I have always liked history and science. The way that the tombs and pyramids were built is truly fascinating. I wish someone would go through all of that trouble for me when I die!

I am going to bring this one to a close today.

05/29/2005

Well, I am back. It is 3:13 a.m., and the breakfast cart just got on the pod. I wonder what is in store for us today. Most likely, it is pancakes. They serve pancakes like four or five times a week! They get real old, real fast!

I know that Richard was to post an article every week. My case is currently in the state courts. Nothing has been ruled on yet, so I do not really have that much to write about, as I do not want to be repetitive. I will be posting articles biweekly, though I will have a few other people post articles so that one will appear every week!

Well, they just served breakfast, and sure enough, it was pancakes! We get three pancakes at a time, and we get them an average of four times a week. So that is twelve pancakes a week. That is 624 pancakes a year. I have been here 2 years and 6 weeks, so that means I have eaten an average of 1,320 pancakes since I came to Death Row! I am sick and tired of freaking pancakes.

Hopefully, something decent will be given for lunch. Due to budget cuts, we only get dessert twice a week. It is up to the prison warden when those two days are. We get it on Saturday and Sunday.

I stopped writing this for a few days. It is 06/02/2005. I made Level 1! Nothing to be too happy about. I mainly came to Level 1 so that I could visit my wife more and get a few visits with people who are trying to help me get off Death Row.

From reading newspaper articles, it seems Texas stands a good chance of getting Life Without Parole as an option for juries. I am sure that will drastically reduce the number of death sentences in Texas. A step towards progress.

I got to knock out a few letters. I am going to wrap this up.

Keep fighting the good fight.

Standing Tall, Fading All, Never Fall,

Clinton Young

#999447

Polunsky Unit

3872 FM 350 S.

Livingston, TX 77351

Uncensored, June 10 to June 12, 2005

Greetings to all!

It is the 10th day of June, 2005. I must say that it is getting pretty hot down here in Southeast Texas. It's starting to actually FEEL like hell in these cages we call home. The sun beats down on the back wall of my cell. So as I type, I can feel the heat radiating off the wall. I am glad that I at least have a fan. I have been on Level One for a week now. A couple of convicts that I associate with said I have broken a record for the time spent on Level One for me ☺ Ha! I normally do not stay long on Level One.

I got a visit with my wife on Monday, 06/06/2005. I was happy to see her. I went 13 days without getting a letter from her. Talk about being stressed out!!!! I could cope with her leaving me for someone else, as long as she is happy. Though I couldn't cope if she got hurt. That is one of my biggest fears. More so since I have grown close to her daughter. It actually makes life on the row a lot harder, as it adds a lot of emotional weight, though I wouldn't trade her for the world. I also got to see one of my closest associates, who is on the row with me—one of the very few people who I would actually call a friend. Well, he is more like a brother. He is housed on a different pod than myself, so I was glad to get to see him as well.

To show how small this world is, the person who comes to see him was married to my wife's cousin! This world is way too small. Anyway, enough about that. I let a few people I associate with, as well as some I don't really know, read the articles that Richard wrote, as well as the ones that I wrote. I was quite surprised by the emotional effect it had on them. One of the guys didn't even know Richard.

I hope that no one tries to hold me to Richard's level of writing, as he had the ability to be humble and was going through a process in the last few months that he was here that no one can comprehend unless they experience it themselves. It isn't something that I look forward to going through.

In other news, Alexander Martinez was executed. He canceled his appeal, so basically, he committed suicide. Once again, I knew him—not too well, though we had talked a few times. For those who haven't read my past article, when Richard was writing these articles, I wrote about the suicides here and how I actually knew every person who has killed themselves by hanging or canceling their appeals.

I could never go that route. I have too much fight in me. At first, it kind of blew my mind that people would give up like that. But after being here for 2 years, I fully understand and am actually surprised that more haven't done it.

The topic of suicides brings another event to mind. The powers that be here at the Polunsky Death Camp removed the weight bar that was on the outside rec yard. It was a bar with a weight welded on each end that was between two rails so that it couldn't be taken out. Not many used it because it was hard to use due to it sitting on the ground and being stationed so close to the wall that it was difficult to use. Well, nonetheless, it was removed from each rec yard.

The reason that I heard was for suicide prevention. I heard that from a good source, and it actually sounds like some stupid excuse this place would give to take something away. I don't think anyone here would kill themselves by dropping a weight on their head!

The fact of the matter is that they just wanted to take something else from us. That is all they keep doing: taking more and more stuff away. I guess they figured since they fixed the coax cables for the radio, they have to take something away from us.

They have officially outlawed pornographic material, which is really going to end up being a very bad thing. Prison rape is already high in Texas. It is only going to get worse, as it appears there are a lot of people without any self-control.

There is a large number of guys with life sentences in Texas, so really, they have nothing to lose. TDCJ always does stuff the hardest and most stupid way that it can be done. I guess they will just use their solution to everything and just lock everyone up in administrative segregation.

Speaking of ad-seg, there was a very good and long article about ad-seg in Texas in the USA Today. It is in the Thursday, June 9, 2005, paper and can be read online. Texas basically admits that they know the cells drive people crazy and make it harder for people to cope when they are released. But they say it is the easiest solution to gang violence.

Now let's think about this. You take an aggravated gang member who already has hate in his heart and lock him in a small cell for several years. That way, he becomes a crazy aggravated gang member, and then you kick him out of prison for the free world to deal with. And as I wrote in one of my past articles, the mental health programs in Texas are not worth shit!

So now this crazy aggravated gang member is free to run around the streets and get his hands on guns to kill other crazy aggravated gang members and whomever might be in the way. I was in a highly violent juvenile prison for 2 1/2 years. Then they just let me go. I still had a 25 high-security risk, which was the highest there was. I was on medication while I was there, and I never got any drug treatment. When I got out, I thought I could handle it. But as time passed, the stress began to overwhelm me.

Little stuff would get me so angry that I would cry! I stopped taking my medication, so I ended up self-medicating with that good old monster itself, Methamphetamine. I morphed into my own worst enemy. When the case happened that got me on death row, I was actually planning on getting my life back on track. I was scheduled to meet with an Army recruiter two days after I got arrested. I just happened to go for a ride that I shouldn't have gone on.

The crazy thing about my case is that two of the people who are defendants in the case that got me here—the actual shooters—I didn't even like them and actually had a conflict with one of them. The first thing that everyone who knew all of us asked me was, "What the hell were you doing with them?" I could only reply, "Hell if I know."

A lot of people have most likely realized that meth abuse has increased in the U.S. There is also an article in the June 9, 2005, USA Today about meth and how President George W. Bush is actually cutting funding for the narcotics team whose main focus is meth and large drug dealers. Doesn't make much sense, huh?

Meth is highly addictive and is spreading like wildfire across the U.S., which results in more crime and violence. Yet, President Bush wants to cut the funding from the people who are fighting it. He wants to tell people that are sick that they can't smoke weed to ease pain and lashes out at pot smokers, but he cuts funding to fight a drug that makes people highly violent and paranoid.

And guess who is controlling most of the meth trade here in Texas? Those good old crazy aggravated gang members who are getting sent home from their cages. So now we have a lot of paranoid, aggravated gang members whacked out on meth running around. But to hell with them, we've got to lock up all those evil pot smokers out there. Maybe put them in cages so that they can become aggravated crazy gang members as well. God bless America!

Well, enough of that topic. I had written in one of my past articles that the food had gotten a whole lot better. Well, I guess I spoke too soon. Lately, we have been getting some B.S.! I am going to start writing down everything we get so that the readers will know what we are given.

There was a case that has been in the news lately. A guy here in Texas was convicted of two counts of capital murder and given two life sentences for aborting his girlfriend's pregnancy, which she assisted and FULLY encouraged him to do. And guess what? She didn't and couldn't be charged with any crime, as it is her right to have an abortion. Yet her boyfriend has to spend the rest of his life in prison. Good old Texas justice!

True enough, he did it in a very bad way—he jumped on her stomach. It just doesn't make any sense that he gets charged and she gets nothing. THEY ALWAYS GOT TO GET SOMEONE! That is all that matters.

Now, everyone has their own personal beliefs when it comes to pro-life or pro-choice arguments. I personally do not agree with abortion and never encourage anyone to do it. Though, who am I to tell a woman what to do with her body? I think it was kind of sick the way they carried out the abortion. All they had to do was go to a doctor or have the kid and give him up for adoption.

It is a real sensitive subject that I am going to get off of!

Well, I'm going to bring this to an end for today. It is June 12, 2005. I was going through all of my paperwork and came across an old article that I cut out of the newspaper. It was in the Saturday, May 21, 2005, paper. The article is out of Indiana. I am sure it can be read online at the San Antonio Express-News website under the Nation section.

Anyway, this article was about a little girl who was killed up in Indiana. The headline is "New Suspect Charged in Indiana Girl's Death." The interesting thing about this article is that a guy confessed to the crime, and the police found out that he had 100% nothing to do with the crime at all! They did DNA testing and found out that another man was responsible for the crime. The police say they couldn't understand why the other guy confessed.

This is actually a common thing. There have been over 170 people found to be absolutely innocent of a crime that they had confessed to! Some of those people were on death row. It's real common among suspects who are mentally retarded. Most people who are retarded feel eager to please others, so they will confess to the police, thinking they are doing the right thing. Plus, the police trick them by telling the suspect the biggest-ever bullshit lie: "If you just confess and sign this here paper, we will help you." Yeah, help fry your ass!

There is a guy here that has a real bad case. He confessed to the crime that got him here. The only problem? The person who actually did the crime also confessed and is serving time in prison for the offense as well. There is no evidence to link him to the crime but his confession, which would be good enough under normal circumstances. But this guy is actually retarded! He said the cops kicked his ass and told him if he helped them, they would let him go home. He has people trying to help him now, so hopefully, Texas won't get to slaughter him.

On to other news. We had pancakes five times this week! It has gotten to the point that when I see a pancake, my stomach starts to hurt.

I went to recreation on the outside rec yard last Thursday. There are a lot of birds' nests at the top of the bars that act as the roof to the yard. So, needless to say, bird shit gets all over the rec yard and lands conveniently on the water fountain that is out there! Now they are supposed to clean the yard with a high-power water hose that is under the control picket every week. They are supposed to clean the water fountain and toilet every day.

I was talking to one of my neighbors about how dirty the rec yard is. He said they haven't cleaned it since he moved to his pod. Now, with bird crap all over the yard, this is a health risk as birds carry a lot of diseases and lice. I am going to put in an I-60 to request that the rec yard gets cleaned up like it is supposed to be. I will turn it in on the 13th. We will have to see how long it takes to get cleaned.

I mean, it only took them a day to remove all the weight bars so that we couldn't use them. So it should only take a day to clean up the damn rec yard. I also talked to someone who was on the pod when I last got pepper-sprayed. He told me that they never even cleaned it up! Another thing to show how backwards these people are.

A while back, the medical staff passed out papers about athlete's foot being a major problem on the Polunsky Unit. So they know there is a problem! The only problem with the picture is they know of the problem, yet they do nothing to fix it but pass out a piece of paper that acknowledges what everyone already knew.

Now, the crazy part about it all is the fact that the prison does not supply shower shoes. So if a person does not have the money to buy shower shoes, then he will have to shower barefoot, which will cause him to get athlete's foot!

The prison system doesn't pass out deodorant. It has to be bought. Nor do they pass out shampoo. They only give out 5 small bars of lye soap, 1 powder a week, and a pouch of bippy, which is like powdered Ajax. That's all the hygiene material the prison gives out.

If a convict gets caught with more than 5 bars of state soap, he can get a disciplinary case! And people wonder why staph infections and hepatitis C are so out of control in prison. A lot of money goes into TDCJ. I don't know where it all goes, but it damn sure doesn't go to us!

The prison has a house on the property for the warden of the unit. It is built with Texas taxpayers' money. It is a nice house! Since I have been here, not one person has lived in it! So all that taxpayers' money is wasted.

We can't even get mail on Saturday—not even our legal mail—yet TDCJ has $80,000 homes just sitting there empty. They stopped letting us get mail on Saturday because of budget cuts!

The director of TDCJ makes well over $100,000 a year. I think it's in the $140,000s. The guards that actually work the runs only get like $1,500 a month, yet we can't even get mail on a Saturday! They laid off a bunch of mailroom staff. It isn't going to get any better.

Karen, I got your email. Thanks. I am going to try to do the best that I can, though I will never be able to match Richard's level of writing. Hopefully, with some of the ideas I have, we can make this even larger. If Suzanne can manage to cope with and tolerate my spastic writing style and militia-based mind. :)

We all just got to keep recruiting more people to fight this war against the murder machine. Well, it is 5:50 a.m., so I am going to go ahead and bring this to an end.

Use the pain to fuel the fire.

Stand tall, fade all, never fall.

Clinton Young

#999447

Polunsky Unit

3872 FM 350 S.

Livingston, TX 77351

Uncensored, June 19, 2005

Greetings to all!

Quote for the week: Mahatma Gandhi, "You must be the change you wish to see in the world."

Another week has slowly ticked by. Not much has changed. It has been fairly calm around here.

On a positive note, the powers that be had the rec yard and pods cleaned up real good! They even used a buffer! Though on the downside, we had to eat Johnny Sacks (a sacked lunch) for the last two meals. Word is that there wasn't enough staff to watch the inmates! Even the Gray Suits don't want to be here! I have noticed lately that a lot of the ranks have gotten lazy—well, I should say lazier! When a convict calls for rank, they don't come. The ranking officers are supposed to come to defuse any potential problem. So if the rank doesn't come, then the problem doesn't get resolved!

Now, we are sent to death row because we are supposedly so messed up that we can't be fixed, so they just have to kill us. That means we have no sense of control or rational thinking. So if a ranking officer doesn't come to handle a conflict, that leaves a convict to handle the situation however he sees fit. If he resolves it with violence, the first question asked is, "What did you do that for?" "Well, if you would have brought your lazy ass down here, we wouldn't have this problem," is the usual answer.

Now true enough, there are a lot of irrational choices that caused them to do whatever got them here. But how can anyone be judged solely by their worst act? For the most part, death row is real passive. Maybe too passive! The majority have never been locked up before! Most were on drugs when their crime occurred and/or were with someone else. So peer pressure can be added. I know that rapists, baby killers, and serial killers don't fit under that category, as those kinds of crimes normally happen alone.

One would expect death row to be a highly violent environment. I read a statement by a guy from Huntsville, TX, in the newspaper. He said that if they opened up death row and let everyone walk around, then everyone would see how dangerous they are! Poor guy. I have to forgive him for his ignorance. He doesn't know any better.

Death row used to be able to walk around freely, with box cutters and scissors! That's right, very sharp metal objects! Nine times out of ten, the supervising officer was a female! No female officers were raped, and no officers were ever killed. Though female officers have been raped by general population inmates! But these death row guys are dangerous!

A guy in population has freedom to look forward to. A guy on the row is waiting to die! He has nothing to lose. So one would expect the death row inmate to be more violent. Yet this isn't the case. So the fact that we are now locked down for 23 hours a day makes no sense.

Human violence is a well-studied topic. In a recent study of five different cultures, it was found that 94% of males and 85% of females admitted to having vivid fantasies of murder! That helps explain all the pro-death penalty people and why they are so bent on us getting killed.

When I first got here, a guy wrote me and told me, in short, to turn my life over to Christ and cancel my appeals! I thought to myself, this guy has to be a complete idiot! Just as a lot of people think the guards who work back here on the row don't really like it. Yeah, right!

They DO NOT have to work back here! If they say that their religious or personal views cause them to oppose the death penalty, then they don't have to work back here. Most work back here because:

A. They think it is cool.

B. They are for the death penalty.

C. They are too scared to work in population.

Several have said they would execute us themselves if they could. Now, there are maybe three or four who don't fit into that category. Most just come to work and don't bother anyone. I have even noticed that overall, the guards don't mess with people like they used to.

Anyway, back to the topic of violence. The Bible says if you think it, then you are just as guilty of doing it! So all those people who have thought about killing us themselves are no better than the men housed in these cages. The same goes for those who try to get death row convicts to cancel their appeals!

Some believe humans are violent by nature and passive by nurture. "Man, biologically considered, and whatever else he may be in the bargain, is simply the most formidable of all the beasts of prey, and indeed, the only one that preys systematically on its own species." That was William James!

The thing that I find to be the most interesting aspect of the mentality of the average pro-death penalty individual is that most are very self-righteous. So they feel they have the ability to judge and punish. Friedrich Nietzsche stated, "Distrust all in whom the impulse to punish is powerful."

All-or-nothing thinking is the product of a simple mind! Most people who are pro-death penalty hold that ideology as a result of being conditioned to be pro-death penalty. Confucius stated, "Only the wisest and stupidest of men never change." Anyone with an all-or-nothing mind frame is surely not a wise person, i.e., "He killed someone, so now he has to die!"

"An eye for an eye leaves the whole world blind!" If you thought about killing someone, no matter who it is, you are just as bad as the irrational person who carries their thoughts out.

Now a lot of people judge others by their worst act. "Men's evil manners live in brass; their virtues we write in water." – Shakespeare.

What should be considered is if the worst act represents a pattern. People can change, even the worst of the worst. Paul, from the Bible, slaughtered lots of people, yet how often is he praised and quoted today? He was forgiven and changed his life around. Can a man on death row not be forgiven and change his life around?

As I wrote earlier, a lot of people are self-righteous and think they are important, so they feel that they can judge others.

I'm going to share a personal story with everyone. When I was a child, I didn't have any other kids to play with in my neighborhood. My mother and stepfather were actually the youngest couple in the neighborhood.

We lived in the northeast Texas region called Piney Woods. We lived by Lake of the Pines. So when I was a kid, I would always go in the woods and run around with my dog. A lot of times, I would sit, think, and watch the animals.

On one particular day, when I was around 8 or 9 years old, I was sitting in the woods, watching two squirrels play. I began to think: If I died right now, would the squirrels stop playing? What would change in this world? Who all would miss me?

My baby sister was too young. She was only one or two, so she would not really miss me. I don't know my aunts, uncles, and cousins that well. The only person who I felt would be truly hurt by my loss would be my mother. Though she would be able to carry on.

The world wouldn't stop turning. So I realized that day that we are not actually that important. In the big picture, we are like a speck of dust in the middle of the ocean.

The truth is that most people who pass away are forgotten by the next generation. If people would realize that they really are not important and would humble themselves, this world would be a much better place to live.

How many people can you name who died in this war in Iraq? I mean right off the top of your head! Most likely no one, unless a relative or friend died. Yet we all can say who started the war.

How many presidents can you name right off the top of your head? I can only think of 15 off the top of my head, and history is one of my favorite subjects! Most couldn't name that many. I guess they just aren't that important, huh?

The point of all that I have written is actually a message to those who claim to be pro-death penalty. What makes you more important than myself to the point that you can judge and condemn me? If you died today, the squirrels wouldn't even stop playing!

Now on to other things. There is a guy who has been on the Row for about 25 years. Since he came, his mental health has greatly deteriorated. His name is Cesar Fierro #000650. You can search his case and mental condition online. His lawyer stated that even when told of some good news from the courts, he raged and rambled incoherently and banged the phone against the glass partition of the visiting room. The guy has lost it. He is actually too crazy to be executed.

I was his neighbor for a little bit. I had some interesting conversations with him :). He never gets any mail. He just sits in his cell talking to his reflection in the toilet. Sometimes he yells at himself. Other times he laughs at himself. For the most part, he seems to enjoy his own company.

Though seriously, I wanted to make a request of some of the readers. I stated the dude doesn't get any mail. So if someone out there wouldn't mind taking the time to send him a card or something to give him some type of pleasure and mental stimulation, I would greatly appreciate it. I mean, 9 times outta 10 if you are reading this, you really don't have anything much else better to do. So if you all got an extra stamp, drop the guy a few lines.

He really is "not all with us," so he won't be responding. Though to my knowledge, he can read. And for any jackass out there who thinks they will be able to get him to cancel his appeals, you might as well give it up. A. He has a FACTUAL innocence claim. B. He is too crazy to cancel his appeal. And C. He is a Mexican National, so he won't be getting executed anytime soon. So all those who fit under the jackass label, don't waste your stamps!

On to other topics. Marina, I got your e-mail, book, and shoutout. Thanks for all three! Also, thanks for all the help you are giving to Janice. I know she appreciates it. Sarah, I got your e-mail as well. You have a letter coming.

I wrote in a past article about how the judge in my case placed an illegal "order to seize assets" on my inmate trust fund. Well, I filed a Pro-Se Motion with the help of another convict. He wrote it; I filed it. Well, the judge denied it, though, doing so, he actually gave me what I need to show he is biased against me. All the legal information regarding what I have written about will be posted on this site and others.

There for a little bit, the mail service was getting alright around this camp. I sent a letter to a P.O. Box in Houston on 06/06/2005. I got the person's response to that letter on 06/08/2005. I was very surprised. Though it seems to have gone back to the usual service as of late, which is like depending on a billy goat on crack to pass out the mail. Or maybe it is just me!

After all, these cells can make a person go crazy. Last night an officer who worked the pod, who really does not have much sense—I don't know her name—gets hell-bent when she shakes down! She took a guy's bippy (cleaning powder) because he had too much and then threatened to write him a case for excessive paper! He had some news publication she said was too old and confiscated it.

So I can see that my time on Level 1 is very short. I asked the officer if she felt obligated to bother people. Her excuse was the porters need the bippy to clean the pods! Yeah, right. I just looked at her crazy and walked away from the door. My mind will not allow me to even try to comprehend some of these people.

I am listening to the "Shout Out" show on KDOL. It can be heard on the internet. I believe that Suzanne has the web address posted. It is just what these people do. They allow people's voices from all over the world to be heard and help keep up the spirits of convicts on the Row.

To all those out there fighting the good fight, stay focused, stay united, and stay strong. I focus on the entire system because the problems are not just based at the Polunsky Unit. It stems from the courtrooms, prosecutors' offices, legislation, the governor, and all the way to the White House. If we can organize enough people to the point that our voice is loud enough, then a change will come about.

Hopefully, President Bush and Governor Perry won't be able to do much more damage before they are out of office. It will not be easy. So take pride in the ability to attack the difficult. More and more attention is being shined on the system. Though we can't stop 'til Victory.

To repeat a quote I have written in the past by Winston Churchill: "Victory at all costs, victory in spite of all terror, victory however long and hard the road may be; for without victory, there is no survival." Use the pain to fuel that fire that burns within you. Channel that energy toward success.

I have a question to all pro-death penalty people out there and American patriots who love this country and its Constitution. The Constitution states that a defendant is entitled to a fair trial. Would you not agree? If a person didn't get a fair trial, don't you think he or she should be granted relief and given a new trial so that his or her constitutional rights are upheld? You can't have the 2nd Amendment right and not the 6th. It all goes together! All or nothing, right?

I leave as I came. Stand tall, fade all, and never fall.

Clinton Young

#999447

Polunsky Unit

3872 F.M. 350 S.

Livingston, TX 77351

Uncensored, June 27, 2005

Greetings to all!

Another week has ticked by. A pretty productive week to a degree. Governor Perry finally decided to comply with the Supreme Court and commute the sentence of the 28 guys who received the death penalty for crimes committed when they were 17 to life in prison.

He also signed into law a measure allowing Life Without Parole. This law will come into effect on September 1, 2005. This is good news. Well, I would say it is bittersweet. It will result in people receiving the death penalty less. Though life in prison is a death sentence in itself, more so in a Texas prison. People always tell me they are sickened by the conditions here. Well, Death Row gets a lot of attention. Think about the other 100 or so prisons in Texas that don't have the public attention the row gets. It is a hard life that only gets harder. There have been cases of guards raping male inmates, killing inmates, and everything in between. Some are a lot worse.

It is way harder if a person doesn't have anyone to help him/her with the basics of mail, stamps, and hygiene. On the topic of mail, on June 20, 2005, the pod I am on only had about 10 letters for the whole pod! There are 84 people to a pod. Usually, there are at least fifty to seventy letters a day. Plus, we do not get mail on Saturday, so there is twice as much mail on Monday! Yet that is the day we get the least amount passed out. Some days everything is golden and on time. Other days everything is backed up and mixed up. I swear the mailroom is more spastic than hanky-panky in a goat pen! :)

I was aggravated earlier today. I was supposed to have a visit. The person didn't show up. This causes a lot of stress because I automatically think the worst. Well, I decided to sit down and write something. Here is the result:

Living Hell

I see it simmer in the distance.

I feel the heat as the sinner seeks repentance.

I hear the screams of agony and beggars of forgiveness.

I smell the pain of the sulfuric flames.

I taste the fear of the not-so-near end.

All together, I experience the life of a living hell.

I live it in this cell.

Welcome to Polunsky Unit. Death Row!

My living hell.

Clint Young

I was feeling kind of miserable when I wrote that. This environment helps increase these unwanted feelings! "Abandon all hope, ye who enter here!" It is easy to latch onto hope in this place. We are so surrounded by the negative that we latch onto any positive we can find: hope, love, faith, and so forth. To me, love is the greatest, and hope is the worst, as hope more often than not leads to despair in this place. But what we call our despair is often only the painful eagerness of unfed hope.

Some days it is easy to stand tall. Some days I can feel the weight of my situation pulling me down. There are some days when I wake up, and right when I open my eyes and see these walls, reality fully kicks in, and dread consumes me. The first thought that comes to mind is, "Damn, I am going to die." Then as I get up and start listening to the radio, talking, and doing stuff around my cell, the thought of death fades away.

It is starting to become too often that I have to make myself get out of bed. The reasons that I have been fighting for seem to be fading away. While I was in the County Jail, my family, associates from the street, and even ex-girlfriends all wrote me, came to visit, and helped in any and all ways they could. When I got convicted, they all cried. When I got the death sentence, they all disappeared! This happens often, as life is just too hard on the row for all involved. True enough, there are people who write, visit, and provide assistance. Though it just is not the same as if it was family and those known from the free world.

I have my wife and a few people I write who I have developed a strong bond with. I can see the strain this place puts on my wife. It eats me up inside. I try to channel the pain into productive action. However, with the way the judicial system is and the penal system, it makes me feel as if I am a drowning man grasping for straws. The courts seem to have this tigerish lust to annihilate. Depending on a lawyer who I do not even know does not help matters any.

Seeing those around me get slaughtered, dealing with incompetent guards, sitting in a cage all day—so on and so on—all of this adds up to a lot of turmoil, which manifests into anger. It gets real hard to keep channeling this anger in positive ways. I try to stay focused on the prize, which is getting off of the row. The system is so corrupt and bloodthirsty that it makes the fight seem pointless.

One of the things that I have thought about that needs to be done is placing more focus on the Court of Criminal Appeals Judges. Their profiles can be read online. I don't have the web address, but I will get it. Anyway, these judges are voted in, I believe. A voter block needs to be formed in Texas. Not that many people actually vote. So if we could rally all the anti-death-penalty people in Texas to vote against certain judges, district attorneys, and the governor, things would get better.

That will be the only way we all can have an effect on the Death Penalty. If we form a big enough voting block, then who knows? Maybe the right people will be put in place to end the Death Penalty in Texas! All it takes is a little effort. I think it can be done. Between family members, friends, and pen-pals, we could create a loud voice. We just have to unite for the common cause. When the bloodthirsty judges and politicians realize that the public will no longer tolerate the injustice, a change will come about. Injustice anywhere is a threat to justice everywhere.

I want to change the subject for a little bit. A grub worm was found in a guy's food! It was a big one. Instead of the officers no longer feeding and calling rank, they, of course, kept feeding. They have at least fed fewer pancakes this week. They have been feeding this axle grease-thick gravy and biscuits. I took a spoonful and turned it upside down. It stayed stuck to my spoon for a little over four seconds! It is that thick. I chose not to eat.

I wrote about the Rec yard not being clean, and the next week I wrote about it getting clean. Well, they only cleaned half of the Rec yard! Lazy-ass people! I don't even want to go outside anymore. I have been on all the pods! This pod has the trashiest and dirtiest Rec yards! They keep the pod freshly painted and clean because A and B pod are show pods for tours and auditions. But the rest of the pods get neglected. Some are painted like three different colors! It looks like trash!

On to other things. KDOL Radio 96.1 does a "Shout Out" show for the Polunsky Unit. I want to remind people of this. You can send an e-mail "shout out" to someone on the row at kdolradio@hotmail.com. KDOL can also be heard on the internet. This is a really good thing for people on and off the row. People call in from all over the world to give shout-outs by phone and e-mail. It means a lot to all involved.

Well, I am going to bring this to an end. I leave as I came.

Stand Tall, Fade All, Never Fall

"Only when the sense of the pain of others begins—does man begin."

Clinton Young

999447

Polunsky Unit

3872 FM 350 S.

Livingston, TX 77351

Uncensored, July 15 to July 16, 2005

Greetings to all!

Welcome to another journey through the mind and chaotic life of Clinton Lee Young. Today is the fifteenth of July. I missed a week due to certain events.

Last week, a female officer by the name of Hadnot wrote me a case. I had my towel hanging on the screen of my door. I was talking to the guy in the cell above me. Well, Hadnot said, "Take this towel down." I replied, "What, you can't ask me to take the towel down? If you ask me in a respectful manner, then I can grant your request." She then got an ugly look on her already bulldog-looking face and said louder in a smart-ass way, "Take your towel down."

I got aggravated and replied, "F### you and that towel. If you can't talk to me in a respectful manner, then don't say shit to me and get away from my cell." Well, as expected, at about 5:50 a.m., a sergeant woke me up asking for my statement on the case Hadnot wrote me. It was a "Refusing to Obey a Direct Order" case.

We had a talk about playing the system game and all the other wasted B/S. I told him if she would have come at me with some respect, I would have taken my towel down. Well, time goes on, and I get moved to C-Pod around one of my associates, a very close friend of mine. Close like a brother.

Well, I decide to half-ass work the program. So I shave and all that good stuff. Then, on Sunday, they come to get me for minor case court. For major court, a person goes in front of a captain and everything is recorded on tape. Well, for minor case court, a person goes in front of a lieutenant and a sergeant. No due process.

Well, I go expecting something small, like a 10-day commissary restriction. Lt. Bryant is running the hearing. He is a mini-Captain-Wickersham. Well, he asks me how I plead. I go ahead and plead guilty with no statement. He then says, "I am giving you 15 days commissary restriction, 15 days cell restriction, and downgrading you to Level 2."

When he said that, my jaw dropped! I said, "Hold up, Bryant. You're bullshitting, right?" He said, "No, you are placed on Level 2."

Me: "So you are dropping me for a fucking minor case?"

Him: "Yes. I have to be consistent."

I give a little laugh and say, "Get off the B/S. You ain't serious, are you?"

He says, "Yes, I am. You don't need to put your towel in the door. I have to be consistent."

I replied, "You are sure right! Then I have to be consistent as well." Needless to say, these articles are about to get a lot more interesting and action-packed. :)

Speaking of action, one of my partners in crime, Mr. Steven Woods, was gassed and run in on. I was asleep, and I woke up to the smell of smoke. I look out my door and see the whole pod full of smoke. In my mind, I think, "Steven must have started a fire." Not a second later, I hear, "Look out, Young."

I yell, "What's up?"

Steven says, "I am about to fade the team." :)

Me: "What for?"

Him: "I started a fire, and now they are trying to take my property."

I laugh and yell, "Go hard, Lil Wood!"

Then, a minute or two later, I hear the stomp, stomp, stomp of the cell extraction team stomping onto the pod. Steven is on another section than I am, so I can't see him or the team. I am in a corner cell, so I can't see much of anything!

They gas him twice, and in they go. I hear stuff banging around and the sergeant yelling, "Stop resisting, stop resisting!" Now they put him in another cell. He says he is okay. He will write about it soon.

Steven only weighs like 120 pounds, if that much! The first man on the team weighed more than 300 pounds! Five men total. I really cut for the dude. He has a lot of heart. He is real smart as well. He will be posting an article.

You see, they dropped me to Level 2 without any due process or anything. Another officer told me, "Man, Lt. Bryant must hate you." Truthfully, I think the cat hates himself.

Oh well. I have laid quiet this week so far because I have a visit Saturday. I believe my wife is coming to see me. My birthday is on July 19th. I was hoping to see my little sister, but now that I have my level dropped, I can only get two visits a month. When I go to Level 3, I will only be able to get one a month. It is the price we pay for the game we play.

I've received some emails from a few people. Miles, thanks for the compliment. As you know by now, I do know Rob. Rev. Amy, I will have a letter heading your way soon.

I see Steven has told you about Punk Rock Mike and the Young Prince. :) Haha! He informed me that he is waiting on a letter from you.

To the behind-the-scenes type of gal from Australia, thanks for the email. Paddy, I sent you a letter. You should have it by now. I received your emails as well. Irene, I got the emails. Thanks.

Sarah of New Zealand and Karen, I received your letters. Thanks. I will reply as soon as I get some stamps. Patricia of Germany, I've got your card and letter. Thanks! Oh, yeah. Miles, I like that memorial site you did for Richard. I was told you were good. Viktoria, I got your letter. Just keep doing what you are doing. I greatly appreciate your friendship. I also would like to thank Scott for helping Suzanne with the article.

Anyway, to the rest of the story. I am working with a friend of mine on getting a non-profit organization going. This friend is in the free world and runs my e-group. Hopefully, we can get everything going to help save my life.

It will take money to get it going, but once it gets going, it will be self-supportive. I've got a lot of good ideas.

In other news, my trash lawyer, Gary Taylor, moved to Nevada and dropped his caseload. So, at this time, I do not have a lawyer. My state writ is pending in court, waiting on a response by the state.

Just another strike toward me getting slaughtered by the state. Now I will have to wait until the state picks some other person to aid in their killing process. This person will know nothing about my case and will be at a severe disadvantage.

Gary Taylor recommended someone. Gary Taylor is nicknamed "the Grim Reaper." I have some very good claims that could get me a completely new trial, but the idiot filed everything just to get me a life sentence! Well, right now, I do not even have a lawyer! Oh well, not having one is about the same as having the one I had!

One quick note to all the English readers, especially those from London: to any who lost a loved one or suffered any pain at the hands of the terrorists, my heart goes out to you all.

There was another good article about methamphetamines in the USA Today on Friday, July 15, 2005, in the Money B Section. It shows how it affects the brain and all that good stuff.

There was another issue that has been in the news recently. The Republicans are trying to do away with the Federal Habeas Corpus for death row prisoners. It will most likely pass the House. If it becomes a law, then a lot of men and women are going to die.

See, the pro-death penalty people form tight bonds and focus on the goal at hand, and that is to kill, kill, and kill. Most of the anti-death penalty people just sit around complaining about Bush and this and that. If everyone would unite and consolidate resources, the anti-death penalty movement would have a louder and stronger voice. It takes money. The pros line the pockets of politicians. Until people are ready to put forth full effort, unite and organize, then the fight will keep going downhill for us.

I have some ideas that I will present once I get the assistance needed in getting the planned organization going. The more people who get educated about the death penalty, the more who will join the fight, and then a voting block can be created, and we will have a loud enough voice.

Say there are two million people in Texas who are able to vote and are against the death penalty. Well, if all those people would unite and present the governor with a list of all the names and told him, "You promise to work against the death penalty, and we will all vote for you," I guarantee you the death penalty in Texas would come to an end.

Though I do not see it happening anytime soon. More so since the Republicans are trying to pass that Streamline Act of 2005. If the bill passes, a lot of people will die. The federal courts act as a safety net when the state system is broken, which all can agree the Texas judicial system is. Without the Federal Habeas Corpus, a lot more people would be dead by now.

It was the federal courts that let Ernest Willis go. Without them, he would be dead as well. But thanks to federal review, he is able to be at home with his wife.

Everyone needs to focus on the political aspect of this fight. If the senators feel it is a good thing to be anti-death penalty, they will be, even if they are truly pro-death penalty. Now that Bush is able to place a Supreme Court justice, it will get a lot worse!

People think Bush will listen to what they have to say. This is not true! The conservative right is trying their hardest to influence who Bush appoints to the Supreme Court. Though he has said he will appoint who he wants to appoint, I give him his care. He sticks to his guns.

07/16/2005

I just got back from a visit with my wife. It was a good visit. I sent out some legal papers to be posted. They show how I got railroaded. They also show how I didn't do this offense.

It felt good seeing my wife. I go through a lot of stress when I worry about her and my stepdaughter. When I see them, it is the only time I am truly happy. Damn, I hope I beat this shit. I can't see dying for another's actions. More so when that other person didn't mean anything to me. I am referring to the co-defendants in the case.

All I can do is fight as long and as hard as I can. Right now, I've got to deal with some in-house issues concerning those people putting me on Level 2. They all wear gray, so they are all part of the same gang. One officer even told me, "I am in the TDCJ gang, and we are a large gang." Haha!

Anyway, I saw Robert Shields at the visit as well. It is good to see that he has some family support to help him through this time in his life. I have only gotten to speak to him at visits, though we do associate with a lot of the same people.

Well, I am going to bring this to an end.

I leave as I came.

Stand Tall, Fade All, Never Fall

Clinton Young

#999447

Polunsky Unit

3872 FM 350 S.

Livingston, TX 77351

Uncensored, August 02, 2005

Topic: Justice

Greetings to all!

Another episode of Clinton Young Uncensored. I am going to step back into the realm of politics for a few moments. I have touched on the fact that Texas does not have the best mental health services. Well, I would like to get into that topic a little more. There was a case in the news last year, May 2004, involving Kelsey Patterson, 50, of Palestine, TX, who, even though he suffered from documented severe mental illness, was executed by the State of Texas.

One of the interesting aspects of his case is the fact that he was granted clemency by the Texas Board of Pardons and Paroles. This is very, very rare. As a matter of fact, his case was the only one I know of where the T.B.P.P. granted clemency. Then the great governor of Texas, Rick Perry, exhibited a prime example of the tyranny of political power over justice and mercy. Governor Perry shot down the parole board's rare vote and ordered Kelsey Patterson to be executed. His reason for doing so was that Texas did not, at the time, have life without parole.

Now, the real interesting thing about Perry's reason is that Texas did not have life without parole because the governor himself had strenuously and successfully opposed the introduction of life without parole! Other states and nations back up the mentally ill to treat them. Texas kills them. Though we are dealing with a state where the highest criminal court has ruled that innocence does not matter so long as the defendant got a fair trial.

In 1980 and 1983, Patterson was ruled mentally incompetent to stand trial for two previous non-fatal shootings. He was not prosecuted for those shootings because he was found to be delusional. Yet, as soon as he committed capital murder, he was found competent to stand trial and given the death penalty. Kind of a "kill him so we do not have to worry about him anymore" type of thing.

"Bubba, go out back and shoot that damn dog so he will stop barking!"

At the time of his execution, Kelsey mumbled incoherently. His statement was, "Murders…no kin, no kin." "I'm not guilty of the charge of capital murder … acquitted by the court of criminal appeals." When he was asked for his final statement, he replied, "Statement to what? Statement to what?" He rambled for a couple of minutes and stated, "They are doing this to steal my money. My truth will always be my truth. No kin to you…undertaker…….. murder. Go to hell. Get my money. Give me my rights. Give me my life back." The flow of lethal chemicals stopped his mumbling.

The victim's daughter said it ended how she "prayed" it would. Those types of people are fucking ill. How can anyone indicate, "My God is a loving and forgiving God," and then proclaim that the same loving God has slaughtered the one they "prayed" to be killed?

I will get off that topic for now.

Back to the subject at hand. At least six people with claims of mental illness have been put to death in Texas since 2002. In 2001, Texas ranked 46th in the nation in mental health care spending. In 2003, the Texas legislature slashed millions of dollars from the state's 2004 mental health care programs. Under the 2004 budget, Medicaid no longer paid for adults to visit psychologists, licensed counselors, social workers, or marriage and family therapists.

Groups have been trying for years to get the courts and legislature to focus more on the state's policy for mentally ill and mentally retarded criminals. The answer to everything is kill, kill, and kill. If we can't kill, then lock them up for as long as we can.

Texas even sends drug abusers to prison. No treatment, just idle time in prison. A lot of state facilities in Texas refuse to hospitalize people unless they are violent. Kelsey Patterson's family tried to get him committed to a mental health facility. He was rejected because he had not harmed anyone. He was on death row for the murder of two people.

The same thing happened with Larry Robison, who has also been executed. The state refused to keep him hospitalized because he was not violent. The first time he displayed violence, five people ended up dead. If Texas would have focused on prevention, then nine people would still be alive in those two cases alone.

A mentally ill man cannot provide as much assistance to his lawyers as a mentally stable person. This is just a good example of one of the many ways that the system is broken.

This is why people need to unite and form a voter's block. This is the only way a change will come about. "Unity" is the key.

This is 2005; it is about time for a change. We need to focus on the state government and make changes in our system like education and treatment of the mentally ill. If the mentally ill had appropriate medical treatment, then maybe we wouldn't have to lock them up and kill them later.

The Texas prison system is overcrowded. It holds 152,000 people. The doors of the death chamber do not stop spinning.

Voters could halt the building of these super-segregation prisons that do nothing but increase mental illness, psychosis, suicidal behavior, and a plethora of other aberrant behaviors.

It has been said that America has the world's largest penal system. That is interesting considering the most well-known statue in America is the Statue of Liberty!

In the course of a year, 13.5 million people pass through the system. The U.S. prison systems now hold around 2.2 million inmates. Texas is trying to build even more supermax prisons.

Now people in Washington, D.C., are trying to do away with the federal writ of habeas corpus. This is the checks and balances for the state judicial system, which means that without a federal writ of habeas corpus, a lot of people in Texas will be slaughtered by the murder machine.

This tigerish lust to annihilate displayed by the courts and government seems to only be growing. Who knows what it will manifest itself into? Death penalty for robbery!

"Oh – you didn't pay your taxes? Get a rope!"

Just like the old west days. It seems for every step we take forward, we fall two steps back. The government can take your house to build a hotel. The government can tell women what they can and cannot do to their bodies. The government even wants to tell people when they can die.

"You can't kill yourselves, but we can kill you!"

The question is: how long will the American citizens let this go on?

I believe it was 1884 when the Supreme Court gave itself absolute powers over the final say-so of the law.

Where are the checks and balances of the three branches?

The three branches of government were created so no one branch would have absolute power.

The President gets to appoint the Supreme Court Justice. This gives him a chance to have an influence on society based on his ideology for the next, say, 25 years. Power corrupts; absolute power corrupts absolutely. Power will only take a step back in the face of more power. Citizens have the power. They have the power to vote.

If all the citizens of Texas that were against the death penalty got their names together and put all their names on a petition and then a representative for the Anti's went to the person that was facing the Governor in the next election and said, "If you promise to work against the death penalty in Texas, along with better mental health care, education, and drug rehabilitation programs, we will all vote for you," I am willing to bet my money that it would happen.

Then those people could help fund his campaign.

Hey, this is America; it will take money to get anything done! A change can come about.

Texas Death Row is the way it is due to legislators, in part. To improve conditions on Death Row, more heat needs to be put on the government of Texas.

The warden doesn't care what the voters think. The Director of TDCJ doesn't care what the voters think about Death Row. He doesn't have to get voted into office by the public. Though the public can put pressure on him and help get him out of office, especially if the public was aware of all the wasted money and insanely high salaries.

Yet we cannot even send out legal mail on a Saturday! We cannot even get deodorant, shampoo, or shower shoes unless we have money sent to us from people in the free world.

Yeah, the system is broken!

People like Richard Cartwright, Kenneth Foster, myself, and many others are placed on Death Row to die under the law of parties. Yet if someone has a full-scale I.Q. of less than 70 or was under the age of 18 when their crime was committed, they cannot be executed. But a person under the law of parties that did not even kill anyone can be slaughtered by the state. A person could kill 100 people, but if his I.Q. is 69, he cannot be executed. But a guy that was a getaway driver in a robbery that goes wrong can be executed! Does something not seem wrong with that? I mean, the death penalty is supposed to be for the worst of the worst (for people that are so irrational and homicidal that they have to be killed)! Kind of like a rabid dog—there is just nothing you can do with it! The truth is, people are not like dogs and can change and be fixed. From medication to tightened security measures, those found insane (I am referring to murderously insane) should be placed in psych wards and treated for mental illness in the hopes of rehabilitation.

I am not insane! So why can they not let me go? I didn't even kill anyone! The guy that shot Reagan was found insane. I believe he gets to leave the psych hospital and visit with his family. Didn't he kill a man and shoot a couple of others? In Texas, that is murder in the course of a felony. That is capital murder. If John Hinckley had done that in Texas, he would be a statistic in the number of people executed by the state of Texas! It is just another point in why the death penalty makes no sense. To say that this person's life is worth more than that person's life is the foundation of most fascist beliefs. If you make an assumption that a murderer's life is worth less than that of the victim, then you go and kill the murderer, that would make your life worth less than the murderer's. You yourself murdered. If a person indicates that they are able to judge the value of another person's life, then they are concluding that they are superior to that person. The scales of justice are supposed to symbolize equality, though history teaches us that symbol is a false representation of our current judicial system.

We all need to stand up and fight the injustice of the system. From the inside, we need to resist against the murder machine and oppressive system. From the outside, a political group needs to be formed. One not bound by age, race, or gender—one that includes people of all religions: lawyers, ministers, teachers, students, taxi cab drivers—all united for one cause: JUSTICE! Martin Luther King Jr. stated, "Injustice anywhere is a threat to justice everywhere." This is true! Unity is the key to success! Most people just do not know the truth about the death penalty or death row. Most believe that we have TVs, CD players, and all kinds of crazy stuff. This is why educating the masses is very important. The T.C.A.D.P. (Texas Coalition Against the Death Penalty) has a good setup on their website.

A lot of people bash George W. Bush. I do not waste my time writing about him that much; plenty of others say enough. I like to use his own words against him, though. When the case of Terri Schiavo was going on down in Florida about pulling her feeding tube or not, President George W. Bush expressed his belief that "we should stand on the side of defending and protecting life." That is a good statement. Yet he does not practice what he preaches. He does nothing to ensure that an innocent man or woman does not get executed. If he wants to protect and defend life, then he needs to enact laws and guidelines that help ensure that NO innocent person gets slaughtered by the state.

I was at visitation on July 28, 2005, when David Martinez was escorted out of the visit to go to the Walls Unit to be executed. He seemed in high spirits, and the warden and other ranks acted like they were escorting him to the barber! As he walked out of the visit, I said, "Another sheep led to slaughter!" You see, I do not agree with just walking to the execution. I have had a gun to my head before; I know what it is like to face death. At that time, I thought, I can die by getting shot in the back of the head, or I can die from running away, or I can die by getting shot in the front of the head by fighting. I am alive today because I fought.

I fight the system in all ways that I can! I maintain my sanity by resisting the oppressive tactics of the system. I fight the courts. I fight the guards. I fight the stereotypes. I fight to live! I am alive!! I am alive mentally and physically. I suffer in some areas due to my resistance, but I would lose the substance of my existence were I to submit. I will die before I ever bow down.

When people walk to their death, it eases the pain because people feel that a person is ready to die. That pain should never be eased! Use the pain to fuel the fire!! If I lay my head beneath the guillotine, then I have committed suicide. If they "place" my head beneath the guillotine against my will, then they have murdered me!! I never feel more at peace than when I am on Level 3 with fellow comrades. Commissary does not control me, property does not control me, and recreation does not control me. If I lose all of those as a cost for standing up for what I believe in, then it is a debt well paid.

People are under a false illusion that our behavior has an impact on our pending execution. There have been numerous people executed that have gone 8, 9, or 10 years with not one disciplinary case. However, I can as well name people that have gotten off of death row who fought the system, stayed on Level 3, and had some major disciplinary cases! So being a passive prisoner on death row does not mean that the person's execution will be halted.

How can we sit idle while people on the outside fight for us? We have to fight hand in hand. I am not saying we need to be violent and hurt people, of course not! To do that would only support the accusations of those that wish to punish. I am very thankful that those I write and have developed bonds with do not criticize my choice of existence here on the row. At first, it was hard for them to understand, though once educated, I believe most people can appreciate my resistance.

Anyway, I have gone on and on and on. Hopefully, at least one person will gain something from this uncensored article. I seek to motivate more people to join the struggle. To unite and fight against the injustice.

"The true measure of a man or woman is not where he or she stands in moments of comfort and convenience but where he or she stands at times of challenge and controversy." —Martin Luther King Jr.

Where will you stand?

Stand tall. Fade all. Never fall.

Clinton Young

#999447

Polunsky Unit

3872 FM 350 S.

Livingston, TX 77351

Veni, Vidi, Vici.

Uncensored, August 18, 2005

Well, I am back! I know that I have not posted an article in about two weeks. I have been going through a lot of stress lately. I haven't felt like writing. It seems that nothing goes right! I have a lot of good ideas, but not enough people willing to help. Here is a poem I wrote about the despair caused by nothing going right and dealing with fake people.

"Despair"

I am cloaked in despair, enshrouded in misery.

I cover my head to envision the dismissal of reality.

I hear the voices of saints, crying, "We care."

I see the smiles on demons; they laugh out there.

The iniquitous declaration of adequacy spews from the hypocrites' lips.

The beautiful face—a mask of the imps.

They pledge to share my pain and free me from this place.

It seems insane to be defeated by this despair.

Even worse is the belief they care!

It gets really stressful sitting in a cell all day, knowing that unless people on the outside help, the system will win. I have gotten a couple of letters from people who have read these articles. They all say the same thing: "I know you must have tons of support and help. I am sure you get flooded with mail." This leaves me confused. I can't figure out where the tons of support are! I have only gotten like eight people who wrote me since I started these articles. A few have sent supportive emails.

I know that some may choose not to write due to me being married and so forth. That is not where the despair comes from. The despair comes from me needing help and not being able to get it. I have a handful of people who are trying their best to do all they can for me. It gets depressing not being able to get all the help I need. I am so used to doing stuff myself. Now I have to depend on others. Well, that gets stressful.

I don't know; hopefully, things will fall into place.

Anyway, onto other events. On the eleventh of August, I had a minister visit. A lady from Dallas, TX, comes to see me about once a month. She sees a few others as well.

Anyway, Robert Shields was out there. I saw his mother walking around. Well, when my visit was over and I was getting escorted out of the visit, I had to walk by his visitation cage. I just said, "What's up, Shields," and kept walking. Well, when I got outside of the visitation building, it dawned on me that I didn't stop to talk to him. I had a lot of stuff on my mind, and the guards were talking to me about something. I wasn't paying attention! I still regret not stopping to say something to him. I had intended to!

I can only blame it on the ADHD. Because from the time the guards got me out of the cage I was in to his cage, I had my mind on something else! ☹

Maybe it was a way to cope and avoid the reality of his situation. Plus, his mother was there. Ever since Richard was executed, I do not like to see the family members. Seeing Richard's daughter, Ricki Marie, used to be hard. Plus, after reading all that his mother, Irene, wrote, it made me not want to see anyone's family!

My mother and I used to be real close. We have no communication now. Well, I got a card from her on my birthday! The only family member I have any contact with is my baby sister. That is far and few between.

See, my mother was real close to my grandfather. He passed away in September of 2004. It was a long, drawn-out ordeal. At one point, my grandfather was in ICU, and then my stepfather had a heart attack. So my mom had a son on death row, her husband, and her father in intensive care! A lot of stress on anybody.

Well, a couple of months later, my grandfather passed away. Since then, my mother and aunt have drifted away. They went through the death of my grandfather day by day. It is just like going through this day by day. So I guess they figured it would be easiest to just lay low on my situation.

I don't know what to think about it really, but I understand. I don't respect it, though, because they know I didn't do this crime, yet they...

So I have to depend on people I don't even know. I haven't even seen before to help me save my life. That is some stressful shit. Plus, not knowing what's going on except through letters, emails, and visits—and the time it takes to get those—adds to the stress.

Don't get me wrong. I do appreciate very much all the help I get. It's help needed to save my life. I tend to compare people to myself. When I believe in something, I do everything I can to support that belief.

Just as I believe in being treated a certain way, if someone treats me in a manner that I don't want to be treated, I end up on Level 2. Oh well! I am on Level 3 with pride that I stand up for what I believe in.

People say they are against injustice and the death penalty, yet they do nothing to stop it or prevent injustice.

"The true measure of a man is not where he stands in moments of comfort and convenience, but where he stands in times of challenge and controversy." – Martin Luther King

Action produces a reaction. Without action, there can be no results. Well, there will be a result, but not a good one. If people don't stand up and act as friction against this machine, it will keep on rolling along and picking up speed as it crushes those placed in its path.

Who knows? Events might take a turn for the positive. I still do not even have a lawyer! The courts haven't informed me of anything. I might get a letter from the court tomorrow.

Back to Robert Shields. I tried to get a visit set up for the 23rd so I could be out there to speak to him before he gets executed! Unfortunately, I was unable to. My comrade, Steven Woods, tried to as well. He was unable to.

I haven't done much lately to disrupt the system. I started a fire; that was it. I was trying to get an inmate-to-inmate legal visit with an associate to help him on his federal writ to make sure all important issues were filed by his lawyer. The captain denied it and indicated I was a threat to the security of the institution. ☺ Ha! I like that.

I have been quiet, so I can't wait to see what he has to say when I get loud!

I am going to go ahead and bring this to an end. I just wanted to drop off an article. A better one will follow up.

Stand Tall, Fade All, Never Fall

Use the Pain to Fuel the Fire

Unity is the Key to Success

Clinton Young

#999447

Polunsky Unit

3872 FM 350 S.

Livingston, TX 77351

Uncensored, August 20 to August 26, 2005

Greetings, everyone.

Welcome back to another chaotic walk through a week at the Texas Death Camp, starring your host Clinton Young, with a guest appearance by Steven Woods, my partner in chaos (his Mohawk included!). Well, this week has been fairly interesting. Starting on the 18th of August, 2005, I was awakened by a sergeant instructing all Level Three prisoners to pack up all personal commissary-bought clothes, which include boxers, t-shirts, gym shorts, socks, and tennis shoes.

Now, the death row plan, which governs how we are treated, states that Level Three prisoners can have these items unless put on property restriction for a disciplinary case. Well, Warden Hirsch, who is the death row warden, decided he is not bound by the rules and guidelines of T.D.C.J. Steven and I decided that if the warden breaks the rules, then there are NO RULES. So we are not bound by the rules of T.D.C.J. either. If those of the law are above the law, then there is NO LAW. Ya dig?

Warden Hirsch just took it upon himself to take everyone's clothes. The only clothing item we can buy on Level Three is gym shorts during the summertime, so we can wear them to recreation. We are allowed to have them by federal guidelines that govern state prisons, the same guidelines that allow us certain hygiene products and correspondence supplies. It is our (death row prisoners') right.

Well, Steven and I informed the rank that we would not be giving up our property because we are allowed to have it. If they want it, they will have to come and take it. So we began to prepare for the use of force (pepper spray or tear gas, whichever they decided to use, and a five-man cell extraction team). We put on our homemade gas masks and all that good stuff. We waited for six hours, until shift change at 6:00 PM, for the team to show up. They never showed up! This was aggravating because I sleep during the day. Instead of being asleep, I was pacing my floor waiting to get pepper-sprayed and fight five guards in riot gear just to defend against the theft of my clothes!

They are trying to take them without my permission, and according to their guidelines, I am allowed to have them. I look at it as if they are stealing my clothes. They never showed up, so I went to sleep.

The next day, on the 19th, I went to recreation in my section's dayroom. I had my shoes and gym shorts on. Smile. I walked around proud that "I" was the only Level Three with commissary shoes! I could have kept my stuff longer, but I said to hell with it and jacked the dayroom and made them come take my clothes! (Oh yeah, "jack the dayroom" means to refuse to leave the dayroom.) Needless to say, I surprised the rank!

While I was in the dayroom, pest control came around to spray people's cells for bugs. We can choose to let them do it or not. When they got to Steven's cell, he said he wanted them to spray it. The guards cuffed him and opened his door; he stepped out and then sat down on the floor and refused to walk back into his cell. They had to carry him back into his cell. Smile. He will write his own account of that incident.

After they finished with Steven, they went to get a team to remove me from the dayroom. The team showed up, and the sergeant was armed with a .37mm grenade launcher. I was ordered to strip out of my clothes and exit the dayroom. This happened several more times as I continued refusing to comply.

Next, the sergeant locked and loaded the CS gas grenade, aimed, and fired. BOOM! CS gas was everywhere. The second time they went to shoot a grenade, the damn thing didn't work. Smile! They quickly got another one ready, and it worked! Frown!

After the second grenade, they popped open the dayroom gate, and in came the team. I made contact with the shield and the first man on the team. BOOM, BANG, BAM!!! We all wrestled for a short time, and they got me down. After I was cuffed, they stole my shoes off my feet. They cut my clothes off—damn perverts! Instead of walking to my cell, I made them pick me up and carry me. I told the sergeant, "Since you cut my clothes off of me, you all are going to have to carry me to my cell." So they picked my naked ass up and carried me to my cell. Smile.

The next day, Steven and I started a fire. We actually started it right in front of the fire exit door! Smile! It was a big one and burned really hot because of the air draft that comes under the door from the hallway. The building is all steel and concrete, so it isn't like we can burn the building down. However, we did catch the paint on the door on fire! The paint is part of the building, so as we see it, we "officially" caught the building on fire! Smile! A first! The door got so hot that the metal started making popping noises and was still hot two hours later. Needless to say, I am quite proud of that one!

Earlier that day, Steven again laid down on the floor and made them carry him back to his cell. They have to use a camera to record it because any time an officer touches us outside of medical assistance, it is considered a use of force. Steven will also write about that event.

Aug. 26, 2005-

I am feeling much better this week than I was last week. I have moments here and there. The stress just becomes too much at times. The article I wrote last week was written when

I was in a bad mood. I have all kinds of stuff that shows I was wrongfully convicted and sentenced to death, yet I can't seem to get the help needed. It does get frustrating!

We all sit in these cells all day. That is a lot of time focusing on ourselves. At times, I only think about how events affect me, and I also tend to gauge people on a level with myself. Not many can live up to that, because not everyone sees the world as I do. In here, Richard did, Steven does, and a few select others do. It actually gets to the point that I want to cuss people out around here. I just feel like yelling, "You stupid coward, why don't you stand up for yourself?" to some of the guys in here.

The machine is already taking our lives—why let them have more? I know that society has its warriors, educators, and so forth. If everyone was a warrior, then society would fall under the weight of chaos. Steven and I were the only ones who stood up and protected our clothes from being taken. I am not mad at the others because that makes Steven and me stand out. I like to be unique, and so does my comrade Steven! That is why he has his hair cut in a Mohawk—the only one on death row. Smile!

I use my warrior spirit in positive ways. Well, I actually consider all my actions positive, even if others see them as negative. My truth is not always going to be the next man's truth. Although I do understand what is socially accepted as positive and negative, I focus my warrior spirit in socially acceptable positive ways as well, such as the fight against the death penalty. Not many have the drive that I do, and that is what is upsetting.

On another note, I got a letter from my mother. It seems that we might be on a productive path toward developing a positive relationship again. I was thinking that maybe I am too hard on her. She has been through some hell, with plenty from me! Like the song goes, "I turned out to be the only hell my Momma ever raised." To those who don't know, that is from an old country song. Smile. My mom tried to do all she could do for me. I gained and learned a lot from her. Being raised by a strong-minded, independent woman has its benefits, especially when it comes to all the lovely ladies. Smile.

On the topic of lovely ladies, a lot of people who write always ask what I miss most. I would have to say the feeling of holding a lovely lady in my arms, more so one that I have feelings for. I never felt comfortable around other guys because of all that has happened between my stepfather and father. True enough, my stepfather is a much better person than my biological father; however, we did have our moments. Anyway, I never felt close or comfortable around other guys. But my mother was always my safe haven, so I have always felt comfortable and at ease with women. I was extremely close with my ex-fiancée. She was the one I was with when I got arrested on this case. Her uncle was also the first victim in the case that got me on death row. (She knows I didn't do it, and that is all that matters to me!)

Well, I have to take something back. There were two guys in the free world that I had a tight bond with—one was my grandfather, and the other was an associate of mine whom I spent a lot of time with and even shared a house with. When someone would ask one of us about the other, it was always "Where is your brother?" Well, he got caught up in a mess and got charged with murder. He didn't do it—a guy he was with did it. He was with two brothers when the crime happened. Well, he testified against one of them for the prosecution.

Seeing that the same thing happened to me, I don't have much love for a snitch. So now this dude means nothing to me. In my eyes, he is complete trash! Some people want to be big and tough when they are getting away with stuff, but as soon as they get caught, they roll over. One of the co-defendants in my case cried when he got caught. When I saw him crying on his video statement, I said, "Why is he crying now? He wasn't crying when he was shooting people in the head. He was a Billy the Kid badass then." He wasn't confessing on tape, so he was not crying out of remorse! He was crying out of fear of what was going to happen to him. Nothing bad really did happen to him. He testified for the prosecution and only got a 15-year sentence for robbery, even after admitting on the stand in my trial that he shot the first victim.

Well, he did say I held him hostage. You know the biggest flaw in the story that I held him hostage? It was the fact that he had a loaded pistol! He helped the prosecution; I didn't. He goes home in somewhere between 2-5 years, maybe 10 at the most! I wait to die. The cops told me when I first got arrested that I was going to get the death penalty. Well, the chief's exact words were, "You will get strapped to a gurney with a needle in your arm, and you will die unless you help us." I just gave a nervous smile and said, "I want a lawyer." I thought at the time he was just trying to scare me. Well, someone give the man a trophy because he is a prophet! I never thought I would actually get convicted. I guess I was too naïve.

Anyway, back to the home front. My baby sister just turned 15 on the 7th of August. Damn, how the years fly by. I still remember when she was in diapers and would stand up on her toes and start dancing to Billy Ray Cyrus' "Achy Breaky Heart." Smile! Ha! Ha! She would stand on her toes when she danced. That was back in 1991 or early 1992. Sadly though, for a third of her life, I have been locked up.

Well, on to other events. For the record, for those who do not know, c/s means "change subject," and CS gas is a type of chemical agent used to gain control and disperse riots. Well, guess what? I am sure most can remember one of the past articles I wrote about the government of Texas trying to make ex-district attorneys, also known as prosecutors, automatically qualify as death penalty lawyers. Well, my lawyer dropped his case.

I'll be damned—I should have kept my mouth closed. The judge appointed a lawyer from near Midland, Texas, which is where I was tried, convicted, and sentenced to death. This lawyer was a prosecutor for eight years. He, of course, knows all the puppets in my case, prosecutors included. I didn't even know he was my lawyer. He has not written to me. The judge did not let me know or anything. I found out by writing my direct appeal lawyer, asking him the status of my first appeal. It has not been ruled on yet. Well, he wrote me back and told me about my new prosecutor who will act as my lawyer!

Then a couple of days later, I get a letter from my old state habeas corpus attorney—the one who dropped my case. He informed me that he was not aware of who my new attorney was! So basically, the only people who know who my new lawyer is are the judge, prosecutors, and my direct appeal lawyer. The court didn't bother to inform anyone else! These assholes are trying all they can to kill me.

Well, now I have to write the Court of Criminal Appeals to let them know that I haven't been informed of my new lawyer. I was told who it was, but not properly informed by the courts. That way, I can object and protest this new pawn for the prosecution. So if I ever get a good lawyer to represent me in the next phase of my appeal, he will have plenty to raise hell about.

I am going to bring this to a close so I can get started on my other letters. I've got to work even harder now. Effort is the path to progress. Unity is the key to success. Use the pain to fuel the fire.

Stand tall, fade all, never fall.

Clinton Young

#999447

Polunsky Unit

3872 FM 350 S.

Livingston, TX 77351

Uncensored, August 27, 2005

Welcome to another adventure on the Polunsky Unit death camp. I am feeling a little sore right now. Steven and I refused to leave the outside recreation area, which is basically a big box with steel bars going through the middle, with steel bars for a roof to let sunlight in. We can see and talk to each other, but we are divided by the bars. We refused to exit the recreation area in protest of having to be in extreme heat while wearing state-issued jumpsuits.

See, Warden Hirsh took all of our commissary-bought clothes, including gym shorts, which we wear to recreation. So we had to suffer in the heat due to not having any shorts. Well, here comes the rank with the camera woman. They dealt with Steven first. Surprisingly, they sprayed him with LA-10 crowd control pepper spray. The furthest point from the door to the recreation yard is only about 20 feet, so the pepper spray covered him. They only hit him with a 2-second burst. They gave their orders, and five minutes later threw in a smoke tear gas grenade. It bounced across the recreation yard and — boom! — smoke went everywhere. It then started spinning and spraying tear gas everywhere. It was a light blue smoke. For a moment, Steven disappeared in a cloud of smoke, kind of like those magicians do.

Well, five minutes later, in comes the team. They got Steven down, cut off all his clothes, and carried him back to his cell. He will write about it. The team and rank all then left the pod.

I heard my fellow Level 3 comrade Lizerd yell that they were going to start over, meaning they had to get another use-of-force video tape and record the team suiting up and coming back to the pod. I walked around for a couple of minutes, and all of a sudden, I heard people kicking on the door, letting me know the team was coming back. One side of the recreation yard has a big wall of windows so the control picket and officers can see the people on the yard. Plus, there is a big exhaust vent on the wall above the door to the recreation area. That's how I could hear Lizerd and everyone letting me know they were coming back.

Here comes the rank giving me the orders to submit. HA—yeah, right! I saw they were about to spray me with the LA-10 pepper spray, so I stood in front of the door as far away as possible. That way, when they sprayed me, it would all be on one side of the recreation yard. They sprayed me; I turned my back, and when they stopped, I walked to the other side that I wasn't going to fight them on.

Well, five minutes passed, and in comes the grenade. Bounce, bounce, boom! Smoke went everywhere, and tear gas kept spraying out. I ran over to the grenade and kicked it as far away from me as I could. I walked around for a little bit. The sergeant kept trying to get me to submit to hand restraints. Well, after five minutes, I heard the sergeant say to the camera, "Chemical agents appear to have no effect on the offender, so at this time additional chemical agents will be utilized."

I'll be damned — they threw another grenade at me. Bounce, bounce, roll a little, and boom! I was standing right beside it when it blew up. The grenade itself doesn't blow up; it just blows the top off. It is a handheld grenade. Well, they had the team ready to come in when they threw the second grenade. It shot tear gas everywhere, and here comes the team.

I charged the shield. I hit the shield and pushed it up and to the side. I lost traction and fell but was back up in a blink of an eye. I grabbed a team member, and the fight was on. It all started about 10 feet from the windows and ended up with my head slamming into the window. I had a helmet in my hand. I yanked it off and yanked and broke off the officer's gas mask as well. The grenade was still shooting tear gas, so he got it bad! I then broke another officer's gas mask.

By then, they had me in a position where I could not fight back, so I let them put my hands behind my back and handcuff me. I told them, "All right, I am down," and they pulled my homemade gas mask off. Remember now, the grenade was still smoking! I could not breathe. Tears started pouring out of my eyes, and my nose was pouring mucus. The mucus kept building up in my throat, so I was choking and had to keep spitting it out. I was gasping for air like a fish out of water. My body kept trying to ball up — I guess from lack of oxygen. They cut all my clothes off me.

I yelled out, "I can't breathe." At that time, I could because I had adjusted to the gas. But it was still burning my throat, so I was trying to get them to take me off the yard quicker. It didn't work. They still cut my clothes off on the yard. They did it really fast, though, as I could hear an officer choking. The officer whose mask and helmet I ripped off ran off the recreation yard choking and coughing. The other one with the broken mask stayed on the yard. They were moving fast for his sake, not mine.

I then made them carry me back to my cell. I am housed on F section, which is the section where the door to the outside recreation yard is. There are two outside recreation yards to a pod — one for A-C section and one for D-F section. The pod is shaped like an octagon. I can see D-section while on the yard. The floor of the recreation yard is concrete.

A-C section is divided from D-F section by a wall running through the middle. Half of the control picket is on one side, and half is on the other. There are crossover doors for access to both sides. It is hard to explain how it is built.

Anyway, I got back in my cell. They took the restraints off me and backed out of my cell. I then got up and gave the handcuffs back to them out of the food slot.

A couple of hours later, I went to sleep and woke up for chow, on fire! It was hot outside, so I was sweating. Well, that caused the pores in my skin to open, and the gas reacts with sweat to cause a burning sensation. I fell asleep on my side, on top of my arm. So the body heat opened my pores up, and it felt worse than when I got gassed! O-well, it's all a part of it. I am okay now. Just anytime I take a deep breath, I start coughing.

Now, onto other topics. I want to clear something up. In, I believe, my last article, I wrote that I felt all my actions were positive. By that, I meant all my actions in the struggle against the system. I do not feel that every action I have taken in my life was positive. I regret a lot of things I have done and didn't do. Though in the struggle against the system, I feel that none of my actions are negative. I just wanted to clear that up, as I assumed some might take what I wrote the wrong way.

Now that all of that is out of the way, I want to get into something personal. I have been going through a lot lately: wife, family, and the system. Plus, I have already been through a lot—friends killed by the state, neighbors killing themselves, and so on and so on. Over time, it has taken its toll. I find myself losing control of my emotions and becoming consumed with anger and stress. I am even starting to push away those trying to help me. The last time I lost control and allowed something to control me, I was with two idiots who did something stupid, and I ended up on death row. For those that do not know, I am referring to my past drug addiction and case.

Plus, I am becoming self-absorbed. I mean, I am starting to think only about myself. One of the main personality traits I was known for prior to coming to death row was being compassionate. That trait is slowly fading away. These cells are meant to break people down mentally. Plus, spending so much time by myself makes it easy to focus only on myself.

So I am going to take a break from writing for a couple of weeks to gather my thoughts. I need to climb my own personal mountain. That way, I can redirect and focus my thoughts and feelings before this place makes me lose my mind. I posted a message on my e-group to those I write to and the ones on there that I do not even know that I am not doing any writing at all. All my friends and pen-pals can still write me. I will respond when I come down off my mountain.

Thinking about the future all the time gets to be too much and starts to eat a person up. I used to only focus on the present, and that is what kept my mind clear. So I got to get back on that path. Fighting the battle against the death penalty needs to be done with love and purpose—love and dedication to the belief that the death penalty is wrong.

I do suggest two books for people to read. One is Tuesdays with Morrie by Mitch Albom; the other is The Alchemist by Paulo Coelho. Read them in that order. Both are small books with a large message. I strongly suggest everyone read those books, especially Irene and Robert Shields' mother. Anyone reading this who has a loved one on death row—Tuesdays with Morrie is a must-read.

I am now starting to read both parts of The Celestine Prophecy by James Redfield. As everyone is most likely aware, Robert Shields was executed. Steven and I lit a big fire the night he was executed in protest of his execution. Two days later, I went to recreation in the section dayroom, and another associate sent me a message that Shields sends his love and respect. Evidently, he was there at visitation with Shields before he left.

I tried my damnedest to get out to visitation on the 23rd. I just couldn't get a visit set up. I regret not stopping to speak with him the last time I was at visitation. I know he expected me to. Hell, if I did and the officer complained, I would have just sat down right in front of his visitation cage! When Patrick Knight gave me Shields' message, it was on the 24th. I just realized that. I thought it had been longer.

Anyway, it had more of an effect on me because I got the message after Robert was killed. It had a "message from the grave" type of effect on me. To Robert Shields' mother, if she is reading this: your son was well-liked and respected. I wish I could have gotten to know him better. Though honestly, part of me is glad I didn't know him better. It is easier that way—for me, at least. Because if I had known him better, it would have been harder to see him go. Good people sometimes make bad choices. It is a shame that one choice affected a good man's life, as well as those who love him.

I admire your strength in standing by your son. The same with Richard's mother. Robert helped people out whenever he could. He was the first person Steven talked to. He got Steven out of his cell and active. Steven used to be a hermit and could never leave his cell. Now I can't get him to stop for nothing.

The first time I met Robert was at visitation. We were talking about a mutual friend, Jasen Busby, who has since been executed as well. I was on F-Pod Level 3, which means I couldn't have any commissary. We didn't even know each other, but Robert still got some commissary food to me. To some, that might not mean much, but to me, it spoke a lot about the type of person Robert was—a good man in a bad place.

If you find the time, you should read the book I mentioned. I will warn all who read Tuesdays with Morrie: it had me wiping my eyes.

I forgot to mention the reason that they used two tear gas grenades on me might have been due to me running around playing basketball. I think that upset them. I actually got hit with three grenades—the one they threw at Steven and the two they threw at me. Ladies and gentlemen, that is a lot of tear gas!

To address a few people: Karen, I sent you a letter. Yes, I'll help you with your project, even while on my mountain. Flavia, I got your letter and responded. I will be sending you an additional letter as well. To everyone else, you all will receive word in the future. I just got to take a mental vacation.

I also wanted to ask the readers of Uncensored for a favor. Suzanne provides a loud voice from death row, pen-pal advertisement, and a whole bunch of other stuff. I would ask you, the readers, if you could help Suzanne with some small donations to help cover the cost associated with running Uncensored, 1prison.com, and 1prison.net. I am asking this on my own. I look at it like this: people pay for newspapers and magazines. Uncensored is free, but I know I am more interesting than any newspaper. HAHA!

Seriously though, I just wanted to see if you could help Suzanne out a little bit with the cost of stamps, ink, internet fees, and so forth. NONE of it would be for me. I appreciate any and all help.

O-yeah, if anyone is wondering why my guest Steven didn't post any articles last time, that is because I forgot to mail it out. It will get sent this time.

Use the pain to fuel the fire. Focus on the goal. Walk in faith of success.

Veni, Vidi, Vici,

Clinton Young

#999447

Polunsky Unit

3872 FM 350 S.

Livingston, TX 77351

Uncensored, December 02, 2005

Well, it has been a while since I wrote an article. Suzanne was MIA for a short period due to an accident in the family. So I capitalized on her absence in order to get my thoughts together some more. Of course, the murder machine did not slow down any. I believe the last execution I wrote about was Ron Howard. Several more have taken place. I did not know any of those executed. To be honest, I never even saw any of them before! Well, no, I did see one before, Shannon Thomas. Hell, I never even heard of the others. Just goes to show how isolated we really are! I have been on every pod on the row. There are people here who have been Level 1 since death row moved to this Unit, and they haven't been on more than three different pods. (There are six pods: A-F).

Several more executions are scheduled into the New Year. One of them is Jaime Elizalde. He is the first guy I met here. He was in the cell next to me. We spent a lot of time talking. Through time and conversation, my respect for him grew. While looking at his name on the "Pending Execution" roster, I started to think back to my first day here and all that has happened in the past 32 months I have been here. Damn, it has been that long?! Almost three years. It has been a roller coaster ride, that is for sure.

On November 2, 2004, Deon Tumblin, my neighbor, hung himself. On February 4, I believe, Christopher Britton hung himself. Both on E Pod. One in 58 cell, the other in 59 cell. You want to know something else that is crazy? Another guy killed himself in 60 cell! But they brought him back to life. He had flatlined though, meaning he was officially dead, but they were able to bring him back. 58, 59, and 60 cell are all right beside each other! All were on Level 2.

E Pod now houses death row Level 2 and Level 3. F Pod is now for Administrative Segregation of General Population inmates (non-death row). Well, here it is a year later, I am on Level 2 on E Pod. On November 2, 2005, I was on Level 3. I got woken up because of an officer yelling out, "Where's Britton?" I sat up in my bunk and said, "Who did you just say?" He replied, "Chad Britton, where is he at?" My response: "Hell if I know, but if you're gonna find him, you're gonna need a shovel. The dude killed himself! He killed himself in February of this year, over in 59 cell!" The officer said, "Well, he has a letter right here and it has 59 cell on it." He showed me the letter in his hand. I just said, "That's a damn shame!"

Now think about this. He killed himself nine months prior, and they still sent a letter to the cell he killed himself in! Well, at least we know the mailroom is passing out all the mail! What freaked me out was that this happened on November 2, exactly one year from when Deon Tumblin killed himself. I just thought that was kind of weird.

Anyway, I am sitting here looking at the "Offenders No Longer on Death Row" list. It was printed out in May 2004, so it is an old list. You can see it at the TDCJ site at (http://www.tdcj.state.tx.us/). You can also see "Final Statements" of executed offenders. It is under the title "Executed Offenders."

Well, going over the list of those no longer on Death Row, 77 people on the list got off death row by winning their appeal and showing they were wrongfully convicted of Capital Murder. Fifteen of those 77 won acquittals on new trials and/or charges that were altogether dismissed. So by May 2004, 15 innocent men had been released from the clutches of death! Fifteen innocent men put away to die for crimes they did not commit. How many didn't get away?

Really, all 77 were innocent of Capital Murder! Murder and Capital Murder are different. Murder only carries 5 years to 99 years or a life sentence with parole eligibility after 40 years. So all 77 were wrongfully sentenced to die. 77 is a lot of people since the death penalty was reinstated in 1976. Only three states have killed more than Texas—355!

So Texas has released more innocent men from death row than other states have killed in 30 years! Hell, some states' entire death row population is in the single digits. This brings me to an article that was in the Houston Chronicle (newspaper for Houston, TX) recently. Everyone, please go to http://www.chron.com/disp/story.mpl/metropolitan/3474407.html), and you will see the story titled "CANTU CASE: DEATH AND DOUBT—Executed man's co-defendant says years of guilt have led him to try to clear his friend's name."

It is an article about an innocent man who was killed by the State of Texas. Even one of the victims states that Ruben Cantu was not even at the crime scene. A guy who was there and one of the victims said he was innocent. So one comes to light. How many others are still in the dark? Cameron Willingham, Gary Graham, so on and so on.

This really has an emotional impact on me, seeing how I am currently in a battle to show that I did not kill anyone, was wrongfully convicted, and did not receive a fair trial. Some more good news has come to light in my case. My trial attorney gave an affidavit (sworn statement) that he made an error in my trial.

Now the error that the statement applies to is he didn't object to the prosecutor's unethical tactic and prejudicial act during trial. The prosecutor was waving a book with the title "Serial Killer" in big bold red letters in front of the jury. There were two victims in the case. So the prosecutor waving that book in front of them was his way of saying, "Hey, you all need to convict and kill him because he's a serial killer!" This book was waved in front of the jury during both portions of my trial.

But that didn't hold up, as it didn't make sense nor apply to the case. Ted Bundy is a serial killer! Anyway, this statement reflects a BIGGER picture—the unprofessional tactics used by the prosecutors to do whatever needed to be done to get a conviction and death sentence.

It also shows the mistakes made by my trial lawyers. Don't get me wrong, I personally liked both of my trial lawyers! I still do. They are only human, thus prone to error. I still write to one of my trial lawyers off and on.

The prosecutor's misconduct was all calculated and intentional, as they wanted the conviction and death sentence. The affidavit I mentioned will be placed on the legal defense organization, SAIL, website at http://www.saveaninnocentlife.com).

Well, onto other issues. I would like to get into something that was brought to my attention. I often ask people around here to ask their friends and pen pals what they think about these articles. I, as well, ask my own friends and supporters. I have had about three or four tell me that these articles seem to be all about me.

I re-read a lot of the articles. I don't see it like that. Then again, I know my reasons. I write about my life on death row in Texas. How can I write about what the next man is going through? That is not possible! I write about the errors of my case. If I write about others' cases, then the prosecutor could try to use my words against them. How would that look?

Plus, it is disrespectful for me to discuss someone's case and/or life without their permission! If someone is willing to write about it, I encourage them to write an article, so long as it is done with honesty and integrity. A lot of people will not write or talk about their case.

Some are paranoid that someone might use their words against them. Others because their lawyers instructed them not to. Then there are a few that will, but I don't feel confident that they will be honest. So I don't ask them to.

It is easy to focus on myself, as I do live in a single-man cell, by myself, for 23 hours a day. I do have to take a shower alone. I do have to go to recreation alone. So 24 hours a day, 7 days a week, I am physically alone.

I can talk to others, but while in my cell, I can't even see them! Only when a person goes to the dayroom can they see every cell on the section. We are so isolated that I have been on every pod in the almost three years I have been here, yet I still have never even seen or heard of a majority of those executed this year or waiting to be executed!

The only ones I have actually met who have been executed this year are James Porter, Alex Martinez, Lonnie Pursley, Richard Cartwright, Ron Howard, and Robert Shields at visitation.

I did a documentary with Ron Howard, which is how I met him. I can't remember if I knew anyone else executed this year.

I have only met one of the people scheduled to die, and that is Jaime Elizalde. When I say we are isolated, I mean we are isolated! I do have a few others lined out to post an article or two in the future.

Well, onto the rest of the story.

1,000! That is the number of people executed in the United States of America. Home of the free. A land of liberty. A land of liberty with over 2 million people locked up! 18% of which are serving life sentences!

That doesn't include the ones with "year-titled" sentences such as 99 years or 150 years and so forth. 1,000 people executed in 29 years. That is like an average of one execution every 10 days. 355 of them swiftly slaughtered by Texas.

1,000 people killed! Thirty-eight states have the death penalty. Texas has over a third of the total number of people killed. On the list of offenders no longer on Death Row that I have for Texas, 77 have been released from Death Row for being completely innocent to being innocent of Capital Murder.

With those numbers and the Ruben Cantu case, I am willing to say that most likely at least 10 to 15 innocent men have been killed. No telling how many were killed that should not have been charged with Capital Murder!

That is why the death penalty needs to end, which it doesn't appear will end anytime soon. 1,000 just doesn't seem enough to some politicians.

Especially Senator Jon Kyl, R-Arizona, and Rep. Dan Lundgren, R-California, who are the original sponsors of the Streamlined Procedures Act of 2005, which can be read at http://www.uscourts.gov/rules/legislation109.pdf.

If the bill would have gone into effect as it was first introduced, the US would have hit 2,000 executions in a quarter of the time it took to hit 1,000. Plus, it would have greatly harmed non-death penalty cases.

It would have all but totally stripped the Federal Appeals Process. Some changes have been made to it. About the same as painting a rabid pit bull's toenails pink to make it look pretty!

When the Federal Judges themselves complain about the bill, which affects their courts, you know it isn't anything nice.

More and more cases are coming to light that have shown wrongful prosecution and execution. Two or three times a month, I see in the newspaper about someone getting released from prison because of new evidence and/or DNA evidence finally tested that showed a person was innocent.

Yet they are trying harder and harder to kill us faster and make it harder for a person to prove they are innocent.

It goes to show that the government does not care about its citizens. It only cares about its money. Several changes have been made since the early 90s to speed up the death penalty to so-called "save" taxpayers money. Yet, have taxes gone down?

More pending.

Clinton Young

#999447

Polunsky Unit

3872 FM 350 S.

Livingston, TX 77351

Loud & Clear, May 18, 2006

Greetings!

I was going to wait a few more days before writing an article, but I was reading the newspaper and came across an article that incited me to write. In USA Today on May 16th, there was an article about China and the death penalty. China is known for executing more people than any other country—actually, more than all other countries combined! China has taken steps to increase the rights and judicial oversight of people facing execution—a step toward progress!

Several weeks ago, the Philippines eliminated the death penalty. The president of the Philippines stated that she would commute all future death sentences, sparing some 1,200 people from death. China—progress. Philippines—progress. America—?

America continues to slaughter dozens of people a year, including innocent people ensnared in the corrupt so-called justice system. Many reports have been printed about Cameron Todd Willingham's execution. Gov. Perry knew that when he refused to halt Mr. Willingham's execution, he was doing so based on bad science. Interestingly, Ernest Willis was released from death row and is free now as you read this. Cameron Willingham and Ernest Willis were both convicted using the same faulty science. The difference? Lawyers! Ernest Willis had a better legal team.

Mr. Willingham had a very controversial case that might have discouraged some from taking it on. He was accused of killing his three children by setting fire to their house. So, four innocent people died in that case.

There has been much attention brought to the fact that the manner in which we are executed in Texas and other states is cruel and unusual. I think media reports should regularly mention that the veterinary association refuses to put animals to sleep using the same chemicals used to execute humans! It is not okay to kill a dog with these chemicals, but it is okay to kill a human being.

The death penalty is slowly gaining more scrutiny. In the past year, reports have circulated about two innocent men being executed in Texas: Cameron Willingham and Ruben Cantu. In Cantu's case, the only living victim and a participant in the crime stated that the man executed was not responsible! The prosecution used its power to threaten charges against the victim and other participants, effectively silencing them! Will justice ever come for Ruben Cantu? Only time will tell.

I have recently sent a request to the judge overseeing my case for access to the vehicle involved in the crime, so that unperformed testing can be done. Two shell casings were found inside the car. The prosecutors in my case told the jury that this was proof I shot the victim while inside the car. Ballistics testing recently showed that I could not have been the shooter. The expert stated in the report that the car could be obtained and easily tested.

The shell casings came from shots fired into the car's dashboard. If the dashboard were removed and the bullets recovered, they could be tested to match the firearm, proving the shell casings did not come from when the victim was shot but from when the dashboard was shot later.

I am still waiting to see if the judge approves or denies my request. If he approves it, I will have to cover the cost of the tests—but I know 100% that the findings will support my claims! Just as the ballistics testing already has, supporting exactly what I have been saying for five years!

I have tried to get five different lawyers to test this evidence. I had to raise the issue myself. If I had not written to the courts with my concerns and complaints, I would have been procedurally barred from presenting this scientific evidence that supports my innocence. I will have a long and difficult legal battle over the next few years due to errors made by my lawyers.

The main problem is that part of the state appeal process has no constitutional protection. This means a lawyer could file no appeal, and the only person affected would be the condemned inmate. Maybe one day, the courts will catch up with the times. They want to shorten our appeals to save money. I guess they never considered all the time and money that would be saved if they just stopped the death penalty altogether.

I read an article a couple of weeks ago about a death row inmate here who was granted DNA testing. The prosecutor in the case stated that they were willing to allow the testing because they were confident it would support the verdict. But if for some reason it doesn't, the inmate should be taken off death row, as "justice is not killing an innocent man." I found that very interesting—especially coming from a Texas prosecutor.

I wonder if I could get the prosecutors to allow all the testing in my case. I doubt it.

S.A.I.L. was established to bring more attention to the judicial system and the death penalty. It is made up of people who are sincere and want to make a difference. With each new member, its voice will grow louder and louder.

I was asked how Loud & Clear is associated with S.A.I.L. Loud & Clear was originally going to be a printed and mailed newsletter for S.A.I.L., but the choice was made to make it an online article instead, helping us reach more people—even those who do not speak English. So to answer the question, Loud & Clear is the newsletter of S.A.I.L.

It will address the cases of those sponsored by S.A.I.L., as well as other cases reported by media outlets. If any reader has a question about the appeal process, a case, or the rules governing the prison system (Texas only at this time), they can forward their question to my email address set up here on Loud & Clear. I will answer questions in the next article.

Anyone wanting to send a question directly may do so as well. I always enjoy mail. ☺

Progress is propelled by the force behind it! The more people who join the fight, the faster the goal will be achieved. Join the struggle. Unity is the key to success.

Until next time...

Veni – Vidi – Vici

With unity strengthened by solidarity, I remain,

Clinton Young #999447

Polunsky Unit

3872 F.M. 350 South

Livingston, TX 77351 USA

Loud & Clear, June 10 2006

"Nearly 7 Million under correctional supervision in the U.S.A.," read the headline of an article in the May 2006 Prison Legal News. Imagine, at year-end 2004, almost seven million people were in prison, on parole, or on probation in the United States. 2.3 million were in prison. Each year, the numbers go up. With these kinds of numbers, everyone knows someone in America who has been involved with the justice system. The higher the incarceration rate, the more likely the chance for an innocent person to be wrongfully imprisoned.

America is a nation that was formed with the basic rights of life, liberty, and the pursuit of happiness. These rights were classified as "God-given" by the founders of the U.S.A. Through time, more and more laws have been formed that slowly degrade these rights. Being one of the world's leaders in executions, it seems that this country is a system of contradictions. The nation's prison population is serving life sentences, with over 230,000 people expunged from society for the remainder of their lives. Some states offer the chance to make parole. In Texas, it is 30 years into the sentence (capital murder now carries life without parole).

Now, this offer is kind of like putting a new paint job on a wrecked car just to make it look good. On a positive note, death penalty sentences have declined each year. I believe this is due to the increased media attention on the death penalty. It has put the issue into the homes of Americans, prompting them to think about it and search their souls to figure out exactly where they stand on the issue. Most say, "If someone killed someone I loved, I would want that person to die." That is nothing but revenge. Aristotle, in the Nicomachean Ethics, stated, "Men regard it as their right to return evil for evil – and if they cannot, feel they have lost their liberty!"

Some argue that revenge is a product of humans' natural propensity for violence, tied in with having become passive by nature. Meaning, violence is in the heart, but due to social constraints, it is presented only in a justifiable manner, i.e., revenge. A study showed that 92 men and 85 women admitted to having fantasies of murder. The fine line is when a person decides to act out these fantasies.

Now, I am sure all can agree that the "psychology of a killer" is not black and white. There is a very large gray area. A man high on drugs who robs a store and, while doing so, panics, shoots, and kills the clerk cannot be put in the same "killer" category as a man who commits the most unfathomable crime of all—the raping and killing of a child! Yet in America, all are put in one trash bag and thrown away. No rehabilitation, no attempt to understand the problem to achieve a solution. Kill him, bag him up, and throw him in the ground.

Now, a man high on drugs is in an altered state of mind. True, he made the choice to do drugs, but what caused him to get to that point? People drive above the speed limit to get to where they want faster. People use drugs to get away from what they are running from, faster. Sooner or later, both get into a wreck. Both can lead to innocent lives being lost.

It isn't always what you look at, but how you look at it. It is all in how you perceive it, and since perception is reality, your reality is how you perceive a needed solution to a problem. In simple terms, if you open up a newspaper and see a story about a fellow human being committing a crime and you automatically think that person needs to die, then in reality, you are a killer.

On the basis of this thought, for every ten humans executed, there are 120 killers given amnesty by the state to kill. Twelve people sit on a jury, and twelve people order a fellow person to be killed. So, in reality, they are killers! Over 1,000 people have been executed in the United States since 1976. So, that means there are 12,000 killers walking the streets of America. Throw in the prosecutors, prison officials that help bring about the executions, and the executioners themselves, and the numbers grow. Something to think about: 12,000 people got to live out that fantasy under judicial immunity.

GOD BLESS AMERICA. Home of the brave and land of the freedom to kill.

In other news, I found out my current attorney doesn't want to take my case and my next appeal if I need one. He wants me to get someone who has more knowledge of the federal appeals process. So now I have to try to do just that. I have asked a couple. Both said no. It gets very stressful. Though I can't stop; submission is not a choice, so the fight goes on.

I have had some problems with people that claimed they cared and wanted to help, yet their actions show otherwise. Though, for the most part, S.A.I.L. is moving in the right direction. The membership is growing, with more and more people stepping up to help. Many have brought some very good ideas. So we continue to move towards progress. We have had some minor setbacks. This only lays a foundation for major comebacks.

Thanks to all who embrace the struggle. The fight goes on. Progress is propelled by the force behind it! The more people that join the fight, the faster the goal will be achieved. Join the struggle. Unity is the key to success.

Until next time,

Veni – Vidi – Vici

With unity strengthened by solidarity, I remain,

Clinton Young #999447

Polunsky Unit

3872 F.M. 350 South

Livingston, TX 77351 U.S.A.

Loud & Clear, June 28 2006

I was given some bad news a few days ago. My lawyer informed me that the judge will NOT allow the testimony of the ballistic expert into my appeal record. In short, the judge is trying to limit how I can use the evidence that shows I am innocent! The town where I was given the death sentence, Midland, Texas, is the hometown of George W. Bush. It is something that Midland is very proud of—they even had a large sign with the image of George W. Bush and the words, "Welcome to Midland, Texas, Home of the President." The majority there are just like him. So, the judge is going to try to please the public and help the prosecutors kill me.

Now I have to fight harder. I am currently obtaining my trial transcripts so I can help my lawyer and post portions of my trial on my website to show everyone just how I was wrongfully convicted. One of the future tests I would like conducted is a forensic test on the gloves worn by my co-defendant, David Page, who is serving 35 years for kidnapping. The gloves he wore have his DNA on the inside, and he admits they are his gloves. When the gloves were first tested, the expert for the state testified that the glove had "lead residue but could not identify the source." He told my lawyer during cross-examination that the pattern of the lead residue was consistent with the blowback pattern from a pistol being fired. A chemist should have analyzed the residue to determine the source. That is one of the many tests I want to have done.

A guy in jail with David Page testified that David Page told him, "They can't prove I done it, because I had gloves on." The recent ballistics reports show I could not have been the shooter and indicate the shooter had to be outside the car. David Page was the ONLY person standing outside the car and on the driver's side—the side where the victim was. During my trial, the forensic pathologist who conducted the autopsy on Doyle Douglas testified. When questioned by my lawyer, he stated that one of the gunshots was consistent with someone walking up to the car and shooting Mr. Douglas. The second murder in the case was clearly committed by David Page. He failed a lie detector test when questioned about the murder. By his own statements to the police after being arrested, only he could have been the shooter. Yet during trial, he changed his story. When my lawyer asked him why he changed his story, David Page pointed to the prosecutor's lead investigator and said, "Because he told me to." So, he admitted on the witness stand that the police had him change his story.

The judge is aware of ALL of these FACTS, yet he still does not want to admit the evidence that clearly shows I am innocent of murder! One day, the lawyers, prosecutors, and judges are going to have to embrace the integrity of their profession. They are supposed to uphold the law—not only when it pleases or benefits them, but in all matters.

Power takes a step back only in the face of more power, which is why I, along with others from around the world, built S.A.I.L.—to be a united voice, a united power. We are taking some positive steps toward progress. Progress is propelled by the force behind it, and with each new member who joins, the force grows stronger. Make a difference; join the struggle.

In other news—a lot has been before the courts lately about mental illness. I have noticed the courts are very quick to side with killing mentally ill inmates. Scott Panetti was given approval to die. The truly crazy aspect of his case is that the judge in his trial allowed Mr. Panetti to represent himself—with no lawyer. During his trial, Mr. Panetti tried to call the Pope, Jesus Christ, and assassinated American President John F. Kennedy to testify. He dressed in cowboy costumes and picked his jury by flipping a coin. The fact that the judge allowed a man who is clearly mentally unstable to represent himself in a case where the death penalty was being sought speaks volumes about the mindset of Texas.

It's an even bigger problem when the appeal courts also find no issue with this. Now they say he can die. The main reason the judge allowed Mr. Panetti to represent himself was to save money on trial costs by not having to pay lawyer fees. So, we kill the mentally ill. Judicial eugenics is what I call it. "He is no good for society, so let's kill him!"

In other news, the U.S. Supreme Court ruled to uphold the Kansas death penalty law. I was disappointed to read that, as I had seen another media article stating the Kansas law had been ruled against. The main issue is how juries deal with what is known as "future dangerousness." The jury essentially makes a "guess" and rules that they "think" the person will be dangerous in the future. So, they kill him. I didn't know we had so many psychics in the U.S.A. Must be something in the water.

I was asked why my lawyers brought up drug addiction, child abuse, and so forth if I was innocent. Lawyers do this after a person is convicted, during what is called "the punishment phase." The jury finds a person guilty either because they believe him to be or because they feel that person deserves to die. So, a lawyer will present evidence to show the jury that the person they just found guilty has had a troubled life, in an attempt to reduce the moral culpability of the defendant and save him from receiving the death penalty. Needless to say, this does not work very often—at least not in Texas.

I am going to bring this article to an end. Thank you for your time. The struggle goes on. With unity and solidarity, we shall overcome. Use the pain to fuel the fire that burns inside you.

Veni Vidi Vici

Clinton Young #999447

Polunsky Unit

3872 FM 350 South

Livingston, TX 77351

Loud & Clear, July 13, 2006

Greetings to all!

Why try? What's the point? We will not win! That is the attitude of a few people, which is upsetting. My question is—why not? If a person gives up, they will never know what they could achieve!

An example could be my past resistance against the prison officials—a five-man team with riot gear and pepper spray. How can I win? Do I think I will be able to beat all of them? Of course not! But you know what? I damn sure try!

I was subjected to not one, not two, but three handheld CS/tear gas grenades, as well as OC 10-round control pepper spray. I was the first on Death Row to be hit with that much and not give up. The grenades are made for 12,000-square-foot areas—one of them! I was exposed to three in a 300-square-foot area, if even that much space! Did I give up? Hell no!

If I am going to fight, it will be to the end! The opposition matters not! I try to win, but I don't worry about whether I will lose. If you spend your energy thinking you might lose, then you will lose! All my energy goes into winning!

The last time I was in a "Use of Force" with officers and they used all those grenades and pepper spray, I was able to make two of them run off the recreation yard—two out of five! That is good. In my mind, I won that battle. Maybe not physically, but psychologically, I did!

The same goes with my fight for my life. I don't think I will lose—I KNOW I CAN win. But to win, I need help.

The whole point of using the pain to fuel the fire that burns inside of you is that it means using the pain as motivation. The harder I am pushed, the harder I push back!

Give up? What!?!? I cannot even begin to fathom such a cowardly act. A five-man team, 10 rivals, or the State of Texas—I don't give a damn. I am going to fight as hard as I can, all the way to the end!

To quote Winston Churchill in a 1940 speech: "Victory at all costs, victory in spite of all terror, victory however long and hard that road may be; for without victory, there is no survival."

I use Veni, Vidi, Vici as my sign-off because it reflects how I think. It comes from Julius Caesar and means: "I came, I saw, I conquered"—not "I came, I saw, I felt there was no hope, so I gave up!"

My second appeal was just denied. That motivates me to fight harder!!!!

It really aggravates me when people write or talk about "we will not win" or "we will not accomplish anything." To say such a thing is to undermine the entire struggle. Progress is propelled by the force behind it. The more people in the struggle, the faster progress will be achieved—so long as they are putting forth all their effort.

If anyone who reads these articles wishes to help, please feel free to write me or email me, and Sarah or Khim will forward the email to me. (Also, if anyone has gone three weeks without receiving word from me—please let me know!)

The point of this article is to help motivate each of you. YOU can make a difference! You just have to have the will to do so and take the step toward making it happen.

It was just discovered that a third innocent man was executed by the State of Texas! I am NOT trying to be a part of that statistic!

Make a difference—join the struggle.

I leave as I came.

Veni, Vidi, Vici

Solidarity Strengthened by Unity

I remain,

Clinton Young #999447

Polunsky Unit

3872 F.M. 350 South

Livingston, Texas 77351

Loud & Clear, August 14, 2006

Greetings!

"Like Red on a Rose" by Alan Jackson plays through my mind. I start to think about different girls and women that have crossed my path in life. My mind fades back to my first love and attraction. She was 17. I was 5. I sat beside her on the church bus. I thought she was the most beautiful person in the world. Just seeing her made me smile. Then she moved away to go to college. She gave me a watercolor paint kit as a going-away gift. I cried and cried. I felt as if my whole world was coming to an end. I don't recall ever again crying as much as I did that day.

I have thought about her often throughout my life. What amazes me now is that I was able to experience such strong emotions at such a young age. Love is a mystery. How can something so beautiful cause so much pain? Like a thorn on a rose.

The majority of those I write to know about my fascination with the "feminine nature." What else has the ability to be so beautiful, cunning, and treacherous at the same time? (I am not saying all are like that.) All my life, women have been my weakness. I believe part of the reason I have such a deep appreciation for women is because of my mother. She was my best friend when I was a child. We have had a few rocky years lately, but that is a story within itself.

Back to the subject. I was speaking to an associate about women the other day, mostly about how some women I cannot even imagine being touched. Like a masterpiece, they need to be put on a pedestal to be admired so one can take in the quality of their design. Society blurs the concepts of beauty. Every other page in a magazine is an advertisement for a "beauty" product. Hollywood is mostly to blame.

It has always made me sad to read about women who starve themselves or induce vomiting to remain skinny, as the media associates being skinny with being beautiful. I have seen women of all shapes and sizes that just totally amazed me. There have been a lot of women that have made me take a double or even a triple look. But the only woman that ever made me actually stop and stare was in flip-flops (for translation purposes, "sandals"), no makeup, hair in a ponytail, and pregnant. The fact that she was pregnant made her even more beautiful. The whole combination of the power of life, beauty, and her self-security captivated me.

Now I sit in this cage torturing myself with memories. If anyone is wondering what caused me to get on this subject, well, I got a letter from my friend Sarah, who does my Loud & Clear articles and a Myspace site for me. She sent me messages with photos from the Myspace page. I was looking at all the photos of different women, while shaking my head and thinking, "Damn, I want to go home."

I then sat down and wrote a poem called "All I Crave." I will share it with you all:

All I Crave

I find myself thinking of her constantly.

Her beauty tortures my soul.

Her mind consumes me.

Her heart is what I pursue,

With my fate in tow.

The picture of her in hand.

This agony I cannot stand.

So easily her smile melts this man.

I hear her whispers floating through the wind.

It wraps around my body.

A driving force that pulls me to the source.

A single touch, a single kiss, a night of love.

All I crave, from this lonely cage.

– Clinton Young, Aug 14, '06, Death Row

Most of my poems are about emotion, which is interesting as I don't get viewed as an emotional person. I just try to set aside emotion so I can make rational choices. Most people make their choices based on emotion. In this place, it is best to set aside emotion. At least for me, it is.

I have taught myself to detach. A book actually influenced me in that manner. It is called Tuesdays with Morrie by Mitch Albom. I recommend it to everyone. It made me shed a tear towards the end. But don't tell anyone, as I am a dangerous killer, and dangerous killers aren't compassionate! (The "dangerous killer" part was me being sarcastic!)

I know that this article was different from my others. I just wanted to express a few thoughts, plus give people a chance to learn a little more about me. I will be writing more about my personal views and thoughts in the future—not all the time, though, as the purpose of Loud & Clear is to focus on the system.

I am on Level 3 with my comrade Steven Woods, same as this time last year. The smell of pepper spray is in the air. Big smile. ☺

Well, let me get to the messages I received:

Kaila, please feel free to write me! Thanks for the thoughts. Tell your aunt I said hello.

Savannah, I appreciate your words of support. Thanks!

Mandy, hey sweetheart, you should have received my other letter by now.

Christina of Dublin, Ireland, you wrote of getting one of my friends to let you know what you can do. Well, you can write to me. I would like for you to. I would prefer to discuss things with you than have others do it. So drop me a few lines.

Shay, Tania, and Emily, the same goes to each of you. Thanks for your words of encouragement.

Melissa, thanks for having me in your prayers.

Catherine, I greatly appreciate you putting a banner for me on your page! I need all the attention I can get. Thank you!

Scouse and Jennie, I appreciate the words. I have a letter on its way to you, Scouse!

Mel from the South, thanks for your thoughts.

Melissa and Scott, I hope that it works out for you both. I know how Scott feels!

Thanks to all for the photos!

Well, I need to end this one. Progress is propelled by the force behind it. Unity is the key to success. Use the pain to fuel the fire.

Veni, Vidi, Vici

Solidarity strengthened by unity, I leave as I came.

In solidarity, I remain,

Clinton Young #999447

Polunsky Unit

3872 F.M. 350 South

Livingston, TX 77351

Loud & Clear, October 2, 2006

I have discovered that my Use of Force videos played in more places than I thought! The sad part is that it leads people to misunderstand life in here and me. The reporter presents me as violent and as liking to fight. I wrote about this in a previous article.

Well, I received some Myspace messages. A child called me a killer and said I liked to fight. Well, she is half-ass right. I do like to fight against those who wish to oppress me—those who wish to take my life. A killer? No, I can't say I am that. I mean, I haven't killed anyone, so I can't carry that title.

I do not seek pity. I do try to get others to empathize with my situation. I no longer get Use of Forces, not because of concern over how it makes me look or whatever. There are different reasons. I want people to see the world through my eyes.

Imagine being thrown in a cage and told: "You are gonna die, boy! Now you sit there on that bed and be a good prisoner until we kill you!" Ha! Yeah, right! What would you do if someone took you hostage and locked you in a cage? Would you comply? Would you give them the satisfaction of being able to control everything about you?

You know they are trying to kill you. You have seen them kill your friends! You have had people living next to you kill themselves because they couldn't handle it! You ever looked into a little girl's eyes as she smiled and waved at you while visiting her father, who will be killed in a couple of days, and wondered if she understands? Magnified by the fact that her daddy didn't kill anyone, but he will still die due to a lawyer's mistake?

You ever been dragged through the media before society, branded a demon, an evil cold-hearted killer unfit to live? Classified as everything you're not?

You ever been 19 and told to stand while a motherfer looks down at you and orders you to be killed for the actions of another?

You ever been addicted to a demon? You ever been a victim of child abuse, to where you grew up and have a real problem with another man telling you what to do? Now, have you been through all of this by the time you were 21 years old?

No? Well, judge me not until you have been down the path I have.

I wrote another poem earlier today. I will share it with everyone. I was going to sleep and words popped into my mind, so I got out of bed and put them on paper. I can't think of a name for it. Maybe one of the readers can give me a name for it? Email me a suggestion.

Here it is:

I lie in this empty bed, with so many thoughts running through my head.

A heavy soul, so full of dread.

Twenty-three years old and half-dead.

Ah! But I am as well halfway alive.

My heart beats to the rhythm of the world.

Fast and steady, I strive to rise above those who despise.

Adversaries surround me; they try to pull me under.

Their dreams I do plunder.

A will to live.

A will to fight.

A warrior's soul.

A warrior's might.

A tortured heart, a mind eager to know…

You don't understand?

Is that a reason to hate me?

To cheer when they cage me?

Look into my eyes and tell me what you see.

Now search within your soul at who you strive to be.

A fool amongst greatness.

Love me as a wise man amongst the wicked.

—Clinton Young, October 2006

Well, let me get to the messages I got.

Wayne in Canada, thanks for the words! Tell Terri I said hello. Well, I am sure she is reading this. Hey Terri! ;)

Frauke, I am glad that you enjoy the articles. Please tell a friend or two about them!

Jenny (the one that called me a killer), I appreciate your opinion. I really do! Adversity builds character. The more against me, the harder I fight! Don't be so hateful though. Life is too short. Smile and give someone a hug.

Onto others:

Liane, hey, I really appreciate your help! I need all I can get! Thanks!

Beth, I am very grateful that you are willing to donate. Thank you! Any and all donations are very much needed and appreciated.

Kat "Katja," thanks for subscribing. Please tell a couple of friends about the articles.

Andrea, I liked your messages. Let me state something in reference to what you wrote. That is good to know.

You wrote that I have a very extensive background with crime and drugs. Actually, I don't! A lot of my past charges all happened on one day when I was a juvenile.

See, I went into my mom's house while they were on vacation and took some of my stepfather's guns. Me and a guy went joyriding in his stepmom's car with my girlfriend. I was staying at his stepmom's house, as she was a friend of my mother! We were going to another state. The guns were going to be sold to a guy I knew so we would have gas money to get back.

You can tell by a previous poem that I did not care too much for my stepfather when I was younger. Well, we got caught. My mom wanted me to learn a lesson, so she pressed charges. I got a burglary charge, a theft of a firearm charge, and an unauthorized use of a motor vehicle charge! I was 14.

I had gotten in trouble when I was 10 over some flutes that were stolen at school. I had one of them and would not tell where I got it from. A guy that I went to school with stole them. Now, I did know they were stolen; I just wouldn't tell on him. So I got probation for six months.

The other charges I got were while I was locked up.

As for drugs, I did a little when I was younger—weed and beer, mostly. I did have a full-blown methamphetamine addiction right before I got this case!

At my trial, I had twice as many people testify that I was a kind and loving person than the state had to say I wasn't! The only ones that the state had were people that worked for the state—co-defendants and an ex-girlfriend.

The media doesn't report all the stuff that makes me look good. They report about what a juvenile prison guard said. Yet I had four guards testify on my behalf! All said I was a nice guy.

I did get into fights and all that, but that is a product of life in prison!

See, a lot of it looks bad as that is how it is presented. But when you look into it, you realize it isn't what it seems.

I don't want a life sentence!

Gov. Rick Perry cannot give clemency. He can only delay an execution for 30 days! So asking him for anything is a waste of time!

My focus is a new trial so that I can beat all the murder charges—capital murder and even regular murder. That has to be done in the courts. That is why I need a lawyer and all the forensic testing.

I told everyone for years that if I could get the ballistics tested, they would show that I was not the shooter, and they showed just that! I was able to get the report thanks to donations from others. Now I am trying to get others done.

Writing the governor will not help me at all. Not Perry! He is with the state, and he will help the prosecution. He is just like George Bush!

My case has to be fought in the courts! That is the only way.

The guy that was charged with capital murder goes home in 2008—if he isn't out already!

I appreciate your help and words! You are right—it will take a lot of effort.

Anyways, let me get on to others.

Kat, I would like to know more about how PA works.

Mandy, did you get my letter? I will have another coming your way soon.

Katie of Alabama—yes, you! Your hand broke? No? How come you haven't written to me? Long sigh! I am waiting!

Anthony, what you wrote was very interesting. Maybe one day your theory will be proved.

Emily, thanks for your willingness to donate. It is very much appreciated. The best investment you ever made!

Thanks! Well, I am going to close it down for now. I am trying to not write the articles so long.

I will address the other messages when I get them. If anyone has any questions or comments, please feel free to write or send an email. When I get it, I will respond!

I am going to wrap this one up. I leave as I came.

Veni, Vidi, Vici

In solidarity

Clinton Young #999447

Polunsky Unit

3872 F.M. 350 South

Livingston, Texas 77351

Loud & Clear, October 8, 2006

Greetings to all!

The cool thing to do now is to go into schools and shoot a bunch of little girls! There were three such acts in the USA in one week. One resulted in 5 Amish girls getting killed. At another, sexual abuse was involved. The cops stormed the school. Guy shoots girls, guy kills himself. A cowardly act at its best. I feel that copycat, outlandish acts such as school shootings occur (more than three in one week) due to the media coverage. Most of the individuals that do extreme killing were people who were not widely accepted by their peers and generally unrecognized in society.

America, with its celebrity worship, has spawned another type of celebrity: killers that seek to be famous. To hold the nation's attention, to get what they can't get in everyday life—recognition! Recognition and attention are needs of the human psyche. If not met, they lead to unwanted feelings and insecurity. A person will then engage in actions to ease these unwanted feelings and to gain what they lack. How some choose to do it is the problem.

But why the kids? The kids always pay. Mom kills kids! Dad gets mad at Mom, kills Mom, kids, and self! Guy wants to end it all, goes to school to rape and kill some little girls, and kills himself. (Long sigh.) You want to kill yourself that bad? Cut to the chase and just do it—no need to take someone with you. If a person wants some attention, do it in front of the White House or something! But leave the kids alone! I am not advocating suicide; I'm just saying… And the world turns!

The American Bar Association issued revised guidelines for the appointment of defense attorneys in capital cases (death penalty cases). The new guidelines require that two attorneys be provided, along with an investigator and a mitigation specialist in every case, with full funding to the defense. No state has yet set standards that meet these minimum requirements! That is a key problem in capital cases: lack of funding!

My lawyer had to pay for several experts in my trial because the court would not do it! It is very rare for a lawyer to do that. My trial lawyers didn't want to see me get executed. They spent most of their time trying to prevent me from getting the death penalty. Because of that, a lot was overlooked in the establishment of my innocence. Lawyers understand how dangerous the Law of Parties is. There is just almost no way to win! So they felt that if they saved my life, that was a win.

We had many arguments about that! I kept saying, "To hell with the punishment phase; I want all focus to be on getting a not guilty verdict." That is why there is so much wrong with my case in regard to evidence that shows I couldn't have done it. Plus, a lot of people would not talk to my lawyers! FBI agents wouldn't, prosecution witnesses wouldn't. They couldn't get the money that was needed, and so on!

In other cases, it is a lot worse! One person who was executed in Oklahoma had a lawyer that had never tried a capital case and was only paid $800.00! Both of my lawyers got around $70,000, and that was with an agreed pay cut! I was given just one lawyer at first, and he told the judge he would take a pay cut if another lawyer was appointed. He knew there was NO WAY he could have handled my case alone. Even with two lawyers, they were overwhelmed because my case is so complicated.

Anyway, the point is that the majority of cases would end in not guilty verdicts or life sentences if the defense was properly funded. The prosecution has unlimited funds! On appeal, federal lawyers are given only $35,000. My trial record is over 8,000 pages. Psychological records and case records, as well as family history together, are around 7,000 pages. So my federal lawyer would have to go through 15,000 pages, interview dozens of witnesses, and have several forensic tests conducted—all for $35,000! What's even worse is that the state writ attorneys only get $25,000! That is the most important part of the appeal.

That is the part of my appeal that was recently denied. That is the part where I had to file everything that shows I am innocent because I couldn't get my lawyer and the crack-smoking investigator to do it! (For those just tuning in to Loud & Clear: Yes, my investigator smoked crack with witnesses and filed numerous false statements in my appeal, which led to it being denied and destroyed some of my appeal claims. Please read all my past articles.)

Northwestern University Law Center on Wrongful Convictions documented at least 38 executions carried out in the United States in spite of clear evidence of innocence or reasonable doubt of actual guilt since the death penalty was reinstated. And those are just out of the cases that were studied! A lot of guys get no attention. What about the mentally impaired defendants who can't cry out?

The law says that a defendant is responsible for their lawyer. If the lawyer makes a mistake, the defendant has to pay for it! For example, if a lawyer doesn't file something, the defendant can be procedurally barred from presenting the evidence later in the appeal and could be executed! What if the defendant is mentally retarded? There is no safety net for such cases!

The courts have said that innocence does not matter so long as the defendant received a fair trial. Uh, okay! If a person is innocent and was found guilty, how is that a fair trial? There is a quote by the United States Supreme Court that basically states the same thing—

that innocence does not justify an appeal or something along those lines. I will find it and post it.

The point of it all is that the system is stacked against us. Help from people outside is a necessity! If it hadn't been for such people, I couldn't have gotten the ballistics report that shows I couldn't have been the shooter. Now I am trying to get a lawyer—not one that is court-appointed! It is an uphill battle, and time is not on my side.

Well, on to other topics. In a past article, I wrote about selling crack cocaine and associating with a street gang. The factor to pay attention to is how I said it. About selling crack, I mentioned that reality set in real fast. That means I had a change of heart and gave up that business pursuit. About the gangs, I wrote "I have..." That means that I did at one point in time but no longer do.

It was really only a short time period in my life. When I went to another state to stay with my father in Texas, I spent most of my life in a small town. That was the whole point of me mentioning emulating media figures. I just wanted to clear that up, as a couple of people mentioned something about it to me.

Anyways, topic change. If I wrote all about how good of a person I am and all the good deeds I have done in my life, most would cast doubt on that claim. If I wrote about shooting people, selling drugs, stealing, and so forth, the majority would be quick to believe it.

But the factor to focus on is that the majority would want it to be true. Why? Because if I am a kind-hearted, compassionate guy, then I am not evil. If I am not evil, then it is hard for someone to want me to die, thus causing one to reflect on their own morality. "Why do I want another human being to die?"

It's easy to convince oneself to support the death penalty and want someone to get executed when that person is a cold-hearted killer. No one likes to be questioned—more so, to have to question themselves.

I am sure at least one person reading this is thinking, "I don't need a lesson in morality from a guy on death row!" ☺ If you think that, it's because you are becoming defensive. This means that, in your heart, you know I am right! That is also why people are so quick to believe the media. After I read all the articles on me, I got scared of myself! ☺ Ha! It was hilarious though, as they presented such an image to be socially conscious. Even though every single person that has known me my whole life said I was a kind-hearted, loving person and all were totally shocked when they heard I got arrested for murder! Something to think about.

The Midland newspaper supported Rick Perry as governor and supported George W. Bush! So, it is safe to say they are biased and favor the prosecution. One reporter said I stole a car and kidnapped the neighbor's young children. When I read that, I thought, "Damn, when did I do that? I must have been on some good drugs!" Ha! Not really! The "kidnapped two children" were my girlfriend and the owner of the car's stepson, all of whom were running away from home!

They also reported about a riot that was started by me in juvenile prison. However, they didn't report why it started. It started because two guards attacked me and were kicking me while I was on the ground. A lot of other inmates came out to jump on the guards. Then other guards came to assist those guards, and it turned into a free-for-all riot!

Why did the guards attack me? I threw a phone, and it almost hit a guard. I was not aiming it at the guard, and she knew that. The two male guards just overreacted. The female guard even cussed them out for being stupid! (Nothing happened to her.) There is always more to the story.

I am going to start wrapping this up. To everyone that would like to have the articles emailed to them, please send an email to my Loud & Clear email and request such. I might write an article once a week. I might write one twice a week. So if it is emailed to you, you won't miss one.

I am going to try to write more articles so they are shorter. I have been meaning to write one about the "me" before I got this case and the "me" now. I am going to start writing one article about the system and then the next about myself, life as I see it, and life in here. This way, the articles will be shorter.

With that, I leave as I came and will be back next week, so tune in, lock it down, and tell a friend.

Veni Vidi Vici. Till the end and back, I remain.

Clinton Young #999447

Polunsky Unit

3872 F.M. 350 South

Livingston, Texas 77351

P.S. If you think that you want to email me a question or suggestion or write me with such, because someone else most likely will—well, guess what? That someone else is thinking exactly what you are thinking! Get the hint?

Attention: Hunger strike is underway on Polunsky Unit Death Row. Please see [www.anarchyinchains.com] (http://www.anarchyinchains.com) for details. Sadly, I am not participating in it. I lost 20 pounds on levels two and three, so I can't afford to lose any more.

Tell a friend!

Loud & Clear, October 19, 2006

Greetings to all!

I just wanted to republish an old article I wrote in February of 2005. I will do this with a few that had errors in them and where certain parts were missing. No need to get into why, but I figured my old articles can help clear up some people's thoughts about this place. Richard Cobb, Steven Woods, and Stephen Moody are still going strong in the hunger strike! Mr. Woods was gassed with two of the new grenades and LE-10 crowd control pepper spray—WAY TOO MUCH! Anyway, here is the republished article. Enjoy!

2/06/2005

I have been here at the Texas Death Row now for about 22 months. After my first week here, I began to wonder how or why someone would or could stay for years in these boxes we call home. I know men who have spent years in these cages of oppression that we are housed in. Some are never the same after they were released.

You see, the single-man cell that we are housed in on the row, along with the program we live under, was designed solely for the purpose of dehumanization and psychological oppression of the prisoner in order to break down resistance so that the offender can become dependent on the officer (AKA turn us from a man into an obedient dog). It was developed to be used for an average of six months, which is what the officials believed would take to modify the negative behavior of violent prisoners housed in general population.

Now, because of politics, money, and fake stereotypes, death row inmates are forced to live in these cells. The sensory deprivation, inadequate food, and thought of dying become too much for some, as it did for Deon Tumblin (AKA Spotlight) and Christopher Britton (AKA Psycho Bob). Both of these human beings killed themselves by hanging. I knew both of them. They killed themselves within three months of each other.

Three months before Spotlight killed himself, another guy tried his damnedest to kill himself. I want to discuss Spotlight for a short period. He had certain traits that I didn't like about him, though we had a mutual respect for each other. Two of the good traits about Spotlight that stand out in my mind are his humor and overall willingness to help others. He lived two cells down from me when he died. I have lived on the same section and pod on six different occasions with him, which is not a common thing. Anytime I needed anything, he would give it to me.

On November 2, 2004, he hung himself. We had been laughing and joking among ourselves and with Tiny and another neighbor the night before. We were mostly picking on Spotlight because he got a fake case. A sorry-ass, piece-of-trash, loudmouth female officer wrote him up. It really wasn't a funny matter, because the case was going to prevent him from getting a long-awaited special visit from his mother.

Now, several ranks told him that they would throw the case away and let him go from level 2 to level 1 so he could get his visit. Well, on November 2, 2004, I was in the dayroom and two officers brought Spotlight back on the pod from court on the case that was supposed to be thrown away! I asked him, "Spotlight, what the hell's up with that case?" He just shook his head and said, "Everything will be alright."

After about 30 minutes or so, I went back to my cell and started to talk to my neighbor. I called Spotlight a few times. When he didn't answer, I yelled, "Oh hell, Spotlight done killed himself!" I was 100% playing. I had no idea that, at around that same time, he actually was killing himself! I assumed that he was just asleep or mad. I went back to talking to my neighbor.

Well, they came by with the food, and when they got to Spotlight's cell, I heard the guards calling his name, "Tumblin, look out Tumblin, you're gonna eat?" He had a towel over his door screen so that the officers couldn't see in his cell. They then said, "Tumblin!" and began beating on his door. "Tumblin, take the towel down if you're gonna eat. Alright Tumblin, I am about to knock the towel down!"

She then instructed the Control Picket to turn on all cell lights. As soon as the light came on, both officers screamed, and one dropped the pitcher of juice she was holding (it was two female officers). Now, from that point until they finally cut him down was almost ten minutes. About 15 or 20 officers came running to the section. Instead of opening his door and cutting him down, they violated procedure and sprayed him with pepper spray. HE WAS HANGING!

I then lost control and began yelling, "You fucking cowards, cut him down!" They, being the guards, started choking, so I took a deep breath and yelled, "That gas ain't shit, get the fuck in there and cut him down, the dude is hanging, you stupid-ass pigs!" They looked at me like I was crazy. They had to wait until another officer brought gas masks for five of the officers to go into his cell. No shield, no armor, just gas masks.

They didn't have the common sense to get the masks before they violated procedure and gassed Spotlight! They finally cut him down. Then the nurse decided to show up. I heard her tell them, "There is nothing I can do for him." I saw them pick him up and put him on a gurney. I looked right at his face and saw his tongue sticking out and nose bleeding.

Every night I go to sleep, this sight creeps into my mind. When they were wheeling him out, I yelled, "Y'all some cowards and, 'long live Spotlight!'" I went to my bunk and crawled up into a ball in the corner and didn't talk for a while. It just seemed so unreal that a man I had just talked to killed himself because of this place and the program became too much for him. I did not sleep for two days nor have I been the same since.

The very next day, a female officer came by my cell and said, "Hey, Young, you okay?" I said, "Yeah." She then said, "Hang in there." And after a pause, she added, "I know Tumblin did." And she gave a stupid little grin. I could only reply, "You stupid swine, get the fuck away from my cell." I heard several guards make jokes about it throughout the week.

Some may wonder how they could do such a thing. It is this program. It causes them to believe that we are less than human. This is a fact! A man will resist. A dog will submit.

Now I learned that Psycho Bob killed himself. I can only wonder when, or better yet how many, have killed themselves before the prison officials and government stop the torture. They know that these cells drive people crazy. That is why they send a psychologist around every 90 days.

Oh yeah, I almost forgot, James Porter, who was a close associate of mine, killed himself on January 4, 2005, by canceling his appeals and getting a lethal injection. He did so because he couldn't take this place. I can't believe I forgot about his suicide. That is three in the last three and a half months! I think that is a record!

Now, it isn't normal for me to know all these people. There are like 450 guys in here; I don't even know half of them. I know or have met only about a quarter of the death row population. So for all three of the suicides to be people I know has had a major impact on me.

Another guy I know tried to kill himself with pills, and then a month later stabbed himself through the neck with a slender piece of metal. He did this a month before Spotlight killed himself. I actually just remembered about him as well. It is a damn shame that the more I write, the more I remember people who killed themselves or tried to.

There are a few others, but I do not know them, and I believe their effort was more for attention, as they were the ones who informed the guards of this attempt. The sad part is that it seems that no one on the outside cares. The newspapers aren't printing these facts, and there hasn't been public outcry. But not many care about low-life death row inmates! Hell, most believe we need to die anyway.

Some scream "an eye for an eye"; others yell out "It's murder." I believe that Mahatma Gandhi said it best: "An eye for an eye leaves everyone blind."

There is a quote by Shakespeare that I would like to share with you. It goes, "The quality of mercy is not strained, it dropeth as the gentle rain from heaven upon the place beneath. It is twice blessed: it blesseth him that gives and him that takes."

I would like to add that by having the mercy to join a struggle to make right a wrong benefits all involved. You can make a difference. Together, we can create a change. All it takes is a little mercy and compassion.

Long live Spotlight. RIP Psycho Bob, Spotlight, James Porter, and all the rest!

Clinton Young #999447

Polunsky Unit 3872

F.M. 350 South

Livingston, Texas 77351

Loud & Clear, November 13, 2006

Greetings to all!

Why are human beings the only creatures that have to get their wisdom teeth cut out of their heads? I found myself asking that question last week as I waited for the dentist to do just that.

In the early morning hours of Nov. 9th, I was told to pack my property because I was going to the prison hospital in Galveston, TX, which is actually the University of Texas Medical Branch. The hospital has floors set aside for the prison. Outside of the holding cells, it looks just like a free-world hospital on most floors, besides the electronic gates. I got there and was not told to not eat. So when the dentist found out that I ate, they couldn't do the surgery since they had to put me under anesthesia.

They admitted me and moved me to another floor. When a person gets actually admitted, they get a cell with a TV. The first thing I thought about was how this was going to mess up my mail—and it did! Anyway, they put me in the cell, and I looked up at the TV. There it was, all nice and pretty, with the damn cord hanging down as it had been cut in half. I just started laughing. It fits my luck perfectly to be placed in a cell with a TV that didn't work!

A few hours later, a nurse came by, asked my medical history, and told me the operation would not be until Wednesday. So here I am in a cell with no property, no hygiene, and a TV that doesn't work for at least three more days. They brought me half a small bar of soap, a toothbrush, and some tooth powder. I paced my cell, worked out, and went to sleep.

The next morning at breakfast, which was served at 7:00 AM instead of 5:00 AM like at the prison units, I got my breakfast plate, which had eggs, bacon, two biscuits, peaches, and buttered grits with sugar and milk. It had been a long time since I had bacon. I love me some bacon! The food is the same as the regular hospital food, so that was a plus!

Then two sergeants showed up at my door to move me to another cell with a working TV. Now, I didn't ask to move. I knew another cell was open, but I wasn't about to ask them for anything. Plus, TV isn't important to me. Turns out there was a fight between two inmates that are actual residents there. The sergeant made sure to let me know that they were moving me for their benefit. I just shrugged my shoulders and told him, "It don't matter."

I must admit that TV has gotten even worse. Most of the shows are just totally stupid! I even found shows that I used to enjoy simple and tedious. I ended up just watching the Discovery Channel and Animal Planet. I watched a few other shows. Of the new ones, the best I think is That '70s Show—that one is funny. That, and South Park.

I decided to watch the news. A guy comes on and says, "Breaking News!" Now, when he says this, I am thinking a disaster happened or some fraud was exposed in the recent elections—something important! Then the jackass says, "Britney Spears seeks divorce!" I wasn't on the entertainment channel! It was the regular evening news. My jaw actually dropped, and I said, "What?" out loud. As a nation, what have we come to when a washed-up pop singer that prances around like a slut, even though she knows a lot of little girls look up to her, decides to leave an idiot with an identity crisis, and this is Breaking News? I am quite certain that time slot could have been filled with information about a child that was kidnapped or some rapist that was on the loose—some type of information that can benefit society! I didn't watch any more news.

Wednesday gets here, and they come to get me for surgery. Well, hold up—let me tell another part. Tuesday night, a nurse brought me a hospital gown and hairnet to wear when I go into oral surgery. She told me I had to wear that and to take everything off when I got ready for surgery. I said, "Hold up, you want me to get completely naked and just wear this gown?" She said yes. I just smiled and said, "I am just having my tooth pulled!" It didn't matter. Damn perverts will look for any reason to get you naked in hospitals! Go in for an ear exam: "Oh, take off your clothes and wear this gown!" Ha, ha!

Now I am actually a modest individual. So I made up my mind real quick that I wasn't getting my tooth pulled butt-ass naked! I didn't have to. I wore pants and the gown. I think the nurse was just confused.

When they started getting ready to do the surgery, they hooked me up to the heart monitor and stuck an I.V. in me. I couldn't help but think about how we get executed. They use anesthesia first. The doctor had like four needles. When he started getting ready to put one into the I.V. line, I could hear the beeping of the heart monitor start to speed up as my heart started racing.

I found out on Monday that they were going to put me to sleep to do the procedure. So until Wednesday, I kept having paranoid thoughts that I was going to wake up or would have some type of reaction to the drugs and end up dying. It was really bothering me. I didn't sleep worth a damn! Some of the guys that had the best chances of going home have died of natural causes in here. One guy died of hepatitis C, and he was about to go home free! Ever since I finally got the ballistics that show I could not have been the shooter, I have had a deep paranoia that I am going to get cancer or something. I have no diseases or anything. So when I move into a new cell, I disinfect it fanatically.

Anyway, they wake me up and show me the tooth. They had to cut the tooth in half and cut it out of my head. In mid-operation, I woke up slightly and heard a noise. I remember thinking, "What are they cutting?" And back out I went! I am still all out of it, so after they showed me the tooth, back out I go. I don't know how I got back in bed and all the restraints off of me.

About eight hours passed, and I started thinking, "Why hasn't a nurse brought me some pain medication and antibiotics?" So I told an officer to let a nurse know. Thirty minutes later, an officer brought back a little cup with a pack of Tylenol—regular Tylenol! Two 325mg pills. I took it, thinking maybe this was to hold me over until pill call in a few hours.

I finally saw a nurse walk by and told her about my medication. She came back with a little cup with two pills in it. I shook the cup and asked, "What are these?" She said, "Tylenol." I asked, "Tylenol? Like a regular pack of Tylenol?" The nurse replied, "Yes. I'm sorry, but we lost your chart."

The surgery was done at around 8:30 AM on Nov. 8th, 2006. I did not get any actual pain medication or antibiotics until 2:00 AM on Nov. 11th, 2006!

I got back to the row on Nov. 9th. A nurse here thankfully put in an order for me. I'm glad that I have a high tolerance for physical pain. I learned a long time ago that it can be blocked with the mind. I got bad luck, huh? Well, it gets worse.

I only got mail one day in the week of Oct. 30th to Nov. 3rd. I was gone from Nov. 6th to Nov. 9th, so they sent all that mail to the medical unit in Galveston. I came back here before they gave it to me. So now I got to wait until the medical unit has something coming back to this unit for me to get it, as it gets transported by a prison van. So basically, it will be about a week before I get all that mail. If anyone does not receive word from me in the normal time, that is the reason. When I get my mail, I will respond.

I was going to make this article a really long one, but I am going to cut it short. I will have another article that will be very interesting in 3 to 4 days, so please tune in. It would be best for people to send their email address to my Loud & Clear email clintloudandclear@yahoo.com, and Sarah will just email the article to you.

I just wanted to tell everyone about my wonderful trip to have a tooth cut out of my head!

To those that sent me letters about Mike after he killed himself—had it been a different situation, it would have disturbed me. We talked a lot when we were around each other. He did what many wouldn't because they stand on hope that the courts will give a favorable last-minute stay of execution. Oh damn, that reminds me—the press release of his suicide was total bullshit! He didn't even die as I thought he did. His cell was covered with bloody messages like "I didn't kill him" and "I didn't shoot that man" and so forth.

See, what did disturb me is Mike got a stay of execution before! This was his second date! Well, he got a stay because a signed confession was found that his co-defendants made. The prosecution had this 30 days before Mike went to trial, yet they still let the guy say on the stand that it was Mike that did it. They knew that was a lie. Yes, that means Mike did not kill anyone, and the prosecution knew this.

He got a stay of execution back in 2003 or late 2002 because the signed confession was found in the file of his co-defendant. He received another execution date because the court ruled that the evidence was procedurally barred as his lawyer did not file it on time. In a nutshell, the court said, "Fuck the fact that you didn't do it; you've got to die because your lawyer didn't do his job!" Welcome to the American justice system!

This fact is why I need to obtain forensic experts and an actual paid attorney for my next appeal. People do not realize how flawed the system is. They are too worried about Britney Spears getting divorced!

That's all today. Tune in next time and tell a friend.

I leave as I came,

Clinton Young #999447

Polunsky Unit

3872 F.M. 350 South

Livingston, TX 77351

Loud & Clear, November 20, 2006

Greetings to all!

I have been wanting to write this type of article for a long time. A pen pal from Israel gave me a boost by sharing a personal experience she went through at 17 years old. She is originally from France. Here is her story:

I was in Paris, and my grandmother was ill. She had to be taken to the central hospital. This is also where they take people before they go to jail, to check their health. When I entered, I saw policemen with two people in handcuffs. The two people were hurt, with blood all over their clothes, like they had been in a fight. They started to curse each other and threatened each other with death and all kinds of scary and violent things. I had never heard anything that violent before, so I looked at them in amazement and shock! I could not move. Then one of them asked the policemen for some water as he was thirsty. The policemen told him very coldly, "NO!" It was summer, and I had a bottle of water in my hand. I swallowed back my fear and approached him very slowly (I was so scared), and I had to bring the bottle close to his mouth, for he could not handle it himself due to the handcuffs. He got the bottle in his mouth and drank it all. Then he stared at me and thanked me in the softest voice and gentlest manner, exactly as if he were a perfect gentleman. I got a second shock that I could not translate into words. I ran to the metro and went back home. When I got home, I went to sleep for a few hours. Later, I was able to translate the situation into words.

It was the contrast between violence one minute and then the soft voice the next minute of the very same man that shocked me so much. It was as if suddenly I had a flash opening my eyes and my spirit to what had happened to this man and what he had been through in life to be this violent, bloody man in handcuffs. How much violence, humiliation, and degradation can a human being suffer before he becomes a monster? I felt horrified that humanity could be assassinated by the difficulties and tragedies of life. I felt even more mortified that all it took for this man to become the soft man I heard was a little bit of humanity and kindness, that was all!

That is her story. I did shorten it some, just a few words.

Now here is a piece from Shakespeare:

"The quality of mercy is not strained.

It droppeth as the gentle rain from Heaven upon the place beneath:

It is twice blessed; it blesseth him that gives and him that takes."

To have the mercy and compassion to fight against injustice benefits all involved.

I am going to redo another old article that was on another site. A lot was edited on it. Well, this will be another version of it with parts tied in. This article is basically about violence, dangerous people, mercy, and how some people can change.

One would expect death row to be a highly violent environment. I read a statement by a guy from Huntsville, TX, that was in the newspaper last year. He said that if they opened up death row and let everyone walk around, then everyone would see how dangerous they are! Poor guy. I have to forgive him for his ignorance. He doesn't know any better. Death row used to be able to walk around freely when it was housed in the Ellis Unit. These inmates had box cutters and large scissors! That's right, very sharp objects! Nine times out of ten, the supervising officer was a female! No female officers were raped, and no officers were killed. Though female officers have been raped by inmates in general population, just as all the officers who have been killed were killed by general population inmates.

A guy housed in general population has freedom to look forward to. A guy on the row is waiting to die. He has nothing to lose. So one would expect the death row inmate to be more violent, but this isn't the case.

Now true enough, a few death row inmates have seriously injured or made attempts on officers' lives since we have been housed on the Polunsky Unit, where we are all locked in single-man cells and have to shower and have recreation alone. Every time we leave our cells, we are escorted by two guards and handcuffed behind our backs. All the doors have little slots that we get handcuffed through. So how can an inmate still assault an officer? Human error and determination.

Anyway, the point is that when death row inmates were treated in a more humane manner, they were more passive. But as they have spent years in these cells and this oppressive environment, with the little we get slowly stripped away, they have become more aggressive, which is actually a product of this environment. This is well known and well documented by psychologists. They give us nothing to look forward to and nothing to gain. If you have nothing, then what is there to lose?

As much as people try to candy-coat death row, the reality is that there are some very dangerous people down here who have done some very disgusting and evil things to get here. I am not writing articles to make us all look bad. I am not writing articles to make us all look good. I am writing articles to show the world who I am and that not all of us fit into these stereotypes placed on us.

Most on death row rank far from being dangerous! Most are extremely passive. I heard about one of the guys that got off death row and is going to go home. He is supposed to be all violent and dangerous, yet he pays inmates to protect him from other inmates so he won't get raped or whatever!

A lot of guys here are rational people who just made an irrational choice. They got on drugs and got a gun. Then they ran out of money and needed a fix. So they rob and kill a store clerk! They never before did anything violent in their lives. Well, a tough-on-crime prosecutor sends the guy to death row! Yet he is supposed to be the worst of the worst?

Now another guy rapes 10 women and shoots 3 of them, but none die. So he gets like 60 years or a life sentence (parole can be made on a life sentence, as long as it is not a capital life sentence. Capital life is for Capital Murder). Now who would you say is the worst of the worst of those two?

Those 10 women will have to live with their pain for the rest of their lives, with the emotional and mental suffering, the distrust, fear, and anger of being violated. The guy that caused all that can go to general population and be around other weaker inmates and female guards. So he can attack again!

Let me give you another example. A guy can walk up to someone in a store and chop that person up with an axe into little pieces. Just a violent, brutal, and bloody murder. He can plead out to 30 years and be home in 15-20. Now a guy can walk up, shoot a person one time, and take his watch. Then get the death penalty. See how it doesn't make sense?

That is what is wrong with the system. A person that commits one act that can be considered violent is not necessarily a dangerous person! A fistfight can be considered a violent act!

Now there are people here who have committed several violent acts in their lives that do classify them as being dangerous. Though, after being here on the row, they become extremely passive and become new people. Why? Because they get shown mercy and compassion from others, such as pen pals. They get shown a different side of humanity.

Growing up, they might have been surrounded by hate, violence, and crime. Yet through correspondence with people, they learn love and peace. They educate themselves and strive to be better people, even though they know they will be executed. The thought is: "I have lived the last 20 years in violence, and I am tired of it. I want to live the remaining five in peace."

If they had been shown mercy years ago, they might not be here in the first place. The most common themes in the backgrounds of death row inmates are divorced parents, child abuse, and low income. All of these cause an imbalance in the psychological development of a child, often leading to a low self-image, which is gasoline for hate!

Murder is not murder. There are different degrees. You have the old man who sneaks into the hospital and pulls the plug on his wife of 55 years to end her suffering, or he might even shoot her at her request! That is still murder.

In Texas, the punishment for murder ranges from five years to 99 years or a life sentence. On life, parole can be made in 30 years! Probation can be obtained but no more than 10 years! So the old man could face life but would most likely get probation for 5 years, which is the minimum amount. He will still be charged with murder, though. Then you've got the 17-year-old kid that is out with his friends, drinking and having a good time. He gets into a fight with a bigger guy, so he pulls a knife and stabs him. Doesn't want to kill the guy, just slow him down and hurt him. Hits a vital area or artery, and the guy bleeds to death. He is now charged with murder and will get around 30 years. Then you've got the guy that rapes and kills this woman, robs and kills that man, and just kills a couple of other people. Well, since there is a felony in the course of the murder, he gets the death penalty. Now on that spectrum of these three examples, that would seem like a fair system, huh? It doesn't always work that way. You cannot place all killers in the same basket. A guy that does the most unfathomable crime of all—he rapes and then kills a small child—cannot be compared with a guy that kills two rival gang members! The child is innocent. To hurt a child to that level goes against the full nature of humanity. Most of us humans, when we see a child, want to pick it up and make him or her laugh, give him or her a toy, or something. Well, I know I do! So to hurt a child on that level goes beyond just a desire for power, which is the case with child abuse. One would have to go against all levels of social constraint and morality to violate a child and then take its life.

The gang member is living a way of life. He could have been raised in a neighborhood that makes life in that manner a reality. He joins a gang that his brother and friends are in and starts to sell drugs. One day, he is going to a girlfriend's house across town. As he goes through a rival's neighborhood, he sees two rivals. They recognize him and start throwing gang signs at him. That is considered an act of aggression, so he thinks they might pull a gun next. The mentality of "I got to get you before you get me" sets in, and he shoots both of them! In his mind, it was self-preservation. He knows that win or lose, life or death is determined by who draws the gun first. Now, if he were taken out of the neighborhood, put through gang prevention programs, taught additional education and job training, relocated to a stable low-crime environment, and given a job that has decent benefits and offers growth, that gangbanger would be more likely than not to live a productive life and never hurt anyone again.

Then you've got the guy that breaks into a home, rapes a woman, and then kills her. Now that takes a lot of time and effort! It is a cold-hearted and cruel murder. These are people that can't be fixed. True enough, most of your wrongful convictions in prison are guys that got charged with rape, and 15 years later, they find out that he didn't do it, which is a very bad jacket to have in prison! I have been charged with a sex crime before. When I was 14, I got charged with indecency with a child by exposure. I thought my life was over! My lawyer told me I could get 10 years. At 14, ten years looks like a life sentence. Not only that, but the social embarrassment of being labeled a sex offender was totally unnerving to me. Now, in that case, the "child" was 5'9", 260 pounds, almost 15 years old, and was a member of the MS-13 gang (he was Hispanic). MS-13 has been talked about on 20/20 and other major news stations. It has even been focused on by Congress and Homeland Security due to its growing size and violent history in the drug trade from South America to the U.S.A., where the gang is spread from. I was 14 years old, 5'6", and 145 pounds. We were both in an anger management placement. We were friends and got into a fight. I made some comments to degrade and embarrass him. He wanted to get me kicked out, so he said I exposed myself and told him to perform oral sex (he used other words, but I am trying to keep the foul language out). Because he was under 17, he was considered a child. Fighting would not get me kicked out of the placement. Sexual behavior and extreme violence would. They could not risk it, so they kicked me out, and I got sent to Texas Youth Commission for the charges. He testified at my trial, and on the stand, he said, "We was friends and got into a fight that got carried away. Wasn't nothing sexual; he was just trying to embarrass me!"

Now, when I was 14, a probation officer came to see me about the charge (I had other charges, which is why I went to the placement). She read me the charge of indecency with a child. Part of the charge states sexual gratification. I jumped up and screamed, "I ain't no homosexual. How am I gonna get gratification by exposing myself to another guy?" So needless to say, it was a traumatizing experience for me. But thankfully, we were able to work a deal with the prosecutor's office so that I was not convicted of it. I know I got sidetracked there, but I have been wanting to write about that because a newspaper article makes mention of me being charged with it. When people see the word "child," they think of a baby and so forth. I had people stop writing me behind that. They said they cared about me, then just stopped writing and didn't even ask me about it. On top of that, she told another person I wrote about it in a manner to make me look bad!

Back to the matter at hand, today, with DNA evidence, convicting the wrong person is not as likely as it was 20 years ago. But what if a case really doesn't have DNA evidence, such as mine? Then co-defendants' testimony becomes even more important. DNA has no reason to lie. Ballistics has no reason to lie. A guy facing the rest of his life in prison has a reason to lie! So when you look at people on Death Row, do not automatically recoil with fear. Do a little research. You can actually see why every single person is on Death Row. Just go to www.tdcj.com/deathrowoffenders. At the TDCJ website, you can also see all that we can get in the mail and so forth. There are people here that didn't even kill anyone! They were just with a person that did. They wait for death, while a serial rapist or axe murderer waits to go home! I am sure everyone can agree that doesn't sound like a fair and just system. The fact is that people can change. What gets me is the vast majority of the pro-death supporters are Christians! A religion centered on redemption and forgiveness. Paul was a serial killer—he wrote part of the Bible (he killed more than one person, so he is a serial killer).

This article is getting way too long, so I am going to start wrapping it up. If you do not understand something, take a little time to learn about it. Being ignorant is understandable; to ignore takes effort, and there is no excuse. I have been meaning to write about how I changed from when I was 15 years old when I got this case.

In the next article, I will write about victimization and how crimes affect the direct victim, indirect victims, and society, and how I have changed. China has taken even greater steps to improve its death penalty to make sure innocent people aren't killed. They have improved the appeal system. With that, I am gone.

Veni, Vidi, Vici

Clinton Young #999447

Polunsky Unit

3872 F.M. 350 South

Loud & Clear, January 1, 2007

Greetings to all!

Well, I received a wonderful Christmas present. My appeal was denied. I am now waiting to find out who my next court-appointed assassin is! Ew-We man! Twelve months till my next appeal is due. A new year, a new approach. I have decided to join the hunger strike. I am mentally ready to do it until they have to hospitalize me! As I always say, mind over matter. You don't mind, it just doesn't matter!

A lot of guys are protesting the conditions here. I applaud them and will assist in any way I can. Though, a few others and I who are joining the strike also want to focus on the law! I am more concerned with what got me here and what is keeping me here! The state of Texas has said that I need to die, as all of my state appeals have been denied! I killed NO ONE, yet they are ready to kill me! Damn, I can feel the love!

One of the portions of the law that I am protesting is the Law of Parties. The law of parties in Texas states that if a person commits a felony with another person, they should anticipate that another felony would occur. Okay, so I am supposed to read another person's mind!? Really, the law of parties should not even be a factor in my case. I am the ONLY ONE in prison for murder. I have shown that I could not have been the shooter. If no one else got charged with murder, then where is the party at? Hell, it is just a one-man show. That ain't no party. That isn't even a date! (Though I do enjoy my own company. But if I had done something with someone, then that would be a party! Or at least a date.)

Anyways, here is a list of things I am protesting:

1. The Law of Parties needs to be corrected. No one should be held responsible for another person's actions, more so, to die for them, when the actual killer is not going to die and will get to go home very soon.

2. In Texas, prosecutors do not have to turn over evidence to the defense attorneys until trial! How can a lawyer properly defend a client if he cannot even get the case file? Channel 11 News did a special on TV about this law. Channel 11 is out of Houston, Texas. In Houston, the prosecution would make defense lawyers look at the case file with only a pen and notepad! They would not even allow the lawyer to make a copy of the offense report!! This is in death penalty cases! One man was in jail for six months before his lawyer was finally given a copy of a statement that showed that he was innocent. Then the lawyer was able to file the proper paperwork to get his client out of jail. This is how Texas works. They do not give a damn about justice. As long as someone pays!!! They

treat this like a chess game! Let's see who can win!! But instead of pawns and kings, they are using human lives!!! This is 2007 in the United States of America. This is not 1956 Russia!! It needs to be made so that as soon as a prosecutor gets ANY information on a case, they need to make the defense aware within 48 hours! And allow the defense to obtain a copy. Isn't it supposed to be FAIR, right? Plus, we are supposed to be innocent until proven guilty! At least that is what the LAW says!!!! This is supposed to be a country that is governed by the rule of law, not the law of rule.

3. The law needs to ensure constitutional protection on the state writ of habeas corpus. This is the most important appeal!! It is often called the Great Writ! Yet this has NO protection based on the constitution. So a lawyer is free to do what he wants, which is why the state writ has often been where the worst appeals are filed! The C.C.A., which is the Court of Criminal Appeals, just recently put in place rules that will hold the lawyer accountable. If they file a trash appeal, they can be removed from being able to do a capital appeal. Okay, that is a start. You know what the problem is, though? That is just a show! As right after they put that rule in place, they denied my appeal. I had an investigator that was smoking crack with witnesses and filed all fabricated statements! The lawyer knew that she had a history of mental illness and had been informed before about her drug use and mental illness, yet he let her work on one more case. Guess who the lucky one was?? ME!!!! The C.C.A. was aware of this, yet they still denied me any relief! Damn, I feel the love!!! Good ole Texas Justice!! The taxpayers paid around $30,000 for my state writ, for what?? NOTHING!!!! They just fueled a drug addict's habit! A change must occur!!!

4. The current timeline for a writ in state court is inadequate. It is due 45 days after the state files its response to the direct appeal. (The direct appeal is the first appeal. The defendant files his, then the state responds. Once the state responds, the defendant must file his second appeal, even if the first one has not been ruled on yet! This is to speed things up!) Well, 45 days with a possible 90-day extension!! That is not near enough time! My case has over 15,000 pages in it. My trial record has 8,000 alone! So how can a lawyer go through all that in 135 days? The law needs to change to at least a year! A timeline should not matter when dealing with a human life, more so one that might be innocent.

Also, some type of rules need to be put in place to block prosecutors from seeking the death penalty for political gain! They are supposed to seek it for the worst of the worst. They often seek it for when the best of the best is killed. That is not how it is supposed to be. Some counties only seek death when a cop is killed. I applaud the men and women that serve to protect society. But is their life worth any more than the black crackhead on a street corner? NO, it isn't!! A human life is a human life! There are numerous laws in place about political campaign funding! But there are no guidelines for when a prosecutor wants to kill someone! Something must change.

Several innocent men have been executed. People focus on race as an issue. It is more of a class issue. If I had the money the state had, I would not have been convicted! The same goes for the appeals. They give the state UNLIMITED MONEY!! Yet, put limits on the defense. Oh hell, it is just a sorry ass inmate, who cares!

Also, there was a recent article in the USA Today newspaper titled "INMATE SUICIDE LINKED TO SOLITARY," and guess who is number two in the nation? TEXAS!! Damn, for once they weren't number one! Oh well, I guess you can't always be number one in all the inhumane, oppressive categories. But Texas did come in number one in suicide attempts! Cells make people so crazy they can't even kill themselves right!

Texas had 24 suicides in the year 2006, with a prison population of 150,000. The number one cause? Being housed in the same kind of cells that death row is housed in! Texas and California prison systems have created environments where violence is a form of communication, even among the officers. So, in the mid-80s, gangs exploded throughout the system. Numerous people join these, not only for a sense of belonging but a sense of protection.

Texas has the HIGHEST cases of inmate prison rape—over 500 in one year! What would you all do if you lived in a town where 24 people killed themselves in one year, and over 500 people were sexually assaulted? There have been numerous stories in the news about people suing T.D.C.J. for not protecting them from prison rape and violence. Then, when an inmate joins a prison gang so he has someone to watch his back, the prison official confirms him and then puts him in a prison cell, just as we are housed in on death row, and won't let him out unless he snitches.

Well, what happens to a snitch in prison?? See, there is no positive recourse! Damned if you do and damned if you don't. It doesn't matter if an inmate acts in a violent manner, or even if he is just a member. If they find out that a person associates with a known gang member, then that is it! Off to lockdown you go. What do you do if you've got a life sentence and get locked down? The rest of your life in segregation! That is why suicides are so high. The entire system is broken—inside and out!

My goal is to fix the outside problem, the "Judicial" problem, as that is what gets people in here. Don't get me wrong, I do not think that if someone does something wrong, nothing should happen to them. We need laws to govern society. But damn, if a man didn't do anything, don't lock him up! Damn sure don't kill him!! I say man, but it happens to women as well.

I will be sending in an article every day or two. Another guy had gone 27 days, and they had not hospitalized him. I will see if I can make it 30 days!

I never claimed that I have always been a law-abiding, upstanding citizen. I have done my wrongs in life. Though I never killed anyone! I have grown since I came to death row. I try to be a man of honesty and virtue. I am honest with people, even when that honesty may cause them to turn on me. But I always try to do the right thing.

I did not kill those two men, nor did I intend for them to die. I can prove that I did not do it. So why do I have to die? The struggle must go on! Give me liberty or give me death!!! Well, damn, they already gave me death—looks like I have nothing to lose, huh?

Join the struggle.

Veni Vidi Vici

In solidarity,

A very hungry,

Clinton Young #999447

Polunsky Unit

3872 F.M. 350 South

Livingston, TX 77351

Loud & Clear, November 11, 2008

Greetings!

It has been a long time since I wrote an article—over a year! So much has happened. I had a few more use-of-force incidents. I will go into that first.

They got a new toy—a paintball gun that shoots powder-filled balls instead of paint. The first time, I refused to come off the outside recreation yard (actually a room with bars for a roof to allow sunlight in; we are not really outside). They shot me several times, hitting me once or twice, then a crowd-control smoke grenade was thrown at me. It filled the entire rec area with smoke to the point I could not even see the other people watching through the observation glass.

A funny note: The major, that is the rank of an official here, well, his gas mask did not work correctly, so he started to choke and beat on the door to get out of the recreation area. So the warden got the paintball gun, came in, and shot at me. A barred gate-style door separated us, so they shot through the handcuff slot. The warden shot me maybe three more times, and then the five-man extraction team with the riot shield came. When they opened the gate to rush me, I ran to one side and charged after the team. I attempted to kick the shield out of the way. I kicked too low and late! My kicking the shield too low caused the top of it to tilt down and hit me right across the eye and nose! It looked like a murder scene, there was so much blood. I went to the infirmary and got seven stitches on my nose. Two weeks later, I did it all over again! Only this time, no stitches!

The video of the use-of-force incident that resulted in the stitches is available by emailing Vera at info@saveaninnocentlife.com. It is being added to others, so it is not exactly ready yet. But you can email Vera, and she will help you with the information. To those who have expressed a desire for a copy so far, please be a little more patient. There were some minor problems that have since been worked out.

Also, another matter I want to address: People posted stuff about having written me and not receiving a response. How do you know I even got your letter?! If someone writes to me and is serious about doing so, then I will write back. Some people write me and tell me all of what they aren't going to do and all this stuff. I will not respond to a letter like that, as it means you already have some formed thought of me. I don't like being placed in a stereotype. Just because I am forced into this situation by a backward, corrupt legal system doesn't mean I have to expect people to place me in some kind of stereotype! Cool is the rule!

Onto other matters. I recently got to read the stuff some people posted on my petition. It seems there are a lot of idiots in this world. Some girl was acting like she knew me. She stated I shot some Mexican in a Hastings parking lot (Hastings is a bookstore). I have never been in or at a Hastings! Hell, if I had been there, I might not have been doing meth and hanging around the idiots I was! Better than that, I never shot no Mexican. So, little girl, you got me mixed up with someone else.

Another lady wrote that after reading everything and going over my case, she fell out of her chair laughing that I could make such a claim. I hope you got insurance and didn't hurt yourself, as you're only laughing at your own stupidity! See, I couldn't get my past lawyers to help me. They simply had no desire to, so they only hurt me! But that has changed a little.

Now I have been able to get forensics on both murders I was convicted of. Guess what? It showed I could not have done both murders. Also, I now got statements that the prosecutors had my co-defendants lie on the stand and were making all kinds of backroom deals with them. This didn't only come from a co-defendant, but also from the lawyer of a co-defendant.

One of the three co-defendants that testified against me was never arrested. While free, he was picked up for possession of marijuana, traffic violations, and aggravated sexual assault on a child. Guess what? All those cases magically disappeared when he testified against me. Jury members have signed statements, stating that they basically would not have convicted me had they known all this. The judge in my case signed an order for the prosecutors to reveal any and all deals they were offering or negotiating. The prosecutors just plainly ignored the court order!

What will happen to them? Nothing! In Texas, prosecutors are granted immunity. So they can just get away with sending innocent people to death row!

A lot of change has come about recently with the election of America's first black president. So maybe Texas will soon catch up with the rest of the world in properly understanding what it means to have liberty, equality, and most importantly, justice.

The revenge policy of the death penalty is an outdated and greatly flawed policy. I will be writing articles again, though most will not be this long-winded! We have been on lockdown status for a month now, so we have been getting a peanut butter sandwich for every meal with some other kind of sandwich. They ran out of regular bread, so now they are putting peanut butter on hot dog buns and biscuits to feed us. For breakfast, we get the hot dog bun with peanut butter and a biscuit with one egg! Damn, I am hungry!

We are on lockdown due to them finding cell phones. They even canceled visits. Hopefully, that will pick back up soon. Really, we've all been quiet, and they just passively keep us without visits. Hopefully, that will change as well.

I am going to go ahead and wrap this one up.

Until next time.

Vini, Vidi, Vici

Clinton Young #999447

P.S. They let us off lockdown today.

P.S.S. Song of the week: Jamie Johnson - "In Color"

Loud & Clear, January 26, 2009

Greetings to all,

I know there's been a delay in the planting of my words. I just have had a lot going on in my personal life, as well as the stress caused by my forced living arrangements. I have had a lot on my mind nonetheless. On January 30, 2009, the state responds to my federal appeal. I am eager and nervous to see what is filed. No matter what is filed, the state is still actively pursuing the end of my life. One would think that their ethical code would require them to correct a miscarriage of justice. Instead, they will make excuses and try to use "technical legal jargon" to justify killing me. I guess their impotence in life requires them to feel a need to defeat my lawyers and me. My life is worthless to them. Only success matters.

Is one life worth more than another? To say one life is worth more than another is utilitarian logic in full form and the basis of most fascist ideologies. To even suggest that a victim's life is worth more than a murderer's, and then you yourself go and kill that murderer—does it not then make your own life less worthy than the murderer you murdered? If you are able to judge the worth of a human life, you are then superior to that life. So what allows one person to be superior to the next? If it is applied to the system, does a vote make that prosecutor superior to the criminal? Prosecutors and judges at a state level are voted into office. The majority of votes declares the winner. So the majority decides the worth of a life?

What if that majority is kept ignorant due to a pathetic education system? If so, then it is safe to say that the voters can't make an intelligent choice. They are ignorant of the facts. The 'poor' criminal's weak voice, a media focused on who Paris Hilton is having sex with, and ridiculous education programs are to blame. Though the prosecutors are aware. The lawyers are aware. As are the judges. So what is their excuse? They all are supposed to be fighting for the law and order of this country in accordance with the Constitution. A country designed on the rule of law, not the law of rule.

In 2009, is it socially acceptable for a lawyer to allow his investigator to run around as she pleases, fabricating reports, smoking crack cocaine with a witness, trying to have sex with a witness, manipulating witnesses, and deceiving the courts, all while funded by the taxpayers? Midland County District Attorney thinks it is, as they refused to press charges on the investigator in my appeal. Her name is Lisa Milstein. She is enjoying her life in Florida, while I try to convince the courts not to kill me because of a procedural default due to her and a previous lawyer not properly raising my claims in my state appeal. Had they done their job, there is a very big chance I would already be back in court for a new trial.

She has a MySpace page. Everyone can look at it and see how she is enjoying her life. She didn't only royally screw up my case; she also did it to four or five others. Those are the ones still alive. A couple have been executed where she worked on their case. Evidence has been found where she messed over them as well. Her MySpace promotes her as a personal fitness trainer. Nowhere does it mention her death penalty work, theft conviction, career as a stripper, or rehab stays. She refuses to help my lawyers. The prosecutors do not want to prosecute her, as doing so will strengthen my appeal. So they allow a crime to go unpunished for the sake of political gain. That gain being from my death. The attorney general of Texas also allows her to get away with it. So it isn't just the local prosecutor. It is a collaboration of judicial officials, including Midland County Judge John G. Hyde.

This judge sent letters to the members of my jury after convicting me, telling them I am dangerous and deserve to die. He then acted as if he is not biased, by reviewing and rejecting two of my appeals! These people all feel their life is superior to mine. I understand they've got a job to do, though that doesn't mean covering up injustice. If they see a wrong, they should correct it—especially since I have evidence that shows I am innocent of capital murder, strengthened by the fact that the police didn't investigate two crime scenes.

It's 2009. God Bless America.

Anyways, onto other matters. I am slated to make level one in a few days. I have been on levels 3 and 2 since May 15, 2008. I have lost forty pounds. So I am ready to eat some commissary! I want to thank Regina for typing up this long-winded ass article. Ha! Ha! I also want to thank Vera for her dedication to both myself and my cause. She spends countless hours and dollars trying to help save my life. A beautiful and headstrong woman. I am forever grateful. I thank and love you for your commitment to me and my struggle.

Leigh of New Zealand, I just found your letter! It got mixed up in my paperwork during a cell search or when I moved to a different cell. You have a letter coming.

To those that write me with a post office box, if you give me a fake name, when I write, they will return the letter. If you are worried about me knowing your name, then don't write me. I am locked in a cage in a building that is surrounded by a 50,000-volt electric wire fence and very bright stadium lights. This building is part of a complex that is encased by two additional separate fences covered in razor wire. All under the watchful eye of guard towers armed with AR-15 assault rifles. The point is, ain't no one leaving that doesn't want to leave! So there is no point in not giving a proper name. Plus, if a person did get out, why in the hell would they go to your house when they've got family and personal friends from the free world they would go to? So if you are scared to put your name, then don't even write. I am a human being, not a hobby.

I guess that about does it for this issue. I will try to write again soon. I thank you for your time in reading this. Take care.

I leave as I came,

Clinton Young #999447

Polunsky Unit

3872 FM 350 South

Livingston, TX 77351 USA

Loud & Clear, February 11, 2009

Here I sit beating up my typewriter, listening to Carrie Underwood—'Just a Dream.' I tell ya what, that little girl can sing! Though she doesn't have anything on Miranda Lambert. But I am biased seeing how Miranda is my favorite. I got to hear her new song, "More Like Her." It's good, though not better than "Kerosene" and other hits that she has.

As most can tell, I am finally on level one again. I was level two or three since May 15th, 2008! I just made level one Feb. 6, 2009. Normally it only takes three months, but I am not normal, so I always stay way longer than average. I just refused to shave and got use of force and other cases. Nonetheless, here I am on the great level one. ☹ The only thing about level one is visits and commissary food items. Both are items used to control us. Oh, and this radio that plays the same commercially promoted songs over and over again.

I would rather be resisting my captors' attempts at control of me until they murder me—which is their desire—thus separating any affection and understanding of their job and/or rules. Though Vera, who has done so much for me, has asked me to try to stay out of trouble and stay on level one as much as I can. So I decided to give it another try. I normally can tolerate level one for about two months. So we shall see.

It never ceases to amaze me how most of the hostages of this place are clueless to their fate. They know they got a death sentence, but they really do not know! They usually don't fully realize it until they get an execution date. Most have this hope that they will get some relief from the courts, though that really is a stroke of luck or divine intervention. It depends on the lawyer the condemned has, as well as the judge over his trial and the federal judge that he gets once getting to his federal appeals.

I have been given some good lawyers that really did a lot for my federal appeal. There was much more they could do and wanted to do but ran out of time. My appeal is 1,300 pages, which is like four times larger than 90% of the federal death case appeals filed! It really could have been way larger. Yet the state is still trying to kill me. Damn this stressful life! ☹

The state files their response tomorrow. I am really eager to see what all was filed. I should be able to speak with my lawyers in a couple of days as they have a deadline of 12 days to file some papers. So I will have an idea of the next step. I got good people on my side. The three lawyers I have now are better than I ever had on my appeal. The other clowns that I had were doing nothing more than sharpening the needle for the state. I actually get along with these lawyers. I mean, during a legal visit, I can actually laugh and leave with a smile. Before, I would be so mad I would be shaking, due to the past lawyers.

Because two of my lawyers work for the federal public defenders office, I got really nervous when they first got on my case, as it was a federal judge that appointed them. I am the only Texas death row inmate with such. But I was also given Donald Vernay out of New Mexico. He has a good reputation as well, so I really don't know what to think. Then I met with my lawyers from California, with the public defenders office. I gave them the usual speech of, "No one listens to me. If you will just listen to me, I promise everything I say will prove to be true. I am not going to waste your time and bullshit." They said they would look into it. I just thought, "Yeah, I heard that before." But then as time progressed, I saw they were really looking. Everything I said they were able to find to be true.

See, the best thing about that is that in a hearing to remove my old lawyers from my case, I stood up and told the judge, "Every claim I made in my personal letters to the court, I can prove if I just had a lawyer that would listen to me and do something." Well, my appeal helps to show everyone that I was not lying. So just a few more steps and a little more time, and I will have a better idea of how my future will be.

I have been meaning to get some more of my legal work posted, but I have had some other issues to contend with. I should have it posted on my SaveAnInnocentLife site soon. Anyway, onto other things. Due to the great Texas cell phone scandal, they have moved everyone on death row around. I actually moved like three times in a week! Though that was more due to level status change. Most have not been able to get commissary because of moving around to other pods. Plus, since commissary is used as a means of control, the powers that be are limiting it.

Maybe it will help break the hold it has on most people here, and they wake up one day and think, "You know what? That commissary is trash. They keep screwing us over. To hell with passive level one shit." I just mostly care about stamps so I can get my letters mailed.

My thoughts are kind of jumbled right now. I got a lot on my mind, and I even got a headache. I used to never get them, though lately I have been. Maybe it is stress. I had some complications with the nerves in the left side of my face, though lately it has not been bothering me. It was just a sensation in the left side of my face. It was not Bell's palsy or whatever it is called.

Plus, I had a spot on the inside of my left thigh. It matched all the characteristics of skin cancer, at least from the descriptions in magazines. When a nurse saw it, he raised his eyebrows and said, "You will see a doctor tomorrow." Well, this clown of a doctor comes to my door. Now, I was on F Pod at the time, and F Pod has doors with two metal screens and plexiglass on the doors. The glass has grime from fire and pepper spray on it. Basically, it is not the clearest thing to see through.

Well, the doctor says, "Let me see the place." Now, he is standing like three feet away and looking through the glass and two metal screens. And just as soon as he sees it—not even a split second later—he says, "Oh, that's just a skin tag. You're okay." So I said, "Well, what about the redness and the fact it is sore and bigger than it was a week ago?" Well, the clown said, "Oh, it's just infected!" and walked off. So I said out loud, "How the hell is a skin tag going to get infected?!"

As he left, I called him an assortment of idiots, dumbass, and commie doctor, etc. There is another doctor here; I am going to try to get him to look at it. It hasn't gotten any worse since, and I don't exactly get sunlight that much…more so on the inside of my left thigh! I mean, free, I have been accused of keeping my clothes off more than on… Haha. But this is prison! Plus, I don't have a family history of it. So the doctor might be right.

There is another doctor here I am going to try to get to look at it. It hasn't gotten any worse since, and I don't exactly get sunlight that much… more so on the inside of my left thigh! I mean, sure, I've been accused of keeping my clothes off more than on… Haha, but this is prison! Plus, I don't have a family history of it. So the doctor might be right. It just pissed me off that he didn't take a better look at it or order a biopsy. Though this is the product of contract healthcare. T.D.C.J. doesn't have any power over the medical branch. I think this was set up as protection from liability.

Some of the people that have been around for a while or have read my old articles on my saveaninnocentlife site know about my last trip to the prison hospital in Galveston, Texas, to get a wisdom tooth cut out of my head. Well, they lost my chart and didn't give me any pain pills or antibiotics for like a week! Since they only took out one wisdom tooth, I get to go back for removal of another. Hopefully, I get antibiotics a little faster this time. I got a high tolerance for pain. Maybe from all the spanking I got as a kid and all the pepper spray here. But I don't want to get an infection in this place, that's for sure. We shall see how it goes.

Onto other issues. Some people get into relationships with people here or in prison. If you are real about the relationship, then you actually are putting yourself in prison with that person. I mean, if you're being faithful and all that. It isn't something to take lightly. Plus, in a relationship of any kind, both people bring all their past with them. The pain, fears, scars—it all comes to the table. This, at times, makes it tougher on the couple to make it. Then add in all the haters that want to try to destroy the relationship. The good thing about rocky starts is that it helps to lay a solid foundation. The adversity can help make the relationship stronger as you get a better feel for each other and a better understanding of each other's limits.

Most people, during a rocky situation, just give up and walk away. There is no substance within themselves. They lack the strength to overcome. They fear adversity.

These are generally the sheep in the world. Everyone has to have their limits, but at the first sign of trouble, you don't just run off. In my own relationship with Vera, there have been a lot of ups and downs. We are both hard-headed and have complex situations that define our lives. There have been people that don't like me or her, and they try to cause division between us. Though, as my mother can tell all, I don't listen very well, and I will do what I'm going to do! My mom used to spank me and say, "Clint, do not leave the yard!" As soon as she opened the door and turned around, I was gone! Haha.

Anyways. Life is short. I want to see all and do all. I know I am a difficult person to deal with. Life ain't been easy for me, so all that comes to the table when I get close to people. I will say this: no matter what ever happens, Vera has done a lot for me and done her best to try to help me, no matter the odds. She has sacrificed countless ways to help me—something I will forever be thankful for. Just as I am for all others that have helped me, even ones I am not in contact with anymore.

Now to MySpace messages. Jo of the U.K.—long time, no word! I am waiting on your letter. Glad that you made contact again. Rusty, I haven't been able to get your letter to you. I am low on stamps. As soon as I can get commissary, I will get stamps! Helia, thanks for the messages! Words are better than pictures, so don't worry! ☺ Simone!! Yes, you—the one from Austria—did you get my letter? I wrote you but haven't heard from you. I see from the message you're still alive—write when you can. To Jaxon's mommy: I see you can write, but can you actually mail that letter? RaK, thanks for the words.

Well, I got to wrap this long-winded mo/fo down. I am going to try once again to write once a week. Now that I am level one, I will be able to, as I need something to focus my stress on. To all, thanks for your attention. I leave as I came—solid and united.

Respectfully,

Clinton Young #999447

Polunsky Unit

3872 F.M. 350 South

Livingston, Texas 77351

U.S.A.

P.S. Song of the week is: "Ladies Love Country Boys" by Trace Adkins.

Loud & Clear, March 5, 2009

Greetings,

Well, the last week surely has been emotionally draining. I had a special visit with Vera. It shocked me how much energy it took out of me. Plus, I was consumed with worry every night and could hardly sleep. I always seem to think of the worst situations! I wanted her to come, have good visits, and then get back home safely. Something about flying over a big open span of water makes me nervous!

Anyways, it was truly a joy to get to see her. Time flew by SO FAST! Then came the last visit and having to watch her leave. (long sigh). As I said, the visits take a lot out of you. Though I did enjoy the fact that I could report good news to her, as well as to all of you reading this. The federal judge sent me back to state court to refile some unresolved appeal issues. The Texas Court of Criminal Appeals has to accept reviewing the claims. If they do, then I will go back into the district court, which is the court I had my trial in. This is a very good thing, as it helps me get my claims that were not presented due to the screw-ups of my previous lawyers presented to the courts in a proper manner.

This article will be short, as I am very tired and need to get some sleep. The battle only gets more intense. Hopefully, the people holding up the completion of my DVD will stop doing so, so I can get it sent out and moving forward! I always have some delay due to other people.

I will write an additional article in a few days. Also, my sister Christy will be getting more of my legal work posted here for people to see more of the errors in my case, as well as on my website: http://www.saveaninnocentlife.com/.

Thank you for your attention,

Clinton Young

Loud & Clear, March 9, 2009

Greetings!

Well, I finally got some rest and have been playing catch-up on my backed-up letters, as well as going over my legal work so I can send some ideas to my lawyers. I do want to cover a few things real fast—things people have written.

Judi, hey, Vera sent me your words. Thanks! On Radley, I used to get Reason magazine, and I really liked it! It is good. The article you mentioned, I actually had it on my DVD, but Vera is having to check to make sure it's okay for me to use—you know, copyright and all. (I liked the article as it points out these forensic mills that the state uses. Same with the Houston crime lab.) Hopefully, Radley will allow me to use his article; if not, maybe I can post it on my site. Hey, what part of North Carolina are you from, Judi? I used to live out there. I even met Dale Earnhardt's mother!

Anyway, I doubt that Oprah will do anything, but we do have a better shot with Drew Carey and Reason, namely if the focus is on the state writ (appeal) process in Texas. If the legal work from my appeal on Lisa Milstein is posted on my sites, then you will see what I mean! If it isn't posted yet, it will be soon!

I also wanted to write some stuff about my DVD again real fast. As I do know there are many who are waiting on it—some have already paid for it. Well, some of the delays are because some footage wasn't properly transferred, such as films of me as a child, plus breakdowns in communication with people. (Always something.)

Anyway, I was also going to add the police chase video; however, that was sent to someone to help transfer the footage and—what do you know—more delays! Hopefully, by now the footage has been sent as requested to my sister. Anyway, the point is that the delays are not my fault. Nor are they Vera's. There have just been one problem after another.

Hopefully, it's all sorted by now. However, due to time delays, a desire to get the DVD out as fast as possible, and the need to resolve issues, the DVD will not have the footage of the police chase or the childhood videos. The disk isn't exactly a book—it's a collection of my poems and some articles. I called it a book to simplify things.

I am trying to get it done as fast as possible. Hopefully, people will put aside ridiculous personal problems that are only harming me and work together so that I can get it completed. To those who already ordered it, I am again sorry for the delays. I wanted to make it as good as possible so that each person feels they got their money's worth. Hopefully, in six weeks, it will be complete!

Now that the judge has sent me back to state court, I am pushing harder for it to be completed. My goal is still to try to get the other videos on the disk, plus some additional information.

Hopefully, the CCA will accept and allow me to go back to the district court I was sentenced out of so that I can refile some appeal issues. It will put me one step closer to a new trial. (As I said to everyone, please bear with me on the DVD. Maybe it's already out by the time this is posted! If not, then hopefully soon. The deadline is six weeks.)

Jessi, please make a copy of that disk and get it to Vera. Thanks.

Well, it seems that the powers that be have limited our trips to commissary, so now we cannot get as many stamps! This is part of the reason for the delay in me responding to people. They used to allow us to buy food items and hygiene one week, and the next week buy more stamps. But they haven't been doing that. There's no real reason to not let us buy stamps like this, only retaliation.

You know, this is what doesn't make any sense. TDCJ is always talking about how little money they have, yet they don't allow us to hardly ever get commissary. The more money they let us spend, the more money they make. Yet they would rather oppress us and limit us than make money to implement the security ideas they cry about not being able to afford.

They also complain that there's nothing they can do to us since we are on death row if we hurt an officer or whatever, yet they don't want to give us access to telephone programs like population inmates get. This could be a means of control for them as well as revenue! A person acts up, they get phone restriction!

Also, they could sell us TVs. They say no because they don't sell them to the population. This is bullshit! Population—even close custody—has TVs! Plus, they sell the population all kinds of stuff they don't sell us: craft items, multi-outlet plugs, and even other kinds of shoes and jump ropes. The only reason for them not to sell us TVs is to oppress us. However, all the officers wish they would so there would be less interaction—plus another control tool.

If there were TVs and also better access to phones, TDCJ would make more money and have better control tools to reduce rule violations. They say they would have to do it for ad-seg—not true! Ad-seg is in such a situation due to violent acts or being confirmed STG gang members. The only gangs they lock up are Aryan Circle, Aryan Brotherhood of Texas, Mexican Mafia, Texas Syndicate, Texas Mafia, Barrio Azteca, and Raza United. So, seg inmates are there for a reason.

It's easy to justify not giving them access to TVs and telephones. But death row has to be in this environment. We aren't locked down for rule violations. There's some rumor that there are officers and ranks trying to get us TVs—not to help us, but to better control us. Several officers wish they would give us group recreation. However, there are a few who are scared and don't want that.

The ones who don't want it are, for the most part, the dudes. I just want to be able to buy some damn stamps! I came up to this stupid Level One and can't even hardly get any stamps.

Well, enough ranting this time. I will make sure that all are updated on the progress of my case. Once again, I'd like to apologize to those who already ordered the DVD. It will be out soon!

I also want to thank the many of you who put forth effort in getting the word out about my case, even though you don't know me. My goal at this time is to get my DVD completed, get as much promotion for it as possible, and also get some additional media attention.

The song this week is Brad Paisley's "I'm Still a Guy." It's a funny song—well, humorous.

That's all, folks! I leave as I come.

Respectfully,

Clinton Young #999447

Polunsky Unit

3872 F.M. 350 South

Livingston, TX 77351

Loud & Clear, April 1, 2009

I was thinking about something the other day. Life is a box. If a person is arrested for a capital crime and given the death penalty in Texas, from start to end that person will never leave a box. The jail cells are shaped like boxes, and a casket is a box.

I was talking to a guy about post-execution desires. He said he wanted to be cremated and his ashes spread over a location in Africa. I said, "Hell no, I ain't trying to get burnt up, and I don't want to be buried in a casket." He pointed out I had a real dilemma. He asked why not a casket. I pointed out that it was going from a single-man box to another! I want to be made into a statue, like how a taxidermist does deer and bears and other animals. I think that is illegal in the U.S., though.

For some reason, death has been on my mind lately, maybe due to the different direction my case has taken. I have better chances, so death is more of a concern. When I didn't have lawyers that actually cared, death seemed more certain. So there was an acceptance of it, so to speak. It is really hard to explain, though I am sure most understand.

Friedrich Nietzsche said, "Hope is the worst of evils, for it prolongs the torment of man." In my current situation, these words ring true. It is easy for people to say, "Be positive" and all that. Sure, I can have hope for a positive outcome, but I am faced with a stark reality. Texas killed four people in two weeks! Last year, China killed at least 1,718, Iran 346, Saudi Arabia 102, the United States 37, and Pakistan 36. A good crowd we run with here.

I went back to UTMB hospital to have my other wisdom tooth cut out. I didn't have the problem I did last time with the medication, though I was ten times more nervous. They put us to sleep for oral surgery. Well, they hooked me up to an IV and an oxygen/pulse and blood pressure monitor. When she turned it on and the guy started the IV, my heart rate jumped from 53 beats per minute to over 80. She asked me if I was okay. I just said, "Hell naw!" The doctor was cool, though, and that helped. I think he understood my concern about getting put to sleep, so they did not use as much of the chemical that puts you out. I was in and out all through the surgery, whereas the first time, I was out cold. I woke up in my cell bed.

This time, I was talking to the guard about death penalty issues in post-operation monitoring. I also noticed a huge difference between the prison hospital and the unit nurses. The nurses all work for UTMB out of Galveston, Texas, but they are stationed at units around Texas. The nurses in Galveston acted like free-world nurses. The doctor and nurses were nice, polite, and treated me like a normal human being. Whereas here, most have snotty attitudes. I guess that could be related to having to deal with all the inmates?

THAT can get on anyone's nerves, as there are some unique individuals in prison, to say the least.

I don't like being on meds, as it's just more that I have to deal with… I have had to jack the food slot and all kinds of stuff for my pain meds. The guard I refused to let close my food slot saw me later playing basketball and eating ice cream on the rec yard, as it was commissary day. She pointed all that out the next time she saw me and said, "Your ass wasn't in no pain!" I just laughed and said, "It's about getting what I'm supposed to have."

Now my struggle is over the medical mouthwash I'm supposed to get twice a day for 14 days. There's this nurse—I don't know her name, I just call her Clown Face as she wears an ungodly amount of makeup and has a very poor and ugly dye job on her hair. My mom was a cosmetologist, so I pay attention to these things. Haha.

Oh, a note to all ladies: dudes really prefer less or no makeup on you. With hardly any makeup on, it makes the woman more confident and more approachable. A little makeup shows you care about your appearance but are not trying to alter anything. So less is best.

Anyways, back to Clown Face. She never brings my mouth rinse. As you can guess, this really, really bothers me! She is the only one who does not bring it and gives a bullshit excuse about it. Long sigh. Always something.

Oh yeah, before I forget, they gave us spoiled beans again. I spoke up, and a couple of others on my section joined me in it. Rank said we would get a supplement. They lied! We didn't get shit. So now I got lied to, which upset me more than the beans. When that working shift came back to work, I tried to talk to rank, though they had numerous use-of-force incidents, so I waited till the next day and jacked the slot. The officers were like, "Man, that was a week ago!" I said, "I don't give a damn, there isn't no statute of limitations on you people messing me over!"

Another reason I pushed the issue is a guy popped off, "I see you still waiting on them beans!" So I said, "I'm gonna get mine!!!!" So ego came into play ;). Long story short, I got my supplement again! Which I promptly pointed out to my fellow inmate who made his snide remark. Haha.

My lawyers recently filed my appeal in state court. They had only 30 days to do so. I received my copy two days ago. I liked it. Now comes the wait to see what happens next! Always the wait.

Some good news is that portions of that are to be added to my DVD, which should be on its way to the needed people. I swear such a simple task has turned into a 2-year project worthy of challenging the attempt at democracy in Iraq. I figure I would have a better chance at getting peace in the Middle East than getting my DVD done and ready to go. Hopefully, Vera gets everything soon!

Nothing else really going on in life. I read The Kite Runner, then The Old Man and the Sea, and now I am finishing up A Thousand Splendid Suns. I really like this one. I am not finished, so I can't say if I like it better than The Kite Runner, but so far, so good. There seems to be a problem with some of my websites. I am trying to get more and more legal work posted. Hopefully, all that gets sorted soon.

With that, I am gone. I leave as I came.

Respectfully,

Clinton Young #999447

Loud & Clear, May 27, 2009

Greetings!

I guess I can start this with the most exciting portions of my past week. Friday, while kicked back writing a letter to Heather, I was disturbed by an officer coming up the stairs. I saw he had a pipe chase key in his hand to shut off the water to the toilet. This is to keep us from flushing contraband. Well, I knew right away: shake-down time. When I saw him look towards my end of the run, I thought, "Well, just great!" Then, when he opened my pipe chase, I uttered, "Man, what the fuck?" To which his response was, "Special shake-down," meaning that the higher ranks had sent them to my cell due to some form of information they had received.

So, I was stripped out and taken to a legal booth cage, then stripped out again by a rank. They then stood there looking at me until the metal detector chair could be rolled down the hall. It is a chair that you sit in, and it detects if there is any kind of metal object on you. Well, I was just in boxer shorts when I left my cell. So, the only way I could have had something is if it was 'inside' me. That was the whole point of the chair.

Well, I sat in the chair. Nothing! I put my face on the platform, to detect anything in my mouth. Still nothing. Well, they put me back in the cage, and at the same time, the commissary officer was asking me about my ice cream, as we got commissary on Friday. She wanted to know if I wanted it in the booth or to credit my account, as if they put it in my cell, it could melt. I looked at the rank, and I could just tell by the number of officers that I wasn't going back to my cell. So, I said, "What's up?" He said, "Got to make another trip!" So, I asked, "Medical?" He replied in the affirmative. So, I just told the lady to put it in my cell.

I got stripped out again, and then off to medical I went. They x-rayed me twice! Once while lying down and once while standing up, to see if I had anything 'inside' me. An inmate here had a cell phone up his ass, and the chair didn't detect it, but the x-ray, of course, did. This is why they started using the x-ray machine.

Now, after the x-rays were processed, they hung them up, and the rank and nurse were standing there debating why they couldn't find anything in me. I stated, "Look, I ain't about to stick nothing up my ass. Nothing is worth that much to keep!" This, of course, brought a round of giggles and smirks from the officers. The nurse then asked me, "So, what do you got?" I said, "I ain't got shit! If I did, I wouldn't hide it up my ass. Y'all ain't about to have me out here pulling nothing out of my ass, pointing and giggling at me."

Well, after all that, they finally let me go back to my cell. They also x-rayed all my property. They have this machine here that is like an airport screener with a belt-fed system. So, back to my cell I went to unpack all my stuff. Well, I didn't until today, so my cell looked like a tornado hit it. ☺ These people were really convinced I had something. Maybe it was just random. Inmates have hidden things inside them for ages. It is called "keestering" it. Hey, to each their own, but homie don't play that!

As for the x-ray, I don't consider it to be really out of line. I don't like the x-rays, as I don't want to be exposed to that. The nurse told me it is harmless. I somehow doubt that medical x-rays don't add up to some harmful amount. Anyways, a prison does have to maintain security, so I can understand it. But when they do it all the time, that is something else. I have only been x-rayed twice though. But I've never been caught with anything 'in' me, so I really don't think it's fair they go that route. You can read about the guy that got caught with the cell phone in him. Just look up "x-ray turns up cell phone."

Anyways, still no word on my case, though several recent rulings out of America's top court, the United States Supreme Court, are helpful to my case! So that is good. I haven't smashed on the system so much lately as, well, to be honest, I am nervous to. ☺ I ain't trying to piss anyone off as far as judges and etc. c/s.

But there is a case out of Pennsylvania. Two judges there were removed from the bench for sending kids to juvenile prison camps for profit. They were getting paid and, it's said, made millions off of sending hundreds of kids to prison camps for kids. They fucked off all them kids' lives for some money. Now, in America, we look at judges as "THE LAW." A judge is the closest thing to a dictator America has. After all, it was the court that decided the election of Bush and Gore.

Now, it's not fair to look at judges themselves in a negative manner. But they are human just as lawyers and prosecutors are. Most judges, if not all, are defense lawyers or prosecutors before they become a judge. A lot of defense lawyers started out as prosecutors, which can be good training experience. One judge was in the news for using a penis pump while sitting on the bench conducting court! ☺ I swear! People would hear a weird pumping noise, and no one could figure it out until an assistant stumbled across the penis pump. (To those not knowing what that is, it's a cylinder that a guy puts on himself and squeezes a pump. It is supposed to help increase size.) I mean, that is out there! I just can't imagine some old judge sitting on the bench during court using one of these! ☺ Hahaha Damn it!

Another judge in El Paso, Texas, was recently removed from office by the U.S. Marshal for some sex offense, like using his capacity as a judge to try to gain sexual favors. There was even an article in Newsweek recently titled "When Judges Go Bad."

("I Wanna Know" by Joe is on the radio. That's one of my favorite R&B love songs, though I am not really in the mood to be listening to songs like that.)

Anyways, as for my DVD, well, as of my last visit with my sister Christy, she reported that the other videos to be placed on it were received by her and sent to Vera so that the DVD can FINALLY get finished. To be honest, several times I have thought about saying to hell with it and canceling the damn thing. Two freaking years I've been trying to get the thing done!! ☹ I am not holding my breath, that's for damn sure. Vera has had the cases and design ready, just not the videos. Now that she has them, hopefully, finally, all will be done.

There was much more I could have added to the book part. I actually thought about doing that. But due to all the delays, I just want to get it done. I will have the other parts that I was going to add posted on my website. Part of the reason I didn't put all on the disk is I wanted to encourage those that order the disk who haven't seen my site to actually visit it and read all my blogs and etc. This way, they can read up on my case and etc.

Oh yeah, Louise Driver, hey, I got your letter, but I can't make out the complete address! I can't find your original email that had the address, so please send me your address so I can get this letter mailed to you! Thanks!

Next subject: music. I have mentioned songs several times here. I can actually recall the exact moment I heard some of my favorite songs. When I was a kid, I was at my Aunt Pam's house with my dad, sister, and twin brothers, as well as an assortment of other relatives from my dad's side of the family. Well, of my brothers (Dino and Dano—no lie, that's their names), I always felt closer to Dino. He was always considered the compassionate one. Dano was the asshole. Me and him have had a rocky past few years due to his testimony against me. He had no facts on the murders, but the fact is he got on the stand for the prosecution. I always felt it was because he didn't want to go back to jail and risk losing this trash he was with at the time. She is the one that Amber's statement makes mention of her kids.

Anyways, no D.A. could ever get me on the stand. c/s. Back to the point: my dad had his truck radio blaring. I was messing around with one of my cousins or something when "Bad to the Bone" by George Thorogood came on the radio. Dino yelled out, "Bubba, there's your song!" So I just took off running and climbed up into my dad's truck cab and twisted my head towards the speakers and just listened to each word. Afterwards, I just smiled from ear to ear. Haha Somehow, I think that song had an impact on me. Haha

A few years later, while in the garage with my stepfather during the winter working on something, I can't exactly recall what, but I do recall bending over using a grinder on some assortment of metal when "Shooting Star" by Bad Company came over the radio. I stood up staring at the radio, listening to the song play. I actually never knew who sang it until I got here!

The same sort of situation played out with "Simple Man" by Lynyrd Skynyrd. But that day I even remember what I was wearing and the way I was standing. As the radio was to my left when Bad Company came on, but it was on my right when "Simple Man" came on (different days of course). The radio never moved until my stepdad got rid of that garage, and it always stayed on the classic rock station.

Now, I'm sure I heard these songs some other time, but they never registered. I mean, I actually froze while listening to the song! I do have an unnatural ability to remember things in detail, but it always amazed me that I can recall the exact moment where I heard so many songs. I was sitting in front of the TV watching MTV in Gillette, Wyoming, when "Runaway Train" by Soul Asylum came on. I was 9!

When I came back to Wyoming, I was walking around the trailer park where my dad lived with his girlfriend, her daughter, and my sister Christy, when a guy was working on his radio. He was putting some house speakers into his car and was trying to get them wired up. He was listening to "Enter Sandman" by Metallica—the first time I ever heard it.

Sometimes I like a song for the lyrics, sometimes for the beat or the voice. My favorite female singer, as far as lyrics and just her nature, is Miranda Lambert. As far as voice, it's by far Sugarland, with songs like "Stay," "Come Home Soon," and etc. Well, I'm not sure if she sings "Come Home Soon." I haven't heard it in so long. But "Stay" is better, as it's mainly just her voice.

Reba McEntire (not sure how to spell her last name), but I like the country twang in her voice. A pair of OLD songs that always make me tear up are "Giddy Up Go" and "Teddy Bear." Both are by Red Sovine. I am just guessing on the spelling of his last name, but it sounds like Soulfine when they say it on the radio. The songs are from the late '60s, early '70s. Way before I was born. ☺ But if you can listen to those songs and NOT have to wipe your eyes, something ain't right with ya. Anyways, I had listed some songs I like to a friend, and she pointed out that I like mainly the lyrics of songs. I never even thought about it. But she is pretty much right. I often wonder if my favorite songs are a reflection of my psyche. I mean, I do like songs based on some sort of manner that I can attach myself to. Just like with the song "Dear Mama" by Tupac. For those that don't know, he's a dead rapper. Now parts of that song don't apply, but lots do. The basic theme of it did. I mean, my mom wasn't a crack fiend, not Black, and never been on welfare! But other than that, it's on point in most areas. One thing I noticed is that "Dear Mama," "Simple Man," and "Shooting Star" all involve a guy and his mom. When I was younger, my mom was always the most important person in my life. So I figure that is what made those songs stand out so much.

A side note: My next few articles are going to be longer than average, as I am going to tie in parts that I was going to put in my book—life story stuff, favorite books, music, and such. I know Brandi, Regina, and Christy are going to be cussing me out at all the typing they are going to be doing. Haha. As I said, my sister Christy came to see me last week. Had a good visit! I just got a lot on my mind lately. Stress through the roof! A highlight was that she mentioned one of my ex-girlfriends had located me. A girl I was with when I lived in North Carolina with my dad and Christy. This, of course, brought up all kinds of stories and people that Christy and I knew. I tried to be 10 years older than I was, so I associated with older people, which is how me and Christy knew the same people. I thought it was pretty neat that Randi had located me, as like three or four days before I had my visit with Christy, I was talking about childhood war stories with my friend. We were talking about ex-girlfriends, wild nights, and the sort. He had mentioned some event that made me tell a story—one of those, "man, that reminds me of the time" kind of stories. He mentioned some girl that was crazy or something. I think the base of our stories was about girls that hit dudes.

The story I told about Randi was the time I was just out-of-my-mind drunk in a motel room. Well, when she came in the room, it was just me and two girls. So I know how it might have looked to her, but it just so happened that all the other dudes in the room had gone outside. One of those "perfect storms" kind of moments. Well, she didn't like me drinking. There were personal reasons that had to do with another person. Anyways, there I was in a chair, just toasted, and she came in the room calling my name. I opened my eyes, and all I could see was a "Myrtle Beach" t-shirt with a smiley face calling my name. So I replied, "Who the hell are you!?" Hey, I thought the smiley face was calling me! Well, as soon as I said that—BAM!—she hit me. After she hit me, I shook my head, looked up, and said, "Oh, hey, Randi!" She then grabbed me by my hair, and I guess you could say she helped me out of the motel room. Haha.

I, of course, repeated that same story and many others while visiting Christy. I just thought it was neat as I've been reading this book, The Secret, and it talks about how things get willed into existence. So it was neat—I was talking about her, and then she pops up. All the memories that came flooding back! I used to get out of school and walk her home along with a couple of school friends. If I wasn't at her dad's house, I was at the Food Lion near my homeboy Robert's house. Well, minutes before five, I would take off running home. That's it! Me and my friend here were talking about running as a kid, and that led to stories about old girlfriends, etc. Anyways, it amazes me now, thinking back on it, how I could run at full speed from the Food Lion to my dad's house. That had to be a good two miles! It was the Food Lion in Kannapolis, North Carolina. My dad's house was right off North Cannon Blvd., across from the KFC. So if all that is still in the same place, I guess Google Maps could tell the distance. The road I ran went right in front of A.L. Brown High School. Anyways, I would run in the house, jump on the couch, and then a couple of minutes later, my dad would walk in the door. I, of course, acted like I'd been there the whole time. Haha.

That made me just think about the arguments my sister Christy and I used to have. Ha. I remember one time she told me to "shut up" as I kept saying some assorted word or another that was cool—or I thought it was at the time. Well, she started going off on me, so I replied, "Yo chill out, you're cramping my style." She responded with, "You ain't got no style, you're a dumbass!" Haha! God, ya gotta love older sisters! While there were many highlights in my life at that point, there were many dark moments as well. My relationship with my father started getting even more chaotic. I was associating with older, more aggressive people. So I, of course, picked up personality traits. Well, my dad was an abusive person, so I was getting to the point where I was getting tired of being a victim. Then the event took place where my dad beat me with the 2×4 board (a two-inch thick by two-inch wide board), all because of a school prank. That single event had a profound effect on me. The next time he put his hands on me, I fought back. I didn't see him again until I was 17.

I tried to tell myself, "I only got one dad; he only knows how to do what his dad done to him." But that event always popped into my head. I was working with him. Well, that didn't last long at all. He fired me on my day off over an argument I got into with Dano's girlfriend! That's just the kind of idiot my dad was. Well, I was mad, and he had been drinking, so I popped off and said something, and somehow my mom got brought up, and he called my mom a bitch. So I jumped to my feet and said, "Don't talk about my mom like that." So he got up, and I started toward him. I mumbled, "I ain't a kid no more." So he started toward me and made some comment about, "Oh, so you wanna be a tough guy." I just stopped, walked away, and yelled, "Man, fuck you!" I really wanted to just beat his ass that day! My dad, while older, wasn't weak. But I was worried about killing him. I didn't feel like going back to jail. He had had two heart attacks by this point, so when I started toward him, I thought, "Man, I'm gonna beat his ass, and he's gonna have a heart attack, then I'm going to end up back in jail." So I just walked away. After that, I rode back with him and my brother and his chick to East Texas. I didn't say a word really on the way back. I left my oldest sister's wedding with Dino and Dano, went and got my car, came back to watch my sister get married, and then I left. I didn't see my dad or sisters again until court on this case.

Back to North Carolina. Well, during this time, I was dealing with the events of my dad and was facing a turning point in my life. Plus, I was not taking the A.D.H.D. meds I had been, as a kid, taking for years. So when I ended up back at my mom's, here in Texas, I wasn't trying to hear what my stepfather was talking about—or my mom, for that matter. I ran away a few times and then ended up beginning my journey through the juvenile system. I think, really, I just became aware! When my dad done what he done with that board, I became aware that I had been a victim far too many times. The shit I dealt with from my stepdad and my real father—I just became aware of it all. I think my mom caught some of the blame as she's the one that had me with my father, and she was the one married to my stepdad. That's how I looked at it. She no longer could control me, which is how I ended up in the placement, which led me to going to T.Y.C.

The prosecutor tries to use my juvenile record against me. Well, what they never pointed out is that it was my own mom that got me sent to juvenile because there's no way she could have controlled me. And to be honest, I wasn't even mad when she took me to the police station. As we were on our way back from Louisiana, where I had just been arrested in a stolen car with two others, me and another kid took his stepmom's car, along with my girlfriend at that time, Tasha. Well, my stepdad told my mom to do something with me, but not to bring me back home. When she told me this, it only set me off even more. My thinking was, okay, make HIS ass leave! Well, by the time we got to the police station, I had told her I would rather be locked up than live with them. I even tried to jump out of the truck. I told the cop, when he told me they were taking me to juvenile, "I don't give a shit!" Well, after two weeks of being locked in that damn cell, I changed my mind and wanted to go home. Ha. Something about jail sure does make that happen.

I was doing good. Everything was all right on the home front until two dudes I was with broke into a neighbor's house. I stayed outside. I didn't go in the house, as my probation officer told me I was going to go to T.Y.C. if I got into any more trouble. Well, the IDIOTS I was with showed their mom the stuff they stole or something like that. My mom found out, and somehow or another, a cop ended up at my house. I ended up going to juvenile lockup for that. I was riding in the cop car, and the cop told me, "Your buddies blamed you for everything." I said, "Yeah, that's what you all say!" Well, the cop replied, "No. I am serious. I am not trying to get you to snitch. Your buddies really did blame everything on you!" So I just said, "Well, who had the most stuff?" and we took the rest of the trip in silence. That was Dec. 15, 1997.

I will get into my journey through the juvenile system in greater detail in another article. This one is getting too long! ☺ A side note is that every time I got in trouble with others, I always ended up being the only one that didn't say anything! So who gets the worst of the deal? Yours truly! This article has covered shakedowns, ex-girlfriends, favorite songs, juvenile chaos, and child abuse. Needless to say, it's been all over the place. It's kind of like me, I guess. I just go with the flow and adjust as it comes at me. I didn't mean to sit down and make this as long as I did. But when I started, I just got in the mood to keep going. Oh well. Anyways, I need to wrap this up so I can get some letters ready to go out. Tune in next week. I leave as I came. Peace out!

Respectfully,

Clinton Young #999447

Polunsky Unit

3872 FM 350 South

Livingston TX 77351

Loud & Clear, July 29, 2009

If it's not one thing, it's another! I had a visit with my lawyer last week on the 22nd. As of then, the judge currently dealing with my case has still not appointed me a lawyer. When pressed as to why my lawyers have not been appointed to my case—without them being formally appointed, they cannot file the things I need filed in my appeal and for future issues—the judge hinted that he was looking to appoint a different lawyer.

NOW this makes NO sense at all! It means that another lawyer would have to spend time getting to learn my case, thus costing the county more money. The lawyers that were on my case and got me sent back to state court are fully aware of all the issues and have still kept working on the issues I'm focused on. What it is, is that the trial judge is trying to figure out a way to screw me over and stick me with some trash-ass lawyer from West Texas that will play puppet to the local prosecutors, just as my past lawyers have done. It's clear as can be that the judge is NOT wanting my lawyers, who are from outside of Texas, on my case.

I have the federal public defender's office out of California. I am the only Texas death row inmate with a public defender on my case. I also have Donald Vernay, who is from New Mexico. He is on the approved list of lawyers to work on Texas state appeals (the federal public defenders have to sign on through Don as co-counsel, so Don has to be appointed).

The judge might have already appointed them, but as of today, I haven't gotten any letter stating otherwise. So, if the judge does appoint some local counsel, I will have to begin the fight to get him off my case.

Now, I have easily proved that I did not commit the murders. They did not properly investigate the crime scenes—the ones they actually did investigate. Two crime scenes were never investigated. It has also been proven the prosecutor gave backroom deals to the witnesses in return for their testimony against me and had the witnesses lie about the deals under oath. There is also much more. Yet instead of doing the right thing and acting according to justice, they are trying to cover up their errors and would rather have me die for something I did not do instead of admit they are wrong.

Man, these people are ruthless. The fact is that all scientific proof shows that I COULD NOT have been the shooter. All they have is a co-defendant that I can already prove lied for the prosecution. Yet, to hell with me—just kill me.

You know what really bothers me though? Most people who read this act like they would rather read about events from my childhood than about how these people are trying to judicially slaughter me.

If push comes to shove, I might have to retain a lawyer for this myself. So, I am asking anyone willing to please donate to my defense fund. I ask that everyone please order my DVD. It's finally, truly complete, and the order information is on my website, www.saveaninnocentlife.com. If there are any complications with this, please send an email to Randi, who operates the Christian site, or directly to my sister Christy Jetton. The PayPal and mailbox information is on my website and pages. I appreciate any and all help.

For those new to my MySpace page, please go to my sites and read over the additional information associated with my case and past articles.

My mail has been slow this week—the days I get mail. See, that's the problem with this place: everyone has to kick up dust to get any act right. Lately, they haven't even been mopping the runs at nighttime. All kinds of fires and shit have to be started just to get the floor mopped. It makes no sense at all.

Then, with the meals, we get milk at breakfast only five days a week. The days we don't get milk, we are supposed to get a vitamin C supplement drink—basically some weird orange juice stuff. They haven't been giving that to us. Yet none of these badasses here say anything. They brag about being this tough and that tough, yet they allow themselves to be systematically fucked over by the officials.

Unless it's about commissary. They keep us from being able to buy the snack items, coffee, and stuff the prison sells us, and people raise all kinds of hell. But what can be expected from a majority population that willingly lays down to die?

Long sigh.

Sometimes the section that I live in is the only section that gets mopped. There is a total of 36 sections in this building. Sometimes they try to get away without cleaning the shower. There is one shower for every seven cells—one on two row and a second one on one row. Each row is seven cells. Each section is separated by a wall with a crossover door. So, seven men share a shower, one at a time ☺ (it's not a group shower). Some of these uncivilized idiots do all kinds of stuff in the shower. So yeah, I get concerned with it being cleaned with bleach and scrub brushes.

It's population inmates that do the cleaning, but it's an officer that escorts them. So, it's on the officer to make them do the work.

I am still trying to get my stuff all situated. My life got turned inside out there for a minute. People putting their nose in other people's business and others responding on emotion and doing counterproductive acts haven't helped any. Life goes on.

Anyways, I once again ask that everyone please order my DVD. There is lots of content on it. Even the police chase is included. People ask, "Why did I run if I did not do it?" Well, I was on parole from TYC, young, been up for days on meth, and they shot at me. So, in short, I didn't want to go to jail. Guilty or not, murder or no murder, I still would have gone to jail even for the parole violation.

As all can most likely tell, I am frustrated. I am just tired of people focusing on stupid B/S and frivolous drama. Stir up some drama, and hundreds have an opinion. Ask about helping to prevent my slaughter or any ideas, and only one or two have something to say.

Anyways, I am going to wrap this one up.

Catia, your letter is on the way. Natalie, I haven't heard from you in a while. I wrote you twice. I also want to thank Dominique for operating my Facebook. I do need the messages, Dom—thanks.

I leave as I came.

Respectfully,

Clinton Young #999447

Polunsky Unit

3872 FM 350 South

Livingston, TX 77351

Loud & Clear, August 26, 2009

This is going to be short and sweet. I don't feel much like writing. I haven't heard from my sister since she last came to visit me on 8/8. Of course, if something happened to her, I couldn't exactly depend on my family to inform me. Anyway, I don't want to get into that can of worms.

As for my legal situation, I finally got one of my lawyers on my case. I'm having to fight to get the other two appointed. The judge denied them for a bogus reason. I didn't get a lawyer on my case until I wrote, telling the judge to allow me to represent myself if they weren't going to appoint my lawyers, as it had been over 60 days. A few days later, he appointed the lawyer. It's a fight every step of the way.

If some of the posted articles don't make sense, well, that's because one wasn't supposed to be posted, and two other articles Christy had, so the order was all messed up. Plus, as far as I know, an article that I sent Randi in July wasn't posted.

Anyway, I don't feel like going into much else here. To anyone that has ordered the DVD but hasn't received it yet, please just hang tight until I get everything figured out. Keep an eye on my site, as I will inform everyone of the changes and such.

I leave as I came.

Respectfully,

Clinton Young #999447

Polunsky Unit

3872 FM 350 South

Livingston, TX 77351

Loud & Clear, September 8, 2009

Topic: STRENGTH!!

How strong is a man supposed to be? What is the measure of a man? In a way, the measure of a man is like the concept of reality—it's according to the person and culture. Reality is based on perception. I had someone who is a close friend write me in concern about some of my previous articles. She wasn't amused by them and thought I was stronger than that. I am in no way condemning her words! It isn't about that, but her words got me thinking, and that is what inspired this article.

I honestly don't know which article she is talking about. I have been under so much stress lately that I can't even recall what I wrote in my articles the past few weeks. I was in an emotionally displaced mind frame, I guess you could say. Though it did get me to thinking: how strong am I supposed to be? Can my strength be measured by my resistance against the system, or by my ability to maintain my humanity and contain myself?

In a recent article, I pointed out the story in the New Yorker about the kind of cells I am housed in. Let me tell ya, those thoughts and that rage are true. For the longest time, my resistance is what kept me going. The fact that I had to battle my previous lawyers at every turn—it was like I had no win no matter which way I turned. So my foundation was built upon my struggle.

Then I got new lawyers on my appeal. Instead of being happy, I felt sad and kind of lost. It was the first time I ever had thoughts of harming myself when I should have been rejoicing. I didn't have to fight that struggle anymore, my resistance against the system. I never felt more alive than when I was fighting the system with others. The struggle, the adversity—it motivated me. I felt alive.

Against the odds! Me getting run in on by the guards and pepper sprayed often confuses people. Some here report how scared or nervous they feel when they get a use of force. I commend them for fighting through their fear, but I never felt that. I felt energized. Right when the door opened and they started coming in, I felt a sense of calmness. Afterwards, I would feel so relaxed and in a great mood. I never slept better than the night after a use of force. I think that is due to the release of so much pent-up energy.

Not all my moments have been strong, though. I have felt helpless. I have been so consumed with rage at the guards and just life in general that I was on my knees in the middle of my cell floor with my head pressed against the floor, biting my knuckles so hard they bled. Thinking of nothing else but lashing out at the guards.

I have laid in bed thinking of just not writing anyone else. Going to Level Three and never writing another person! The oppressive nature of the system. The tigerish lust to annihilate shown by the courts and prosecutors. The ignorance of the people. And mostly the lies and pipe dreams of those that should be by my side or claim a desire to be. As well as the drama games that take place in here with other inmates. It all adds up.

More so due to my personality. Some people are able to survive in here because they have no ability to guide themselves. They are satisfied with letting others run their lives. Their whole life has been spent as sheep, so their weakness helps them survive. My strength has helped me to survive and, on the other hand, almost destroyed me.

I had to deal with lawyers trying to kill me. An investigator that blew one of my appeals due to smoking crack with witnesses and filing false statements in my appeal. Then an investigator was hired by a friend of mine for "a lot of money." It was all wasted due to my lawyers at the time refusing to even speak with the investigator. The lawyers sent me paperwork to sign to give them permission. I signed it, and they got it!

Well, they just started to refuse to return the investigator's calls. They didn't speak to my investigator until ten days before my appeal was due. When they did speak with him, they had him look into a bunch of frivolous bullshit that only burned up the money—matters that they knew were baseless and false! Basically, they diverted the investigator from anything that pertained to showing I was innocent.

You don't believe me? Well, the friend that was dealing with the investigator is still around! It isn't my place to put her out in public. She was shocked by it all.

Then I was able to finally get these lawyers off my case. I got appointed the federal public defender's office from Los Angeles, California, as well as Donald Vernay of New Mexico. I was the ONLY Texas inmate with a federal public defender's office on his case. The Fifth Circuit region of the United States—which is Texas, Louisiana, and Mississippi—I believe those are the only three states in the Fifth Circuit. Nowhere in the Fifth Circuit did any other inmate but me have a federal defender's office on their case.

This rarity did open some doors and upset some people. The result of having them on my case is me being back in the trial-level court with proof that the prosecutors hid evidence and had people lie. They also helped to get the ballistic testing that shows I didn't commit both murders. Before, I was only able to get a report on one of the murders.

The murder of Samuel Petrey is the one that mattered the most, as his death is what makes it a capital murder. I had two counts—two murders for one count and murder robbery for the other count. Samuel Petrey was listed in both counts. So without his death, there is no capital offense. If I prove I am innocent of his murder, I prove I am innocent of capital murder. I have done that.

The state's own experts show I couldn't have done the murder. They also uncovered that the judge over my trial—who is also the very same judge I am back in front of—sent a letter to all of my jury members telling them I am dangerous and deserve to die. He then turned around and denied my motion for a new trial and then denied my state writ of habeas corpus. The appeals court found that there was no harm in him sending that letter to my jury and sent me right back in front of him.

For 67 days, he would not even appoint me a lawyer. I had to write him and request to represent myself if he wasn't going to appoint my same lawyers. It would have been more complicated for them to let me do that, so he appointed Donald Vernay back on my case. The lawyers have to be reappointed at every level of appeal.

Though he refused to put the two lawyers working on my case from California. The reason given was not a valid one, so my lawyers filed for reconsideration and provided proof that the judge's reason was invalid. He still refuses to appoint them. I am starting to think that this judge is a tad bit biased. What do y'all think?

Also, to make things a little more interesting, guess who gets to investigate the prosecutors for presenting false testimony and withholding evidence? THE VERY SAME PROSECUTION OFFICE! That's right. The Midland County District Attorney's Office gets to investigate the Midland County District Attorney's Office for misconduct! The current head prosecutor is one of the prosecutors listed as withholding evidence. So I have a judge that has openly stated that I deserve to die and the same prosecutors who withheld evidence investigating themselves and dealing with my case. I mean, please really think about that! NOW you all see why my stress level is so high? Why I try so hard to get the funding raised for future legal costs and try as hard as I can to get media attention?

I had to fight like hell to get the previous lawyers off my case. I finally get decent lawyers, and I've got to fight like hell to get them back on my case! JUSTICE AND FAIRNESS? Time ticks on… In the meantime, I strive to stay strong.

Next issue. I have previously mentioned the case of Cameron Todd Willingham. I recently got some articles on his case, old and new. I BEG you all to go to www.chicagotribune.com and look up the article posted August 25, 2009, by Steve Mills. The article I got in the mail had three of the comments posted. It shows an indicator of (34) comments by the date the article was printed for me.

The top comment of the three that got printed cites his final statement. The next comment cites Willingham v. State, which is what the appeal judge wrote out. They take the words of the prosecutor and repeat them in their opinion, making the defendant look as bad as possible.

Well, in the opinion listed in the comment, it makes it seem like Willingham had no concern for his kids and was only worried about his car. He just sat there watching it burn. Well, the VERY NEXT comment was taken from the New Yorker in an investigation they did. It says that while talking to a fireman, another fireman carried out one of his kids, and Todd ran over to her, saw her, and then tried to run into the house. They had to put him in handcuffs and tackle him to keep him from running into the house after his other two kids. He even punched a cop, giving him a black eye while trying to get back into the burning house.

A fireman even said that prior to all that, they had to also hold Willingham back, as it was too dangerous. So you see how the opinion by the state court paints this image of an evil person who just sat there watching his house burn up with his kids in it while only worrying about his car. Yet upon further digging, it gets revealed that "Oh, what do you know," he had to be restrained, not once but twice, and even assaulted a cop to try to get inside the house!

The first fireman on the scene had to keep him back. Yet the court's opinion says that Willingham showed ZERO concern for his kids and no remorse.

See, what people don't realize is that when a prosecutor files a response to an appeal, they ONLY pick and choose and present the bits and pieces that absolutely support the prosecution's position. So the whole picture isn't presented. Then, if the court (which in the past more often than not has) accepts the prosecutor's findings of fact, the court adopts that finding and presents it as their ruling.

An example from my case: the court says I shot a man during a home invasion, yet this VERY same man that was shot says that I didn't even have a gun. I got his testimony! He says it in his testimony and in the initial police report. Yet the state doesn't quote that.

Well, since the defendant's lawyers file the appeal first and then the state responds to it, we have no idea what the state will say. So there is a guessing game on what to raise and what to say in the appeal. The cards are stacked against us, is what I am saying here.

Willingham's situation is a prime example. The prosecutors make me out to be some violent, hell-bent-on-total-destruction guy when I was free, but when a person looks a little deeper, it all starts to fade away.

The media often doesn't help, as most Texas media caters to the prosecution. When you read the words "the state's position," well, the state is the same as saying the prosecutor or district attorney. They represent the state. So when we say the "state" does this or the "state" does that, more often than not it is about the prosecution when referencing something filed in an appeal.

I just thought it was interesting how the comments posted about Willingham's case (on the row, we called him Todd) show how the state propagated one perception, yet there was a totally different reality.

There was another media report from Texas. I think it was in Waco or the Houston Chronicle, where one of Todd's lawyers—his trial lawyer—just totally smashed on him, calling him all kinds of liar and names, and went on about how he saw the house and believed it was started by Willingham.

Now this lawyer doesn't know anything about forensic science. People will read those articles and think, "Wow, Willingham must be guilty and deserve what he got." What they will not think about is that this attorney is trying to cover his ass and the fact that if he had done a proper job, Willingham would not have been executed.

So if he let an innocent man die, it is bad for business. So this lawyer gets out in the media and, in a totally unethical manner, just slams Willingham's character and says he is guilty.

When the nine different experts that have reviewed Willingham's case say the fire investigators totally blew the investigation and testified in a false manner that was more fantasy than reality. Now an actual state committee is reviewing the case.

If they rule in a manner similar to the other nine experts, then it will be the first time ever that a state committee openly admits an innocent man was executed. So it will be interesting to see if they do it or try to cover it up. Time will tell.

It is little specks of light that shimmer in all the darkness that help to provide strength. The thought of being able to hold on a little bit longer. My websites are finally getting shaped up. So maybe some progress can be achieved.

To all those helping and focused on what matters, I truly appreciate it. A couple of people have stepped up to shape things up. Their help was a godsend, though they need numbers and assistance.

Time ticks on…

I leave as I came.

Sincerely,

Clinton Young #999447

Polunsky Unit

3872 FM 350 South

Livingston, TX 77351

Loud & Clear, September 14, 2009

Topic: FORGIVENESS!!

Forgiveness. Most of us seek it out. More of us try to be better people by giving it. Do you know the elements of forgiveness? Sympathy? I have a friend, actually two, that 'preach' to me about it. A book was recently being discussed by my neighbor and me. The book is Belly of the Beast. It's about prison. I didn't read all of the book as the guy the book is about is a Marxist (a follower of Karl Marx, the author of the Communist Manifesto). I also disagree with the writer's understanding of prison racism, which is different than everyday racism in the free world. Anyways, I drift.

In one part of the book, he writes about a person who is locked up by the state from a young teenager to adulthood and how that person can't truly understand forgiveness, sympathy, and such. He will be aware of these things, but the application of them is foreign to him. The reason is that prison life is built around the Alpha Male complex—who's the toughest. As a result, forgiveness and sympathy are not often shown. If they are, they are perceived as weaknesses.

Even something as simple as saying "I am sorry" or "thank you" has too much of a formal air to it. This often causes conflicts with some of the people I write. I was told once by someone during an argument that I was ungrateful. She went on about what she had done for me and such. Now I would say, "I appreciate it." I didn't realize there was a difference. "Thank you" carries a deeper meaning. In prison, we often just say, "Appreciate that." She was pissed at me, so it was really more about her strengthening her position in the argument and looking for reasons. But it got me thinking.

Having been locked up for so long conditions me towards certain behaviors, some even positive. For example, at the motel I always hung out at before I got this case, there were several couples that lived there as well as others who were a common presence. So there was, more often than not, some drama at one time or another. When someone would make a comment about it to me, I would respond with, "Say, that ain't my business, huh." This, in general, caused others to have more trust in me.

In prison, getting into other people's business is a way to get hurt. Humans are naturally curious. We keep up with others naturally as part of the tribal system or social structure. There is a difference between being aware and speaking on the matters of others. Speaking on it is associated with gossip. Gossip is associated with women. Anything associated with stereotypical women's concepts is seen as a weakness in prison. It's the Alpha Male complex. Forgiveness, sympathy, compassion, and such are considered traits of a woman.

I am speaking in regard to the beliefs in an environment that is run by the Alpha Male ideology.

To understand a system, you have to understand the foundation and creator of that system. Who creates the prison systems? The government. Who operates the system? The government. Why would the government enjoy an Alpha Male environment? Very simple: If the inmates are too focused on the pecking order among each other, how can we focus on them?

The United States has the largest prison population. It is one of the VERY few countries in the world that locks up juveniles for life without parole. The system will have a hearing to certify a juvenile as young as 14 years old as an adult. That juvenile will then be able to be sentenced under adult laws. A 14-year-old gets none of the adult privileges, but as soon as he/she breaks the law, they get the punishment of an adult.

Thousands, tens of thousands, of juveniles are thrown into juvenile prisons, then conditioned while there as a means to survive, and then released to the public. Many officers in TYC would state, "We just get them ready for TDCJ" (TYC: juvenile system; TDCJ: adult system).

In the trial testimony that should be posted on my website, saveaninnocentlife.com, Rachel Polk makes a comment about fights being such a common occurrence that they get numb to the violence.

Now, to sum it all up, the conversation about the book helped me to realize how the system conditions us against having forgiveness and remorse—the ability to understand how to apply it. In prison, if you see someone getting bullied, the proper thing to do is stay out of it, as it ain't your business.

The only real difference in TYC and TDCJ was how the inmates would unite against the guards. In TDCJ, unity amongst prisoners is almost non-existent, unless they are mutual gang members. In TYC, unless you were a sorry lowlife or child molester, if the guards did something foul to an inmate, everyone would unite. There were numerous times that gangs were in full war and would halt their conflict and go after the guards. Then, when the conflict with the guards ended, they would go back to their war.

BUT if the conflict was inmate-on-inmate, you stayed out of it.

Now, I myself understood and appreciated the concepts of forgiveness, sympathy, etc., but only towards certain groups, such as the innocent, the elderly, women, and children. In the Alpha Male environment, that is who you respect and protect. But emotion still isn't proper to be shown. It took me a year to really get comfortable with my trial lawyers and not keep up the tough guy image. So they had seen the tears and fears. They had seen the tears I shed about the murders—more so Samuel Petrey's murder.

But in the courtroom, more so in front of the prosecutors, I didn't want them to see me sweat. I didn't want them to think that they had me scared. So I carried on as if it was no big deal. What I wasn't thinking about was how others, not understanding all I had been through, would fail to understand my actions. So the victim's family looked at me as arrogant and without remorse.

Now I didn't kill their loved one, though I still felt pain and regret over the event and the loss of their loved one. One of the few times I lost control of my emotions during my trial was when they showed the photo of Samuel Petrey and his granddaughter. So emotions aren't totally alien to me.

Though the conditioning I received by spending so many years in a violent Alpha Male environment, I had lacked the ability to properly understand how to apply and read these different emotions. So the very system that creates these behavioral patterns uses it against us to condemn us.

My neighbor is an old-school Black dude who has been in the system for decades on the row. We have known each other and lived around each other off and on through the years I have been here. We have daily discussions on different matters—more so political arguments. Though there is lots of self-reflection on my part, so I will engage him in conversation about thoughts of myself and different events. It is taboo, due to some of the personal conversations and interaction I have with him—prison politics concerning race. Anyways, I digress, but still am feeding the point.

The United States of America. One of the so-called superpowers. The so-called "greatest nation on Earth." Leader of democracy. How is it that such a great place destroys its youth? Condition us, then kill us.

Why is it that this great nation, in rankings of the Organization for Economic Cooperation and Development's 30 free-market countries, has American 15-year-olds coming in 21st in science and 25th in math? OUT OF THIRTY!

We lead the world in incarcerated youth. We trail the world in educated youth. Many politicians are currently in an uproar from both sides about health care, while the very fabric of our nation is being destroyed. The future of our nation depends on those that the government seems the least concerned about.

We lock up our under-educated youth, condition them towards remorseless behavior, and then we kill them or lock them up again, condemning them as sociopaths or demons for being victims of their very own system.

California, Texas, and Florida. What do these states have in common? The largest death rows in the nation. What else? The worst juvenile prison systems in the nation.

Florida's juvenile system is designed like TYC. In the halls of Marlin State School, which was the orientation unit for all TYC offenders (it is now Mark State School in Mark, Texas), on the wall were all kinds of newspaper articles about Florida setting up their juvenile system like TYC.

Guess who was governor of Texas? George Bush. Guess who was governor of Florida? Jeb Bush. Yes, they are brothers.

The connection to focus on is the link between the worst juvenile systems and the largest death rows.

Now something I want all to do—hopefully, many of you do it. I want you to read The Unmaking of the Criminal Mind by Bobby Delgado. He was a gang leader that became a Christian. So the book contains religious concerns, but a good deal of it is about the prison system—the design of it. Trust me, it is a must-read! His full name is Robert Vallejo Delgado, though the book is most likely under Bobby Delgado. Read it, and you will have a much better understanding of this world we call prison.

There are many books that contain his writings, but the one you need to read is The Unmaking of a Criminal Mind.

To wrap it up by drifting back to the beginning of this article, there is always more to know to properly understand myself, as well as why the prosecution does and says the things they do.

A perfect example is from the New Yorker article about Cameron Todd Willingham. They used Led Zeppelin and Iron Maiden to make Todd a demon. He didn't testify on his own behalf, so the prosecution gets away with it.

If listening to Led Zeppelin and Iron Maiden makes you a sociopath and means you're into satanic behavior, then between the U.S. and Europe, we've got about one hundred million demonic sociopaths. More so since Led Zeppelin was one of the all-time greatest-selling rock bands.

Prosecutors are elected. When are you going to break your conditioning and stand up for justice?

What's the name of Beyoncé's last CD? What is the name of the three top-selling clothing brands? How many children drop out of school in your state? How many children go to jail in your state?

Which two questions can you answer?

I am trying to improve my ability to forgive. I try to increase my ability to be more open. It is a journey.

I leave as I came.

Sincerely,

Clinton Young #999447

Polunsky Unit

3872 FM 350 South

Livingston, TX 77351

Loud & Clear, September 23, 2009

The past week has been a journey. I took a trip back to Midland County to attend a hearing to secure the judge in my case. The judge that presided over the hearing ruled against us and allowed the judge to stay on my case. That was expected. It is almost impossible to get a judge removed from a case. Part of our complaint was that the judge refused to appoint my other lawyer to my appeal. Recently, they obtained a clearance from the Court of Criminal Appeals, and there is also a Supreme Court ruling that supports our position. So they are going to try again to be appointed. They did get to assist in the hearing to secure the judge.

I did get a smile from the hearing. In the final argument, the prosecutor really had a great argument on why the judge was not wrong in refusing to appoint my other lawyer. At least he thought he did. That was until my lawyer had his turn to speak, and he demolished the prosecutor's argument. The prosecutor was so sure of himself that he repeated his same argument twice and even looked at the head prosecutor in the audience and nodded at her, and she gave him a thumbs up! The fact that he repeated himself only allowed my lawyer to point out how the prosecutor was "talking in circles." So that was enjoyable.

The ride there and back was long but okay. Two of the officers I know from the county jail. They were corporals there. They left the jail and now do SWAT and warrants. The fact that they know me helped them at least be polite. Before, when I went back, I had to deal with dumb-ass rednecks; one even chained me to the divider in the car. So it was at least nice to have respectful officers.

The state has already responded to my appeal. They did not address directly any one issue in my appeal. They did not even deny lying or having witnesses lie at my trial, nor did they deny withholding evidence. Instead, they just filed a bunch of stuff that supposedly points to guilt that was presented at my trial. So basically, the prosecutors are saying, "So what if we lied, withheld evidence, and had witnesses lie under oath at trial? None of that matters because he is guilty."

I would also note that no additional or new evidence was presented that deals with my ballistic reports and other related issues, which are all new. I am not sure when the hearing on my appeal will be. It will be before 2010.

In additional news, the saga of Cameron Willingham continues. Governor Rick Perry was in the media denouncing the "so-called" experts. OK. Who is right? The at least seven top-rated-in-the-nation experts or Rick Perry? One of those experts was retained by Rick Perry's own commission. So he attacks his own expert? OK.

What about the cases of Ruben Cantu, Carlos DeLuna, and Gary Graham? All from Texas. Then we've got the case of Larry Griffin. What about the mentally impaired inmates who lacked the ability to speak out on their behalf? See, that is the problem with most hyper-conservative politicians. They refuse to admit error, even when faced with the clear truth.

It would have served Perry better to admit the mistake, tighten up on these errors, and review other cases. Instead, he charges ahead. All this does is scare the population. What happened to Willingham and Ernest Willis could have happened to anyone reading this. Though Willis got lucky. Fires happen all the time. So yes, it could have happened to you.

Then we got Supreme Court Justice Scalia saying proving innocence is not enough to free an innocent man. Keep in mind what I said about hyper-conservatives. That comment was made by Scalia in the Troy Davis ruling by the Supreme Court. Thankfully, Scalia was speaking for the minority, and Mr. Davis was granted relief.

In additional news, in the past three months, two former death row inmates in Texas were freed. One guy from the Austin Yogurt Shop killings and Michael Toney. I was surprised the press didn't pick up on that fact. I guess they didn't know to put the pieces together.

I am going to wrap this up. To all reading for the first time, please go to saveaninnocentlife.com and read my prior articles and case information. I greatly appreciate your time and attention.

I leave as I came.

Respectfully,

Clinton Young #999447

Polunsky Unit DR

3872 FM 350 South

Livingston, TX 77351

PS. Thankfully, the commissary manager was nice enough to allow me to get stamps. The pod I am on bought them a day before I got back. Though since we are on lockdown, we can only get $10 worth of stamps. They didn't have to allow me to get stamps, but thankfully they did.

Loud & Clear, November 16, 2009

I know that I just wrote a blog, but I wanted to take a little time to tell everyone about my hero.

My hero is a two-year-old baby girl. She, sadly, is no longer with us. Her name is Riley Ann Sawyers. She was murdered by her mother and stepfather, both of whom have received a life sentence. She was known to the world as Baby Grace before the authorities were properly able to identify her.

It is actually the reason that she was killed that caused me to have so much admiration and respect for her. Her stepfather was mad at her for breaking some rule, and she would not tell him "yes, sir" or "no, sir." No matter how many times he spanked her, held her underwater, or whatever else, she would not give in! No matter how much the punk-ass dude tried to make her, she wouldn't give him what he wanted. She would not call him sir.

I wrote about this case when it first happened. I actually wrote a poem that is included on my DVD set about her. The poem was read, in part, at an international meeting about youth violence in France a while back.

No matter how hard it gets, Baby Grace gives me inspiration to keep on truckin'! Had her life not been so tragically cut short, with the spirit that she had, there is no telling what she could have accomplished in life. There is always some story in the newspaper about a child being killed. The story of Baby Grace is the one that stood out the most due to the circumstances of the case and the way that she died.

It is hard to explain. The story, of course, made me cry, but there is also an element of it that energizes me—that's from the spirit of Riley. It's hard to put into words. In a way, I feel a connection with her. It's that refusal to stop. It's that warrior's spirit.

No matter what is thrown at me, no matter how many people try to screw up and undermine my campaign, post BS lies about me, no matter how many lawyers say it can't be done, or judges rule against me, laying it down isn't an option. It's the can't-stop, won't-stop-until-the-casket-drops mentality. (I also wrote a poem about this as well.)

It's why I use the phrase "Veni, Vidi, Vici," which means "I came, I saw, I conquered." It's why I had use of forces. No matter how much pepper spray or tear gas they used, I refused to submit! When a barrier pops up, the flame inside flares up to give that boost to go harder!

This little baby girl clearly had the warrior's spirit and more courage than hundreds of grown men that I have met! While her life was cut tragically short, her spirit lives on! Her life should encourage others to never give up.

You see it, you want it, get it! No matter how painful the journey, defeat hurts even worse. Use the pain to fuel the fire inside of you! As the saying goes: "I would rather die on my feet than live on my knees."

There is a portion of a book that I really like. It goes: "You do not drown simply by plunging into the water; you only drown if you stay beneath the surface."

So if times get tough, and you feel like giving up, think about Baby Grace. It doesn't matter even if it's an educational goal, physical goal, or whatever. Use the pain to fuel the fire.

Veni, Vidi, Vici

Clinton Lee Young #999447

Polunsky Unit

3872 F.M. 350 South

Livingston, TX 77351

USA

www.saveaninnocentlife.com

Loud & Clear November 29, 2009

Well, this Thanksgiving Day had a dark cloud over it—not just for me, but for the Petrey family as well. Nov. 26 is the day that Samuel Petrey was killed and the day that I was arrested. In 2001, the 26th was on a Monday after Thanksgiving Day. I was discussing this with my neighbor, about how I know it was affecting the widow very hard. This fact motivates me to fight even harder to show that I am not the one that took her husband from her!

The prosecution propagates a ridiculous version of the events, and sadly, this is what she believes. Eight years. This shit hasn't gotten easier. It has actually gotten harder. The last Thanksgiving I was free, I went to my mom's house and ate turkey and such, then had her take me back to my friend's house. She begged me to stay home, but I wasn't trying to hear it. Long sigh.

The establishment holding me hostage feeds us a little better on the holidays, though it gets smaller each year. I guess we really can't complain. Some didn't even get as much as we did. At least they did something, though.

Holidays normally don't get to me. I have spent so many locked up, it is just another day—but one without mail! Though, as I said, this one had a dark cloud over it. I did use my spare time to do much-needed thinking. I recently found out that one of my former friends that helped with my saveaninnocentlife.com site messed it up. Grrr. Thankfully, it is getting fixed, and I still have copies of all the legal work that was posted.

It does give me a chance to have it better organized and also have a detailed list of what all is on there, as I wasn't sure before. So maybe it getting screwed up is a blessing in disguise. Who knows?

As many will see once they look at my site, there is a special raffle ticket sale taking place—an awesome skydiving trip for two! All the listings and how to take part in the raffle are listed on my site. Anyone willing to take part in it, I truly am grateful for your help.

I am happy to announce that Katie has received 95% of the material needed to fix my DVD! So all is on track with that. She should have the rest and have the DVD fixed within the next three weeks. So starting Jan. 2010, it will be ready to go. I previously posted about the pre-orders for it. So that is good news.

To all that sent me messages of encouragement, I thank you! A common mistake is that people see all those that are a part of my Facebook and MySpace page and assume that I write them all, or the majority. With this thought, the person decides not to write me. I assure everyone I DO NOT write all or even near any kind of worthy portion of those that are a part of the social networking sites dedicated to me. Most of my day is spent with me laying in my bunk looking at the ceiling, trying to figure out how to pass the boredom. So if you want to write me, then please do. If, for some reason, I get to where I can't write someone, I will let it be known.

The hearing for my appeal in January 2010 is getting closer. I am getting a little nervous as so much is riding on it. I mean, if my appeal is denied at the current level, I still have other appeals to file. Though matters will speed up.

It is late, and I am tired, so I am going to wrap this one up. I thank you all for your attention and time.

I remain,

Veni, Vidi, Vici

Use the pain to fuel the fire.

Clinton Young #999447

Polunsky Unit

3872 FM 350 South

Livingston, TX 77351

Loud & Clear, 12 August, 2010

This is going to be short and to the point on an important issue. I have some things that I need to get done on my case. My past lawyers have not been able to locate some people, etc. I need to get a civil lawyer involved in an aspect of my case and also an investigator. The lawyer is only needed in a few minor ways. The main cost is everything, as I am not trying to give the prosecution a chance to get there first! They have already done so much corruption!

I am faced with the task of needing to raise ten thousand dollars to retain the investigator I need! He is top-rated and is well known for producing results. The main problem? I've got like 20 days to raise it! I've got everything in order for what he needs to do and where he needs to go, so he will not have to work for long on my case.

The main problem with my case is how spread out it is and everyone in it. Texas is just too damn big! Midland County and Harrison County are 500 miles apart! So an investigator has to travel that area!

I never have and will never lie to anyone about what I need in my case, as it would undermine my entire efforts. (I really ain't into playing with my life.) In the past, when I told people if I had the funding, the ballistics would clear me. Now all can see the report on my website: saveaninnocentlife.com.

I guarantee if I am able to obtain the investigator I need, it will be fruitful. Ten thousand will cover everything I need him to do. When I retain him, the contract will be posted online and all this for people to see.

I've got to keep this one short, as I've got much to do.

I leave as I came,

Veni, Vidi, and hopefully Vici!

In Solidarity,

Clinton Lee Young

#999447

Polunsky Unit

3872 FM 350 South

Livingston, TX 77351

U.S.A.

Loud & Clear, August 24, 2010

I finally got married again. I know, to many, this comes as a surprise, as I'd never mentioned being this close to that level with anyone. I'm a private person like that. Sadly, we are already having problems. :(It seems as if a divorce is in the near future; I married myself, and it seems we just can't get along! Me and I are always fighting! Hahaha :) I have gone to look for myself, and should I return before I get back, please keep me here! Ha! No, I haven't gone crazy yet, though I am pretty damn close. I figured with all the talk on gay marriage and such in the US media right now, I would just file to marry myself. Then I thought it would be best not to do it, as we would just end up fighting all the time. :)

Seriously though, it's interesting how this issue is being raised at the same time everybody is up in arms over Washington getting too big. People say the government has too much control and is too big, yet they want the government to control the bedroom and lives of certain sectors of society. See, the thing is that when you give power over something to the government, it may be applied in one sense while a specific group is in power. Once that shifts, however, the law is open to be applied how the next group of people in power deems fit.

An example: back in the day, interracial marriages were outlawed in certain states. People supported the state having such a law. Okay, with the state having this power, it then has the power to enforce such a law. They could make mandatory blood tests to check the DNA of each person getting married, under the premise of "racial purity." So if an individual falls in love with a woman/man but comes to find out through the state's in-depth testing that the person is 1/16th Native American, the state could possibly ban the marriage whilst keeping the files of such people to make sure that they would not try to marry interracially again. The point is, government has no right being in people's personal lives. If I wanted to marry three women, and all three were of proper age and knew/agreed with such a union, why does the government have the right to say I can't? Why would these women and I be denied our happiness?

I understand and believe in a social moral code; however, I don't think our government should involve itself in marriages. The government shouldn't give tax breaks or privileges for married people. Marriage is personal; therefore, it should retain no favor or loss from the government. There is a growing movement created by the Christian Right. I listen to American Family Radio every day. These people rally about big business this and that and how Obama is trying to screw big businesses over. They preach about how Washington is tearing up the Constitution. It's interesting to hear how they outline their arguments. They yell about the government's attack on limiting their freedom of public practice of religion. They then yell about the Constitution for freedom of religion, then say things like, "It supports Muslims being able to build mosques," etc. Though this is ONLY so that they don't appear to be aiming to promote a specific agenda.

These are the same people that, when the US Supreme Court banned the execution of minors, called Justice Stevens, who authored the court ruling, "a spawn of Satan and a threat to America," and so forth. The sad part is, when it comes to shows like this one, the average listener is not one to methodically read between the lines and see where a potential argument may be headed, as they are looking for advice and guidance. If people want to know where these arguments are headed, they need to read a book called The Handmaid's Tale. I read that book and understood the dangers of such an influence. American Family Radio supports the death penalty, saying "an eye for an eye" and that the law of the land is to be followed. If these people have power in government, then they make the laws… and death may become applicable to many more offenses.

I was listening to a show on AFR, and a man was ranting about Obama and Washington, D.C. He was comparing the administration to a dragon up on a hill watching over a village while the villagers have to slave and give the dragon gold. I'm sure everyone knows how all dragon fairy tales end, and this man was talking about having to "slay the dragon." Of course, he would add in, "… Come November," since that is when the elections are drawn out. Strangely, he would say "slay the dragon" three times but said "come November" once. He also mentioned that all this is "God's will," and such. A fanatic listening to this program would get the impression that it would be an act of God and country to slay this "dragon," clearly a metaphor for Obama. I haven't heard that guy on the radio anymore, so maybe even they thought that he was walking that line a little too close.

I am not 100% against the politics of such shows. I am a conservative on many issues, though my whole slant is common sense and personal responsibility. That being said, on some issues, I am more of a liberal as well. What offends my sensibilities the most about shows such as these on American Family Radio is that in one breath, they scream an originator viewpoint, meaning that they believe in the Constitution in its ORIGINAL form. Then, in the next breath, they rally against the treatment of Muslim women, which leads to random women calling in to support their battle cry. Sometimes I want to grab these people and ask them if they're seriously that stupid. If the Constitution was in its original form, a woman could not vote, own property, or have equal rights/respect as men. If women wanted to gather anywhere, a man would have to be involved, so there couldn't even be an all-female organization.

The "founding fathers" made the Constitution so it would be amended, and it was designed to be changed by expansion when future issues developed. It took such a change in 1920 when women were given the right to vote. They scream states' rights, which is a part of the Constitution, but they yell for Washington to stay out of the state's business. I want to ask if any of these women played high school sports and if they enjoyed it. If they did, they should thank Washington for going against states, in Title IX, ending gender discrimination in school sports.

In the state of Texas, up until the 1970s (!!!!!), a husband could legally RAPE his wife. Any husband accused of raping his wife would be free from prosecution, and if a woman killed her rapist husband, she could not claim self-defense. So just 40 years ago, if you were married in Texas, that "honey I have a headache" talk wouldn't fly. He could rape you, and there was not a damn thing you could do about it legally. Companies didn't want to give women equal pay, as big businesses tried to cut corners where they could. It was Washington that made it so that if you were a woman, you were entitled to equal pay.

There are women that vote for the Republican party just because they are against abortions. People have to stop voting over one single issue. People need to vote, period. In Texas, if you are a felon, you can still vote if you are OFF of parole. People constantly ask about what they can do to change things. In Texas, the people vote for a county prosecutor as well as judges, so don't ONLY vote for senators/governors/presidency. Start locally. Most people don't even know about the officials that run their own county! Another thing I would like to mention is that women come on shows about activist judges and the Supreme Court making rulings they don't concur with. It took the US Supreme Court to make it legal for all women to be able to use birth control pills, because contraceptives were illegal.

People need to comprehend that when they listen to a specific political program, it is pushing for its own agenda. Everyone should educate themselves AND think for themselves. The people preaching this aforementioned fear of Washington are the same ones that cite "to serve and obey" in marriage vows. They are the same people that support individual states' rights when some states have laws that condone raping wives, denying females contraceptives, and underpaying employees that are women. The only reason these people put a focus on women now is because women voters play a powerful role in politics now, and they are merely trying to expand their base to have more power.

Observe history and see WHO you are really giving power to. Ask a Southern Baptist church leader why it is called the "Southern" Baptist Church. Why did the "Southern" part of said church break off? I will give you a hint: it happened around the time of the US Civil War. Ignorance is the greatest key to self-destruction. I am not against religion. Not at all. I am against using politics to advance religion and using religion to advance politics. More so, when you say, "God gave me the power of choice."

Veni vidi vici,

In Solidarity,

Clinton Young #999447

Loud & Clear, September 9, 2010

This will be a long blog, though it is important. Thanks for reading it. There is so much I desire to write about, though the most important issues come first. I will have a couple of blogs posted back to back within the next week.

Nothing these people do has ever really amazed me, though they have managed to reach a new low. On August 30th, the cell search team arrived at my door. I saw that they had property boxes with them. All of our personal property, excluding electronics and shoes, goes into this box. It is 2 square feet. They mainly use it during unit lockdowns. Legal materials always stayed out of the box.

Suddenly, policy changed during the last major shakedown in July. (During a unit lockdown, they search the entire prison. We call it a "shakedown.") Some people had conflicts over their property. They were told that they had to submit a request for a legal box. This is a box given to an inmate to hold excessive legal material that doesn't normally fit in the allowed space. The allowed space has always been the property locker under the bunk in our cells.

Recently, inmates were told to submit requests for legal boxes. Only a few did. I was NOT told to. I heard people discussing the legal boxes. Death row inmates weren't allowed to get them for a couple of years. I decided on my own to try to obtain one. I requested a legal box from the law library, which controls such matters. They sent me a five-page document to fill out and return to them. NOWHERE on the document did it say I had to return it in 45 days.

Some parts of the form made no sense to me, so I asked an inmate who worked in the law library. He told me that if my legal material did not fill up the big locker under my bunk, I would be denied. At the time, I did not have the proper amount of legal material. I knew I had transcripts and exhibits from past court appearances, as well as legal books coming. I decided to wait until I received all of that to file the paperwork, as I would then be able to be approved. Because I filled out the paperwork but did not turn it in, the cell search team showed up at my door.

It was determined that I was denied the legal box, EVEN THOUGH I never even turned in the paperwork. That fact earned me a denial. As a result, it was determined that I could only have 2 square feet of property, period — be it personal or legal material.

The cell search team got to my door. I thought they were only going to measure my personal property — that's the impression they gave me. I threw out some stuff I didn't need, got everything else in order, so it would fit easily in the property box, and avoided losing any of my property. After all was in order, I got strip-searched, handcuffed, and brought out of my cell.

One of the officers began putting legal material into the box. I asked why, as legal material had always stayed OUT of the box. He said I could only have two square feet. So I thought, "OK, no big deal. I get two square feet of each." What made me also think this was the fact that they actually carried two property boxes with them. One turned out to be a prop.

After they got my legal material into the box, they started cramming personal property into the same box. Now my mind was spinning. They all started to look at each other, then one officer, rubbing his head, said, "Man, Young, you got too much property." So I stated, "You got my legal material in there!" He THEN informed me that it ALL had to fit into the box.

Now I'm getting mad. They called for the ranking officers. A sergeant and lieutenant came to the pod. The lieutenant was trying to make jokes. So I just stared at him. He told me to relax; he was just trying to make the situation light. I told him, "Ain't a fuckin' thing light about you taking my property!" He told me it wasn't up to him — it was the higher rank.

The ranks go in this order from low to top on a unit: Sergeant, Lieutenant, Captain, Major, Assistant Warden, and then Warden. I announced that I could get in trouble and get the same punishment now, even though I wasn't getting in trouble.

We went back and forth. A sergeant started talking to me, explaining the situation like all I had to do was fill out an I-60 (a form inmates fill out to communicate with various officials), and he would take it to the law library. Once I got approved, I would get my stuff back. He gave me a timeline of 48-72 hours.

So now the choice had to be made. Do I send out most of my legal material, all of my personal property, or what? I thought in my mind that I had a much better chance of getting my legal material back than my personal property, as we have more rights when it comes to legal material — at least we used to. So I had them take most of my legal material, though ONLY under the belief that I would get it back soon.

The next day at mail call, I got my I-60 back. The official in the law library said I was denied, that I had 45 days to submit the paperwork. So I wrote him another I-60, telling him I was never told this, asking him to send me the paperwork again, and promising I would submit it. He responded to that I-60, saying I had 45 days and to RESUBMIT in 90 days.

This means that I cannot obtain ANY more property for 90 days! 90 DAYS! The officer, who is nothing but a law library official, has basically put me on a form of property restriction.

Now here is where the fuel for my anger comes from: I was lied to! Had I known all this in advance, I would have handled the situation differently. The cell search team lied to me. They manipulated me to get me out of my cell. Then the sergeant lied to me.

See, I also lost my hot pot, as the bottom had broken off when it fell off my sink. So I just lost all the way around! I could have refused to come out of my cell. They would have pepper-sprayed me and sent five officers in riot gear into my cell. I would have gone to Level 3, meaning I would have been on disciplinary level for 90 days. While on disciplinary level, we cannot have commissary items, etc.

So I would have only gotten my legal material back. After 90 days, I would have been able to get my personal property back. Once I made Level One, the 90-day point would be met for re-filing for a legal box. So, in short, the ONLY thing I would have lost would have been my hot pot. Though they would have earned taking that with being covered in pepper spray with me and having to do a whole bunch of paperwork, as I would not have made it easy on them!

So now I am having to argue and go back and forth with ranking officers about my property. No one told me I had to file for permission to have extra space. Here is what is so stupid about it all: If I got approved, they STILL would not have given me the stupid box! Only permission to use up more of the space that is ALREADY in my cell! It makes no sense! I have an ongoing appeal, so I need all of my legal material. It is a direct attack on us on death row. Others faced the same situation. However, mine was different in that NO ONE told me to file for any paperwork for a legal box. Plus, I was lied to. I do not like that at all.

So now I have one of my most vital appeals up and coming. Also, in the near future, I am going to have to meet with the investigator I need to complete some tasks and possibly a civil lawyer. And guess what? No legal materials to be able to present to them. However, thankfully, I am kind of a smart guy. I already predicted that a situation could develop that would end with me separated from my legal material, be it due to me protesting and getting pepper-sprayed or whatever. So, I always had copies sent to Katie, as well as a copy of my trial record. It does hinder me from helping my lawyers with my appeal, though not with the investigator and such. I am not done with this situation, so I shall see how it all turns out.

Onto other topics: the investigators. It was posted that I needed the funding to help cover the cost of the investigator. He has been in contact with Katie. There are two investigators that I need, as one lives in West Texas. So actually, due to the complex nature of my case, it's CHEAPER to retain two than to just use the one, as he would have to travel more. Plus, the other investigator knows me personally and knows my case. She sat through my trial. She was a legal assistant on my case while going to trial. The prosecutor of Midland threatened to press charges on her. He was indicating that she was doing work she was not licensed for, which was the work of a criminal investigator. She was not doing anything wrong.

What's worse is she knew and had worked with these prosecutors for years, though she worked for defense lawyers. She is well-known in that region's legal community. She did nothing different on my case than on any other case she worked on. The difference was how hell-bent the prosecutors were on sending me to death row. They were trying to block my lawyers at every step in fighting my case. She even testified to this fact at previous hearings years ago. Though as a result of the prosecutor threatening her with criminal charges, she went and obtained her investigator license. She attended my recent appeal hearings to be able to keep up with everything and talk to me.

I have a lot of love and respect for this woman, and I trust her. It is extremely rare that I ever state I trust anyone. I normally just say I have faith in them. My time to achieve the desired results is getting slimmer.

Let me focus on the amount of funding I am seeking. If I didn't need it, it wouldn't be asked for. It is that simple. One investigator I am in contact with isn't the cheapest, though quality doesn't come cheap. He is from Houston, Texas. Now, my lawyers and others read my blogs and such. These are people whose opinions I value. People I care about and who also care about me. If I were asking for something I didn't need and lying, then I would have to sit in front of my lawyers and personal friends and explain why I would do such a thing. More so when they respect me for my honesty and have faith in the choices I make when it comes to my case.

To me, that is not an option! I might, in the end, lose my life; I can't control that if it happens. Though I can control how I carry myself. I am not going to lose the respect those that care about me have for me. My lawyers cannot deal with anything outside of what they were appointed for. They can lose their jobs if they did, as they aren't normal attorneys. They are employed by the federal government. So, in order for me to get what I need done outside of my appeal they directly deal with, I have to get that help elsewhere.

After the investigators obtain the information that is needed, then the next step begins. An additional development is this: a human rights lawyer has agreed to look at my case. He is able to do work with human rights counsel with the Geneva Convention. I have to be able to cover his traveling expenses, as he needs to meet with me. That's all why I need the funding.

I really do not like to go all into details out in the open of all I am working on, though I want those reading my words to have confidence in me. My mail has been extremely slow. I only received one JPay today (Sept. 9, 2010). It was from Sandra and dated the 7th! So I was supposed to have gotten it on the 8th at the latest. I received no letters today. On Wednesday, I received no JPays at all. I did get a couple of letters.

There have also been some positive developments in France with some key figures taking interest in my case. Stephanie has really worked hard, as have all the others. Sandra got the human rights lawyers to look at my case. I am waiting on word from two other lawyers to look at my case here in the U.S.A.

My book is three-quarters of the way completed. I will be done within two weeks. Then it has to be edited, which should take a month. I might send half to one person and half to another so that they can get it finished faster. As they complete portions of it, they will email it to others to be translated. I might not meet my October 15th deadline. The first week of November seems more likely.

The company I am going through will make it available on Amazon.com and such eventually. My other book is partially done. I am fighting my case, writing two books at once, reading three different books, writing my friends, and also trying not to go insane. And women say men can't multi-task! Though, I like to get things done fast. I believe in taking my time with only two things in life: making love and holding babies! :)

Time is ticking, so I got to get back to working.

Veni, Vidi, Vici!

In solidarity,

Clinton Young #999447

Polunsky Unit

3872 FM 350 South

Livingston, Texas 77351

Loud & Clear, September 21, 2010

It's one thing after another! Now we are on unit lockdown again! Last time, in July, they only locked down and searched death row! Though this time they locked down the whole unit! Last time General Population got to go to recreation and etc., but death row didn't! Yet death row doesn't get the same privilege this time, even though death row hasn't done anything wrong on a scale to warrant such treatment compared with other prisoners. Everything they keep doing targets us! ☹ Throw us in a cage, tell us we are going to die, then sit there and poke sticks at us!

Anyways, to make matters worse, the pod I am on has not been to commissary in 18 days. I spoke to a ranking official, and he said that because we are on lockdown, we have to wait 14 days to go to commissary. On lockdown, we can only get stamps and hygiene products. We can only buy 30 stamps at a time, no matter what. Actually, on lockdown, it is less. So needless to say, I am not going to be able to do much writing!! ☹ I have to keep what few stamps I have for key people in my campaign and my lawyers until I can get more. Though I can still get letters. As soon as I get more stamps, I will respond. Now you see why I stay pissed off?

Here is something else. I wrote in a previous blog about them taking my legal material and the issue about the property space. Well, guess what? Since then I got more legal material again! They are going to be trying to take it! I am tired of these motherfckers!

Anyways, on a positive note, my friend Stephanie, who oversees the France portion of my campaign, has informed me of an offer to provide me with funding needed for a civil lawyer or for them to have a lawyer take up my case in concern for the civil law concerns. Hopefully, I can get the civil lawyer to assist me in what I need. This will be a huge help as well as save a lot of heartache from the fundraising attempts. I still need the investigators, though, so got to keep working towards that.

Oh yeah, also something else to point out to people—how expensive things are. Yesterday morning, I received the transcripts of the recent appeal hearings (court appearances), as well as a copy of the exhibits admitted before the court. It is a total of about 700 pages. Guess what the cost is? Go ahead, in your mind, try to guess what these 700 pages could cost if I went to the courthouse to buy myself a copy. What did you guess? $200, $600? Somewhere in that range? I mean, it is only roughly 700 pages. How much can a little over 700 pages cost? Try $7,451.53! Yes, that is seven thousand, four hundred fifty-one dollars and fifty-three cents!!!

My trial record—just the transcripts without all the pictures and exhibits—was over $8,000.00. So, say I was convicted of capital murder and wanted to attain an appeal lawyer myself right after my conviction. I would have to pay over $19,000 just for the copy of all the paper records. For what you pay for a new car, I would have to pay for about a three-foot stack of papers! That doesn't even count the additional files, such as reports and etc., that weren't put in the trial. I would have to pay a paralegal to get all of that and a lawyer to read it all. That would push the amount up to over $30,000 before any direction would be started. God bless the almighty dollar!

When I have the transcripts posted from the appeal proceedings, I will have the official page posted that shows the cost, so you can all see for yourselves. Since I have court-appointed lawyers, I don't have to pay for it. Hell, just to copy my TYC records, which are 1,200 pages, to get a copy from the court reporters would be $100.00. Anyways, thankfully, I have a copy on disk, so a digital copy can be made and provided to whoever I need it to be! God bless technology. ☺

Anyways, I got to get back to reading over all of this stuff so I can write my lawyers about it all. I just wanted people to know the good news, bad news, and shocking facts! No wonder why the police didn't investigate two crime scenes! They couldn't afford to. I'm gone!

Veni, Vidi, Vici!

In solidarity,

Clinton Lee Young

Loud & Clear, September 29, 2010

Last week a correction officer died in a car wreck. Her name was Ms. Miers. An older lady, I would say mid-fifties, maybe early sixties. She was hit by an 18-wheeler that crossed into her lane. I am known for not being the most appreciative person when it comes to correctional officers, which I more often than not simply refer to as pigs. Though I did like Ms. Miers.

I liked her because she was an honest person. She was aware that she worked at a correctional facility and didn't fall into this 'wannabe-mobster' mentality dictated by all these so-called unwritten rules officers are supposed to follow. Most think rules and laws only apply to prisoners. She was no pushover; she would hold her ground.

One memory of her that makes me smile: Another inmate had upset her and then tried to raise his voice. She got irate!!! I heard her yelling and cussing. She then ended up walking by my cell. I stopped her and said, "Hey lil' lady, what's going on?" and she just grinned and went talking to me like everything in the world was perfect. That's what I liked about her. She didn't carry her problems over to the next person.

She looked the part of a grandmotherly schoolteacher, a small woman with dark gray hair. She had the same hairstyle since I have known her—short cropped, somewhat curly. I wouldn't call it a perm. One day on the recreation outside yard (it is not really outside; it's a room with bars for a roof divided in half by more bars), she and another officer were taking the other inmate off his side in the recreation area. The male officer made a comment about how hot it was. The inmate they were taking out said, "Ms. Miers gots it hot like that."

When he said that, I started snapping my fingers and singing the Toby Keith song "Hot Momma." Ms. Miers, without missing a beat, smiled, patted her hair, and said, "It's not easy!" I roared with laughter. She had a youthful spirit about her; one could tell she was a good woman.

After spending so many years looking at guards like my enemies, it becomes difficult to sympathize with them. This place has a way of taking away that aspect of humanity for both prisoners and officers, but I was sad when I heard the news about Ms. Miers' death.

Her passing is an example of how little control we have over our lives. A truck driver fell asleep, and then she's gone. Her funeral was yesterday. It just shows how fast life can end, yet people choose to waste it on petty crap. Life is too short for all the bullshit.

Yeah, I liked Ms. Miers. I hope that she left this world as rapidly as possible without suffering.

On to other simpler matters... Well, no, I don't really feel right combining anything else with such a serious matter as this. I will have another Loud & Clear posted in a day or two. In the meantime, enjoy life and make your days count.

Veni, Vidi, Vici.

In solidarity,

Clinton Young

#999447

Polunsky Unit

3872 FM 350 South

Livingston, TX 77351

Loud & Clear, September 30, 2010

Seems every other day I've got a new blog; just got lots to write about. I have some soon-to-be-made changes to write about. Katie is simply only human and thus unable to handle everything pertaining to me, more so with two kids and law school. She will still be over my defense fund and working on many other aspects of my campaign, such as my website and communicating with my legal team. Though others will deal with the social networking site and blogs.

In the near future, SAIL will be established as a registered non-profit organization. This way, any donation is tax-deductible. In the past, I never worried about getting it registered with the government as it's a bunch of hassle. Plus, I do not do anything with the funds donated outside of the intended purpose of such. In the past, the funds were just sent to Katie. A problem with that is taxes!

I decided it would be best for all to just go ahead and get it all established as a legit non-profit. All the paperwork is getting put together. After all is set for the U.S.A., then I am going to get SAIL registered as a non-profit most likely in France for European donations.

Michele is going to help me with the U.S. Facebook. I have some other ideas currently being developed. Once all of that is sorted, I will post about it. Tali will be maintaining my currently being developed blog site, as well as other 'feet on the ground' activities.

We are still on lockdown, so stamps will be limited for a while. I ask that those I write please bear with me. People can still write me. I will get my response written, though I cannot mail it until after lockdown. So, please write as normal, and I will respond as soon as possible.

Magazines—I started to get many of them that were ordered. It seems some ordered ones I already get. I have gotten Yachting, G.Q., Details, Outdoor Life, Rolling Stone, Wired, and Psychology Today. I already receive Time and Newsweek. Some just take longer than others to arrive.

So if anyone tried to order me any of those magazines within the last two weeks, please cancel the order, as I certainly see no need in getting two copies. Thanks.

My case: I spoke with my lawyers last week. That was a good thing. No news other than they have two more lawyers assisting with my current appeal. I finished reading some transcripts from the hearing and other legal papers that weren't stolen from me, which I am still trying to get the rest back.

Anyways, I actually came across something very good. I can't write about it yet; I will when the appeal is filed, as all will get to see a copy of it. Though when I read it, I literally started to shake with excitement, laughed out loud, and said out loud, "Gotcha!" It, within itself, is not profound, but the way it all came together. By the end of October, you all will be able to read it for yourselves.

I gotta go. Take care.

Veni, Vidi, Vici.

In solidarity,

Clinton Young

#999447

Polunsky Unit

3872 FM 350 South

Livingston, TX 77351

Loud & Clear, October 18, 2010

I've been meaning to sit down and write a blog for over a week now. I've been too stressed out and focused on my appeal. I didn't even write letters all weekend. I have to deal with some frustrations in my personal life, though mainly this case has had my mind on "lock." Let me back up with some positive news. I was able to get my legal material back that was taken from me. During the lockdown, I was called out to an office so that it could all be sorted out in front of me, basically to make sure that I needed it all and that it was actually legal material. I got all of it except for a copy of a rally flyer from last March.

What bothered me was that the law library supervisor kept making smart-ass comments. He would look over at the property officer like she was supposed to cheer him on. After about 75% of the stack, he rolled his eyes, looked at the property officer, and let out a deep breath. When he did this, the property officer said, "Oh, he knew what he was doing. That's why he said," and in a mocking voice, she said, "I'm going to get my shit back." I knew right then that they had some series of discussions about me and my legal material. I did say, "I'm going to get my shit back!" but not to the property officer or the law library supervisor. I guess it bothered people that I was so sure of myself.

When they went to take it the day I was searched, one of the officers asked me what disposition I wanted. When property is confiscated, the inmate has the choice to: A) Destroy it, B) Send it out through visitation with a person on the approved visitor list, or C) Pay to have it mailed out to someone. Normally a person has to check one of the three, though to me, none of these was an option. I told the officer, "Ain't no disposition of anything. I'm gonna get my shit back," and then walked away from the door. What upset me was how they seemed to take my statement personally. I just want what I need in order to fight my case!

Many people write about their horror story-esque experiences with the property officer. She does get mad easily and makes some out-of-line comments. It isn't always unprovoked, though! The main problem is most guys here simply aren't aware of what is truly policy and what is myth. Then, they complain that "this" policy is not followed and then complain that "that" policy is followed. Ignorance is the root of much chaos. I, knowing the policies, simply refused to sign a disposition of my property because I knew that once we check one of the options, we cannot get the property back. If this place has taught me one thing, it's that communication/social skills paired with some good old-fashioned education can go a long way.

There are only a handful of people in this world that can cause me to truly lose my cool. They all happen to be women! :) Ha-ha! Anyway, I got my legal material back, so that was good. I had to listen to some shit-talking while I was getting it back. That's alright, because while he was talking shit, he was handing it back to me, piece by piece.

Last week I was worried about my legal situation as one of the lawyers working on my appeal didn't show up for a visit. He was supposed to bring my appeal so that I could read over it and then talk to my lawyers via a phone call the next day about it. I did get the phone call. They informed me that they rushed it to me via FedEx, which I received the next day, on Friday. I spent Friday and the weekend going over that and the rest of my legal files. My lawyers told me on Friday that they were going to set up another legal call for Monday (today).

1:00 PM came around, and the officer in the control picket did not call out to me that I had an attorney phone call. I started to worry. A few minutes later, officers showed up to escort me to make the call. I was worried that I wouldn't get to talk to my lawyers before the appeal was filed, as I saw a few changes that needed to be made. Once it is filed, that is it—no changes. Also, it has to be filed by the deadline. No excuses.

I went to the phone call anticipating having to argue my points in order. However, it didn't go down like that. I pointed out the areas I had problems with, indicated the changes I wanted made, and then explained why I wanted such. A few things took a little more explaining, though 95% of what I said they agreed with. One of the lawyers had to leave the conference call to get started on the changes. I then spoke with my lead counsel for a few minutes. When we were hanging up, she said, "Clint, we love you. Keep your head up and be good." After hanging up, I felt a moment of happiness. It's been a while since I felt good like that. Knowing I have lawyers that genuinely care about me and will listen and follow up on suggestions made me feel really good.

Then a guard came by and said something really stupid and pissed me off for a few minutes, but I eventually brushed her off and went back to smiling. My lawyers could have filed whatever they wanted to, sent me a copy, and said, "Here ya go, good luck!" Some people's lawyers do not even do that much! It is certainly a world of difference from the lawyers I have had in the past.

The only thing I hate is the fact that my lawyers cannot work on anything but my actual appeals, as they are federal defenders, meaning they are employed by the federal government. The actual name is "Federal Public Defender's Office." This is why I have to get the civil lawyer and investigator myself.

A friend who attended my court appearances in January and July made a comment about how a person could see how much love my lawyers have for me, including my old trial lawyers. My trial lawyers are very good people that I am fond of. They were just overwhelmed and stonewalled by the corruption of the police, prosecutor, etc. The difference between my trial lawyers, my current appeal lawyers, and the other lawyers I've had is the fact that my current lawyers and my trial lawyers took the time to get to know me and speak with people who know me. My other appeal lawyers just read the paperwork.

I believe I wrote about this in a former blog. When one of my past appeal lawyers first came to see me, he made a comment about knowing I'm not "firing on all cylinders," which is a reference to a car motor that didn't completely work. Like saying "the elevator doesn't go all the way to the top." The dude was basically saying I was retarded. I looked at him like he was crazy and said, "Dude, I have ADD; I ain't a fuckin' retard." That was the first time a lawyer had accused me of being stupid. I knew right then and there he and I were not going to get anywhere. Sure enough, it worked out that way. He was one of the lawyers I was able to get removed from my case and thankfully got the lawyers that I currently have.

My appeal was officially filed on Tuesday. I will know what the judge decides by the end of November. Sadly, the judge was not shy about being open to the fact that he was very pro-prosecutor. ☹ All I can do is wait and pray. Friday I didn't receive any mail, so I got Jpays on the 18th from Zandra, Angela, Michele, Tali, and Jenn. The dates of them spanned the 15th, 16th, and 18th. I did not get much writing done at all last week. I have been so consumed by my legal matters and also some other issues. I haven't even worked on my book, which disgusts me, as I could have been done with all three that I am working on right now.

I wrote out a couple of short stories. I'm doing a book that is a collection of them, as well as my life story book. I will get it done soon. My appeal and the transcripts from the hearing will be posted on my site soon. I am having a copy sent to someone, and then I will write out some stuff explaining everything, plus add in some other facts that show and expose the lies.

The annual anti-death penalty march is taking place in TX on Oct. 30, 2010. If you live in the area but need information, just Google Gloria Rubac, and you will easily locate her information. You can get all the details from her. I ask that anyone that is able to attend please do so. The bigger it is, the louder the message it will send to the politicians and media.

I am going to wrap this one up. I appreciate your time and attention to my words. Please tell ten friends about my website. I leave as I came and remain.

Veni Vidi Vici.

In Solidarity,

Clinton Young #999447

Polunsky Unit

3872 F.M. 350 South

Livingston, Texas 77351

USA

Loud & Clear, November 7, 2010

The death penalty has been heavy in the news due to Anthony Graves' release. I know Anthony, but not too well. He was always quiet and stayed to himself mostly. The media hasn't reported how others on death row have gotten out. In the last year and a few months, three people have been released from TX's death row: Anthony Graves, Michael Toney (he died a month after getting out due to a car wreck), and another guy from Austin, TX (who got out due to being 17 at the time of the crime). He got out of prison and is currently free. How the media overlooked all of this is beyond me. One would think all the anti-death groups would be heavily pointing these facts out to the media to help show how screwed up the process is in Texas. I mean, three different people in just barely over a year—that's a lot.

Two of these people had their charges dropped; the other one didn't get his charges dropped. Although he is out on bond, his bond was free, and it was just a verbal guarantee that he would appear in court. If they think someone is guilty of murder or any violent crime, their bond would generally be in the hundreds of thousands.

I can't think of the guy's name who was from Austin. His case was about three people killed in a yogurt shop in Austin. Two guys were arrested in the case, and DNA has cleared them. There are also two others from the Houston area who stand a good chance of being released within the next year. The two are personal friends of mine. They already have DNA proof that would clear them. One is just waiting on the tests, which even the prosecution knows will clear him. Yet they drag the process out.

There sure are a lot of people getting off of death row, considering how Texas supposedly has a 'perfect' jury process.

There's nothing really new to report about myself. Just been working on some new elements in my campaign. I had a visit with Michele yesterday, and I am supposed to see her over the next two days. It was a good visit.

I got word from my lawyer. I swear it's like every time I hear from them, I get some form of good news. See, I'm not complaining!!! ☺

I got a few more donations as well. To the doctor in Norway: Thanks! I also got donations from Sarah in France, Stacy, Carla, and Zandra for a total of $130.00. (That's the total of all the donations combined.)

I know that there are several people I haven't responded to. I have a lot to deal with right now on many different fronts. I haven't done much writing at all. I am going to get started back on my book, though.

See, here is the deal: I need to help people get a little more insight into the person that is me. I don't like having to ask for help, so I thought, 'I will just write a book! This way, I can get all the help I need.'

As I wrote my book about my life, it caused me to relive many moments and also made me think about the fact that it's as if I'm selling myself, in a way. I basically was faced with a double-edged sword, so to speak. I decided that I already came this far with it, so I might as well just get it finished.

I will have another blog posted up soon. This blog is a short one. I am tired… just exhausted all the way around.

I would like to ask those from Norway that are on my Facebook page to PLEASE attend the City of Lights event on November 30, 2010, and encourage others to join, too. I'm sure that Sandra will have all of the event details posted on the 'Clinton Lee Young Norway' page.

I am not going into detail about my lawyers' good news, as I need to double-check something first. After I do this, I will share it with everyone.

I shall return in a few days. I thank all that participate and assist.

PS- Simone, I wrote you. I haven't gotten your JPay yet, though I did get a letter from someone I write to from Germany who said she hasn't gotten my letter. I guess all German-speaking postal carriers got a conspiracy against me or something! ☹

I leave as I came,

Veni vidi vici,

Clinton Young #999447

Polunsky Unit

3872 FM 350 South

Livingston, TX 77351

USA

Loud & Clear, March 11, 2011

Topic: Part One of the Series.

Today marks the 8th year since the jury handed down the guilty verdict. I was devastated, as it was certainly not the verdict I expected. We (my lawyers and I) anticipated verdicts pertaining to lesser offenses; however, we thought that I would beat the capital murder charges.

What many people don't understand is how truly complicated a capital case is. I was found guilty of double murder on one count and murder, robbery, and kidnapping on the other count. There were two victims: Samuel Petrey and Doyle Douglas. They used Samuel's murder in both counts, meaning the double murder was for supposedly killing Samuel and Doyle. The other was for the murder, robbery, and kidnapping of Samuel.

If I prove I didn't kill Samuel, it destroys BOTH counts of capital murder. Capital murder is the only crime I can get the death penalty for. Murder carries a sentence of 5-99 years or life with parole available in 30 years, same as aggravated battery, robbery, or kidnapping. Just a little legal information there.

Now I have—I repeat, I have—proven that I did not kill Samuel Petrey. I haven't proven this yet in the court of law, as it has not been ruled on by the judge yet. It is on hold while I deal with my current appeal issue of prosecutorial misconduct.

Now, I prove it by showing that the only "witness" to the murder of Samuel Petrey, the co-defendant David Page, was:

A.) Lying in his testimony at trial.

B.) He failed a lie detector test, though in the USA a lie detector test is not allowed as evidence in a trial. The jury cannot hear about it, as it is not always 100% accurate.

NOW—and I beg for your attention to this specific fact—WHEN DAVID PAGE GAVE HIS POLYGRAPH EXAM, THE INSTRUCTOR INFORMED HIM THAT HE HAD NOT BEEN HONEST ABOUT HIS INVOLVEMENT IN THE MURDER OF SAMUEL PETREY!!!! THE INSTRUCTOR NOTED THAT WHEN INFORMED OF THIS FACT, DAVID PAGE TOLD HIS LAWYER AND THE INVESTIGATOR, AND I QUOTE THIS: "I KNOW WHAT IT IS."

Okay, if you are telling the truth, then why, when someone tells you, "Hey, this machine says you're lying," would you say, "I know what it is"? If you did not do the crime, you would say, "I don't care what your trash machine says, I did not do it!" You would not say, "I know what it is!"

The part he specifically failed was to the questions: "Did you kill or fire a shot into Samuel Petrey and/or Doyle Douglas?" He showed clear deception at all parts involving Samuel Petrey.

While the polygraph is not allowed before the jury, the court is aware of it, and you, the people, are aware of it. It is a piece of the puzzle. By itself, it is weak, though when added to the rest, it weighs heavily.

C.) Page bragged about getting away with the murder. He did so to Raylonda Ray Villa. This sworn affidavit is on my website under his name.

(There is also a picture of the victim on the autopsy table. It shows gunshot residue. I took the picture down as it shocks people. In addition to this, the victim's family complained, so out of respect for them, I removed it. Though it can be provided for individual viewing upon request, if the request is sincere—I ain't got no time to feed no morbid curiosity.)

The proof the gloves offer is they support McElwee's testimony and also explain why Page would lie about gloves that had his DNA and residue consistent with the blowback pattern from a gun if he didn't shoot anyone.

You see, it all starts to add up against Page. The gunshot residue on Samuel shows he was shot at close range. Page admitted to standing about four feet away, and that I was over ten feet away from Samuel.

G.) This is something only I can speak on and can't prove as much as I wish I could—and that was motive.

Page was the only one that thought he was wanted by the police. He lied and stated we were both wanted, but that is not true. Amber Lynch and her father are the ones that informed me the police were looking for Page. He at first said, "They are looking for you and Page." Amber yelled, "Stop lying, Dad, you know they aren't looking for Clint!" He then said, "Well, they didn't say nothing about you, but they are looking for JR" (which was Page's nickname).

While I was asleep, Page told Samuel the area he was from, as well as other details. I did not know this until later. Page is the only person that had a reason to kill Samuel. I was the only person who had all the reasons in the world to keep Samuel alive! If he was harmed, everything would come back on me!!

H.) I can prove that the gun was empty and that I emptied it. I did not know that Page got more bullets later on! The cops could not prove who bought them or where they were bought. However, there were no fingerprints on the box. The only person with gloves on was Page! He also admitted to disposing of them, though he lied and said I handed them to him.

I.) Page's lies about having the gun in his possession and his claims that he was held hostage by me at my trial. There is an 11-minute video that shows Page driving up to a store and getting me out. He admitted to Detective Kent Spencer that he had the gun and keys in the truck with him.

This is proof of who had the gun before Samuel was killed. Kent Spencer's testimony is on my site. It is under "Gregory Kent Spencer." (There is a part that is missing where Kent Spencer testified the second time about the fact that Page told him he had the gun and keys. I thought that testimony had been posted, but it was an oversight by the person helping me. She did not realize his testimony was in two parts. It will be posted soon, and all will be informed of such.)

This disproves his lies about being held hostage and fearing for his life—which is something it seems every other criminal claims when arrested as they try to get out of trouble. The two top lies: "I was just the getaway driver," and "I was afraid they would kill me." Those are two Hollywood-classic excuses given by criminals.

J.) The law of parties.

Page is in prison for kidnapping. No co-defendant went to prison for murder. I am the only one in prison for capital murder. No others were convicted or given plea bargains for any crime of murder or capital murder, meaning that there is NO ONE for me to be a party to murder or capital murder with.

The prosecutors at trial indicated that I was the shooter. The law of parties was just a way to manipulate the jury into convicting me somehow! Though the form of the law of parties jury charge I had in my trial was that I had to be a direct actor in helping to bring about the commission of the murders. Meaning I had to know Page would kill Petrey and have helped him to do so. There is NO evidence of that at all. I did not know that he would do any such act. He claims that I did it, so there is no proof that supports the law of parties.

K) To convict me of double murder, the jury was misled to believe that Doyle and Samuel were both killed for their vehicles so that we could travel to Midland. This is incorrect. I did not kill Doyle or Samuel, though beyond that, the murders were in no way related. Only Page made that claim; others gave different reasons initially for Doyle getting killed. However, they were allowed to read each other's statements prior to testifying. This is so the witnesses can "fill in the gaps," so to speak. (This happened with another witness in my punishment phase, though that's for another day to discuss.)

I have given you not one, but 11 different reasons that show I did not commit and am not guilty of capital murder simply pertaining to the murder of Samuel Petrey. As I wrote, showing that I did not kill him destroys my conviction of capital murder, which means I would need a new trial and could prove this.

In a criminal case, there is what is known as factual and legal insufficiency. (I think I spelled that word right!) I have to prove one or the other. I am still, 10 years later, STILL trying to gather up all the evidence. My point of this blog was to lay out more details about why I am innocent of capital murder.

I can give you ten more reasons why I never had a fair trial—from the sloppy police work (which I go into on my site) to the secret deals, to the unethical actions by the prosecution that directly hindered my lawyers from properly representing me at my trial, to lies told by witnesses. Even IF you do not think I am innocent, the fact that I did not get a fair trial should be enough for you to support me in having a new trial. That is what I ask for. It is what I fight for. I want a new trial so that I can clear my name.

I will soon post the testimony from the recent legal hearings I had. You will see, with a police officer admitting this fact, that my co-defendant was "charged" with capital murder at the time he testified, and they let him walk around downtown Midland, Texas, with free-world clothing on and NO HANDCUFFS! He ate at a public café with his mother and father. His family admitted it, he admitted it, and a police officer and prosecutor's investigator admitted it happened!

But guess what the former prosecutor tried to claim?!?!?! He lied and said it never happened, though his very own investigator said, "Yeah, it happened." This co-defendant acted like he was getting death, yet he knew he had a secret deal. He only received 15 years non-aggravated. He made parole after 7 and one-half years and is free today.

My plea is: give me what I am supposed to have! If you believe in this system and the U.S. Constitution, if you hold the foundation of this country near and dear to your heart, give me what the Founding Fathers entitled me to have, and that is a fair trial.

If you're the right-wing Christian that believes an "eye for an eye," and that you believe that the Founding Fathers were influenced by divine guidance and biblical influence when drafting the Declaration of Independence and U.S. Constitution, one of these ten basic human rights is a right to a fair trial. Just give me what I am supposed to have and have yet to receive, and that is a fair trial.

It is difficult to place all information from my case up. There are over 13,000 pages! My juvenile record is over 2,200 pages. My appeals all combined are over 2,500 pages. The hearings I have had all combined are over 1,000 pages. There have been five different hearings since my trial. Thousands of pages have never been presented to the courts, as not everything is used as evidence. This means it does not get placed into the "trial record."

Though I now have someone who is personally covering the cost of my site, this is good! We are waiting on her to get back from vacation and to be able to sit down with her friend and all that and get a game plan developed. I am also having all legal documents from my trial and from outside the record put in the hands of one person to coordinate it. There are also more videos to be posted. Much work to do!!

In the meantime, my sister-in-law is helping me get my defense fund lined out as I want it—the actual bank account and etc. Information for donations will be posted soon. I also have been sent the information I needed to show the medication I was forced to take while locked up as a juvenile is known to cause psychotic behavior in youths. When I started to have negative reactions to the drugs, instead of taking me off the medication, they upped my dosage and the strength of the medication!!! I can prove this!

Then, when I got into more fights and altercations with the increase, they labeled me as psychotic and with antisocial personality disorder—the same thing they label serial killers with! Yet, when they took me off the medication, I had no problems and was able to properly function. This information will be posted.

Much to do! I thank you all for your time and effort—those that continue to support me and those that will start to support me. I thank you, and it will pay off! I fell off for a little bit, though as the saying goes, I am back in the saddle again.

Veni, Vidi, Vici.

In solidarity,

Clinton Lee Young #999447

Polunsky Unit

3872 FM 350 South

Livingston, Texas, 77351

USA

Loud & Clear, July 20, 2013

Topic: Vaughn Ross

On the 18th of July, Vaughn Ross was executed. Through this strange journey that is life, his and my lives intertwined beyond our both residing on death row. Before that entanglement is revealed, allow me to discuss my experiences with Vaughn. People here called him Ross, which is common. Most people who do not have a nickname are simply referred to by their last name. In prison, the officials categorize people by last name and prison number. I don't know if that stems from the prison system's connection with slavery—last names indicated ownership—or from the military-esque ranking structure the system uses to classify ranks below the warden, e.g., Sgt. so and so, Captain, Major, etc. First names are more personal and reserved for those outside these walls.

The way the state portrayed Ross is 100% the opposite of the man I have interacted with all these years. He was, as his friends described him at his trial: calm, cool, and a peacemaker. He smiled easily and was quick to laugh. I have met some killers. Vaughn Ross was no killer! There is a difference between a killer and a murderer. All killers are murderers, but not all murderers are killers. There is a reason they call them serial killers and not serial murderers.

The first time I met Ross was on disciplinary level two—his one and only time on that level. He had gotten in trouble for some ridiculously small reason. Back then, they would send you to level for anything. I think he refused to allow them to take blood from him, saying that they had already put blood on items of his that didn't have blood on them and that he wasn't going to give them any more to use. I was a couple of cells down from him. The cell I was in was located in front of the dayroom. He would come to the dayroom and work out. I struck up a conversation with him.

Back then, I was far more militant in my resistance to this place. I was always looking for more people to join the "good fight." I could tell right away that Ross was passive. When he talked, he sounded like a country-club white guy. After we got cool with each other, I would jokingly say, "Look out, ole black-ass white guy!" The catch was that I, due to my past, sounded more stereotypically black than he did because of the slang I used. My associates would tell me, "You sound pretty fly for a white guy."

Oh, I forgot—there are people out there who claim I hate black people. I guess I'm not living up to my image! Ha, anyways!

One of the issues I was always raising a fuss about was how little this place was cleaned up. TDCJ does not allow death row prisoners to have a work detail. Instead, they bring prisoners from general population back here to do the work. Since they don't live back here, they don't personally care if it's cleaned or not, even more so because they don't get paid for the work. Many of them get upset at us for wanting the place clean. They say, "I don't get paid for this shit." I respond, "Lay it down. Don't work back here. The fact you all work back here gives these people an out to not allow us to work."

As a result of them not cleaning worth a damn, I would tear up paper really small and throw it all over the floor in front of the cell I was in. Back then, part of the door, at the bottom, was open on the side—a 4x4-inch hole. I would get handfuls of shredded paper and flick my hand so that it went everywhere. I yelled down to Ross to ask him to do it. Ever the pacifist, he declined. I told him, "Dude, these fuckers don't give a damn about how dirty the run (walkway) is." Not wanting to waste my time and honestly feeling he was being weak, I left it alone. I just threw even more paper out the door.

That night, I didn't know it, but Ross stayed up and watched the night crew of working inmates come through. The ONLY place that was actually swept up and cleaned was the area in front of the cell I was in. After the guy with the broom cleaned it, he pushed the broom straight for the door to the next section. This whole vast area of the section was left unswept and unmopped. Feeling proud that "my" little area was cleaned, I went to sleep.

The next night, when the SSIs (that's what the working prisoners are called; it means Staff Support Inmates) came through, my area was already nice and trashed for a good sweeping. I was sitting on the bunk when I heard a noise. I came to the cell door and saw Ross slinging trash on the run. I laughed and said, "Hold 'em up, Ross! What are you doing down there?" He responded, "Man, I saw last night. They didn't even try to sweep anywhere else on the section. That guy just zipped right through here with the broom."

My response was, "Dude, I told you—they don't give a damn. You've got to force their hand." Every night after that, he had some trash to toss. Though he certainly wasn't ready to be the next Che Guevara! :)

Ross was educated and had a good sense of right and wrong. Again, anyone who knew him would say that the way the state said the murders took place just isn't the Vaughn Ross that anyone knew—not even remotely. You can go to www.executionwatch.org and listen to the interview and show that was done during his execution. Ray Hill does the show along with lawyers. He also did an interview with Ross. You can hear his voice and listen to what the lawyers say about the case.

Now, how our lives twisted together. How through his life, my very own may be saved. As I have often written about, the investigator who smoked crack with witnesses and filed false statements in my most important appeal also did the same in his case. She made up all kinds of stuff and presented statements to the same lawyer I had for his appeal.

She made up all kinds of stuff and presented statements to the same lawyer I had for his appeal, supposedly from Ross's family. When he received his appeal, he wrote his family asking why they said these things. He quickly learned that they didn't. BEFORE Lisa did ANY work on my case, Ross had written to the lawyer telling him that Lisa came to see him extremely high, something even the officers noticed. He also said she was talking about things that weren't true and had never happened.

Knowing this, the lawyer still allowed her to work on my case without properly following up. The lawyer himself had even noticed her bizarre behavior. He claimed he thought it was due to family troubles, which still doesn't excuse letting her keep working on death penalty appeals. As a result of her actions, Ross had his appeal—the most vital appeal—destroyed as well.

I told my new lawyers that he had the same lawyers as me on the state writ of habeas corpus. The lawyers I now have from California spoke with his family, even flying out to Missouri to meet them all in person. They also met with Ross. The lawyers and the investigator all took an immediate liking to him. When we spoke, they always asked, "How is Vaughn?"

A unique twist. I told them that Ross seemed like a good dude who needed better lawyers. Long sigh. Here is where it shows how far perception can be wrong. I had the lawyers out of California, the Federal Public Defender's Office. I also had a lawyer out of New Mexico who was licensed to practice in Texas. I needed someone with local connections, which is why that lawyer ended up on my case. It was believed he was a great lawyer due to working with the Canadian consulate on another case out of Montana, plus the way he had openly criticized Texas appeal lawyers.

Now, because it cost so much to make a trip to Texas, and due to some very political activity that was going on behind the scenes, it was not taken very kindly that the federal lawyers ended up on my case. Some powers that be tried at different times to get them off my case. See, the 4th and 5th Circuits (Texas is in the 5th) do not have Federal Public Defender Offices, mainly because these types of lawyers have the same type of resources as the state does. They work for the federal government. (Well, they did have the resources, though due to the government sequester, funding has been cut back.)

When Ross's case was discussed, the head of the office in California decided it wasn't good to ruffle any more feathers by taking another Texas case. They all decided it would be good for my other lawyer to take the case, with everyone thinking Ross would be in good hands. Ross himself also thought this. Long sigh. Needless to say, everyone's beliefs were off point.

The lawyer is no longer on my case. He had no active role in it, and the little he did do, he either messed up or damn near mistakenly ruined any chance I had at getting new evidence reviewed. Thankfully, what he filed wasn't ruled on before my other lawyers caught it and filed to have it removed. Ross should have been able to win a new appeal. Had the political bullshit not gotten stirred up about my case and my current lawyers taken his case, I am very confident in saying Vaughn Ross would still be alive.

I didn't know what all had happened in Vaughn's case with the investigator until it happened in mine. My current lawyer and an investigator went to speak with Lisa, who had the audacity to rant that I destroyed her career due to all that I posted on the internet about her. She claimed she wouldn't do anything for me. My lawyer pointed out that it wasn't even me who said anything about her—it was the people she smoked crack with! She still went on about me destroying her career by my actions of posting everything about her.

Well, Lisa Milstein, I am glad that my "actions" ended your career. While my actions ended your career—one that you certainly should not have had—your actions ended the life of Vaughn Ross, one that he certainly should have had.

Rest in peace, ole black-ass white guy. At least you don't have to endure the bullshit of this place anymore.

Veni, Vidi, Vici

In Solidarity,

Clinton Young #999447

Polunsky Unit

3872 FM South

Livingston, Texas 77351

U.S.A.

Loud & Clear, January 17, 2014

Greetings to all! I am finally getting back into blogging. Lately, I have not done very much beyond thinking about my case. Due to several new developments, much more work is required. This blog will basically be an update. I have proven that there is no proof of guilt: no fingerprints, no guilt-relevant DNA, and no confession to the murders by me. No gunshot residue on me or anything. Plus, several people have come forward, providing testimony about one of the co-defendants bragging about getting away with murder and how the police couldn't prove it was him because he had gloves on.

There is a request before the judge right now to test the gloves, as they have never been properly tested. Once they are tested, they WILL show that he shot a gun while wearing the gloves, which only have his DNA inside them. I have now PROVEN:

1. That there were hidden secret deals.

2. That I did not kill anyone.

Also, my lawyers were unable to properly investigate the case, as they were court-appointed and provided limited funding. The full story was not told at trial. That is changing now!

1. A juvenile prison guard testified that during a fight, I assaulted her when she went to break it up. At the time of trial, I did not think the D.A. or my lawyers had her actual report written about the event. Turns out they did, though it wasn't used. Only a summary of her report was presented. She said the assault was detailed in her report. IT ISN'T! This is the Jaqueline Timmons testimony that should be on my site in the legal material section.

2. Another guard said I assaulted him. He and I had personal problems and argued often. Two other guards and a prisoner said I did NOT assault him—they saw the entire fight. As a result, no new charges were pressed against me. At trial, NONE of these people were called to testify. They will be now, as they have been located, just like the other officer's report was.

3. A first-grade teacher used to call me stupid in front of the class for failing a spelling test. I was only 6 years old! She attended my trial and said that I bit and hit other kids and tried to cut students with scissors as a child. When asked why there was no report, she stuttered and said I did it in kindergarten when I was 5 years old. My lawyers failed to object. That testimony should not have been allowed, as she was NOT my teacher then. However, the teacher I had then—you guessed it—is coming forward to state these events never took place. This teacher cared about me, and when my home burned down when I

was 5 years old, she bought me clothes, etc. This shows that the one schoolteacher they could get to testify against me lied—all because my mother cussed her out for calling me stupid?

4. When I was going into the juvenile justice system, other inmates told me that if a person had a bad gang and drug history, they would go into a placement instead of the much-feared actual lock-up facilities. The Texas juvenile system was rocked by scandals in recent years for staff physically and sexually assaulting kids and allowing violence to exist in extreme forms. Thinking this myth to be true, I made up all kinds of stuff. I told people I did all kinds of drugs, some of which I had never even seen before! I made it seem like I drank beer and did drugs every day. I also invented all kinds of gang activity from stuff I saw on TV. Even the gang I claimed to be part of was made up! (Now, I did later join a gang, which I have since dropped out of and signed up with the G.R.A.D. program. This is the Gang-Renounce-And-Disassociation program operated by the Texas prison system. It means I denounced all gang activity and walked away from it.)

The social historian who helped on my appeal even contacted the police in another state I had lived in about all this. They informed her that they had never heard of the gang I made up. I told my trial lawyers, yet they never presented it. All of this is being filed and will soon be presented on my site!

There are also people who follow my case who were around me in North Carolina. When I wasn't with my sister Christy, I was with my then-girlfriend, Randi. A simple fact as to why I didn't drink beer all the time is that Randi didn't want me to. Her father had a very bad drinking problem, so she was 100% against it. Now, I did smoke some weed here and there, though I barely did that, as I have a very low tolerance for it. That was it! Nonetheless, I will be able to show, not just through friends and family who knew me as a teenager, but also through police agencies, that I made up all this stuff. Finally, for once, the police are helping me! Ha ha!

In short, within the next month or two, all of this information will be posted. I will be completely destroying that state's entire case against me: that I am a future danger, and that there were numerous others who could have testified about knowing me as a teenager, friend, boyfriend, and student but were never called by my trial lawyers.

When entering juvenile prison, everyone goes through the orientation unit. This is where an assessment is made on each person. They do sociological, psychological, and criminal assessments to best determine placement of the youth. Depending on the needs of that person, their classification is determined. Past history also determines the limited length of stay, as each person was sentenced to their 21st birthday at the time. However, the juvenile system sets a Minimum Length of Stay (MLOS), unless the person was sentenced by a judge or jury for a specific time. Most plea-bargained for the undetermined sentence, and the juvenile system then set the MLOS.

It was during this process that I was told the myth of how to get to a placement. Placements were better as they were far less violent. The person could wear clothes from home instead of prison uniforms and, after a period of time, could go home for the weekend. The other facilities were maximum or minimum-security facilities that were worse than adult prisons, as they allowed fewer privileges. This is when I made up all this stuff, based on things I had seen in movies.

Again, these reports were not factual—police, psychologist, or court reports. It was just stuff I made up due to an incorrect belief in this myth that a bad gang and drug history helped get one to a placement. This myth turned out to be a bad reality, as instead of going to a comfortable placement, I went to the worst maximum-security unit for the juvenile prison system.

It was these words I made up that the prosecutor used to go after me for the death penalty. Had they actually bothered to investigate one bit, they would have seen it was all untrue. Though they did struggle with my background investigation, as they couldn't find teachers or prison guards to testify against me beyond the lying first-grade teacher (which I can show lied).

You know that other free-world teacher they used against me? A woman who was an aide for the school. She testified that she saw me walking down the hallway with a wallet chain hooked to my belt loop. She claimed that she told me to put it away, as it wasn't allowed. She testified that I then gave her a mean look—if looks could kill—and slammed the door. That's it! I was such a horrible, mean, psychopathic youth that that was the worst they could get!

To those who don't know, prison slang for the outside of prison is calling it the "free world." And I never wore wallet chains! Not my style.

So, to answer an often unanswered question of what made the prosecution go after me over the others: They simply read stuff I made up out of a desire to avoid going to the much-feared juvenile prison units, which have been rocked with scandal after scandal for extreme levels of violence. I told my trial lawyers this, though they just brushed it off and said, "The jury isn't going to read all that paperwork." Guess what? Yeah, they read it! As I said before, I can completely destroy the state's entire case. If I was such a horrible child, why could they only find THREE people to testify against me? I now can prove 100% that they lied! I actually still write to my 5th-grade teacher! Again, as is posted in the legal material on my site, I had two guards against me, four for me! I could have had many more! Other teachers have given affidavits stating that I was not a bad child, just really hyper, and that they believe there were more problems in my home than were revealed.

Another element that I find a bit of a relief is that it has been discovered the state knew the first victim was not killed for his car. They had to use that theme to make the crime a capital offense. This was the only way they could get a death penalty. I have always been very embarrassed by this idea that I would kill someone for a damn car! Murder is bad, but to kill someone for an object or to rape a woman? That is sickening! It shows the lowest view of life. I never proclaimed to be an angel, though I damn sure am NOT the demon they claim I am. And guess what? I can now PROVE IT!

Just keep an eye on my site: saveaninnocentlife.com. More and more evidence will be posted in the next month or two. My friend Renate and the journalist Jessica Villerius, who made the film Code Red: Death Penalty, got to see some of the new material before anyone else due to the film being made and work being done on my website. I am having to rebuild the site. As a result, many new things have not been posted. Plus, it's why I really haven't been blogging. Though much is coming.

I will also be showing more of how the police DID NOT investigate the two crime scenes. One was where the victim was shot at. As I said before, to this day, NO police officer has gone to the area. The state does not even dispute this! They cannot. There is NO police report on it at all! They only went to where the body was located. The victim was shot in a residential area, in someone's driveway! Blood and bullet casings were in the driveway. NO, I repeat, NOT ONE police officer of any type went by the house!

The store where the second victim was supposedly kidnapped, I can also show there was a booth in the parking lot, where the clerk would be facing the store where it supposedly happened. NO police officer questioned her from that night! There were numerous cars in the parking lot. If a guy ran up on another person with a gun in the middle of a parking lot, does anyone think that everyone would just ignore it?! Hell NO! More so in a very small town, as it was. The police went by the scene 16 days later and only took two pictures of the storefront! That's it. They never even got out of the car, nor was any call for help made.

The co-defendant said I did this act. However, I can now show I was inside the store myself! The co-defendant also has been found to have bragged about details that only he could have known to two others.

I feel energized. Ten years of battles are finally coming together. The way I feel, actually—when you were in high school, was there ever that kid growing up, who was always faster than you? You could never beat him in a race. Though one summer, you work out real hard! Push yourself that extra hour. Then the big day comes, and the starter gun goes off. BANG! Everyone takes off. This guy who always beat you, he gets the early lead. You just know he is grinning, thinking he's going to win again. Slowly but surely, you're catching up to him. Until you get to that fourth turn, and when he looks at you, you see the look of shock as he sees you're running right beside him. As you're going down the final stretch, that feeling comes over you as you start to pass him and see the finish line. That you are winning. That you WILL win!

For the first time in 10 ½ years, that is how I feel! The prosecutors threw a party to celebrate getting me the death penalty. Soon—real soon—it will be my turn to party!

Veni, Vidi, Vici – I told you all, it's a way of life for me!

P.S. Those who have followed my case for years, they know when I have stood up and said that I can show something. Show it, I do! Just keep the faith and keep your eyes on the site. I will be blogging every week again.

In solidarity,

Clinton L. Young #999447

Polunsky Unit

3872 FM 350 South

Livingston, TX 77351

U.S.A.

Loud & Clear, January 26, 2014

Code Red: Death Penalty Film

When Jessica Villerius showed up to interview me, it started out with a bunch of unexpected turns. I did not expect it to be an on-camera interview. She did not expect it to be as openly received without controversy. No one expected it to be as popular as it was!

When I did the first interview, I was very nervous—not so much about how I would be portrayed per se, but more about how my portrayal would reflect on my friend Renate Bouwmeester, as she is the one who reached out to Jessica after returning to the Netherlands from the U.S. The experiences Renate had while working on death penalty cases and being part of my life left her wanting to do more—just something bigger.

Being a fan of Jessica, she emailed her the story of how our lives intersected. Renate had also mentioned to me before that she had spoken to a magazine journalist, which is what I thought the interview would be. Living the last 10 ½ years in a controlled environment, unexpected events aren't well received, which is why I was uncomfortable at first.

My worries were, as I wrote, not so much about me. I do not live in the Netherlands. I am here on Texas Death Row. If I am presented badly in the media, it doesn't impact me as much as it would someone living there. Renate has told friends and family about me and my case of injustice. I was concerned that I would somehow reflect badly on her.

I actually wrote to Renate, thinking the interview had gone badly. However, I was overreacting, it seems. One thing I quickly noticed was that Jessica had done her research on me and my case. She asked a few questions I did not expect, though that is what journalists do. I told her, as I tell everyone: Do not believe me—I will show you.

An interesting thing is that I told her during the first visit that there were going to be some upcoming investigations. During our second interview (which had to be 90 days apart due to TDCJ policy), the investigator was traveling through Texas meeting with people. The following week, I was able to have a copy of what was found emailed to her by my lawyers. These were reports that matched what I had told her during the first interview over 90 days prior.

When the film aired, I expected it to get a small wave of attention. I certainly did not think it would be the hit it has been. Due to the lack of internet access, I am sadly unable to see all the reactions. However, from all accounts, it was overwhelming.

I want to extend a big thanks to Jessica Villerius and her film crew, as well as the never-ending dedication from Renate. In addition, I want to thank the people of the Netherlands who, upon seeing the film, reached out to Jessica, Renate, or myself. You all could have just gone on about your lives, but you chose to get involved. Thank you!

I have had many struggles over the years—legal, personal, and emotional. Everything that has happened in this struggle has started to wear me down and take its toll. One has to wonder how many times a person can get knocked down and keep getting back up. It seems I have another round left in me, as the positive reaction has encouraged me to attack my struggle with renewed energy.

I am proud that Jessica was able to gain a positive reaction, especially considering the amount of time, money, and risk involved in making such a film. She treated my friend Renate with a level of kindness and courtesy that makes her grade-A in my book!

A bit of inside information: The scene showing me getting handcuffed almost didn't happen, as I do NOT like to be seen in handcuffs at all! I find it embarrassing, even after 12 years of going through it. Some get accustomed to it; I have not and will not!

When I realized I would be leaving the visitation area before Jessica and her crew, I almost told the guards that I wanted to wait for the media personnel to leave first. However, I knew it would be a scene she would most likely want to include, as it provides a view into how life is here on Texas Death Row. The only physical contact comes when guards handcuff me to be taken to another area.

The fact that something as simple as getting handcuffed still impacts me in such a way shows that this place hasn't affected me to the degree that I would be unable to readapt upon release.

I also want to thank the film crew personnel who worked behind the scenes—even though they shined that bright-ass light in my face! Ha ha.

Until next time,

In solidarity, I remain.

Veni, Vidi, Vici

Clinton Lee Young #999447

Polunsky Unit

3872 FM 350 South

Livingston, Texas 77351

U.S.A.

Loud & Clear: February 20, 2014

Down but not out

I readily admit that the way my appeal was denied surely knocked me down. Though they didn't knock me out! Not yet, at least. As long as I am breathing, I have a fighting chance. Fight I shall do.

Maybe I let myself get lost in hope. I normally do not, as my life experiences have taught me that it can be a dream. Though I did not, at all, expect the ruling that was handed down—more so the way it was written. I was denied in the worst way possible! Each claim was denied in three different ways. The way the courts are structured means I have maybe a 1% chance to get such a ruling overturned. Justice, truth, right or wrong—none of that has anything to do with it. All of that is for the lower courts to sort out.

Due to my past appeals not being filed properly by lawyers, it adversely impacts me now, as I am procedurally barred from review by higher courts. I can show 1,001 ways to the United States Supreme Court that I am innocent. It would not matter unless I could show a specific U.S. Constitutional violation. The claim would have to be shaped by saying the prosecutors violated my right to due process or that a lawyer was ineffective.

Now I am sure everyone is thinking, "Of course, it would be all of that if you are on death row and innocent!" No one disagrees with that. However, if the lawyers do not "structure" the claim properly, the court cannot review it. That is the law of the land. My past lawyers made mistakes. Sadly, only I will suffer the consequences of these mistakes and intentional flaws.

One of my previous lawyers was trying to help the state get me killed. That is why I got him off my case. Another lawyer on my most vital appeal filed an appeal around statements that were gained from an investigator who was smoking crack cocaine with a witness. She also forged signatures on other false statements. The lawyer did not independently check all the statements. He built my State Writ of Habeas Corpus around her statements. As a result, my entire state-level appeal was destroyed. This is the one appeal that allows a person to get new evidence that was not presented at trial into the record. The blog I wrote about Vaughn Ross—R.I.P.—the investigator that got him killed, she will add another tombstone to her collection!

There is still a way to sort out a way around the recent ruling, though it is going to be very difficult. What will need to be done is to have new lawyers and investigators go over the entire case again. Then, anything new that is discovered—re-filing last-minute appeals. I have not gone over the entire ruling yet. Though something that makes it all even worse—the ruling was 445 pages. You know what I get to respond to that? Ten pages! My lawyers made a request to get extra pages. I am unsure if it will be granted or not.

Now on many things that it is claimed my lawyers improperly filed the claims on, I disagree with the court on this. All they did was, when filing the new claims in, they only cleaned up the other claims. Basically, they were making the appeal more organized. The basis of the claim, nor the fundamental structure of the claim, was altered.

While I cannot yet go over the way each element will be addressed, as I do not want them to be aware of how we will fight back, I will address a few comical elements.

An officer from juvenile prison testified in my trial. He claims that I hit him during a fight as he was trying to break it up. I was charged with assault on staff at the prison. I went to court and beat the charge. Officers and other people in prison testified that they saw the entire fight and I never hit the guy. I was actually attacked! A gang had issued a hit on me. When the guy attacked me, I just wrapped him up and went to the ground. I had my back to the officer that claims I hit him. He said I turned around, looked him right in the eye, and punched him.

If you saw how small the areas are that we had to sleep in, you would right away know that this is not humanly possible. My jury never got to see this.

This same officer said that I was over several violent riots that resulted in prison staff and other prisoners getting assaulted. The problem? No such disciplinary reports were in my record! I had a disciplinary report for playfully popping a guy with a rubber band! Does any sensible person think that if I started a riot where people were physically harmed, the prison would say, "It is okay! No worries, just go on about your day, good fellow!" No way would that happen!

Here is the really comical part. He claimed that I was a gang leader over 5-2 Hoover Crips out of Houston. First off, 5-2 stands for 52nd Street in Los Angeles, California, crossed with Hoover Boulevard—a gang started on Hoover Blvd. It then spread to 52nd Street.

Okay, this is a Black street gang. I am not, nor have I ever been, Black or in this gang! One would think I wouldn't have to explain the Black part!

Now here is the real kicker! Ready? I AM NOT, NOR HAVE I EVER BEEN, FROM OR EVEN IN HOUSTON, TEXAS!!!!!! How then am I, a white guy from the Lake O' The Pines area, going to be a leader of a Black street gang, be it a chapter from anywhere, much less a chapter out of Houston, Texas—a city that I have never even been to in my life!

Now, anyone that knows the smallest detail about gangs knows that Crips and Bloods started in California. Though they have spread across the U.S., I want everyone to google Lake O' The Pines area. Look up Ore City, Texas, Jefferson, Texas, Avinger, Texas. These are places I went to school as a kid. When I was older, before I got this case, I lived in Longview, Texas, which is much bigger.

The town I spent the majority of my first 15 years in? Mims, Texas. Look it up! Now google prison consultants, advisors, and such. Ask this simple question to them: "Could a white guy from a small country town be the leader of a Crip gang inside a prison environment in the 1990s and year 2000?" Please ask someone! You know the response you will get? They will laugh at you!

They will say the only way a white guy would be a part of such a gang as that is if he was "owned" by that gang—meaning the sex slave trade that exists in prison. That is generally the response you will get once they stop laughing at you. Prison is a VERY racially segregated area. Then, to top it off, the guy said that during a disturbance, where he was attacked, I and a Blood joined forces to attack him.

So here I am, a WHITE leader of one of the largest BLACK street gangs, united with the sworn enemy of this same gang, attacking him. Which, by the way, that attack was not written up either! Also, ask the prison experts if this same white guy could be from a small town in Northeast Texas and be able to speak for or lead any gang based in Houston, Texas. They are going to say, "Hell no!" As he isn't even from the city.

See, now they have this trend in Texas prisons called Tango, which is Spanish for "town." It is people clicking together by the towns they come from, as prison gangs have declined due to the members getting locked down in segregation. If I am not from a specific city, then I would NOT be able to speak for it. PERIOD!!

That was one of the reasons they justified me getting death. Another was they claimed I shot a guy during a home invasion. A co-defendant that testified for the state said that I shot the guy and wanted to kill him. The VICTIM—yes, the VICTIM in the case—said that I did not even have a gun!

Another common theme in the ruling is my "underage girlfriend." Every time they mention my ex—the girl I was in a relationship with when I got this case—they always label me like I am some kind of diaper sniper or something!

First off, this was never a theme in my trial. They act as if she was 12 or 13 years old or something. When I was arrested, she was less than one month away from being 16. I had just turned 18. I met her when I was 17. It was not common for me to be with women younger than me. Once I turned 18, she was the only one I was with. Every other woman was my age or older.

Though with her, I did think about doing the whole "settle down and build a life together" thing. I know that people overseas see the idea of getting married at 18 as something odd. It is not so uncommon in the southern portion of the U.S. The second victim in this case was 19 when he met his wife. She was 14. They were together 35 years before he was tragically killed. No one would blink an eye about that, as it was normal back then.

Beyond the fact that it was not a theme of my trial, it could not be! I had lived with her at her FATHER'S house! Texas law is parental consent at 15. Again though, I met her when I was 17! Actually, she was the only person in that crime-riddled, drug-infested, godforsaken area that had any sense! Therefore, the presentation of "underage girlfriend" is simply a character assassination attempt.

Coupled with the police chase, I was a Black street gang leader, underage girlfriend-dating, speed-violating, rabid terror of a guy!

They also go on about me being violent since kindergarten. I have already written before about the testimony of Debbie Barton, the first-grade teacher who hated my mother and used to call me stupid in front of the whole class when I failed a spelling test. First grade for my European readers is 6 years old! She testified that I used to try to stab other children with scissors.

The problem with this? There is NO report in any file of such an event taking place. She claimed to know about it from when I was in kindergarten, which she was NOT even my teacher for!

As I was 5 years old, her speaking on that is a violation of court rules! It is 'hearsay' evidence, as she had no DIRECT knowledge of it. Also, another teacher from when I was 5 said I was NEVER violent—just really hyper and a follower.

Again though, I was NEVER written up for this. Even the prosecutor asked her about how I stabbed kids with scissors in kindergarten, as he knew that didn't make sense, though he allowed/directed her into correcting her words.

Everyone remember the scissors you get at 5 or 6 years old as a child in school? The PLASTIC scissors! That are made big and PLASTIC so kids cannot poke their eyes out with them.

Again though, I was NEVER written up for it, and she was not even my teacher, so she never saw such an act.

I must confess though to one event that was talked about. They said I was kicked off the bus for biting another student. Yes, I did this! The problem? He was 16 YEARS OLD!! I was 6! I had to bite him to get him to stop pulling my hair so I could take a nap. That's right. I led a black street gang from a city I have never lived in. I had an underage girlfriend whose father let me live with her. I lack proper driving skills.

In some other universe, I supposedly stabbed other kids with big plastic scissors. I shot a guy who says I didn't shoot him! I started riots that were miraculously never documented, even though these riots supposedly resulted in employees of the state getting hurt. What happens if a person gets hurt on the job? They have to report it for workers' compensation. Not to mention the criminal charges that would be pressed for the act itself.

These acts are the reason that the state of Texas is seeking my death. Along with two murders that ALL ballistic evidence shows I could not have been the shooter for. As well as having NO confession, NO fingerprints, and NO gunshot residue on me. Only a co-defendant saying I did it. A co-defendant who failed a polygraph exam, repeatedly bragged about getting away with murder, and was wearing gloves when he killed the man. These same gloves I was refused the ability to get tested, which would have shown him to have fired a gun while wearing them and that he lied about how long he had the gloves.

The murderer has been given permission to write the Gospel of Clinton Lee Young by the state of Texas. If the prosecutors have their way, he will have three victims!

Now, as I wrote at the beginning of this, they knocked me down but not out. The fight goes on. The unique element about me is that making me have fear is the worst thing they can do. The pain must be used to fuel the fire! It shall NEVER be a brake. Since then, my mind is clicking faster than ever. When I spoke to my lawyers, I was pointing out stuff left and right. They were taking notes as fast as they could, telling me things like, "You're right. You're right! I cannot believe we did not think of that!"

It is going to be a real hard fight for the home team, though it is a fight that we can win! I really need people focused and helping, most importantly working together. Any and all donations are greatly needed. This way, I can retain another lawyer to go over my entire case for any last-minute appeals, which I will need to avoid getting executed.

The PayPal donation link is detailed on my website: www.saveaninnocentlife.com. For those in The Netherlands, my dear friend Renate has an account to collect donations. The account information is:

Clinton Young Foundation

IBAN: NL66 INGB 0006517329

BIC: INGBNL2A

Web: www.clintonyoungfoundation.com

Please do not send donations to the inmate trust fund account with JPay.com. Midland County gets a percentage of all money sent to my prison account, as they are charging me with having to pay the cost of my trial. Yes! Not only did they wrongfully convict me, but they are also making me pay for it! They do not get all the money sent to me, only a percentage IF it is sent to the Inmate Trust Fund Account. There are five people on death row that this happens to. However, "I" am the only one charged with not only my entire trial costs but my appeals costs also.

You recall the investigator that smoked drugs with the money she was given? Yeah, they say I have to pay for that also. That truly is insult to injury. If funds are sent to the account Renate has, or the PayPal donation account that my family operates, this can NOT be touched. I am allowed by law to raise funds for my defense.

Thanks for everyone's time and attention to this matter. I have to break up with my underage girlfriend and take driving lessons! ☺ Haha. It is so insane that I can't help but laugh about it. If I didn't, then I would go insane!

Take care!

Veni, Vidi, Vici

In Solidarity,

Clinton Lee Young #999447

Polunsky Unit

3872 FM 350 South

Livingston, TX 77351

USA

Loud & Clear – Insane Opinion

I finally finished reading over everything and find that it is even more insane than I first perceived! As I have to detail a few things, I will get to the point. As I have ranted about for YEARS, I have wanted to get the gloves the codefendant wore tested properly.

When I was first arrested, I refused to talk to the police—not because of any guilt, not at all. It was a matter of the "code of conduct" for the trash culture I then adhered to, plus a general disdain for most police, shaped by life events. Like the ones I saw take advantage of drug addicts, beat up people, sleep with underage girls, or drive past my mother while she stood in the middle of a street asking for help after getting the hell beat out of her by my stepfather.

I also knew the story of her being pregnant with me and my dad beating her up. She called the police. When the officer showed up, instead of talking to my mother, he ignored her and walked past her to ask my dad what was going on. When my dad assured him that everything was okay, he walked off, again ignoring my mother. Then again, this was early 1983. (It was just the 1970s when the law that a husband could not be charged with raping his wife was removed from the books. Yes, in 1970s Texas, a husband could NOT be charged with raping his wife, as she was considered "his.") These things helped shape my viewpoint of the police in general.

After learning that the codefendant was putting it all on me, I thought, "To hell with letting him do that!" I asked to speak with detectives in the case. I then told them to "take my DNA and hair samples and test the gloves!" That "I did not kill that old man." However, not knowing that the others were putting everything on me for the first murder, I refused to talk about that one. The police at that point HAD NOT EVEN FOUND THE GLOVES!

This is detailed on my website. It should be under Kent Spencer and Paul Hallmark's testimony, which the JURY complained about due to the poor police work on my case. I got that in black and white!

Okay, when the judge wrote the opinion, he quoted the detective at my trial saying that I told them that Page was wearing the gloves at the time of the shooting. The judge writes: "The detective does not say that I told him the codefendant shot the victim while wearing gloves." My jaw dropped! WHY THE HELL ELSE WOULD I MENTION THE DAMN GLOVES!!!!!!! That is exactly what the detective was saying. He then goes on about the codefendant changing his story.

Okay, but he twists it as a way to not help me. Now I ask every rational person reading this: If you are dealing with a person, and every time you talk to them, they change the story, what will you think???

There is only ONE person in this whole case that has NEVER changed his story. That would be Clinton Lee Young!

Next up is the plea bargain. See, there are time restrictions for when evidence can be presented to the court. If you have the money for investigators, experts, and lawyers, then this is okay, as you can do all that you need to do. If you do not, then this can truly be a killer!

A previous investigator went and talked to one of the codefendants, now free, in 2006. He refused to talk. In 2008, I got new lawyers on my case. They went back to speak with him. By this time, he had been granted parole, so he was not scared to talk. He then admitted to the deals. He wrote a statement for me that he had lied at trial about the deals.

Taking that statement to his former lawyer, that lawyer handed over his file, which then produced more helpful evidence about the secret deals.

At the court hearing about it all—excuse me, let me back up—the prosecutors and police knew that the codefendant was going to expose their dirty deeds. He was at the Hilton Motel to stay for the hearing. He went right outside the door to smoke a cigarette. They CLAIM that his ankle monitor, which he had to wear as part of his parole, had gone off. TWO police cars showed up and arrested him.

Okay, he gets really nervous now, as he feels that they will violate his parole. Now he is afraid to testify for my lawyers, much less admit that he lied in a capital murder trial. He gets on the stand and talks about the deal but then says he didn't lie at my trial.

The judge then later calls him BACK onto the stand. Wanting to clear up everything, the judge tells him, "I am going to ask you two questions. I want to separate the trial into only two parts.

#1) The deal.

#2) The facts of the case.

#1) Did you lie about having a deal at trial—yes or no?"

He answered, "Yes, sir."

The judge asked him, "Did you lie about the facts of the case?"

He answered, "No, sir."

(Now I personally disagree with that, but that isn't the point right now.)

It is now CLEAR that he admits he lied when he said he didn't have a deal.

Okay, in my trial, he had said not once, not twice, not three times, but FOUR times that he was facing the death penalty and getting ready for trial on capital murder charges. That he was testifying for free.

A point that the prosecutor highlighted to my jury. The prosecutor told the jury that they would be "facing trials back in East Texas." This was NOT true!! Everyone knew it. The codefendant's lawyer said over and over again at the hearing that he was not facing death. That he was not even a death-penalty-qualified lawyer.

The fact that he was even on the case proves it was not a death penalty case. The prosecutor and lawyer denied that they ate lunch with the codefendant and his parents. Yet the codefendant ate at a cafe in regular clothes, with NO handcuffs on. He then, while charged with capital murder, walks across the street, gets on the stand, and tells the jury that he is facing the death penalty!

The prosecutor and his lawyer denied this happened. The codefendant, his mother, and TWO police officers testified that the lunch did happen!

The trial lawyers for my case both said that if they had known about any deals or talks of deals, they would have conducted my entire trial differently.

THAT and THAT alone is supposed to be a MANDATORY new trial!

The judge over the court hearing found that the prosecutor did have talks about a deal with the lawyer. That the lawyer did tell the codefendant—yes, you read that correctly! They had talks, and the lawyer told the codefendant, yet the codefendant did not lie!

The codefendant SAID he lied!

My trial lawyer even said I have always maintained my innocence and that there was no actual evidence besides the codefendants' testimony.

As a result, they would have even picked a different jury!

Okay, so now the judge, in his recent opinion, cites that the codefendant, who said he lied, did not lie! Also, that it wouldn't alter my trial—even though BOTH lawyers said it would.

He also said that even though the evidence does not match what the codefendant said about the second murder, that doesn't matter, as the codefendant said he had his head leaning on the truck.

Again, that is ridiculous, as at the trial, the codefendant clearly detailed where everyone was standing. My lawyer acted like he was me and said, "Is this far enough away from where the victim was standing?" The codefendant said, "No, back up more." Which put the lawyer 10 feet away and the co-defendant 4 feet away, at point blank, as the gunpowder burned the skin and the powder that had not burned tattooed the skin! Meaning flakes of it got under the skin. That means the gun had to be under 6 inches from the victim. NO WAY a person 10 feet away (3 meters +) could be the shooter!

When my lawyer asked him why he kept changing his story about the shooting, he pointed to the prosecutor's lead investigator, who had just come into the room, and said, "Because he told me to!" THAT is why the jury barely convicted me. One of the jury members, who would talk to my lawyers, said that had he known about the deals, he wouldn't have convicted me of capital murder. This is a man who sat through the entire trial and watched every person testify. Not every single word is in the record, like the statement about the prosecutor's investigator. ☹

The judge also dismissed the ballistics report by Richard Ernest. This is CLEARLY posted. The judge said that the expert could not make the finding that the victim could have been shot inside the car because it was not in that expert's field. The expert I used found I could not be the shooter. He was a police officer for decades and is the expert's expert, meaning he trained other experts! He has been to other countries and trained their police forces. He isn't just any man with ballistic training; he is THE MAN when it comes to ballistics. Plain and simple.

Plus, you do not have to be an expert. If I am sitting in a car, in the passenger seat, how could I shoot the driver, at a distance of greater than 3 feet (1 meter), IN THE LEFT SIDE OF THE FUCKING HEAD!!!! HOW??!!!!! While inside a small two-door car!!!???? If that expert was going against me, that judge would have been praising him from the rooftops about how he is one of the top experts in the world, which this guy IS! He is one of the best in the WORLD!

The saddest element of it all is that my previous lawyers, including those at trial, failed. If they had done better, the judge would not have been able to do as he did.

Example: The TYC guard that said I hit him. He said I started two riots. The problem? NO REPORTS ON THEM! He is the same one that said I was the gang leader of the black street gang. There were two people who testified for me at the hearing in TYC, where I was found NOT guilty. My lawyers didn't call those two witnesses.

Another unique factor: One of the people locked up who testified for me at the hearing stood 6 feet away (2 meters) from the event. He is on death row with me.

The other officer that lied in my trial testified that I hit her. Her report should be posted on my website, www.saveaninnocentlife.com. The judge found my claim that she lied was baseless, as "some" officer was hit. Okay, that is NOT what she testified about. She said at my trial that I HIT HER!!! My lawyers pointed out a synopsis of her actual report. It just listed an officer and another prisoner were hit. Okay, in her ACTUAL written report, it does not say I hit her. IT DOES NOT SAY THAT!! Yet the judge twisted this to say that while it doesn't clearly state she was hit, it says "an officer was hit." Okay, that is not what the damn woman testified about under oath!

Plus, the guard who "was" hit refused to press charges.

#1) She was hit as she violated procedure. She jumped right in the middle of two guys fighting. We were both 16 years old and swinging as fast as we could. It is kind of hard to stop in mid-swing. Though I didn't punch her, as I saw her coming. The other guy hit her.

What I did accidentally do is that when she jumped in the middle, I sidestepped her and went to kick him in the head. She stuck her hand out, and I kicked her hand and broke her finger.

Now, that would have been an automatic new charge and an extra year locked up! Though she knew it was an accident, and she should never have done as she did. It violated all protocol for stopping a fight. She could have testified for me.

When it comes to the ballistics, they should have retained an expert. Instead, the lawyer tried to explain it himself. He got it mixed up, and the prosecutor told the jury that he got it wrong. My lawyer then failed to object. The jury looked at him. When he didn't say anything, they took that as him admitting he got it wrong.

When that happened, it popped into my mind to jump up and yell that I objected to the prosecutor's lies. I regret not doing that. The logic that is used to explain all of this is truly baffling to me.

The worst part? He is considered the fact-finder. That means the next court I go into, I can only argue based on what was filed and his ruling. His ruling is considered as good as God's law! Though instead of getting depressed and letting it overcome me, I see it as the path to freedom! I see exactly what I need to do.

While the next court is going to be hard to overcome, more so because of how the case was ruled on, I can file last-minute appeals. I just have to locate some people. I cannot write about all that will be done, as I do not want to expose my hand to the prosecution.

On to other matters. In a recent blog, I used the term rage. No one made mention of it. Though, being as there are many new readers, I wanted to explain that terms are used to express raw emotions. When I use rage, I use it as a prolonged feeling of anger. That burning propellant moves me forward and helps me go through the barriers. People are trying to kill me. I am sure everyone can understand that it is an emotional roller coaster.

It is interesting—all these firsts in history that have happened in my case. I have the first trial of its kind in Texas history. The longest federal judge opinion in a death penalty case or any criminal case. Every lawyer who has heard about it, their first words were "WHAT?!" or "Oh My God?!" when they hear about the 445 pages. Though when there is no quality, one must resort to quantity!

The fight isn't over. Just bear with me, as I need numbers on my side, and we can win this! As long as that needle is not in my arm, there is still a chance! Others who won have been to this point also. Some had one or two execution dates! Though I do not want to get that far. I thank everyone who is stepping up to help. The fight goes on.

Veni, Vidi, Vici

I remain,

In solidarity,

Clinton Lee Young #999447

Polunsky Unit, Death Row

3872 FM 350 South

Livingston, TX 77351

USA

Loud & Clear, Never ending confusion

You miss me? Yeah, I know that I have been gone for a couple of weeks. Everything adds up and really frustrates me. There is something that I want to point out from the appeal opinion. The expert that did the reports on my case — the reports that show I could not have been the shooter.

Okay, now read my words slowly so you can follow me. I want to make this insanity make sense to SOMEONE! In 2002, Midland County had the state crime lab analyze the evidence they tested in preparation for my trial. Again, this is the crime lab for the STATE OF TEXAS. These people WORK FOR the police and prosecutors. It is THEIR experts. These experts issued reports based on the evidence.

When you take the STATE'S EXPERTS' reports and combine them with the autopsy reports, any regular person can follow the pattern and see that I could not have committed the murder. It is physically impossible for me to have done the first murder. The second murder, I could not have plausibly done it either. Plus, the co-defendant failed the lie detector test and repeatedly bragged about getting away with murder.

Now taking all that — taking the state's, I repeat the STATE'S, star witness co-defendant and the STATE experts — just with that, it is easy to see I did not kill anyone. It was important to go beyond that. This importance is why an independent expert was needed. We then went to the best.

I want to share a story with everyone about this expert. It is about the report that is posted on my website www.saveaninnocentlife.com. In 1993, there was an event known as the Mount Carmel Disaster. MANY stories can be found about it online. The way the federal government handled that is why Timothy McVeigh blew up the federal building in Oklahoma. It was because of the Mount Carmel Disaster and an event known as the Ruby Ridge Disaster, where federal police killed an innocent woman holding her baby and killed a man's son. They went to arrest the man on bogus charges. At least that is how the story goes. I wasn't there, of course. I only know of the stories.

Okay, back to the point. When the federal police were dealing with the David Koresh followers, they were worried about what they were encountering. They wanted to know exactly the kind of weapons they were facing. Who did they call upon? Out of ALL the experts in the world, who did the U.S. government call on to make 100% sure they knew what they were facing? They called Richard N. Ernest. Who did the ballistics reports in my case that help to show I am innocent? Richard N. Ernest!

The appeal opinion states that the evidence shows I am guilty and that the experts are not skilled enough to find what they did in their reports. Then it makes up evidence. The appeal opinion in my case stated that the STATE'S EXPERTS and THE BEST BALLISTIC EXPERT IN THE WORLD are wrong!

I do not think the judge wrote this monstrous opinion himself. Judges use law clerks to write these opinions. He might have scanned the appeal and response, though I do not think he wrote all 445 pages of the opinion. (This is what my lawyers filed the [59e motion] about.) At least I do not think he did. Maybe due to them going to such extremes, it can help me later on.

The BATF (more commonly known as the ATF) and the FBI, known as the world's leading police force — when other countries struggle with something crime-related, they call in the FBI. The recent event of the plane missing, Flight 370 from Malaysia — the pilot had a flight simulator and computer in his house. Out of ALL the police agencies in the world, who did they call in to help? The FBI!

When the directors of the ATF and FBI, in connection with the U.S. Department of Justice, needed the best expert, they called in an expert because lives were on the line. They went outside their own inner officer experts and asked another for help. You can take it to the bank that this expert is hands down the best in the world. They did just this with Richard Ernest.

He has testified in hundreds of cases all over the U.S. He had, at the time, over 31 years' experience and worked over 10,000 cases. He isn't a defense expert. He is a police expert! The court is saying this man is wrong. The state has not offered up ANY expert to counter his report. You know why? Because they can't! As soon as another expert sees who wrote the report, they will say, "If he said it happened, then it happened!"

This expert has testified in cases that resulted in guys coming to death row and being executed. In all THOSE cases, he was considered God's word. Yet in mine, he is wrong? When his own report only confirms what the state's other experts themselves found? Again, the STATE'S experts testify for them.

Man, this is a new one! The court calling the prosecutors' experts liars! The crazy thing is the prosecuting lawyer working my appeal did not challenge it on factual grounds. He just tried to dance around it because he knows it is shaky ground to cross. Do not get me wrong — he still tried. Though they did not attempt to get their own expert because they know what it will show.

Thinking about this all really aggravates me. ☹ It has gotten to where every little thing really upsets me. I get mad because there is no room for error. It truly is David versus

Goliath. I got one stone left. If I do not hit the mark, then it is a wrap. I will write more later.

Vini Vedi Vici

Clinton Young #999447

Polunsky Unit

3872 FM 350 South

Livingston, TX 77351

Loud & Clear, May 2, 2014

Topic: Lethal Injection

Due to the botched execution of Clayton Derrell Lockett in the state of Oklahoma, the death penalty has come under greater scrutiny. Recent news indicated that the United Nations is investigating. In a rare turn of events, even the White House has spoken out about the execution.

It is good that the death penalty is getting more attention, though I have mixed thoughts on this debate about lethal injection. It is a given that the execution of Clayton Lockett went horribly wrong. Pro-death penalty news commentators seemed dismayed at the uproar, saying that he was sentenced to die, and he did indeed die, so there should not be any problems.

While on the surface that is true, in a nation that prides itself on proclaiming to be the world leader for governmental ethics and the rule of law over the law of rule, there is a bigger question that must be debated. We do not rape rapists, as we deplore that behavior. We wish to show that it is wrong and to punish it. While we do kill those who kill, the intent is to do it in a fashion that separates the state from the killer.

Clayton Lockett shot a woman for her vehicle, then buried her alive. She died a very horrible death, one consumed with pain and fear—a helplessness of being unable to flee or defend herself. The same feelings that the state of Oklahoma caused Clayton Lockett to experience. He died a very horrible, painful death while partially paralyzed, though feeling everything due to the deficient performance by the state executioners.

Ironically, Clayton Lockett had, prior to his execution, attempted to sue them over their execution protocol. The state became equal with the killer. The "noble defender" of the rights of the people became the "predator" they profess to disdain.

The United States of America is a very polarized nation. There is this "us versus them" thread that intertwines throughout society—left vs. right, my team versus your team, Texas versus the rest of the country. There is a sense of pride in being on the side of a greater sense of morality than the "other side." That is why we do not kill killers as they kill. It is why we do not allow honor killings. It is why the police are not supposed to be allowed to kill (though they damn sure seem to get away with it often enough!).

Now the issue that has kind of faded is all the political action that took place before the execution of Clayton Lockett. Oklahoma, like Texas, has two branches of court systems—civil and criminal. The Court of Criminal Appeals refused to halt the execution. The

Oklahoma Supreme Court issued a stay of execution as Clayton Lockett and another person sued over the execution protocol and lethal injection drugs.

The state governor, Mary Fallin, along with several members of the state legislature, went up in arms over the Oklahoma Supreme Court halting the execution, stating that they had no right to halt it. I am sure this will create a new legal battle, as people on death row have the right to sue. A civil matter should be addressed in the civil courts.

Even the spokesman for the Court of Criminal Appeals in Oklahoma stated that they had no say in it, as the Supreme Court of Oklahoma issued the stay of execution based on a civil suit. From the view of someone with a working understanding of the law and politics, that statement is significant, as it expresses that the state's top criminal court acknowledges that the state's top civil court had the legal right to step in given the circumstances.

This would mean that by the politicians stepping in, the civil rights of Clayton Lockett were indeed violated.

This doesn't mean that someone on death row can file a suit about mistreatment in prison and then not be executed, as that would destroy the concept of the "finality of justice" used to justify executions and not allow undue delays. However, if the lawsuit relates to the case evidence or execution method, the person can challenge this.

If a person sues in state court, it would take a different path than if they sued in federal court. Most file suits in federal court, where the standards of law are different to a degree. Plus, it is deemed to be less politically interested than the state courts, as federal judges are appointed by the U.S. President for the life of the judge. State judges are not. Some are voted in or appointed by legislative boards.

If a person on death row were to choose the state court route, leading to the state Supreme Court, that is a proper legal path. It does not mean it is wrong. There could be something in the Oklahoma constitution and/or state laws that I am unaware of, which would challenge what I write here. I can only go by the available information I have from news programs on the radio and two newspapers to which I subscribe.

However, the simple fact that the Oklahoma Supreme Court previously halted the execution shows that the ability I expressed here is plausible, as the state Supreme Court would not have taken such a controversial action—especially in a state dominated by pro-death penalty politicians—even more so with a case such as the one that Clayton Lockett was on death row for if it was not legal.

How will this impact Texas? It will not have any direct impact beyond simply putting a greater spotlight on the death penalty in general, as Texas does not use the same execution drugs as Oklahoma. There have been no problems detailed in previous executions this year. The courts have refused to accept challenges on this matter in Texas.

I have no desire to upset anyone, but if you have a loved one in Texas and think this Oklahoma event will impact Texas, that is like saying something in China will impact something in Iceland. It might create a discussion, but it will not change the course of "business as usual" in Texas.

Now, something that I personally want to address as a person on death row: Since the death penalty became legal again in the United States in 1976 (which, ironically, was the 200th anniversary of the independence of the United States), there have been 1,379 executions as of April 30, 2014. Of these, 1,204 were by lethal injection, 158 by electric chair, 11 by gas chamber, three by hanging, and three by firing squad.

Not one of these methods has been outlawed. Not one! People get caught up in this fight against the death penalty due to lethal injection. In my opinion, it is a misguided fight. If lethal injection is removed, then they will use hanging or the electric chair.

The U.S. Supreme Court has already ruled that lethal injection is not prohibited. People who are on the fence about how they feel concerning the death penalty often express more concern about an innocent person being executed than about how they are executed.

Being both innocent of the crimes I am here for and also a victim of a fundamentally flawed appeals process—all due to corrupt prosecutors and ineffective appeal lawyers—my mind is not focused on how they want to kill me. Instead, it is focused on them not killing me.

I have changed the minds of countless people in the United States about the death penalty. Prior to the film Code Red: Death Penalty playing in the Netherlands, 35% of the country supported the death penalty. I imagine that number has dropped to around 5% now, as people have become more aware.

What shocks people are the flaws in the system. It is the people in the U.S. who matter when it comes to voting. Changing their minds will change the system. To do that, they must be educated about the realities of the judicial system, as most operate on myths created by tough-on-crime politicians and some media outlets.

The flawed execution of Clayton Lockett can help shine a light on the overall flaws of the death penalty system.

I thank you for reading my words. On the website for my case, http://www.saveaninnocentlife.com, it mentions not to share content without permission from me. This is because, in the past, people would copy and share my blogs but sadly remove my name and website information.

I gladly welcome everyone to share my writings with anyone they wish, as long as my name is attached and the writings are not altered from their original form. By all means, please spread the word.

I thank you for your time and attention.

I remain,

In solidarity.

Veni, Vidi, Vici

Clinton Young #999447

Polunsky Unit

3872 FM 350 South

Livingston, TX 77351

Loud & Clear, May 29, 2014

Topic: When I'm right, I'm RIGHT!!

As I wrote in my last blog about the botched execution in Oklahoma, states would adapt by stepping away from lethal injection. The state of Tennessee has passed a law allowing execution by electric chair. Other states avoid the dilemma by offering a "choice" to the person being executed. I doubt states would go back to hanging. A couple still have it as allowed on the law books, though they do not use it. It wouldn't be that they are averse to hanging—Texas was known for swinging the ropes freely. Though, in modern times, being that the vast majority of executions occur in the southern portion of the U.S., the "image" of a bunch of white prison guards standing around a Black man being hung would NOT be a good publicity image for Texas.

It is good that a discussion is being had about the death penalty, in any form. Though this is a topic that is up close and personal for me. If it came down to a "one drug" lethal injection that Texas does—which is simply an overdose—versus the electric chair? Fuck that electric chair! A person could not even have an open casket for the funeral. They put the hood over the person being executed due to the horrible effects of the electricity. I mentioned before that states would adapt to the controversy. That is being done. The conversation is good! Though the end result must be analyzed. After all, it is not you all being killed.

I had a discussion with guys back here that are around me. The common theme is, as I said: Fuck that chair! Really, I wish people would ease up on the subject and actually focus more on the horrible legal representation many get and the ones with legit concerns that have been executed. The injustice is what changes people's minds. I do not speak for everyone here, though the people I have discussed it with think the same. Groups will raise nine ways of hell about the injection drugs and harass these companies, yet remain silent against the lawyers that refuse to write their clients and file bogus appeals. That's just my thoughts—Loud & Clear.

Now that I have someone that will help me type up my blogs, I will be posting more. Also, my book reviews and the online story that I am working on. It also helps me feel better, as it gives me more of a solid foundation to operate from. Lisanne was more than willing to continue helping with the blogs. As a mother and dealing with the effects of brain surgery, I didn't want to add extra stress to her.

To everyone that has ordered a shirt and/or a bracelet that Alexandra made, thank you! Also, with the funds raised, I have been able to get the investigator retained and started. After the first part is completed, then hopefully additional funds can be transferred to finish the second part. The first part is matters relevant to my innocence. The second part deals with the punishment phase issues, which was simply a matter of a life sentence vs. death. I am NOT working towards such. Though, it is important that the relevant information be presented to negate the adverse image created of me by the state. Hopefully, soon I can contact and come to an agreement with the proper experts that I need. My goal is to get the best! This way, they cannot be attacked.

I will get back to blogging about personal issues and not the heavy legal issues, as I know this topic wears on people. Just please understand that I went from planning my life after death row and enjoying the reaction from the film to trying to figure out how to get an appeal and not be executed! Words cannot explain the emotions that entails.

As of May 28th, the judge has not issued a ruling. That was unexpected. Though the areas my lawyers pointed out where the denial ruling was clearly wrong, they were correct! I think a law clerk wrote everything, and the judge assumed it to be true. However, my lawyers pointed out the opinion error about my ballistics reports, which clear me of the murder. The state said the judge was wrong also! So, we both agreed! Which is unheard of. ☺ However, the state said that it doesn't matter. ☹ While I disagree with the insanity of the state's thoughts—that a report showing I didn't kill someone doesn't matter—the judge sees that both my lawyers and the state said he was wrong. That will, I believe, encourage him to go back personally and review the records, which I hope that he does.

See, a judge has many cases and deals with a great deal. As a result, law clerks write the opinions, and the judge signs off. Due to the chance of an error, lawyers are able to have a legal filing pointing out errors of the opinion. This is for federal judges. In the lower state courts, the judge actually writes the opinion. Time will tell.

Thank you for reading my words, and please encourage others to do so. Please share my blogs and also post a link to my website: saveaninnocentlife.com. Thanks! Take care, smile, and strive for all that you desire.

I remain,

In solidarity

Veni, Vidi, Vici,

Clinton Lee Young #999447

Polunsky Unit

3872 FM 350 South

Livingston, TX 77351

U.S.A.

Loud & Clear: Major Disruption

I found out on the 18th that the additional legal filings were rejected. Some parts of the legal reasons for my appeal denial were altered. It will help me make a better argument to the next court on why I deserve another appeal. The rejection highlighted the fact that my lawyers did wrong. Now I surely need to raise the funds for a new lawyer.

It will take an extra day or three for me to finish typing my series of blogs about my supposed bad acts before my arrest. I am having those posted so people can understand the dynamics of my case. It will also give me a chance to show later that the claims are false.

Now that my website is fixed up, I am also going to start posting my autobiography. A few pages will be posted each week. One of my co-defendants has admitted that the first victim was not killed for his car to go see a girl. This is very important, as it means there have been other developments. I will post about them soon.

Thank you to all who have donated and ordered bracelets and t-shirts. I need all the help I can get right now. I need another ten grand to get a lawyer started on the case. Hopefully, I can find one willing to work out a payment plan.

I guess another good thing from the past legal filings is that I got four more months of life, though my desire and plan was surely more than to delay my stay. Thanks again for everyone's help and those that write me. Please keep an eye on my site. More will be posted each week. Take care!

Veni. Vidi. Vici.

Clinton Young #999447

Loud & Clear: Why the Death Penalty

Many have asked me why I received the death penalty. I told them in letters that I would write a blog about it, though I've delayed it some. Why? There are people who want to see me dead. Pro-death penalty types. Hell, I think some of them do not even care at this point if I am guilty or not. They just cannot endure the thought of me. I can be a bit arrogant at times. I used to have messages sent to them from me :) Others want me dead because of their involvement in the case. If I win, it really looks bad for them. Then there are just some others who simply do not like me. And then there are two women who just want to see me fail. I also like to stand back and have others do things to attempt to discredit me, as then I can step up and chop it up.

I am going to attempt to make this as short and to the point as possible for the long-winded guy that I am. :)

Why the death penalty:

I was arrested after a high-speed police chase. I have written about this in other blogs, so no need to repeat.

The alleged murder weapon was in the truck, though it was under the passenger seat. (REALLY A BAD LOOK THERE!)

Juvenile prison records contained reports of alleged extensive drug use, gang activity, and numerous fights in juvenile prison, including some riots and assaults on officers.

I had a few prior cases—the ones that landed me in juvenile lockup.

A guy gave a statement indicating that he and I had a shootout with another guy, plus a gun store was broken into.

There were two murders.

The biggest factor: I refused to talk to the police when I was first arrested.

I readily admit that it all stacks up to be a bad look for me. Though what it is, is a complicated, tangled mess. When you first see it, it overwhelms. Though as you start to unravel it, it all quickly falls to pieces. This is why the legal support I have is so very critical.

Point A: The gun in the truck

This gun did not have my fingerprints on it, nor did any other gun. It didn't have anyone's prints. It couldn't have been expected to, as the co-defendant wore gloves—which he bragged about to others. (That testimony will be re-posted. For some reason, it was removed years ago, and I just found out about it. :( )

I requested that DNA testing be done when the police blamed me for the murder. It was never done, though it wouldn't have been a big factor, especially since the police were seen in a picture holding the gun with their bare hands. It was handled by several officers, thus destroying anything of value due to the sloppy work. What is of value is that the gloves the co-defendant had on have gunshot residue that has not been properly tested.

In one of his statements to the police, he admitted that he told me to get rid of the gun and truck, as I had, in short, removed him from my presence.

Point B: The police chase and the shooting

I have already addressed the police chase and the shooting of a Hispanic male. The guy involved blamed me. However, the victim said that I did not have a gun and did not shoot him. He testified to this.

Point C: My prior cases

The priors I had were petty for the most part. One was a burglary of a house. I did not go into the house. The woman who owned the house believed that I did not break in. Two other guys I was friends with went in. I refused to go in and didn't want anything to do with it, as I had just gotten out of juvenile lockup, where I spent two weeks.

The probation officer I had was threatening to send me to juvenile prison (which I did not want to go to!). Both were older than me; one was 17, so he was able to go to adult prison under Texas law.

An old barge had washed up behind my mother's house. It had been floating in the lake due to a storm. It was in really bad shape. Myself and others used to hang out in it and do what teenagers do. From the house, they stole some guns and stuff and put them in the barge—which, when they spoke to the police, conveniently became my barge! Funny how that works.

They blamed me, as I was the youngest, I guess, and they thought I would get in the least amount of trouble. When the officer came to pick me up, the first thing he said was, "Clint, you know they are putting it on you. Now, I know that is all a bunch of bullshit. You going to give a statement?" I replied, "No, sir." The cop replied, "I didn't think so."

We rode in silence until the officer said, "I understand you not saying anything, but I'm not going to let them get away with it. I'm going to make sure their asses go down too. Being as you don't want to talk, you know you got to go also." I just responded with, "I dig it."

It was a small-town area. This officer knew me. He had questioned me about a store that was broken into. It was a beer store. Again, I was the only one who refused to talk. The store was broken into two times. Yes, one time I did do it. The other time I didn't, though I knew who did. However, I did not say anything. (I wasn't alone when I did, but I didn't tell on the other person.)

I broke into the store because the owner got drunk with someone she knew. She then gave this person my mother's telephone number. That person called my mother's house, leaving threatening voice messages on the answering machine. I got mad. I broke into her store and stole beer and candy. I was 13. Then me, my stepsister, and a couple of others got buzzed at the lake. They couldn't figure out who did the other break-in, though they "cleared the books" by charging me when I was signing for my time.

They actually couldn't prove I did the first one, but I did.

Another case was when I was mad at my stepfather. I wanted to run away from home. I took some of his money and a few of his guns that I was going to sell. The police gave the guns back to my mother and released me to her. My stepfather and I—to say we didn't get along would be an understatement. He didn't want to have me back at the house, and I didn't want to be there.

I had just recently left my father's house, as he was arrested for hitting me. She couldn't send me with him. My mother seemed to think the only solution was to turn me back over to the police. The fact is, had my mother not taken me to the police station (I was arrested in another district), then it all would have gone away. I never would have ended up in juvenile prison.

Myself, a girlfriend, and a friend of mine—who was the son of my mom's friend—we ran away and took his mom's car. We were going to bring it back! She did not want to press charges when we got pulled over. This happened when the guns were taken.

Guns are all over the place in the U.S., and outside of jewelry, they bring in the most money. Also outside of drugs, but it takes money to get drugs!

The state was going to drop all charges if I completed a six-month program. They sent me to a mental health facility. They declared that I was mentally ill due to severe ADHD. Basically, it came down to this: I was a smart, good-looking kid who could have achieved anything I wanted.

The school was actually fighting the hardest for me! They all wanted me to get situated. I was hyper, though most of the issues came from the whole "divorced parents bouncing back and forth between them—emotionally abusive stepfather—no male role model—too immature to properly deal with the pain I was feeling" combo going on.

At the placement, I was placed on very powerful stimulant medication: Dexedrine, Adderall, and such. As I mentioned in previous blogs, these medications now carry warning labels that they cause psychotic behavior in some minors. Guess who was "some minor"?

I am sending the pages to be scanned and posted with this blog. I have written about it for years, though never posted it.

My behavior spiraled out of control. I was accused of manipulating the treatment team when I begged them, while crying, that it had to be the medication or something. I would just snap, and the next thing I knew, I would be restrained on the ground, not fully clear of all the events that happened prior to that point.

Two times I had to be sedated.

I then got into a fight with another guy there. He was a gang member. He was 15, and I was 14. He was 5'9" and 260 pounds. Yes, 260! I was 5'4" and 145. I have written about this in the evidence/legal part of my website.

He told the staff that during the fight, I told him to perform oral sex on me, and I would stop beating him up. Here is how the events unfolded: We had been joking around, play fighting. I told him to stop, as I had to get ready for an event. The placement had girls. As a result, I had a girlfriend there. When I say, "I have had my share of crazy girlfriends," I mean that literally! :) Haha. No, she wasn't crazy, just came from a messed-up situation like myself, and at 15, she got classified as bipolar. I think she was just a teenage girl! They all act a bit bipolar at times! Anyways, she had bought me a necklace. I was sitting on a bed next to the guy, as we shared a room with another guy. He was also Hispanic and in some kind of gang.

The place was for troubled youth with some kind of mental problem—or a daddy with enough money to say they had such, to keep them from getting a criminal record. It was a nice place, though the chief psychologist was TRASH! She was a very despicable, low-life of a woman. She was made for Hollywood films about evil psychologists. Anyways, I went to get up, and the dude grabbed my shirt. In doing so, he also grabbed my necklace (he grabbed me by the collar of the shirt). He broke the necklace. I got mad. He said he would pay for it. I told him it had sentimental value and that "I told his dumbass to stop playing." He told me to "shut the fuck up." I told him, "Bitch, make me!"

He swung at me. I ducked, and the next thing I know, he is on the ground, and I was hitting him in the head. Again, I was in my boxers and a T-shirt. He went to get up, causing me to fall forward. He SAID that he felt my penis touch his ear. I don't know if that is true or not, though it did fall out from the slit in the boxers. The other guy, as I was standing back up, said, "Ahh man, put your dk up!" I looked down, and when I was fixing myself, just to talk smack, I told the guy I was fighting, "Stop looking at my dk!" I then made some comments that would call into question his sexuality.

Now the other guy was, as I said, also Hispanic, and both were part of a "Hispanic-only street gang." When I had backed off, as I was done, he hit him also and told him to keep the gang out of his mouth—basically meaning do not speak of being associated with it. He was an embarrassment due to losing the fight to a white guy, and I had "clowned him." When we stood up, he didn't want to fight anymore. ("Clowned" means to embarrass.) I even stopped the other guy from hitting him anymore.

Several factors came into play after this. First, the dude did not want to have me around. Outside of the fight, there were some jealousy issues due to the girl I was with at the time. She really was pretty! Anyways, I considered the fight over with and gave him his space. Though he couldn't get over the fact that now the only other Hispanic there did not want to talk to him. He had a large bump on his head, though that was from him getting hit by the other guy.

Staff talked to him. It became that I caused it and that I told him I would stop beating him up if he performed oral sex. Everyone knew that any aggressive sexual behavior would result in automatic removal from the placement. I was removed. The psychologist classified me as having antisocial personality disorder, which meant there was "no help for me." Instead of going to another facility, I was sent to juvenile lock-up, then prison. (That classification is meant for 18+ years old, not a 14-year-old child.)

Before I went to prison, they allowed me to go home. Once for a couple of days, then for a week before I was to appear in court. NO ONE ELSE got to do that. NO ONE! The psychologist at the facility had labeled me as a homicide precaution, stating that I should "remain in a secure facility" and that I posed a risk to myself and others. She even added that I indicated I would hurt my baby sister. (That was a personal twist to it, as she knew who two of the most important people to me were at that time.)

If the probation officer or anyone else believed that, they would not have let me go home! Anyone that knew me knew that Jessi was my heart. (Jessi is my baby sister.) While at juvenile lock-up, they knew me, as I had been there before going to the facility. They opened the door and allowed me to walk around. One even made a joke about "who I had pissed off." They knew all the "homicide precautions" were bullshit!

The lock-up gives different levels. If a person is good, they get points. So many points, more privileges. My probation officer checked up on me and found out they had zero problems. She let me go home. Matter of fact, my mom, baby sister, and stepfather were taking a trip to Ohio to visit his family and Brandy, my stepsister. They were going to release me to take the trip "OUT OF STATE" with them. After the trip, I was to come back. Though the paperwork was messed up, so I didn't get to take the trip.

When I went home, my mother called the probation officer and told her, "There is nothing wrong with this boy!" You know the ONE AND ONLY thing that was different? I was taking ZERO medications! Since having been on ADHD pills since the age of 6 years old, I was taking no meds.

Now again, I was 14 years old. The guy told my trial investigator that I was just trying to embarrass him. It wasn't anything sexual, just two boys that got into a fight that got carried away.

I will finish this subject in another blog, as this is way too long. Though it is important that all this be explained. It will all come together in the next blog, along with some recently filed new statements. After this next blog, I will get off the legal topics and onto other matters. I know all this stuff makes people's heads hurt reading it, though it is important that I clear it up and show the proof that I am being honest. This way, I can counter the bullshit! If I've done wrong, I admit it.

I am 30 years old. On July 19th, I will be 31. I am having to tackle stuff that happened when I was 14! Though it is important to show that the reasons the state picked to go after the death penalty are flawed and incorrect. Plus, with my ability to destroy the bullshit tossed out by the state, it helps to gain the faith of people that cross my path.

If I can show I am being honest and am able to repeatedly disprove the state, it helps support my innocence claims. Plus, more importantly, it shows I am not the person they claim I am.

More posted soon. Please bear with me, and thanks to those that have recently purchased the bracelets and T-shirts.

Clinton Young #999447

Polunsky Unit

3872 FM 350 South

Livingston, TX 77351

U.S.A.

Loud & Clear: A Dutch Tragedy

Today, I was standing in the middle of the cell, thinking about what I needed to do. A radio show I listen to mentioned the plane crash in Ukraine. When he said the flight was from Amsterdam to Malaysia, my heart sank. Some of those I write to in the Netherlands have made references to flying to Malaysia for vacation. Since the film aired, I have written back and forth with so many Dutch people that it has become a sister country to me. With all the letters, cards, and help given, I cannot help but feel a kinship with the Dutch.

I have been glued to the radio today, listening to the updates. The tragic event is made worse by the fact that it will most likely turn out to be the result of some dumbass shooting at the wrong plane. My thoughts and prayers go out to all those who lost their loved ones. The Netherlands, being such a small country, would find it hard for such a loss of life not to impact everyone in one way or another.

I folded my mattress up and stood on it to look out the cell window. I can see the sky and a highway. My thoughts went to how quickly life can change. Tomorrow truly is not promised today. I am in this situation, and I have a slow pace of watching death approach. It is vastly different from a sudden loss—more so when I didn't exactly make all the best choices in life. Though people on a plane feel safe and secure, they are on a journey to have fun and relax.

The reports were that the plane was 30 minutes behind schedule. It creates so many thoughts of "if this would have happened," "if that would have happened"—it would all be different. A woman I write to asked before why God would allow the suffering of innocent people. This tragedy would seem to be the perfect storm of a "Why!?" I do not profess to have the deepest, most secure faith. Though I know that Man has the power of choice. That power bears the burden of responsibility, to be held accountable.

It doesn't matter if they thought it was a military plane from Ukraine or not. These foolish political power games have cost the lives of almost 300 people—all innocent. The governments cannot claim to have been ignorant of the threat, as the U.S. and the U.K. issued warnings to their pilots not to fly over the region over a week prior to this happening. The majority should not have to live in fear of the few. Hopefully, the stupid political games are put aside, and the international community acts swiftly, forcing peace in that region so that at least some positive can come from this.

I was telling a guy near me that from my writing to the Dutch, it is clear they are not 'hawkish' people. They are laid-back—cool is the rule. All is good as long as no one gets hurt. They do not bother anyone! If that had been a U.S. flight with 150+ Americans on board, U.S. Marines and Special Forces would have been on the ground before the smoke cleared. Over half the country would have been screaming for all-out war.

Though that is the difference in a country whose identity has been shaped by military might in its young history, versus one that has had its thumbprint on history, has calmed with age, and accepted its role as the party hat of Europe. I imagine the media in the Netherlands made it seem as if hell on earth was coming forth—a plane shot down, Israel invading Gaza. Peace seems to be a chore!

Hopefully, the families of those whose lives were lost can get some kind of justice, and the people who fired the missile and those who made it available are taken to task and held accountable. I was looking around the cell while thinking of how to wrap this one up. I had to laugh. I've got letters and cards lying all over the place with 'Nederland' postal stamps.

On the bunk beside me is the book The UnDutchables. On the floor by my feet is the book New Visions of the Netherlands, along with a GIANT birthday card from greetz.com (Thanks, Liz). I was even listening to the Netherlands play in the World Cup when it was on, hopeful they would win (only if the U.S. lost, of course). So yeah, the Dutch consume such a large part of my heart.

I know that the lives of so many people have been turned upside down. I pray that their pain eases and that they are able to find peace. I'm not really good at dealing with emotional topics unless it is anger. I just hate to think of the pain that a people I have come to love are going through. My thoughts are with you.

In Solidarity,

Clinton Young #999447

Polunsky Unit

3872 FM 350 South

Livingston, TX 77351

U.S.A.

Loud & Clear: Bird Shit and Toilet Water

A unique topic, though one worth discussing. On the Polunsky Unit, there are various buildings. The 12 Building holds those on Death Row and administrative segregation. Each pod has four outside rec yards—two on each side of the pod. The two rec yards are actually one big room, with bars down the middle and across the top. There are two doors for each side of the bars.

The bars over the top act as the roof. It is considered an outside rec yard due to the bars being an open roof that allows in sunlight and weather elements. The walls of it are over 25 feet high, with a concrete floor and a floor drain. There is a sink and a urinal toilet on each side. Over the top of the bars, there is supposed to be netting fastened to keep the birds off the bars. When birds gather on the bars, they turn the rec yard into "their" personal toilet. They always congregate at the bars near the walls. On one side of the bars is the area where people walk into the outside rec area, and on the other end are the sinks and urinals.

With the netting up, all is good, and the birds stay away. The officers have the general population prisoners clean the rec yard once a week with a water hose. There are no birds, so it is just washing off dust. They are supposed to clean the sink and urinals each night. The key word is supposed, as they certainly do not, which is the problem with not allowing us people on Death Row to do it. Since it is seen as the environment we live in, we would keep it clean—or at least some of us would.

The general population prisoners who work to clean 12 Building are known as S.S.I.s, which stands for Support Service Inmate—a fancy term for janitor. In Texas, only a very small number of prisoners get paid for the work they do. S.S.I.s do not. I am unsure of the actual number of prisoners who get paid. There was an article I read years ago about prisoners and free labor, which mentioned a small minority. Though that article could be wrong, as I know of none that do. "You get what you pay for" rings true in here. They do not get paid, so they really do not want to do it. They have to.

When slavery was banned, the wording was that it did not count as slavery if the person was convicted and sentenced to penal servitude. Basically, they redefined what 'slave' meant. The government then expanded what was known as 'criminal laws,' such as drug offenses, so they could lock more people up. The prison population exploded. Many want to blame hard-nosed Republicans; however, that is not true. The largest prison population expansion in U.S. history happened under former Democrat President Bill Clinton. All politicians try to get elected on 'tough on crime' platforms.

The point is, people do not get paid to clean up. The officers do not have to live here, so it doesn't get cleaned. Many people on Death Row just turn a blind eye to it and do not complain or take the initiative to do it themselves. The showers are a prime example. Only a few people here take it upon themselves to clean the shower at the end of the row of cells where they are housed. Each pod has six sections. Each section has two rows, and each row has a single-man shower.

When I moved to the pod I am in now, I went to one row's shower one day (I am on the second row). The sides of the shower base were black with mold and gunk. I had to go back to one-row shower with a hairbrush sold on commissary that I use to clean with. I also took detergent and the cleaning powder that the prison passes out each week. It is called Bippy and is similar to Ajax cleaning powder. (This has happened a few times when I moved to different areas.) The detergent is also sold on commissary and is made by TDCJ. TDCJ has several industries where prisoners work, producing goods that TDCJ then sells for a profit on free labor.

I yell out when coming out of the shower, "Yeah, you all are welcome for cleaning your nasty-ass shower!" No one says anything, though they usually start to wipe it down themselves here and there. Ninety percent of the people here complain about everything, though very few do anything about it. Many will not even file a complaint with the administration.

Back to the topic of the outside rec yard, which is another example. Every six months or so, the officers get on the roof to hit the bars with a hammer to make sure they are still secure. When they did this, they needlessly removed the netting but failed to put it back. I cannot go up there and fasten it back myself, or I would. Now that the netting is pulled back, the birds have returned. The S.S.I.s have failed to clean it for over 2.5 months! Can you imagine how bad the rec yard looked? The sink was covered with bird droppings. It is 95°F outside. The sink is nasty, so there's no way to get fresh water to cool down. One sink was so bad that it was plugged up and didn't drain properly.

I ended up going to rec with a guy who is like-minded when it comes to this place. He is a guy I associate with. Friends is a strong word rarely used in here. I have a couple of friends, though he and I would be considered good associates. On the outside looking in, people might consider us friends due to the way we associate. I know all that seems technical. I just want people to understand that when I indicate someone is my friend or that I love someone, it is a valuable statement—more so in my older years.

To satisfy your curiosity, it is Paul Story. We were at rec, and since it was Monday, the rec yard was supposed to have been cleaned the previous Sunday. It wasn't. Both of us have a long history of protesting and making the officers suit up in their ninja turtle gear and use tear gas and pepper spray. That is where the talks started to head, as my special visits had not been set up yet and I was tired of being exposed to bird shit! The pod officer called and asked for the sergeant to come to the pod and speak with us. The one working knew us both, so he came. He called and spoke to maintenance about fixing the netting, and then Sunday the rec. yard was sprayed down as it should be. The netting still has not been fixed yet, though. They say they are ordering new netting, which isn't needed, as the netting is bundled up on the roof.

I wrote a grievance about all of this. The response from the warden was that he spoke with a lieutenant that works in 12 building. That this ranking officer said the netting was over the rec. yards, which is NOT true. All it takes is for anyone to walk onto the pod and then go to the windows that allow observation to the outside rec. area. Then look up and see the netting is gone. Then look down and see the bird shit everywhere. This is the area we are supposed to work out in! Also, there is NOWHERE to sit besides the ground.

Okay, being that the netting is not fixed, it was a week before the rec. yard was sprayed off with the water hose. I decided that I would take it upon myself to clean it up. I went to the rec. yard with Randy Halprin on Wednesday. It is the usual outside rec. day for the section we live on. Not everyone goes to rec. We were going to work out, though I couldn't find a spot clean enough to do push-ups.

I started to try to use a hand towel to knock the bird feathers out of the way. The dust kept flying up, so all I could think about was breathing in microscopic pieces of bird shit and parasites. That pissed me off! I used a bottle to pour water on the ground to stop the dust. I then just said, "Man, I am tired of this bullshit!" I told Randy that I was flooding the rec. area.

I then took what is known as a Chill Towel (a green deal that is sold to us. It holds lots of water and is supposed to help cool a person down. They started selling them after being sued repeatedly for heat-related problems in the summertime). I got it wet, folded it in half, and covered the drain. I then grabbed some trash that was laying on the filthy-ass fucking rec. yard and stuffed it in the drain of the urinal.

Now these are not weak urinals. These are some industrial-strength urinals! These things spit out like 3 gallons of water a flush. Come to think of it, it is really a HUGE waste of water when half of Texas is in a drought! Anyways, I plugged the drain and started flushing. Randy looked it over after I explained what I was doing. He decided to join in.

The rec. yard ended up with like 4 inches of water in the middle of it. It drains to the middle, so it wasn't that deep all over the yard. The side of the rec. yard I was on is the window side, meaning one wall is these big windows. They cannot be broken. It is so the officers can see all of the rec. yard.

Now it isn't every day that people see a guy flooding the rec. yards! Haha. The commissary officer came on the pod to deliver a commissary care package. As she was walking off the pod, she had to walk past the window to get to the exit door. She did such, as I was running to the deep part of the water, and I side-kicked it in a sweeping motion. This huge wave of water flew up into the air and hit the window. (I do this so the water will hit the edge and then come back to the drain, pulling all the dirt and filth toward the drain.)

She saw this wall of water hit the window, stood there stunned, and yelled at the officer. The officer then looked and ran over, and she started beating on the window telling us to stop. She thought we were trying to flood the area so the water would go into the pod. Some do flood the cells and such to protest, though she calmed down when she spoke to us and figured out what we were doing and saw no water go into the pod itself.

I just wanted to clean the rec. yard. When I yanked the Chill Towel off the drain, there was this whirlpool in the middle of the rec. yard. It was a loud roar as the water went down the drain. That was cool! :)

The rec. yard is a fairly large area. I did this twice. By using my foot to knock the water to different areas and let it drain back, it actually cleaned the rec. yard. Though it also ended up knocking a great deal of the bird shit to the area the officers have to stand. Hey, that is just the way it worked out! ;)

So yes, I had to use toilet water to flood the rec. area so I would not have to sit in or work out in bird shit! Needless to say, I took an extra-long shower and scrubbed the hell out of the cool-down towel. Twice!

I am sure people are wondering what I consider Randy. We are closer than me and Paul, though I connect with both in different ways. Now, do you all see the "shit" I've got to put up with here? It turns out that when I say that, it is meant quite literally.

Loki vs. The Birds. A short battle won by Loki. :) Haha.

Stop by and see me next week. Until then, I remain,

In Solidarity,

Veni, Vidi, Vici,

Clinton Lee Young #999447

Polunsky Unit

3872 FM 350 South

Livingston, TX 77351

U.S.A.

Loud & Clear: November 18, 2014

I know that I've been silent for the most part. Several factors have come into play, one of which has adversely impacted my efforts. A bit of good news is that I was able to get the other lawyer I needed started on my case!

I have several issues to blog about. They finally put the netting over the rec yard. ☺ The birds were none too happy about that! I fight to win all battles, though.

I also had another interesting trip to the hospital to blog about. I will write all of this over the weekend.

On a more serious note, November 26th marks the 13th year I've been locked up on this case. However, for one of the victim's family, it marks an even worse date—the day they lost their loved one. The situation is complicated even more, as it is so close to the U.S. holiday Thanksgiving. It's just a bad time all the way around.

With my appeal, the state obtained more time to respond to my filing, which means there will not be a ruling until after the new year. I thank everyone who has continued to support me, even though I haven't been active.

All the stress and frustrations add up. I have been fighting so hard for so long, yet the hardest part is still to come.

Veni, Vidi, Vici

I will be back blogging after this week.

Take care.

In solidarity,

Clinton Young

Loud & Clear: January 26, 2015

Updates

I was just thinking about how I never updated about the rec yard and the birds. I did win the battle. The rec yard was covered again with netting to keep the birds off. However, after being able to have the run of the place for so long, these terrors with feathers were not willing to go down without a fight! When they returned to the rec yard to do as they pleased, they were met with a shock. The netting hindered their free flight. No longer was the world their own personal toilet. Angered, they attacked with a vengeance. Finding a small hole that was left in the netting where it was tied down, they entered. Feathers and bird shit were scattered about, as in their fit of rage they were unable to easily navigate their way back out of the rec yard.

A few of the braver souls laid in wait, their plans to unleash an unholy jihad on those that restricted them. A guy who went to rec first in the morning, he and another guy were walking around talking. (The rec yard is split in two; you can see each other and talk, though there's no contact.)

When the demon on wings swooped down, releasing his load on the unsuspecting guy's arm, ☺ haha! When he told me the bird shit on him, I could not help but laugh out loud. I told him, "Ha, the bird got you with a shit hit!" I swear to you all, that happened! I tell you, we are not dealing with normal birds here! Though they faded away as they were unable to roost in peace.

I was then moved to another pod. Upon getting to this pod, I went to the shower for the row I was on. The walls were black with mold! Sadly, this is far too common. The inmates that come back here to clean up do not do anything beyond the bare minimum, as they do not get paid for the work and the officers do not force them to do it. Some of us use supplies we buy from commissary to clean it. I had to go to the shower the next day with a hairbrush to use as a scrub brush and a bottle of liquid detergent. After spreading the cleaning chemicals all over the wall and scrubbing it down, I used my hand to direct the water to the wall. It was like a brown waterfall going down the wall. Being that the walls are supposed to be white, it was finally bright in the shower since the walls were white again. Sadly, few people take the steps to change their environment, at least beyond the cell they are in. People will complain all day and ask the people they write to file complaints, yet they will not themselves take any additional steps.

As the world spins! Again, thanks to all that have ordered shirts and bracelets. Some ask about funds. Any and ALL funds raised from donations and the sale of items are strictly for my defense. None of it is used for anything else. So yes, the funds from the t-shirts do go to me, same as the songs.

While on the topic of the shirts, I developed an idea to create a form of protest with the shirts. I would like everyone that has ordered a shirt to please wear it three days each month. The three days are the 3rd, 12th, and 25th. These days are picked because of the letters they represent in the U.S. alphabet, which are the C, L, and Y, which, of course, are my initials. When wearing the shirt on these days, please post a picture wearing it on the social media pages. Not only does it show support for me, but it also increases the idea of community, as a group of people working together towards a common goal in solidarity.

A new form of gaining attention has been developed. Large window stickers have been designed to help advertise my website, with both the website and a slogan that I developed. I know that many might not use the slogan, as it is heavy. So the stickers are separate. This way, a person can just post the one with my website on their car window, though using both is best. The information to order these will be posted on my website, Saveaninnocentlife.com. It is a way to turn a person's car into a mobile billboard, helping to reach people who normally would not be reached.

I know that some might not like such a direct approach. Many worry about what others will think. If you do not speak up, then who will? If you believe in something, then you should represent it. True, some will try to drag you into the death penalty argument with all the different examples of why they support it. However, my site is not about the death penalty. It is about the basic desires of humanity—fairness and justice. The death penalty only highlights the injustice, as they are trying to kill me for something I did not do. Even if a person is not 100% sure of my innocence, NO ONE can reject my claim that I was never given a fair trial or appeals. That cannot be disputed.

It is my desire that people around the world order these stickers. The stickers go across the back of the car window. An example will be shown on the site.

As for my case, all the legal filings have been presented. Now we wait on the court to decide what happens next. It is my desire that they grant oral arguments. This way, the lawyers for both sides can argue before the judges. It is easier to get more across with speech than writing it out. There are several options of what can be done. They can reject everything, which is the worst-case scenario!

I have seven issues that I can be granted an appeal on. Then I will have to do more filings. However, I have GOT to be granted an appeal on at least one of those seven to win an appeal in the current court. Hell, I've got to win one before I can even file an appeal! The other matters are due to the new evidence. There are three different filings. These filings can result in me being returned to the lower courts to file a new appeal on the new evidence and/or my innocence claim. I should get word within six weeks. Time keeps on ticking.

I am going to wrap this one up. Another blog will be posted next week, as there is lots to write about. I plan to get back to working on events and all that good stuff.

Please spread the word. Thanks! In solidarity.

Veni, Vidi, Vici.

Clinton L. Young #999447

Polunsky Unit

3872 FM 350 South

Livingston, TX 77351

USA

Loud & Clear: A new year

I was sitting here thinking of a good start to the new year. Then the breaking news interrupted my daydreams of how I would accept my Grammy award for songwriter of the year. Okay, maybe that is a stretch of the imagination. Though the reality of terror was not. The shootings in France and the manhunt that followed. Suddenly, my song seemed a bit trivial. I actually was hopeful for a visit on Friday from one of my lawyers or someone. This way, I could have had the release of the song delayed. These kinds of terror acts really do go against the grain of humanity. As terror is meant to cause fear, to change the course of behavior. Though when it is used to attempt to silence people, it is a bit worse. As the voice is the key to freedom. A baby fresh from the womb lets the voice cry out to announce one's arrival.

Free speech is so ingrained in the concept of freedom for the West. In the U.S., it is the very first amendment in the U.S. Constitution, which no other constitution has lasted as long. So important is our belief in free speech and the freedom of religion that not only was it listed first, but the very next amendment is our right to own guns. The symbolism being to the government that it shall never attempt to silence the people.

In a way, the freedom of speech is like a religion of the West. The terrorists telling the West that it cannot speak as it wants to would be the same as the West telling them they could not worship as they want. To support my position on this, I need only to quote Stephane Charbonnier himself: "I would rather die standing than live on my knees." When refusing to be silent. It really impressed me how the people of France turned out after the attacks. Though there should have been such turnouts all over the world to that degree. To see newspapers and media run the same images that pissed the terrorists off. That is how terror is defeated. To stand up and say "Fuck you!" It shows the tactics do not work.

It does not matter what someone says or does. We are responsible for how we react. I do not agree with every religion, nor do I like what every person says. I am big into politics; I listen to many political talk shows. Of course, some say what I do not like, though I would not dream of depriving them of their right to say it. The line, "I do not like what you say, but I will fight for your right to say it," sums up the mentality of the Western embrace of free speech. People make fun of Jesus, Buddha, Shiva, Jews, Muslims, and all in between. Personally, I disagree with attacking what people believe in. I do not care what it is. Though I cannot dictate what others say or do not say, as then there is no freedom.

When acts like these happen, people get into the Muslim terror acts vs. Christian terror acts, etc. Some even go back to the horrors of the Roman Empire. One guy on the radio even used the example of the mass shooting in Norway. Now, if I were the host, I would have entertained his position and asked, "Okay, what else you got?" As in modern times, there have surely been more acts of violence by those that wish to twist Islam. However, it is nothing modern. Social media just makes it more personal. Plus, it is impacting the West more. It has been going on one way or another in the Middle East since the 1100s. Just read about the Nizari Ismailis. Though their struggle was different than the modern terrorist. The modern terrorist is not fighting for preservation. Instead, they have a desire to conquer, to force others to accept only their ways.

I write to Muslims in Europe. They are grateful for the tolerant nature of the West. Though people get a knee-jerk reaction to these vile acts, they then use it to justify themselves in becoming vile. Hating billions of Muslims for a radical twist of some. All it does is serve to create a greater divide, which then becomes a breeding ground for the very illogical thinking we wish to defeat. To cure cancer, we attack the tumors, not the person. However, we surely should not, in any form, tolerate those that wish to go against the core of our existence and the freedoms that we enjoy.

This world we live in! Long sigh.

Anyways, I am back to writing more and blogging. There will be a series of blogs written about my past few months. I am also going to be getting back to work on events. My days might be numbered, but I will not spend them laying on my back. Stay tuned! Stand tall, fade all, never fall.

In Solidarity,

Veni, Vidi, Vici

Clinton Lee Young #999447

Polunsky Unit

3872 FM 350 South

Livingston, TX 77351

U.S.A.

P.S. When writing the address for me on the envelope, PLEASE make sure it is written correctly and clearly so there is no delay in me getting your letter. Thank you.

Loud & Clear, March 1, 2015

General Update, Relationships, + Who Will Lead My Campaign

There have been a couple of blogs I started or wrote, though I had them trashed as I was not in a very good mood. When I get upset, I make it pretty clear! Then I got sick. Glad I got over that, as I had a radical cough that I thought would never go away! It finally has, though it surely wasn't thanks to these people. I went to medical one night as I was coughing so badly I could hardly breathe. My fever was 99.6°F. I had sweat coming out of my forehead, and it was certainly not warm outside. They gave me some "Non-Aspirin." What the hell kind of shit is that!? It isn't named for what it is; instead, it is named for what it is not! The main ingredient is what is in Tylenol. I threw that shit away.

Another update: I got on a vegetarian tray. It surely is not salads and fruits! It is beans or black-eyed peas as the main course, then a peanut butter or cheese sandwich. Since I am on the diet tray for high blood pressure, I get fruit at nighttime with the tray. Though it is applesauce or some kind of canned fruit, which they also give to diabetics. I fail to see how bread with every meal and canned fruit soaked in high fructose corn syrup is healthy! There is a portion of another vegetable, though by weight, there is more food on the diet tray/vegetarian tray. I got on it as I was sick and tired of these mystery meat hamburger patties they give on the diet tray 22 times a month! I swear to you all, this hamburger patty—when you look at it, you can actually see pieces of bleached veins. It is a gray-colored patty speckled with bits of whitish veins. If the burger is not cooked properly, it is pink and gray. Just horrible-looking. Other times, it is soaked in grease. Again, it is supposed to be a healthy tray! I said to hell with it and got on the veggie tray. It's not so bad.

Today, I got a mix of ranch beans and black-eyed peas, a cheese sandwich, and two pieces of buttered toast—which I surely do love me some buttered toast.

Hmm, what else… If you have not yet seen the shop on my website and the window sticker, please give it a look. It was made to turn the car into a kind of mobile billboard. Yes, I know it is big and all that, though I must ask this question: "How else will you get a person's attention unless you stand out? Stand out and represent what you believe in!" I would like to be able to get 50 people around the world to get them, as it will help us reach many who never think about the death penalty. Got to educate the masses, or no change can be had.

Hmm, oh yes! There are also maybe 48 shirts left from the original batch that was made.

Nothing really new. A court ruling that I at first thought would be really helpful to me—sadly, the way the Supreme Court justice worded the opinion, it limited it way too much so that it would not impact really any other cases. There is this idea that court rulings in death penalty cases have to be very narrow so as to not open the door for everyone to slip through and "delay justice." What it does, however, is cause a few select cases to get stuck out in the rain.

The guy whose case it was will be getting a new punishment phase, meaning he will either get life in prison or death again. My claims are focused on conviction, not "punishment." To explain that: As for what my claims are, I basically have 15 ways something can happen beyond a total rejection. I can win permission to have an appeal at the current level on 7 claims. There are 3 other specific claims that were presented that can cause me to go back to the lower courts, one of which is new evidence supporting innocence.

Of the 7 appeal requests, 5 of them could return me to the lower court I was last in. This way, certain legal questions can be sorted out.

Now, there was another case recently ruled on in January that I had been giving no attention to. However, the Supreme Court ruled in the guy's favor, and the 5th Circuit, based on that case, returned another guy to the lower court. This happened 3 months after the same 5th Circuit judges had totally denied the guy's appeal requests. They overturned their denial and sent him back to the lower court due to how the Supreme Court ruled in a different case.

My case is much more complex, and I believe I have a stronger legal position than the other guy. However, I might not have the same 3-judge panel that he had, so as a result, I could get a totally different ruling. ☹ The panel is a secret until a ruling is given. Right now, I only know of one judge.

Beyond all that, I am in a better mood. I don't know if I was depressed so much as I was just burnt out!

A woman that I write recently sent me a letter. In it, she mentioned something I never thought about, as it was not my intent. She stated that the way I wrote some stuff gave the impression I wanted a relationship.

To be clear, she and I did not start on the best of terms. Why is not important, though it was not my fault, and she got caught up in another—I will call it—"improper approach." So, it was not her fault. Anyways, all is good now, and we get along great. Though what I took as just generic conversation pieces, she perceived as something different.

It was not my intent for her to get that impression, but I thought it was a good push to make something clear. That being: I am not getting into any relationship while here unless it is my ex, whom I told to get on with her life after my appeal was denied. This is a complicated, difficult, and truly unique situation. The state is trying to kill me. I am married to my case.

Now, this does not mean I would not develop stronger bonds with people. However, that as well takes some time. This is why my initial letters are generic, as I am not going to blindly trust someone right out the gate! Hell no! Plus, some write and expect me to write all about myself, yet they write nothing about themselves! This is supposed to be a two-way street.

Also, I do not want to write about my childhood in the first letter. I understand the curiosity, as people wonder what brought me to this point. My position is this: If you are not going to walk up to someone and ask them about their childhood, then don't ask me. I will sum it up: It was fucked up. I do not like thinking about it, as I get aggravated.

Keep in mind, I am stuck in a box with little to occupy my mind. Negative thoughts get amplified. Also, I am 100% averse to people discussing my letters. I really do not like it when people even post that they got a letter from me. Not saying it is meant as bad; just keep in mind that I did not grow up on social media. All that came out after I got here. Plus, I was raised in a culture of "what is said in the house stays in the house." It takes time for me to develop a bond with people. Cool is the rule.

Anyways, I am not going to sit here and try to overanalyze every word I write. A compliment is not a marriage proposal! Plus, to be honest, it takes a really unique woman to be on that level with me, more so due to other women that came before. Each impacted me in different ways and shaped my views further. I readily admit I have had some great women in my life! Each one raised the bar higher.

Why would I still not be with one of them? For the most part, it has been my fault. I did not "cheat" or anything like that. Anyways, another reason why I would not go to that level with a woman unless I really got to know her is there are some crazy-ass people in this world!

Let me give an example: A guy that was here before—he has since gotten off death row—has a wife from overseas. Where doesn't matter. He thinks she is highly educated, very wealthy, and all that, with a great job. He thinks she made some financial moves to help him in the future. Everyone else that knows her knows she is full of shit. A guy here was reading off comments people made about her from a Facebook printout. I felt bad for the dude, as his wife is a nut. He has no clue at all of the truth.

I could give some specific details, but it would make it easier to identify her. It is not my interest to get into all the bullshit. Point is, a damn fool Clinton Young will not be!

The main people helping me all have met one or the other in person. I mean those helping with my campaign. Jorunn, Alexandra, Camille, Louise, Catia, and Anna—they are all solid, good people. Same as Alex and Renate. Alexandra was picked to be the "go-to" for my campaign, as she is a go-getter with multiple skill sets that suit such a role—

from being able to speak multiple languages to creativity and having a solid foundation in life.

Plus, we see eye to eye on several matters. She is also in contact with my civil lawyer/investigator, whom she recently retained. The funds from the shop sales are being used first. She made the shirts and bracelets. Linda made the window stickers. (Let me be clear: There are other great people who help, such as Linda, who has met others in person. I just did not mention them, as they do not have the primary, main role in my campaign as the others do.)

As everyone is interacting with those involved in different elements of the campaign, it requires people to have faith in them and know I have faith too. I just want to be clear, so it doesn't seem like I am leaving anyone out.

Alexandra and Jorunn are great examples. Both are go-getters. They came up with shirt styles. Jorunn has gotten shirts made, as well as calendars and such, which she sells out of her business. Due to currency differences and shipping, the main focus of her work is Norway. Beyond that, they both treat me damn near like family. Jorunn sent Christmas gifts to my nephews, which really touched my heart. (Also, my baby sister is selective about who she interacts with that writes me, as she has seen some of the crazy dumb stuff people did in the past. She does not have much tolerance for nonsense or drama.)

Alexandra, right out the gate after she saw the film, started making moves. She got the shirts made and sold a huge portion of them to people she knew. She did not profess to be my friend or anything; she just truly believed that I did not deserve to die. My bond with Alexandra was sealed when I saw her in December. We had to have a visit which, sadly, was mainly about business, as another investigator messed me over. Now, we have to sue her because she lied on her billing. Thankfully, I have a much better person helping now! Still, there were questions that needed answers, and the easiest way was a visit.

During our visit, she voiced her position on something. She looked at me and said, "I am not your friend; I do not know you. I just started to write you. Yet I am pissed off about this problem." It was about a complicated situation involving how some others reacted to something. Anyway, when she said that to me, I wanted to give her a hug! If the glass hadn't been there, I would have. The visit was good for both of us, as we were able to discuss more in eight hours than we could in 100 letters. I believe the visit helped her too, as I could elaborate on some matters, including how I think and so on. We are friends now.

I'll put it this way: I have NEVER said anyone could fully be my voice. I have always held the position that it's my life, my choice. It doesn't matter if it took extra time. However, Alexandra is so on point that she is now over my campaign. Instead of waiting a month for word back from me due to the slow pace of mail, just ask Alexandra!

To elaborate, it wouldn't be practical to have ten people from Norway and ten people from Italy contacting Alexandra, as she would do nothing but respond to people. Jorunn handles my main FB page and is in contact with Alexandra. She is also over the Norway page. Anna and Catia deal with the Italian part of my campaign. Someone from Italy would contact them, just as someone from Norway would contact Jorunn. If someone from France needed something, they'd contact Camille, and so on.

I am trying to expand my campaign to be more successful. I cannot have Jorunn focusing on all corners of the globe, as that takes away from her ability to solidify our efforts in Norway. If I had to give a title to make it simple, Alexandra would be the president of the S.A.I.L. campaign. For example, Camille would be the director of my France arm of the campaign, and so on. Appropriate emails will be set up for them and easy to identify on my site.

Alright, to sum up this blog here: Not looking for a wife—Alexandra runs the show—hold up! On the "not looking for a wife" comment—Charlize Theron, if you are reading this, I would surely reconsider! Haha. Though I'm sure Sean Penn would have something to say about that.

Seriously though, I am feeling better, ready to get back to blogging more, and even get my book reviews and song reviews posted. Plus, my Mr. Pig! Yeah, buddy—you all are going to love Mr. Pig! ;) He is a bubble-butt-loving, Budweiser-drinking, honey-bun-eating pig. I swear I don't know where he got such interests from! Be back next week!

In solidarity,

Veni, Vidi, Vici.

Clinton YOUNG #999447

Polunsky Unit

3872 FM 350 South

Livingston, TX 77351

U.S.A

Loud & Clear, March 5, 2015

Clear up my previous blog, update.

I got to thinking about my last blog that I wrote. As happens when I am frustrated about something, I do not explain in the best way. I wrote something about relationships. The way I wrote it could seem kind of like I was being an arrogant asshole, which was not my intention, plus I did not properly explain my position. I wanted to better explain why I was frustrated.

Because of my looks and the fact that many women follow my case, some think it goes to my head—that I might think a person has more of an interest in me than they do. That kind of thinking could cause someone to read more into my words. As I often say, in life there is presentation and interpretation. There are stereotypes attached to guys in prison. Sites about prisoners often mention guys trying to find a "wife."

I have had numerous women write and, in the first letter, include the words: "I am not looking for a relationship." Even seeing that upsets me, as it means right out of the gate we are on the wrong foot. I do not find solid friendships or relationships beginning with a series of what a person will NOT do. Plus, when I see that line, I want to write and ask: "What makes you think you would qualify to be the better half of Clinton Young!?"

The fact something like that would be written means they already assume it would be a focus of mine. I mean, sure, I am a guy. Yes, I do have an appreciation for the ladies ☺ ha. Though the reality is, I could be dead within a year if all goes bad. Not saying I will be! Though it is the reality I face. My number one interest is fighting my case.

Now, it is true I have some wonderful women in my life. Also, I have found that I do tend to have people who become a part of my life who never would have written to someone in prison. My ex, for example. She was actually searching for something she had read in a book when she came across my website. A large sum of funds had been sent back then to make the site have great search engine results for different terms. This was in early 2010, I believe.

She was shocked by my site and wrote me a small letter, basically telling me she had seen the site and had seen people suffer at the wrong end of the system. She had friends who had been in and out of prison. She understood the lifestyle I once lived. That understanding helped us relate better, and over the years, we developed a stronger bond.

Though we had our ups and downs. It became harder and harder for her to deal with. We would split, patch things up, and repeat the process. Basically, it had been off and on.

When my appeal was denied, I expressed that that was it—get on with life. One thing I always appreciated with her was how she was one to see a situation for what it was.

Once, she visited me when my last state-level appeal was denied. It was my second round of state appeals due to winning a new appeal because of newly discovered evidence. She saw me and had known my appeal was denied before I did. When I went out to visit, the officer told me I had an attorney phone call later that day.

Then, when I sat down for the visit, I could tell by the intense look on her face that something was on her mind. She asked me if I was okay. I said, "I take it my appeal was denied?" She said, "Yeah." When I heard that, I gave a kind of laugh and said, "On with the next fight."

That just totally blew her mind, as she could not understand how I was able to act like it was a simple matter. So her mind started to hyper-analyze everything. She went home and stayed in bed for two days. It just overwhelmed her. She misunderstood my laugh. She started to wonder if I ever thought I would actually win. That called into question if I am being honest about my situation.

It just all became too painful. She couldn't handle it. While it hurt, I was not mad at her. This is some radical shit! Though the reason I laughed was because the state court denied me. No one here really ever expects much from the state courts, as they reject us so much, sometimes for the most simple of reasons.

Every person who was on Texas Death Row that is free now was rejected by the state court on at least one of their appeals. Anthony Graves had been rejected by all the courts and was given an execution date! Now he is free and paid by the state for the years he spent in prison.

We on death row see the nature of the beast. Anyways. A woman putting her life on hold and falling in love with a man she did not know while free—more so, one who under any other circumstances would not have ever thought of writing to a guy in prison she did not know personally—that is a hard pill to swallow.

I cannot speak for others. Everyone is different. As I have gotten older, I cannot see putting a woman through the pain of this shit. It is hard enough on friends. That is why I say, I will not go to that level. As a result, no one has to worry or even consider such.

Now, if my case turned around and it looked as if I was standing a chance and had victory in sight, yeah, I could see a mutual interest developing in that way. Though I got one foot in the grave right now. Maybe not one foot, though I damn sure am on the edge of it.

Yeah, sure, I might joke around, flirt, and all that. I am a guy! Though I am married to my case.

On a side note. Now, what I meant by other women in my life raising the bar. I have had the privilege of having that emotional and mental bond with some good women. One of which, well, we are not really very fond of each other anymore. However, I can say that she never would have cheated on me.

She would have been solid. I can say that about several. Plus, take my ex, for example—she never tried to tell me what to do. I am against control with my whole being when it comes to a relationship.

Love, within itself, is control. It will dictate the proper course of action. More so when paired with a solid moral code.

There are guys who boss their partners around. That shit is crazy to me. I would not respect a woman who allowed me to boss her around. A child is bossed around. I am a grown man. No one is going to boss me around.

A relationship should be bound by a mutual love and affection for each other. Both respecting the other, and when that person is not sitting beside them, they act as if the other is. A dedication and solidarity.

I mention that to dovetail into another matter. It bothers me that sometimes how I look is allowed to overshadow the injustice of my case.

Someone had recently made a comment about "having a soft spot for this handsome…" Now, to be clear, I am not trying to single out anyone. Nor do I misunderstand her words. I believe she takes my case very seriously. I am not mad at the words, though I find it as offering a chance to have a good example.

I would prefer someone to post: "There is a soft spot in my heart for this innocent man." I just worry that outsiders viewing in could get the wrong idea. Maybe not take my campaign as seriously.

I am not trying to be a cute corpse.

To better explain how little my looks factor into my concept of self when I was younger: When it came to my looks, I felt it made me appear weak. Being that I had the adverse interactions with my stepfather and real father, I was stepping into the world from that foundation. Then I had experiences such as:

When I was 11, I was at a placement for a couple of months. Supposed to be for a couple of months. There was a trade day near the placement. Various people had all kinds of booths set up. There was just me and, at first, two other boys at the placement.

One staff member. They could take us places with them. The school had paid for me to go there as they knew there was something else going on that was not getting told. My mother and I always acted like home life was all great.

When I got to the placement, they told me what MHMR meant, as I had seen it on some paperwork. As soon as they told me the "R" stood for Retardation, I went off. It took them a whole bunch of explaining to get me to accept that they didn't have me there for being retarded—that MHMR was a type of catch-all.

The problem was, I still thought they were labeling me as some kind of crazy. Being too smart for my own good, I thought, "When in a crazy house, do crazy!" ☺ I could always justify it. This one Black lady was a staff member working there. Now, older Black women from the South have a personality type that white women usually don't.

One day, I was bored. "When in crazy, act crazy" came to mind. I jumped up, took off running around the room with my hands in the air, yelling: "Raw, raw, ree, kick 'em in the knee!" and so on. If a white lady had been working, she probably would've said, "Now Clinton, you need to calm down and take a time out." An older Black lady, though, would say, "Boy, if you don't stop acting crazy, I'm gonna beat you!" Ha ha. That's basically what she told me.

(She wouldn't really beat me. Though my mom, raised on old Southern Baptist principles, gave me plenty of spankings!)

Anyway, when I was asked, "Boy, why you actin' crazy!?" I responded, "Well, I am in a crazy place, so I must be crazy!" I stretched out the word "crazy" and rolled my eyes around.

Ms. Paddy, the older Black lady, told me: "Boy, you ain't crazy! You just need to be beat. Go sit down." ☺ I really liked her.

Back to the point: We went to a trade day. Even though I was 11, when I was just sitting around talking to the staff, they no longer looked at me as 11. Not having kids my age around, I often spent time with adults and older kids. The head doctor at the placement described me as "an angry 15-year-old," even though I was 11.

At the trade day, after promising not to get in trouble, they let me walk around by myself. This one guy had a table full of sports cards, electronics, and stuff kids would like. I started talking to him.

The next day, I went back with a different staff member. She was talking to the guy, and he was giving her a spiel about having a rich accountant who got messed over—a guy ran off with all his money. She was buying into it, but at 11, I could already tell he was full of it!

I had been around enough low-end workers and construction types to recognize one. My dad worked with iron, welding and all that. My stepfather worked at a steel plant. They knew other blue-collar workers. My dad had friends who were what people called "poor white trash." I had friends whose dads worked construction. Nothing wrong with it at all! It's an honest day's living and deserves appreciation, as they help keep the economy running.

But I knew that fool wasn't a Wall Street type. I didn't care, though, because I wanted the staff member to leave me alone so I could be free to wander around. Sure enough, she wanted to go look at other stuff. I expressed wanting to stay and look at the cards and such. She said okay and walked off.

Long story short, the guy let me behind his counter and had me sit in a chair while I played with a remote-control car. Brave little me said okay. I sat down, but I felt his hand on the chair when I did, so I jumped up.

My mother always told me never to let a guy touch me in certain areas. If they did, I was to tell someone. If it was a boy my age, I was to hit him in the mouth. Momma didn't have to tell me twice.

I told the guy to move his hand and slapped it away from the chair. I thought he was just being goofy. I sat down again, but it happened again. This time, I grabbed the remote-control car and raised it over my head. I told him, "Do it again, and I'll hit you with the car."

He laughed and explained it away as just playing. This time, I sat down while keeping an eye on him. We talked about other things, and he asked me to go into his trailer (RV) to get a box—he wanted to show me something.

I stepped inside and asked, "Which box?" He pointed to one clearly too high for me to reach easily. Then he stepped in behind me. I looked up at the box and thought, "If I try to get that box down and it's heavy, it'll fall on me."

I turned around and looked up at the guy. The look in his eyes and the way he said, "Go ahead, get it," set off alarms in my head. A voice in my head said, "If I reach for that box, it will fall, and he'll use that as an excuse to hit me and knock me out. Then anything could happen." I felt scared, thinking, "If that happens, I may never see Momma again." I pushed him and jumped out of the trailer. As he came out, I walked backward and said,

"Stay away from me." I grabbed the remote-control car. He let me, probably thinking he could tell me to bring it back the next day. I didn't say anything to the staff. That night, I ran the car until the battery died. Then I grabbed a screwdriver from the toolbox and slammed it right through the middle of the car.

The next day, we went back for the final day of the event. I walked up to the guy to return the car. He reached for it, and right before he grabbed it, I let it drop at his feet, making him pick it up. He looked at me, saw the smirk on my face, and knew I did it on purpose. He told me, "You sure are a little asshole!" I responded, "Yeah, and you sure are a big faggot!"

(A side note: Growing up in that region of Texas—well, back then, really the majority of the country—being gay was not something people were open about. Not at all! I didn't even meet an interracial person until I was 12. The area at the time was only Black and white. They stayed on one side, and we stayed on another. People got along, though everyone operated on invisible lines.

I did know a gay woman—she was a friend of my mom's. It was just a different time back then, and I was taught that gay men were pedophiles. I know now that it's not true.)

Anyway, fast-forward to when I was 13 in North Carolina. In just a few months, three guys tried to kidnap me. This blog has gotten too long. I will explain those events later.

Another guy, older than me, that I met shortly after, I thought was a bit weird but cool. I was never one to avoid strangers, as I didn't see myself as a little kid. If someone tried to grab me, I was just going to make them let go. That was my mindset. Anyway, the guy gave me a ride somewhere for something. We got to talking. I had started to smoke, and he agreed to buy me a pack. So I was thinking, "Hey, cool, here's a guy old enough to buy smokes and beer, and he's willing to. Plus, he has a car. Cool deal."

We spent time together here and there. I thought he was just odd and bored, so I hung out with him occasionally. I could always depend on him to help me out when I needed it. I didn't know the fool was a prolific pedophile. I mean, we would talk about women and all that like normal guys, so I just thought he was a square.

At the time, drinking cough syrup was becoming popular with teenagers. I would pop NyQuil gel caps sometimes, as I felt the effects but avoided the nasty taste. NyQuil actually has chemicals that can make a person hallucinate, but it also has other chemicals that make you throw up if you consume too much. Anyway, his method was drinking cough syrup to pass out. So when it came to slamming a shot of NyQuil and chasing it with whiskey, I was all for it. He joked about me not being tough and bet I couldn't do it again. I poured it out and slammed it.

Of course, later on, I passed out. I felt weird, so I opened my eyes. There I was at 13, and this dude had my penis in his mouth. I pushed his head and kicked him off the bed. I was trying to fix my pants and get my head straight, cussing him out. He walked toward me, trying to calm me down. I grabbed a souvenir baseball bat—a smaller version with a logo on it, like the ones sold at various events. I threatened him with it and my knife, telling him to take me home.

The whole car ride home, I held the bat raised, warning him in so many words not even to look at me. I'm shocked we didn't get pulled over; it damn sure looked like one of those "need to be pulled over" situations.

When I got home, I took a shower and stood there looking in the mirror. All that shit came flooding back: the three dudes, at different times, who tried to get me in the car with them; the guy at the trade day event; what happened that day; my stepdad's mental abuse that I couldn't understand and him always calling me names to talk down to me. I thought it all came down to how I looked. There I was at 13, looking in a mirror with my knife in my hand, thinking of cutting my face up. Thankfully, I didn't.

After thinking like that, it's why I never did PCP or hallucinogenic drugs. I always heard of guys getting high on that stuff and doing crazy shit, like peeling their face off to feed to the dogs. True story—it happened in New York City.

Shortly after that event was when my real dad beat me with a 2×4 board. It's also when I started to fight back. The next time he hit me, I hit him back.

Now, those events are a big reason why:

A) My looks are not relevant to my concept of self.

B) I've always felt much more comfortable with females.

C) I have very few friends that are guys.

The ones I did have in my life share a common trait: aggressive and rough around the edges. I've got rough edges, and I'm real direct, which some people seem unable to deal with. Life and prison made me that way.

Anyway, the point of all that—which I had no real desire to share with people—is simply to express that I don't get egotistical or vain because of all kinds of women in my life. I never have, as it's been a common thing all my life. I don't care if 10,000 Victoria's Secret models wrote me. What would it matter if I'm strapped to a gurney? It doesn't mean shit.

My case should be the focus.

Also, to make sure no one gets the wrong impression: I know not all gays are pedophiles. I actually write to a gay dude—well, a dude who just so happens to be that. The point is, I don't care. When I was free, I knew a guy who was gay, so I was sensible enough, as I got older, not to start gay-bashing or anything like that. I don't give a damn who sleeps with who, as long as it's not a child. I've got a real big problem with people who hurt children in any way.

Up until this point, only a few people knew about some of these events. I really didn't want to write about it but want people to finally understand how little I care about my looks and that I want people to focus more on my being wrongfully convicted rather than on how I look. That jury damn sure didn't care about how I looked when they sentenced me to death.

I gotta go.

Veni, Vidi, Vidi,

In Solidarity

Clinton Lee young #999447

Loud & Clear, March 10, 2015

Topic: Dirty Showers & Music Reviews

Two weeks ago, I was moved from B Pod to A Pod. The only difference is that A Pod is where the section for Death Watch is—those with execution dates. A Pod A Section is Death Watch. I am currently housed on B Section. Also, on this pod is where those with severe disabilities are housed, which is on F Section.

There are a few guys who have to walk around with a walker or be in a wheelchair. The disabilities happened after they got to death row. Four of the guys got so bad they had to be moved to 10 Building, which is the medical building. It's like a small drama center. One of the guys over there is around 80 years old. His name is Jackie Smith. He can't read or write, cannot control his bodily functions, cannot even walk anymore, and has to be in a wheelchair. He cannot even shower himself—the nurses have to wash him.

Yet this dude is still on death row waiting for execution. Though the state would not execute him, the publicity of having to execute someone so old and broken down that they would literally have to carry him to the execution gurney to kill him would not be worth what they like to call "the cost of justice." Max Soffar is also over there. He has a very strong claim of innocence, though he is dying of cancer. I guess if he dies of cancer, Texas can still stick to its position that it never executed an innocent person.

Back to the point. I moved over to this pod and went to the shower the next morning, the one for the row I am housed at. I stepped into the shower, and behold, another black wall that is supposed to be white. It was blacker than any previous shower I have been in. ☺ The other side wall was not as bad. One side, though, was black and brown.

The next day, I took the trusty hairbrush and liquid detergent to the shower. After I scrubbed the wall and deflected the shower water onto it, as it ran down the wall to the drain, it made me think of old oil from a car—just that color. The next day, I went to recreation with a guy who has been on the section for several months. He lives near the shower.

(Outside, the rec area is split in half with bars. We can see and talk to each other but not touch. The roof is bars to allow in sunlight and all that—for those reading my blogs for the first time.)

For those curious about the birds: actually, only half the netting is up there, and the rec yard is in good shape. It appears the birds on this end know how to act. Must be birds from the suburbs, as them birds down on F Pod—which, ironically, is where people go when in trouble—are straight out of the ghetto! ☺ ha.

While walking around, the guy was telling me he was sick the past two months with bad allergies. He blamed it on some negativity in his life, saying it weakened his system. I yelled out, "Ain't no damn negativity! It's all that fucking mold in the dirty-ass shower that you have been breathing in for the past nine months!" He responded, "Yeah, it was in bad shape." My reaction was, "Yeah, I see no one else thought to take the time to clean it."

Now, here is the deal with the showers. It is a very small room that we are locked into—1 meter by 2 meters (3 ft x 6 ft). Ventilation is poor, and the shower water is hot. Okay, picture the scene here: locked in a small, hot, steamed-up shower for 15–30 minutes every day, breathing in this steam that has floated around nasty-ass shower walls. People wonder why they have sinus/breathing problems.

A couple of days later, I went to the shower. I was standing under the water, thinking of a remix I want done of a song I wrote. I was standing there with water hitting my head, eyes closed. I happened to look toward the shower door and saw two different flying bugs of some sort. Not sure of the type, as I've never been into bugs. I looked back at the wall that was previously really bad with mold. I saw a spot that I didn't clean good enough and thought about how it would grow back. I then closed my eyes again.

Though I had an urge to look to my right, so I did—and I'll be damned! There was a centipede climbing the wall, and it was at eye level. I thought out loud, "I'm not in a shower—it's a damn jungle!" I then started to sing the song from The Lion King: "In the jungle, the mighty jungle, the lion sleeps tonight…" ☺ ha. I swear, people, it's wild in this habitat.

Though let me dovetail into my song reviews. I have been meaning to write about several of my favorite songs, though I need to get the lyrics of them. I cannot say that I have always been a huge fan of music in the sense that it occupied my time. Most of the songs I like, I cannot even tell you the name of them—never kept track of it.

Though interestingly enough, many songs mark different points of my life, like when I first heard the song. I remember the first time I heard the songs "Simple Man" by Lynyrd Skynyrd and "Shooting Star" by Bad Company. I was actually in the shop with my stepfather. He had an old radio that he kept on the classic rock station.

I am sure I heard the songs before, though I wasn't aware of it. When the songs came on, it made me think about my mother, who I was really close to back then. The fact that

I was in the shop with my stepfather, who represented a main conflict element in my life at the time and factored in on my reeling behavior—the symbolism was not lost on me.

I remember actually turning and staring at the radio as the song played. It has been maybe 20 years, yet I can still picture everything—even the clothing I had on that day. My favorite Metallica song is "One." The first time I heard it, I was sitting in the room of my friend's sister. I had always had a crush on Melissa when we were younger. We were all sitting in her room when she played the song.

I do not remember when I first heard the song "Dear Momma" by 2Pac. Though when I hear the song, I remember the time I got my mother to listen to it. She was laying on my bed on her stomach, facing toward my radio. I was sitting on the floor by the radio. We had been talking when I suggested she listen to the song.

My mother was no fan of rap music. Once, she found a Snoop Dogg CD, and she threw it out my window. She did not like hard, heavy metal either. She was messing with my radio one day, and I had a Pantera CD in it—Far Beyond Driven. She pressed play and listened to about three seconds of it. Matter of fact, I was in the shop with my stepfather that day. She came storming in and yelled at me, "You are not going to have this trash in my house." She then snapped the CD in half, threw it down in front of me, and walked back to the house. I shrugged my shoulders and went back to doing what I was. (This was not the same day I heard the previous songs in the shop.)

My mother was always very unapologetic about her positions on matters. ☺ As time went by, she stopped trashing my CDs.

The picture on my website of me in the blue shirt with my arm around Jessi—she is in the yellow shirt. I had the bowl haircut, and we were sitting in blue chairs. Okay, that picture was taken when I was 14. I was in Waco at a placement the prosecutor agreed for me to go to, to keep me from going to TYC. That is a whole blog in itself!

The facility was co-ed, though, of course, the boys and girls were housed separately. There were two girls there who were some kind of good-looking. One was Lacy, and the other was Lindsy. Lindsy had rich parents and had that kind of personality. In the U.S., it's called preppy.

Lacy, though, was the opposite—and was the best looking. She got there not long before I did. When I first got there, the dorm I was on went to the cafeteria for the place. All the dorms went at the same time. I was talking to a guy and happened to see Lacy walking on the other side of the cafeteria. She had on these tight pants. She was built like a mini-Iggy Azalea.

I asked the guy who she was and if she was hooked up with anyone. He said no. I said, "Lord have mercy, I know I'm going to try to change that." Of course, he later told her a whole bunch of something else, so she had this attitude toward me.

Okay, there is a sidewalk that if a person was at a certain privilege level, he or she could walk on it. The reason it was required at a higher level was that it was considered a co-ed area. Me and this guy who fancied himself a cowboy were sitting on a picnic table in front of the dorm we were housed in. There were different dorms for different stuff. I was on the anger management dorm, which was dorm 4. Dorm 1 was all girls. Lacy was 15 at the time.

Okay, so Lacy and this goth girl named Emily were walking back and forth on the sidewalk. We had a boom box outside, and Chris was playing Garth Brooks. We were talking, and I was watching Lacy. She was going through all kinds of effort to intentionally not look at me. That's when I knew I just had to create the right moment. Chris changed the radio over to a mixtape. After a bit, the song "Nice and Slow" by Usher came on. I told Chris to turn it up loud.

Lacy and Emily were walking back towards our end. They could hear the radio. I jumped on top of the picnic table and started to dance like Usher does in the music video. That made her look. When the part of the song where he sings, "Good loving, don't keep me waiting," came on, I pointed at her as I was singing that part. She busted out laughing. I knew right then it was a wrap! I ran over to her, found out why she was all attitude with me, cleared that up, and boy, I got the girl.

Actually, even with Garth Brooks and the song "Rodeo," I was 10, living in Gillette, Wyoming, with my dad, my sister Christy, and my dad's girlfriend. I had a girlfriend named Holly. She had a twin sister. It was hard to tell them apart—I had to look at their hair length.

Anyway, Holly was big into country music, horses, and all that stuff. I kept the TV on MTV. Holly lived a couple of blocks down the road. It was like a really nice trailer park outside of the city limits. She and her sister came over. My dad was gone somewhere with his girlfriend. I knew he had some country music CDs, and I knew who Garth Brooks was. I wanted to impress Holly.

My mom had bought me these tight Wrangler jeans and cowboy boots that I never wore because I didn't want to be some little cowboy. I couldn't stand wearing tight jeans—I hated it! But wanting to impress Holly, I put all that stuff on and put on a Garth Brooks CD. The song "Rodeo" seemed like an appropriate choice since it dealt with horses! I selected it and pushed play.

I actually really liked the song, and it's now one of my favorites by Garth Brooks. Though it was all for nothing. When Holly came over, she looked at me all crazy. I guess she was into the whole opposites attract thing. Holly's sister later lied to me about Holly, so I broke up with Holly for a girl named Heidi.

Every Heidi I met while free seemed to have a ... 'fun personality.' She was the first Heidi I met and was no exception. I found out she kissed all the boys on the baseball team. Heidi had the little blonde beauty pageant look. I wonder how many kids she has now? I should have stayed with Holly! ☺ They were both 11, and I was 10. Too damn young for all the complex interactions.

Thinking back to all the stuff I got into when I was young, if I had a daughter, I know damn well I'd be a complete nervous wreck! Ha-ha.

I remember, while living in Wyoming, a guy I was friends with. We would do stuff like sit under a bridge/overpass watching cars go by, smoking Camel brand cigarettes, and looking at a stolen Playboy magazine. He was 14 and a runaway from Tennessee. Both of us were too damn young.

Alrighty then, I'm going to bring this one to a close. I will, hopefully soon, be posting more song reviews under that part of my site. I thank you for reading these words, and I'm grateful for any and all support.

Until next time.

I remain,

In Solidarity,

Veni, Vidi, Vici

Clinton YOUNG #999447

saveaninnocentlife.com

Polunsky Unit

3872 FM 350 South

Livingston TX 77351

U.S.A

Loud & Clear: March 30, 2015

Another Week, Another Battle on Death Row

It never fails in this camp. Always something! This time it was the inmate kitchen workers and 12-building officers double-stacking breakfast trays. Breakfast is passed out at 2:30–3:30 in the morning on average. The majority are asleep. Some do not get up for breakfast unless it is something not normally given, such as coffee cake or a cinnamon roll. As a result of this, they do not give attention to the tray cart or tray carrier as they would during the daytime.

I will explain how the food is delivered to the pods on 12-building. Being that we cannot walk to the chow hall like those in general population, the food has to be brought to us. The main kitchen puts the food in holding bins to stay warm. It is carted to 12-building. The carts are plugged in to keep the food warm. Trays with food are placed on a line. As the tray slides down the line, food is placed on it in individual slots. It is then placed on another cart. These carts are also to be plugged in. Each cart holds 42 trays. It is wheeled to the pod and plugged in. The officers then use a handheld carrier. They place seven trays in the carrier. It is seven, as there are seven cells per row of cells.

That is how it is SUPPOSED to happen. At breakfast time, the punk-ass inmates working in the kitchen were putting 84 trays on the cart. This means the bottom of one tray is on top of the food of another tray. I mentioned the tray sliding down the line, being held by different people... Okay, I am sure you get the idea. The officers were then putting 14 trays on the carrier—all so they could feed quicker, and the inmates could get back to their living area quicker.

Due to being asleep, I did not know that for a long time now, this had been happening. Wonder why I got sick a couple of months ago? A little over a week ago, when I got my tray, I happened to see the carrier and saw the trays double-stacked. I had gotten my tray and did not see it until the food slot was closed. I said, "Hell NO! What the fuck are you all doing!?" The female officer looked at me like I was crazy and said, "What?" Maybe they have been doing it longer than I thought, and she assumed that was the norm. The male officer said, "Young, that is how the kitchen has been sending them."

The next day, an officer worked that I had previously discussed this kind of issue with. I did not bother making an issue of it, as I did not expect it to happen. At breakfast time, I got my tray and was walking across the cell when I looked at it. I saw the indentation of another tray on my bread. I grabbed the bread and threw it across the cell. Then I told the officers, "You motherfuckers done lost your damn mind!"

I then asked if all the trays were double-stacked. A guy who has been here for at least three months said, "Yeah, they always are." We had an exchange, which I was none too calm about. The officer went to the chow cart, called out the cell I was in, and opened the door so I could see that the kitchen had double-stacked the trays like that.

Now here is where it gets to the usual bullshit. I wrote to the kitchen captain the next day about it. I got NO response, though I know how this camp works. See, I got no response because I put specific times and officers. If the rank writes on it that she investigated and it didn't happen, I can use that to prove otherwise, as there is a multi-million-dollar camera system here. Two cameras actually cover the area where the cart is plugged in. It can easily be seen that the trays are double-stacked.

I asked another guy to write the kitchen captain a simpler I-60 (an official form for TDCJ), just indicating the trays were double-stacked. Now I asked this guy because he has a rather popular blog. Of course, like most around here, it is easy to write online about something and hide behind the women they write to complain to—then not do something their damn self.

After I laid out my idea to him, he made this excuse and that excuse. I just laughed. I wanted to say, "Yeah, if the laws beat your fuckin' ass one day, I will be sure to react the same way." Another guy who overheard the conversation wrote the message I was mentioning. While I did not expect him to, he wrote it as I wanted.

The next day, I was talking to another guy about the tray situation. He then yelled out, "Hey, Loki, I wrote the kitchen captain. She wrote back!" The message was EXACTLY what I knew it would be: "I investigated this matter. No one is double-stacking the trays." See, that morning it was not done because I had been making such a big issue about it. So the rank can say they checked the cameras. Yeah, THAT day, but what about the previous day and beyond!?

I was getting ready to write a long letter to the kitchen captain, outlining what I was going to have done—from writing a grievance to having my lawyers call the Huntsville headquarters and having friends and family call and complain until it stopped. Though the next night, an officer worked. This officer has been here for years and knows me. He expressed that it was being done on his cart also. (There are two carts. Each cart has two shifts. A cart is a set of officers working.)

He expressed that he hated the trays being double-stacked because it gets food everywhere. He mentioned that he was going to talk to a rank that night. It ended up that he spoke to the rank over the main kitchen during the night shift. Other building ranks had told him to report it to the kitchen rank. (The unit holds 2,900 people—that's like feeding a small city!)

The nighttime kitchen rank came back to 12-building and told the working inmates, "Don't give a damn what officer tells you to double-stack trays. If you do it, you all are getting disciplinary cases." A disciplinary case can be the difference between a person getting parole or not!

The next night, I mentioned something to a different rank. This was a female rank who had been an officer back here during the daytime. She acted with disgust about it and said, "Oh no, that is unsanitary! No, that is not going to happen."

At breakfast on this pod, the cart and carrier were as they should be. The next day, I asked the officer working (the officers rotate on pods and do not work the same pod every day) if the pod she worked on the night before had a cart with double-stacked trays. She responded, "No, not the pod I was working. Though a couple of pods did, and they had to send the carts back." That meant the kitchen workers had to remake the trays on all of the carts.

Thus, this has brought to an end this awful, disgusting practice! Veni, Vidi, fucking Vici! HAHA

It took me a damn week to fix a problem that should have been relatively simple to fix. Now I've got to make sure I mention it here and there to keep it from happening again.

As I have mentioned, it is common to have to clean them myself. There are other guys here who do the same as me, though we are a minority. However, I wanted to point out that I was placed in the shower for the section that holds death watch, as the officers could not get the door open for the shower on the section where I am housed. (The electronic locks sometimes do not work, and the officers did not have the keys.)

The shower was in good shape on A-section (death watch). I noticed a washcloth in the shower, so I yelled to a couple of guys on the section about it to see if someone had forgotten it, as it was hanging from a string. One guy yelled back, "That's our cleaning rag, to clean the shower." I yelled back, "Right on!"

I couldn't help but smile. These dudes are waiting to be executed—all have execution dates to die—yet THEY are taking the time to clean the shower. People never fail to amaze me.

No news on my case at this time. I was shocked for there to be no word in March, though I was going by the timelines for other guys in my kind of situation. The difference is that the opinion by the previous court was FAR longer than normal, plus all the other filings my lawyers made. It would naturally take more time to sort through it all.

With Easter being next Sunday (at the time of writing this), the courts will be on a holiday vacation. I expect it will be a few more weeks or so. In the meantime, my lawyers are trying to get some forensic testing done. Once all the paperwork for it is sorted, I will have a copy posted.

I am really slacking on getting new legal papers filed on my site. I have been dealing with so many issues. Though in April, my focus will be to get new legal material posted. There have been three or four blogs posted in the past three weeks. If you missed one, be sure to check the previous blogs posted.

Though it seems no one reads mine, as no one comments to me about them. Actually, one person did. Maybe people make the comments on my Facebook pages. I wouldn't know, being as I do not have access to Facebook.

Also, people, please keep in mind the possibility of typos. I am not stupid, so if something does not seem right, then it is more likely than not I made a typo that I missed when I reread my letter or blog. That or the person posting it missed it.

There have been times in letters I wrote that I meant to write, "I might not…," though I mistakenly wrote, "I might…" Like on a Facebook message, I had accidentally referred to Santa Claus as Satan Claus. ☺ Haha. I type so fast, I just missed the error. Plus, typewriters do not have spellcheck. Haha. My politically correct typewriter autocorrected Santa to Satan. Haha.

Alrighty then. Thanks to those who downloaded the songs and all that. I understand that many expressed there was not a shirt in their size. I am trying to get this fixed. With that, I am gone. Another blog next week.

I need to expand on a point I missed about the relationship topic! Also, go over some ideas. Take care.

In solidarity, I remain,

Veni, Vidi, Vici.

Loud & Clear, April 7, 2015

Topic: Please give your undivided attention!

There must be some typos in some of my recent blogs. That, or I did not put enough effort into explaining my point of view. That, or some did not read it correctly. In recent blogs, I mentioned relationship matters and those that handle my campaign. Someone used the term Empire. I like that! Emperor Clinton! ☺ Haha. It fits the topic of the books I am currently reading. To those not getting it, I mean that as a joke. It's a fucking joke!

Though to be clear on something, I wrote about people helping me. I listed some of them that are key players in my campaign. The word to lock onto in that line is "KEY." Okay!? These are the main people behind my efforts. I wrote about how they had proven themselves to me. I actually received a couple of Jpays about this matter, one of which I was more shocked to get than the other, as this one I have had much more contact with, etc. I expect I might get some regular letters about it.

I want to take the time to clear it up. Just because I did NOT mention someone's name, it does not mean that they do not hold any value for me. I repeat: it does NOT mean they mean less to me. My blog was not a roll call of all that have helped me. As there are surely those that have donated often, I did not mention them. Is one to be foolish enough to assume that I do not value these people?

I did not mention Amy. She visits me often, is a friend of mine, and helps out as I need. Did I mention her? No! Why? Because she is not over a particular area of my campaign. I mentioned Alexandra and went into detail. Why? Because I was, for the first time, proclaiming an individual as being able to be my voice, something I have never done before. I have always made sure I had a firm grip on my campaign, as it involves my life. Plus, I had never, until now, met a person that was, in some ways, a woman after my own heart.

Meaning, we see things in a similar way when it comes to business, etc. It does not mean we see the world through mirrored eyes! As we certainly have positions we disagree on. That is because she is an individual, as I am. Now to break it down even further.

I ask people to donate money to help me—people that have not known me prior to coming to prison. People that do not know Alexandra, Jorunn, Renate, etc. For them to want to donate, they must:

A.) Believe in my cause,

B.) Have faith in my efforts, and

C.) Have faith that the person over the account will handle it in an ethical manner.

How smart would it be for me to pick some random person that wrote me to handle thousands of dollars? This money people give due to believing in me, which is something I value. I take the trust people put in me very seriously.

As not only do I have to protect the interest of my life-saving efforts, I have to protect the people that help me. I am obligated to them. As a result, does a person that has a pivotal role in my campaign have to prove themselves to me? You're damn right they do!

What kind of fool would just ask some random person to hold thousands of dollars? There have been men that write to guys in prison and act as if they are women. Pro-death penalty people act as anti-death penalty activists. People have headed over others' campaigns and then kept the money raised.

My previous blog was about the people, what people help with, and to reaffirm the faith I have in them. That I have met them, or they have met each other. That they took independent efforts to help me.

Alexandra had 500 shirts made before we really even got to know each other. She sold 350 of them herself at 25 euros each. She took it upon herself to raise funds in other areas. When the funds were needed, there was not a second of hesitation in transferring these funds. (Not all of it has been used! Though she retained a civil lawyer/investigator to help out with areas in my case.)

Beyond that, in other areas I needed help in—commissary, etc.—she has never wavered in helping. Jorunn is the same way. She made shirts, etc., to sell in Norway from her own shop. She reached out to family and friends to help me. There are many months I would not have had enough funds for stamps or commissary had it not been for Jorunn.

During Christmas, she sent gifts to my nephews. She has never hesitated when needed. She and Alexandra have treated me as a member of their family. When I say they have proved themselves, I mean that! I say it so that all can know that these are not random women pen pals. Both have had successful lives and families. Both are very active in my campaign.

I say all that so I can stand up and tell people that they can be trusted. It is to do with two things: honoring those that have given so much of their life for me and also for the benefit of my campaign. That all can know these people are sincere, honest, and dedicated.

I have written to Renate, Camille, and Catia for many, many years. They have seen people come and go. They have seen the crazy bullshit I have had to deal with. They have gotten to know them. I have met them, and others have met them. Katia and Anna handle the Italy portion of my campaign. They interact on a daily basis and have met each other.

I did not mention Amy, for example, as Amy is not over any element of my campaign. She is just my friend. I am sure she would be willing to help if I asked her, though I never have in that area as of yet.

Amy is called a friend because she has proved herself to me. By that, I mean she has shown her sincerity. She has me all mixed up in the family! ☺ Simple matters, like when she went back to Mexico to visit relatives, she had a picture of me cut out and enlarged. Her family was having Christmas dinner and had the picture positioned as if I was in the family photo with them.

It was just something simple, though it showed I was not seen as an oddity. I was embraced like part of the family. Anytime I needed her, she was there for me.

There are others that I write to, as well as other members of their family. My blog isn't meant to be a roll call of who I like and dislike.

Now maybe some people use the word "friend" more loosely than I do. I understand social media has made the term far more common. Friends demand loyalty by simply being who they are—a friend.

My using the word "prove" is a simple saying, meaning their actions have spoken louder than any words. That is all. It in no way means that I am on this pedestal that a person has to clamber up to.

Again, I mentioned them so the world would know these people helping me in these key roles are trustworthy. It is me giving my word that I have faith in them and that others can have faith in them.

Now others have made little comments about the relationship portion of the blog and past women raising the bar for future women.

The funny thing is, I wrote a blog about child molesters and being emotionally impacted by some encounters, thinking my looks made me a target when I was younger, so I wanted to cut my face up. No one besides Amy mentioned that part of the blog! (At least in the mail I have received thus far.)

Though allow me to clear up the relationship and raising-the-bar comment, as then maybe people will finally realize that I cannot be viewed through a simple lens.

Long sigh. It's fucking stupid that I even would have to clear this up. I should have stuck to blogging about my case.

Nonetheless, here is the deal. I was having a conversation with a couple of guys here. One is married, and I believe him to have a sincere relationship both emotionally and mentally with his wife. His wife is from the U.S. (NOT that that matters!), but they get to see each other often. Also, they got in contact with each other in a unique way. With time, it grew.

We were talking about the benefit of having a great woman beside you and how some guys mess over women. The other guy is single but also was talking about one of his exes. This conversation went on about people in life. I, of course, talked about my experiences. I got to feeling a bit sad for myself and lonely, thinking about how I missed that unique bond. I reached out to my ex. Sometimes the past is too much, and the present too complicated. It simply will not work out. I was frustrated with myself, as I felt I acted in a moment of weakness. It takes nothing away from her. We have had an off-and-on interaction over the past couple of years. We split; she would go on with her life. We write here and there, get closer, and then repeat. ☺ This situation is hard to deal with, though that chapter has closed.

Anyway, my words were not meant for anyone that I currently write to. In a moment of frustration, I wrote what I did. Mostly, I was frustrated with myself. Also, so that anyone in the "future" wanting to write with the idea of such developing wouldn't. If they do write with such an idea and it doesn't happen, they might feel let down. I would rather avoid all that there. It does not mean that everyone who writes to me has such in mind. My words of "a compliment" are not a marriage proposal. I meant that in two ways. Meaning just because someone compliments me or writes to me, I do not have any preconceived notions about them. I take each person as they present themselves, and we go from there. Some develop stronger bonds; some do not. Again, it was just a general statement.

As for the relationship comments, they were due to frustration with myself. I am only human. I am sure none can blame me for wanting love and affection! Though I just want to avoid any bullshit.

Now, as for my words about "raising the bar." If anyone took that as a vain statement, then you do not properly understand me. To explain: there have been some in my life that raised the bar, as they have shown me the essence of a great woman. Others have shown me what to avoid. The bar is not one placed in a position that all others have to overcome. That would not be fair! Though past experiences do help to shape future desires. Everyone looks for certain qualities in a person if they are thinking of the person they would want to spend their life with. I do not think anyone reading this would just marry some random person.

Some have had a man in their life with certain traits, and that person hurt them. As a result, if she meets a guy who shares such traits, it will be a turnoff. It goes both ways. I made a joke about Charlize Theron. However, most guys will say looks do not mean anything if she has a shitty personality and messed-up attitude. Hell, even the Bible warns about such! I doubt God could be wrong. ☺ (Not saying Charlize does).

I have had a woman who never tried to control me. She accepted me as me, was independent, and had a proper sense of right and wrong. I have had a woman who was insanely smarter than me—masters in philosophy and business, very dedicated to her faith. Just examples. When you experience people with certain qualities, it forms an attraction. Does it mean that I expect my future wife, if I have one, to have a PhD? Hell no! Though I want her to have a hunger for learning. It doesn't have to be in the collegiate sense.

I damn sure am not about to marry some crack whore! Not that I am against crack whores; I just do not plan to marry any! Ha.

To wrap it up, my words were NOT from vanity. It was a mixture of personal frustration and also to exemplify that I have met great women in my life. As a result, I have come to appreciate just how wonderful it is to have such standing beside me.

I discussed some of this with one woman, and she surprisingly asked me why I would settle for just one. My belief is not for everyone to know everything about you. That is why I have always liked having that "one" beside me. Anyway, it has been on my mind more, as I am faced with a potential end. Such causes me to think about all I have missed out on and could miss out on.

To wrap it up, I can only be the man I am. Life has caused me to develop rough edges. I am going to wrap this one. Take care and strive for all that you desire.

I remain, in solidarity.

Veni. Vidi. Vici.

Clinton YOUNG #999447

Polunsky Unit

3872 FM 350 South

Livingston TX 77351

U.S.A

Loud & Clear, April 24, 2015

General Update, Life on Death Row

Weeks gone by, no answer. Though when I last spoke with my lawyers, they indicated that the local prosecutors in Midland would not agree to allow me to do the testing of the gloves, which means we have to fight it out in court. I really did not expect anything else. Sure, I hoped that they would go along. However, it just would be abnormally unnatural for me to get something done without a fight. Which is a stupid position for them, as if I had an execution date, for example, I would be able to get a stay if the gloves had yet to be tested, as the law is on my side.

On to other matters. I was recently asked why I get so frustrated by others and why I need to justify things. I get frustrated as all I have is communication. If that communication is distorted, it causes chaos, which hinders the advancement toward the goal, more so if it is someone that should know better. If this person knows me better than others and still sees it wrong, how can I expect others to see it right?

When I write something, it is not always directed at those that already write to me. It is to clear up potential misunderstandings, like the line, "A compliment is not a marriage proposal." I just want to make sure that new people are not misunderstanding my tone and/or words, as many write me but do not respond to my first letter. Some write multiple people, and some guys will do anything to catch a person's attention. I would rather have one person beside me that the hands of time have helped to shape into a solid friendship than to have 100 standing on a platform of lies or manipulation.

I do get frustrated when my words get twisted, as they are all I have. I cannot touch anyone. I cannot walk down the street with anyone. I cannot have them view my interaction with others they know. All I have is the spoken and written word. My words are the basis of my existence here. If these words are seen for something they are not, this creates chaos.

Beyond that, I have to battle the words of others that wish to distort the person I am, such as the state prosecutors. People that do not know me will not understand why I am so direct. I recently had a conversation about this with my friend Amy. Many people do not get straight to the point.

Think about manipulation. It is not always with evil intent. The way a person writes or talks can soften the defenses of another. I can write you a ten-page letter to ask one question, or I can just ask the damn question or make the statement. I am polite and well-mannered, which is why I do not ask 1,000 questions.

Being here has given me a sort of complex. For example, if I ask about a person's children, I worry they will think something bad because I am on death row. Everyone has boundaries and limits. Some make sense; some are very irrational. Their perception of my situation clouds their vision of me as the man that I am.

I have always been interested in other people. When I was a child, I never met a stranger. I would talk to people and find out more about them. When I was 13 in North Carolina, I would talk to homeless people. The girls I was in relationships with, I would lay in bed with them or sit outside and just talk for hours sometimes.

I enjoy conversation. I have read about how men will sit around in cafes in France and converse, like how they do in philosophy clubs. In the Southern US, especially in the more rural areas, talking is associated with feminine traits, which I do not think is a bad thing, as I believe in a balance. A balance equals stability.

My grandfather, stepfather, and father were not men of many words. Well, my father would talk, but it would be mostly lies and bullshit. As a result, I would always sit with my mom and discuss different topics, from women to social issues. My point is, no one should ever assume that I am not interested, as I am.

Being that Renate has visited me many times, we have a more natural friendship. We have talked about her boyfriends and everything else. Though when I write to someone new, I never know how they will react. Plus, I have been through so much stupid shit since I have been here. I am talking about people that seem to have escaped from the damn crazy house!

I admit that this place has given me some insecurities. It is much, much easier to interact with a person that you can look at eye to eye. With the written word, a person can fill in the blanks with whatever they think in their mind. That is why I write that the more a person writes about themselves, the more comfortable I feel.

I do not get bored by what people write. I would rather have a five-page letter about the happy times or even sad times in a person's life than a one-page letter being all about me. Many think I do not want to know about such times since I am in this place. While I do not really like to discuss death, for obvious reasons, I have never been against a person venting to me how they feel over the loss of a loved one.

Though when I respond to such a topic, it will be short. When you know about 270 people that have died, it has an impact on a person. A soldier in war does not know that many people that died, as the groupings are not as big. The generals are far removed from the battlefield.

There are some here that have known over 500 that have been executed, not to mention friends and family. Point being, death is not an exciting topic for a guy on death row—at least not for anyone here that is half as normal. Some here will not write to anyone under a certain age because they cannot get help from them.

I have never objected to anyone that wanted to write, as maybe I can help a person accomplish something greater in life. This way, if they do kill me, I can at least have some kind of positive legacy (though this does NOT mean I will connect with everyone).

When I was a child, I wish I had more people to actually listen to me, instead of just trying to classify me. I have had people write me from ages 11 to 90! All have a story and all have a journey. Naturally, anyone at such a young age, I expect for their parents to approve of that, as there are certainly some guys in prison that no young child should try to interact with.

The 11-year-old, I write to her mother. Even her grandmother has written to me.

A teacher from Holland would have her students write something after watching the film that Jessica made. I always enjoyed getting the little notes from them—all the clever comments and art.

While on the topic of children, I recently saw my baby sister and brother-in-law with my baby nephew. He turned 3 last month. He is full steam ahead! ☺ I was talking to him. Being there has no concept of talking on a phone system. When we would stop talking, he would tell me, "Okay, I'll call you later," and would then hang up the phone. He stood in the chair and once said, "Come play with me, Uncle Clint." When he was leaving, he told me, "I love you, man!" That really tore me up. It was great seeing him. Little dude is cool as can be.

Anyways, to wrap this up: I am in a situation that defies common sense. You cannot read about it and grasp it. Experience is the only educator. More so if someone knows how European prisons are versus the barbaric nature of U.S. prisons—it is shocking to those contained within the walls. It defies understanding for those that have never been on the inside.

In many ways, it reverses time, which mainly applies to the general population areas where people can be in physical contact with each other. As we are all locked up in administrative segregation, the isolation has an impact. Though what I think gets to some in these cells is that they have to live with themselves. That includes thinking about their past, what they did in their case, etc.

Another way is from having to depend on everyone or from the isolation. Some get paranoid! The hardest thing for me is having to depend on others. Beyond making sure a person is legit, it is also the worry of how others will react in the future.

My site had to be rebuilt, as it was messed up by someone that had previously helped me. I just found out that 40 blogs—NOT 4, but FORTY!—were not on my website. Some others were incomplete. Plus, some legal papers were messed up. There were a few that I wanted removed, but there were only like 3 or 4! Now I've got to sort through everything and see what is missing.

The thing is that people never really comment on my blogs to me, so I don't know if I reference something and it is no longer posted. Once, my ex came to see me, and she told me that some of the legal papers I wrote about were not on my site. Long sigh.

That is exactly why I've said what I have in a couple of past blogs. If Catia had never told me about it, I would not have known. Alex did not know, as these blogs were written before he knew me.

Didn't I say I would wrap this up? ☺ I apologize if my words seem off-putting lately. I just have a great deal weighing on my shoulders. It is compounded by the fact that I am next to death watch.

Being on other pods helps to kind of ignore it. Being on A pod, it is more in your face. Plus, being that death watch is now A pod A section—which is the section that I was in when I first came here. Back then, it was A pod F section. It is not lost on me that it could also be the last section I could be on.

Though the way things are going, I think my chances are better now. That possible nine months—I do not think it is relevant anymore. There has not been a ruling in the 5th Circuit yet, though I feel a little better about everything.

Recently, some legal papers were posted. In a week or so, more will be posted. It shouldn't be longer than weeks. I have to get copies and cannot post it until it is filed.

Alrighty then. I hope that everyone has a joy-filled day.

Veni. Vidi. Vici

In solidarity I remain,

Clinton Lee Young #999447

www.saveaninnocentlife.com

Polunsky Unit Death Row

3872 FM 350 South www.theclintonproject.com

Livingston TX 77351

Loud & Clear, June 7, 2015

Topic: The Gloves Be Tested

I felt a need to properly explain the situation with these gloves, as people keep writing about DNA. Some have even reached out to forensic institutes, again with the theme of DNA. So let it be very clear: I DO NOT NEED DNA TESTING ON GLOVES!!! None. Nothing. Nada. Zip. Zilch. Zero!!! It has already been done. TWICE!

To explain the history of them: The co-defendant bought these gloves at an EZ Mart in Longview the night of the murders. Fast forward to after the murders—the police had everyone. The police tried to question me. I told them I wanted a lawyer. I was so exhausted from lack of sleep over a two-week period (the longest I slept was during most of the alleged offenses). When the police sat me down in a chair, I passed out. They even tried to get me to drink coffee.

The lifestyle I was living had rules: do not talk to police. Beyond that, I knew better than to try, as I was so out of it from lack of sleep and crashing after being high on meth. After being put in a cell, I went to sleep. I was so tired and dehydrated that I slept for two days. When meals were passed out, the guards had to keep opening the door and physically shaking me to wake up. I didn't even want to eat.

I write this just to explain how out of it I was, as people often ask me questions about why this and why that. As for poor choices being made, half the time I was asleep during the events that led up to me being arrested, which the co-defendant has now admitted. In the new legal filings posted on my site, saveaninnocentlife.com, the co-defendant also admitted to others that I was asleep when he committed the murder.

Okay, back to the gloves. After I woke up, I heard a guy talking about the newspaper articles on my case. I yelled out to him to read to me what was printed. When he finished, I could tell that the co-defendant was putting everything on me. (The police told me that when I was first arrested. Though they always say that, so I just ignored them.)

After the article was read to me, I thought, Oh hell no! I asked to speak to the detectives on the case. They came and got me. I then told them: "Take my DNA, take hair samples, do gunshot residue testing. I didn't kill that old man. Test the gloves."

They then asked, "What gloves?"

We then got into an argument, as I thought they were bullshitting me. Turns out the crime scene tech, whose job it is to map out the crime scene and collect any evidence, had overlooked these gloves!

The detective agreed to go back out to the crime scene. When he drove up, he saw the gloves lying right there in plain view. He then got on the phone and called the crime scene tech to come out to collect them. He testified about this at trial. My lawyer asked, "Did he come out?"

The detective said, "No."

My lawyer asked, "Why not?"

The detective looked at the prosecutor, then dropped his head and said, "He said he didn't want to."

All the jury snapped their heads around toward the prosecutor with a look of shock. They complained about it all to the sheriff after my trial, as the sheriff oversaw the detective and CST who worked on the case.

Now, back to when the gloves were finally collected. The detective put them in a bag and brought them back to the office. The CST then sent them to Austin, Texas, to the Texas crime lab there.

Now think about this. You've got a murder. The word is that the killer was wearing a pair of gloves. You've got two people, both saying the other did it. You can do DNA testing and gunshot residue testing at the lab. What do you do?

Hopefully, everyone reading this thought: Test the inside for DNA to see who was wearing the gloves and then test the outside of the gloves for gunshot residue to see if a gun was fired while wearing them.

If you thought something else, then you might be able to get a job with the Midland County Sheriff's Office. As the CST there did the dumbest move that was the opposite of that! He requested DNA testing on the OUTSIDE of the gloves and requested NO testing on the inside of the gloves.

The thing is, he was trying to destroy the gloves. With DNA testing on cloth, the lab tech has to cut away parts of the cloth, then soak it in a liquid and all this. What happens then is if there were any unburnt gunpowder particles on the cloth, they would dissolve. His request was an attempt to destroy the gloves. Plain and simple!

When the crime lab got the gloves, the ballistic expert got the package first. He looked over the gloves for lead residue and powder burns. Even though he was not even requested to do such, he sprayed the gloves with a chemical that makes lead show up. A special light is shined on the gloves, and the lead residue will show up. It did and was in a pattern that is common for what a gun would leave when shot.

BUT lead is only one part of gunshot residue. Plus, it can come from many different sources. At the end of the day, it doesn't hold much value as an actual gunshot residue test. It doesn't hurt me but barely helps me.

Okay, DNA testing was done on the OUTSIDE of the gloves. It showed the co-defendant, the first victim, and myself. Though that holds no value, as it just means he touched me with the gloves and/or touched something else. I know what it came from. He wiped off a Sprite bottle I had drunk out of, as he was wanting a drink. The Sprite bottle had both our DNA on it.

The point is, the DNA on the outside of the gloves for anyone had zero guilt relevance. So it was pointless to test. My trial lawyers then had to request DNA on the inside of the gloves. It came back on the co-defendant. It EXCLUDED ME. There was NONE of my DNA on the inside of the gloves, which makes sense, as I never wore them.

Okay. Now that is why there is 100% NO need to test the gloves. Also, to top it off, the co-defendant admitted they were HIS gloves and that he had them the whole time! However, he lied about his reasons. He said he had worked in them, moving scrap metal and tree limbs. That was an attempt to explain away the lead residue.

Okay, now. One can look at the picture of the gloves and see they look brand new and clean! If you worked in cotton gloves with scrap metal and tree limbs, there would be wear and tear and organic material stuck to the gloves. They would be dirty—all of which these gloves were NOT.

Okay, to the current testing. The gloves have been sent to the world's premier expert. Living in the United Kingdom? He trained your Forensic Science Service. From Canada? He trained your Royal Canadian Mounted Police. Been in the United States Army? He trained the U.S. Army Criminal Investigation Laboratory. North Carolina, Louisiana, New York City, Illinois, California, U.S. Customs, the corporation 3M—you guessed it. Trained and taught for all of them. Oh, don't allow me to forget TEXAS!

He was once employed as an Intelligence Analyst for the United States Army Intelligence in Stuttgart, the Federal Republic of Germany. The point is, when he says, "This is what it is," then other experts would, more likely than not, agree with him and not even attempt to challenge his findings.

Many times, the state gets an expert that says this, and the defense gets an expert that says that. That complicates everything and leads to long, drawn-out processes and the risk of the court picking who they believe. It is a blessing that I was able to get such an expert.

My lawyers located him. Let me explain about my lawyers. One has been on my case since 2008. I truly adore her. She is a great person and cares about me. I am the only client she has ever sent her family newsletter and family photo to. She has been working on appeals for a couple of decades now.

My other lawyer puts about 90% of her time into my case. They care about me, believe in me, and appreciate and value my opinions. We do not always see eye to eye, though that's not abnormal. I get frustrated and rant and rave. Like I sometimes write, "I am going to cuss them out." First, I would never cuss them out! They have fought too hard for me.

They have done more for me than any other lawyers I could have gotten—with the exception of paying for my own lawyers. Now, some stuff was not done properly during the last court I was in. Well, it was not so much improper as more could have been done. They were accustomed to dealing with the courts in California, which are not as harsh as the courts in this region. So it was more of a cultural difference in the courts that they were not considering. The best lessons in life are taught by experience. ☺ As now they've gone from being Golden Retrievers to being German Shepherds. Texas will do that to a person. haha

Now a very interesting twist. My lawyers had filed a notice with the current court that the gloves are being tested, with a motion to halt my case and send me back to state court for a state appeal. There are state and federal levels. They filed a copy of the letter from the Midland prosecutors agreeing for me to do the testing.

Now the state's lawyer responded to it, saying I shouldn't get to do anything as I never mentioned the gloves before. So I have the prosecuting lawyers for Midland agreeing to let me test the gloves, though I have the lawyer for the state of Texas fighting against me on it. In a weird kind of way, my lawyers and the Midland prosecutors are on the same side, with the state on the other. I think that is a first! haha

Though in his response, he said I never mentioned the gloves. I do not know why he made such a claim, though my lawyers chopped it up, as the detective testified about the gloves and how the only reason they did any forensic testing was due to my request.

My trial lawyers testified I wanted the gloves tested, though they just never got around to it, as with the gunshot testing. Then more importantly, I filed numerous legal filings in my previous appeals going on and on about the gloves.

There was also a copy of the letter I sent to the state appeal lawyer asking him to get the gloves tested. Basically, I have done nothing BUT rant about these gloves since Nov 29, 2001!

The gloves, as of this week, still have not been tested. They are being tested for gunshot residue and gun primer residue. Hopefully, the bullshit that the police did back in 2001 was not successful in destroying all the traces of it. That is what I am nervous about.

Though it can be shown that the steps they took back in 2001 could have destroyed the traces of gunpowder and such. While it would not help me as much as the actual showing of gunshot residue, it would help to show that the actions of the police hindered me from being able to properly defend myself.

Nonetheless, we will know something this month, and they will show something!

In addition to this, there was a court ruling back in April that can help lower the bar for me to win a chance to re-look at one of my appeals. As a result, more filings were presented to the court in May.

Time will tell! We are doing all that can be done at this point.

To those that donate something each month, thank you!

To those wondering how to help out, donating something each month helps. It slowly but surely adds up. This helps me to navigate future obstacles, be it through additional investigations, testing, experts, or raising greater awareness of my case.

I shall return soon. Thanks for reading. Please encourage others to view my site.

Take care.

Until next time.

Clinton Young #999447

Loud & Clear, June 9, 2015

Topic: Part Two of Last Blog "Gloves"

I wanted to add some to my last blog to help people get a better idea of everything. I was a bit shocked about the current District Attorney of Midland agreeing to let me test the gloves. Not because she is corrupt, but more because I believe she genuinely hated me! We exchanged some verbal jabs here and there, though she was not the prosecutor over my trial. He has since retired. At first, I was a bit paranoid, but as I have thought about it, I remembered during my trial when the co-defendant was testifying against me. He claimed to have been kidnapped by me, which is just ridiculous. I remember sitting there thinking, "They cannot believe this bullshit!" I looked over at her, and she had a look of disgust on her face. She knew he was lying.

Though she was not the head prosecutor, he was the one who did all the secret deals, and his investigator, who is also retired, was the one who coached and threatened people. Now, there is a difference between a prosecutor that hates a defendant versus one that is corrupt and unethical. It was easy to dislike me. I was arrogant and had the bullshit mindset of the "streets." Though sitting in a cell, waiting on a trial where life hangs in the balance, it makes you start to wake up and see bullshit for what it is. Plus, there were several pieces of the puzzle that were simply not true. It fueled the false impression of me, like most of the psych report from TYC. I made up all kinds of gang and crime stuff that I had seen in movies. I listed all kinds of drugs that I had never seen.

The myth there was that if a person had a bad gang and drug problem, instead of going to the gladiator units, they would go to a therapeutic placement. Acting like I had a drug problem, I listed every drug known to man—half of which I only knew about from school anti-drug programs, like Angel Dust, various pills, mushrooms, and heroin. I have never even seen heroin or Angel Dust. Hell, I don't even think Angel Dust has been around for the past 25 years—maybe? I don't know. I wrote it as a "myth" because it was just that! Instead of going to some nice placement, I went to one of the worst juvenile units in the U.S.! One thing everyone was able to agree on was that the violence was unreal and off the charts. However, that is not my fault. I did not create the facility. I did not operate the facility. I was just forced to survive in the environment the government allowed me to thrive. I did not make the officers pick favorites or bet on us fighting each other. I did not create an environment where gangs truly ran everything and the power-playing tactics the guards used with that. I just survived.

Though the prosecutors read the psych reports, and not knowing better, they believed it. I can now show it all to be false with people who knew me at the time in question before I went to TYC and even the word of police officers from the area I used to live in. I now have statements that show TYC guards who testified against me lied. My girlfriend at the time was saying I had hit her, which is total bullshit. As I have mentioned before, yes, I did grab her by the face and pushed her away from me. I was high, and she was saying hateful things. It doesn't make it right, but a clear picture needs to be told.

One of the times she claims I hit her in the back of the head, I can now show, with a person who was in the car at the time, that the way she claims it happened, it did not. I was teasing her. She sat in front of me. A song came on that I liked, so I started drumming on the seat. As I was sitting behind her, I was beating on the headrest, just being juvenile and teasing her. She got mad and yelled at me to stop. I started hitting the back of the seat like it was a punching bag. I knocked the headrest forward, and my hand slipped forward and caught her ponytail. She acted like I hit her with an uppercut. She started crying, and I said, "Are you fucking serious? It was a damn accident. I was just fuckin' with ya." The other person in the car later even expressed that she thought it was an accident.

My ex has, since my trial provided a statement, which should be included on my website, about the kind of person I was. That was great until I started messing with meth. I do not blame the meth. I blame myself for doing meth, which I stupidly started after an argument with my ex. She told me I had better not ever inject meth. My half-brother offered me a shot, and I said, "Fuck it, come on." So yeah, I started doing meth because I was mad at my girlfriend, and then my being on meth made us fight more. It doesn't make much sense, though I was 18 years old at the time!

Now, I did stop doing meth. I chose to leave it alone. The last time I did it was a day or so before the case happened. It was to be the last time, as I promised her I would stop. Another fact the prosecutors did not know: I was actually making plans to get my life together and back on the right path, as I was scheduled to meet with an Army Reserve recruiter two days after I was arrested. The appointment had been made a week prior. I hung around with a bad crowd while growing up due to events in my childhood. I felt more at home with the rebels and outcasts, though I have never been considered evil or violent.

However, the prosecutor surely believed me to be. Now, all of this could have been brought to light over a decade ago, though on my state appeals, well, I have often written about how they were destroyed. I could have gotten the gloves tested and everything else. Also, the very medications I was forced to take as a child—it is now known I was basically allergic to them. They made me worse. This was not known when I was a child.

Then there is the first-grade teacher who lied in my trial and basically said I was an evil child who tried to hurt other children with scissors. The problem is she said it happened in another grade and that she "heard about it." Since there were no reports to support it, she lied! Plus, she should not have been allowed to testify about events she had no personal knowledge of, as that is hearsay and forbidden in court. My lawyers mistakenly did not object to silence her. The reality is my kindergarten teacher adored me. Yes, I was hyper, though I never once got in trouble for trying to harm another child, beyond a playground fight and the time I bit a 17-year-old on the school bus because he kept pulling on my hair. I was 6 years old! I know where he is now, and when a mutual friend told him they used it in my trial, he laughed and commented about how he used to tease me on the bus.

Anyway, I do not claim to be perfect, though the image that was painted of me was not true. Plus, there was the co-defendant making just off-the-chart lies about me. He said I threatened to cut the victim's throat and forced him to buy stuff, all of which he now admits was a lie. A LIE! Another thing is the theme of the case. The prosecutor said the case happened because two people were killed for their vehicle to go see a girl, which is 100% TOTAL bullshit! All the co-defendants, everyone involved in the case, have said now that the case did NOT happen to go see Amber (my girlfriend). I have never said it, and the three co-defendants admit it did not happen. A fourth said it happened because the first guy was an informant for the police. So no one but the prosecutor is claiming the two murders were connected to that ridiculous theme.

Anyway, the point is it was easy to demonize me. My trial lawyers tried to dispel most of it, though they could only work with the funding they had. While they cared about me, some things were not done that should have been done. For over a decade, I have been fighting for more than proof of my innocence to the capital murder charges. I have been fighting to show I was NOT the type of person they claimed I was. Basically, I have been fighting for my legacy in many ways.

I cannot know what the prosecutors in Midland think, though I can say that if they did not have at least an interest in the letter of the law, they would have fought me on the gloves. (The police are also to blame, as they did such a horrible job. When the co-defendant showed up blaming me, all investigation stopped unless it was done to support his lies. Even the FBI dropped the ball!) I am just glad they did not fight me on it. In the end, I could have won and gotten them tested anyway, as the law is on my side. It does get looked at a bit differently if the prosecutors agree for the testing to be done.

Anyway, I just wanted to explain a bit of why they were against me and also to explain that the current prosecutor, who is the Chief Prosecutor for Midland, while she worked on my trial, was not the head prosecutor back then. He was the one they said made the deals, etc. The co-defendant's lawyer, who admitted to the deals, even expressed that she was not the one he dealt with and that she was not in the room. This is all from before my trial. So, in all fairness, I cannot say she is "corrupt" like the previous prosecutor. Though it is still to be seen how they will react if the gloves come back and show exactly what I have claimed they would. We will soon know.

Anyway, I am not going to be writing about my case anymore, so no one ask me any questions. Anything I discuss in the future will only be done in the blogs. Alrighty then. Until next time, take care.

Veni vidi vici

In solidarity,

Clinton Lee Young #999447

Polunsky

3872 fm 350 South

Livingston TX 77351

U.S.A

Loud & Clear, August 2, 2015

Topic: Appeal denied, gloves, & etc.

This place is truly an emotional roller coaster. Last week, I found out the gloves showed even more favorably for me. Then this past week, on Monday, I got a copy of the report. After reading over it for the third time, I was feeling great. Then Friday, I talked to my lawyers and found out my appeal was denied.

To make it worse, I had been doing a fast and was at 4.5 days, so I was not feeling at my best. I was sitting there trying to formulate the game plan for the next round, though I was having trouble focusing. It was just a bad go!

Now, the appeal that was denied was all about my previous appeals. It has nothing to do with new stuff. See, the way it goes is that a person is locked into what was previously filed. This is why the quality of work by a lawyer is so vital. A mistake or failure to file a claim all the way back in the first appeals impacts the appeals all the way up the line.

(I have not read the actual opinion yet. My lawyers told me it is bad. I should receive it by Aug. 4th or 5th.) However, they did rule in such a way that goes against previously established law. They applied legal standards to me that are not supported by previous Fifth Circuit rulings or U.S. Supreme Court rulings.

This means I have a legal argument to ask the whole panel of judges for the Fifth Circuit to review my case en banc, which basically means "in whole" for the entire panel. See, each case is heard by a three-judge panel. As can be expected, not all judges operate on the same ideological lines. I could have gotten a different three-judge panel and possibly gotten a different ruling.

I happened to end up with three of the most, what they have been labeled as, conservative judges on the court. By ruling as they did, they are saying it is okay for a prosecutor to tell a co-defendant, "I will consider 10 years instead of giving you death or life if you testify," though not put anything in writing.

Okay, that is a HELL of a carrot to hang in front of a guy. The PROMISE of a deal is stronger than an actual deal, as it encourages a guy to make sure a person is convicted. If the guy is not convicted, well, he no longer gets the sweet deal. He is stuck facing harder time.

So, can you see how a PROMISE of a deal is a more dangerous threat to the integrity of the process than a SEALED deal? The court is saying there is no deal. Yeah, they are right. There was NO "sealed," legally recognized deal. Instead, there were a bunch of backroom deals!

The damn prosecutor himself said that he would "consider" a deal in the 30-year range. Plus, they hid it from my trial lawyers, even though the trial judge ORDERED them to reveal ANY talks of deals, not just signed deals. So, they violated a court order.

Okay, and the previous court, the federal judge, when addressing my ballistics evidence, said that the victim could have been turned around in his seat. Turned around in his seat?! In a small-ass Pontiac car? Hell no!

Plus, NONE of the others said that. They all said very clearly that the guy was leaning forward, getting ready to let Page into the back seat with the driver's side door open. Anyone that has ever allowed someone into the back of their car knows exactly the kind of motion: lean forward with the seat so a person can get in the back.

No one turns around in the seat, much less a grown-ass man that weighs like 230 pounds! So, this judge invented evidence, and the Fifth Circuit says that is okay! Operating on this premise, there is no longer the concept of rule of law.

There is no longer a fact-based justice system. Instead, it means that the government can operate as it desires and speculate as it wishes when considering so-called "facts." Ha ha. Man oh man.

Even though my previous state appeal lawyer royally screwed up, there was a ruling from the U.S. Supreme Court, Martinez v. Ryan, that opened the legal door for me to file a claim about my trial lawyers in federal court if my state writ lawyer messed up. It is more complex than that, but that's the gist of it. It's all complicated.

So, for what happens next, we ask the entire 5th Circuit to review my case. That is due in 14 days. My lawyers have lots of other stuff to work on. They will request the allowed possible 14-day extension. So, the en banc hearing request will possibly be filed in 28 days (if granted extra time).

Then the state will file their response in 14 days. The court will then issue a ruling fairly quickly. They will not allow it to take very long. Within 2-3 weeks, they will issue a ruling. They can agree to hear my case and allow oral arguments where the lawyer and state's lawyer will argue the various positions. Then within 2-3 weeks, they will give an opinion.

To accept, I would need a majority in my favor. Though, if they refuse to hear it, then it is off to the U.S. Supreme Court. That whole process usually takes 3-6 months. That is if a person is rejected. It is extremely difficult to get the U.S. Supreme Court to hear a case.

I have to present the claim in a very specific way, and it has to be relevant to the whole nation, not just Clinton Young.

The fight goes on. What bothers me on a personal level is that I just started really taking a greater effort to connect with my nephews. I wouldn't want them to feel close to me, and the worst happens. I also started to put more energy into others and the bonds I have with them.

I got the gloves tested. I was thinking the Midland prosecutors would do the right thing. After the glove test results came back, my lawyer called the prosecutor a couple of times asking to speak with her. She didn't return my lawyer's call, at least by the time I spoke with my lawyers. Maybe it has changed by now. If not, then we will have to fight that fight.

Now to be clear, this ruling has NOTHING to do with all the new stuff that I have. There is still a way for me to appeal that. I just have to wait until my current appeals are done with. As the Fifth Circuit refused to hear my request to go back to the lower court based on the gloves, which is not abnormal for that court.

So, as this process goes on, I just need to get more work done. Make sure I use the time to the best of my ability. Gather up as much as I can to present in the future. The fight goes on.

More will be posted soon. I am going to get a copy of the gloves report made and all the related documents. This way, when it is posted, it will present a clear picture for everyone.

I thank everyone for sharing links to my website, saveaninnocentlife.com. Please feel free to share my blogs and poems. I just ask that my site be credited. Thanks!

Also, a special thanks to everyone who donates or orders a bracelet, shirt, or window sticker.

Until next time.

Veni, Vini, Vici

In solidarity,

Clinton Lee Young #999447

Polunsky Unit

3872 FM 350 South saveaninnocentlife.com

Livingston TX 77351

USA

Loud & Clear, August 16, 2015

Title: Daniel Lopez & the Death Penalty

Daniel Lopez, no matter how you cut it, committed suicide on Aug. 12, 2015. He canceled his appeal—not because he was guilty, as he was not. He just knew that no matter what, it would be a prolonged struggle. He expressed that his loved ones were drifting away as they could not handle it. I guess he just felt it better for all.

If anything funny can be brought from it, there was a scene during Daniel's legal proceedings that seems straight out of Hollywood. His lawyers knew that he was not guilty of capital murder, which is required to get the death penalty. See, he was running from the police. A cop jumped in front of the SUV he was driving. He swerved away from the cop, but the front corner clipped the officer. The officer died from the injuries.

Now, I do not think there is anything in police procedure that says to jump in front of a speeding vehicle. The cop simply was not thinking and reacted on instinct. Daniel was not wanted for any violent crime. It was a traffic stop that went wrong, and he took off. Not surprisingly, the proper angles to show what happened during the chase were not available, as the police car cameras that would have seen that angle were "supposedly" not recording. I guess it is better to say an officer was murdered than that he made an ill-fated error.

Nonetheless, Daniel was innocent of capital murder and guilty of involuntary manslaughter, which only carries up to 20 years. I will get away from this part and opinions, as it will just get me in trouble. Back to the funny kind of part, which really shows the insanity of it all.

Daniel had a court hearing to cancel his appeals. There he is in court, his lawyers beside him. He was not fighting the state; he was fighting his lawyers. He wanted to cancel his appeals. The lawyers did not want him to. There they are, standing before the judge, and the judge asked Daniel what he wanted.

Daniel said, "I want to cancel my appeals, man!"

His lawyers said, "Your honor, he should not be allowed to cancel his appeals. He is not even guilty of capital murder."

The judge: "Mr. Lopez, did you do it? Did you intentionally kill the officer?"

Daniel responded, "Well, no! I didn't mean to do it. He jumped in front of me. I tried to swerve, but it was too late."

Now it went on. He told me that the judge said he couldn't cancel the appeals if he was not guilty. Though I moved to another pod, so I never found out how he managed to get his appeals dropped. It is a head-shaking kind of funny. An "I thought I had seen/heard it all" kind of humor.

He was trying to die. He had no reason to lie. He said all along, since he got down here, the same story. He was just tired of the bullshit. Being that it was a cop case, he knew they would drag the fight out and would not be willing to accept anything less than death.

The fact that almost every person who kills a cop has prosecutors seeking death shows that all are not equal in this country. As there are people who killed two or three gang members or drug users and were given life. If all lives are equal, then all punishment should be equally applied.

It is another reason why the death penalty system is flawed and unjust.

Then, when he was being executed, some bikers revved their engines so loud that it drowned out his final words. When I heard about that on the radio… yeah, I think this is one of those extremely rare times that I will think it best to keep my words to myself. Yeah, it's best.

I was not friends with Daniel. We had been on the same pod from time to time and communicated here and there. I can honestly say he was sincere in his desire to go!

So few states use it, so few areas of Texas use it. There are only very few counties out of the (I think) 206 counties in Texas that use it. It is a political tool that is easily misused. People are aware of how pointless and costly it is.

It does not deter crime. For that person dying—people who use that position, they are dumb.

There are like 30,000+ people locked up in Texas for murder! There are thousands of murders a year in Texas alone. Hell, the major cities top out over 200 every year (that is Houston, Dallas, and San Antonio, on average).

There are, I think, over 500 people serving life without parole since it passed a few years back. There are only like 230 on death row, for the exact same type of crimes. Not one of those 500+ has killed anyone in prison.

Before life without parole was put in place, a person could get life with parole in 40 years. Well, a chance for parole in 40 years. There are thousands serving that sentence or the one before that from when it was 35 years. Has any of them killed anyone in prison? No.

Majority of all murders in prison are committed by people serving under 50 years for a non-murder case. Ah, there was a guy several years back that was serving life for rape/murder. He was just serving life for rape. Though he raped and killed a female clerk, then he killed himself. One case out of thousands. It shows that people can get a sentence other than death.

It is almost September, and no county in Texas has sent anyone new to death row. That is historical. A few counties tried, but juries voted for life. It wasn't because they think death row is so hard because we do not have TV.

It was because of all the exposure to innocent people being executed, prosecutors hiding evidence, and chaotic courts. People are losing faith in the system. If you highlight the flaws in the system, then people lose faith. The powers that be, they know their system is on the way out.

As a result, they are in a rush to kill as many as they can. What happens when you rush, though? You make mistakes. Mistakes get exposed, and the system falls apart even more. Money wasted, pain dragged on, and chaos reigns.

Back to Daniel. Some here, for some stupid reason, get upset when a person cancels their appeal. It's that person's life. The gurney only has room for one. It was his choice. Not one I would make for myself. It was his fate to govern.

Alrighty then. I will have another one posted soon, hopefully.

Until next time, take care and keep on keepin' on.

Veni, Vidi, Vici

www.saveaninnocentlife.com

I remain,

In solidarity,

Clinton Young #999447

Polunsky Unit

3872 FM 350 South

Livingston, TX 77351

USA

Loud & Clear, August 18, 2015

Topic: My Last Appeal Denial & What's Next

Maybe it was a bit of wishful thinking on my part, though I surely had high hopes that:

1) The court would grant me a C.O.A. (Certificate of Appealability)—basically permission to appeal, as the federal district court (lower court) denied me such a right.

2) Being that the gloves came back favorable to me, the prosecutors in Midland would do the right thing.

At last, they still were not responding to my lawyers. The Fifth Circuit denied me and further expressed the insanity that has plagued this case.

Take my ballistic report by Richard Ernest. This report shows that I could not have been the shooter for the first two shots into the first victim. The claim by the state: Doyle was sitting in the driver's seat of his 2-door Pontiac Grand Am car. I was sitting in the passenger seat. (This I do not dispute in the filings.) The state claims, by way of the co-defendant's words, that I shot Doyle twice in the head. (This I SURELY dispute.) Doyle was then taken to another location, where his body was left, and Mark fired a third shot into Doyle's head.

Mark claimed that he was under duress and in fear of his life from me. Now, Doyle was shot in the left, back, and right sides of the head. The ballistics show that the gun the state claims I used was responsible for the shots to the left side and back of the head, at a distance of greater than 3 feet. The gun Mark used was responsible for the shot to the right side of the head. Now, the forensic pathologist found all three shots, due to the paths taken, would be fatal, though the first two shots were 100% fatal.

Okay. Mark says I held up the gun about 6 inches away from Doyle's head and shot him. (NOT supported by forensics!) Darnell McCoy, who was in the back seat also, said I held the gun in my lap, angled up, and shot Doyle. (NOT supported by forensics!) Matter of fact, the forensic pathologist at trial said that method was not possible due to the angle of the bullets.

Darnell said I had one kind of gun. Mark said I had another. How do two people, sitting right beside each other, not 3 feet away, see a totally different version of events? Not just a little different—TOTALLY different. The only thing in common is the claim that I shot the guy! Both stories are not plausible forensically, as I, in the passenger seat, could not have shot the driver in the left side of his head at a distance of over 3 feet.

Okay. What the forensics are supportive of is someone walking up to the car and shooting Doyle. That person would have to be standing outside the driver's side. The co-defendant David was.

Now, the federal judge, when faced with the forensics, in an effort to explain them away, said that Doyle could have been (or he said was—I will have to double-check the exact wording)—though the federal judge, who did NOT "watch" the trial and was NOT present at the crime, with 100% no testimony supporting this—claimed that Doyle was turned around in the seat, facing towards the back to allow David into the back seat.

Now, what grown man who stands 5 feet 11 inches tall and weighs over 230 pounds turns around in the front seat of a small 2-door car, to the point his body is facing the back seat, just to allow a person into the back of the car? A 16-year-old hyper teenage girl, yeah! A big grown man that is also over 50 years old? Hell NO!

We appealed his revisionist history of the events. The Fith Circuit (all the circuit courts are the 2nd most powerful courts in the U.S., with the U.S. Supreme Court being number one) said it doesn't matter, as the ballistics are meritless, due to the fact that the co-defendants said I did it.

Which, legally, is not the law. Co-defendants are to be deemed "corrupt" witnesses—not trusted—and a jury cannot convict unless their testimony is supported by corroborating evidence.

Which, in the case of Doyle, another co-defendant in a different crime who was high on meth and expressed a desire to kill me, said I told him I shot Doyle. (I did not tell him that!) Again, he was a co-defendant in another case, high on meth, and mad at me! Then the Fifth Circuit went on to say that it still doesn't matter due to the "law of parties," as I could be found responsible for Mark's actions.

Now, they also said Mark fired a shot into Doyle's dead body. Key word there is "DEAD" body. Okay. How can I be guilty of a crime that Mark is not even guilty of? You CANNOT murder a DEAD BODY!!!!

It should also be pointed out that Mark was indicted for capital murder of Doyle when he testified, which was a manipulation tactic. The state argued throughout the trial that I shot Doyle unexpectedly, held Mark hostage, and threatened his life.

Okay, by the state's very argument, Mark cannot be guilty of capital murder, as he was under "duress and threat for his life." As a result, following the state's logic, Mark could NOT be guilty of my actions, by the state's own reasoning. If I killed Doyle unexpectedly and then threatened the others, they are in NO WAY guilty of any crime.

Does everyone understand the basics of the law? No plan to kill + taken hostage = being under duress, and thus excused under the law.

Okay. So, by the state's words, Mark is innocent of any crime. Period! No ifs, ands, or buts about it. There is no debate if the state's position is to be deemed true.

Now let's present it this way: They lied, and David shot Doyle, which the forensics support. There was no plan for this. That means no one can be guilty of his act. If Mark then shoots Doyle's DEAD body, he cannot be charged with murder. Thus, I cannot be a party to his actions, as he did not commit a crime.

Also, it should be noted that Mark was not sent to prison for murder. He was sent for non-aggravated kidnapping of Doyle. Which, again, Doyle was not kidnapped!! No one said he was in any way! They just had to find something to charge him with to keep him in prison for a while, and Mark foolishly pled guilty. He has since said that if he had not, he would have walked! Period!

As I refused to talk to the police and the others' statements helped him, really, his lawyer let him get messed over. Mark surely did not properly know the law. Most people do not, as it is all so complex.

Bottom line: Forensics clear me. The Fifth Circuit said it doesn't matter, as I can be charged as a party to murder for a guy shooting a dead body. So it is official! You can kill a dead body now!

I cannot help but laugh, as this is so insane!

Now the 5th Circuit, in regard to a previous appeal issue about the gloves testing—which the federal judge denied me permission to do (though later Midland prosecutors agreed for me to do it)—said it would be procedurally barred.

Not so!

1) The prosecutors allowed me to test it.

2) Under Texas Senate Bill 344 and Code of Criminal Procedure 11.073, advanced testing can be done that was not previously available at the time of trial.

This is bolstered by a case known as the Robbins case, which is a Texas court case ruling. The testing was new and advanced and also showed what I claimed to be true.

So, it is good to go, and there are still other matters being done. These I cannot get into yet and will not until my lawyers are finished with it and it is before the courts.

So, on that front, it is not the end of the road for me. However, it is by no means easy sailing. It is an uphill battle—harder than before.

Now, what is next? My lawyers filed a request for the entire panel of the 5th Circuit to review my case, as they expressed that the 3-judge panel ruled in a way that "conflicts" with clearly established law and previous 5th Circuit rulings.

The state did not oppose me having an extra 14 days to file the en banc request. (En banc is Latin for "the whole" or something like that. It means the whole panel.) Before the extra 14 days were granted, I only had 14 days. Being that the state did not oppose us on the extra 2 weeks, the primary judge granted it. (Thank you! I'll take an extra 2 weeks of life.)

So, at the end of August, the REQUEST for the en banc hearing will be filed. Again, this is a request for a hearing. First, the request has to be granted, then the case heard, and an attempt made to get them to overturn the ruling. Then, if it is overturned, we have to file something else.

See? Complicated!

If the request is denied, I have 90 days to file with the U.S. Supreme Court. The state will, after so many days, respond to what we file. Then, after so many days, we respond to that. Then we wait on the USSC. It takes 4 justices to hear a claim. 5 to win. U.S. Supreme Court officials are not called judges. Their title is justices. If you call them judges, they get upset. There are some key bits I could mention that would strengthen my claims. I mean mention them here and point out the paperwork and images. But this is not the time or the place for that.

The gloves testing came back as I said it would. The report will be posted very soon. There is a very valid reason for the delay in my posting it. Believe me, I am EAGER to post it to show I was telling the truth again.

Every time I made a claim and it was looked into, and the testing was done, it has come back as I said it would.

Too bad the prosecutors at the trial never once bothered to communicate with my lawyers to get my side of the story! They only did the bare minimum work needed to bolster the co-defendants' claims. But after a bit of light was shined on it all, it has started to crumble!

It is my hope that after I post the report on the gloves, those reading this will believe in me—whether for the first time or even more—and feel a desire to become more active. That you will believe this is a struggle worthy of your time, effort, and, if able, donations, as you feel comfortable with it. I have always asked to just be given the chance to show I am telling the truth. Claims I have made over the years in my blogs and before the court in filings I had to make myself, when proven, have shown me to have told the truth! I have been open about the not-so-good choices I have made in my life. I have never sought pity or to be seen as some white dove to be freed from the cage. What I have asked for is help in the pursuit of truth and justice. To help me get what the law of the land, the U.S. Constitution, and international law allows and even mandates: a fair trial. A trial without backroom deals and coached false testimony. A trial on equal footing of funding.

I am stuck in a box. I cannot get out and fight for myself. I need help. I can win, and every person reading this can help me in some way.

I hope that you are willing to join the team.

Until next time.

Veni Vidi Vici

In solidarity,

Clinton Young #99447

www.saveaninnocentlife.com

Please visit my site & share my blogs. Thank you!

Loud & Clear, March 16, 2016

Topic: My book & general update

Seems there is some confusion about stuff that should have been posted in February. Hopefully, it is all resolved by now. I was planning on writing a blog going into great detail on a few things. Though am dealing with some frustrations. I have finally, after years of going back and forth, made up my mind to write my book. I debated with myself about if I wanted to write two books. One is my life story and the other is about death row and the system. Now, due to my long-winded nature when I write. :) I could write very long and detailed books. I think in the future I could gain more with two books. He is on the best sellers list TWICE! :) Haha No, seriously, it is appealing to put out two books. Though two books mean more effort is required by those that help me. More to keep up with and all that. As a result of that, to simplify it. I am putting out one long book. It will cover my life story and death row. It will also have special chapters and a forward by another person. It will have a few pages of pictures in it. My goal is to write a book such as has never been written before. I have already sent word out to people about finding a place to get it printed. Also who will type it up, edit it, and all that? The first portion will be mailed soon. As a result, it should all be ready to go within 8-12 weeks. I am aiming for a window of 6-10 weeks. Though what I want and get are not always the same. It is very possible though. I have a few people willing to help, so I think it can be accomplished. Plus, technology has advanced to such that it makes it so much easier to get everything in order. When the book is 75% completed towards 'ready to ship'. Then a page will be set up on my website for advanced orders. The rate of advanced orders will help me understand the number of copies that I will need. Hopefully the book is completed before the second film airs. Also upon digging through all my stuff to gather the pages for my book that I already had written. I've had the first 13 years of my life already complete) I came across my first chapter of The Adventures of Loki and Mr. Pig. Tomorrow, I am going to go through it and edit it. Then, send it out to type it up. There are Music Reviews and life story postings on my site. Suppose you have not seen them. Please do. Thanks! I was overcome with frustrations and truly considered not posting anything else. After years of dealing with this stuff. It often gets to be too much. The frustrations, that is. I am a go, go, go, type of person. At times, I feel like I am spinning wheels.

One of the reasons I decided to go ahead with my book. Time restrictions force me to.

The state has responded to my filings in the US Supreme court. My lawyers responded to that. The case is now circulated amongst the justices. Really it is their clerks. They will review everything and see if I get the 4 votes needed to accept the appeal. It takes 4 to get a claim heard. 5 to win. They can take it up and just direct me back to the lower 5th circuit court and order them to do a re-do. Or they could hold oral arguments, have a hearing and then issue a reasoned opinion.

Or they reject everything and it's off to plan B. Alrighty then. Tell others about the site. Thanks!

Clinton Young #999447

Polunsky Unit

3872 FM 350 South

Livingston TX 77351

USA

Loud & Clear, March 23, 2016

Topic: 90 days to live

When a person receives an execution date, it is for no less than 90 days. Many counties will give a date of execution that is 90 days away. Some will set it at a 4-6 month range. 90 is the worst case. Since the US Supreme Court rejected me. When I wake up in the mornings, the first thing in my mind is I have 90 more days to live. As if I got a date that day, that is what it is. I plan on what to do. How to fight it. Who I have in my life, that I know that I can depend on. Now, the prosecutor has ot indicated, at this time, that they will seek a date yet. As I previously mentioned, they are aware of the forensics and etc. In my previous appeals, I was fighting against a Texas attorney general. He is not from the country and only deals with the matters of the record of the case. He doesn't know all the side stuff. What is frustrating is that the Supreme Court had JUST 2 weeks ago given a guy on death row a whole new trial. He is from Louisiana. As a result, he is in the 5th Circuit Court of Appeals region, just as I am. My positions are stronger than his. Though he filed first and they rejected me. However, I can still use the law in future filings. Due to new forensic testing, there are legal avenues that I can file, also with newly discovered evidence. As a result, it is not a dead end road for me yet. Though I do not have time to be overly optimistic. My thinking must be: Expect the worst, hope for the best, be ready for all!" It is now a Wednesday. I am a bit shocked by how few people I got jpays from about my appeal being denied. Only two people, Jorunn and Susanne, made any mention of it. Others sent jpays and did not even make any mention of it. I do find that a bit alarming. As I don't know if it had such an adverse effect on people that they shut down on me or what. I am big on communication. If I post a blog, story, or music review. I want to know people's opinions. I do not care if they hate it. I am not offended by people that think differently than me. Though when hardly anyone says anything. It frustrates me as I am left to wonder if it was even read. Suppose it was posted in some cases when no one said anything. I can not just hop online and see who is there. I am stuck in a box and have to wait for people to write to me. People wonder why I get so frustrated and stop writing stuff. Then they will ask me," How come you have not blogged?" Even if someone is reading this, that does not write to me. There is a simple rule in life. Communication is the key to success. In this situation. It requires far more communication than normal. The more words you can use, the better it is. Imagine a piece of paper as being a canvas. Words being the paintbrush and paint. You got to paint a picture with words. If you just draw a line, how am I supposed to know it is a street? I need sidewalks, curbs, and all that good stuff. Also, I am not frustrated with everyone. I am in a high-stress situation that just got more stressful. Then there are a couple that add to it and I get frustrated. As many can tell by now. When I get aggravated. Everyone knows it! Don't assume I do not want to know. Comment, ask questions, state opinions, and all that good stuff. You know, communication!

As I might not be able to do much communicating, for very long. Alrighty then. I am going to wrap this one up. Be back soon. Hopefully less frustrated.

Tell others about the site. Thanks!

Clinton Young #999447

Polunsky Unit

3872 FM 350 South

Livingston TX 77351

USA

Loud & Clear, May 16, 2016

Topic: Case update. The death penalty, Death Row

A heavy weight upon my mind. Was a date set for early this month. My lawyer was due to meet with the prosecutor in Midland. The topic of discussion revolved around my future. It was a life or death discussion. The hope being that with all the new evidence. The prosecutor would agree for me to be granted a hearing/appeal on these matters. They would not concede to such. Only stated that we need to file the appeal and they will look over it. The hardest obstacle it seems is the police chase. Everyone from the prosecution/police side of things. They seem to take it as a sign of guilt. That is so very far from the truth! I had no idea I was named in the murders at that point. As I was told they was only looking for David, The co-defendant. I was pulling over to stop. Video of the chase shows just that. Then I take off. The reason that is not detailed in the video. It is due to a conversation I had with my girlfriend at the time. I told her "Well babe, looks like I will be going back to jail for a bit." She then told me that if I went back to jail, do not bother writing or calling her. Now, I was on parole. It's a wrap. I will be going to jail! Though I was thinking for some months or like a year! Not death row and all that stuff. When she told me not to bother contacting her anymore if I went to jail, I was pulling over so I would not get in any extra trouble when she said that. I told her. "You know what? You sure right! I aint going to jail." Then I took off. They started to shoot at me. The police that is. That was an extra reason to go in my mind. I went to get on the west bound lanes. A super-shot-cop took out a back tire that caused me to spin out. The truck was spinning down the interstate. when I got control of it and it was lined up, I was facing oncoming traffic. I HAD to take off/to move so I did not get hit by an oncoming car. Then I had to swerve away again. The police are back chasing me. Now, to avoid hitting anyone. as I seen an older lady and a kid in a red car. I saw the look on their face. I didn't want to hurt some kid or old lady. I yanked the steering wheel, hit the ditch service road. went airborne and almost hit a parked van, went through a trailer park and back onto the road. Cop shot the truck some more and I let it roll to a stop. I got out of the truck and did not resist arrest any further. Now, in no way shape form or fashion does any of that equate to guilt. The jury nor the DA never knew this. As I did not testify and the prosecutor never bothered to ask why I ran. This story I have told is the same one I have told from day one to every lawyer, every media outlet, in every blog I mentioned it in. It has never changed. A cup of gasoline was found in the truck with a lid on it. There is NO fingerprints from me on this cup. It got put on me, as David claimed I was going to go blow the truck up. Again though. That is HIS words. There is no video of me putting fuel in any cup or truck. Matter of fact, David was really great at telling the police every store he stopped at. Yet the two stores he was never able to tell the police we were at, was #1) where the bullets was bought. #2.) where fuel was obtained. It is simple as to why. I was asleep when he stopped and got fuel and put the fuel in the cup. It has been said by him and me that I was sleeping on the way to Midland. I did not kidnap anyone, did not threaten anyone, did not put any fuel in a cup, or any of that. The fuel and the cup has never been talked about before. Hell, I never discussed it with my lawyers. As I did not put it in the cup. Plus, there was no talk of blowing up or burning Petry's truck. As Mr. Petry was not supposed to be harmed. Only thing I thought David said about burning something up/was the first car. At trial, I think he said the truck though, which I did shoot the side of that car up. I did that so as to empty the gun. It is frustrating/as in order to kill me. It has to be capital murder. The murders were not related. I never threatened, seen threatened, or any sort of thing by anyone towards Mr. Petry. There was no kind of plan to harm Mr. Petry. NONE! In 13+ years I have not thought anything about the cup of fuel. No matter what though. The police threw it away, which means it is to be deemed favorable to me. Anytime the police or such destroys anything that can be considered evidence. It is presented to the jury. that they are to deem it favorable to the defense. (me.) As if it wasn't then the police would not have destroyed it. Hey, we could have requested DNA on the cup, additional fingerprints, looked for the store it came from and sought out the store video. All kinds of stuff could have been done. The police could have took a sample of the liquid inside. Then emptied the cup, let it dry out and then bagged and tagged it. But NOOO, instead they throw it away and then say it shows I am guilty of Capital Murder. Really!? That cup of fuel does not even support David being guilty of anything. Not by itself. He will say I done it. I will say he done it. Too bad the police THREW IT AWAY. As now it cannot be tested. So, it is his word versus mine. The great cup conspiracy will continue. Look I get the 'idea'. The 'idea' behind the cup and chase. is that it is the actions of a guilty man; People always ask "why did you run, if you was not Guilty?" I was 18 years old-, been through all kinds of crazy stuff, was arguing with my gal, and at the bottom of it all. The culture I adhered to back then. The culture shaped in some ways how I responded to critical situations. The police was seen to have an adversarial role. What I am aware of as being wrong today was seemingly right back then. Police chases are also glamorized in Hollywood and the media in general. DVDs can be bought of the "Wildest police chase". The glamorization of such was around way before I ran from the cops. Media impacts culture. A bad choice simply does not equate to being guilty of killing someone. I run from the cops = I am supposedly guilty of murder. I supposedly get mad at a teacher aide when I was in 8th grade. I slam a door = I am a future danger and monster? No bullshit! They used a hallway monitor/teacher aide lady. One that I could not have pointed her out or told you her name. She said I had a chain hanging down my side. Like from wallet to belt loop as Bikers and skaters wore according to her. She told me to put it up and I got mad. looked at her mean and slammed a door. That is one of the people they used against me in my trial.

1.) The event did NOT happen.

2.) I never even dressed that way! NEVER!!!!! My mom would not allow me to leave the house with something like that. I was not a 13-year-old Biker gang member. I did not ride skateboards. I listened to hip hop and hard rock.

I just do not fucking get it! Even if I did get mad at the teacher and slammed a door, I was a damn teenager!!!!!! What teenager has NOT slammed a door? I am sure I would have slammed a door had she told me how to dress. After I would have told her: " You buy my clothes, then you can tell me how to dress." Anyway, the fight goes on. I have until August to file my appeal. On to other matters. Death Row. As many know, there was a social media ban by TDCJ. Being that it is just a Facebook thing. It is not so bad. When the first impression being given from wardens and etc. It was that we could not blog. I aint never been good about letting people shut me up. :)

TDCJ just wanted to have a control tool for people using Facebook to cause problems and etc. That is all that it is. (like writing protests and such) Me or any other guy having someone tell an old friend or sick grandmother they are thought of and loved. That is not going to get someone in trouble. Just cannot be as interactive as was before. A major pharmaceutical company stopped providing execution drugs. They did it for legal reasons more than moral reasons, I am sure. Unless their stockholders started to complain. However, that does not matter as Texas uses compound pharmacies that are not regulated by the FDA in the same ways. People in the anti-death penalty movement have focused on Compounding Pharmacy from the Woodlands, which is in the Houston area. The evidence cited is the huge donation the owner made to Greg Abbott. Now it is possible that this guy is the supplier. HOWEVER, one does not give a 250.000$ donation to a governor just to keep a lock on supplying and executing drugs. That does not add up. Execution drugs cost, what, a couple of hundred dollars. 250K would never be made back. A person wants a profit if they are donating for a return. Do the math. If execution drugs cost 1,000$ an execution. It would take 250 executions to break even! There are not even 20 a year. So he would need 25 a year for 10 years to break even. That is Not a good investment numbers! No one supplies 250K as a political donation to be able to provide execution drugs. Compounding pharmacies are regulated by the state in many ways more so than the Federal government. 250K is a donation to say: 'Please continue with soft regulations.' Compounders provide all kinds of drugs to hospitals and etc. There are many major hospitals in the Houston area. Sure the guy makes millions. The last thing he is going to care about/is being able to supply drugs for executions. It would not be about the money, it would be about the political favors. No matter who it is. Anyways. Bottom line is that the choice by Pfizer has no impact on Texas, though good deal. As I mentioned before. If they don't kill us one way, they will find another way. My focus is more about the people being aware of the injustice in the system. THAT changes hearts. But hey, what do I know. Back soon!

In solidarity.

Veni Vidi Vici

Tell others about the site. Thanks!

Clinton Young #999447

Polunsky Unit

3872 FM 350 South

Livingston TX 77351

USA

Loud & Clear, June 6, 2016

Topic: Ramadan, death row

Today is the first full day of Ramadan. The Islamic holy period of fasting, which is a simple way to explain it. Now, as to why I mention it. I was on the rec. Yard with a guy here who is a Muslim. (There is a different dynamic with black Muslims in prison hare in the US, than everyday Muslims in the free world). We were discussing prison politics and different groups' world views. We got onto the topic of Ramadan and the fasting. What he eats and doesn't. While having this discussion, I think of my beautiful friend Karima. She has helped me in various ways. I decided that I would observe Ramadan. As a way of having a hit of solidarity with Karmia, who is observing it also. After starting it, I got to thinking about the idea of suffering for another. Many people lack the ability to sacrifice for anything. As all they think about is the instant gratification. To themselves. They will not even sacrifice for their own benefit, much less another. Today being the first day. I thought about the days to come. I actually felt a bit closer to her as I thought of her going through the same thing. A common thread between people a world apart with totally different lives. While on Ramadan, I can not drink or eat anything during the sunlight hours. Texas being the humid and hot place it is during this time of the year, the no drinking part starts to add up around 5 pm! ☺ The minor suffering gives strength to the bond. It is a small way to feel closer to a dear friend. Though there are surely many in this world suffering far worse than I. I wrote about it, to maybe get someone to think about sacrifice in their life. In whichever way they think of. Beyond the feeling of a stronger bond with her. There is the benefit of fasting. I am limited to what these people feed me. Sure, I could get stuff from commissary, though I am planning to just eat the trays the prison serves. Healthier than the processed junk they sell. All who are observing Ramadan get fed after everyone else. The section I am in will eat at around 3 am. I will get a tray at around 4 am. I don't get lunch. Last chow, they eat around 4 pm. I will not get a tray until 10:30 pm/11 pm. (on the 7th, we were fed at 02:30 am and 9: 30 pm) This lasts 28 days. As for everything else on death row. They are writing up petty cases on people. Officers are saying they have to write 2 cases per shift, no matter what. As a result some are making things up. The bad thing is that when a person gets a case, they lose stuff. Like, I got one and got 15 days rec. Restriction. I had some paper rolled up, like a pole. Now I can't rec. for 15 days. Well once a week/I get 1 hour of rec. The guy in the cell next to me. He got 15 days no rec. and 15 days no commissary. For the exact same thing. Only he had a case a couple weeks ago, so he got the added commissary restriction. He can not buy any food or clothing items for two weeks. Only stamps and limited hygiene items. These people are just not satisfied with a passive death row population. The crazy thing about the 15 days is this. There has been people who murdered another person in prison. You know what they got for the disciplinary case? 15-day cell restriction! Of course they then also got the criminal charges. But my point is, that I have some rolled up paper and I get the exact same restriction that a person gets when they commit murder!? These people see nothing wrong with that. They do not see the failure in not prioritizing punishment. I really was expecting like 5 days! They want people to be on cell restriction. As it is less work for them. It is really amazing that some in the state wonder why people go so crazy here, they can not be executed. The real shock is that mute don't go crazy! Anyways. Hopefully the 15 days pass by quickly. There is no real way to get it off. As a grievance takes 38-45 days to be resolved. I will file on it, but what is done is done. Long sigh. I just got to keep my eyes on the prize. No word from the legal arena. Waiting on word from my lawyers. Alrighty then. I am going to wrap this one up and get some sleep.

In solidarity.

Veni Vidi Vici

Tell others about the site. Thanks!

Clinton Young #999447

Polunsky Unit

3872 FM 350 South

Livingston TX 77351

US

Loud & Clear, August 23, 2016

Topic: Quick chat

Hopes all's good out there. Just a quick rundown. No real news yet. Filings will be maybe next month or October, due to developments. Though, expect no court action due to docket length and holidays coming up, until after the New Year. Nov./Dec. Both have prominent US holidays. Thanksgiving and Christmas. Which removes a couple of weeks of activity with a non-execution date filing. The response time from the court is generally 4-6 months at least! I haven't blogged much. Been writing longer letters though. I know some have gotten them and thought: "What the hell?" Haha. :) I was just doing a great deal of thinking about life, love, and connections. Along with how little freedom people have. More so when it comes to their interactions with others. What I wanted from life, what I did not have and how fucked up life has been. Thinking about all that, I just got on a kick about connections with others. Then to add to it, everyone that has read my book so far and works on it. (It is not done yet) They make similar remarks about common theme and etc. Ha! Haven't even got to my Juvenile prison/lock up years. Really, I am not even sure now if I want to even finish it. Reading over it all, always brings the question. What am I fighting for? It damn sure isn't for the life I had. I really think it is about the fight. It is all I know how to do really. It's all I have been doing in one way or another. Anyways. Will write another blog soon. It will be long and go into some things that I have thought about lately. Take care.

In solidarity,

Clinton Young #999447

3872 FM 350 South

Livingston Tx.77351

USA

Loud & Clear, September 26, 2016

Topic: Little of this & little of that

Prison Life

Penitentiary –

A petty paradise,

no wise served twice.

Life lost for losing lives.

Given freely. What cost?

Dreams. Schemes all jumbled.

Rumble tumble in this fuckin jungle.

Sum total of the end result. Aint no kris kringle.

Gotta be from the occult.

Punks poppin like pringles. Look at Mr. Splinter jig that jingle.

The police don't police the police.

Its a long time to a quick release.

Hold down that pride, less no reason why shorty died.

Expression given through halls of depression.

Snap judgement!

Wrong day right mail call.

Rignt day wrong mail call.

To live or die.

Never know as ticks tick bye.

Broken clocks, torn calenders.

No time piece, no time for peace.

Strife leased life from grief.

Pain, misery, & sorrow.

No price, rent free.

Un-taxed to borrow.

Penitentiary –

a petty paradise,

Sellin hope, buyin lies.

Ink coats Fear.

Hangin onto soap, byes in a lope.

Prison livin. Given a rope a dope.

A dumbass genius & tough ass coward

Walked into a bar. Walked into a bar.

Walked into a bar.

Now wrapped up & planted afar.

Zapps, caps, no maps. Living life by the

Petty mishap.

Bullshit ass penitentiary

Loud & Clear, January 2017

Topic: Jpays/mailroom

Am finally getting back into writing, though right now, need to focus on a more pressing matter.

Many that write use Jpay, An email service that your letter gets emailed and printed out by mailroom. TDCJ makes a profit from this. So short and simple. PLEASE post this on all pen pal forums and share with others. An idea that I developed and others are putting it forward. These people always say: "File a grievance." When a person files a complaint with tdcj.gov/ombudsman, they are told that the prisoner has to file a grievance. Okay that is bullshit, that these people want us to do, as it is THEIR system. Why would I complain to the Devil about the temperature in Hell? He wants it hot! With jpay, there's NO need to file a grievance. ZERO! I don't give a damn who, what, or where you are told that. Don't care if ombudsman office, TDCJ director themselves or any so called death row/prison advocate expert tells you that.

Here is WHY.

#1. A prisoner does NOT set up the jpay account in Texas. It's done by a person who is FREE. In signing up and transferring funds, the person enters a form of contract. The other party has an obligation to complete their part of the deal. Here is example: You hire a contractor to remodel your kitchen. You pay said person agreed amount of money. Yet the contractor does NOT do the work. What is that called? Fraud. Theft. PERIOD. You pay Jpay for a service to be done. TDCJ gains a percentage of the funds. Due to this fact and because they are the end party responsible for the delivery of the jpay. They then shore in blame. As they act as agent for jpay and etc. So the prisoner is simply an interested party. As the prisoner benefits from the contract you have with Jpay/Tdcj. When a prisoner does NOT get the jpay. He then is a witness also.

#2. Solution to the problem. I came up with idea to have people report missing jpays as a crime to the Texas Attorney General office. As it is! With many doing this, the attorney general office then will have to investigate. This will then cause TDCJ to/take the matter much more serious (the Texas Attorney General is the TopCop and prosecutor in Texas). It also gets others involved, such as the actual director, which then lights a fire under the ass of the lower ranking officials. It's a way to think outside the box. It hasn't been done before. Grievances have been done and guess what? The shit don't work! In addition to this, people should email and complain to Ombudsman office. BUT do it in connection 'with' complaint to Attorney General office. ALSO file a complaint to Jpay.com and the parent company for Jpay that is Securus. It is a Dallas based company that helps keep people locked up! So every time you use jpay, the very system many of you fight, profits from it! You think that money TDCJ gets is used to help us? Make our life better? Hell no! it is used for pepper spray, execution drugs and etc by TDCJ. Goes to their pocketbook. It is used DIRECTLY for execution drugs? Who knows, BUT it all goes in the same piggy bank! One thing is sure. They aren't feeding us better. Many units still are without air conditioning or heat.(Texas death row has air conditioning and heat. Any says otherwise are lying! Might not be perfect temperature. But its there. Other units don't have such.) Now the mailroom is not giving us mail faster. They make more money yet it gets worse for all of us!? So please file complaint with Securus and Jpay and inform them that you are boycotting jpay. Inform Ombudsman this also. See then they begin to lose MONEY. It is the Dollars and cents that makes SENSE to these people. They don't give a fuck about pain and suffering. Tall they care about is can they make money from it or save money with it. Period. Politicians invest in Securus and other prison companies, when they start to lose money they get things done. You have to think outside the box. Other states have a tablet. An actual Jpay tablet that the jpay email can be sent to and can also respond with by the prisoner. It is sold on commissary and ALL is routed through mailroom. But is faster and easier. Has NO outside connection to internet or anything. It is a closed system. Mailroom hits send and it goes to the tablet. The person in prison can then type up response and hit send, it goes back to mailroom, they then forward it to jpay who posts it on your account. Real simple. TDCJ does not have this. TDCJ chose to keep this print email system. They do more than that. They steal your money! They give your jpays to the wrong people How many of you have had a loved one/friend write to you that their mail was given to another person locked up or they gave them another's mail? Countless. The guards do not give any attention half the time. They just give it to whoever and sometimes mailroom sends mail to wrong pod and etc. Doesn't happen ALL the time, but far to many times it does! It needs to stop. Only way to correct it is by everyone taking the time to file a complaint with TDCJ, Jpay, Securus and Attorney General Office of Texas. Request that the mailroom start passing out the jpays as they do legal mail books. when a person orders an ecomm care package commissary passes it out. Why then can not the mailroom pass out jpays?! It is PAID for! TDCJ MUST accept responsibility and stop this behavior. Conservatives that control Texas pride themself on Law and order!!! Well lets get some damn Law and order and stop this theft. Here is another fact. Jpay pays for ink, paper, and computer. Texas nor TDGJ as agent of Texas spends NO money on any part of the jpay process. Yet they get money from EACH page. Texas ALSO to add insult to injury charges more than any other state for jpay. Another fact that must be complained about also! They make more yet, but do less!? I was told before that Texas makes 15¢ per PAGE. So a 4-page jpay is .60¢ TDCJ gets. They get free money and say fuck the people and fuck those locked up. You want words from your loved ones correct? You want them to not stress correct? Okay then you must fight for a solution. Hell Jpay doesn't even tell you all, that the pictures are printed only in black and white trash quality! They make it seem as if it is color. I am telling people to write me with jmail, and not jpay. That are regular mail. I am serious. Many guys here on G-pod are joining in. Some who are fuckin idiots lost in their fake sense of self will always resist, because it is not THEIR idea. Happens all the time. People cut their nose to spite their face. I will leave why to the DSM-5 experts. In the meantime. People focused on solutions/are pushing forward. One thing I know is how to fights. Been doing it all my life! Spent far too many years locked up in Texas prisons. I know what works. I ask that people PLEASE show solidarity and address this matter. They are punishing us for crimes. They then commit crimes and use the money from their fraud to oppress us. To fight us in lawsuits. They do NOTHING for us. NOTHING. Our lives have gotten worse! Or sit on your ass and cry.

3 kinds of people in this world.

#1. Those that make shit happen.

#2. Those that watch shit happen.

#3. Those that ask what the hell just happened!?

Which one are you?

I can't speak for everyone here. Each is his own man. However, if a person is not going to fight beside and or for me, they do not need to be in my life then!

BECAUSE SILENCE IS CONSENT!

Veni, Vidi, Vici

Take care.

In solidarity

Clinton Young #999447

3872 FM 350 South

Livingston Tx. 77351

Loud & Clear, March 1, 2017

Topic: Past, present, & future-Death Row, executions

The past few months, while not being very active. I did a great deal of thinking. About the relationships of my life. The way with some, I overlooked things I shouldn't have, which it never gets better when such is done. People have to hold each other accountable, along with themself. With others, I did not focus enough on the bond with them for who they were. I focused so much on winning the fight I often failed to focus enough on the fighters. Not everyone can be fueled off of an idealistic position. Some fight for principle, others based on emotions and desires. I am steadily go, go, go, and go a little more. It is easier to be that way while looking down the barrel of the gun as I am. Plus my fight response seems to so vastly outweigh my flight response. Tied in with the conditioning of spending so many years in prison. I lock on to the fight and just keep pushing forward and forward. This often overwhelms others, as they can't keep up so to speak. As they fall behind, I then would doubt their sincerity. Some that have known me have told me things like. "You can't expect everyone to be able to meet your standards, if anyone can." I would take such a statement with pride before. As I seen it as just reinforcement that I could fight longer and harder than others. Though I also now realize the foolishness of it. That I allowed some really great people to slip away. The problem with always looking forward to what's over the horizon. You often overlook "what is right in front of you and who is beside you. I have even argued with my lawyers, because I felt they was not being aggressive enough. It resulted in one lawyer and I have a couple heated arguments during legal calls. Once I hung up on her. The next she went smooth off on me! I was speechless, though I realized she was right. I was being an asshole. For years I was on outside rec. only, which farther isolated me. Which made me digress in some ways. After getting off of it and after lots of thinking. I realized the ways I was so rigid and locked on that I was becoming my own destruction. A lesson to be learned from the classic Moby dick is how one's obsessions can destroy himself. Also don't be a moby dick! Ha. A balance is always best. Not reducing my desire and passion. Though am trying to be much more understanding and empathetic. To see the world through another's eyes. It doesn't mean that I have to lose my own vision. Another thing that I messed up, is not properly expressing all that I was going through. People that write are clueless about prison life and or really my own life. Sure can read some blogs etc to get a general idea. Though can not properly understand my way of seeing things. They way I constantly think about various stuff. The way things in here impact me, be it small or large. I remember reading somewhere about how some with great minds, suffer depression and such. That often their own minds work against them. Guess that is why people say ignorance is a bliss. I am not the smartest person. Though I have my talents. However, forcing myself to be an island was self-destructive. So often we focus on more and better that we overlook the blessings in life that we do have. Anyways. Point is. I feel better now. Even have gotten along so much greater with lawyer. (this lawyer is one of my main appeal lawyers. She is not featured in any media. All will understand why I say that when film airs. I have appeal lawyers, plus an investigative lawyer that was retained by my supporters). This place is not designed for mental and emotional growth. Though it can be overcome by staying focused and being self-aware. I have seen many spiral into mental chaos! Seen people give up. Totally lose their will to live. Ready to die. Never want to be that way. As long as I can make it through tonight, tomorrow is a new day. It can get better, more so if I can still fight for it to be. Back to one last part of what I was writing. I know that many I pushed away, I was just in general an asshole or gave up on. I do sincerely apologize. Some I do not have address anymore. As a result just decided on a public apology. Now there was many that I cut ties with for being bullshit ass people. Believe me, I have had some crazy ass people write to me, pathological liars and just down right twisted. I could go on and on about that! Got to sail forward though. Anywho. The future. I am not so certain of the future at this point as for timelines. Waiting to see if will have to fight it out on some testing. I shouldn't have to, with all I have in my favor. Will find out this month. At least that is impression I was given. You know I wrote something to someone recently. I am going to add it here. While here, when I first got here. I expected certain people that held certain positions in my life to help fight for me. To stay involved. As years passed and they faded away and or did not live up to expectations. I depended so much more on those that wrote me. The more I had to depend on them, the more it made me think about who I should be depending on. It would cause me to be frustrated. That is natural, though the problem is I focused my frustration on the wrong people. That is why I apologize. This place is on lockdown. Seems to be a month-long lockdown. The meals are given in sacks. Tonight regular meals. They got one sandwich and 1 baked potato. Just a plain potato. I swear that is IT! One fucking simple sandwich and one plain ass potato. That was the meal. Years ago dudes would be willing to riot behind that shit. One thing I noticed about this place. So many do not want to appear to be 'Following' someone else. Yet so so so many will not take the first steps on their own. It was always the same ones leading the way. We now all have the same thoughts "I am tired of being the only fuckin person!" Now I am on the diet tray list. I got two sandwiches and fruit. On lockdown the fruit is raisins or prunes. At lunch the regular meals got ONE cookie and one sandwich. I wish I was lying. Sure, lets blame TDCJ. Though I blame also the people locked up here. We allow these people to get away with this bullshit. Normally people have commissary saved up for lockdowns. As we get placed on it every 90 days. I didn't, as didn't get much last time when got commissary. At first, I was like "damn I am hungry?" Though my stomach has adjusted to the smaller meals. Plus really we do eat too much. Its why Americans are so fat in general. Most here got high blood pressure and all that. In some ways glad for the forced diet! ☺ Oh, I get the diet meals for having high blood pressure. Though the word diet is deceiving by TDCJ standards. Nothing healthy about the meals. Executions. Renaldo Ruiz was executed recently, after 11 pm. Never heard of an execution happening that late. People look at it as he had to wait until after 11 pm. See? That is the fuckin problem right there! The problem is not that he waited until 11:27 to be killed. No, the problem is he was 33 minutes from LIFE! 33 minutes. A fight. A resist. Anything. 33 minutes later the death warrant expires. They can't execute when the death warrant expires. A person has to get a new execution date. All dates have to be at least 90 days from now. Plus lawyers have to be informed, so it's 93 days extra life at the least. In 93 days, new evidence can be found, new laws pass, new court rulings develop. All of which can cause one to live out his natural life. 93 days allows lot of possibilities. 33 minutes away. Every person I spoke to about it expressed about how they killed him so late. No one said "33 minutes away." It's the first thing I thought! I really do see things often in different ways than most. Though it's been that way through out my life. As a child in church, when the story of Adam and Eve is told. I heard that the rib was taken from Adam and that Eve was created after Adam so she could serve him. Another version was that the rib was taken so that she would be at his side. That they walk side by side in life. I asked. "Couldn't it be that Adam came first so as to prepare earth for her and to protect her?" I got silent stares. Back then I felt stupid for saying it. Though now I understand that they were all thinking "never thought of it that way." Maybe even the implications of the history of humanity if the wise men of yore had seen it that way. Hey in life there is presentation and interpretation. 11:27pm or 33 minutes. Mail situation. A way is being developed, which should be by time this is posted or shortly after, to reduce jpay errors. Hopefully everyone will take the extra minute to do it the way I request, so I do have the added stress of delayed mail and missing letters. After a couple times it will become routine.

Veni, Vidi, Vici

Take care.

In solidarity

Clinton Young #999447

3872 FM 350 South

Livingston Tx.77351

Loud & Clear, March 1, 2017

Topic: A Little Bit of Everything

Last year about this time of the calendar I was thinking I could face an execution date 90 days later. When one has battled a system for so long and so hard, it is hard to have faith in doing something other than fighting. My case has had many new twists and turns. Then to say the least, I was exhausted! Years of this has worn on me a bit. Then I had to deal with stupid shit because of others dumb ass ways. It all adds up. Most days, I just laid back in the cell listening to the radio. A bit of good change. For years, I was on outside rec. restriction, meaning I could not go to the day room. A good thing about going outside was the sunshine, though I was further isolated. The outside rec yard is a room with bars for the roof and bars in the middle, so two people cannot have contact. The sunlight is why I look so dark sometimes. Due to the times Jessica seen me, I know in some parts I am lighter and in others I look like a blue eyed Arab! More so with my beard, huh Michelle? ;) Being further isolated in a place that is built for isolation…Not always a good thing. What ended up happening is my ability to move around was further restricted, causing me to lack the small degree of independence that is allowed. Thus, having to depend on others more, which is hell for me. I was restricted due to past acts from the day room. Use of forces were years ago in my more rebel days. A fellow locked up with me decided to say mean things to hurt my feelings by calling me a bitch as he walked by the day room bars, which resulted in me slapping him through the bars, causing me to lose my day room attendance abilities (the bars are big enough to reach through). The ranking officials here, due to my years of good behavior, allowed me back into the day room. I could literally feel the difference. The ability to move around more. It is hard to explain, really. It was like I felt more alive. I got my old edge back. That was the minor highlight in an otherwise stressful past few months. November is always stressful due to marking years locked up, then the usual holidays and such. Only have had two visits since November. One of the visits being a special visit over a few days. Others had things going on in their lives. The mail situation is still horrible for me. I got mail twice in over two weeks. No letters since like the 13 of February. Jpays on two occasions since the 10th of February. Today is March 1st! I haven't heard from my lawyers in a month. So yeah, I can safely say I am not in the best of moods right now. Only jpays I have received since the 9th of February is two from Michelle, one from Amy, and one from Laura, one from a lawyer who is not on my case, and a funds deposit notice. I got those all in one of the two days in over two weeks, so if any sent me something in that time period, well, I haven't gotten it. I got 2 valentines day cards. One from Jessica and Meike. Which just goes to show just how commercial Valentine's day has gotten! They got cards for siblings, etc. now. I tell everyone there is a million ways to make money in this world! I am NOT saying I wanted more Valentine's day cards! Ha, let me make that clear. Just making a statement of fact!! Oh, I did get another one, a funny one from Alex. Write that just in case any others sent one, you know I didn't get it. In my last blog, I ranted about jpay. Amazing how few people complained. People do not have to use jmail to write me. Regular letters are great. Or you can still use jpay. Just if I don't get the shit, don't get mad at me for not writing. Nothing new in my case. Again, haven't heard from any damn body. Do know the lawyers etc. are supposed to meet sometime between last week and the next couple of weeks. I do know that something is going to happen somewhere! At least I know that! I myself have not been writing very much, though I am back at it again. Been writing and reading more. Right now the unit is on lockdown. It is going to be a long lockdown. They are searching through everything piece by piece. Long sigh. Time keeps on ticking. I might get back into doing song reviews, etc, but not sure yet. An idea I had, a couple were on board to help with it. Hopefully it sorts out sooner rather than later. Oh, before I wrap this up. Most of the longer than expected wait has been due to prosecutor on the case having to deal with some other cases awaiting trial. Not complaining. Just explaining as I had previously expressed a different time period of events that was expected. I am at least able to express that I am grateful the case is being looked at from all angles. Nothing else really to write about. Waiting, waiting, waiting. Time ticks on.

Until next time.

Take care, strive for all that you desire.

I remain,

Veni vidi vici

Clinton Young #999447

Polunsky Unit

3872 FM 350 South

Livingston, TX 77351

USA

Loud & Clear, March 23rd, 2017

Topic: Death penalty, death row

People are acting like the new appointee to the US Supreme Court is some horrible thing. The reality is he is as close to the exact way a Supreme Court Justice should be, by way of the intent of the court. Does not matter if you agree with his politics or not. The intent of the court and his qualifications match up. Now, will he be great for people on death row? Who knows. He, like most Americans, support capital punishment. Just like them, great liberals out in California who overwhelmingly voted for Hillary Clinton. They were given the option for California. End it or speed it up. They said speed up their death penalty. Another state that ended the death penalty by legislative action. The people voted it back in. So the people support it. When I got here, was told that in 10 years it would be gone. Well, I say about ten years from now it might be gone. Doubt it. As when dealing with the arguments like the suffering of a person on death row. Most do not care. Sure, media figures and such might make some noise about it. Though if you go to the average person and say" Hey this guy right here. Yeah, he raped and beat to death a couple teenage girls. When we kill his ass, he might feel a bit of pain and suffering." Most Americans will say, "I hope he feels all kinds of suffering!" I have said it for years and I say it again. The people do not give a damn about execution drugs or if we can't watch some TV. I have heard guys here say "If the public knew how bad the health care is, there would be an outrage." No, the hell there wouldn't! Not when people who never committed a crime struggle with health care costs. As often happens when people spend their lives in a bubble. We all associate with like-minded people. We listen to the talk shows that support our line of thinking. Follow the politician that votes our way. As a result, we do not see the world outside of that bubble. Most do. Which is why I make it a habit to read, listen and discuss a variety of topics with a wide range of people. To end the death penalty. You have to show the system is broken. If media would focus on the cases down here where dudes was wrongfully convicted, then it would show the people how their money is getting wasted. For example ,how Harris County / Houston Texas would spend hundreds of thousands of dollars to send a guy to death row. Yet over a thousand rape kits (the test done on a woman after a rape). These kits was left to sit in storage for years. No justice for the woman. The attacker left to roam the streets and hurt others. Huh, never heard of the mass marches by feminist over that. Wasn't just in Houston. Was in several cities like that, with untested kits.

Got to show the system is broken and that money is being wasted. People did the lethal injection fight. I get it, but well with current political environment. Yeah, that's out the window, because laws that help the state are going to be passed. Most people are totally clueless about the laws of the land, much less the roles of government and what the constitution dictates. Right now due to republicans controlling the congress and senate, along with president being republican and deep majority of the states being controlled by republicans. They can change the constitution! They can right now say, it is now the ah I can't recall if there is 25 or 26 current amendments. Anyways, they can say it is the 25th amendment of the US constitution that all persons who commit rape OR murder, that they are to, upon conviction face execution. It then would be the law of the land and COULD NOT Be challenged. Now because not all republicans think the same, that's NOT happening. Point is though, that, if you are going to fight the system. Learn the system. Also get the media to focus on the wrongful convictions. As has been shown, most do not care about the media's opinions. Trump being president is prime example. The way US media is, most do not trust it and haven't trusted it way before Trump came along. There are several people that fight hard as individuals. Sure I do not agree with all, but applaud their energy and efforts! What needs to be done is to get the media to focus on the way the system is broken. To through highlighting several cases current and past. THAT will change people's minds. Not just 'telling' the people the death penalty is wrong. You got to show people. The Supreme court will be 5/4 split on most issues like it was with Scalia before he passed away. Chance is it could end because of the swing vote on the court. That is possible! Though if it does not end within 2 years by US Supreme court. It will be 10 years at least before it ends. Unless Trump and the republicans fuck everything up, then it will be 6 years. To clear up the Media comment so no one thinks I contradict myself. The media tends to 'tell' people the death penalty is bad. That will not work. The media needs to SHOW the people it doesn't work the way it currently is and that both money is being wasted and innocent people are being executed. You know why Texas leads the nation in criminal justice reform? Because even though they will not admit it. Everyone knows Texas has killed innocent people. Todd Willingham's case and the coverage it got more to change the system then any march, blog, story, and or poll result. Alrighty then, as can see I will be blogging more.

Take care,

Veni vidi vici

Clinton Young #999447

Polunsky Unit

3872 FM 350 South

Livingston, TX 77351

USA

Loud & Clear, April 20, 2017

Topic: Death penalty, death row, & those that fight for justice.

(To make a correction/stash addition I forgot to do before mailing my last blog. I wrote about republicans being able to change constitution. I mean if they win more seats in this upcoming election in 2018. As with 2/3rds majority they can do whatever they want to. Death penalty got extra news due to all the executions that was scheduled then stayed. Short term solutions, to a much larger problem with the system. Though as long as we can all talk about easy topics like lethal injection drugs. Why focus on the harder topics- of prosecutor misconduct and layers misconduct. When it comes to the fight for justice with those locked up. Be it on death row or elsewhere. It has often been the odd that gets attention. Such as the way media will do a story on a woman that wants to marry a violent offender. Then to cheapen the overall debate, other women get cast under such a light. This topic came up with a friend. Okay, what about the men? So all the women have to be one of those women'. I guess the men have to be what? Rational beings in the pursuit of justice? If a man attempts to cast all women through a single lens. I think there is some name for that. What do they call that? Oh, yeah that's right. Sexist! In their dualistic simple black or white thought process. They see how I look and automatically assume that has to be some kind of sexual attraction. So women are such simple beings, that such is the only option? What about lesbians that write me? Forgive me, that I do not see it that way. Though maybe it is just that the guy that thinks that way is projecting. Maybe it is him having these thoughts. Aw, you are attracted to me? Aw, that's cute. While I would not want to impose on your lifestyle. I got to let ya down. As I am all about the ladies. I really, really, really love women. They are just so wonderful. Or maybe it is some men are so insecure, they feel threatened by me, so they have to attempt to shame others away. I understand that my comparative/analytical thought process tied in with a wealth of knowledge. That this can be intimidating. Or maybe you heard of the unofficial motto of Texas" Everything is bigger in Texas" Maybe you don't realize this is due to the vast size of the state and think it to mean some form of phallic representation. I mean…Alright, I will stay away from that one. Haha. I can just imagine some that know my sense of humor, sitting there thinking. "Please Clinton, don't go there!" ☺ ha. Hey, I am just trying to help these insecure dudes. That try to paint all women with such a brush as they do.

Seriously though. If I was mentally retarded and physically deformed. Then would not be such a thought. So basically, due to how I look, I am not allowed a free group of people to fight for my LIFE!! I am supposed to just be at the mercy of the government and die for some-shit I didn't do? No one is supposed to be moved by the 'situation?' True there is some people that write to prisoners for an objectified reason. Though what I have noticed is how they come about -writing is the indicator. While not absolute and I surely would not say every person is this way. As many people just like the idea of writing and most that are free do not have the time or desire to do. Everyone does everything with email and text. What I noticed from most that wrote me from seeing "media stories" on me. It is the shock of the situation. Not some rooted desire for something odd. Yet when the topic comes up and is debated in public forum for example. Dudes ALWAYS go there. Stupid fuckin idiots. It is really more of a show as to the way THAT guy thinks, versus the person writing. It is not like I am Trick Daddy. The rapper, "My name alone been known to break up a happy home." Ha. That's a rap lyric. However, with the new film coming out. I want to give guys a warning. I got to see some stills from the film. There is a part from during the summer when I had been out in the sun a great deal. My beard is looking all perfectly sculpted. I'm dark and it makes my eyes stand out more. Hair slicked back. I had been working out a bunch. So had a bit of my size back. LOOK, now here is what ya do. Get the TV remote and remove the back. Get one of the batteries a bit loose. So when it gets to that part, you can 'accidently' change the channel and then drop the remote so the battery falls out. Then you can fumble around with it for a bit, so as to buy some time for that part to pass. You DONT want her seeing that part. I'm trying to help ya out. As you have established that women are simple creatures. That are unable to grasp concepts such as empathy, sympathy, and a sense of justice. Long sigh. The sad part is you get to vote and have a say in things like public policy. ☹ Now what really gets me is the women that want to get involved and want to write. Though they are afraid of what others will say. I am glad that some other women were not like that. Such as you know Mary, Joan of Arc, Oprah, Jessica, Rosa Parks, that little girl was shot by the Taliban for going to school, Sabatina James, and etc. It does always amaze me at how worried such can be about what another thinks here in the West. You got little girls in Indonesia getting their genitalia mutilated, baby girls forced to be married in Yemen, stoned in Syria, sold in Iraq. Yet your feminine nature ends at what another thinks? I write about all of this, as it comes up anytime a woman is attempting to spread word about my case. Though it is more than just about me and my case. It's to a bigger point in life. I am here on death row. I have a very limited ability to live any kind of life. I am totally dependent on others. You got one life to live. Do not allow someone's opinion to keep you from striving for what you want. Fear is a concept that is more often than not constructed upon a baseless thought or feelings. If it comes to what another thinks. People have their own fears, mental illness, insecurities, jealousy and etc. Sometimes, we build up people based on an idea. The reality is they often fail to measure up.

People get amazed by stars. Guess what? Stars fall! They burn up. If you believe in it, fight for it.

People always see me as being this super strong person. Strength does not mean that I do not feel anything such as pain. Doesn't mean that I do not get knocked down. What if I told you that I thought of killing myself before? What if I mentioned there was a time where I thought of it every day. People would maybe not be super shocked. It's a hard situation and I have went through some hard times. What if I told you These thoughts was just a couple weeks ago? It is not about the difficulty of this place. It's about the uncertain waiting. The way I have to keep asking for help. The way some people say one thing and do another. (Don't be confused, I have some great people in my life) After I quit blogging, you know how much was donated to the Dutch account? 10 euros a month. With another donating here and there. That's why I became so against publishing my book. I am not selling my pain and struggles. Though, what weighed on me so much, was how for so long everything has been a fight. It's not the system so much as it is my lawyers and some people in my life. Its a fuckin struggle just to get someone to tell me they made it home safe after visiting. My uncle died. I found out from Jessie, who is not even related to him. Never seen him. She came to visit and said," Ohh, did you know Tony died?' Well, no, I fuckin didn't. Hadn't seen him in a long time. Wasn't close to him or anything. It is still the fact, though. Some people I don't hear from. Others because they do not hear from me, stop doing certain things. I guess I am not supposed to have down moments. Then my lawyers. I could already be on my way to having an idea of what will happen, with appeals filed. Though they want to wait on the prosecutor. Never mind what the fuck I go through every day. So I just languish here in this fuckin place. I really wish they would have given me an execution date. I mean. That with everything in me! Not because I would be executed. Hell no. I would get a stay, but it would force the appeals to be done quickly. If back in May 2016, they had set a date. I would have a ruling by the court already! Yet here the fuck I am, waiting on- waiting. What gets me is the fact that they feel some kind of right to hold off. Like I have no right to what's going on in my life! It is like everything has to be a fucking struggle. I just want some peace. That's all I want is some peace. People do not see the pain I go through, as life has taught me to channel it into anger. I am so tired of being angry. We all face barriers in life. Don't fear the barrier. Don't fear getting knocked down. The only thing to fear is when you lose the desire to get back up. The only thing special about me is that as long as I am breathing. I am always going to fight back. People are always going to attack what you do. You will always get knocked down. What matters is that you believe in what you do and that you always get back up. It is okay to hurt, worry, feel a bit lost. As long as you keep putting one foot in front of the other. You will find the way. Even God weeps.

Veni vidi vici

Clinton Young #999447

P.S. Blog extension.

This morning I mailed off blog to be posted and then couple hours later I received legal mail, from my lawyers. Turns out they have been pressing the issue plus working on everything. Also, the DA refused to allow me to do some additional testing. They will leave it to the court to decide. Which is better than nothing. As now the fight begins. I feel WAY BETTER! I couldn't stand still after reading the letter. As now I have something to fight. The sitting here with the unknown was pure hell for me. I want to be clear, I have great lawyers that care deeply for me. We have a different philosophy about how to approach the fight. They naturally feel it is best to not stir the water. Me, I say flip the damn boat. First one to shore wins! ☺ The sitting here with almost a month of silence from them. It created a void that allowed doubt to creep in. I have been fucked over by lawyers so badly in the past. I just do not trust people. One starts to expect it. It is a lesson I guess. Try to have more faith in people. Also. for you all in the free, never just assume everything is okay. I often gain energy from those in my life. There is people in my life that can totally flip my mood. Another point for those here in Texas. PLEASE, if you are from Texas. Reach out to the politicians that represent your district in the Texas House and Senate. The ones in Austin Texas, not DC. Tell them to support House Bill 316, Which will end the law of parties. Tell them no one should be executed when they have not killed anyone. DO NOT make an anti-death penalty remark. Keep it on point. Just say you think it is

1. A) against sound morals to kill a person who has never killed anyone.

2. B) a sin. Doesn't matter if you are religious are not.

Ask others to also call and email. Speak about the matter at church and etc, give the info out and say that the state should not be killing those who have never killed anyone. The law of parties needs to end. Classmates and etc. It doesn't matter your age. Try to get 5 people to call and email. Next-An idea I have, hopefully can gain enough help to wage a proper campaign here in Texas. I got a several point plan about ways to gain attention to my case here. The mailings, billboards, media ads and etc. Sitting on my ass doing nothing. That I cannot do. That is just horrible and depressing for me. Fighting? That I can do! Fighting for my life. Yeah, I can do that all day. It is crazy. Hours ago I was so depressed. Then I get a letter saying they will leave it up to court. ie, fight on it. It is like new life has surged through me. Now glad that things are moving along. Everyone is going to discuss filing dates. So then I will have a time line. Trying to get some other things sorted will post about it. Alrighty got to go.

Clinton Young #999447

Loud & Clear Topic: follow up.

I wanted to farther explain my previous blog while the emotional rollercoaster I experience shined through. My words about lawyers did not fully detail enough to give the proper image.

Since I have been here. Well, since I was first dealing with the judicial system really. My experiences have not been the best with lawyers. As a juvenile, my lawyer made no real effort to fight for me. Just explained the motions we would go through. Never asked me if I was innocent to some of the charges. He only told me that if I didn't accept a plea deal, I could face 10 years! His words scared me into pleading guilty to a couple crimes I did not do. Then I get this case. My first appeal lawyers really messed me over. One refusing to explore my claims, as they would have reflected badly on the prosecutor and trial lawyers. The other let a woman smoke crack and file all false claims in my appeal. Which resulted in my having no appeal basically. The court refused to give me an out over it. I was held to bear that cross. Then again, lawyers that actually plotted to keep me from doing something with some highly qualified investigators. They delayed and played phone tag, until the one-year deadline to file my appeal. What ended up happening was a dear friend lost the $10,000 she had paid the investigators. As my lawyers got them to look at some dumb shit. I could have won at trial or at least won in 2007. Versus being here still fighting in 2017! Another 10 years of life gone, all because of lawyers. Then here I am at this extremely vital point. I have lawyers that one of which I have known since 2007. Which I have documented in blogs how close I with her. That I was treated like a friend versus purely a client. Had a rocky relationship with another lawyer. Which came to a head last year, with a couple of very heated arguments. One of which I hung up on her. (can have legal phone calls.) After the last argument. It was like everything cleared up and we then got along better than ever. Now what fueled that fight was my feeling lied to. I was given the impression that filings would be pushed. It wasn't done when thought would. Nor was there a plan to. They wanted to do what most lawyers do. Wait. Which is what I want the least to do! As waiting just means staying more in this god forsaken place. When I went off about it, the lawyer I was closest with. It seemed she was trying to avoid me. Which in all honesty it is easy for me to point at that and yell, "BAD!".

Though I understand. She is scared that I will get executed. Being aggressive in a state that she has seen do things that made her jaw drop in shock. That in 1.9 years prior she had never seen in a court room. It un-nerves a person. So to them the wait means being alive. Also, I readily admit that my approach can be a bit too aggressive. Okay fast forward. Had a visit a month ago with lawyer. One that I had argued with. After our fall out. As I wrote it was like a cloud lifted from our interactions. We got along way better than ever before! Really enjoyed our interaction with each other. She is super smart. I got a decent brain also. We make a great team. Plus, I have more say in my case than any other client they have. It is very rare for any client to have the voice I do in my case. One of my biggest honor badges is that they have come to trust me and respect me and my mind. As I wrote, we work as a team on equal footing. When I last seen my lawyer, felt we was on great ground and that she was going to push the issue. In doing so thought would be speaking with her again soon and or get a letter from her. As days became weeks. I thought "here we go again!" Doubt creeped in and I felt like it would be more of the same hurry up and wait bullshit. It all hit me, along with some other personal matters, when I wrote the last biog. Then a few hours later I get a letter detailing how she had been doing all she said she would. She just didn't tell me sooner. I am sure her thinking was that since all is good with us now, that I would have faith in her. One of the downsides of everyone seeing me as strongest person they know. It is often thought 'he will be okay.' It is hard to fight the courts and prosecutors. Having to fight lawyers and people I know. It becomes overwhelming. Though as I said, I am getting along great with them now. I overreacted. Surer while my experiences would make it that none would blame me. I shouldn't all that did me wrong in front of everyone else. It isn't fair. Though when in a relationship with anyone. Each person brings their past to the table. It has to be shifted through, so as to see each other properly and the relationship can prosper. No matter the type of relationship it is. A bit of understanding goes a long way. As for me personally. I fight to win. Not going to stop fighting until I win. Really wish I could take that blog back. It is very rare that anyone beyond my baby sister or a woman that I am really close to, get to see such raw emotions or thoughts from me. My strength comes from past pain. The adversity I have been through. It is why I developed the saying." Use the pain to fuel the fire that burns- inside of you." We all worry, get scared, have doubt, and etc. What matters is how you deal with it. The saying, it doesn't matter that you get knocked down 9 times, as long as you get back up 10. It is very true. Also, I hate being defined by this place. I always tell people do not call me a death row inmate. I am a man on death row. Beyond the case struggles, over the 8 months or so. A topic about myself and this place have developed. Which took an emotional toll on me. Several projects I was wanting to get done didn't get completed. Let me be clear the projects are pertaining to my songs. It is not due to lack of effort by Alex, Meike, and Jorunn have tried. Want to make sure that my words are not seen as reflecting those that lead my campaign. Anyways. this is a complicated situation that is not easy for anyone involved. In some ways I make things harder for me. As I worry about everything. I attempt to fight every battle. Like in here have had to deal with some issues. Becoming even more frustrated because of so few, that actually will stand up against this system. Shame really. You all will see/have seen one of the use of force videos where I am all bloody in the film. I have chronicled many of the efforts we have taken here to protest the system. A way to disrupt and resist. Guess it can kind of be seen as like the monks that would set themself on fire. As that pepper spray felt like fire. :) The paintball gun shoots a special kind of ball that has CS powder in it. Cs powder burns and eats up oxygen making it harder to breath. The same as the smoke grenades. Two weeks after that use of force, I made -them run in on me again after the stitches was removed. As wanted to make sure they understand, while they broke my nose, they didn't break Clinton Young! Alrighty then. Gonna wrap this one up. To all that step up and help. Thanks! Its needed and I am grateful for all Also with all I worry about, it is why I stress so much about my mail. So when writing me PLEASE follow the steps I outlined. As I want to make sure is no problems or hang ups in my getting it. I understand life moves fast out there. I get it, the ease some things. Just please take that one extra moment to make sure all is done right. As otherwise I risk not getting your words and that causes delays, doubts on both end and etc. Thanks

In solidarity,

Veni vidi vici

Clinton YOUNG #999447

Polunsky Unit

3872 FM 350 south

Livingston TX 77351

USA

Loud & Clear, May 1, 2017

Topic: Thank you.

It seems the film was properly received. Glad to know. There is still so much to be detailed. Plus, there is currently some activity in my case. Lawyers do not want me detailing it all yet.

This blog will be short. Though will write another one soon. I really just wanted to send a thanks to all that watched and shared the film. During the course of last week. I also found out that two of my poems was indeed made into a song. I did not know the band had done this. One of the poems, it was important to me that a Dutch band done it. As the poem "Final Flight" is about the MH-17 tragedy. Also, I found out that a rapper from Houston will be doing the three hip hop songs I wrote. Which is really good as I specifically asked for this rapper to do it. I had just wrote a blog where I expressed frustrations about not getting the songs done. Then within two days I get word about the songs getting done. :) My blog had not yet been received. See, this is a great example of how the frustration and stress of not knowing what is going on and or having to wait on mail. It adds up. It is why I stress communication so much with people and encourage those that write to me, please write the address exactly as I ask. If sending a jpay to make sure to send your name, letter ID number, and date to Alex letters@saveaninnocentlife.com. NO ONE will be able to see the letter. Don't send the actual letter, just this info. This is just so that I can get a list and know what I am missing if any. Please see portion of site dealing with my contact information. Had thought jmail would be good way to go, though others are expressing frustration with it here. So guess will have to stick with regular mail and jpay until something else is sorted. Just please keep in mind I do not have access to a computer, phone, or such. While you all have everything in an instant almost. It is a far slower pace for me. Which is a source of never ending frustration for me. :) ha Enough of that. Again, I thank all that have visited this site.

When it comes to my writings. I like knowing what a person thinks about them. Guess the same way a painter would with art. When I write something and get zero comments from it. My thinking is 'to hell with it then.' I will be writing more book reviews, music reviews, death row blogs and the Loki & Mr. Pig story. Disappointed in myself for slacking. As mentioned before, just had so many frustrations pile up. Two of my friends that read my autobiography, they keep telling me I need to finish it and get the book published. I might. Not sure exactly yet. Or I might just get a newsletter type thing set up on my site and have it forwarded to people that help. Which is what I have thought of doing with my blogs. The people that write and help. It really is like wind in my sails. It might be soon that I need people more than ever.

Thanks again,

I remain,

In solidarity,

Veni Vidi Vici

Clinton Young #999447

Polunsky Unit

3872 FM 350 South

Livingston, Texas 77351

USA

Loud & Clear, May 2, 2017

Topic: My pending execution

Well, shit just got serious. Spoke to my lawyers today. The prosecutors filed for an execution date. This has been known that they would for over 2 weeks, was hopeful to avoid it. They tried with talking. The real catch is the head prosecutor only sought it as the appeals court sent a letter to them asking for a status update. Which being that I had no appeals, it is not the judicial branche's place to do such! Such would be from executive branch such as the governor's office or the legislative branch such as senate or house in Texas. If no appeals are due, then a court shouldn't worry about it. It is purely up to the Prosecutor. The impression we had was that would not have to worry about this from the other prosecutor. Hell, even the former head prosecutor that was a part of my trial, she did not even seek a date of execution. Though the real jab to the stomach for me was finding out the judge that was over my appeals now. He was the same one that was a visiting judge and was over my appeals in 2010. Yeah, not good at all. I will find out the exact date in a week or two. I think will find out the 18th or 25th. Well one thing is for sure, my appeals will be filed faster. Though that can be done without a date. The judge does not have to sign for the date. The prosecutors are leaving it up to him. That's my impression. Though I certainly do not have high hopes, that he will avoid setting a date. Hopefully he does not. Just because I get a date, does not mean it is the end of the road. It is just my Lawyers and I did not really expect this prior to 2 weeks ago. I need help, I know that. All is greatly appreciated. I will be writing a great deal more blogs and etc. Airtight then. Got to do some thinking. One other thing. As someone mentioned to me about this. Page and etc. says that Doyle was alive in the trunk. That he was breathing and making noise. That is physically impossible. The forensic pathologist testified that the path of the bullets would have made him immediately unconscious. The third bullet had No blood pooled around it. Which means the heart was not beating. That is how they know that Doyle was dead before the third shot was fired. My expression of the 'hospital' was not about that Doyle was alive in the trunk of the car. It was about 'where do you take people when they are hurt'? I will get the pathologist testimony to post with autopsy report that shows this. The first shots crossed a path that would not recover from and would remain unconscious.

My thinking was, it's a bad situation. What do we do. It was not my first thought "hey lets go throw a person in a ditch'. Darnell mentioned security guard. Page said "he's already dead". Page knew the 'outside of town' area. I just want it to be clear that I was not sitting there ignoring the pleas of a dying man. Darnell said he heard a noise in the trunk. There was all kinds of tools and other items in the trunk while driving down a road. Page tries to make it seem like Doyle is still alive and that Mark the one that actually killed him. This is in a way self-serving to Page. Thanks again.

I remain,

In solidarity,

Veni vidi vici

Clinton YOUNG #999447

Loud & Clear, May 4, 2017

Topic: Ways to help

Hope that this finds all is good for all. With myself, just waiting to see what is up. Here is the deal. As I wrote in the last blog, they filed for a death warrant. Which is where the prosecutor files to a judge and asks him to sign an order telling TDCJ to kill me. They asked for no less then 91 days. Which is the law. They can ask for a specific date. Though they left it up to the judge. They seem to be on a angle of just leave everything up to the courts. Fuck it I live or die. Fuck prosecutors discretion. Just set a date for me to fucking die and let me roll the dice and see what comes of it. For some odd reason, that doesn't sit good with me. Look, I need help. I need donations to help with both the spreading of word about me in the USA and more importantly to help with investigative costs, experts, and legal fees. I know that not every person can do a large amount. If people can do just a set amount each month. It all helps. Also, to keep things organized. I am going to get a specific email and text list created. This way can issue call to actions basically. Instead of everyone doing random things. The idea is to get an organized list compiled. That a mass email/text can be sent out to people to do a specific action needed. Such as, 'sign a specific petition.' As I do not want anyone's effort wasted. Haha, I smiled at thinking about a name for the email. Being from Texas and the stereotypes of Texas and horses and cowboys. Haha yeah going to have the email as Saddle Up. Sure would have a strong emotional impact with some harsher name. Though might as well find some form of humor in this fucked up shit. Saddle Up is a play on what the cowboys/posse would do. Everyone would saddle up to ride towards a common task. :) Now to be clear here. I only rode one horse in my life. It had no saddle, I had been drinking. The louder I yelled, faster it ran! Mind you, I did yell in the most manly way! (PS. After writing this and giving it a thought... it is better to have a more serious title. So will not be saddle up. It will be action(@saveaninnocentlife.com). More info to follow.

Oh yeah. Can not recall if I wrote this in last blog. Though my lawyers was trying to get the notes from the prosecutors that worked my case from east Texas. They have had them all this time. We asked for them. All of a sudden they have thrown away the entire file. So the entire file on my case for the Doyle Douglas murder, in the area it happened. They threw it away! Gone.

When I got proof to show a detective threw away other evidence before my trial. When other stuff came to the surface all of a sudden what would have shown even more the deception by prosecutors and etc. they threw it all away. I am supposed to see this and accept this as some random fucking accident? All of a sudden huh. Look there is some stuff that has yet to be publicly discussed. Jessica could make another 90 minute film with all of it. Now, the judge does not have to sign the warrant. Lawyers will be fighting to prevent it. With this judge, I do not have high hopes. The date could be 91 days from when he signs it or 12 months away. Which is highly unlikely to be that far. To those that know me and feel some form of attachment to me. If you want to walk away, due to thinking that you can not handle it. Do so now. I understand how hard this shit is. It will be harder in many ways for those that care about me, then myself. As I been here for years. Plus most of my life has been full of turmoil. Do not wait until a few weeks before I am due to die and then all of a sudden wake up and realize this shit is real and you can not handle it. This shit is serious. Motherfuckers are about to attempt to kill me. For some shit that they can not even say for sure what happened. If you are going to stay. Then stay locked in and ready to go. Don't hesitate. Don't sit down and cry, because that shit doesn't accomplish anything.

The only way to victory is to keep fighting Forward! We came, we saw how fucked up it all is. There is only one thing left to do. WIN. Veni, Vidi, motherfucking Vici! You got to look at the situation and say what it is. You got to look at it and say," That is fucked up!" It should make anyone mad. You hold on to the anger and you fight. If you cannot handle it and want to walk away. I will not be upset. There is people that have grown to care about me. I don't want people, more people, getting hurt. Though here is the thing when you walk away. When you give up. Later on the questions rise of "what if I done more?" Doubt is a evil fucker! At least for me it is. If there is ONE good thing that anyone can ever say about me. Those that know me. "There's no give up in me." I give up, it is suicide. These motherfuckers are going to have to kill me. I do not want to make it easy for them. I damn sure do not want them to win! So I need help. Not everyone can do everything. Though everyone can do something. For those that want to donate the account information is

The Clinton Young Foundation

IBAN: NL66 INGB 0006 5173 29

There is links and such on this site: http://www.saveaninnocentlife.com/donation-corner/

Please share the link. I am also getting some songs made. I went to get these done by a very good artist from Houston who agreed to do it. I informed him would pay for it. He is a locally known artist. Though he is talented. For lawyer to do work needed for all that and him to do songs. It will only cost $2K for 3 songs that I wrote to be produced. The songs are good as they can be used to also raise funds and is a non-controversial way for people to spread word about me and raise attention. The goal to have many ways to reach people. If you want to help, you can donate for the songs via PayPal, using PaypalUSA@saveaninnocentlife.com. Everyone loves music! Other songs are being done by other artists. I am going to get more campaign gear, such as window stickers for cars and etc, ads, billboards, shirts and etc. for here in US. This way people can help advertise my site in different forms. The more numbers we have the stronger we are, then the easier it is to accomplish things. Not everyone that gets an execution date is executed. Many that have gotten off death row, first had such dates. Though the more I have the better my chances of winning are. I need peoples help. Until next time. I remain,

In solidarity

Clinton YOUNG #999447

Loud & Clear: May 16, 2017

Topic: Death Warrant

PLEASE SHARE THIS BLOG

Now, I want to make clear something. At times people have an emotional reaction to something and they lash out and make comments that can be deemed as negative. Do not do such. Use the emotion towards a positive, legal, and productive manner. I have previously detailed about the action@saveaninnocentlife.com email list. Alex has been in Vegas, so not sure if he has gotten it done yet. Though I encourage everyone to share this blog then join the listing. Actually, Alex might post a message here with this blog about an app or some other form of alert type system. I been locked up-for 16 years. There is computer stuff I do not know. So if Alex adds a Post Script message, that is a better way than the action@... idea. Please follow it. (Alex: At this moment, the Action@... idea is active. If you want to join, let me know!) I have expressed an idea about an app, so can get computer and mobile updates rapidly when needed. I myself will detail the specific ways to help, that maybe a person reading this can do. First things first. Here is motion for execution date. – link to motion will follow- -When I first read it, it was ... fuck I do not even know how to explain it. The language of the forms are not unique. It is just written so as to reflect my case. My lawyers filed a motion to oppose it. Plus request for additional testing.

Now things to help with. Again, thanks to all that donate to the Foundation. Donations can be sent to The Clinton Young Foundation NL 66 INGB 0006 5173 29 OR you can use the Crowdfunding page: http://fnd.us/clintonyoung?ref=sh_06cYF4

Now for ideas I have. As I detailed before. There are songs being made to help spread awareness. Just a different way to spread the word. There will be heavy metal, rock, and hip hop. 2 of the rock songs have been completed. I have an idea for an EDM track. Someone reading this blog knows or is a person that is considered one of the best from the Netherlands with big name recognition. Could you please see if him or her would work with me on the EDM idea? If said person does not want to interact with me directly. They can reach out to meike@saveaninnocentlife.com. Meike is one of my most trusted friends. She is from The Netherlands. Even if willing to interact with me directly, please also inform Meike so as to speed things up. I could have days only! :(

Next. Being that I have music being produced. I would like to know if anyone has a building/field/venue that can be donated for a day to host a Justice-music event concert. If you do, then please contact or have said person contact Meike. Again meike@saveaninnocentlife.com. Next. Anyone that has a high level of computer skills. No matter the specific field you are skilled in. Please contact Alex at alex@saveaninnocentlife.com Please provide him with your contact information and expressed intent to help as needed.

Next. Theater. I have long desired to work on a Play of some sort. If you are involved in theater, be it acting or directing. (Naturally, I prefer both) If you are willing to create a stage play with me. Then please contact Meike meike@saveaninnocentlife.com Next. Art/Museum. I have a desire to do an art exhibit. If you work at and or associated with any kind of museum and you are willing to explore this idea. Then please inform Renate at info@clintonyoungfoundation.com

Next. I would like to write articles about justice/death penalty issues. A non-controversial break down of the topics in a newspaper. It will be translated in Dutch. I would like it to be in The Netherlands largest newspaper, online and or print. If this is something you would be interested in reading in said paper. Then please email them about it and ask that they contact Renate at info@clintonyoungfoundation.com to inform her that the newspaper is willing to allow me to contribute such writings, once approved by their editor. Next. Anyone that is a lawyer no matter the type of profession. If you are a lawyer then please contact Merel at info@clintonyoungfoundation.com. Please contact her and express your interest in helping where needed. Next- Anyone that is associated with the media. Be it music media, or whatever. Any form and you would like to do an article, be it about the role of music for us here on the row. As I can have a radio. Though no Mp3s. Just am/fm. Plus the creation of my own songs. Life style media, psychology, whatever. If you have an idea for a story and would be willing to allow me to participate in such story. Then please contact Renate at info@clintonyoungfoundation.com.

Next. Fashion. If you are involved in fashion/clothing/jewelry in any form. Please contact Merel at info@clintonyoungfoundation.com You might be sitting there curious, wondering how I could link with such. Trust me, the world has yet to see the extent of my creative mind. Just contact Merel at info@clintonyoungfoundation.com Next. Anyone that is an exotic dancer or hiphop dancer (women dancers) First, please contact me directly! ☺ ha Seriously though, please contact Meike at meike@saveaninnocentlife.com Why? I am going to need someone to perform the dance moves for the music video idea I have! Next. Anyone that is a part of a band. No matter the genre. If you are willing to do a song with me. Please contact Alex at alex@saveaninnocentlife.com. Just express to him your desire to work on a song with me and the genre of music you are a part of. I have outlined the many different areas that I need help in. If you are affiliated with these various subjects. Then please reach out to the friends of mine. Once they have compiled a list of those willing to help. Then they will inform me. I will have my ideas outlined and forwarded to each person. Once this happens, if you have no desire to help/ be involved. Then cool. Just please give me a chance to be heard and to express my ideas to you. Of course anyone can write to me directly. It is just easier when my friends have such information, so as to properly coordinate. Also to make sure each person is who they say they are. I might have 90+ days left. Not exactly dealing with time to waste! If you are from Norway and are associated with any of these areas I list. Then please contact Jorunn at jorunn@saveaninnocentlife.com If you are from France and share a desire to assist in the listed areas. Please contact Camille at Camille@saveaninnocentlife.com. Anywhere else in the world, contact the listed people from the Netherlands in the specific areas detailed. Merel, Meike, Renate, Alex all communicate greatly in English. My sister will be working on other local matters with appropriate figures. In addition to this I want to detail that going forward, legal developments might happen at a much faster rate. Renate and Merel are the Legal Advisors for the Clinton Young Foundation. Both have worked on Death Penalty cases in the United States. Merel also interned at another law firm in New York City. These will be the 'only ones' who speak about the legal developments in my case. They will post the news and or speak with the media. This is to avoid any confusion. US Media or where needed Joaquina, the lawyer for the Clinton Young Foundation, will speak in connection with Renate and/or Merel. These are my most trusted people. People that I love. My time can be limited and I have no access to the Internet. Don't even have a TV, much less computers (I write on a typewriter the prison sells.) They make sure all is legit and then get with me. They are my eyes and ears and part of my voice. As I wrote, if you are associated with the specific areas I detailed. Please get with the appropriate person. Just give me a chance to be heard. If you do not like my idea, no harm—no foul. If you do, then we can work on something great together. I think all will be receptive of my ideas though. Again, beyond donating to the Foundation. If you are not associated with the listed areas. Then please help spread the word and also if you see a performer/band etc. that is supporting me. Please support them. For example the band (see http://clintonproject.com/rock-songs/) produced the song Loves Gone Missing and Final Flight, based on one of my poems. Show them your support. Download or advertise their music. Show your support in being a part of a community of people that believe in justice. In doing show you show others they do not have to be shy to get involved. Instead of buying a song from some mega commercial group, support the smaller artist that is willing to perform music they believe in. Call into radio stations and request their music. Help them as they help me. If you see a newspaper is willing to allow me to contribute writings to it. Then share that papers information with others. Encourage people to visit that newspapers site and respond to its ads, if this comes to be possible for me. So, for everyone reading this, there is a way for you to help. NO one is weak. All have a voice. No matter how you speak, you can be heard! Please help me be heard and reach out to my friends if you can in the listed areas. Thanks. And please share this blog.

Until next time.

In solidarity

Veni Vidi Vici

Clinton YOUNG #999447

Polunsky Unit

3872 FM 350 south

Livingston TX 77351

USA

Posted at Saveaninnocentlife.com Please Share.

Texas Department of Criminal Justice
Correctional Institutions Division
Notification of Execution Date

Date of Notification: __June 7th, 2017__

Offender Name: __Young, Clinton__   TDCJ #: __999447__

The Office of the Texas Attorney General has notified this agency by order of the Court, your execution date has been set for after the hour of 6:00 p.m. on __October 26th, 2017__. *Can we talk about this?*
The following information will be requested from you two weeks prior to the scheduled execution. A current copy of your Visitors List has also been included, review it and make changes as necessary. Changes to your approved Visitors List will not be made within 24 hours of the execution.

1. Attorney Name, Address, and Telephone Number: *Whoever O.J had, the first time!*

2. Spiritual Advisor: *See below* (If they wish to witness your execution they do not need to be on your Visitors List).

3. If executed, it is my request that disposition of my remains be handled by: *7 Dwarfs*
   Relationship/Address: *No kin / Where Snow White camped out.*
   Telephone number: *1-800-Bring-me-back*
   I would like my remains to be donated to the Texas State Anatomical Board for medical education and research. ☐ YES ☐ NO

4. I would like for _____ to pick up my personal property.
   The property will be picked up from the _____ Unit.

5. I have $_____ in my Trust Fund Account. I would like my money to go to: _____

6. Contact staff if you request the preparation of a Last Will and Testament. If you have less than $500, State Counsel for Offenders shall assist you with this request. However, if you have more than $500, you should arrange to hire a personal attorney. *So if I have $501.00 & the attorney cost me $500 & the money order cost 1.29, I die in debt. Take that government!*

Witnesses to the Execution (include addresses)

1. *Jesus - Damn Homie, can't get to be rich? I told you!*
2. *Muhammad - Do I pick the 72 Virgins or you? Hotster!*
3. *Buddha - So much for "get what you put in" Huh?*
4. *Clinton Young from 2018 - God damn, the Dwarfs done it!*
5. *Kendall Jenner - Can a dying man get a final wish? ;)*
*6. *A Deaf, Blind, & dumb dancing Monkey.* — Spiritual Advisor

Clothing Size
Pant Size: *¥ ?*   Shirt Size: *¥ ?*   Shoe Size: *10½ 3E*
**How the hell I know, I been locked up for 16 years!*

Execution Procedure *IS supposed to be date Form went into effect. Duh - Typo!*
Form I (October 2014) *What Year is 2014? Aw man. 20+1+4+1 = Oct. 26th. ;)*

Loud & Clear, May 18, 2017

Topic: Blogs, case, help

First to those I have recently written to I know in The Netherlands, 'Greetings' is used last in a letter. I start letter with it as such is common in the US. Now to business. My past blogs and legal papers are momentarily being taken down. This is because over the years people have had access to the previous web sites I had. Some have out of spite removed certain things. I can not be sure that everything is properly reflective of the facts as I have detailed them. My case will be coming under greater scrutiny. I want to make sure everything that is presented as being my voice is true and correct. A simple missing "NOT" can change the whole tone of a blog and etc. I have always greatly valued those that put faith in me. I need to make sure all my ABCs line up with the 123s. I will continue to blog and fully encourage others to share the future blogs. After I sort through all, then old blogs and etc. will be brought up again. My plan is to also get the legal filings put in proper order. My old blogs are going to be printed off and mailed to me. In a blog to he posted after this, or reposted. I detail the ways to help right now. More details will he presented as needed. I got many plans. With current and existing funds the 3 hip hop songs are being produced. Fund raiser tools in various forms will be developed in the coming days. T-shirts, more window stickers, unique advertisement ideas, and etc. I will not detail all my plans openly right now, though as the weeks tick by. People will see the way their help has been used. Got lots of ideas. Been gearing up for this moment for 15+ years. Throughout the years, every time I have detailed what is needed. It turned out as I said would. The ballistic reports and etc. I thank everyone for their help. There are many parts of case that have never been publicly revealed yet. As lawyers want it filed in court first. Please stick with me and have faith in me. The fight goes on.

Until next time.

Veni Vidi Vici

Clinton YOUNG #999447

Loud & Clear, May 22, 2017

Topic: A bit of this & that

There are people that express ideas' pertaining to petitions.' Here is the deal. Overall petitions do not work. The 100K signatures was an Obama thing. Some have read about it, for the White House. The President of the US cannot tell a state what to do. There are limits to his power. The USA-system is very complex. Sadly, many in the USA do not even properly know it. There can be some success for specific type of petitions. Though it is not needed right now. For example: an overall petition. With say 3 million signatures, having people around the world sign it. The governor of Texas would not even blink at it. I got some plans. Just need people to stand with me, stay tuned in, and express a willingness to help where can. PLEASE, by all means. I 100% encourage everyone to forward their ideas. No idea is stupid. Though there has to be a time and place for all, or else we will be entrenched in chaos. For example, with 5,000 people trying 5,000 different things. It becomes a real mess. I will outline ways I need help. Who to contact. Just please contact the person I list. They can make a contact sheet with a who's who in the areas we need. This way we can accomplish the most with the least amount of effort. Everyone has a strength and something to offer. No matter the age, education, or place. When it comes to raising funds. Jorunn, Renate, and Merel be the only ones. Jorunn has in Norway. Renate and Merel Pontier are over funds for the Foundation. If there are events then a person will be publicly named as to who will be at the fund raiser. It is important that those that help me know who's who and that no one 'acts' like they are helping me. Alex and Camille was also able to. Though I wanted to shrink the number of people, so as to make sure all stays smooth. A smaller group of people means a more controlled setting basically. Alex did express about help for the songs per my request. Though from this point forward. Will only be as said. Jorunn, Renate and Merel. Now to other matters I need help with. I have a poem titled Arabian Lovers. Being that Ramadan is soon to begin and I observe it here. (doing so out of solidarity with a woman that is a friend of mine. She is Islamic. I am not.) I have detailed before why this poem meant so much to me. So I want it as a song. I received a wonderful letter from a woman there in The Netherlands. She translated this poem into Dutch. Reading her letter got my creative gears turning. I need help! I need a woman of Middle eastern or North African ethnicity. Prefer a woman of Arabic ethnicity. Though naturally doesn't have to be! Can be Persian, Moroccan, etc. I want the poem to be turned into a song. I want the first parts in English, last portion Arabic or which ever. With the music being traditional to your ethnicity. Example, basically if your Syrian. Want first parts in English, last portion in your mother tongue, and with the music being traditional Syrian music. Has to be a woman that can sing with the passion this poem requires. More so since it is about the plight that sadly many women endure. If there is a well-known singer that can do it. Great! If you are a single mother that works at McDonalds but has a beautiful voice and can sing it as I ask. Then wonderful, the world will get to hear your beautiful voice! I just need it done NOW. So if you are willing to do it or know someone. Then PLEASE have contact or have contacts Alex at alex@saveaninnocentlife.com If due to traditional paths prefer to contact a woman. Then contact Merel at info@clintonyoungfoundation.com This way her or him can communicate with you, making sure all is as needed. Also I recently wrote a new poem. A Dutch Rose. It is more than a poem though. It's a new saying. I detail in the poem, can see in the poem section of my website. Now I could have wrote it with maybe some greater word structure here and there. Though what people should notice from my poems. Not only what I write/hut how I write it. Life is not perfectly aligned. It is full of ups and downs. My poems are more then the words they are detailed with. Just as an artist uses different medias to draw/paint/color a picture. The way that I write the poem. It is why I will at times explain what I write and why. This is so that the reader can get a glimpse of the world through my eyes. I am confined within these walls. So having a person see it as I meant for it to be seen and read. Then it is a way to make sure my creation is seen as I meant for it to be. In a way to have control over my life in the limited ways I can. As I am placed in a situation where I am meant to have no control or power. To those that have written me and have done so as I requested with the address. The 447, young, DR in red ink. Rest in blue or black. With this being unique to only me. It surely helps prevent error. Helps to ease my mind, as it is an extra step to avoid mishaps with my mail. Mail is my lifeline to the world. With Jpays. The most problems seem to be from the weekends. I guess the most logical solution to that problem is for people to only send me jpays Monday through Thursday. The mailroom is not here Saturday and Sunday. So, they print them off on Monday. Others also seem to have problems with such days, on the weekends. Alrighty then. Again, just please stay tuned. Encourage others to follow my blogs, so that as I detail the areas of help I need. People can help. Please visit my site daily.

My lawyers are working on my new appeals. I think the world is going to be really interested in what is contained within it. Much I have never written about, for obvious reasons. If I do not get an execution date this week. Then my appeal will be filed in about two months. If I do, it will depend on how long away the date is. I thank all again who have donated and or reached out to the listed people and expressed interest in helping. I am thanking people in advance, as I have not yet been told the list of people if any. If I do get a date, I am going to write a different type of blog beyond my loud and clears. Alrighty then. Will write again in a day or two.

Until next time.

In solidarity

Veni Vidi Vici

Clinton YOUNG #999447

D.R-Polunsky

3872 FM 350 South

Livingston TX 77351

U.S.A.

Loud & Clear, June 17, 2017

Topic: Life & death watch

People often ask me what I would do if able to get out of here. I normally cite the little things I would do. Though to top of the major events. It would surely be to go to The Netherlands. I would have to! As I would need to go there so as to retrieve my pet Moo Cow! Yes indeed! What is a moo cow? People often ask me after failed google searches. It is a cow that goes Moo! Any cow can be a moo cow. Though not any cow can be MY pet moo cow! My pet Moo cow will specifically be a highland cow. After seeing a picture of such, I fell in love with this magnificent beast! It has all this hair. Sadly, in most pictures the hair is messy. Mine would not be victim of such. What makes it so great? It has hair on its head. I could run my fingers through its hair and pat it on the head while saying "That's a good moo cow!" It is not so huge that I could not put a leash on it. So, there I could be walking my neatly trimmed and brushed Moo Cow with a leash down Canal Street in Amsterdam, with me wearing nothing but cowboy boots, cowboy hat, and shorts while drinking a nice cold Budweiser. With Mr. Pig trotting behind me. Mr. Pig would have one of those cone shaped party hats on his head. I tell you, good times had by all!

People often are shocked by my pet choices. All this petist pet discrimination I personally do not appreciate! My moo cow is just as equal a pet as your stinky ass ferret or squawking parrot. Though some pets are more equal than others. None as equal as Mr. Pig of course. Now I want a hippo. This woman sent me a picture of her in South Africa giving this hippo some tea from a big bottle while kissing it. That is fucking amazing! I always thought hippos to be far too dangerous to have as such a pet. Though this means I could have a big swimming pool for the hippo and also to swim in. I could float around the pool laying on a float on a hot summer day, drinking an ice-cold Budweiser long neck. My hippo, which I would duly name Fat Ass, could swim up to me and open its mouth so I could pour it a drink of Budweiser also! How cool would that be!? It is great! These people, from South Africa also had pet cheetahs. Which are the fastest land animals. Can it be trained to go fetch a fresh beer? Hm, I must explore this idea more, so long as Mr. Pig has no obvious objections!

I got many adventures to go on. Though it seems that the Midland prosecutor wanted to send me on an adventure of her own making. She was insistent on setting an execution date. The judge thought about it for almost a couple weeks. I guess after whatever, he decided to go ahead with it. He did give us some additional testing, against the protest of the prosecutor. Her whole angle seems to be that I was convicted by a jury, so just kill me. Never mind all the facts that show I was robbed of any chance to have a fair trial by the prosecutors and police. Nor did I have any kind of fair proper appeals in state court. The fight is not over with yet. I spoke to several lawyers last week. Will talk to others this coming week. All the lawyers have worked on my case /currently do so. These aren't new lawyers, to explain. While I thought testing would be done this month. Due to some other developments, it will be mid-July before testing is done. I wish that I could detail what all is going on. However, I can not. It is not due to concern for the prosecutors knowing. As they know. It is due to a couple that read my blogs. Believe me, there are some people hoping that I am executed! As things develop, those that need to know will know. When appeal is filed, then it will be posted.

As for how I feel. When I first heard about the date being set. I worried about Jessi and other people in my life. That it would be hard for them. I been here for 14+ years now. In April of 2003, when I stood before that judge and he told me that he was sentencing me to death. I took that very serious. (The judge does it based on jury's recommendation, based on how they answer three questions in Texas.) The only time this whole situation really got to me, was when I was convicted. I was devastated then. As I was 19 years old and a jury told me I would be either spending life in prison or getting executed for something I did not do. The next day I walked into the courtroom. Everyone kept looking at me, to see what I guess my reaction was. I was laughing and telling jokes. What was done was done. I have an execution date. Okay, that is done. I am not going to sit down and cry about it every day. That would be a pointless venture. I only worry about people not doing the things I need done. As I know if everything is done as I need it to be, then I can win.

After the May 25th hearing. I got to sit down and have a long talk with my lawyers. Most times we only talked during a limited time. This time though we got to sit down for a couple hours without my feeling pressure from the clock. I was able to explain some of my ideas and positions on a few matters. Many things are happening very fast. Legal front, personal front. At times some matters have gotten crossed up. Trying to make sure things do not tangle up. I am very grateful that people are positive about my ideas and working towards making them a reality. Music is developing as planned. So good things are happening. I really need someone that works at an art gallery or something of the sort. There is an art exhibit idea I have. I do not want to simply display art for people that already want to help me. I want to be able to reach a new crowd of people.

Now to make some things clear. The reason the crowdfunding for the song was posted about. (Songs have been paid for) I wanted the song paid for with funds from the foundation. As the songs will be used for fundraising, just as t-shirts would and etc. Renate and Merel did not feel comfortable with it. Which aggravated me to no end. Though I understand their line of thinking. They both have integrity which is why they are over the foundation funds. If I thought otherwise, then they damn sure would not be responsible for such. Though I also know that people have donated funds there for campaign related matters, and also even for me to use for commissary items. To avoid confusion that is why I posted on my site for people to send funds for commissary to my inmate trust fund account via ecommdirect.com or jpay.com, Which I prefer the ecommdirect.com transfer funds option, as it is cheaper. I just generally am not a fan of jpay. Anyways. I was sitting here pondering this problem. I am all about finding solutions. I remembered something from the printout of some donations that was made. Renate sent me a couple pages. I noticed something with the donations. A Dutch word "Omschrijving" and then sometimes Dutch words like; "Ik hoop dat het niet te laat is voor Clinton". Other times the words were English 'pray for him.' BAM! Solution. When donating a person can put "legal defense only". Or "defense and campaigning funds". This way in the future if something comes up. Like for example wanting to order a bundle of t-shirts for an event, Merel or Renate can search through the donations and have a better idea of the budget available for such a matter. Helps to avoid any confusion and keeps things moving faster as days are a bit precious lately.

    I am currently housed in the death watch section. It is A-pod A section. A bit of irony. When I first got to death row I was housed in A-pod 3 cell. This section I am currently in R cell. Every time I go to rec. or visit, I have to walk past 3 cell. The symbolic nature of it is not lost on me. When I first arrived to death row. Death watch was housed in F-section on this Pod. Though after Richard Cartwrights execution. Due to all the attention to his blogs and those that wrote with him. It was highlighted about how Death Watch people could watch someone being loaded in the van, to be transported to be execution. They also would hang on the windows with cups and etc as form of solidarity. As a result of this, death watch was moved to A. section across the pod. When I got this date, the pod I was on C. pod. I could look out the window and see A pod A section and B section. So I could See the death watch section. I would often look to see what all cells was open over here. I could tell by what cell lights was on at nighttime. Now I look out the window and when looking to the right I can see C. pod E section Windows. Which is where I was when I got news of the date. The pods are separated by 20 feet. There is grass in the area between the pods. Like a green moat. Such a short space, though a world of difference. It feels weird having looked from that way to this way. Now I am looking from this way to that way. All the death watch cells have cameras IN the cell. This came about due to Mike Johnson killing himself before his execution. The cameras are badass! Infrared, regular camera/ lowlight night vision camera. We are not supposed to cover them up no matter WHAT we are doing. There is a monitor in A pod control picket, so that the officer can pick a cell and zoom in and all that or watch all 14 cells at once. Also, they can see other cameras around the unit. Though they are supposed to stay on this section cameras only. 12 building control picket has the same thing but multiple monitors. Also every ranks office. So at any given time, could be 20 people watching me in this, cell no matter WHAT I am doing. Does that make me a porn star?! ☺ hahahaha! The ranks have said that we can masturbate (well thank you for the permission!) so long as we do not do it while looking at the camera... I am serious! This shit can not be made up! If the guy does it while looking at the camera, he can get a disciplinary case, which means that someone else would have to be watching the camera at that actual time. So, they can look at me with camera and watch me. But if I look at the camera, the same one I am being looked at with, I get wrote up!? I kind of can't help but feel that steps into some range of sexual abuse type area. Now I get the idea behind it and while many in prison have lost their sense of humanity. I haven't, so I have no desire to stare at an inmate object with the thought that someone might possibly be watching. It might be the wrong thing. That is not my kind of kick! Though it just shows the absurd nature of this place. The last 7 days or 3 days I forget. They have to watch only the cell of the guy about to be executed. Every 15 minutes, ANYTHING a guy is doing has to he written down in a log. The next morning the higher ranks look over everything to make sure all is legit and correct. A guy kills himself, people get fired. Multiple people check in throughout the days. They want to keep us alive so they can kill us. So, the logs could literally read like this. NO BULLSHIT!

6 pm: pacing cell floor

6:15 pm: eating

6:30 pm: using restroom

6:45pm: sitting on bunk

7pm: looking at magazine

7:15pm: masturbating

7:30pm: washing off

On and on. Also, I can only rec in this area. This is also the area where they do the tours. Politicians, prosecutors, and etc from here and other areas of the country can come and tour death row. Being on death watch I get to be a main attraction now! Anyways. As for how I feel. Frustrated really. As the date was not needed. It could have been waited on. It is hurting people that care about me more than it does me. I thank everyone that is helping out in any way they can. Also, thanks to everyone that writes my name, number and address as I detailed. Helps make sure there are no problems with my getting your mail. Under Write Clinton. I believe it details exactly have to write my information. This is important as undelivered mail gets destroyed by US postal service after 10 days if they do not return it to anyone. Alrighty then. I am going to wrap this one up. Shall return soon. Until next time. Take care, smile, & strive for all that you desire. Use the pain to fuel the fire.

Veni Vidi Vici

I remain.

In solidarity

Clinton YOUNG #999447

Polunsky Unit

3872 FM 350 south

Livingston TX 77351

USA

Loud & Clear, July 15, 2017

Title: Red October

It seems that they are determined to take out a white guy in October! I was telling people how I did not really have anyone to truly associate with on death watch. Then they moved a friend of mine, Robert Pruett over here. The ironic thing is prior to my getting a date. It was known the state was planning to set him one. I was hopeful to get moved to A pod so could at least be on the same pod. Then, I ended up with an actual date before him. I made a joke when I found out. "Guess we will be on a pod together after all." Now Shore has shown up, his data also being in October. I barely know him though. Robert and I joke about when we will get stays. Him October 11th and me Oct. 25th. A day before our dates. This way can get all the visits. Plus, 14 days before the execution date, a person can make their final spend. Normally, we can spend 95$ every two weeks on average for commissary. Though final spend is 150$. It used to be more. At one point they would let you spend as much as you wanted to. I learned that Shore had a date for October also. They are trying to make sure they get a white guy in October! What stood out before Shore got over here. There were 2 white guys, 2 black guys, and 2 Hispanics. I do not think that to be by accident. I can see them doing it as a way to keep from stacking the numbers one way or another and avoid additional racism accusations.

When the prosecutor was trying to get my date set. They asked for at least 91 days, but the attorney general told them the next available date is Oct. 26th. As Robert's was already pending for the 12th. But then here comes Shore for the 18th. Relieve me, them white folks in Austin aren't stupid. There is a method to it. Anyways. Next issue. Look, I am getting really tired of all the depressive shit over the date. I know when my date is. I do not need a reminder. At this point it is not a serious threat. It isn't, as I still have testing being done and etc. My point is the data is real. Yes. However, the testing can change things. If the prosecutor still wants this to be the case, she fights. Then things will be a bit more serious. I thought the testing will be done July 12th for some reason, but my lawyers said no. It will be end of July beginning of August/ as the prosecutors wanted to do another test with something. I could write about it, but not going to. Will discuss it with some media and blog about it. Just right now I am not going to detail it. Time and place. These people are trying to kill me. It's like a high stakes chess game. One that I aim to win.

I seen a woman that is from the Eastham Unit. She is a parole officer. They see us for the board of pardon and parole. Many guys with a date refuse to see them. As they rarely ever grant clemency. She went over all the records from trial. We spent about 20 good minutes talking about everything. I noticed a couple things. One was when I would start going into more detail on some things, she would move on. I let her control the flow. After she got done. I told her, "you don't mind, I would like to comment on one thing." She said okay and asked what it was. My response was, "I noticed the one question you did not ask me. That was you didn't ask what I would do if I was NOT executed." She was not expecting that. The obvious way she was not expecting it. It told me all I needed to know. Her report to the board will not be a Let Clinton Young live report. I have asked to speak to one of the actual board members. Which I have been told is a right. Shockingly no one really does it. I damn sure am. I want to live!

I went over the blogs that was on my site. They should be getting put back up by now. It has been a long time since going over them. What stood out was how someone that once helped me added some lines to some. I know my style of writing! I know what the hell I didn't write. I also noticed that many blogs was not up there. There was 84 blogs sent to me. There should have been about 120/130. Also, I noticed was that the pattern of blogs. The early one posted make me look so much more aggressive as some other blogs was not there. See this is why I wanted to go over everything. Will be getting legal papers put back up soon. I wanted to get that done before everyone started to write everyone. This way, all could be broken down. Though seems was a bit of what they call miscommunication.

People ask me how I feel. I feel good. I actually feel more relaxed than I have in a long time. When I first got the date, I was angry, had that back to the wall feeling. Which is good as I started to think better about everything. Thought up some different angles. It will all be detailed in August. Also, I will be soon posting who all I picked to witness the execution if it did come to that. Will post that in a week or so. I get to pick who visits, witness to the execution, and who I get to talk on the phone with that final day. The day of a person's execution here. It is the most organized and planned day in a person's life. The only unknown is the courts, if something is pending. If a person does not have anything pending in the courts. At 6pm the process of the execution begins, with a team escorting the person to the gurney. I do not plan to reach that point. As I have many good things in my case. When you are innocent such things develop.

To those that write me with jpay. Casey, Amelie, and etc. If you do not put your address, I cannot write you back. Please read the guidelines and etc. Ya know, I recently found out that Jpay supposedly in their contract agreement state that anything sent through jpay they have the rights to. If that is the case; words, pictures, and etc. They claim to own if sent through them. Jpay is owned by a police service agency Securus. If they sell goods and services to prison and police. What would stop them from selling information that can assist in profiling? Guess no one reads the fine print these days. People can look over terms of agreement portion and let me knout if that is true or not. On my song about Arabian lovers and one looking for someone to sing it. Look, writing me telling me you have friends that may do it. That takes too long. Get with Meike, let her know who, so she can get it done. Here's the slogan for the next 91 days. "Make it happen."

You know, I been really thinking about my idea to have a pet hippo. Them damn things get to be 8000 pounds! That would be a hell of a feed bill. These damn people set out to de-masculate me! AS they robbed me of my beard. :(They do it every year around a person's birthday, so as to take a picture. It is not needed. they just do it to harass us as they only take pictures once every five years for guys who do not have a beard. It is alright, as I am re-masculating! (FYI – I know the right words. I just say it how I want to.) Look, people have tried to get me to shave by choice. Aint happening! I had grew it out and then trimmed it down. There was male and female officers making comments after I shaved. Called me baby Young. The barber that I always have cut my hair and trim my beard. He said, "Damn homie, we done put so much work into it!" ☺ Ha. After it was shaved off, I looked in the mirror. I looked like I was 19! I was rubbing on my face trying to get it to grow faster! :) Ha.

As for camera in cell. There was only one time it really got on my nerves. This year I started out observing Ramadan, out of solidarity with a friend of mine. Though being that I hadn't heard from her. I kind of gave up on it. Though one night, I was asleep and they brought my tray after 10 pm. I woke up to get it and went back to sit on the bunk. A guy called my name, so frustrated I get up and go back to the door asking, "What's up man!?" He asked me to walk back to the bunk. So I am standing there / thinking what the fuck is this As I feel like 1 am being bothered. Back to the door I come asking, "what the fuck?" Turns out he could see the monitors reflection in the control picket windows. He noticed the movement when I got my tray. He told me that she had me on full screen. Normally the screen has all 14 cells on display. Which makes the displays small like 3inch by 3inch. Normally a person doesn't get full screen display until 7 days away from execution. When he told me she had me on full display. I looked at the picket and said "Yeah, it don't surprise me." Then went back to eating. As I was eating I thought about being watched and I got mad as fuck. I wanted to throw the tray at the damn camera. I was being watched as I slept and then ate. Long sigh. Anyways. I am going to wrap this one up. Will be back to writing more. I got to as I had been not doing anything but thinking about my case. Also court ruling in favor of us with social media! So that's good.

Veni Vidi Vici

I remain.

In solidarity

Clinton YOUNG #999447

Loud & Clear, August 20, 2017

Topic: Love

The world needs more Love! It seems like today civility has gone to the garbage heap. Everyone is so mad about everything. Half the time they do not even really know why the hell they are mad. They are just mad! People protesting this belief. Protesting that political group. Driving cars into people. Killing in the name of hate. Killing in the name of religion. Everyone just needs to chill out! The future does not seem bright. These terror groups that keep driving into groups of people and blowing things up. I doubt they even have a real goal about what they want. At least not a realistic one. Though to show that no matter the foreign policy of the country. They will still attack it. It is not an attack on imperialism or political thought. It is an attack on the way of life in the west. Spain withdrew the troops after the Madrid train bombings. Being that they are not in the middle east, why attack Spain? It just goes to show it is 100% about attacking the very way of life that westerners live. Attacks have taken place in Sweden, Finland, and etc. The reality is that there is no way they can win. At least not in the sense of bringing any of these western powers to their knees. It will farther divide the cultures. These attacks are not going to stop.

More so as long as funds continue to pour into countries that support it. Prisons in the US are, more often then not, laboratories of hate. The division amongst those locked up. It is something that the administrations desire. It allows them better control. In California all the prison gangs put aside their differences and united for common goals. These are groups that have slaughtered each other for pride and power, over the past 30/40 years. The violence didn't scare the system. As they can deal with violence. Buy stronger weapons. Build more solitary cells, pass tougher laws. Violence helps the system thrive, as they can tell the public. Look at these dangerous super criminals. We need more money, we need more prisons. Vote for me, I will keep you safe." No, what struck the system at its core is when they all united and in a peaceful way expressed a political desire. They won to a large degree. Unity was key. When it comes to love. People can always appreciate what is done from love. I have always seen hate as a weakness. People ask me if I hate my co-defendants. No, I do-not. They are not worth hating. A snake does what a snake does. Side step for a story that happened here. I was on the outside rec yard with another guy (as I have explained, the rec. yards are split, by bars. So no contact.) We made up a game by using a tight-rolled up sock, with some rice in it. Would throw it like a baseball. It would bounce off walls and such and the other person had to catch it. It would sometimes bounce outside of the rec. yard gate. I would then have to use a t-shirt to get it back. During a game there was a wasp walking around the rec. (Wasn't flying) I didn't want to step on it, so I started to try to blow it out of the way. I was trying to shoo it away.

Once it got out of the way, I went back to playing. The ball went out of the rec gate. I grabbed my shirt to get it and BAM! Felt a pressure then sting. It got me on a callous on my hand. I yelled out 'damn it' and then shook the wasp loose from- my shirt and got the ball back. The other guy said "See if you would have killed it when you had a chance, it wouldn't have stung ya!" I looked at him and said: "I'm not mad at it. It just done what a wasp does." The reality is that it only stung me as it felt under attack from me. That is the difference in some humans. They will needlessly hurt and or betray others. Sometimes they are worse than snakes. As a snake is just like a wasp. It's really why as children grow, there needs to be a greater social investment in them. As frustrations often transform into hate. Be it some anarchist, Islamic terrorist, skinhead neo-nazis, black militants, extreme Zionist radicals. Whoever it maybe. Now it is totally different to be proud of a person's heritage, religion, culture, ethnicity, nationality. We often find comfort in the traditions of our nations. 4th of July celebrations, Kingsday parties, Ramadan, Christmas, Chanukah, whatever. People can appreciate the events and dedications to these days and much more. Each nation, religion, culture has its days. A celebration of love is embraced by all. The problem is when people- want to force others to live then way another desires. There is an irrational fear that one will lose something. The big fights over marriage is a great example. In the US it was like half the country was about to have a damn heart attack that gays was wanting to get married. I get it that people have different ideas based on religion and etc. But really, whose fuckin business is it what the next person does? There were even laws about what two adults could do in their bedrooms. From the acts committed via anti-sodomy laws, to laws banning the sale of sex toys. I mean what the fuck is the government doing in people's bedrooms!? The same people that pushed that agenda wanted the government to stay out of churches and schools. That's the thing about giving the government power. It never stops where you-want it to. If a religious institution wants to celebrate certain marriages, okay that is their right. Not the government. If I start a church that only marries Mr. Pig to Ms. piggy. Okay, if you got a problem with the Church of Oink, get the hell out. I don't want any Pigist in my congregation anyways :) Ha! It was once that we could celebrate the exchange of various ideas and beliefs. Now it is as if even thought is under attack. People attack each other over race, religion, environment, economics. and etc. As time has gone by, we seemingly have gotten more divided. When 9/11 took place, the USA for a brief moment became a land of United Americans. It seems that was the tip of the hill because it has been downhill since then. (it has been said that no form of democracy has ever survived longer then 250 years. The USA is closing in on that year mark)

Humanity should not need disasters to stop and reflect. We shouldn't need to have a face for tragedy. Why can not intellect rule the day? How come Love can not be the force that propels us?

Coming into prison at such a young age. It would have been easy to sink farther into a spiral of hate. Many states ban pen pals. Florida and etc. have very strict rules. South Carolina does not even allow people to have online presence. (this really only serves to cover up abuses and promote isolation. Other states have different rules. Texas is not so strict. One thing about Texans, we do believe in the right to express. To have free speech. It's the very reason I can write these blogs as I do) The women that have written to me. They have helped me to come to truly appreciate that Love is control enough. The thing about having people in your life. You become responsible for them, accountable also. They help shape you. People that are well loved, respected, and apart of a social fabric. They do not generally lash out with violence and hate. They do not go into schools and shoot up kids. They do not drive cars into crowds of people freely expressing their ideas. They do not blow themself up. There just needs to be more love. While most modern rap is nothing but materialism and the sexual objectification of women. Which is why I do not like most new rap.

2pac was a genius with the pen. The violence that-consumed the later years of his life, has painted-his image to mainstream society. However, he truly was one the great poets of our time. People that have never read his works, He wrote many poems, essays, and songs. They might not appreciate his talented outlook. Though there was a philosophy that he expressed on his stomach through a tattoo. Many people have copied it, though fail to even know what it meant. 2Pac had THUG LIFE tattooed on his stomach. It stood for "The Hate U Give Little Infants Fucks Everyone." That is so true. Unloved children grow up to destroy the world around them.

As a society women must be our cornerstone and children our foundation. As a man there is that duty to be a pillar. I am a complex person. My life has been a very unique journey. It can be said that I have an aggressive personality. Growing up we did not really talk about emotions and such. Boys play hard, fight harder, and work hardest. Talking was more associated with women. In prison -violence was the form of communication. I have not always been a great person, great friend, great brother, great son. Though as I have grown up, I have strived to be a great man. To make those around me stronger. To use my intellect to guide others toward their own strength. I will leave the nature vs. nurture battle to more sophisticated folk. I know that in my life I have been given plenty of reasons to be evil. Though some part of me. Even as a child, I understood that people hurt others because they can. They attack what's weaker. Once, I was really upset and was walking across the yard. My dog at the time kept rubbing against me and messing with me. He was a golden retriever. I was 7 or 8 years old. I smacked him upside the head. He yelped and jumped back in surprise. (at the time, I was mad at my stepfather) When I done that, my dog looked at me like I was crazy a voice popped into my head that said, "you are no better than him." (him being my stepfather) That never left me. I understood then that it was only out of cowardice that bullies exist as they are. That experience is also why 'The

Art of Racing in the Rain' by Garth Stein is one of my favorite books. (Not saying my dog was talking to me!) I love animals. They just are who they are. Only thing that beats a good dog, is a great pig. As I wrote I am a complex individual. Even my quirky pet choices reflect that. Most people conform to some various pre-designed mold. They rarely carve their own path in life. When it comes to me, so often I have had people shake their head and say, "that's just how he is!" ☺ I am not easily defined. Though one thing about me. I always try to take each person as an individual. Which helps develop a better understanding of people overall.

I am trying to write a great amount as short as I can. As I know my blogs can be long windows. Bare with me. As I started this blog about Love. I will end it on such. By the time this is posted I will have less then 60 days of life left on this earth. Unless something changes. How do I want to leave it. Hopefully someone that has read my words, that had thoughts of hurting others. Hopefully they have came to understand the strength is in being able to protect the weak, not attack them. The strength is in Laver in all its forms in hate. You can be who you are without tearing others down. One of my other favorite books is by Paulo Cohelo. It is about Love, though in a more romantic sense. The love for another love of self. It is titled 11 minutes by Paulo Cohelo. I recently re-read 'The 5th Mountain.' Next week I am going to re-read '11 minutes.' I would have to say Paulo Cohelo is one of my favorite writers as I have read more books by him than any other author. 'The Alchemist' is also really great. Anywho. I am going to-wrap this one up. As I leave I say. Cool is the rule. Don't trip tater chip! Just be cool. Don't worry be happy. Calm the fuck down take a deep breath and enjoy life.

Veni Vidi Vici

I remain.

In solidarity

Clinton YOUNG #999447

www.saveaninnocentlife.com

www.theclintonproject.com

www.clintonyoungfoundation.com

Loud & Clear, August 15, 2017

Topic: Days of life

Greetings! As the days tick on, I have been meeting a great deal with my therapist. He and I are working on my anger issues and obsession with Priyanka Chopra! Alright, alright! I am joking, everyone CALM down. I do not have a therapist! ☺ Well beyond Robert that is! While prefer to be housed on a different section. It is good having someone that can really talk to. Being that we are on death watch and not allowed to rec. Around any others. We are able to get outside 3 or 4 times a week. Could be more, however they shut the rec. Yards down at 1 pm due to the heat. :(Which really upsets me. As I love the sun and heat! If it is 100°F. Then I am happy! Not sure what the Celsius is for 100F. Anywho. They shut the outside rec. Yards down, as people have sued over the heat levels. As most prisons, the general population areas do not have air conditioning. As a result, guys sue not to work. The powers that be say no work no rec. Now for death row I am totally clueless as to why that applies. We cannot work! The outside rec. Yards have water fountains. Officers do security checks every 30-40 minutes. Plus when we come in, the building is air conditioned. Look I know you all read that we don't have air conditioning, never get vegetables and all this other bullshit. Its just that. Bullshit! Is it some ideal temperature for some specific person? Maybe not. Though I got cold air coming from my vent. I normally block the vent as I don't like the cold! The air would blow harder if they would change out the filters more often. They used to do it once a year I think. I haven't seen them do it in 10 years! Gets clogged, reduces air flow. Plus there is cross section vents that are in the wall that separates the pod in half. A,B,C section on one side and D,E,F on the other. Before with these vents and the wide space under the doors for the cross avers. Air would flow better, but they wielded some plates on the bottom of the doors to keep people from passing things under them. Being that not all vents are open on the cross section. It makes it where one side gets more air than another. So for example. A.B.C on A-pod is warmer than D.E.F section. Even with cross section vent open, as it is on this pod. But the air doesn't blow as hard. Meaning the filter needs to be cleaned/changed out.

Beyond Randy being a friend. Why would I give it to him over my other friend, William Irvin, who is one of my best friends. I never write about him, as he doesn't seek out pen pals and such. Though the people I am closest to here are Randy Halprin, William Irvin, Robert Pruett, and Harvey Earvin. So these are the four that crossed my mind. William is innocent. I know his case in and out. He is innocent! Just had some shitty lawyers. He will be able to beat the case. Harvey has a chance to navigate the system and get off death row. Once off death row. I think he would have a good chance to get parole. I got a lot of love for Harvey and know that he could get out and be a productive member of society.

The brief moment that so defined his life is not the sum total of the man he is. Not by any stretch of the imagination.

Robert and I have not always been so close. Though, over last couple years have gotten closer. We been cool for years. Other people's bullshit caused some distance in the past. Though in recent years have developed a great deal of love for him. We have become good friends. He got majorly fucked over! He was given 99 years as a 16-year-old kid. Certified as an adult for a crime he had nothing to do with. There is a BBC film about Robert. About his life and being innocent. Now he awaits death based on inmate snitch testimony. NO DNA or anything from him. No prints! nothing! He didn't do the case, but an inmate said he did, so he gets sent to death row. Bottom line is he should have beat this case long ago. In Texas the hardest cases to beat are any that involve law enforcement. Be it police officers or guards. To put into context jailhouse snitching. There were guys who was NOT EVEN AT THE SAME PRISON trying to say they had information. Prison truly shows how some will sell their own mother) if it would benefit them. Robert can eventually win his cases. Randy, due to politics of his case, has the hardest fight. Beyond that factor. I know Randy and have spent a great deal of time over the years discussing different things. He is a good dude. Plus, if released, Randy would not hurt anyone. When he first came to prison, he was a teenager, going through a lot of shit, and high on drugs. He had done something really stupid that he deserved not only to go to prison over. He also deserved to have someone beat his ass for it. (I have told him such before and he even expresses such.) Though this is so that they can be up to date on all. However, it cannot be shared at this time. I have no desire to give the people trying to kill me any advanced warnings as to what will be filed. The day it is filed, it will be posted on here. On contacting people. Again, thanks to all that sent the letters to the Dutch government. I mention the Dutch as clearly I have more attention in The Netherlands than anywhere else at this time. Though, I encourage others to do the same for their government. Here is the deal when it comes to writing people from Texas.

Texas has a standalone mind set. Which is why it is called: the Lone Star State. It was its own country for a bit at one time. Texas politicians, more so the republicans that dominate the government of Texas. They will give an ear to a C.E.O. or foreign leader they trade with. (From an economic position Texas is a world powerhouse) There are major connections between Texas and Netherlands due to energy sector, shipping, and also many companies are listed as headquartered in Amsterdam as The Netherlands actually has a lower corporate Tax rate then the USA. (People rant about tax laws that help the rich. It is not the US corporate tax rate/ as it is listed at 35% and is one of the highest rates in the world! I think it is highest in the G8 or G20 groups.)

That is why I say if you are an average Dutch citizen. Greg Abbott, the Texas governor, will never think once, much less twice about what you write him. He will not even see the letters. Instead of writing Mr. Abbott. Write to politicians, and C.E.Os, from your country, that does business with Texas. Alrighty now. Things are going to be moving faster now. I will be posting more. Know that I am very grateful for everyone's help. There are ways that all can help.

Going to wrap this one up. Till next time. Take care! Oh, I made mention about social media. I misunderstood a comment made on radio. I thought a court ruling applied to people in prison. It was about convicted sex offenders. Ooops!}

Veni Vidi Vici,

Clinton YOUNG #999447

Loud & Clear, September 14, 2017

Topic: Humanity & etc

NOTICE: I have gotten back into groove of writing more. I ask people to please bare with me. Thank you. Greetings to all! Many times, people write to me about losing faith in humanity. It is easy to water that though then viewing the various forms of media. My case surely doesn't equate to an indictment on humanity. While there is an injustice, I always say, I made a series of stupid choices. Though the way media is in today's time, it is so easy to get locked into your own little sub group and then start to see everything as adversarial. People go after each other's throat over these issues that divide, be it politics, religion or whatever. We build up these fences.

That's why we need storms. To cause people to have to stop and reflect. To look around and re-evaluate whats important. With so much energy put into material items, we often overlook the people around us. We have become masters at developing ways to ignore each other. To fill our lives with distractions. Then the storm comes and you realize those fences are not so high after all. You are forced to look up and see the people around you. Hurricane Harvey stormed in the state of Texas, then suddenly the impossible became possible. With so much destroyed, it would be hard for any to have hope. Though from the shadows of destruction. The storm showed that not all is lost. As Harvey raged on and the floods ripped through southeast Texas people left the comfort of their homes. They loaded up supplies and hitched up boats, driving into harms way to help others.

Houston is a very diverse and heavily democratic leaning city. It is not hard to guess who those men in jacked up trucks and fishing boats voted for in the last election. It damn sure wasn't Hillary.

There was a reporter who interviewed an older gentleman She was not from Texas. She covered natural disasters and as she expressed she had never seen people respond as they did. As she interviewed the older guy you could tell he was just an old country boy. She asked him why he came down to help people. He paused for a couple of seconds. It was clear what she was asking was 'Why do FYOU come help THESE people.' He responded in a slow southern draw. "Ma'am, today we're all Texans." That touched me so much. It's why I love Texas; the spirit of the state. Texans will fight each other 6-days a week though if on the 7th your drowning; they will reach in and pull you out. Texans are a passionate and fiercely independent people. They absolutely hate people not from Texas telling them how to live or act. Robert and others always express amazement at my affinity for the state. Though that's viewing it from prison. The state is not trying to kill me. It is a few select people that know nothing about the case truly or one that simply doesn't care.

Though when people are educated, they see the problems. It is why I tell people do not react with animosity. If someone says I need to die, ask why and then ask about fairness and justice and then educate them about the facts. People then will change their mind.

Rage with rage just equals more rage. Anyways Having lived in other states there is often a dislike of Texas. Texas has always been seen as rowdy and a bit uncivilized. :) I would go to other states I Like when I went to Wyoming. First day of school A kid tells me "My daddy says only steers and queers come from Texas. You don't look like you got any horns!" Which is a line from a movie Heard that line so many times in other states. Having to fight because of being from the state, it increased the passion for the state. Back to my point. The storm showed that there might be these one or two issues that we disagree on. We hyper focus on that instead of the 8 or 9 issues that we share common ground. It is sad that we need these disasters to stop and reflect.

Though with disasters, you also end up seeing the worst in people. Some decided to go scam and steal from people. It takes a special kind of shit to rob people while they are drowning.

Stores were jacking up the cost of fuel. One store went from $2 a gallon to $9.90 a gallon for fuel. Which is illegal in Texas. During natural disasters crimes get enhanced to harsher punishments. If I lived in a community and a store started to triple the cost of fuel and water (one tried to sell water for 30$ for a case of water!) That store would not be able to operate in my community. They would have to sell or shut down. I would have people boycotting it.

Running a business is one thing. Taking advantage of people in need When they are going through hell and have lost damn near everything. To hike up costs on important items, yeah, that is just foul. Bottom line is we often look at storms for the destruction they do. Like this case. With the way it has impacted me being that I was wrongfully convicted) Now yes, the care fact is that there is no silver lining for the families impacted by the case or the victims. That is not lost on me. The scope of it for me personally is that had I not came to death row. If I had walked out of that courtroom at 19 years old, beating a double capital murder case, with all that I was involved in. Back then, While I would have liked to have hoped that I would have gotten out and changed my life, chances are that most likely I would have ended up dead or in federal prison for life. Since being here people around the world have been impacted in positive ways. A woman that had been attacked as a teenager went from not wanting to leave the house. I helped her regain control of her life. She is now married with two kids. Who knows what the children will grow up and accomplish. People –turned away from suicide, got out of bad relationships. Redirected their life towards other goals. In some ways I have impacted the way the world turns. There are people that go through life just going with the flow. Never seeking their own path. That or worse, they are too afraid to carve their own path. I have actually gotten to impact peoples lives. If I end up losing, the blessing is that I was able to love and be loved by some wonderful people. Also, that I was able to inspire others. Plus, I will get to express feelings and love to my friends and family. I think that is one thing that many here overlook. It is easy to only see the world through our own eyes. The situation is viewed for the final result, versus the journey there. (We get to at least say 'bye') The reality of the death penalty is death. Most are here for depriving another of their life.

The system sure has its flaws. I can damn sure name many in my case. If they do get me, I will have impacted so many more people around the world than I ever would have had I not come here. I am not bitter. Now no way in hell am I giving up. I am innocent in this case, and will fight to prove that till the very end. While I was pissed off before, I am not anymore. Instead of seeing what I do not have, my focus is on what I do have. People have shown me a great deal of love.

The storm makes you refocus! I thank everyone that helps me. A special thanks to those that donate something each month and continue to actively help. The filing of my appeal was pushed back one week. Will not be filled until the 25th of September. Please help spread the word, share my poems and blogs and posts links to my sites. Another blog will be posted in a few days.

Take care, smile, & strive for all that you desire.

In solidarity

P.S .*ATTENTION* If you write me for first time with jpay, I have to have address or I can not respond. I can not respond with jpay.

Clinton YOUNG #999447

www.saveaninnocentlife.com

www.theclintonproject.com

www.clintonyoungfoundation.com

Loud & Clear, September 17, 2017

Topic: Ways to help

Spoke to my lawyers last week. Nothing really new. There is a hearing to remove the execution date. Even though the testing came back exactly as I said it would, they do not want to agree to remove the date. The fight goes on. I want to thank all those that have written letters to various officials. Those that continue to donate and spread the word. I wanted to detail additional ways to help. Music- There are several songs that have been made for me. Some will be for download at cost and others will be free to share. The song "Song for a stranger" by ELYA is on YouTube and has a video. (http://www.saveaninnocentlife.com/song-for-a-stranger/) If everyone reading this goes to YouTube to view it and then posts links to it and encourages everyone they know to view it then the higher the view count is, the more attention it gets, the more attention she gets, the more powerful her voice is, will help get other media involved. Reach out to others on YouTube and various social media and ask them to share the links and/or mention it. Music is something everyone enjoys. It is easier to share a link to a YouTube video with a wonderful song then it is to get someone to read lots of pages about a death penalty case and/or to post directly about such.

It is not as controversial. Also reach out to radio stations in your town and ask them to play the song. The song "Death row" by Pyrexx. If you are into hip hop, I wrote this song with the intent that it would be an audio autobiography-esque song. It is free to download and share. Please do so. (You can find it here: http://www.theclintonproject.com/buy/) The more that it is shared, the better. It mentions my site, so it is a way to advertise my case. It details about the case, so it is free. The "Lore of Loki" is a rock song. It is available for download at costs the funds go to my defense. The more downloads it gets, the more attention I can get in other areas. For example, let's use wishful thinking here and say the song gets 1 million downloads, such would catch the attention of media around the world. In covering the song, they would then also focus on my case. So you see how it can be used as a way to raise attention? People download music all the time. It sounds good. If you like music, there ya go. Two other hip-hop songs will be soon available for download. Then hopefully I can get the country song that I wrote produced as either a country song or a southern rock song. I am also trying to find someone to sing the Arabian Song. Next up. A young woman that writes to me, who happens to also be a model, is going to be helping in a few ways. She is from The Netherlands. Her name is Alyssa Traore. I would like everyone to please follow her on Instagram. Now I know you might be thinking "Clinton, how the hell is following a model going to help you?" Simple! The way things are these days, the more popular a model is, the higher her status is. With such allows more doors to be opened.

If you do not have an Instagram account, please create one and get you some family and friend followers. Then follow Alyssa. See here is the deal, if she had say, 10 million followers (I doubt I can bring that many) but if she did, she would have the attention of many, many people around the world. Doors would easily open for her and she then could pull on people's ear and tell them about me. By helping people that help me, you make them stronger. Also, to all in The Netherlands, by following her on Instagram and viewing/sharing the YouTube feature by ELYA, you send a message to other celebrities who might be worried about diving into a controversial topic. That it is okay. An addition to this idea is that everyone reading this in The Netherlands could contact the most popular TV shows, newspapers and magazines and tell them that you would like a feature done on Alyssa and ELYA as to how artists participate in activism. In doing this, the media helps to reach even more people, thus increasing the status of Alyssa and ELYA.

The YouTube views spike, her Instagram followers increase, you don't only help me, but you help those that help me. It is a way to have a form of community support. Each helping the other. The end result is everyone is stronger. Others see and get involved. This is a free way to help, it is a way that no matter your age, you can actively help. Ask others you know to do the same thing.

Reach out to music blogs, fashion blogs, magazines for fashion and music, etc. Famous YouTube stars and so forth. For every person that tells you no, ask 5 others. If they tell you no. You are not harmed in any way. Someone will say yes and then we will help them. To the person that said no, hey so be it for them. These are ways that people can help for free with just a bit of time online.

Last but not least. Due to various problems I have had with mail and due to limitations to the number of stamps I am allowed to buy from the prison, I can NOT get stamps in the mail. They will be denied! A program is being sorted to be installed on the websites for me. The letters will be printed by my sister and mailed to me. I believe it is .50$ per letter, is how the program is. This is to cover the cost of mailing it to me. This will make it faster, cheaper and surer delivery for people that I write overseas. I can respond by sending the letter to my sister and she will scan and email it to the person I write. My sister will be only one with access. This makes it much easier for me to write with people. More so given my days are numbered. It is not required. Not saying that. Though it is an option for those that want to use it. The cost is to cover delivery, US mail is .49$ for standard letter rate. Trying to find ways to streamline everything. Also to increase ways for people to help that only require a bit time.

Also with my poems, please feel free to share them with any and all. Just make sure you add that it comes from me and my website. Thanks! Going to wrap this one up. Will be back in a few days. Thanks to all that have continued to support me. It is not over until it is. If every day you reach out to several people, you are helping. Again, thanks in advance to all that follow Alyssa on Instagram and also view the YouTube feature done by ELYA. Take care, smile, and strive for all that you desire.

In solidarity,

P.S.*ATTENTION* If you write me for first time with jpay, I have to have address or I cannot respond. I cannot respond with jpay.

Clinton YOUNG #999447

www.clintonyoungfoundation.com

Loud & Clear, October 8, 2017

Topic: Anti-Venom, Case & Help

"Keep fightin', got to keep my anti-venom strong because these snakes keep strikin'!" The powers that be in Midland never fail to amaze me. I really had hope that they would do the right thing, however, it seems that the new D.A is just all jolly to kill me. As the testing came back exactly as I said it would, the never-ending list of people coming forward saying that Page bragged about the murder continues. People from various ethnic groups, none that associate with each other, the only common theme is Page bragging about getting away with murder. For a first, I have to thank Midland Reporter Telegram. It was due to their story about the October 16th hearing that my lawyers found out Page was not only back in Midland, but he was also being given "Use Immunity." (Which means anything he says about crimes in Midland, he cannot be prosecuted for.) The idea being that this would get him to tell the truth. Problem with that? Yeah. They gave him that at my trial and he still lied and has admitted he lied in my trial. So that piece of paper doesn't mean shit. But whatever he said, they would use against me. Half of my appeal is about Prosecutor misconduct, yet here the D.A calls Page back in secret. I feel safe assuming they met with him and had private discussions with him. As they have many times before. (D.A is for District Attorney, The Prosecutor.) There was all kinds of stuff that the D.A was doing that they failed to discuss with my lawyers. They call that something… Ah, what is it? Oh Yeah! It's ILLEGAL!! A total violation of my due process rights and is a clear-cut ethics violation. It gets even laughingly worse. The Judge signed the orders for the D.A two days before the D.A filed their legal arguments, which are known as 'motions'. Now how would a Judge or why would a Judge know to sign off on an order to a legal argument that has not yet even been filed? Well, they were clearly discussing the case in private. Oh, there's that word I am looking for again!

My lawyers read the story in the newspaper. They naturally filed with the higher court. Maybe the D.A thinks that if they kill me, it will all end. NOT! Ya know, I am mad at myself. People wanted to do so much with media, protest actions, etc. but I told everyone "No, just chill. I want to wait until the testing comes back." I naively believed that once the testing showed what I said it would, the D.A would come to the table and have a discussion about the most reasonable solution. But that did not happen. Instead, they dug in harder and started doing even more crazy shit. Here are the basic facts:

#1. Over 5 witnesses swear under penalty of perjury that they were threatened, offered deals, etc., by members of the Prosecution before, during, and after my trial. As late as 2010, at a hearing, James Kemp discusses this in the film "Deal with Death."

#2. A letter was found from Mark Ray to Harrison County D.A about plea bargaining. This letter was never given to my trial lawyers. Instead, it was given to Mark's lawyer who put it in his file. Which in turn meant we would never see it before the trial due to Mark Ray's legal rights with his attorney.

#3. The D.A at the time of my trial promised in a letter to turn over all favorable information. They failed to do this. In the TX DPS files it was discovered that they didn't.

#4. The Violent Crimes Task Force met with a witness about Page saying to put the murders on me. This information was left out of the case file until recently. Two Judges ordered everything to be turned over.

#5. Courts found that the Harrison County D.A had indeed discussed plea deals with Mark Ray's lawyer. Okay, that same D.A testified under oath TWICE that he didn't do that. So it has been affirmed that a former D.A committed perjury TWICE! Which is a felony in Texas!

#6. Here we are in 2017 and all the above-mentioned events took place in concern of the October 16th hearing.

#7. That's not all I got. There is something that hasn't been mentioned before. ☺ It will be though.

So they have shown a systematic pattern of misconduct in my cases. I can show this from before my trial, during my trial with allowing false testimony, to after my trial. This spans from 2002 to 2017. Oh yeah, don't let me forget the D.A at my trial filed a false complaint on my mitigation specialist. Also threatened to press charges on my paralegal. He was actively threatening my defense team. He retired after the appeals court denied my first appeal. Damn, also don't let me forget about the evidence in my case that they threw away or 'lost' as they say. I really do not understand why this new D.A is so obsessed with killing me. I really don't. More so, being that I have shown everything is as I said it is time and time again. Two jury members signed statements for me. If all the jury members would have talked to my defense team, I could have gotten more. I was recently approached by a member of the media to discuss the role of Journalism keeping branches of the government in check. It is needed so much because people are so ignorant to the law. People believe all these myths. In Texas there is a HUGE difference in how death penalty and non-death penalty cases are handled. If Robert Pruett was a non-death case, he could have had a new trial 4 times over instead of being 3 and a half days away from dying. Andrea Yates killed all her kids. She got a new trial because a guy lied about a TV episode in her trial! Yet, I can show several witnesses lied in my trial, including FBI Agents and Police Officers. Yet here I sit. ☹

Death Penalty cases are treated so differently. Sadly, this myth does real harm. As even politicians believe some of the myths of the system. This myth that we are getting new trials left and right and that we delay justice… That is so far from the truth! There are hard limits on what can be done and when. It truly puts people's lives in danger! Back to the medias role. Anthony Graves is free in part thanks to something the prosecutor admitted to the media. See, I always try to argue that this is about Justice and what the constitution allows me. A fair trial. I never had that. Just give me what the law says I can have! People want to pick and choose which Constitutional rights they want to give. Everyone wants free speech and guns. Why can't I have a fair trial? It's because they know I would win. Never mind the fact that I never killed anyone. Instead of them admitting an error, they would rather kill me. Take my life to cover up their misconduct. So, the motive to kill is NOT justice. Not in the least. If it was about justice, Darnell would never have remained free, Mark would not have gotten just 15 years and Page would not have gotten only 30 years. To cover up all their errors and misconduct they think that if they murder me, I will become silent. No, not hardly. Too many love me. Too many believe in me. I know too much about the law. My baby sister loves me too much. If they do kill me, she is going to know how to carry the fight forward. Time ticks on. To other matters, I want to thank everyone that attended the event in Amsterdam. Also, a very special thanks to Shanna Nico for her participation in the event. She said she would sing and she did. Forgive me Shanna for not mentioning you sooner. My friends were so focused on getting everything in order I was a bit late in getting all the specifics. To everyone, please download music by Shanna Nico. Post links for her on you social media pages and encourage others to do the same. Help her in response to her helping me. As I mentioned before, the stronger you make those that help me, the stronger I am. Plus, in a way, it is a way to Pay it Forward. Also, if you are a fan of hip hop, please download "Works" by Pyrexx and post links for him as well. He did the song "Death Row", "Hip Hop Song", and is working on another known as "A gangstas death." (the song is critical of that lifestyle). The Song "Death Row" is free to download and it is encouraged that any and all download it and share it as a way to help bring attention to my case. The Rock song "Lore of Loki" by Forsete is good so if you like Rock music please download this one. Also share links with that band with others that like rock.

Many people think that because I have so many hip-hop songs, that is my favorite music. I actually listen to country and rock music more than anything. I like some older hip-hop and some new stuff from the southern region of the U.S. I am Texas made, so mainly I like artists from Texas such as Pyrexx. I will even listen to some Mexican music if it is an artist from Texas. Might not understand a damn thing they are saying! ☺ haha. Will just get Amy to translate for me. See, with the music, it is as I have said before, It is a non-controversial way to spread the word. Also, the more downloads, the more attention I get. I still want to get my country song and the Arab song produced. The reason why I made the choice on having the song "Death Row" for free is because it mentions stuff from the case and out of respect to the victims family, I did not want it to be for profit. I additionally want to thank everyone that has written to the Governor and Parole Board and those who have reached out to other media sources. Every single day reach out to someone. Ask people to share the links and songs also. Every day do something. It will grow and grow. If someone tells you no or rejects you in any way, then ask or tell 10 more. Fear is a brake to progress. You all are my Anti-Venom! This is getting long winded, so I am going to wrap it up. Will be back in a Couple of Days. Thanks to all that help.

Veni Vidi Vici

In Solidarity,

Clinton YOUNG#999447

www.saveaninnocentlife.com

www.theclintonproject.com

www.clintonyoungfoundation.com

Loud & Clear, October 14, 2017

Topic: Robert Pruett

The story of Robert is one that is complex and an indictment both on poverty and prison.

It casts the justice system of Texas in a decade long shadow from a shameful cloud of injustice. Being certified as an adult at age 15 for a murder his father committed, he was given 99 years.

He was thrown away by people that could have and should have redirected his life. He never had a real chance. His dad was in and out of prison. His mother, uneducated. He never even really got to be a child. If we could rewind the hands of time, the person Robert was before coming to prison would be one that few people reading this would admire. He was a product of poverty and prison. With that comes hate and crime. Though the man the state of Texas killed, that man was one that inspired others. A man that was full of love and life. You can see it yourself by going to the site for execution watch, produced by Ray Hill, and see the interview there. I highly recommend that any and everyone watch/listen to the entire execution watch show that was done on Robert. Share it with everyone you can. Robert was very intelligent. Everything came easy for him. He was someone that always tried to make the most of a situation. Like being on death watch together, time flew by because we were having as much fun as we could. (Often to the amusement of others on the section and pod.) So many here are just miserable people. Everything is 'woe is me'. Robert was like me. Just grab life by the horns. He never shied away from a fight, spoke his mind. He was also always interested in the human element, what made a person who they are. We had many common interests, which is why we became so close. We also shared a kind of similar story, both having been in prison for so much of our life. We both dealt with the pressures that come with being young white guys tossed into violent prison systems. Then coming to Death Row at young ages and going through the changes we have. I myself have not always been a person that many would be impressed with. Again, like Robert, the people that came into our lives made us see the world with a bigger lens. One thing truly holds the key to power. It is LOVE. Going through some of the things I have as a child inspired me to want to obtain power. I saw power as my ability to dominate the world around me. To do it in the way it was shown to me, by force. Robert was the same. These common themes are what helped us develop such a strong bond. It is also how he was able to inspire me in ways. He was not scared of death. The morning of October 12th I woke up hearing him talking to someone. I laid in bed smiling, I could tell how hyper he was. He had even expressed a few times how excited he was to see what was next. Growing up in prison, there is not much attachment to this world. When he talked about living life, it was always with Theressa. She was the one he wanted to live for. To get out and build a life with her. One thing that helped make his days easier in the end was how strong she was. After one of her visits, he came back and we talked. He told me, "Bro, she is so much my chick. We really are perfect for each other. She is so strong, I thought I would have to work to comfort her but she is tough." This brought him more comfort and made everything go smoother for him. Everyone deals with pain differently. I always tell people not to cry but to fight! As long as you can fight then you can win. Although, this is a hard situation, It is not natural. It is confusing to most. The important thing is to try to make the most of each moment.

Last Saturday Amy came to visit me. Robert was visiting Theressa and Cenda (forgive me if I spelled that wrong) and I was in a different booth at first but then got moved to the booth next to Robert. That is when the picture of the two of us was taken. We had the most fun we could being in the situation. Amy wrote to me about how it inspired her seeing how we interacted and were just ourselves and enjoyed the moment. When you watch the execution episode you can hear the smile in his words and see it in his face. Make his death worth something. Take from it a better appreciation for life. Do not be afraid to live. You have one life. Make it count! That doesn't mean go out and make life all about you. Many people use such thinking to step on others. No, you can have the greatest life possible just by loving life and the world around you. Do not be driven by always wanting more because you might just overlook the treasures you have right at your feet. Robert was one of a kind. I was out at a visit the day of his transition. I was in the booth that made it so that when he was being escorted out, I could see him. On the day of a person's execution they escort from the visitation booth to the transport van. They place the person in the visitation restroom so he can use the restroom before getting in the van to go to Huntsville. As he turned the corner to walk towards the restroom he yelled out "Loki! I love ya bro." I said the same in return after he was done and cuffed again. As he was walking back past me to leave the visitation area and my head was leaning against the visitation booth screen when he stopped right in front of me, looked at me with a big smile on his face and said again, "I love ya." I managed to get the words "you too" out. I watched him walk out of the visitation area and I sat down feeling the pain of the moment. Then I laughed as the thought entered my mind, "The fucker smiled at me." I was optimistic something good would happen as the slim chance existed that it would. Though on the execution watch show Ray Hill took the call from Dave Atwood (who was at the Walls Unit where executions happen) and he said that Robert's people were crossing the road. This means they are being escorted to witness the execution. That is how people know it is going forward. It didn't really even hit me then. It wasn't until they played the recording of him, then it really hit me. It was the first time I really had someone close to me be executed. Though we had gotten so much closer in recent years, more so this year since we were on C Pod together. Then I got my date and he got an execution date shortly after me. We spent every day talking. We were always going to the outside rec. yard together. We couldn't be on the same rec. yard but we could see and talk to each other. Just imagine being in a room with no roof that had a fence splitting it. That is a rough example which makes it a little easier to understand. One person would be on each side of the fence. We laughed, cried, argued, cussed other people out together, had others laughing with us or at us, hell we even had officers laughing. A bond was formed stronger in a situation that is so unique. Every day was not only a new day, it also marked one less day on this earth. We made the most of it. The storms of life make us stop and reflect.

Robert got into Physics during his time here. He read many books on it while he was here and his belief was that energy never dies. The world is made of energy and as a result we never die. Our physical bodies die, but the energy that is in us never dies. We fear death due to all we hang onto here on Earth. Also, the fear of the unknown. Robert came to not see death as most people do. That is why he did not fear it. As far as his case goes, the lawyers discussing it on the execution watch say it all. Although, something I did notice was when the person from the Special Prosecution Unit spoke to the media on the radio, he did not say Robert was 100% without a doubt guilty. Instead, he said "A jury reviewed the evidence and found him guilty." (5 members of the jury said they regret convicting him.) The evidence that they used to convict Robert was false and flawed. Jailhouse snitches changed their stories and did not have any information until they were offered secret deals or they were in trouble a year later and were trying to get out of it. The forensics they used in his case was flawed and bullshit. They did not kill Robert because they proved on Appeal that he was guilty, No. He was executed because of being legally barred as legal claims were not made on time. See, there is this bullshit ass myth in Texas that people are so fucking wrong on. The myth that we on death row get off on technicalities. NO! That is total fuckin bullshit! I challenge anyone to find a case where a guy is free from death row due to a technicality. Find me ONE fuckin case where a guy got a whole new trial for it and got away.

No, it does not happen. Instead, what happens, is they kill us on technicalities. A lawyer fucks up, we die. THAT is what the fuckin media will not focus on in Texas. It is like everyone has to propagate this myth that we are beating the system. If that is the case, why the fuck is Robert Pruett dead for a murder they cannot prove he did?! But instead, he can prove he did NOT do! Why is Todd Willingham dead? Carlos Deluna? Gary Graham? Etc. Hell, the prosecutors admitted and the Judge and appeals court signed off on it that a prosecutor in my case committed perjury twice. He lied about the plea bargain discussions with one of the co-defendants lawyers. Appeals denied, denied, denied. I begged for a new state appeal lawyer. Then it came out that the investigator was smoking crack and falsified all the documents in my appeal. They tell me basically, Oh Well. Tough Shit. I also want to making something else clear, when I express my love of Texas, it is NOT the prison system or injustice system. Not at all. It is about the mythology and spirit of the state. It hurts my heart that so many people in Texas refuse to look into the systems they support. If they do, they doubt the death penalty. People who read Robert's story, and hear the execution watch show, it will open their eyes. I have some people that gave statements for me. The prosecution says they cannot be trusted because they are criminals and drug users. Hahaha. What the fuck is every witness they have?! Criminals and drug users! So their dope head crook is better than my dope head crook? This is not unique to me, Robert had people who were not even on the damn unit with him, units over a hundred miles away, writing in trying to be a snitch for the state! Yet, the government was okay with killing one of it's citizens based on the word of a person they would not even trust to borrow a single dollar. A persons life is worth less than a dollar to them. The person that the state of Texas killed on October 12, 2017 was by no means the same person that entered Texas Death Row. He damn sure was not the same person as the kid whose life was thrown away when he got 99 years. While his life was not lived the "normal" way, that doesn't mean that it was worth any less. Do not let Robert's execution be for nothing. Robert is a good example as to why we should not write off other people. The people that entered his life helped to make him a better person. As a result, he made other people better.

Learn, Live, Love.

Shield Wall Brother!!

Veni Vidi Vici.

In Solidarity,

Clint Young #999447

U.S.A

Attention My lawyers and a P.R firm started a website: saveclintyoung.com. It is for official info, etc. The Clinton Foundation is focused on international attention and saveclintonyoung.com is geared more towards U.S. Theclintonproject.com is for my music and saveaninnocentlife.com is just used for writings and such. I still use it as have for so many years. Sorry if it is confusing. I didn't know the saveclintonyoung site would be made, or I would have streamlined everything. Just keep this in mind. USA, International, music, and writings. For US media or whoever visits saveclintyoung.com and clintonyoungfoundation.com I am going to get them reduced and consolidated in the future. But for now, there ya go. ☺

Loud & Clear, October 21, 2017

Topic: It ain't over yet

A small battle has been won, but the war is far from over. When my lawyers told me on the phone that I got a stay, they all started to cheer and such. My mind, right away, went to "Okay, what's next?" The urgency has changed, but the dynamic remains the same. I am still on death row. Now is far from the time to take the foot off the pedal. If anything, it is time to mash it harder. Everyone can stop writing to the parole board and governor. The Governor only has limited power in what he can do with a death penalty case and now that I have a stay, it is 100% out of his control. I am back before the court. I understand that some people have been confused about why not the DNA Claim and all that other stuff. DNA is not in question. So to clear it up, I did not have a DNA claim. DNA is mentioned because it matched the co-defendant. My claim was about gunshot residue. An item that had the co-defendant's DNA also had GSR on it. Hence, he shot the gun while wearing the gloves. Now, the way the C.C.A of Texas works, they do not rule on a case in such a way that will open the door for many other cases. They always try to deal with it case by case. They could have granted all my claims, though it would have been kind of pointless really and would have only served to be a case to be used by others on death row. (Which those against the death penalty see as a great thing) However, the judicial landscape of Texas does not cater to an anti-death penalty political climate. By ruling on the claim they did, it helps me to bring everything else into the equation. For example, the gloves. 11.073 is a new appeal angle deal with forensic science. In order to win that I have to meet a set of standards. I cannot just say, "GSR on gloves, I win!" There is a series of standards that have to ALL be met. As a result of this, it is harder to win because there is more to prove. The claim I won on, there was only one thing I had to do, prove the co-defendant lied. In doing so, I can bring in the gloves and everything else without having to do a checklist of standards. The Judges in that court are not stupid. Almost all of them are former prosecutors, if not all of them.

I am going to have to sort a few things out before going back to Midland. They can take me back to the county at any time, but I suspect they might wait a bit. More so since they are currently holding Page hostage out there. Which please, people, stop attacking him. I got a stay of execution based on him admitting to my lawyers on the things he lied about. He came clean on mass majority of everything, except the murders. What matters is that Midland County doesn't do anymore unethical actions like threaten and intimidate witnesses. I think doing it to 6 is enough! Right now I need people to focus on the future. Helping promote my sites, songs, the people I have mentioned that support me, and donating. As I have said before, if someone sees that people support a band that supports me or a model for example, then they will not shy away. Others may come to help through this.

Also, I ask that everyone please share the Execution Watch by Ray Hill; episode on Robert Pruett. More so, people in Texas. People in Texas need to know that a 15 year old kid who never even killed anyone was certified as an adult and given 99 years in adult prison. Then, in turn, execute him for a murder with absolutely no evidence. That a man was killed by the state due to technicalities, that the courts say was his lawyers fault. The only way true reform can happen is if the myths that cloud the justice system are destroyed. People need to understand the realities that plague the system and cause innocent people to be locked up and even killed. Murder has different labels under the law. Manslaughter, both voluntary and involuntary; Negligent Homicide; Capital Murder; and the most recently created one, Justifiable Homicide, which was brought about 11 or 12 years ago. Before this law, when we were "Texecuted", the cause of death would have been homicide. As a result, the death certificate became a political tool for the anti-movement, which was really highlighted under the old school uncensored blogs with Richard Cartwright and so forth. Politicians came up with a new definition for the law, Justifiable Homicide. Homicide, by definition, is the killing of a human. The state of Texas did not carry out a justifiable homicide of Robert Pruett. No. They fuckin murdered him.

The past 2 weeks surely have been a roller coaster. The silver lining of the experience with the execution date is, well, there are actually a few of them. First being my own self-reflection whilst in the shadows of death. As I have mentioned, the storms make us stop and reflect. The last couple of months, I really had the best visits. There is a song by Tim McGraw called "Live Like You Were Dying." I am horrible with song names and artists so hopefully I got it right, but basically it is about a man that is dying and it details how he is living his life. I've always been one that was about the people around me. The concept of 'who can you call at 2 in the morning'? At the end of the day, when all else fails, there has to be a person in your life that you can count on. I have never had to struggle with having people in my life. The blessing of looks, brains, charisma and strength; it attracts people. I took that for granted. When faced with losing it all; it humbles a person. I also got to spend the days with Robert.

Additionally, there was so much more attention that came to my case. It took me a couple of days to really process that I was not going to die on October 26th. I expected someone to come back with some type of bullshit. I was visiting on Friday with Merel when I was told I had an attorney phone call. It was an unexpected call so the first thing that came to my head was the date. Beyond suicide, no one has to sit around and think about the exact date and time of their own death. It was 2 weeks after one of my best friends died. When I was doing my 14 day processing (which is 14 days from the execution date) they took me to the office with all the high ranks of the prison, as they do everyone 14 days prior to their scheduled date, I had to meet with Wardens, asst. warden, Major and Captain for 12 building (death row and ad -seg.). We sign some religious forms for the reason I am not really clear, I didn't pay much attention to it. I think it is about the chaplain that will be at the death house. Then, I signed forms about what to do with my body. I had a message from Robert to the Warden as he was having his final visit and the night before he got no mail. Well, he did get an envelope with no letter in it and no return address. It just had some message on the outside from some Christian group. (Also, if someone from said group is reading this, your idea is fuckin stupid! Whatever idea you had might have been good, but this was a dumbass stupid fuckin thing to do that no one likes, appreciates, or even really gets the point of. So, how about you stop doing it or come up with something better.) Anyways, the experience is crazy! I am sitting there planning what to do with my body in case the state anatomical board will not accept it; I was going to donate my body to science. I mean, with a brain and body like this it would almost be a crime for humanity not to benefit from it. ;) Haha. Seriously though, I am discussing with these people about my body, who will watch me die, and my final visits. All of this on the very day my best friend was set to die. That is such a unique experience. Oh, I forgot to mention, they also took the handcuffs off of me. So the first time a person will be in a room with other people without handcuffs on death row is when they do their 14 day processing to get ready to die. Hmm. Time ticks on.

When I found out about the stay, the investigator asked me if I had a statement about it. I couldn't really focus on such a thing but as I was trying to think up something short to say, which is not one of my stronger points ☺ I expressed a couple thoughts and the investigator said, "how about this…". My response was, "cool, go with that" and we went on to something else. When I was visiting with Renate and Merel later, Merel told me she had told Renate that I didn't make that statement. She knew this because there was no emotion in the statement. That got me to thinking about my words. That my ability to make people feel what I feel when I write is what impacts people, I guess. I certainly never follow all these grammar rules and such. I just thought it was neat. On to other matters. I express from my heart the love I have felt from everyone. To the people of The Netherlands: Dank u wel. Ik hou van jou!

A very important point I wanted to highlight is the claim that I won on in my appeal. The claim involved 2 elements pertaining to Page. One being his statement to my lawyers, the other being his statements to Jessica in the film. Jessica literally helped save my life. (The song Crossroads by Bone Thugs and Harmony just came on the radio…A fitting song at this time. It also was the favorite song of a friend of mine from when I was a teenager. His life ended way too soon.) To the people that have fought so hard for me these past 5 months, Jorunn, Renate, Merel, Meike, Jessica, Alex, friends and family, my lawyers, strangers, and too many others to name. Thank You. The various groups from the TCADP, ICADP and other anti-death penalty groups, criminal justice groups and human rights organizations along with concerned conservatives. Thank you for encouraging your members to speak out. As you all know from experience, the fight is not over with yet. I would encourage people to join these groups. The TCADP does actual lobby work for reform with elected officials in Texas. If you are from Texas and want to be a part of working towards reform and educating others, then I would suggest joining Texas Coalition to Abolish the Death Penalty. TCADP.org is the site I believe. You can be from other states or countries and join Amnesty International also, though of course their focus is much more than the death penalty. The logo for them is a candle and they did help shine a light. Amicus, Reprieve and other more legal focused groups helped as well. These are vital groups that need legal talent that can intern on cases. Being that they deal with death penalty cases, they try to pick from the top of the class as people's lives are at stake. Merel and Renate both interned with Amicus.

Now, I've got to give a special thanks to all those in the Lone Star State that stepped up. More so those that, while supporting the death penalty, recognized the injustice of this case and then spoke up about it. I need more people from Texas; as you pay the taxes, you vote the politicians, prosecutors and judges into office. You should be outraged that over $300,000 has been spent so far on this case just on trial and appeal costs. It isn't over yet! I am going back for a new round of appeals now. Midland county seems so content on covering for the former prosecutor and their good ole boy buddies then what it costs taxpayers, victims families, my loved ones, and pervert the very concepts of justice that is guaranteed by the Texas and and U.S Constitution. None of that matters to them it seems. Thankfully, I get to live to fight another day. I was surely thinking that I was going to have to be hanging out in the big meadow in the sky with Mr. Pig, eating watermelon and watching the video to the song "Honky Tonk Ba Donka Donk" by Trace Adkins on an endless loop. ☺ haha. But instead I get to live to see October 27th and work on additional projects!

The songs I've mentioned that I've written, which Pyrexx performed, I didn't realize they were not yet distributed. By the time this is posted, the songs should be available for download. They are located on my website, that hosts my personal stuff: www.saveaninnocentlife.com. For official case information visit saveclintonyoung.com. This is set up as an official word of my lawyers for US Media and such. Clintonyoungfoundation.com is operated by Merel and Renate and focused on international media and the more 'hit the streets' type of campaigning. Also to raise funds for public awareness campaigns, future legal fees to be saved up so that when I get a new trial I can hire the best lawyers possible. (My current lawyers are only appeal lawyers.) Bottom line is this. Songs, sites, blogs, etc. it is all about one thing. Winning. I am in it to win it! Veni Vidi Vici! ☺

P.S Actually, when my lawyers first asked me for a statement to be released, I did say Veni Vidi Vici! Though I haven't won yet, so got to keep on fighting. Need you all as my anti-venom, because these snakes keep striking!

Keep Fightin'.

Take care, smile and keep on keepin on.

In solidarity I remain,

Clinton Young #999447

www.saveaninnocentlife.com

www.clintonyoungfoundation.com

www.saveclintyoung.com

Loud & Clear, November 5, 2017

Topic: The Saga Continues – Label me this, Label me that

NOTICE

Due to a roller coaster of emotions and such, I was not doing much writing but I have started back. With jpays– here is an idea to help me keep track of the ones I am receiving; number them. The next one you send to me, label #1, this way in the future if I get, for example, #5 and #7 then I will know I didn't get #6 and can write the mailroom about it and get it printed off. If you are writing me for the first time and decide to use jpay, please include the address. I cannot write back with jpay, but once I get your address you do not have to continue to include it in future letters. Due to problems I would always suggest you send me your first letter via regular mail. Details for all of this are included on my website: www.saveaninnocentlife.com. Although the letter program on my website is better and more secure, I just want to make sure I get what people send. Again, I am back on stable ground so I am writing more. Thanks. Alrighty then. It seems that some things change and some remain the same.

What has not changed is Midland. The D.A told my lawyers that she was not agreeing to anything. Some other stuff has developed that makes such a stance even more shocking. My lawyer asked me not to blog about it right now. I really, really want to though, but I will give it a week. I will say this. If ANYTHING about this case has shocked you, get ready, because you haven't seen anything yet. It even shocked me! I can't wait to write about it. I should be able to in a week, just giving my lawyers time to sort everything for the next course of action. I am truly blessed to have appeal lawyers that care so much about me. More so with what I am currently facing. This is going to be where it matters most. I regret being so hard on them in the past. Due to previous lawyers messing me over, I made it harder on them. Though, it is through the struggles that we have gotten closer. I would hope that having worked this case and with me all these years that they would feel it made them better lawyers. Steel sharpens steel. I push them to hit harder, they pull me to tone it down some. I am, as people know, a very determined person. I have a dominating personality, so we knock heads all the time. But I really do love them. Hearing the joy in their voice when I got a stay, that let me know how much they care about me. Margaret even commented to me that day that they seemed happier I got a stay then I did. I was happy, but my mind was clicking over to the next battle. This is not over with yet. More so with the way some things unfolded. The only thing is, if I get a new trial, I cannot have them as my lawyers. They are only appeal lawyers. The bond I was able to build with them over the past years, I will not have the time or opportunity to develop that with new lawyers for trial and such. Since I will not have the best lawyers love can get, I will need the best lawyers money can buy. As it seems I will have to fight for any and all I want. With donations being sent to clintonyoungfoundation.com it is building up to be able to raise more awareness here in Texas and also to save up for future legal costs. The big name lawyers, they charge 300-400+ an hour, usually with a 30-50k retainer fee just to get started. This is the land of the free. As long as you can pay for it! I thank everyone that donates. Everything adds up.

On to other matters. I did an interview with Midland news station. Ah, I think I did horrible. I was mentally and emotionally exhausted from the two weeks prior. The interview was on the 25th of Oct. I was still sorting out everything from Robert's execution and then getting the stay. I was also nervous, as my lawyers told me to hold off on the interview, but the next day they were here! I didn't know exactly when they were coming as no formal date was listed, just that it would be on one of the media days. I was stumbling over my words, didn't properly express myself on some points that I should have. I think it was the worst interview I've ever given. Plus, I couldn't gather my thoughts, so I kept looking down to think and to the side. If they desire to make me look bad, guess they could. Hopefully the reporter understands all I just went through. We shall see how it turns out. Another film with me in it is supposed to air this month also but I'm not sure where. When he lets me know I will have it posted on the sites and such. When I wrote in a previous blog about love versus force, my meaning was accepting people for who they are. To allow them the freedom to be themselves in all ways, not trying to get people to live up to my standards or what I see as right, and that I focus on the bond with those in my life that I have. I write that as it is applicable to a civilized society. For example, if I were to be locked up in a maximum-security prison, I would not walk onto the rec yard and yell out "I Love You All!" No. THAT would NOT happen! ☺ haha. The other guys might not be as emotionally advanced as I am causing them to get the wrong idea. Then I would have to resort to my Viking/Irish bloodlines! Haha. Seriously though, prisons in the U.S are so different than in Europe in so many ways. It is due to how the government shaped the systems. Prison and war have ways of showing the worst about humanity, the ways that people find to hurt each other, how people will turn a blind eye to the suffering of another. People in mainstream media even joke about prison rape. Like it is just something that is to be and because it is men, it's like a pass is given to the weak being attacked. What's even worse is the way guards have made light of it and put a person in a bad situation on purpose.

This wasn't meant to be the topic of this blog. A joke I made got me thinking about it as I wrote this though and also about how I changed my thinking. Before, I had always thought that if a guy was not strong enough to stand on his own two feet then he couldn't stand with me. If he couldn't stand up for himself then oh well, tough shit. That line of thinking has come from having been all alone and had to fight for mine. Having gone through the flames and then overcoming. It was the struggles I had early in life that made me stronger. Not everyone in life is conditioned to fight the same. I used to think that it was something to be proud of, that if I thought someone was going to stab me, I didn't feel fear. Or that I could dominate my environment by any means needed. When I was called "dangerous" by the system that helped shape me, I didn't feel shame. No, I felt a sense of pride. However, outside of the system, I did not want to be seen as this dangerous person. More so while free, I understood the free world was different than prison. I wanted a normal life while free, to be a part of society. Though in prison, "dangerous" is a virtue. Even while I was locked up, I understood how sick that line of thinking was. Not just for me, but the very system that causes it to be required. It is shameful that as a society people are locked up in these environments. Then after they become the person the need to be to survive, we condemn them. The U.S prison systems are a threat to public safety. Prison gangs formed as a way for outnumbered ethnic groups to protect themselves, and now many of those gangs wreak havoc on communities. A reaction to the system. The system then responds for access to votes and funds and builds solitary confinement cells. Thousands go into isolation. As the years tick by, their minds deteriorate, and the weaker prisoners are left even more so and victimization spikes. The result is to pass more laws and create fancy policy labels. With people getting rich from private prisons, then pass laws locking more people up to fill the prisons. Prisons are laboratories of hate and emotionally numbing, they breed the worst in humanity. If people could flip a switch and scan with a camera to see how most prisons are, they would be disgusted.

Prison has shown me just how deplorable a human being can be. Also how, with routine, people can ignore others, no matter the problem. I have seen mentally ill people here. One time a guy had shit in the middle of his floor just playing with it while staring off at whatever he was looking at beyond the walls. The whole side of the pod stunk! It had been 2 days!! (this was years ago) The officers were just walking by, cussing him out as they passed but doing nothing to fix the problem, just following routine. I refused to exit the dayroom and after throwing a fit about it they finally did something. I remember rank coming to the pod asking me what the problem was and I said "What's the problem? You can't smell the fuckin' problem?!" One would think that would have been enough but no, I had to push even further about if having to smell shit I was going to have to smell pepper spray too. One extreme to resolve another. My position to the guards was that they were working in a place where they breathe shit in all day. That concept never seemed to cross their mind, I guess. I don't know why the other prisoners didn't speak up. Maybe they enjoyed it, or were afraid to force the issue or hell maybe they thought it wasn't cool to make the guards go in the guys cell and clean it up, who knows. There were other prisoners who would have spoken u, but at that time none of them were down there on the disciplinary level. I tell ya what, labels are a fucking trip! We put labels on people, then based on that we ignore certain things. Things that a person with a different label wouldn't be ignored. Beyond the 'others', is the prisoner. Often seen as sub-human or worthless.

Labels.

A cheerleader in a small town gets killed and the feelings of outrage are overwhelming to all. Yet, flipping through the channels and seeing a news story about a girl of the same age getting stoned in Syria gets merely a headshake and the channel changed. As 'that's how "they" are'. The labels of "ours" vs. "theirs", "us" vs "them", "we" or "those people."

What is in a name?

Everything, if it is a label.

As soon as we put a label on someone it seems to make it to easy to throw them away, toss them in the trash bin. One for every label. That is, until it hits home. Was terror only terror after 9/11? Was crack and meth only an addiction? Politicians response to prior drug problems was to build more prisons. Now that their nephews, friend's daughter, etc are turning up dead from heroin and pills, well now it becomes a crisis. An illness, see that is a label we can fix. They are sick, not "bad" people!

It is no longer a crime wave or dope feens. Those labels we have to lock up and punish.

The ironic thing is that the current U.S heroin/pill problem is a result of drug companies being unregulated by politicians. As the companies make more money, stock prices go up and politicians and investors get wealthier. Then the problem comes to their neighborhood and now it is a crisis.

Money and Labels.

They way people determine each others worth, or lack of. I wonder how the future will really look. Sometimes it seems like Love is fighting a losing battle. However, it is all the hate that makes us cherish the rarity that is love. To value our bonds as even our human connections are fading. The advancements we make in society with technology, just more ways we do not have to deal with each other, person to person. We seem to be on a journey to remove what makes us, "us". Label it progress! People say the damnest things.

Time ticks on.

Veni Vidi Vici

In Solidarity,

I remain,

Clinton YOUNG #999447

Thank you for sharing my words with others.

-Tell someone you love them-

As tomorrow is not promised today..

Loud & Clear, November 12, 2017

Topic: This & That

The days tick by, the fight goes on.

Thanks for all that continue to spread the word about me and to help. Just because I got a stay does not mean I am safe. Keep in mind, Robert had 6 different execution dates. I have been writing like crazy the past couple of weeks, so I've just been getting caught up on all that. Also, I did not win a new trial, I won a new appeal (for a rare second time). Channel 7 from Midland did a news spot on me and when asked what shows that I am innocent, I am told that the interview that aired it seems as if I just say that I didn't get a fair trial. Hmm… I guess maybe they had to edit it for time purposes?! I believe what I said was that the best experts in the world for the forensic fields pertaining to my case, say I am innocent. I didn't say it in exactly those words, I think I said it as "the best experts in the world, all the forensics clear me." From what I have been told, the interview was not bad, considering it was the media from the town I was convicted in. It is rare that small town media goes after prosecutors as they would in, say, Dallas or Houston. So, I really did not expect that to happen. What really amazed me is that the Sheriff said that he has never been more proud of Midland then when they gave me the death penalty. Wow! The jury that gave me death is not even proud of what they did. Two of them, including the foreman of the jury, have given statements to my lawyers. This same jury also complained about the sloppy work done in my case. It is well documented at how the Midland County Sheriff's office lost evidence, destroyed evidence and failed to properly test other evidence. Look, just please go to www.saveclintyoung.com and read my filings. My lawyers document it very well. My jury today is not even all convinced of my guilt, which happens when someone is INNOCENT! Maybe the Sheriff does not know Page bragged to 6 people that he committed the murder and that the best experts in gunshot residue and ballistics say that I could not have been the killer. I wonder why Spencer doesn't work for Midland County Sheriff's office anymore? Hmm.. I really do not want to have to fight with the Sheriff's office. I've got enough chaos dealing with prosecutors! The Sheriff is just not aware of the new developments and such. To people from Midland that are new to looking up my case, watch the films done on my case and read everything at www.saveclintyoung.com (Even more so if you have had a loved one get railroaded by the Midland injustice system.) I also want to point out to people that this is the 2nd new appeal I've won. Which is rare in Texas…maybe it is because people have concerns about my case.

Anywho, to people that are new to reading my blogs, I do not script these blogs. I just sit down and write. As the words come, they hit the paper, which is why I might cover several topics in one blog. In regards to my last blog, I wrote about being dangerous, as I had been speaking to a guy here that was at the same juvenile prison as me and I made a comment about how we used to beat the hell out of each other for the stupidest reasons. Not Him and I, but all of us there. I mentioned prisons being a threat to public safety, the juvenile prisons are. Point in example, the unit where I was, there are 5 buildings: 1, 2 a/b, 3 a/b, 4 a/b/c/d and 5 a/b/c/d. From 4B, 4D, 5A and 5C (they hold 24 people each) and in a 3 year span, 5 people have come to death row. A 6th would have but the victim survived. A 7th was able to plea out to 3 capital life sentences and 2 others got life for murders (plus another that was involved in a murder but snitched his way out.) The 6th survived a gunshot wound to the head! So it could have been 7 people on death row from just those 4 dorms. Four of these people were on the same dorm as me! These are just the ones I know about. Now, does that not seem like a public safety threat? A culture of violence that was so bad that officers who worked with adults in TDCJ were scared to work there. Guess which unit in all of the system was easiest to go home from? Yep. The same one I was at. A study showed that 72% of people locked up there would re-offend. I guarantee 60% of that number was just from the 4 dorms I listed above. I wrote about prison as it bothered me so much. I was thinking about how one could become so numb to violence. Not that I was "dangerous". I did enough to control my environment as best I could, though I never saw myself as being dangerous because I care. I know some dangerous people. They all have a common thread, they don't care about themselves, much less anyone else. This topic came up as they have reconfigured a cell here for a guy that is going to trial for beating a guard to death. He is at Telford unit. The story should be in the news, it happened at a prison in New Boston, TX. They are seeking the death penalty. You see, I have never focused on harming anyone else. My focus has only been to make sure I was not harmed. That I could control my environment, meaning my space! I should have been more clear about that and explained the time frames.

In prison environments, the people that are seen as willing to cause trouble tend to be treated better than those that never get in trouble. The guards/prisoners will poke at the person that will not fight back. That concept is what causes prisons in the U.S to create a culture of violence. It was heavy on my heart as it impacts so many people. Now and later. It doesn't have to be that way. In Europe they do not have these problems and people actually learn and improve in prison. Yet, here in the U.S, we use these labels and complain about spending money and the person gets out and commit even worse crimes! More so, when a prisoner is released and cannot get a good job since they have been classified as a second hand citizen because they were convicted of a crime, it creates a cycle that only those that invest in prisons benefit from. Maybe that's why they keep it going. I am lucky and blessed because if I were to get out today I have so many people who love and support me that I could land on my feet, be in a stable environment and go on to do great things in life. That is why I say that in many ways coming here has been the best thing for me. Also, I have been able to help others which is truly rewarding. Even if they had killed me, all they would have done is killed my body. My spirit would have remained in all those that I have influenced and who now go on to help others, or the ones that have unlocked themselves from their own prisons and enjoy the freedom of living their life! Tens of thousands have read my blogs and walked away from them feeling stronger or seeing life in a different way. I have gotten countless letters about this. So yeah, I am still dangerous. But now I am a danger to those that use fear to control others. I am a threat to self-doubt, fear, insecurities, bullies and hatred. I only had to suffer the pain and injustice of one life, but I get to help countless other lives. Everything in life has a price. Someone asked me if I could change my past, would I? Sure. We all have the fantasy of what if, etc. Though it is from all that has happened in my life that has brought me to this point. I wish I could eliminate the pain I've caused others. Though each time I get a letter from a kid that felt hopeless and had been told they are worthless but now they've taken control of their life, or a woman that has gotten out of a bad relationship, or a guy that went back to school to go on and do something to help others… Each time I read about someone that was impacted by me and how they go on to make this fucked up world a little bit better live in… It's a cost I am glad I paid. We never know how this journey we call life will unfold, but what we can do is change the way we treat each other while on the ride.

Love is Freedom.

Veni, Vidi, Vici

In Solidarity,

Clinton Young #999447

D. R- Polunsky Unit

3872 FM 350 SOUTH

Livingston, TX 77351

U.S.A

www.saveaninnocentlife.com

www.saveclintyoung.com

Follow the Clinton Young Foundation at Facebook.com/clintonyoungfoundation

Loud & Clear, November 19, 2017

Topic: Bad Anniversary

A few days from writing this will mark the 16th year into this tragedy. The 23rd is Thanksgiving. (A major U.S Holiday) Being that the events of this case took place around the holidays, it does cast a shadow over the season. It impacts all the families. Thanksgiving is about taking a step back and reflecting on what a person is thankful for. I am blessed that I am alive and have the love of so many. One element of my personal philosophy is that life must be balanced. When one is taken from life, then you need to give back. It is from this thinking that I developed an idea. My plan is to develop a charity. With the access to certain people that I have, my belief is that it will be easy to get going. The goal being that funds will go to young girls who want to reach educational goals for the purpose of making the world a better place to live. There is someone who writes to me that could help me sort out the details. I am not sure if she wants to publicly mention her name but the bottom line is I am going to do this. What I need help with is to be able to communicate with someone that manages/owns a printing or card company. I think it is a safe bet that my best chance will be one from The Netherlands, although it can be from anywhere. I want to communicate with such a person to discuss an idea I have. I am also in the process of talking to some about publishing my book. What I will not do is publish it purely for profit. It just didn't feel right. An interesting bit is that Robert had his posted for free; though with the various projects I have in mind the book would help with that. I can take the struggles I have had in life and use it to ease the struggles of others.

The reason I want to start a charity for young girls is because the most important people in my life have been women. The people I am closest to are all women. The sector of life that has helped me the most is clearly women. Plus, education strengthens a person. Many are denied the greatest gift that humans can give or receive. That is Love. Many people are forced to marry for money, social status, and other limited options in life. Those that have followed my writings over the years and/or written to me, know that this is something I have always been sympathetic to. Now that I have the ability to make a difference, I will make a difference.

On to another topic – Writing people here. I have long said that I will not write to anyone that writes to another person here, unless it is one of the few select that I have faith in. However, after some thought, I understand that position goes against my other governing philosophy of allowing a person to be free to be free. As I also believe in balance, I came to this conclusion: I am going to start a penpal section on my website. It will have profiles for people here that I know will honor the two rules I do have when it comes to getting someone to write a person here. #1 is no scams or bullshit. #2 is never give a person's address out unless they give their permission. To keep it simple, we are not all the same here. Many change their ways, many do not. There have been some here that would have the people's information sent to them and then pick out the best pen pal for themselves and pass other ones on to other guys. That is some bullshit! The profiles will be posted on my site and if someone feels a need to write one of them, so be it. It is up to the person. Now, I am not going to accept some random people that I do not know on there. The fact that I do not put a person on it is not an indictment on them. One thing I will not budge on is if someone writes to someone here with even the slightest hint of drama or bullshit of any kind, I will end all contact. I have too much positive stuff going on, my loved ones are working too hard to have to entertain some dumb shit. Some morons here think they can build themselves up by trying to tear someone else down. That line of thinking is why they are here in the first place. It is also why many here will not write to people who write others here. If people would put their energy into legit production, they would be a great deal more advanced in life, versus investing in dumbass plots. Anyways, in a couple weeks everything will be set up on my site. I decided to do this after two guys on the section with me got letters from people that wrote to me. Both are actually people I am cool with and will be listed on my site! They are people here I associate with so when they see a Netherlands address, they ask me if I know the person. Ha.

I am also going to use that sector of my site as a way to highlight various projects I am working on with others here; be it art exhibits, writing a play, etc. There are some very talented people here and I want to help highlight a different side of the people here other than their cases. Some are innocent, some are not, but all are different men today then who they were when they were first locked up. That has to count for something! I ask for people to still continue to share videos, download the music available on my site and spread the word. The fight is NOT over with yet! There are others that write to me and as I get to know them and feel they will focus on more than self-gain, I will promote them also. I am going to make the most of each day while I am alive. I thank everyone that has donated, every bit helps. Thank you for spreading the word as each new person makes me stronger. Also, supposedly there is a case before the U.S Supreme Court about the death penalty being unconstitutional. If the USSC ruled such, it would end the death penalty. The case will be decided BEFORE June 2018. It takes 4 Supreme Court justices to hear a case and 5 to win. There are 9 on the court. Justice Scalia said before he died that he saw the death penalty ending within a couple of years. So few states kill, and even in those states there are only a few prosecutors that send people to death row. Therefore, it has no purpose and is unusual. If a punishment is unusual or cruel, then it is a violation of the 8th Amendment of the U.S Constitution. I'm just saying that you never know… Alrighty then, I shall be back soon. Take care, smile and strive for all that you desire.

Learn, Love, Live

Veni, Vidi, Vici.

I remain in Solidarity,

Clinton YOUNG #999447

www.saveaninnocentlife.com

www.saveclintyoung.com

www.clintonyoungfoundation.com

Loud & Clear, November 28, 2017

Topic: Corrections and Updates

This will be short and to the point. Another blog will be following in a few days.

1. I mistakenly thought the U.S Supreme Court had accepted a case out of Arizona to hear about the death penalty. I misunderstood what was said on a program called The Prison Show, which airs on a local radio station from Houston. KPFT. The radio reception is not very good in this cell so I didn't catch it properly. Danielle and Ms. Linda do a good job trying to keep us updated on new cases, rulings, etc. Myself along with many others here are very grateful that they do this. Many guys here have found out about their appeals being denied from the radio station, as their lawyers didn't even bother writing them. As a result, this volunteer service that these women help with is a good deed. Danielle sent me some paper work on it all. After looking over it, I realized it was set for conference not granted to review. There are 2 questions before the court in Hidalgo V. Arizona, one being the death penalty for that state and the other being death overall. Most likely the USSC will hear about Arizona's death penalty laws. They CAN take on the death penalty as a whole, it is possible to get 4 to agree to hear it especially if enough media attention is given. However, the way the high court works when it comes to criminal matters is that they rarely issue all out rulings striking down a punishment nationwide. They can though, so we shall see if they hear it. If the court grants cert. (agrees to hear it) the question about the death penalty overall, I would bet money it would be ending. If they only hear about Arizona's specific laws, it is just one more step. To my forgotten readers, each state in the U.S is like its own country when it comes to criminal laws. In one state a gram of weed is a fine, in another state it is 5 years! Then there are the federal laws. It is why lawyers make so much money! So many damn laws!

2. The Judge in my case requested to be removed from my case. This was done either because he recognized there was a world of shit that he wanted no part of and his ethics, oath, and Christian values he professes to adhere to all got to him. Or, someone actually thought it would be best for him to step down as him staying on the case could actually help me due to unethical actions between him and the prosecutors in 2010 and 2017 (which clearly display a pattern). So maybe he was advised to step down so that him being on my case wouldn't help me, or so they think. Or maybe he just wanted to go fishing! I would wager on the 2nd reason though. Hmmm…

Alrighty then, gonna wrap this up. I will be back in a couple of days. Thanks for all the help. Keep spreading the word and sharing the films, etc. One little video has over 1.6 million. Lets see if it can get to 3 million.

Take care. Smile. Strive for all that you desire.

Learn. Love. Live.

Veni, Vidi, Vici

In Solidarity I remain,

Clinton YOUNG #999447

DR-Polunksy Unit

3872 FM 350 South

Livingston, TX 77351

USA

www.saveaninnocentlife.com

www.saveclintyoung.com

www.clintonyoungfoundation.com

Use the pain to fuel the fire that burns inside of you

Loud & Clear, December 2017

Topic: Wrapping up a year

It has been a roller coaster of a year. As I write this there is still a few days left in 2017. It has gotten to where so much takes place in a year that it is hard to believe that the event wasn't a couple of years ago. The destructive forces of nature, man's unique ability to be able to develop new ways to hurt each other, so many agendas it is hard to sort out what "right" even means. More so with so many wrongs. It has gotten to where facts do not even hold weight anymore. The means have to matter or the end will always be turmoil. Clearly shown by the tone of the political landscape. The masses are at odds while few get richer and stronger. How big of a storm is needed to wake people up? It's like people cannot even talk to one another. We hold onto our walls that are reinforced by elements that at the end of the day really do not matter. People may have picked up a different tone in my words in recent times. It's simple. I had my storm.

Beyond the date for execution, I went through some stuff with people that I was close to. I directed my frustrations towards the wrong people at times. When I needed people the most, I pushed them away the hardest. I ended up going several weeks without a visit while dealing with the execution date. All of it helped to open my eyes more. Then planning my funeral and final days with loved ones. It makes you re-evaluate life, or at least it did me. I have always thought about what could have been had my life been put on a different path. Though a different path doesn't always mean a better outcome. As a child I had plans of joining the military. When I went to enlist I couldn't due to my criminal record. At least not as an officer. Had life been stable for me, I could have joined, went off to war and ended up another casualty saluted and then forgotten. My life went as it did and now I am here. Before, I focused on everything I didn't have, dwelled on the ways I was wronged. Justified the anger as cause and effect of life. Then I fought for those that doubted to see my victory. The past few months helped me to instead look at what I did have in life. A rich man can sit up in his castle and cry, while a poor man huddles in his hut and smiles. When we always seek for more, we can never be satisfied with what we have. There are people that have never been to prison that live with more pain that myself. When I write that I feel happy, I do not mean that I am fully satisfied, as I am not. There is still injustice that I face. The prosecutor is still trying to kill me, to protect (I guess) the reputations of her past co-workers. (Life doesn't have much value these days it seems). The ironic thing is that she does it at the risk of her own reputation. What is a bit scarier is that I have a group of lawyers fighting for me. Plus, I am educated enough that I am like an extra lawyer. If all took place with me and my team how much more would happen to an uneducated person with an unconcerned, court appointed attorney? (For cases that are not "capital" in Texas the court appointed lawyers have a very small budget and if it costs the county too much, they do not get appointed again. Capital cases, more so facing death, those lawyers get a bigger budget.) My fight is not over with yet. There is surely no time to relax. Maybe they will end up doing the right thing, they are human beings, so I will not give up on them. When it comes to feeling blessed, I have reasons to be. Again, I could sit around and focus on all the things I do not have or I can focus on what I do have and make the most of it. Are my problems so big that I cannot help others? No matter your journey, there is always time to help someone up that has fallen. There have been people enter my life that have had some hard times in their own lives. Many can see the problem, but not all have the vision to be able to see through it, thus allowing it to define them. If I can help someone take back control of their life to then help another, it makes my own life gain a bit more value.

I have been told before that I am worthless. That I would never amount to anything. Do I sit here in a pool of pity and allow that to be true? Or do I make the most of what life has given me?

What really is success? If life has given me the wisdom and strength to make the world a better place, that is a blessing. People that know me personally would not be shocked that I would want to help others. Many testified to that fact in my trial, that I would help people. Only thing is that going through everything with the execution date, it caused me to really think about my legacy. Coming so close to dying I was aware that, had it happened, I would have left this world defined purely by my fight over this case. Since day 1 my fight has been that I did not do it. That I would not have done what they said I did. As I often said, I was so embarrassed in the trial. That they were saying I killed 2 people for cars. Beyond calling me a killer, they said it was for a car to go see a girl. That is total bullshit. So that was going to end up being my legacy. That my life would be defined by that battle. One my enemies created, versus one I created. I don't know about others, but I want more for myself, I expect more from myself and I demand more of myself!

I am aware of my individual greatness and the various strengths that I have. I am strong enough to be able to life others up during my journey and to keep going forward, even beyond the finish line. I can live on through the love of others by the way they go on to help others. It makes all the pain worth it. A person can use the pain inside of them to fuel the flame that scorches the world around them, or they can use the pain to fuel the flame that can then be used as a light. It is all about how you sue what life has given you. You either allow it to make you or break you, to be a master of YOUR life or a slave to the life given to you. Someone comes along and from their own weakness, harms you. To what right do they then have power over your life? Do not give it to them! I have been wronged. I have been hurt. I have also wronged and hurt others. Thankfully I can see beyond the obstacles. I could sit here and write out all the ways life is unfair to me. That is not the man I am. As a child I saw myself in the way that was presented to me by others. I allowed others to define my life by the insecurities that I had adopted from them. Labeled as broken. Classified as bad. What was there left to do but be bad? I mean, it wasn't my fault, I was "broken" after all! As a child other peoples lack of understanding, fear, and weakness defined my world. As I grew up I began to take control of my life. Thankfully, I had a vision to be able to see beyond others; to recognize my own strengths, to be educated so that I could love myself and then in turn, live. Learn, Love, Live. I am happy that I can help others take control of their life, to be able to have the love that allows them to live. That is a blessing. Sadly, my awareness of my own strengths was often forged in the flames of violence. That it defined my courage. Here I am at this place in life. Do not be shocked that a man in my situation could see the world as I do, as that would mean you doubt your own ability. Also, please do not confuse my joy with satisfaction and safety. My life is still at risk. I am far from being out of dangers way, you all are still needed. The battle is not over yet, much less the war. There is much to do. I am going to have to write my book differently and self-publish because publishers just take too long. So that begins, it will be done by summertime. I thank everyone that helped guide me through the storms of 2017. We have to keep pushing ahead. Take Care, Smile and Strive for all that you desire.

Learn, Love, Live

Veni, Vidi, Vici

Clinton Young#999447

D.R – Polunksy Unit

3872 FM 350 South

Livingston, TX 77315

USA

saveaninnocentlife.com

clintonyoungfoundation.com

saveclintyoung.com

"Love is Freedom"

Loud & Clear, February 1, 2018

Topic: A New Year with New Lies

I have been silent thus far for 2018 as I was waiting… Waiting on the State to respond; and they did hahaha. Lord have mercy. Here is the deal: While I had an execution date, they met with a co-defendant and they taped the interview. In doing so he admitted to kidnapping Samuel for the first time and also holding the gun. The D.A kept this from my lawyers while my appeal was pending. So while I was waiting to be executed, they had the very evidence that showed my claim to be true: that he lied at my trial. Yet, they hid this from us until after my stay.

This is against the law. Just like they lied about deals, they with-held the information given by lab experts before my trial about the gun being empty before getting to Midland. I can go on and on. I really do not know what they had in mind by doing what they did in their response. They just openly lied. Lies that I can easily disprove. Like in one part they say about DNA on the gloves and try to act as if I wore the gloves. This is so bullshit! On the tip on the side of the OUTSIDE of Page's gloves, on one small spot on the OUTSIDE, again, OUTSIDE of the glove there was a DNA "mixture" of several people. Again, a MIXTURE of several people. They say I am one of them. Okay, this has NO value at all. NONE! It could be from Page grabbing a sprite bottle I drank out of, which is exactly where it came from. He picked it up to throw away. I guess the D.A wanted to go to such far reaching extremes to attempt to convince the Judge to not hold a hearing. But, by them saying something so untrue, it makes the hearing all the more needed!

Then, they admit they with-held the evidence about Page's admissions while I had an execution date. They try to explain the gloves away 4 different ways. They try so many different arguments it confused me! How can I defend against fantasy? Easy. They have NO EXPERT! The D.A just writing some bullshit and taking stuff from Wikipedia is not allowed in court. Where is their expert? Why can't they get an expert? I got some of the best experts in the world. Microtrace works for the Department of Justice. That is why! You all know who The Department of Justice is over in the U.S? FBI, ATF, DEA. The top ranked law enforcement agencies in the world.

My lawyers get to respond. They will be responding soon. We are going over it all now, but I cannot say everything I want to. Though when I was reading some parts of what the D.A wrote I started to laugh out loud and jump up and down in the cell. Hahaha. They went to some real extremes & stretched some things way beyond what I ever thought they would. Then they try to attack my witnesses, though they ignore how they intimidated them, which Kemp details in the film "Deal with Death." Also, other stuff was NOT in their handwriting. It was something written up by a D.A investigator. Then half of it is not even about my case. They go on and write on and on and on about 2 cases that are not even mine, as if trying to link it or something. I do not know what the hell they were doing. Though really, one part made me laugh as it will help me with a side issue. It is really sad to me reading over it. As these are people who are supposed to be the defenders of the law, to make this abstract concept to be conformed to a fair and just foundation that our society operates from. That a prosecutor will with-hold evidence and do it so easily they openly admit in the filing they did it. They say we could not have had the evidence that Page admitted to them because they didn't give it to us. WOW! They so easily and openly admit they broke the law. They violated my rights of due process under the law. They with-held the very evidence that would have granted me a stay of execution as it proved my claim.

People, please understand that had I been executed, the evidence would have faded away.

Had the appeals court rejected all my appeals, they would have done so because they did not know this evidence existed. Then, to even write the words that make it seem as if I wore the gloves. I got the damn DNA report from the Texas Department of Public Safety crime lab. The crime lab for law enforcement in Texas! The D.A's own expert! So, again, it is clear as day they are lying! I can prove it with experts that testified for the D.A!!! (D.A means District Attorney, The Prosecutor) Thankfully I have very smart lawyers on my case and many others helping out and they love me and fight so hard for me. (What is so scary is, what if I didn't? If you read the state's arguments in Anthony Graves case and court rulings, you would think he is guilty as can be. Yet, today he is free.) They try to link a print from another case to me. Again, experts have discredited this. I mean, it seems that the prosecutor is so accustomed to lawyers not fighting back in the small-town legal arena. Yo' I got a whole tribe of lawyers fighting for me!

Several that hang back in the shadows. They even say I admitted to several witnesses that I stole the truck. I wonder who these phantom people are as no such thing happened. NO ONE SAID THAT BULLSHIT! What the witness said is what I have said all along. "I came out the store and Page was in the truck." They would know this had they actually investigated the store where Samuel was kidnapped. This is fact! They just passed out mail and my sister was saying some are saying bad things about me. Maybe it is from what the D.A filed. Okay, look: For anyone that supports me, do not get upset or argue with anyone. It is pointless. My fight is not over.

My lawyers get to respond to what the D.A filed and respond they will!! Though the difference is, my lawyers will have facts. From the prosecutors own experts and also other experts that work for law enforcement. There is some stuff I want to write about but now is not the time. I have always said to everyone to give me a chance. Each time I am given a chance, I have been proven true. My fight is not over yet. Now, to be clear, none of this is funny with case. There is just a side issue that made me laugh, as they helped me be able to prove something. The sad thing is that 2 people died & they do not want to admit that people of power would abuse it so badly. I worry about those with mental illness and bad lawyers. I really do. The system fails people so much. Look at Carlos De'Luna, Todd Willingham, and on and on. The fight goes on. My lawyers will file their response soon. Let me get to another topic. For a long time the wife of a shooting victim has lashed out at me and expressed her desire for me to die. Her husband was shot in the leg. He is alive. Yet, she wants me to die. Again, he is not dead. Also, I was never charged, indicted, or such for the shooting. Not at all. No charges or anything were filed against me in the case, nor can any due to statute of limitations. Though the victim testified in my trial during punishment, I did not know this man. I held no ill though for him. A guy I also did not know had someone attack him. They wanted to go at night, there is a reason they did not. I stopped them. See, this guys wife was pregnant. So, if Pat and Josh would have went over there at night, they expressed about shooting them. I protested. It is like this, Josh and Pat show up at Hippies, a guy we all knew, Dano, who is my half-brother, is sitting on the couch. Pat is going through bags of stuff he had. Him and Josh discuss some Mexican guy. Dano made a remark about passing a blunt, which is a marijuana cigar. Pat took offense and pulled a gun out asking Josh if he needs to shoot anyone. Pat is someone that is to be taken seriously. Dano is my brother, so I pulled out a gun that Hippie kept in the kitchen drawer. I dropped it on the counter so the thud could be heard. I leaned forward and said "Hey Pat, chill out. No one's trippin, put the heat up." He looks at me and says "No one's trippin?" I say "No." He puts the gun away. They then go back to talking about this Mexican guy. Josh mentions his wife, Pat then brings up the fact that sometime prior he was hanging out when a half ounce of meth, automatic assault rifle and 2 other guns was discovered by the police. Pat and another guy went to jail. I was on parole and didn't. Pat hinted about this. So I point out he admitted was his guns and it was other guys car. What was he getting at? He backed up some on the topic and then said: "I'm not saying you done anything fucked up, I just ya know, need to know if you gonna have my back?" Okay. I express that if someone gets foul with him, yeah I had his back. Him and Josh get back to talking and Josh asks about what to do about the wife. Pat says "fuck it, shoot her." Now, I don't know if he would have, I think he was just talking noise to uphold a ruthless image. I came around the counter yelling "Oh fuck no! Hell no! I ain't down with any pregnant chick getting shot." I looked at Pat at told him "Homie, It aint going down like that." He backed off from it. After that element of the topic, I said "Only way I would go is if no guns are involved." Okay, Debbie testified to this! She was sitting next to Dano. I can name a couple of others who know if this situation. The reason why the events unfolded during the daytime is because the Mexican guy, his name is Carols, I called him "Mexican guy" as that is how they kept saying. I was not trying to not dignify him by avoiding the use of his name. I detailed it as the vents was unfolding. Again, I did not know the man. Well, the events happened during the daytime as his wife was known to be at work. This was, she would not be hurt. The bottom line is this: Carlos was shot. He should not have been shot. People justified it by claiming he was a drug dealer, that he was associated with someone else that was not liked. That is what I was told. None of that matters. The shit we all were into was wrong.

I am ashamed of many of the things I done in my life. I have hurt people. I have brought shame to my family. I was not there for my baby sister as she grew up. I was not there to help my mother when she needed me. I am truly sorry for any role be it directly or indirectly I have played in hurting anyone. I am not the same person I once was. No one owes me anything. If anything wishes to hate me for anything, they will get no protest from me. I never really discuss anything but the murders, as that is the only crime I am on death row for. Nothing else is key in my conviction. When I had my execution date, Carlos actually had contacted TDCJ or someone about meeting with me. I wanted to meet with him. As a man, I believe firmly in allowing a man to have his word said. My lawyers blocked it, NOT ME! I did not shoot the man. Pat lied on me as did Josh. Josh admitted why he lied! Pat told my lawyers he, in short, wanted me to be executed as he told the police information on me and he felt I would retaliate and also his brother held a gun to my head and he knew I was not real happy about that. So because Pat can't kill me himself, he wants to have the state do it. He has admitted stuff to my lawyers also though. Again, I am not making any excuses. I associated with people and lived a lifestyle that ran counter to civilized society. I have spent 14 years on death row. Locked up on this case 16+ years. I have sat in a cell for over 16 years. Had friends die, life has passed me by. What cost am I supposed to pay? I can disprove all the dumb shit the D.A filed recently. Let's take the murders away, let's pretend murders never happened but everything prior to them did. What cost am I to pay? Am I to be executed for Carlos getting shot? He did not die. I did not want him to die. I did not want him hurt. He is alive. Pat lied and said I said something about killing the guy. That is bullshit. Another that was there, Krystal, she admitted that I said nothing. That actually I got in the car and was quiet and that Pat was the one that kept going on and on. Josh has admitted he said the things he did, because of lies the D.A's investigator told him. I was no angel in life. I regret the bad choices I have made. I have suffered in many ways as a result of the bad choices, though others have been impacted worse. I seek no sympathy or pitty. I hope that one day those that I have hurt directly or indirectly can find it in their heart to forgive me. If they don't, they will get no blame from me. To those that wish to turn against me due to some lies told by a prosecutor, Okay. It is cool. You know why? Because when my lawyers respond and outline the facts, people will see how prosecutors lie! Many times a court opinion that is detailed as a finding of fact is simply the Judge signs off on what the D.A files. There is actually a University of Texas Law review study about this fact. That in Harris County (Houston Texas) the Judges adopted 100% of the Harris County prosecutors filings, word for word, in 96% of the capital post-conviction orders. In the other 4% the Judge changed some things in the wordings. They didn't just sign on the dotted line what the D.A filed. This study was published in the case of Anthony Medina. It just shown how hard it is as the Judges generally just sign off on what prosecutors do. Why? Because most Judges are former prosecutors from the very same offices. They protect each other. It happens all over Texas! Every person freed from death row had bad filings against them in state court. Ernest Willis, Anthony Graves, and hundreds of others. Yet, the courts never punish the prosecutors! It happens all over! Hey, the fight goes on. Anywho, my focus is my plans to help others. Am still working on the outline of that. To those that maintain faith in me, your faith will be affirmed soon enough. Will be back to blogging now. Sticking to my previous messages.

Love is Freedom.

Do something today to make tomorrow a better day.

Until next time,

Take Care, Smile, & Strive for all that you desire.

Veni, Vidi, Vici

Clinton YOUNG #999447

Loud & Clear, February 4, 2018

Topic: Addition

I sent the previous blog before receiving the copy of my lawyer's response the next day. My lawyers sent me the prosecutors filing, minus the various exhibits. As a result, I did not know the prosecutor did obtain an expert, if you want to call it that. Now, I do not say that A. Koettel is not an expert, though the statement only deals with what is possible, not what is fact. It is an attempt to provide a distraction. The state failed to even mention by ballistic expert, which they damn sure are not going to get A. Koettel to discredit or attack my ballistic expert. I do not even need to get into the science. The simple fact that the ballistic report was written by Richard Ernes. Koettel works for Tarrant County medical examiner's office. They do a great deal of work in forensics. Though one thing I know is no one in the Tarrant County Medical Examiner's office is going to speak against Richard Ernest. Being that he is one of the best there is when it comes to gun science. He has worked often with Tarrant County. As I wrote before, when the Branch Davidian Waco standoff happened (there is a T.V series out now about this event.) ATF agents were shot. The feds needed the fastest and most accurate to go over everything. They brought in Richard Ernest. The Best! So a funny thing I noticed in the state's response was they make no mention at all of Mr. Ernest and his report. Hmm. What is most telling about the prosecutor's expert is what is NOT mentioned. The expert said as much that could be said without committing perjury or looking like a damn fool. Dr. Palenik, whom is my expert, works with the elites. He is the elite in his field. I have the best of the best. Then the D.A used pictures from an Army training manual without proper judicial notice argument. So, it is basically hearsay and worthless in court. But hey, give them an E for effort. They also made arguments about different stuff they know is false. My lawyers will be responding ASAP. I will put up lawyers filings, states response and then my lawyers response. This way people can see how we detail facts to support our position and also how much the D.A distorts testimony and the record. I think they did it for, well, to try to reduce support for me. As really it makes no damn sense at all for the D.A to file such bullshit documents that are baseless and gross distortions of the record. (The Judge will see this. My lawyers will point this out.) It reduces their own credibility with court and public.

If I was the Petrey family, I would be highly offended. They have no desire to show the truth.

Page admitted to kidnapping Samuel. That then gives him motive to Kill Sam so as to cover up his actions. The reality is that Sam was not even kidnapped or under duress while in Midland.

It will come out. To those who have stood with me, as I have said before, you will be validated.

Though, I was hopeful the prosecutor would agree to something that allows us to resolve this in the best interest for all. After all, the prosecutor had unethical communication with the prior Judge and also with-held evidence while an appeal was pending and I was under threat of execution. I am having all the Bar Association rules and etc. sent to me. Plus, I will be reaching out to various firms in Amsterdam that have offices in the U.S that specialize in civil law. I wanted to resolve this as easy as possible, though it seems I will not be able to. So be it. They also brought Page back to Midland, appointed him a lawyer and then turned around and interviewed him without his lawyer! Again, illegal and unethical act! They filed things in their response that are completely false! They are so obsessed with getting a death under their belt that they ignore their own ethical obligations. Their oath taken. The fuckin' law! They ignore it all! The fight goes on. When it comes to helping, please keep in mind that for future legal expenses the funds go to the foundation. If you want to help with stamps, etc, here then you can send to paypalusa@saveaninnocentlife.com which is also where funds go for the letter/emailing mailing. It helps cover cost of printing and mailing to me. Plus, if I need funds for commissary or whatever it can be sent to me. Alrighty, will be back in some days. Take Care. Thanks for the love and support from those that give it. For those that hate me and stand against me, you motivate me. You encourage me to fight harder. Thank you. I feel more alive and think clearer while dancing in the flames.

Veni, Vidi, Vici.

Clinton YOUNG #999447

Loud & Clear, February 10, 2018

Topic: Case, Clarity, & etc.

I was feeling all bad and trying to be understanding, which is why my last blogs were written as they were. I thought that Janet and Carlos were still married and because a bullet hit his testicle that maybe he couldn't have kids or something. Turns out they have been separated for years. I don't know, for some reason Janet seems to feel she cannot go on with her life until I am executed. Wow. She was not harmed directly thanks to me. I am aware of the indirect harm, however all the others involved are not facing execution. No one died and I guess he can still have kids, so why would a person attach themselves to a tragic event that has in turn generated a great deal of attention? Hmm. Why would someone do that? It is always amazing to me at how people who have been in trouble with the law seem so quick to want to use the law to accomplish something. More amazing is wanting me to die because another guy shot her ex in the leg. The guy that was shot said in a statement, and in my trial that I did not even have a gun. Yet, this woman is online wanting me to be executed. Again, the others involved will be home soon, never went to prison, or have been released but came back to prison for other crimes. You know what, this seems like a story for Dr. Phil! Yes indeed. See, before I became a changed man, I would have been more of an asshole. BUT, I am a changed man now! I have seen the light! I want to help people. So we need to go on Dr. Phil to help her work through this pain. It is so bad that she cannot go on with her life until I am executed. It has caused her to be arrested for deadly conduct and other charges which she states have been dismissed. Great, so was mine! Only thing is, I was never even charged for that shooting case. Huh!? Being serious. If I can help anyone work through any pain that I caused directly or indirectly, be it through my actions or inactions, I am wanting to help. (Beyond being executed of course!)

Now I was thinking that people were trippin' about what was currently filed by the prosecution, but no, instead it is some old ass opinion that I can and have disproved for the most part. I'm not even going to give this much more thought. As if someone is too much of a dumbass to not look at the date on the document, then your thoughts about me really do not matter. My lawyers have filed their response by now to what the D.A filed. The prosecutors filing will be posted and alongside it will be my lawyers filing. The way the D.A lied is amazing to me. I can't believe the prosecutor even wrote that I admitted to several people that I stole the truck. Now they do not say WHO those people are, as will see I did not. What was said is what I have said ALL ALONG! (I was inside the Brookshires grocery store, walked out and Page was in the truck. Told my ex and her dad that before being arrested.) They really grasped for some straws in trying to distort the record. They attack Kemp and all the guys who gave statements for me saying that they are convicted felons. As a result of them being convicted felons, they cannot be trusted. Now seriously, let's stop and think here. Prosecutor: "These 4 guys should not be trusted because they have criminal records. They are nothing more than jailhouse informants and such testimony is unreliable." (Now let me footnote here. I think everyone in the anti-death penalty movement would read a prosecutor saying that line and have their jaw drop as prosecutors have executed guys with jailhouse snitch testimony. Many on death row behind such.) Okay, let's go over their witnesses: Page- 30 years kidnapping, Mark- 15 years kidnapping, Darnell- numerous drug charges, sexually assaulted a 14-year-old girl twice while waiting on my trial as he remained free. Those charges were dropped too because she kept screaming at the nurse not to touch her. As a result, they couldn't do the rape kit. Pat- 35 years aggravated burglary of habitation, Josh- same charges and etc, Pat also had long criminal history.

Well hell, I am starting to see a pattern here that ALL of the state's witnesses were criminals.

So, if my witness is not reliable due to being a criminal, that must mean….?? They use a jailhouse informant statue against some of the guys in my appeal as they heard Page confess while in jail. Hey, I am glad that Midland will never use jailhouse testimony. I have someone looking over current and past cases to see if they are using such witnesses. They cannot attack a person under jailhouse informant in my case and say they are unreliable and then turn around and use the very same to deprive people of life and/or liberty in another case. Now, yes, jailhouse informants for the PROSECUTORS are unreliable as a prosecutor has the power to send people to prison or not. A jailhouse snitch will fake knowing about a case to get time off or beat a charge. They do not go AGAINST the prosecutors as they fear being punished for it like the ones in my case were threatened several times. The prosecutors used their power to intimidate witnesses in my case over and over again. However, the jailhouse informant laws do not apply to those that give information to the defense, as there is no reward. Also, the burden is on the state.

To other matters. When it comes to their expert; again, it is only about vague possibilities. As I know damn well there is not an expert worth their salt in the USA that will go against Richard Ernest and The Paleniks. More so when they are mainly law enforcement experts. They work for the police! Anyways, on to other matters. They executed Rayford, Shore, Cardenas and Battaglia since I got a stay. Played chess and etc with Shore, though I did not care for him much beyond that. Now ol' Rayford, I started to like him. He walked off the unit to be executed using a walker! I cannot see the sidewalk, I wish the media could have captured that image. This damn near 70-year-old man walking towards his execution with a walker. Yeah, they wouldn't want that image shown. Rayford was a big Cowboys fan (Dallas Cowboys are an NFL team in Texas). During more spirited times while on death watch, Robert and Rayford would get to going back and forth about NFL football. Robert would start slapping the door yelling, "You wanna fight? You wanna fight?" and Rayford would yell back "yeah I wanna fight!" During the last few months from time to time as I laid in the cell or paced the floor in the evening times I would hear the silence broken with "Lookout Loki!!! You wanna fight!?" As Rayford yelled over to me. HaHa! JOh no the fight saying started over the Mayweather/McGregor boxing match! Me and Robert were saying Mayweather was going to get his ass beat and Rayford would go on about how crazy we were. Then Robert yelled out the "you wanna fight?!" It kind of became another saying…one that has now faded away with two executions. Death watch is A-pod – A-section. I am in A- pod C-section so it is not hard to see or hear each other throughout the day. More so when at rec. These situations are bad all the way around. Rayford never said he was innocent. People were hurt by the death he caused, people were hurt by the death the state caused. The common theme is hurt, something that human beings have excelled at, hurting each other. John Battaglia. Long Sigh. Where to start? He went by Batman. A play off Battaglia, not his altruistic superhero ways. He didn't make many friends, I used to go to rec outside with him all the time to discuss philosophy and history. If he was anything, he was educated! I don't know if it is that I have an old soul or that I'm just out of place with the culture commonly associated with my socioeconomic status but I have always enjoyed the idea of sitting around drinking whichever beverage and discussing the history and/or ways of mankind. Such would be more common in a French Café than in Northeast Texas. I got along with Batman good enough. The reason he was here always bothered me. For years I wouldn't even talk to people with such a case. In my dealings with Batman, he had some mental issues. It was hard to keep him from going back to the 'Dallas Texas lesbian KKK member coalition that was out to get him.' Never mind the fact that the KKK is not supposed to like lesbians. To him it all made sense. Who knows, there has been stranger things in this world. He was smart and had been wealthy. Though mental illness became the driving factor to a horrible ending. The other victim that was never talked about was his other daughter. He would tell me about her. I would walk around the rec yard listening to him, thinking about how this girl has to be lost in some kind of darkness. Her father killed her sisters and then constantly degrades her mother. Now her father is dead. Death truly is a survivor's affair. The reasons people hurt each other, the way they hurt each other. It is crazy. I just hope she can find love and peace that offers stability. If not, it will be a hard road for her.

Cardenas went by Scooby. He and I had lived around each other many times. We always ended up around each other. For the longest time he was in a cell next to me. I was between him and Harvey Earvin, whom is a friend of mine. We all got along great. Scooby and I would always cook tacos and such that we make with commissary items. He is one of the reasons why I don't like knowing why people are here. We would talk every day, make food with each other. We are not supposed to pass stuff but we find ways and do it. Him, Harvey and I would talk and joke every day. Then I saw an article in the newspaper and was all "damn it!" He swore up and down that he didn't do it. The police beat him up and he signed a statement, which that area of the state is known for that in the 90's. Around that time period I told myself that if I am innocent then others could be too. Don't put stock in what the system says, was not my place. So we stayed cool and talking. I meant to write something about him after his execution. Scooby was an easy-going guy in here. He was quiet. When I first met him, I moved into a cell next to him. It was in my wilder days. His kidneys had messed up so he was on a low protein diet. He couldn't get peanut butter. During lockdown we get peanut butter sandwiches with each meal damn near. He was trying to tell the officers but they would not pay attention or fix it. He mentioned to me that I could have them if I wanted. I just at first thought he didn't like them but when he explained it to me, I told him "hey these laws gonna give you what you're supposed to have. When they pass out the sack, tell them about it. I will do the rest." Sure enough, the officer gave some bullshit "that's what they sent" generic, not gonna help answer. They opened the slot on my door to give me mine and I stuck my arm out of the slot, started to slap the slot door yelling "yall got life fucked up tellin' that man he gots to eat something he can't eat! I'm making it my business!" Amazingly their attitude towards me was 100% different. For the remaining time of that lockdown he no longer had that problem. After they gave him the proper food, he told me "Thank You." I noticed that after living next to me for a while he had a bit more fore in him JHa. I really wish they would have allowed him a chance to do all the forensic testing in his case. His lawyers fought hard for him. Scooby and Rayford surely was not what the system would label as a threat. TDCJ would not treat them as personally dangerous. There are guys serving life for 4 or 5 murders on this unit that get to walk around like everyone else. Their county or city just didn't have the funds to send them to death row. The case about the death penalty is still before the Supreme Court. It is telling that they did not dismiss it yet. They are still discussing it. Most times if a case is going to be dismissed, they do not conference on it so much. Although, we cannot get our hopes up just yet. Will find out by February 16th what their next course of action will be. Alrighty then. Thanks to all that help out.

Hopefully, everything evens out soon.

Take Care, Smile, and Strive for all that you desire.

In Solidarity, I Remain,

Veni Vidi Vici

Clinton YOUNG#999447

D.R- Polunsky Unit

3872 FM 350 South

Livingston, TX 77351

U.S.A

saveaninnocentlife.com

saveclintyoung.com

clintonyoungfoundation.com

Loud & Clear, February 23, 2018

Topic: Jpays/Complaint

Alrighty then, I have several issues to get to, though this one will be about Jpays and the way to complain. These are the ONLY Jpays I have gotten. If your initials are not listed with a date, then I did not get it. If you sent one and I did not get it, then I need you to file a complaint with tdcj.gov/ombudsman. That is the complaint department with TDCJ. File that I posted notice of Jpays that I received and that is how you know that I did not receive it. When you file the complaint, include your name, letter ID#, and date the Jpay was sent. Add in that you paid for service that was not provided. I received the following:

Feb. 1st – J.D.B #8

Feb. 2nd-6th I got nothing

Feb. 7th – C.N

Feb. 8th – C.N, M.M.E

Feb. 9th-11th Nothing

Feb. 12th – E.E

Feb. 13th – M.D.V

Feb. 14th – J.T, C.F #7

Feb. 15th – Nothing

Feb. 16th – R.B, A.S.R, C.D.R

Feb. 18th – C.J

Feb. 19th – Nothing

Feb. 20th – N.W, J.D, M.M.E

Those are the ones I have as of Feb. 23rd 2018. I did not list Merel as I know I got all of hers.

Nancy W., I did not get the jpay from January. Meike, Haven't gotten anything from you since December 24th. Eva K., I got #60 from you. Heather L., I wrote you back thanking you, did you get it? Alice I got one from you in February and have responded. That is that. Jorunn I got the print outs from December 14th that you mailed beginning of January with pictures. Ah, got one jpay transfer funds notice from M. W at the beginning of last month. Alrighty then, I know that many sent me cards and such. As Merel had expressed, I would send a card back to students and etc. I cannot work so I have to depend on others. To order cards I have to do it from my inmate trust fund account with approved vendor. People cannot just send me an order, I have to do it with approval from these people. Also, I have to buy stamps from the prison. I did not have the funds I expected to have, as a result I could not order the cards previously. When people tell me they will do something, it is stuff like this why it is important that they do it. More so since I think they will do it. I don't ask another to help, which I don't like asking as it is, then I end up with just .29 cents in my inmate trust fund account as I do now. Inmate trust fund is controlled by TDCJ and funded by deposits. I should be getting some that will help cover, etc. Though due to order time, etc., this will be another 3-5 weeks before I can get them sent. I do not get upset with anyone for what they are unable to do. It is when I am told something will be done and it isn't that is problematic. As then I cannot do what I am supposed to do. Like I damn sure would not have been getting graphic novels or food stuff had I known I would be in this situation. Now, it is part my fault as I don't really say anything. There is surely plenty that would help as do with foundation donations. I have never really liked asking people for stuff, as I have gotten older the desire has faded even more. To those that donate and such, thank You. I know some just do not understand the difference in accounts due to not knowing about prisons really. I detail all this, so as to explain why I haven't sent "Thank You" cards as Merel indicated I would. I did not previously inform Merel of the problem, so she didn't know. Though, when it comes to doing stuff, that applies to anything. No one should be faulted, at least not by me, for their limitations. Anywho, it will sort out. I should have done better at explaining things and sorting everything. I don't ask sisters and mom because it costs $60-$80 for travel, etc. for each visit, each trip. (In case such crossed anyone's minds) Alrighty, to other topics. People ask about the case and updates.

The State filed their web of lies. My lawyers chopped that up. The State then filed their response to that, which is unheard of. We then filed something pointing out some stuff. Everything that was due to be filed, PLUS some, has been. We now wait on the Judge to decide if there will be a hearing and then, if so, scope of the hearing. Once the Judge determines this, if a hearing is to take place, then the parties involved will sort out schedules for the best time to have the hearing. Basically just waiting right now. Should know something soon, like 30 days or so. The system does not move fast. Plus, we do not know Judges schedule. He is NOT from Midland, which is a good thing. As for prosecutors- When I express that they never fail to amaze me, they then go and amaze me! I'm not going to get into the newest filings at this time. Though they have argued from so many different angles, I really cannot say what they are claiming. I am serious. These pages say this, the pages say that. I do know that a court would never accept defense lawyers doing as the prosecutors have. If the system was fair then the court would reject their filings and I would win on merits and being unopposed properly. But, the fight goes on. Who knows. The Judge will say something soon. Then I will let everyone know what's up. Thanks for those that spread the word. I am still working towards getting some other music projects going. Mainly my country song that I wrote, which has been the one I have really wanted to produce. Got lots on my mind. Will be back soon.

In Solidarity,

Veni Vidi Vici

Clinton **YOUNG** #**999447**

Clintonyoungfoundation.com

Loud & Clear, March 2018

Topic: Update & Explain – Notice

Note At times I will rush a blog and or not express some things. Also, I do not rough draft my blogs. I sit down and go! I feel it is better so I can go with the emotions and just be more authentic, which is how errors will occur like in an older blog once I wrote about Romantic, that to say it as in pro Rome. Well, that would be an incorrect usage, I meant to write Rome-esque. Then go on about a pro Rome view. Though I was writing so fast I did not catch it until I got a copy of the blog in and saw the error. Also, with for example, recent blog about only .29 cents in my account. Midland gets a percentage of money for me sent to the TDCJ inmate trust fund. This is to force me to pay for trial and state appeal costs. It's a fact! They charged me $297,000+ USD. The only way I get stamps and commissary is with funds to TDCJ-ITF. So I have to deal with it.

The $3,000 appeal investigator blew smoking crack and lying in my appeal? Not only was she not charged for laundry list of crimes but they make me pay for her cost when she destroyed my appeal! She and the lawyer were court appointed. Never mind justice. I cannot get basic fairness. So I got to pay for the stuff done that can cause me to be wrongfully executed. That percentage eats away at what is sent. Also, normally my mother does help me. Though needed to cover some additional costs for legal dues related to getting all squared with my past music projects. I didn't want to have her pay for both, so I asked her to help get all the attorney fees related to music sorted, plus as mentioned, cost of visits and travel and such. I did not think about how all would appear in the previous post. No one said anything, I just did not want to present an image as if my family is not helping me. I asked her to help with elements of fees related to music projects that cannot be covered by the foundation. Though I had expected others to do certain things and that was where the problem came in. When writing, we come from our position first. In doing so, we don't always think about all angles and how words could reflect on others. Plus, generally a topic I do not like to discuss is needing others, etc. Back to Midland. I am the only death tow person that was charged at full cost. It is NOT supposed to be like that. Supposed to be just a couple grand for some cost, if anything. Only a few places in Texas do this. Waco, TX; Midland, TX; and a couple of other small places. Though ONLY Midland slams with full cost. LIt really is not supposed to be for death penalty cases. Also, they only get % of the initial deposit in TDCJ-ITF account. They do not keep taxing funds in the account. Okay, for the past month of blogs.

To point out, Oct 8[th,] 2017- I mentioned a few paragraphs in "I feel safe assuming they met with him and had private discussions with him" about Page previously being back in Midland. Fast forward to February blogs "was uncovered Page had secret meeting with the D.A where he admits to kidnapping and holding gun for the first time. They kept tape from us until after my stay." Shows I called that one huh!? Wrote the blog Oct 8th. They met with him on Oct. 4th! As I wrote, got to keep anti-venom strong because these snakes keep strikin'!!! Nov. 5th blog I mention the need for a trial lawyer. Now, I wanted to get some to start looking at cases now, so if I win a new trial I can be ahead of the case. Though, right now I got to see if I get a hearing first. So I don't want to get ahead of myself. But I am looking into law firms for civil support to trial lawyer is criminal defense. I am working on getting other matters sorted for fund raisers. It was not my intention to only have the bikini offered on site. I should have asked about what was up there. We all just been busy and distracted. Being that I support feminism as I do, I am aware of the way 'only' having bikini on SAIL shop can be seen as objectifying. Was no ones intent and just has taken longer to get other items sorted. While none has directly complained to me or anyone else as far as I know, it still bothered me. I apologize if image was off putting. More so being that across board. From lawyers to active family, my team is all women, minus a few guys. Other items will be posted soon. Also, I am aware that I often think about things more than others. Nov. 28th blog I mention 'strong enough to be able to life others up. "If anyone quotes me, it should have been LIFT people up. While 'life' could be poetic, I meant lift. Alrighty then, Blog posted in a day or three.

Take Care,

Clinton

P.S In a week or so I will blog about the case and make corrections to past postings. Nothing big, I just want to make sure I am being honest and correct when critical of D.A. If I make a mistake, I will make sure I correct it.

Loud & Clear, March 4, 2018

Topic: Loved, Free & Safe

I was writing with someone about a matter of focus for them. In responding, I made mention of how they are loved, free and safe. To feel blessed at only having to worry about emotional topics or feelings. That got me thinking. Many of the problems we see as problems, are really struggles of the mind or heart. They are problems that safety and security allow us to dwell on. Safety and Security being the most basic need. Sure, we all need love and affection, though while someone in New York throws a fit behind someone unfriending them on Facebook, the world around them allows them to have the freedom to put worth into such a frivolous matter. Could you image some teenager in war torn Yemen? He checks his phone and sees he was unfriended on Facebook. Then he throws down his AK-47 in a fit of rage and starts kicking up dust about how unfair it is?

That would be a site to see. I have had many that have written to me that felt lost in some way. They are in their 20's and feel a void or questioning the point of everything. There has been no real struggles in life, no real reason to be depressed. Though it becomes a reality for them. A battle of self. This is why they say adversity builds character. The flames strengthen you. Resistance and challenges can be healthy. With many what becomes a crisis is really inflated by a person's own mind. They lose perspective. It is not to say that anyone should feel bad for the blessings that life has given them. Not at all! No one has to go through life feeling guilty, though it is always important to put things into perspective. To see clearly. To not allow yourself to be blinded from what you do have in life. I would only be offended if a person wasted the blessings they have in some pool of self-pity. Even then would only be mildly put off by it, as it is their life to waste. The cost being theirs to pay. Giving or taking no toll on my life. Let me put it this way, many reading this are Free, Loved and Safe. No punishment or guilt is due for this. Though when you face the journey of life it is important to not take this for granted. When something becomes a crisis ask yourself if in the grand scheme of things is it that big? The one problem cannot outweigh the blessings. I know how it is to get worked up over something. To feel slighted and wringed and be consumed with it. When really most times it is foolish over reaction and a waste of the borrowed time on this Earth. I say this with the intent that you be able to get the most from your life. There is always time to step back and take a deep breath so you can re-focus. Honor the blessings you have in life by not taking them for granted. Never get distracted from what is important. Also, no one owes you anything beyond what you are due by agreement. It shouldn't take a storm to open eyes. When you step back and focus on the blessings you do have then your life develops greater value. As you invest in what you do have versus what you do not. Thinking about it. I have never been free, safe and loved.

As a child I felt a threat to certain adults. Then barricaded by insecurities. Eventually being literally behind bars, locked away in prison. After gates opened up I was still in parole, at the mercy of a parole officer. Being on death row. Lack of freedom & safety often combining in life. The flame either all-consuming or fading away, though never extinguished. Always feeling the heat as a reminder. If asked what I would want in life, it is to be free, safe and loved. I know I am loved. However, to be all three is the grand goal. Such seemingly simple words acting as a Holy Trinity for humanity. Something I have fought so hard for. Sometimes fighting by way of an emotionally immature rebellion, other times by physically defining my space. To the very battle for my life. Always having emotionally, mentally and or physically resisted to the point that to fight is to feel alive. The elixir of struggle, revitalizing the soul. What scares me is not that I will give up along the way. No, it is what will I do if I finally win? Will I be strong enough to accept victory? To be Free, Safe and Loved. The elements of happiness. Life's great award. To share it with others is the reward. Be wise enough to recognize the blessings, and brave enough to appreciate the simplicity of life. It all seems so easy does it not?

Veni, Vidi, Vici

In Solidarity I remain,

Clinton YOUNG#999447

D.R- Polunsky Unit

3872 FM 350 South

Livingston, TX 77351

U.S.A

saveaninnocentlife.com

Clintonyoungfoundation.com

Feel free to share my blogs, just please tag my website and credit my name to my writings. Be it the whole blog or quoting me. Thank you

Loud & Clear, May 20, 2018

Topic: Updates & Such

Finally managed to sit down and force myself to write this. I haven't been writing much of anything lately. Was frustrated about many things. Namely some people. I will be so glad when this is all over with for so many reasons. The hearing was granted, which is a good thing. This is not the same kind of hearing I was supposed to have last year. It is a whole different animal, so to speak. Plus, I no longer have that bullshit ass Judge that was acting as if he was a prosecutor.

I am not going to get into the specifics. I previously had blogged that I was not going to post some things. I mean I wrote this in my blog, yet someone still chose to post about it even though my lawyers asked him not to. On to other matters. I am going ahead with my book. It is on pace to be completed by June, then in print by July. I have been conflicted with this as people know. My idea about the charity is out the window as I haven't heard from the people who were supposed to be helping with it in months. At least not in connection with that. Which is cool. I expected such. It is better anyways that I focus on a single goal. The single goal is beating this and having the tools I need to win, if given a new trial. Plus, I should have written the book a while back. Main reason I am doing it is because I told people I would. Plus, someone gave me the funds to cover the cost of printing. It is important that I keep my word. More so to this person, due to some other events that took place. Really I was kind of going at it with a turtle pace. I was thinking that the people I wanted to help type it up that they would take a bit of time to get it done. Damn fool I was! They got it done in a week! Ha. I am going to self-publish so once it is ready, then the pre-orders will be accepted. What I mean is when it is all typed up and edited and sent off to the printer then we can start the orders for it. This way when it is done with the printing, we will already have the initial wave of orders ready so there is not a delay in the future due to having to catch up. I don't know how many will order it. I wouldn't cry if a million did. Ha. I am also still working on some music projects. The country song will be done one way or another soon. I was wanting a specific person to do it, though I am in here and unable to try all the ways to reach the person. I asked others to, hopefully they do. As for Death Row, if the ones I want involved are not willing to do it for free then I will have to use the funds from the book to expand it as I want. I have an idea for the song Death Row. Pyrexx did good, though was unable to do the exact production I had in mind due to budget and time constraints. I have had a vision for how I wanted it done. Naturally I will not stop until my vision is fulfilled. Alex did good with the video for it. Though again, he was limited. When I get it re-made in the future I want it to be MTV music video quality and about 15 minutes long. A kind of mini-film. Lots to do still.

The state executed Castillo. He had someone recant their testimony against him, a jailhouse snitch. That is one good thing about Midland. They do not use jailhouse snitches. Prosecutors know they are unreliable and most are just trying to save their own self from doing more time. (They do use dophine snitches) Sadly many though still use them in trials. Stronger laws related to this need to be put into place. More so since courts do not put much weight in recanted testimony, which is also a problem. They require that we have some other evidence that supports the recanted testimony. Such as how I do in my case. The road goes on forever, the party never ends. Onto the next chapter. I thank those that told me what they thought of the Loved, Free and Safe blog. I always enjoy learning what people think about stuff I write. On the topic of writing, the posts about jpays, as I mentioned before, are just about jpays. Not letters sent to me in the mail. If you wrote my name, number, and address out correctly, as I detailed on my site then I more than likely got it. I have not been writing much, as I mentioned. I was aggravated about several things. Though I am getting back into it and getting caught up. If it has been a long time and I did not respond, then please write again. Just in case. Those that have continued to support me, Thank You. The fight isn't over with yet. The horizon looks much more promising. I have a window in the cell. It is up high, so to look out of it properly, I have to roll my mat up and stand on it. Most people never look out the window, the idea being there is nothing out there for them since they are never getting out. I did not look out of it as much before, at least not as much as I have since April 24th. Today the weather is kind of gloomy. It has rained and is cloudy out. Something I miss is driving on a day like today. It's just done raining some and the highway is wet. Not many cars on the road. Hearing the sound the tires make on the wet highway. Out in the middle of nowhere with trees on both sides of the road. Me and my gal or me and my homeboy J.B going somewhere. The radio is barely playing. Driving like that and the smell of the air when getting out of the car at whichever destination. It is simple stuff like that I always paid attention to. That, I miss. In all I do I take everything in. How a car sounds, the scents at a house, the expressions of people, word structures, everything. Anywho. I had a visit with my mom, sisters and nephews. The baby turns three this month. Last I have seen him he was shy as can be. This time he wouldn't shut up! Jha. He has a huge personality. The glass between us really bothered me. Ready for this situation to be over with. Alrighty then. I will be back to writing more. Take care, smile and strive for all that you desire.

Veni Vidi Vici

In Solidarity I remain,

Clinton YOUNG#999447

D.R-Polunsky Unit

3872 FM 350 South

Livingston, TX 77351

U.S.A

Loud & Clear, June 28, 2018

Topic: Update. Hurry up & Wait

Yeah I just cannot get in the groove of writing. I was thinking about this. Here it is the conclusion I have come to. For so many years writing has been the way I was forced to express myself. To convey my emotions. As a result of that, when I am aggravated and then try to write, that frustration will channel in my writings. As a result, I do not write. It gets hard for me to sit down and write some. More so the person I am pissed off at. As it might start out calm, but as I go it builds up to the point I am ready to sling this typewriter across the cell. Having in the past done just that. I learned not to do that! These things cost $225LIt certainly is not fair for me to tear up something, based on emotions, that others have helped to pay for. Plus handwriting these blogs, more than one letter and legal stuff, to hell with that! Been there, done that and want no more of it. Some of my frustrations are connected with the case. Knocking heads with lawyers and such.

Tired of being here. All that stuff. Add in some stress from in here. To distract, I was focused on reading books. I read the Ganghis Khan series and the Caesar series. Both by Conn Iggulden.

I am reading the Kahn series twice. Plus, I will re-read the Caesar series again. People here have told me about it for years. That I would like them. I brushed it off, as I wrote so much. I did not read much, until I got into comics die to Randy. Randy kept telling me about The Walking Dead and etc. I finally gave them a look and got on a comic craze for a while. As the pictures allowed a visual not offered in this place due to not having a TV. Plus, it was easy to read. Did not consume much time to read them. Though was time consuming for my friend that would order them for me. Plus, costly, so I faded from that. Conn Iggulden is a great writer. I am reading also his War of Roses series. In the past, there was only one other book I have ever read twice. It is from a German author about World War I. 'All Quiet On The Western Front.' It was the first introduction of realism into a war novel. The reality of war over the normal hero worship and grand victors. I believe Hitler had the author killed. I read it the first time when I was 14 and the second time when I was 16. I also started on re-reading 11 minutes by Paulo Cohelo. Ya know, I have suggested that book to people over the years, amongst many other titles. (I always suggest everyone read The Art of Racing in the Rain by Garth Stein. I am going to re-read that one also. That is just a great book.) Anywho. When I started back on 11 minutes, at first I was flipping through it reading certain parts, a line here, a paragraph there, which I always do when I first get a book. I had to laugh as I forgot about some parts. Then to think about people I suggested the book to. Haha. There are some parts in the book that are kind of 50 shades of grey-ish. Though I didn't care about that specifically. The overall nature of the story was the focus. Anyways.

I am writing more about books then I intended. There seems to be a book I am forgetting. O yeah, my book! As said it is not good for me to write when aggravated. I sit down to write about my life and get to parts I do not think about day to day. Yeah, that is just not a good equation. Plus, part of it was not passed on to the proper person. So now dealing with that delay. To include frustration, then another frustration. I sent in the order for the first batch of cards, so I could send them to people. I done this in April. Okay, on June 25th I finally get the form back. To explain: To order cards they have to be ordered through an approved vendor, with funds from a person's Inmate Trust Fund account. This is done by filling out a form, sending stamped envelope and form to the Inmate Trust Fund. Once it is approved on the Unit, it goes there and they approve it. They basically fill out a check and mail it with envelope to company of choice. Company then sends card order. I will include the form for people to see the example. I tore off my thumb print. I do not need a scoundrel using my thumb print to make a latex copy and breaking into my future Iphone 11 when I am free. I joke, as I wouldn't have a damn Iphone. I would just get me a flip phone. Old School! Use it for the only thing I would need it for. Ya know, to TALK on.

Having been framed for murder and having had a partial print be blamed on being mine in another case. Yea I damn sure am aware of ways such things can be used against a person. A cop said they found my thumb print on a doorknob of a place. That I know damn well could not have been found there. Which I got an expert now that discredits that cop. It doesn't pertain directly to the murder case. As was no prints in that case. Isn't that amazing? Multiple guns, vehicles, and etc. Images show clearly I had bare hands. Was no prints. Yet some backwoods ass cop just so happens to match my thumb print to a doorknob. This "after" they re-took my prints.

My prints have been in the system, before I was arrested on this case, as I was in juvenile prison! I was on parole. So if it was my print at the specific location, if they ran my print in the system, it would have made a match. They would not have had to come 18 months later and retake my prints and then all of the sudden make a match. More so if they already had me listed as a suspect and had prints from when initially arrested on this case. So yeah, I don't trust scoundrels. Anywho.

So over two months later, the ITF returns to the unit the order stuff. I forgot to write a "word".

See we have to write the amount like 97.00$ then have to write out the amount. Like ninety-seven dollars. I forgot to write the 'seven' in word form. So they held it for 2 fucking months! Just to return it and tell me I messed up. So for 2 months I been waiting to get these cards. The first set I was ordering that dealt with specific themes. Now I have to do it all over again. Which will add another month to get these damn cards. (They CANNOT be ordered by anyone but me, for myself.) I could get out today and buy an AK-47 with less trouble than trying to order cards while in prison. You know who is responsible for the woes of the world? Three types. Greedy, Petty, and Insecure. I'm serious. There was a bullshit ass dude that was a serial killer. He was some city ordinance y. He would do stuff like write people up if their grass was half an inch too high and such. Just a petty power trip type. Turned out to be a serial killer! Those types, we all have met one in our life. The real petty types. You just know they got some weird shit going on in their life. Like the preacher that never shuts up about the evil homosexuals. He then gets caught in a motel with a gag in his mouth and a well, ya know. I am serious though. Cannot stand petty ass super-whatever adjective applies-people. Same as insecure dudes. Jealousy is evil! The world suffers due to insecure men. Some dude in Canada ran over women in a van. Turns out he was part of some hate women group. That is just the craziest thing to me. They hate women, because they I guess say women will not sleep with them. So, to advance this struggle, they join a group or form a group focused on hating women? For some reason I think that did not increase their odds! Though me, I love women. Love them! Just great. Even on worse days, still just amazing!

I told Thor we had to promote Freyja over Odin. But the dumb brute didn't listen. Well, I was wanting to, due to my love and appreciation, send cards to women. Though no, a petty person prevented me from doing this. (Really I was sending cards to all kinds of people. Just trying to add in some humor and make a point about something that really pissed me off.) So, the lesson is, do not be a petty person. Alright, I got some other stuff to rant about, but this is getting long. On the ITF form it has administrative approval. That means the ranking official here approved it. The green highlighter was from the ITF official in Huntsville. Isn't green the color of jealousy? See, I just give up! The scoundrels are everywhere! Hey, it would not be my life if it was not a struggle! Take care! No news on legal matters yet. Will be soon.

Veni Vidi Vici

In Solidarity I remain,

Clinton YOUNG #999447

D.R-Polunsky Unit

3872 FM 350 South

Livingston, TX 77351

U.S.A

Loud & Clear: September 27, 2018

Today an innocent man was murdered. Daniel Acker was executed over a tragic accident. I didn't previously write about his case, as I never thought he would be executed. The medical examiner in his case was the same one that fucked up in the – now famous – ex parte Robbins case. That case resulted in the Texas legislature to create the new 11.073 writ ruling on science. Daniel's first appeals were messed up due to a dumbass lawyer. Texas changed the rules of lawyer appointment due to Daniel's case. Yet, he is dead. I really can't believe it! The DA in his case distorted facts. Like he said Daniel's truck was a front wheel drive. First off, there ain't a fuckin full size utility work truck that is front wheel drive in this world! Damn sure not a Ford or Chevy. The medical examiner who has already been shamed, he said the woman was strangled. No, she wasn't! The woman jumped out of a moving truck and had a history of this. Listen to the execution watch show by Ray Hill. I am sure they talked about the case. Daniel was innocent. He had been in prison before due to some small petty stuff. He was not educated. Just a big ole country boy killed behind previous lawyer's fuck ups and a technicality.

Look, everyone needs to put focus on the CCA election. Keller is up for election. If he and the other seat opening is changed over, this murder machine would grind to a halt. EVERYONE needs to reach out to Texas Monthly, Houston Chronicle, Dallas Morning News, Austin American Statesman, the New York Times + other media. Tell them to do a joint look into Daniel's case, also Robert Pruett's. Make Texas politicians recognize this. People in Europe protest in front of embassies + pull your law makers to condemn the murder of innocent people. Push it on U.N. etc. Look, in Texas the CCA is the high court for criminal cases. They are elected judges. Yet all I always read people bitch about Trump. Trump can do nothing over a "state" case. He is only over Federal cases. Texas death row is a state matter. So people need to reach out to any and all to focus on the CCA election. Sharon Keller has got to go! T.I.F.A. and H.I.S. + other groups in Texas. Tell everyone. Discuss it on the Prison Show. Tell people locked up to tell their loved ones to vote. To vote against Sharon Keller. Anyone is better than her. Hardly anyone votes in the prosecutor and judge elections in Texas. If all the democrats in Harris County would vote, it would flip the court. Stop talking about execution drugs. No one that has the power to change it will over drugs. It is a death issue + wasted time, at least in Texas. Fuck conditions. Who cares if we got TV, when they are killing innocent people. 100% focus needs to be on the CCA. Let me tell yall something. If Keller wins + a hardliner wins the other seat. After they have killed someone like Daniel, I don't care what fantasy, hopes and dreams anyone here has. They will not stand a chance in hell. As the CCA has said that innocence does not matter! Research his case. The man never had a fair shot on appeal. The media did stories on it years ago. Force US media to look at it. Get people to push the vote. The CCA impacts anyone locked up. If the CCA rejects a death penalty case due to how the law is written, it is hard for any higher court to do anything. The CCA also impacts non-death cases. You all need to do something if you believe in justice. Talking about the problem with like-minded people will not accomplish anything. Posting "The Death Penalty is bad" on an anti-death penalty page is a waste of time. Forcing media, courts and politicians to look at cases of innocent people like Daniel, Robert and Todd Willingham. That is what will bring the death penalty to a halt. So stand up and fight!

Veni, vidi, vici,

Clinton Young

Loud & Clear: October 8, 2018

Topic: Daniel Acker

On September 27th a man that was innocent of murder was put to death. His case was the shining example of the death trap that is the Texas Death Penalty. Daniel Acker never had a fair trial nor appeal. His death shows they kill us on technicalities. We do not get off from them. To the points of fact.

#1. At trial a rookie intern medical examiner testified the victim was strangled to death. Counter- Another medical examiner of proper training discredited those findings.

#2. The Prosecutor withheld those findings until after Daniel was denied by the Court of Criminal Appeals. They then turned it over to his lawyer. Once he was out of state court he was then locked into the AEDPA Act while in Federal court. If the state doesn't review a claim a fact, the Federal court can't review it. IE: Procedural Barred. The C.C.A said in their State court opinion, "But for the damaging evidence of strangulation…" Showing this "false evidence" was seen as value. The prosecution knew this was false. The Law- Texas Penal Code Sec. 37.10 – Tampering with a Government Record. (a) A person commits an offense if he: (3) intentionally destroys, "conceals", removes, or otherwise impairs the verity, legibility, or "availability" of a government record; (2) An offense under this section is a felony of the third degree if it is shown on the trial of the offense that the government record was: (B) a written report of Medical, chemical, toxicological, ballistic, or "other expert examination or test performed on physical evidence for the purpose of determining the connection or relevance of the evidence to a criminal action; so as the law says, the Prosecutor not turning over that new medical examiners report. It is a 3rd degree felony. Which is punishable of 2 years to 10 years in TDCJ. The prosecutor is an unindicted felon. Plain and simple.

#3 Daniel's 11.071 writ lawyer filed Daniel's "letters" as his appeal! The C.C.A enacted policy limiting lawyers allowed to represent Death Penalty cases on 11.071 writs due to Daniel's Case. The Austin American Statesman Newspaper did news stories about these facts! Look them up! I think was in 2004, maybe 2003.

#4 The medical examiner that totally screwed up and said strangulation, she testified on a guy from Montgomery County, Tx. A Mr. Robbins. Her false testimony is why Robbins is free now. C.C.A cite is ex parte Robbins 478 S.W.3d 678 (Tex. Crim. App. 2014) and other filings. Due to the ping pong efforts of C.C.A to avoid giving Mr. Robbins the justice he deserved. The Texas Legislature in the 83rd Leg. Enacted S.B344 effective September 1, 2013. Article 11.073 – A writ to attack false science and experts basically. They expanded the law in relation to the C.C.A not properly following it with H.B 3724 in 2015! So the same lady that lied in Robbins case, lied in Daniels case. Robbins was a non-death penalty case, Conclusion- Robbins – Free. Daniel – Dead.

#5 The prosecutor in Daniels case said tire marks was acceleration marks. The D.P.S- highway patrol said skid marks. The D.P.S investigates all traffic related incidents. They are the experts. Counter to D.A- Daniel was driving a full-size work truck. A Ford F-350 Dully with a 1,000 lbs tool box on the back and additional railing to hold tools and pipes. Please google Ford F-350 Dully work trucks. They have 6 wheels, 4 on the back and 2 on the front. The transmission is geared to haul and pull, not for high speed. With the added weight, a dully truck will not peel out and leave rubber. It damn sure wouldn't with the front wheels. It is not a front wheel drive vehicle. It is rear wheel. If it was 6 wheel drive it still, matter of fact it would even less likely peel out. The laws of friction denounce the D.A's claim. If you had such a truck and it was a manual transmission. You could press clutch in, drops into first gear and floor the accelerator for a full 10 seconds, then pops the clutch. It would NOT burn rubber like a sports car. More so with a 1,000 lbs extra weight on the rear axle. The four back wheels are there to make sure the tires gain grip. DO 18-wheelers burn rubber? NO! Nor do Ford F-350 dully work trucks!

#6 Daniel ran over her. – The physical evidence fails to show this.

#7 The victim was thrown from the truck. – Counters. In a full size truck a person cannot drive the truck at 40 mph, reach across the seat to the passenger door over a meter away! Open the door against the wind resistance and throw a grown woman out with enough force that she hit her head at the top of the passenger door frame.

#8 Daniel forced her in truck. – Counter- he sat her on the ground and she crawled up into the truck. Now, under letter of law, Daniel could not be guilty with non-aggravated kidnapping as indicated. As he didn't restrain her in the truck. Sadly, the way the law is, it traps a case like Daniel's. Now people can say "he made her get in the truck." He didn't restrain her. He sat her down beside the truck. Let me get to cultural norms and such. My European readers might not see it the same. Though small town country boys and girls from the U.S will. See, a country boy that is a decent guy isn't going to kick a woman out of the house and make her walk off in the dark. More so, back when cell phones were not as common. Many of men have told a woman "get your purse and get in the truck." Might even grab her purse and her and carry her to the truck like Daniel is said to have done. She might be crying and saying sorry and all this. He puts her in the truck and then takes her to her mom, or sisters house or such. He gets out at the house, she might still be crying and all this. Her mom comes out, maybe her dad. He thrown her purse onto the lawn and pulls her out of the truck and sets her on the grass. When asked, "what's going on?" He might respond for example, "Bonnie, I put a roof over her head, I put food on the table and all she wants to do is whore around. I'm done with her!" Then gets in his truck and leaves. Her parents then would shake their head and go back in the house, might even say something like "you need to grow up!" A good country boy, he isn't going to beat her or leave her on the side of the road. He is going to get her somewhere safe. Mother, sisters, friends or such. Older folks from the south when seeing that type of action would see him as "a boy that was raised right." Now a low life dude will do like a guy I know did. He stripped his ex naked, took her to the South Side of Longview Texas in a crack infested area. He got her out of the car, honked the horn and when he seen a group of black guys come out, he yelled "yall can have her" and he left. With the idea that a naked white woman in such an area would be gang raped. Now, that is some foul stuff. It is what a piece of shit person would do. My Point is this: Daniel did what countless others have done. Only it had a tragic ending. The physical evidence matches her jumping out of the truck hitting her head and then not clearing the tool box. The side of which hit her on the head, snapping her spine. Marquetta George had a history of jumping out of moving cars. She done it from a patrol cop car and another person's car. Several times! Judge refused to let Daniel present that evidence! She was "NOT" ran over by Daniel. Daniel was going to ask the guy she was with that night if they had slept together. She didn't want that confrontation and tried to jump from the truck.

It was not a capital murder. Daniels case is an example how unethical prosecutors, bad experts, and lawyers can so easily result in a person being executed for a crime he didn't do. Was NO crime! The key is intent. He had no "intent" to kill or harm. I know there is some women on my fakebook or such reading this that has been on a couch crying and her boyfriend or husband has yelled at her "get your purse and get in the fuckin' truck I'm taking you.." People that have been exposed to or a part of the drug scene, they know of a brother, husband, father or such that has went to a dope house or such. Grabbed a woman that was strung out and made her go somewhere safe like home. The letters of the law it is kidnapping in a way. Though any decent man would do it. The "police state" wants everyone to call the cops for everything. Which of you called cops and they bust dope house. Then she would go to jail and drug dealers would be wanting to retaliate! Just worse for all. These situations are real. My point is this: Daniel Acker was a big ol' country boy from a small town in Texas. His actions were not so rare as to be abnormal. The letter of the law does not match up with ways our environment shapes us. The key element is "element." If Daniel was beating on the woman and kicked her out of the truck and another car hit her. I wouldn't have wrote a word. As such just wouldn't be right to do. (He clearly didn't even restrain her.) Imagine you are the provider. Your partner stays out all night and comes home with another. Would any of us not be emotional? The reporter Jolie McCullough of the Texas Tribune wrote, "But there are multiple theories as to what happened." Well, Ms. McCullough, if there are "multiple theories" and all this uncertainty then why is Daniel Acker dead? Maybe you could report the answer to that. Lady Justice weeps for that answer.

Clinton Young #999447

D.R. Polunsky Unit

3872 FM 350 South

Livingston, TX 77351

U.S.A

Loud & Clear: January 8, 2019

Topic: Note of Thanks

I am sure glad 2018 is over, but as the world still spins the same way, 2019 looks to be more of the same bullshit. One good thing is I will finally find out the date of the hearing soon. Trying to make sure that things are all in order for that. I have been meaning to write a blog about Joseph Garcia. I need to. I want to thank everyone who has donated and helped. Thank you. For those that do help, just please keep in mind that funds to the foundation is to my case. To help with stuff like books, comics, magazines etc. then that goes to the PayPal on my saveaninnocentlife.com site by way of the tip jar. This way there is no way of mix up or confusion and such. Once it is in the foundation account, I can't access it for anything that is not legal related. This caused some confusion in the past as I would just tell people to send everything there. When I later tried to do stuff with my songs and such, I ran into a roadblock. So to be clear: foundation = legal/case. Tip jar / US PayPal account = books, commissary and such matters. Thanks! I am grateful for however people want to help. I finally got my card order! Of course I got them all on December 21! ☹ including the Christmas cards I ordered. Being that Christmas was four days later, and mail doesn't get processed here on Saturday, post office is closed on Sunday. Yeah, I didn't mail any Christmas cards. Will use them next year. I have gotten many cards from people. Thanks! It is the 8th and I am still getting Christmas cards ☺

Also, look people I cannot get banners, homemade snow globes etc in the mail! Ha, just letters, cards and pictures. Also, please always make sure you include the TDCJ number with my name (#999447). I asked everybody to write my last name + the 447 part of my # in red ink. This helps the vital information stand out. Also to make my mail unique. I seen "other" letters as guards passed out mail, that was done that way. If you write someone else, please do something different. I know you might be thinking "Clinton, this is a bullshit idea!". I know! That's why "I" came up with it for me! If all do the same, then what is the point? I am missing some mail though. I moved cells many times over the past 3 months. I am missing some official pages from TDCJ, a picture sent via shutterfly.com + what Merel was told at least one letter. I will repeat this, please write my name + address as detailed on the SAIL + Foundation website. If you write with Jpay, if I have never written you before, you have to send your address. I can **not** respond with Jpay. Texas does not allow for such. Once I have your address, then there is no need to include it anymore. Also, just in case anything is ever mixed up with another person's mail at this prison of almost 3,000 prisoners. I will never ever just give out anyone's address. If any person ever gets wrote saying I gave them your letter, they are lying! I value + respect people's faith in me. If I ever thought of having a person write someone else, I will write that person myself and ask them to write whoever directly. I don't care if it is my best friend. So if anyone does get wrote by another prisoner, please inform me. The option of having the mailroom block future letters is available. I repeat this from time to time, due to new people that find out about me and write. So if you sent a Jpay and no contact info, that would explain why no response from me.

Alrighty then. I am going to write out a blog abut Joseph. More so since Randy was denied by the 5th Circuit. Texas seems hell bent to kill all my friends. I am going to wrap this up. Thanks again for all the support!

Veni, vidi, vici

In solidarity,

Clinton **Young**#**999447**

Polunsky Unit – **D.R.**

3872 FM 350 South

Livingston, TX 77351

United States of America

Loud & Clear, February 24, 2019

Topic: Updates and all that

I know that I have not been writing much. I was just not feeling it for a bit. Plus, I had gone to level 2. Then back to level one. I then got sick. Then back to level two. However, I beat that misadventure and got my level one back. I have been reading on another series. It is known as the Saxon Tales by Bernard Cornwell. I read the first 3 books in the series, requested the next two. Not exactly sure how many books are in the series. Another series I read a couple books from, it is by Giles Kristen. They are about the British civil war. The story line revolves around a family that had brother against brother. The Bleeding Land & Brothers Fury. Giles had written some other books about Vikings that I read. His most current work was by far way better writing than the previous Sigurd & Raven series. Anyways. The Saxon Tales are good. It's about the Danes and English having their dispute during King Alfred's reign. The Danes was doing all that rape and pillage stuff. Had I been alive back then, would not have had to do all that. See I just would have put a saddle on Moo Cow. Which being that I would be riding into the English lands. It is only natural that it is done on Moo Cow, for he is a Scottish highlander! I would ride under the banner of Freyja. Flags was kind of heavy back then and it would be a decent size ride. I would just drape the banner over the back of Mr. Pig, as he trotted along with us. As I went town to town, the Englishmen would just give me their women and wealth! Virgins and widows alike would wait for my arrival. The monks would plea "Loki the magnificent, please take our silver!" I would have to correct them. That "my name is Loki the Humble". Men would confuse my title because as I rode away from each village, the elders would say "there goes a great fellow Loki and his magnificent beast!" Though this would not stop the Pope from bestowing sainthood on me. Giving me the Latin name Saint Loki Magnus. As I rode through the land, a highlander heifer would join the caravan along with a plump butt sow, that was quite smitten with Mr. Pig!

Eventually I would make my way across the channel and cross paths with a wise king who felt it best to bless me with barrels of wine and suggest that a fine breakfast could be had if I only headed west. My never being one to turn down a fine breakfast, west it was! When I reached the coastal Marshlands and enjoyed a tasty waffle or three, I decided to settle.

Thus is how the Scottish Highlanders came to populate The Netherlands. Plus, with all the wine and women, this is how throughout history, the Dutch became known as a rowdy lot. I would eventually make my way to Texas and become the founder of the City Nederland, in Texas. It's a true story! You read it on the internet! Hahaha! Someday I will have to tell y'all about the time I got drunk and crossed the Alps by mistake with a hippo named Fat ass. Them damn Romans thought it was an elephant. Some sematic dude thought me to be a tour guide and followed me across with his army. Damn fool he was. I thought I was heading back to Finland!

But that's what ya get when you follow a drunk hippo! Ha! Not much has been going on. Sorting out everything with the hearing, for when it takes place. Reading up on past court rulings. Which has been helpful. You know, really my having went to level two was the best thing for me. Both times was because of wine disciplinary cases. The second time was total bullshit and the result of a guard with an old grudge. None the less, I got to meet and spend time with the same people. One was on that level at the time due to actions of protest. The whole situation with the new warden and the property disputes. Though the warden realized finally that we are dealing with life and death appeals. Thus have much more paperwork than other people in prison. Anyways, one guy has a Law of Parties case. He was going to file his own appeals. Through helping him with stuff, I came across some other court opinions and developed some ideas that will be helpful to my own case. People can look at the situation as I was worse off because I was on disciplinary level. Actually, it was the best thing for me. As I had stopped eating all this bullshit salt and sugar filled food they sell us on commissary. With no radio to distract, I spent a great deal of time discussing the law with others. Which helped them and myself. The downside though, was that I was on the pod with Joseph Garcia before I got in trouble. As a result, I was not there the last three months of his life. He went by Joey or Jedi due to his love of Star Wars. I have long been friends with Randy Halprin, who is tied up in that case. Some of the media coverage around Joey before his execution really pissed me off. As the media has covered the case of the Texas 7 wrong. They make it seem as if Randy was involved in the shooting. He was not. Another guy Mike accidentally shot Randy in the foot. Randy was too busy yelling, trying to hop away from it all. Something we often teased him about. He did not point a gun or shoot a gun. The Sunday before Joey's execution, I was listening to a rock station out of Beaumont called the Big Dog. On Sunday nights, they have a metal show and play harder stuff than what is normally on the radio. More so the bullshit music stations out of Houston that are easier to pick up. Only certain sides of the building can Big Dog get picked up. Sadly, I am not in that side of the building ☹ So I can only get it now if it is really cloudy between here and Beaumont Texas. Even then it is messed up most times.

Anyways, that Sunday I was in a different cell and was listening to the metal show. Someone yelled to me that on NPR was going to talk about Joey. So at 11 PM on Sunday, I flipped down there and listened to that horribly edited fucked up interview. The show was called Texas something. They really presented him bad. When the show is listened to, one can tell just how much of an edit job it was. Joey only met with that guy, because it was NPR and he thought he would get a fair shake. Then that fucking reporter made it seem as if Randy was shooting from the Jeep by the way it was edited. Though it is clear as day how it is edited. These same media outlets rant about Trump and shit. If they would give just 10% of that attention to the flaws of the system, the death penalty would long be over with. So there I was pissed off about how that interview went. I zip back down the dial to Big Dog and thankfully I didn't wait any longer. Sadly, I waited too long after 11:30PM as a song I hadn't heard in a while was playing. I heard this woman singing and felt excited as I realized who it was. It was Marie Brink of In This Moment. The song was 'Whore'. Ms. Brink turned the word 'whore' into this whole acronym and such. It is a bad ass song. She has some really good music and sadly she does not get anywhere near the attention that she should for her talent. I had been waiting to hear that song. Missed a third of it due to that bullshit ass NPR interview on Joey. Due to the complications of the Law of Parties, I will write about all that in a separate blog. Would make this one too long. There are angles to it that many people do not properly grasp and even lawyers fail to adequately argue to juries. Just wanted to drop a few lines. I will be back soon.

Veni, vidi, vici

I remain,

Clinton Lee Young #999447

D.R. Polunsky

3872 F.M. 350 South

Livingston TX 77351

U.S.A.

www.saveaninnocentlife.com

Loud & Clear, July 7, 2019

Topic: Tick Tock

Still no news to report. I had anticipated getting an update, but haven't. Time ticks on. Life around death row has been slow and steady. Not as tense as was around this time last year when we got the new administration. It should be enough that they are trying to kill us. All the extra stuff to stress over is not needed. So glad everything is at least slow and steady. When it comes to writing. People can go back to writing. The reason that I want people to not write when it gets close to the hearing when I leave the unit. The mailroom used to forward a persons mail to the specific county jail. Which is where we are houses when going to court. Now the mailroom only "returns to sender" anything that arrives. That would just result in all kinds of stuff lost.

I will let people know a couple weeks before I am due to go back. For security reasons, obviously, I will not know the exact day for my transport! Anyways. Nothing is even remotely set in sand, much less stone. As to when hearing will be. Could be August or next year. I have not been writing much for a simple reason. I have to get a new typewriter. Wish I could say I got mad and threw it across the cell. Though I messed it up in a much stupider way.

The hammer was barley hitting, so letters wasn't laying down. I thought maybe it was dust or a wire issue. First a little bit on the impact came off. So I get that fixed with string. We aren't allowed tools and such. So I have to go get it. I have to get cave man creative. Well, it messed up again! I clean all and check what I thought was old. Still wouldn't work. Warranty is long expired. So it is just dead. Then I get mad! Then worse gets ripped. I go to set it down and hear something rolling around. I find the noise source. It is the bottom part of the impactor. The impact has a bullet shaped base, with a shaft and nut at the end of the shaft. Well, I see the bullet shape part rolling around. Confused at how in the world the shaft could have broken off. I push the hammer forward and pull the impact shaft out. Soon as I seen the end of it. My heart sank and I felt sick. It had threads on that end also. Meaning, all I had to do was place a small string on threads of the shaft and screw the base back on. The string helps it get a secure grip. So what would take five minutes and a piece of nylon string, became a $225 fuck up. To my defense though. The brand of typewriter that they used to sell. That impacter was all in one piece. Which I assumed would be same w/this brand. I had it for three years. Though only problem was that impacter, which I could have fixed. Anyway, when I finally am able to get a new one. Then I will write more. I also recently found out a pen pal ad a couple of years ago had that I was not willing to write people overseas. I never said that, and it makes no sense. I know some people get frustrated that I don't write back. Several things w/that.

#1 At times my mind is so consumed with my case I toss letters to the side and will only write letters that pertain to action or some that I feel good about writing. Like they make me smile. That I don't have to worry about any bullshit, complaints, misunderstandings, and the sort. That's just cool is the rule. Now that is "NOT" to say all others are. But if getting to know someone new. Due to past experiences there is a feeling out process that takes time. So and is about energy levels. Or I just get focused on other stress.

#2 has at times I just don't get it due to mail mishaps. Though that is a low percentage.

#3 this one I hate to admit. I got mad at lawyers and another person was going to shut everything down and represent myself in court. During this time period I threw a lot of stuff away. That includes letters and such. Which also ties into not blogging for awhile.

#4 some people act like writing me is a hobby or that I have some obligation. I am not here for anyone's entertainment. Nor have I filled out a job application.

Now I have been putting more focus on the US and Texas so as to get a chapter of the foundation set up here and all that. My point is. When I get my typewriter I will get off the bullshit being lazy and stressed out and write more. I am just so tired of this place and dealing with all this. Tired of living it and writing about it. Trying to write more blogs on other stuff. One about the hearing getting cancelled. Should have been posted by now. Not sure if it was properly received yet. Alright then. I shall return. Take care, smile, and strive for all that you desire.

Veni Vidi Vici

In solidarity

I remain

Clinton Lee Young

Loud & Clear, August 11, 2019

Topic: Safe and Sound

You fuckin people have gone batshit crazy out there. With all the fake book conspiracies, instadumb post and violence. I am staying on death row where it is safe and sound! Here I only have to fight with ants, mold, multi-legged roaches, and 2 legged roaches. There was even a tornado in Amsterdam. What the hell? So much for my planned post upon arriving to Amsterdam. "The Texas Tornado has landed. I'm here to tear the town up!" Pfft Ha! I promise I don't pay for these lines. Ha. Oh and yes "instadumb" is an official Clinton Loki Young creation. As Instagram seems to make people dumb. As in dumb criminals that do crimes and then post about it. Thus being "instadumb" "Local guy caught after posting about robbery on Instagram." He was #instadumb.

Caught cheating? #instadumb! I copyright it and declare it my creation. My supporters who are already NOT instadumb people. So they are free to use it against those dummies that it applies to as their heart desires. See I am hip to the times. I still don't understand guys wearing skinny jeans. But generally, I am able to keep up with the cool kids. Still no typewriter, as the unit commissary has not had any in stock. Guess I will have to get one when I get back from the hearing. Not sure if I wrote about this yet. The state had concern about some matters. They had testing done to check. It came back. Do I even need to say who it favors? I mean it is automatically understood. I'm just saying! Will post about it as hearing goes on. Plus people will understand why more wasn't discussed. The hearing almost got delayed again, but judge thankfully said no. Last delay was for my benefit. To make sure my rights were protected. It worked out and is all moving along. Next. I think a blog I sent to someone to forward, was not posted. The Nuts and Butts blog was never supposed to be posted. As after writing it, a couple different set of details was brought to my attention. Which would have altered the way I wrote the blog. The blog that was supposed to have been posted would have explained more hearing etc. more so how the video deposition went. Will just post videos after hearing. Alrighty then. The fight goes on.

Veni Vidi Vici

In solidarity

I remain

Clinton Young #999447

Loud & Clear, Aug 18, 2019

Topic: Thank you

I wanted to thank everyone for the cards and birthday blessings. I will be getting ready for the hearing, by the time this is posted. It will be a short time until I am returned to Polunsky. Had hopes the prosecutors would agree to work with my lawyers, but is seems will fight to the end.

So I will have a longer fight. Will keep everyone updated via Merel. Just wanted to thank everyone for the birthday blessings.

Take care,

I remain,

In solidarity

Clinton Lee young #999447

Loud & Clear, August 20, 2019

Topic: Never fails/Always something

Had an unexpected legal call today. It seems that the main point of the hearing will change.

Two Developments. 1. There was some guys who gave statements in 2003. I wrote a blog about one guys video deposition from April 2019. That D.A. investigator altered/falsified a statement. Then had it improperly notarized. I wrote a long blog on this. No one has commented on it, so I still assume it has not been scanned and forwarded to Alex or Merel. Well last week I was told a guy gave a statement saying that I said I shot Samuel Petrey. This was done in 2003 after my trial and before my motion for new trial. I have been furious all weekend and planning on how to attack it. Lawyer said he was a fugitive from cops, so might not show up if they don't catch him. Well my team found him online I guess and lawyers spoke to him.

He told them "No. Clinton never told me anything like that. The investigator told me if I would help him, he would help me. He wrote that and I signed it. But it was Page that confessed and also told me about his plea deal" and some other stuff. So yet another false statement by a D.A. investigator. Multiple people say stuff about him. It shows a pattern of misconduct. It gets a bit better. It was revealed to my lawyers that the D.A. that worked on the forms given to my jury, handled my direct appeal and my state habeas each time I filed one and the filings around my execution state and testing requests. Turns out that as he was doing this, he also was working for the courts as an advisor for habeas appeals. He thus worked for the court, while operating as a prosecutor. That is what is called a "conflict of interest". He knew he should have got off my case. It is prosecutor misconduct and rendered my previous appeals improper and biased. Which then raises the matter of doing them all again. Which I don't want to do. All the lawyers have been talking I should have still returned to Midland for the other parts of the hearing. If I end up not going that is. The officers are of mind that I am not due to leave the unit tomorrow will find out in the morning at latest. Hopefully still leave in a day or two. Every time I turn around, there is always something. Other matters was discussed, but not going to get into all that right now. As more is to be discussed. Chaos is the story of my life it seems. To my supporters and friends. Thanks for being there for me. Even when at times I didn't make it easy with my frustrations and such. To my enemies. Many assume they are listed as such. When they really aren't worthy of such a title. But to keep it simple. To yall. Well stay tuned. To other more important matters. It seems that positive steam is building for Rabbi Randy. That is what I took to referring to him as, since the stuff came out about the judge from his case. I tend to find some sliver of humor in all situations. Rabbi Randy should never have been convicted.

Beyond all that. A serious question needs to be asked by the citizenry. How many lives are enough? If it was the Texas 10 would 10 be too much? A store clerk is killed or such. The actual shooter accepts deal first so gets life and other gets death. Cases of average people getting killed and plea deals are passed out like candy. 1 cop gets killed, then 7 people have to die. Even those that never fire a shot!? How do we as a society seek justice and equality. When we place the value of one life so high above others? Not only do we treat criminals differently. We treat victims differently. Cop kills a citizen and ends up with official oppression. Yet a citizen kills a cop, or is just there, and he gets death? A cop in Harris County lied on a search warrant that got a door kicked in. This leads to a shootout and 2 people dying with multiple cops shot. So a cop caused events to unfold based on lies and 2 people died. Based on transfer intent / law of parties. He caused 2 deaths in one scheme. That is capital murder. Yet, Harris county prosecutors will never file such a case. Though guys are serving life in TDCJ for just running from cops and a cop said guy point his car at a cop. Didn't hit him. Just supposedly drove towards him. Amazing that some can't understand why parts of the population are upset. I am not saying that special protection should not be given to those that protect the innocent. Though when are the scales even? Why can not mercy be shown and it still be justice? Since the Texas 7 case, people have still escaped and killed. Violence goes on. Killing Randy will have zero deterrent on crime. His story will only serve to make people view their government as heartless. People turn against the death penalty fastest at the notion that we kill people who never killed. It also supports those that hate the system and police. "See look, they will kill anyone. They kill people who never killed." In so many ways the execution of Randy would be wrong and counterproductive. More so when people read about a racist judge. It would only serve to be propaganda for those that hate cops and believe the justice system is only just for the protection of a slice of the population. Our system is built on a foundation of justice. Rooted in the faith the people have in it. This can only be maintained through fairness and the rule of law. The officer's name is honored through fairness, justice and mercy. If Randy is executed then the officers name will forever be tied to a hateful judge and the death of Randy. We should never kill anyone that hasn't killed nor even tried to harm another. We should also not tie the name of one that has sacrificed in the call of duty, to the very concepts that undermine what caused him to answer that call. No matter where people stand on the death penalty. All should stand against the execution of Randy Halprin. Free Rabbi Randy! Still no typewriter. I was told the warehouse for the typewriters burnt down. That one was supposed to have been held for me on the unit. Though another clerk accidently sold it to someone else. Then warehouse burnt down. It is always something I tell you! Shall see how all that sorts as is only one company that makes them. Long sigh. So after I get back from hearing. People will just have to bare with my handwriting. It will grow on ya. Alright, I have carried on long enough. Please keep up support, and spreading the word. Take care, smile, and strive for all that you desire.

I remain,

In solidarity,

Veni Vidi Vici

Clinton Lee Young #999447

saveaninnnocentlife.com

clintonyounfoundation.com

Loud & Clear, August 27, 2019

Topic: Can it get crazier

Was all geared up for nothing. Monday, they wanted to kill me. Tuesday, they offered me life, which I promptly rejected. Thursday, the Midland D.A. had to get off my case. Found out the assistant D.A. literally was working with judges to kill me. So Midland had to get off my case + a special prosecutor will be brought in. The former D.A. that fought all my state level appeals, was paid by judges to advice the court on how to deny my appeals! A major conflict of interest + totally unethical. So all my state level appeals were rigged. It is like the insanity knows no end! Yes, it can help reopen stuff, but I am tired of this shit. The trip to and from Midland was neat. Got to ride on police airplanes. Coming back to this place was not neat. I felt sick! It was like getting locked up all over again. Look, I am trying to stay as distracted as possible. People always ask me how to help. I want to be able to get newspapers + as many magazines, books + comics as possible to keep my mind off of this place as much as humanly possible. So if you want to help me, then please send something each month to the PayPal/Tip Jar on www.saveaninnocentlife.com This way I can just send my people a list of what I want every week. Thank you in advance.

When I first came to death row, when they closed the cell door, I pulled on it and thought "one day I'm walking out of here". This time I just felt sick. It is like it will never end. Each time I get a step closer, BAM! I get kicked back. If it aint lying witnesses, prosecutors hiding secret deals and having people lie at my trial, it is the investigator for my state appeal lawyer smoking crack with witnesses, to D.A. investigators creating false statements, to the judge and D.A. literally working together to kill me. The insult to injury is that Midland takes my TDCJ trust fund account for a % of all funds I get, to make me pay for it all! It is like this shit will never end. I can't get a fair trial. I can't get a fair appeal. Prosecutors and law enforcement commit felonies with no one punished. Yet they got the audacity to offer me a bitch ass life sentence. Motherfackers are smoking crack and eating dog food. I just want all this to be over. I am not writing about my case anymore. I am tired of even thinking about it. Thanks for any and all help. People can start writing me again.

p.s. the clintonyoungfoundation.com site account is purely for legal.

Take care, smile and keep on keeping on.

Clinton Lee Young #999447

Polunsky Unit

3872 FM 350 South

Livingston, Tx 77351

Loud & Clear, September 19, 2019

Topic: My focus

Over the years, I have told people my focus. As to the system and goals. I am not an anti-death penalty activist. I reserve that for those not on death row. For a guy on death row to say he is such. It is really to say he is a "don't kill me" activist. I do not make the fight about capital punishment. It is about justice. It is about the rule of law and all being held to the same standard. Which is the basis of a civil society. We see, far too often, how the system in the U.S. works differently for various people. I have always said, there is a true way to end the death penalty. It is to deplete the faith people have in the system. This is done by highlighting misconduct. My case tops the cake. The level of conspiracy to murder me is breath taking. Never seen before type level. You all don't know the half of it yet! I was smart, young, white, attractive and loved by a wide range of people. All that was supposed to protect me from the death penalty. So I was told, before receiving such. I wasn't from Midland, so no connections. Then there is the lack of wealth. What truly was the defining factor. It was a prosecutor willing to win at any cost. To secure the merit badge of having gotten the death penalty. He retired as soon as the appeal court upheld my conviction. The assistant D.A. Ralph Patty who handled appeals. He had that court's ruling hanging on his office wall. Like it was a trophy. The officials around the prosecutor. Law enforcement, judges and other D.A's. All bound by ethics. All professing to be fighting a noble cause. They stood for nothing and done everything. Damn the law, morals and ethics. They pumped the victim's family with lies. Manipulated their pain to serve prosecutors own end. Denied them surety of legal fact. Them people was fuckin sick! They called "me" the sociopath!? This is why the system needs to be questioned. It is why those in power need to be challenged. I don't need to tell people to deny the government the ability to kill citizens. They come to that conclusion on their own. My focus is on the constitution. The rule of law. What we define as justice. This line of thinking. It is why I welcome pro-death penalty people on pages, as I do anti-death penalty activists. I want a police officer to feel just as welcomed as an outlaw.

As what you feel about a political topic. The moral position you take on a form of punishment. These self-defining perspectives of 'right or wrong'. To each her or his own. My focus is to get beyond that. To instead focus on the moral contract, that we operate by, as a society. The U.S. is not a pure democracy. It is a democratic republic. We elect people to be the voice of the people. In Texas, prosecutors are elected. Judges are elected. The people bind them by oath and trust them with the power to make choices that impact lives. We use a symbol to define our vision of justice. Lady Justice with her scale, blindfold, and sword. A lady because women truly do have a greater sensitivity to injustice. Blindfolded so as to see no difference in the people. The scales to balance out justice equally for all. The sword to feel the wrath. To feel her fury. This is how we define our system. Those who are corrupt overlook a detail. Her sword is double sided. It cuts both ways! At least that is what it is meant to do. Being that she is blindfolded. Man can lead her down the wrong path. Protecting their own from her. They all done everything they could, to serve one prosecutors objective. They committed felonies! Tampering with a witness in a capital case is a first-degree felony. Murder, aggravated sexual assault, and so forth are first degree felonies! It all carries up to life in prison. Beyond the lies and such. They all acted outside the law, to accomplish depriving me of my life. That was the goal. The sole objective. To lead up and result in my death on Oct. 26, 2017. I don't care where you stand on capital punishment. Where do you stand on truth, ethics, morals, the law, and our symbol of justice? I say that cops, prosecutors, judges and the sort should take care of their own. As long as they don't forget their own is the people. All the people as they damn sure aren't supposed to be above the law. To think though, they really don't understand why a part of the country hates them. They create an "us vs. them". Because they treat "us" different than "them". Though we shall see how everything unfolds. It really is not hard to do the right thing. If you believe in what you say you stand for.

That is that.

Take care, smile and strive for all that you desire.

Feel free to share all blogs.

Just please credit me as the writer.

and my sites. Thanks.

Veni, Vidi, Vici.

In solidarity I remain.

Clinton Lee Young #999447

D.R. Polunsky

3872 F.M. 350 South

Livingston, TX 77351

United States of America

Loud & Clear, September 29, 2019

Topic: They like it dirty

TDCJ allocates certain items. 3 times a week can exchange towel, jumper, 2 pair of boxers and 2 pair of socks. On Mondays get 3 pair of socks. Tuesdays can exchange 2 sheets and a cell towel. A cell towel is basically a long washcloth. It can be used to scrub body with or the cell when cleaning. All these items have been used by others. Imagine sharing underwear with your classmates! Now if one is blessed to have someone send them money to the inmate trust fund account. Can buy wash clothes, socks, t-shirts, boxers, tennis shoes, boots, and cleaning supplies. TDCJ only provides 5 bars of cheap hotel size soap, roll of toilet paper and a small paper cup of Bippy a week. Which is an Ajax type cleaning powder. Twice in the past 4 weeks there has been no Bippy. Now today they informed us will no longer be exchanging cell towels. As for a new guy who enters the system and has no money. He has to just use his hand and the tiny bar of state soap. The water is not always the hottest. How can a person truly wash off grime and dirty body oil? Or clean the cell properly? General population have long not been getting cell towels. Though they have access to brooms, maps, and scrub brushes. Things we can't get due to "security reasons". Hence the cell towels. Now by policy, before a prisoner is moved into a cell. It is supposed to be cleaned by the working prisoners. Swept, mopped and areas wiped down with bleach water. As some prisoners are dirty. Psych patients leaving bodily fluids. Additionally, there is the fact of hepatitis C and its ability to live over a week outside the body. Prison is bad with hep C. as many are former drug users, prison tattoos, exchange of blood during fights, etc. A cell tower cost these people 5 cents to make! Hep C treatment cost $80,000. I went to public school and even I get that math makes no sense! Most on death row wash their jumper sheets, and using commissary bought boxers and such. It is easy to tell who washes their jumpers. They are actually white! The ones these people wash take on a dark tan color. Water is not tan, bleach is not tan, detergent is not tan. As how a white jumper turn tan? They stuff the machine to max with clothing, so dirt and grime just gets swashed around. Those that do wash our own clothes, we do so in the sink or in cereal bags. They are large and sturdy. (Some people in prison wash in their toilet). Back to matter at hand. With them not issuing Bippy powder and now no cell towel. How is a guy to clean his cell? I already documented how the showers are. Prisons get access to vaccines, the same as nursing homes. As the people in such have weaker systems than the general public. Plus, the way people are crammed together. It is a perfect breeding ground for a virus to evolve. When the swine flu scare happened in the U.S. Politicians complained in Texas that a large number of the limited vaccines was going to TDCJ. That prisoners should be last on every list. What the idiots didn't think about, was how if a guard brought a virus from home. Then infected a couple prisoners. If not enough on the prison population is vaccinated. Then the virus can evolve and become resistant.

Then pass to other guards. Who then take it home. Can infect children, who then take it to school. A whole new struggle begins. A clean prison is thus about more than prisoner care. It is a matter of public safety. More so given the size of the prison population. Also, guards are considered low wage employees. Poor people take the longest to seek medical help; due to costs. It seems that TDCJ insists on operating on the edge of crises at all times. They are reactionary. As outbreak happens. "Then" they come around washing all the hand nails and doorknobs with bleach. Why not do that before and thus prevent the outbreak?

Additionally, there is a huge staff shortage. They had to shut down recs and showers 2 days in a row here. Some guards are having to work 16+ hours. Normal shift is 12 hours. Some drive an hour to get here. This means they spend 18+ hours a day for work. Add in eat, bath and etc. They end up with maybe 4.5 hours of sleep. Some have slept in the parking lot in their car. The less officers show up for work. The more strain on other officers. If an illness gets passed around. More will not show up for work, due to being sick. Yet now they pick to reduce our ability to be cleaned!? TDCJ is over 4000 guards short. That is a safety risk, due to prison generally being a violent place. They could easily fix financial problems, so they would not have to budget cut cleaning supplies. They can expand commissary spends. Sell TV's which generates money and would be less rec. I mean for the entire system! General population prisoners have TV in the dayrooms. The more prisoners in dayroom. Greater chance of conflict. More so with staff shortage. If a guy could buy his own TV. He could hang out in the cell and watch it versus giving to the crowded dayroom. Death row and Ad-seg would rec less and also help with mental stability while in isolated cells. It would be easier on guards and generate money. The same goes for Jpay tablets or GTL tablets. Most states have these systems. One state sells actual custom made cell phones on commissary for $100,-. It is a flip phone called 'cellmate' with no internet and some restricted applications. All these other prisons, including federal prisons, can have these systems. Yet Texas prisoners are too bad to have them? King pins go to federal prison. Not state prison. So mafia Dons, drug lords, and such can have access to e-mail systems and tablets. Yet a beer store stick-up man in Texas can't? The system fears a baseless and invisible foe. That people in society will complain. So they focus on oppression and stay on the edge of crisis. All under guise of "tough on crime". The reality is, that most people already think we all are sitting in here watching TV and playing video games! Even the cops, that escorted me to Midland. They were shocked, when I told them we didn't have TV on death row. TDCJ keep guys in cells that make them crazy. Which increases conflicts. They keep things dirty. Hmmm. Maybe the prison system is really a giant college study on crises management. We can't blame the wardens always. Warden Perez is actually extreme about wanting everything clean and neat! It is the politicians that insist on slashing budgets and try to outdo each other on who can be the most oppressive.

On Sept 1st a law went into effect making Brass Knuckles legal in Texas. A law is on the books that an 18-year-old can buy an AK-47 with a 100 round ammo drum. He then can walk around town with it openly. Yet I can't have a cell towel or buy a bullshit ass TV? Huh…

Take care, smile and strive for all that you desire.

P.S. several blogs have been posted recently. Make sure you didn't miss any.

Veni, vidi, vici

In solidarity I remain

Veni, Vidi, Vici.

In solidarity I remain.

Clinton Lee Young #999447

D.R. Polunsky

3872 F.M. 350 South

Livingston, TX 77351

United States of America

Clinton young #999447

Loud & Clear, November 10, 2019

Topic: Life on death row

To those that are not on the foundation's social media pages, there was an additional set back. Though my situation is surely the minor point of it. The judge that was over my case passed away recently. A new judge has been appointed. The previous judge had children and had done a great deal with foster care. I do not know how he would have been in the end for me. Though he did grant me a full hearing. Outside of the courtroom he seemed to be a decent person. The new judge is not from Midland, as none can be on my case. He has lots of experience with death penalty cases. Will have a status hearing soon, so as to sort timelines and such. In additional news, my book is being typed up. Well, it has been typed up. It is being gone over for typos and all that. I will add some more to it, as there is some areas that I need to expand on. As people that know me and followed my blogs over the years, I have my own style. Such is reflected in the book. While I am behind schedule on it. It is close to being done and ready to go. Not sure if I have written a blog since Randy got a stay. I know I mentioned it in the messages on social media pages for the foundation. I was glad he got to live. Randy and I got to go outside on Halloween day. Mind you it was freezing cold and jackets had not been passed out yet. Have I ever mentioned how much I hate the cold?! Had thermal top and bottoms, along with shorts and T-shirt. So I only half ass froze. I also had a kufi on my head. It is the head cover some Muslims wear. The previous warden made a big ordeal about guys making homemade head covers. Like do-rags and etc. to cover head. Even if it was simply due to the cold. So I bought a Kufi. It is religious so I could wear it all over the prison and no one can even touch it. There we are on the outside rec yard. I told Randy "Happy Halloween" and have him a mint stick. But to my shock and dismay he did not bring anything out for me. Friends these days! I asked him "What the hell. Nothing for me?". He pointed to an empty water bottle and said "you can have that!". While at rec. and wearing the kufi, my costume character popped into mind. I told everyone that for Halloween I was going as Jihad John. Ha I was going to go to visit like that and take a picture and state such. Someone was of the mind it would be insensitive. No, it wouldn't! Jihad John was the British guy that made the videos for ISIS. He was a real-life monster. People dress up as Jason from Friday the 13th, Joker, Bin Laden, and etc. If I said I was dressed up as the prophet, then THAT would have been insensitive. Though because everyone is so high-strung these days and with no sense of humor, I did not want to offend anyone. So I didn't go to visit like that, for the picture. No really, the truth is I just forgot until I got to visit! Sure some people might have got upset. Though if they did, my response would be that they must accept Jihad John as the representative of their faith. Because if he doesn't, then there is no harm in mocking 'him'. People dress up as sexy Nuns and such for Halloween. Though I missed the chance. Maybe next Halloween I will have something witty in mind. Hell, hopefully I am not here. Though I did use the idea, to have a discussion with a guy here. I always appreciate a good discussion. It is why I like politics. Many people tell me they do not care about politics. If you do not care about such, then you do not care about the direction of your life. As politics impacts everything. Tax, rights, laws, education, and etc. The government controls so much of our lives. In the US, peoples lack of interest in the system. It's why we have courts and prosecutors that do as they do. They keep the people focused on Washington D.C. This way everyone freaks out about the presidents and ignore local level politics. A judge is often elected by only a few votes. Same with prosecutors. People will vote for the president, but no one else. The prosecutor can deprive you of your life in Texas. It is the judges that allow prosecutors to get away with misconduct, that results in you, your friends, or family being locked away. Or even worse; being executed. All these people in arms about Reed and how appeals court denied his appeals. Damn, where were all of yall when Sharron Keller was running for election? Keller is the judge over the appeals court in Texas.

I had friends overseas trying to highlight the election. They were confused by the lack of interest in Texas. Everyone will scream nine ways from Sunday about the death penalty. Yet do not push the vote. When the judge, who has caused so many to be executed, runs for election. Real fuckin amazing! Had she lost the election, the court would have been better suited for actual justice. I understand! I get it that posting on Fakebook, Instadumb and twit-lit is easier then actually getting out and pushing people to vote. For one of the most powerful positions in the state of Texas. Fight on key board Ninja. Anyhow. I am glad that more attention is being placed on Texas death row. Between Randy, Reed, and the unique circumstances with Patrick Murphy. There has been a great deal of focus on Texas. From psycho judges, TDCJ and the way appeals court will kill us on technicalities. The Court of Appeals did not say Rodney Reeds appeals was meritless. They denied it on procedural grounds. Basically saying his lawyers could have done things sooner or that it 'by itself' is not material tot overcome conviction. Well if all things are considered and one knows that if re-tried today, he would not have been convicted. One is supposed to say okay give him a new trial. Long sigh. The fight goes on.

I will know more with my own situation in December. If it was up to the Court of Criminal Appeals in Texas. Anthony Graves would have been executed and Ernest Willis. Todd Willingham wasn't so lucky. Nor was Daniel Acker. If anyone has not seen the film Trial by fire about Todd. I heard it is worth a look. I recently found out the documentary about me was no longer on amazon. Something to do with music rights or some flim flam bullshit. It is still on YouTube and Vimeo under "Innonocent on death row" or "Deal with death". Thanksgiving is coming up in the US. It's a holiday people are supposed to be focused on matters they are thankful for. Be thankful you are free and take time to appreciate the little things in life.

Alrighty then, I have covered a bit of this and that. Oh, lately the focus here on death row for me. It is the dirty ass trays. The bullshit ass dudes that work in the 12-building kitchen prep room. Where trays are made for death row and ad-seg. The person that is supposed to wash them, clearly does as little as possible. One guy found a piece of a ramen noodle season pack of his tray. Other trays have had several pieces of tape on them. They tape a tag to the tray for those that are on the diet tray, pork free or meat free trays. Well, if a guy after getting his tray, does not tear off the tape and tag. The sorry-ass kitchen workers are not doing it. I had one tray that had three pieces of tape on it! I spoke to warden and other ranking officials at every chance. Today instead of taping the tag to tray. The kitchen put the tag in the utensil slot of the tray. That solves the tape problem. Though still does nothing about the nature of the inconsiderate person who is supposed to be washing them (next day back to using tape). They do not care, because they do not have to eat off the trays. They eat in the main kitchen. Though looking at some of them as I walked down the hallway. I doubt they would care period. Just amazes me at how inconsiderate people can be. Though prison is a petty paradise. No wise served twice. I wrote a poem in September 2016 about bullshit ass prison. It was posted under Loud & Clear blog, as it was a blog I wrote as a poem. If someone had not really been hip to life in prison then people would not get it. Prison just shows the worst of humanity. I hate prison!

Alrighty then. Take care, smile and keep on keeping on.

Veni, Vidi, Vici

In solidarity

I remain,

Clinton Young #999447

D.R. Polunsky Unit

3872 F.M. 350 South

Livingston, TX 77351

United States of America

Loud & Clear, December 1, 2019

Topic: Death Row Holidays

This time of year is naturally not the best. It is holidays and when the case happened. So not the best for several families. In here it becomes just another day. A day with no mail. Though they do feed us better. Thanksgiving was last week. It is a US holiday that everyone used as an excuse to eat a lot and get together. Few do the actual reflection the holiday is supposed to be for. TDCJ feeds better on Thanksgiving and Christmas. That is cool to do. Actually, only two times of the year we are guaranteed to get fresh fruit. An apple and orange. Other fruit we get is canned fruit, raisins, prunes, or applesauce. That stuff is given throughout the year. Nothing really much on the legal front. The status hearing got moved again until January. Hopefully no more delays. As the status hearing is to discuss the actual hearing. There seems to be another film coming out about the criminal justice system. I heard a part of a commercial on it. I am glad that the topic stays in focus. This is why it is important to highlight the cases the public will react to.

Some people have been commenting about how some seem to gain more attention than others. Every case is not going to stir people. That is just not possible. Though when certain cases highlight the flaws of the system, that benefits everyone. We care about the people in our lives. That does not mean we can force others to care about them also. There has to be something that sparks the people's attention. This applies to music, art, etc. The death penalty clearly spoken. It is about people facing death for murdering someone for some special circumstance. Be it rape murder, robbery murder, kids, multiple murders, etc. These are not pretty topics. Though we are supposed to have a system that operates based on the rule of law. Not a prosecutor's desires. Sometimes the facts of the case do not make people sympathize with the condemned man. Been other times the guy just did not have the people around him to raise awareness. Daniel Acker was innocent of capital murder. Though he wouldn't seek media as his lawyer was against it. His family was poor and real country folks types. They knew nothing of the law. Put faith in lawyer and god. He has been executed and been silence. If people looked into the facts of the case, he would be seen as an innocent man executed. He did NOT kill the woman. Could not have thrown her from a moving truck, nor force her to be kidnapped. It is not that people would not have raised up for Daniel. He just would not speak out and had no one to speak for him. Then you have a case like Robert Sparks. That case was so fuckin horrible. It made an anti-death penalty prosecutor change his views. No one would rally for Sparks beyond those that are just truly anti-death penalty. As they did for Reed for example. Human nature cannot be dismissed. People generally have to feel something for a person to stand up for them. If a guy here is not willing to properly present himself or fight for himself, how will anyone else? I have tried to get all kinds of people to work together and do stuff.

Most dudes seem to care only about commissary and letting some woman in their life do all the fuckin work. Unless a guy has a hellified team, that aint gonna cut it. People like Randy, myself, and Rodney. We put in years of work. Had setbacks due to other people's bullshit. Though we kept on fighting forward. Carlos DeLuna was said to be innocent and executed. His case didn't get as much attention as Todd Willingham. Though Todd was executed based on same forensics that freed Ernest Willis. Plus, Todd had a friend that never stopped fighting for his name to be cleared. Many times, it is the people in a person's life. Many times, it is the guy. Most times it is just the case. My advice is to just keep working forward.

Now me personally, I do not view this fight as we are all in the same boat. That gurney is a one-man-show. Though I understand the benefit of united efforts. Certain cases I will do something with. Some I wouldn't, as certain cases are just out of place. Though I would never hate on anyone else here. To me that is weak. I am strong enough to carve my own path. I don't cry because someone got a bigger piece of cake than me. I go bake my own cake. We got enough enemies with prosecutors and judges. We don't need to hate on each other. Anywho. I am going over the pages of my book. Need to do a bit more work on it. It is closer to being finished. Should have been done long ago. Though I just did not feel it. Merel can only do so much also. As people know, she came to the US to attend law school here. In the US, if a lawyer is bar certified from Texas. That means something! Though all the work required, where she has to cram 3+ years worth of studies into one year. She has her hands full. Plus, I have lots of people that express desire to be involved. Though they do not follow through. It gets difficult to put tasks in the hands of people I do not have experience with. As a result, I tend to pile on with those I feel I can depend on. Though things are coming along and I am grateful that more people are actually getting involved. For those that have expressed interest in blessing me for the holidays. As usual can send it in via the tip jar on my site (http://www.saveaninnocentlife.com/donation-corner/). Thank you. I am working on some other ideas. What really holds me up, is when will the hearing be! I want to organize an event in a few places. Though it is hard to plan when people cannot seem to agree on a schedule. It has changed three times due to one lawyer or another or the judge. Again this is just the hearing to sort out the actual hearing. The fight goes on. I have not been reading much lately beyond some graphic novels. Have touched on a couple books. I need to finish Solitary by Albert Woodfox. As I get closer to the hearings, I will dive back into the law more. Thanks again for everyone that has been active in sharing information about me and offering help. Keep on keepin on. I am going to wrap this one.

Take care, smile, and strive for all that you desire.

Veni, Vidi, Vici

I remain,

In solidarity

Clinton Lee Young #999447

D.R. Polunsky

3872 FM 350 South

Livingston, TX 77351

U.S.A.

Loud & Clear, December 30, 2019

Topic: Life on death row

This year is finally winding down. Glad for it to come to an end! I wrote a couple blogs but had expressed for them to not be posted, as couple issues I was ranting about was resolved. Though in some ways only. In the past two months we have only been able to get commissary twice.

When we were supposed to have gotten it 4 times. There is no reason why we haven't been able to. Death row used to have over 400 people here, so they had much more orders to fill out and could get it done then. Yet all of a sudden now everything is complicated. What bothers me is that it limits the amount of stamps and such things. Really some bullshit. Plus, staff shortages are getting worse. They will keep getting worse as job market will get better, so less people will even want to work here. As a result more and more days we are not getting rec or showers. This is happening all over the system. They need to come with different changes. More so for ad-seg and Death row environments. If they would allow at least a 2 or 3 person group rec. It would help a great deal, as far less rec to do. It would not be some great complication to do. Plus, with additional mail room rules going into effect in 2020. They could bring the tablets like other prisons have. Yet TDCJ acts as if for some reason their prisoners are somehow worse than every other state and the federal prison system. Never mind the actual fact that kingpins, terrorists and gang leaders end up in federal prison where they have all kinds of programs. So, it isn't about security here. It is all about oppression. These places are having adverse effects on people who will more often than not be free. They have nothing to help them before going home. Which means it helps to create a safety risk for the public. I wrote a grievance about the problem with not getting rec. They actually said that recs were being done properly. Two days after I got that grievance back, I got stuck out of shower and then on the 27th of December didn't get to rec. At least after a month they finally gave us cleaning powder. There ya go. Life on death row. As fucked up as usual. Take care.

Veni Vidi Vici

In Solidarity

Clinton Lee Young #999447

Loud & Clear, February 2, 2020

Topic: Back in the Twilight Zone

A quick turn-around trip to Midland did not produce much results. Though I did find out the DA knew absolutely nothing about the case. Keep in mind this is new DA's that got on the case in August. They didn't even have any of the files. My lawyers had to give it to them, which is not their responsibility. The crazy thing is that when my lawyers spoke to them about resolving the case, they told my lawyer: "No we are too far apart on the issues". When my lawyers asked later on what that meant, they didn't get any favorable response. Though it was then in talking that my lawyers realized they had no clue as to what all had taken place. They didn't even know why they got on the case and seem to think that they will only being dealing with the Chabot issue. Hell no, they got the case now. One would thing they would not want to drag DA's and judges through all that is to come. Whatever. Back here it is the same old bullshit. I got back on Friday. I did not get my property back until the next Friday. Which included all my legal material and etc. The property officer was out sick and these people acted like the property room was some magical portal that only one wizard could access. Ranking officers could have went in there and got it all. Hell, the first 4 days back I didn't even have a jacket and it was cold with the heater going off. It took everything in me not to go smooth the fuck off. I am still mad about it all. Plus, the trays are still trashed out. The sorry ass dudes working in the food prop room for 12-building are not washing the trays right. I filed a grievance on it and others has also. Plus, more will be.

If this shit doesn't get right soon, I am going to go on a hunger strike. I am tired of being treated this way. It is not in my nature to just accept some bullshit. Now TDCJ is making all these changes also. But what do they give us? Oh how exciting another ecomm spend. So basically, TDCJ is taking so much from us, but it is a treat to be able to give them more money to buy some bullshit ass commissary? Also, these rules. They have posted NOTHING in the dayrooms or rec areas on this building. Many guys do not even know about these changes. I am going to write out another blog on them specifically. As people need to file complaints that it is rolling out too fast. They do not have to roll out all the policy changes on March 1st. Like the money issue. Okay they say has to be on a guy's visit list to send money. Okay what if this guy is on death row that only get money from people not on their visit list and can't change their list until after March? Plus, we do not have the OTS list. So population has 30 people that can send money, as 10 on visit list and 20 on phone list. Yet death row and ad seg can only have 10? That is unfair and just fucked up! They going to let us make out a 20-person phone list? They do not have to roll out such drastic changes all at once. They can do it in phases so as to better understand problems and receive feedback. Like the drug dogs. Okay TDCJ can do that.

Though word is the dog will be behind a screen. That people put back to screen and such. Well, I will be suggesting to my people that they request for the dog to sniff screen first so they can see if the dog hits on the screen before they get sniffed. As what if some person came through before them smelling like a dope factory and they leaned on the screen, so now the screen smells like dope, thus causing dog to hit again on the smell. They then would mess off innocent people. Also if the dog hits on someone a high rank should be brought out and have test done again. As what if it is some poor family, where say 3 to 4 people use same car. Say nephew smoked weed in car all the time. The grandmother gets in the car to come visit. She never smoked weed in her life, but car smells like it. Thus her clothing. She then gets a positive hit by the drug dog and gets removed from a guy's list. What if that guy is serving life and the only family he has in his life is her and TDCJ took her from him and he knows his grandmother done nothing wrong. How do you think such a guy might respond towards a guard? Add in race factors. Say it is a black guy and the guard is some redneck. The south has some unique history with redneck guards and dogs. You all see how such drastic actions can lead to violence? This is why on so many fronts they need to slow down on this part of the plan and map out a more plausible idea. As what about medical marijuana users? What about people from states and countries where legal? Weed smell doesn't go away. I get TDCJ has to do something. People are dying left and right over that K2 trash. TDCJ will always be allowed to impose security measures. Though some common sense needs to rule the day. I will write about it all again in another blog breaking all down point by point. TDCJ should have April phase, May phase, and then for money issues, if they will press forward on that, have it for June so guys have time to adjust. After all, the only thing they give is commissary, so they are making it harder for them to use their own control tool. Long sigh. It sure keeps life interesting.

I am going to wrap this one up. Know I await yalls words. Also if anyone gets a return to sender letter. It was due to getting here when I was in Midland. Also PLEASE do not spray perfume on letters. #1 I am sensitive to smells and many give me a headache. #2 they will reject the letters.

Alrighty then. Take care, smile, and strive for all that you desire.

I remain,

Clinton Young #999447

D.R. Polunsky Unit

3872 F.M. 350 South

Livingston, TX 77351

United States of America

www.saveaninnocentlife.com

www.clintonyoungfoundation.com

Loud & Clear, March 16, 2020

Topic: Problem? Solution!

When a problem develops, it is only natural for me to seek a solution. The problem is that currently plaguing the TDCJ is staff shortages. While I would love to solve all that, my main focus is Texas Death Row. The staffing problems have an impact on rec. And time it takes to get to visit. As often they will have one escort team. If some of the 'freedom fighters' on level 2 and 3 is causing 'use of forces'. Then staff have to suit up the extraction team. A couple guys in ad-seg start to express themselves in disruptive ways. This will adversely impact staff available for other areas. With only one escort team for visit, it has resulted in people having to wait an hour, sometimes two. Many people travel long distances to visit. Add in other life responsibilities. This added time becomes a major complication. More so at times a guy here cannot get all of his visit time. Okay, in other states a person on death row can have contact visits (California is working on a program that will have guys on death row moved to different prisons around the state. They will be in general population). In Texas the classification system is G1 through G5. G5 (close custody) being the most restrictive before entering ad-seg (Texas recently changed the name of ad-seg to restrictive housing, a duck is a duck no matter what color you paint its ass!). Death row is housed like the ad-seg people are. G5 is a disciplinary level. Guys being assaultive and such. Mass majority of the problems a unit has occurs with the G5s. Now when a G5 goes to visit, they do so with just one officer while handcuffed. The same thing could be done with death row. They could make it so that death row level 1s can be escorted with one officer. They could even put leg shackles on for extra security during a single officer escort. Or reserve the leg shackles for those with security precaution designators. This would reduce the time it takes to get to visit by a great deal. I prefer they free walk us by ourselves. Though I doubt they would do that. Every part is gated off. It is not like there is this wide range of areas to possibly roam. The restrictive housing plan allows for group recreation if warden and regional director approve it. Guys are in ad-seg for behavior problems or being affiliated with certain gangs. Even if they never been in trouble! They can get locked up for a tattoo and known association. Anyways. The point is that G5s can have single officer escorts. Ad-seg could get group rec. Guys are serving life without parole who are going to die in prison. No hope. They are allowed to get contact visits and such. Death row will eventually be opening up. A lawsuit is coming and Texas death row has a greater leg to stand on than other states. As Texas actually allowed work and group rec by law. The board has just suspended it. I am shocked that the powers that be have not went ahead and made changes and opened up death row before litigation. As once the lawsuit starts, they will be able to have less say in how it goes. Muslims never could win on beards until they had a lawyer and expert sue for them. Death row now has lawyers and will have experts, plus many other states to point as examples. That being said, it makes more sense to start slowly bring different things into play.

There is now this problem of staff shortages and visit. Allow single officer escort to visit. Or allow single officer, well, AND/OR allow single officer on pod escort for rec. and shower. TDCJ knows the prison population with less problems is death row. Most have never been on level 2 or 3. Hell most have never even been in trouble. There is only two full pods of death row level ones. Plus, another section on c-pod. Some productive changes can be made. Better yet, restore at least the group rec. Portion of death row plan. Three people in the dayroom. Can cut handcuff slot in section gate and put slot on outside rec yard door. Officer puts one guy in the dayroom. Secures door. Goes to next cell, gets second guy. Uncuffs him behind section gate. He goes and opens dayroom door, enters and then secures door. Repeat for third person. No one is exposed while handcuffed and officer is never with anyone not cuffed. That is remove the security button on cell door and roll doors from picket, so staff could be off doing other things like escort for visits.

Bottom line is something can be done to better adjust to the new reality. I spoke to officers about the single man escort to visit. The reply I was given always goes back to "yeah, they single man escort G5s!". I hate to offer up this last solution. But it is an option. Reason I hate to offer it up is because I would prefer them opening up more and single man escort. It would just speed everything up and result in less days where pods have to shut down for staff issues. TDCJ allows units with high traffic visit areas to go from 7am to 5pm. Instead of 8-5. Shift change here is 5:30am – 5:30pm. A 7am-5pm visit schedule would not disrupt shift change. Count is 6:30am and 8:30am as far as that starting time range. So a 7am time start would not interfere with count time. The warden could get permission to do this from the Regional Director. I believe the warden here could okay it himself. Though being everyone overreacts when it comes to death row, am guessing he would seek okay from regional. Being that visitation is currently closed, which it should not be for death row! Now would be the ideal time to discuss and put forth these various changes. Start visits at 7am and allow single officer escort. Problem solved! No one would be turned away. All would get proper time. No more complaints. See, a plausible solution. I know y'all are just amazed as how I can always come up with such great ideas. It is not easy being great, though I do my best! Like the old country song by Mac Davos 'Hard to be humble'. It is hard, but I do my best! Give it a listen and smile. Alrighty then. Take care, smile, and strive for all that you desire. Another blog will be posted shortly before or after this one, so keep an eye peeled for that one also.

Veni, vidi, vidi

In solidarity

I remain,

Clinton Lee Young #999447

www.saveaninnocentlife.com

www.clintonyoungfoundation.com

p.s. on visit list printouts, it now lists video visits. It has regular visit, contact visit, special visit, and **now** has video visits. Which means TDCJ will be allowing some class of prisoners to have video visits.

Loud & Clear, April 12, 2020

Topic: The Days of Death Row

Ya know, I wish when I listen to a damn news story they start with how many people recover from Corona. Instead, I get hit with 2,000 people died! We understand people are dying. DUH! That's why the fuckin economy is shut down. Tell us properly how many recover so we can properly plan for the days ahead. The unit done something cool. They have a unit radio station. It is only 15 watts of power. They mostly do religious stuff on it. Though they started to play movies on it so guys on 8 building and 12 building who are not allowed TV can hear it. I am really grateful the wardens done that. Even the religious stuff, while I am not religious, I understand some are. I will always champion for anything that benefits people in prison. Even if I myself gain nothing from it. It is always important to show that positive acts can be done. The good thing about the current head warden for the unit, he has been on this unit before, for a while. Which when we get new wardens, we always het this concern of "what type of new bullshit will we deal with now?!" As usually it is a new warden that is all shell shock about DEATH ROW! Some come in and do some really dump shit. When I heard who it was going to be, first thing I said was: "Good! Someone that has had already dealt with us." Plus the warden currently over death row, I have spoken to him a couple times. He is stable and level headed. He seems to be a decent person. So for a couple years we should be good when it comes to the wardens. As lord knows we have had to deal with some unique individuals. As for what we talked about. I never write about the conversations I have. Yall might notice I never write about individual guards either. If I wrote about everything I discussed with people, who would want to talk to me? I also try to get things sorted internally before I rant online about it. Some might not understand this, but I am strong. I could survive anywhere in the system. I understand there is policy. Though I also appreciate culture. The culture has gotten worse in some ways due to the people on both sides. If TDCj would have been able to stay with the times and adjusted like other systems may have, would have been less headache. There is no reason why California, Federal prisons and etc. can operate the way they do. Yet TDCj could not match such. I want there to be more productive avenues available to people in prison. Jpay tablets, better programs, video visits as an addition to visitation. NOT to replace it. Like TDCj made many changes due to dudes messing with K2 (which that bullshit was killing people, it was horrible). Say they bring in video visit with all ID units. If a person got caught doing something at visit, that visitor could be restricted to video visits. People that don't abuse such, they be able to get regular visitation and video visits. Things that help keep families together. Plus with the tablets, TDCj would make at least 4 million a year if they brought tablets. I think would actually make more! Though let's stick with 4 million. 30% could go to child protective services, 50% to prisoner programs and welfare. Put it towards food, sanitation, education, and activities. The remaining profits go to security. I have different numbers before. Point is to get people thinking about this. The offender phone system is used to help fund victim impact. The Texas Lottery is used to help fund public education. Okay, anyone think that child protective services could not benefit from say an extra million a year? How many foster children would that benefit? Just because I am in prison, does not mean that I cannot come up with a good idea. At times TDCj and politicians worry about a possible reaction that simply does not exist. Like with TV's. Prison and TV's go together like bees and honey! People are shocked when they find out we don't get TV. Have had people that did not believe that was true. As Texas death row is the only one now I think without TV. Was two states. I personally do not care about the whole TV angle. I want contact visits, group rec. and all that. Though if TDCj sold TV to everyone in prison, it would reduce number of people in dayrooms, thus reduce fights and etc. for general population. They do have TV, though in dayrooms. Death row, ad-seg and G5-closed custody do not. Anyways, they need to give people tools to be better people. To have something to occupy time, besides sitting around frustrated all day.

I previously wrote about the color pencils being taken. I also wrote that would be getting them back in March or April. Had people here ready to cuss me out damn near, over trying to debate with me on why pencils was taken. Last time this pod went to commissary, I got me a pack of colored pencils, just to get some. I am grateful that Mrs. Davis allowed us to have them again. While I personally do not draw, others here do and I support them being able to be productive. It is better that guys on death row have positive productive activities to do. It is a distraction. It is better than sitting around thinking about dying all day. Arts allows a person to create. I write, others draw. If death row can use such to help charities and such. That's a good thing. TDCj should always encourage positive actions. If a guy is here for killing 10 kids, he can't draw for shit but slaps some b/s paper and then sells it for 10 grand! Okay, I fully understand the moral element here and why they would be upset. I am here and would never want to see such a person celebrated. Though if guys here, through a legit avenue such as University of Texas, if they can create art and it be used for helping a charity and such. A negative can be used to create a positive. Public reaction matters, so it is all about 'how' things are done. I want TDCj to allow more, that gives a person something to look forward to. Something positive to be proud of. Like in Louisiana they have football league, boxing, and etc. Texas is supposed to bring the Rodeo back. Hopefully they do and have it at more units along with other activities. Anyways, will be back soon.

Take care, smile, and strive for all that you desire.

Veni Vidi Vici

I remain,

In solidarity,

Clinton Lee Young #999447

Loud & Clear, April 19, 2020

Topic: Death Row and the world

It's an outrage I tell you! TDCJ has finally gone too far. Better yet TDC-NO-J for No Justice! Ya know, some of their bullshit oppressive tactics I can understand. Though now they have gone too far. These kind of games can not be accepted by a civilized society! The pod I am in went to commissary and they had NO Cheesy Poofs! What the hell kind of shit is that? It is un-American I tell you! There on the inventory list, in all it's glory, is listed Jalepeno Cheese Puffs.

I fill out my list and put down three bags. Stand at my door for hours on end awaiting their delivery. Only to see my sack void of any big orange bags. They had stopped selling Cheesy Poofs for about 18 months. They started again 6 weeks ago. Though where I am, we was only able to get them once. Though no, I was to be denied the cheesy poofy delicacy that is the BarbCo brand Jalapeno Cheese Puffs. It is a sad day in America when a man cannot enjoy his cheesy poofs. I was told that the warehouse didn't have any. YES, I investigated. Am I not the man I am?! It seems that this damn Wuhan-dirty-bat-insecure lab-corona virus has even halted the cheesy poof business. ☹ Trump needs to get his shit together and get this problem fixed! As I cannot abide the halt of production, when it comes to this matter of importance. Cartman would not stand for it, nor will I! Chaos, I tell you! To other matters. In a previous blog I wrote about media. I should have explained more, I was meaning political media and evening news.

Though I am sure people understood. Just to be sure, I never mean any kind of blanket statement to apply all or nothing. My frustration is that with the economy shut down. All it takes is the wrong spark and civil unrest will occur. I think about this cause and effect on loved ones. Plus society as a whole. (Also the public radio station I could hear briefings on airing them, though started back again.) Sure enough, just as I wrote and told people there was going to be some news story about virus impacting minorities. Then would come the stories that the government is trying to kill black people. Took longer than I thought but they have arrived. Just like when Obama was president and the stories was that he was going to take all the rednecks guns.

Then some mayors and such have lost their damn minds and told people they couldn't go to church. The constitution does not end. No one can tell people they cannot assemble. It is in the first amendment of the Constitution. When I heard that on the radio about trying to halt church service. I knew many would not be trying to hear that shit. I am not religious. Though I believe in the bill of rights. These are NOT rights given by government. It is written they are rights given by God that government can NOT take away. The first is free speech, media, religion, assembly and petition the government. The second is right to own guns. The reason it was put second is to back up the first. I guarantee you there was some churches in the USA somewhere, where the pastor and people had guns and was daring any to try to stop them. Now can we not use common sense? Sure! A saying I thought up. "The good lord created good sense." That is an official Clinton Lee Young quote. Instead of having one big church gathering, could break it down into two or three gatherings. Though the government cannot deny the people their rights. Period.

The thirteenth amendment cannot be abused can it? What if the government came in and rounded up 10,000 civilians and ordered them to work for free for three months during this pandemic. What would that be called? It is Slavery! Okay if we will not allow the government to do this act. Why would we allow the government to violate the first amendment? As a people we cannot allow those in political power to pick and chose which rights they want to allow us. If you allow it today, it could be against you tomorrow. Remember Elmer Fudd, it ain't no fun when the rabbits got the gun. Be very very careful at the power you give to the few. A perfect example in the USA is the Michigan governor. She must not want to be re-elected! You can buy vodka but not garden seeds? Cannot go to vacation homes? Cannot shop in the paint isle? Though I understand the people of Michigan's pain for I am unable to buy cheesy poofs or get visits with my loved ones. ☹ People might wonder my political leaning. I am libertarian, though am not as radical as some. I am more conservative leaning on some issues. Like I would say it is not good for prisoners to be shooting up heroin and having sex with each other. Just doesn't seem kosher.

I'm just saying. A site for the main libertarian magazine is Reason.com. They have done some great stories on criminal justice. I subscribe to their magazine. To that one jackass that never wants anyone to joke about anything. Don't be a jackass. The police state continues to worsen. Now officials are calling on citizens to snitch on each other by reporting quarantine violators.

From the DARE program having kids reporting their parents for smoking weed, to the corona that has a dad getting arrested for throwing a ball with his daughter. In Colorado a father was playing catch with his daughter in a local park. Police showed up and placed him in handcuffs.

Shame on the filthy PIG that done that. That is the kind of cop that the people of the city should demand he be fired. To place handcuffs on a man in front of his daughter. For her to have to see that. More so for such an innocent act. Hell with the rate of children who suffer absent fathers on the rise. Such a man should be celebrated. Major events like what we are currently dealing with. It has a lasting change on society. I fear that it will adversely impact our concept of humanity.

Such as some saying we should never shake hands again. We already, as a people, have enough that keeps us apart/distracted/divided. It is bad enough we have images of people out together at lunch, yet both people are looking at their phone. To remove the initial connection of shaking hands for example. It would cease to be a human-esque gathering. It becomes even more pointless and robotic. Instead, we need to use this to be better. To eat healthier and practice better hygiene throughout the day. If I was King, I would decree that all should eat healthy and be active. What about cheesy poofs I hear you asking. That would be the royal snack, forbidden to the likes of the common man. This way I would never be void of their delightfulness. Though I will share with the ladies, as cheesy poofs are good for a woman's hips :-P. Alrighty then. I have blessed you with the ramblings of a true stable genius. I shall wrap this one up. Corona has caused a couple more executions to be halted/dates moved. That is good. Would be great if lawyers were able to use that extra time to uncover something new and helpful. Though Government Abbott is getting Texas back going. So no telling how long will last. Texas has the worlds eleventh largest economy. When oil was booming it was eight. Something else I told people, when this first started. The world cannot handle a shuttered Texas. People that never been here, really do not appreciate how large and diverse Texas really is. It is way bigger than cowboys, oil and the death penalty. Alrighty then. Y'all take care, be nice to each other and do not allow the few to strip you of the rights that do not belong to them.

Veni, Vidi, Vici

In solidarity

I remain,

Clinton Lee Young #999447

facebook.com/clintonyoungfoundation

saveaninnocentlife.com

Loud & Clear, May 6, 2020

Topic: A new month, the same b/s.

They locked the unit down. We have been told so many versions as to why. The thing I don't understand is why they treat us like we have to be punished. They limited commissary to same we get on behavior lock downs and such. They would not even allow us to buy over the counter medication on commissary. Yet sick call requests are not being allowed if not an "emergency". I can't get basic medication from medical. Yet also can't get it from commissary? Where the fuck is the logic in this shit? During a pandemic, no less! They say we could get $10 in correspondence materials, yet refused to let us get typing ribbons or greeting cards that are sold. Next week or the week after they say we can get $15 worth of commissary, any items like food stuff. At least the pod I'm on did get to buy stamps today. First, they acted as if would have to wait 2 weeks. (The bad thing was pod hadn't been able to get any for 2 weeks already.) Look, some officers tested positive of antibodies. No one on Polunsky had the corona when they locked u down. Still the way they treat us on this lock down, is as if we done something wrong. Though an oppressor only knows how to oppress. Next Issue: Some blog was recently posted. There was a delay, I did not expect in them getting posted. I would not been have blogged on certain topics had I known, as the moment changes and emotions switch. I finally finished going over my book, is maybe 3-4 pages to add. I will do that tomorrow. When get someone to properly edit it and all that for me. Also if someone writes with Jpay and you have never written to me before. How am I supposed to respond if I do not have your address? Also do I ever post anything about anyone I write? No I don't, because privacy is something I highly value. HINT! Nothing new on the legal front, still waiting.

Take care, smile, and Strive for all that you desire.

Veni, Vidi, Vici

I remain,

Clinton Lee Young #999447

www.saveaninnocentlife.com

Facebook/ClintonYoungFoundation

Loud & Clear, May 18, 2020

Topic: The Saga Continues

The lock down they had us on was short lived. Though it seems my pain must be long term. The pod I am on got to get the commissary on the 14th. Still no Cheesy Poofs. :(I tell you these people are evil! They do sadistic shit like sell Jalapeno Cheese Puffs. Get everyone loving them, only to yank them away. I never seen a group of people that always claim about being short of funds, yet do nothing to make funds. The oppressor knows nothing but to oppress. Long sigh.

Word is that visits should resume soon. Shall see how that turns out. They did give us masks. Actually gave it to us really quickly. Which makes sense, as they can't have dozens of people, on death row, in a hospital. They also have been coming around with bleach. They spray a rag and also allow us to use a handheld spray bottle if need be. Something they never done before. Really, someone's lawyer filed a pointless lawsuit on the masks for death row. As after the judge ordered the other unit, TDCj gave us masks. They spray everything with bleach & giving us bleach. Sure, could always be better. Though they are taking proper steps. Now the visit cancel was out of line. However, that was the Governor that done that. He just should not have done it pertaining to death row. Due to, as I detailed, Code of criminal procedure 43.17. Actually, people's family and friends could have sued. As the right to see the condemned, equally applies to them. No right or privilege under the law can be denied absent due process. C.C.P Article 1.04

They started back with Phone calls. When visits start back, the phone calls will go back to 5 minutes every 90 days. For death row and ad seg that is. ☹ In a previous blog I made a remark about news coverage pertaining to the corona virus. The way it impacted blacks. To be clear, I didn't dispute the numbers. Just the way news is "reported". Instead of saying Americans in general eat unhealthy and this is more common in the south. Plus, that blacks tend to be poorer and in more close knit communities. Thus, more susceptible to cross contamination. Most go to same local church, shop at same local community store, and such. PLUS fact that New Orleans is a majority black city. Instead of detailing such facts when reporting the news. The news gets told as if basically the government is killing blacks due to inaction. Which is geared at creating fear and animosity. I do not like it when politicians or media figures use fear. As I believe that is a form of force. I believe that with Love being Freedom, force is evil. I would love to be in politics if I was free. Though I would focus more on being a statesman than a politician. At times when I write things, I do so with expectation that people can properly fill in the blanks. Though that is unrealistic on my part. As not everyone knows me, my personality, and or how system works. More so with many not being from the US. So when reading blogs. If read something that is a question mark for ya. Then just ask me to explain or such. I always operate with good intentions. To mail. Ah the saga never ends. I got the list of all the jpays sent to me in April. From April 1st to 18th I was missing no jpays. From 19-30th I was missing 11! Tonight I got a letter from the State of Georgia and it was post marked April 24th! Though I believe that is more about the way post office has reduced workers during the corona crisis. The jpay issues was these people somehow some way. But the letter delay. I just do not see these people just sitting on it that long. Nothing about the letter would require any extra scrutiny. Just a new person writing.

I have been writing a lot more. I asked Merel to take the letter option off of the sites. As she has enough to do, beyond playing secretary for me. Plus, she is not working, so forwarding messages and such adds up. I just prefer people to write me directly. I am working on other goals that will require more of Merel's attention. TDCj has added to the policy of cards. Can not send cards in the mail directly. Though can use a service such as shutterfly to send a card. Would design the card and shutterfly has to print and mail directly to person that is in prison. There are other services. Though I always ask people to send pictures with shutterfly. So would just suggest them for cards. Can download the app and sort all that. As long as my name, tdcj #, and address is put in as shipping address. It gets mailed to me with no issues. Something I have always wanted people to do that are on my social media pages. Is to take a picture of them and photos of the city they live in. A kind of photo tour. I never been outside of the US, though have traveled to other states here in US. I always liked to see new places. Can receive up to 10 pictures per envelope. As I mentioned, am working on book to finally get it out there. Plus a couple other projectes I think people will like. One is a legal defense organization here in Texas. The other is a charity I have long wanted to get going.

I also, once I get something else waiting on, will write some more of my online story. The Adventure of Loki and Mr. Pig that is posted on my saveaninnocentlife.com site. Lots to do. No news on legal front. Will find out something this week if hearing will still go on. At least I think I will. I am going to put some stuff together to better explain to you all the misconduct that took place by prosecutor and judge. It doesn't matter if anyone thinks I am innocent or not. What was done to me by these officials. It was so extreme. It offends the basic concept of justice. It truly undermines the core design of the United States of America. Which is the separation of powers. And that these powers be separated and used to protect the God given rights of the people. Stay tuned! Alrighty then, Take care, smile, and strive for all that you desire.

Veni Vidi Vici

In solidarity I remain,

Clinton Young #999447

facebook.com/clintonyoungfoundation

Loud & Clear, May 28, 2020

Topic: Needed Changes

Being that so many units are shut down due to the Corona. All of these prisoner rights groups, TIFA, anti-death penalty groups, and the family/friends of people locked up. Everyone should be working collectively towards encouraging TDCj to bring about the tablets that so many other states allow. The GTL tablet would be the most secure, as it allows unit activity. Such as filing grievances, commissary lists, and etc. Which means less contact between officers and people in prison. That means a more secure prison. Plus, with law library on the tablet, TDCj could reduce law library staff. No telling how long this corona shit will last. Plus with the economic loss. It is a guarantee that TDCj will suffer additional budget cuts by the state. If ever was a time to get tablets it is now. Plus as I said before, a percentage of funds could go to Child Protective services, which will surely also suffer from this pandemic. More so with parents unable to properly take care of kids due to side effects of pandemic. It is only smart, but hey what do I know. The hearing will take place in September. So glad that all is getting on the go. The jpay machine is all glitched and messing up, so they are working on that. Am sure it will be fixed by time this is posted. I had two letters returned to me due to people not putting address properly. One Texas and another Utah. Hey, why do people say they want to help or be active. Yet when a simple request is outlined, nothing gets done? Is it so hard for a yes to be yes and a no to be no? anyways. I will have some of my ideas detailed next week. Which really, I will just wasting my ink and time. Though I got to keep trying. Take care, smile and keep on keepin on.

Veni, vici, I tried but peoples bullshit ways held me back.

I remain.

Clinton Lee Young #999447

Loud & Clear, June 1, 2020

Topic: A world in flames

A crazy world we live in these days. You know I often will add different twists to my blogs.

What has always amazed me is how little people comment on them when writing to me. At times I was left wondering if a certain blog was even posted. I know the cheese puff one was as people made comments about that. Though I guess it's easy to talk about cheese puffs. Yet nothing about media, politics etcetera. Though I understand generally do not like such topics. Though the world now sees the great divide of the United States. Not just the race issues with police. The police state in general is a problem. The misconduct by police and prosecutors has gone unchecked for far too long, as it didn't involve all people. We know these problems that plague the system.

Here is the bigger question. Why are so many people, NOT protestors, so willingly destroying the country the live in? The country that everyone in the world wants to come to? Why would so many people have so much hate for each other? Who conveys information to the people? Who creates the idea of how a situation has taken place? Why will so many people openly rob, attack others and set fires? The country that allows the most opportunities. Something to think about.

Sadly illegit protests are being high jacked by anarchists. Me and a guy here who is black. We were listening to a program and a reporter had caught an exchange of a black guy telling someone: "You white people aren't welcomed here, this ain't your space." He said he wasn't feeling that. The other guy here said that to me. That the black guy should not have said that tot hem others. I took up for the black guy and said: "Listen, that guy knows his neighborhood. He knows they don't belong. Watch and see how shit starts." Two days later he told me how I was right. Little white dudes parking their BMWs, dressing in all black, talkin about how they are disenfranchised. Then throwing rocks and setting the community on fire. The very community they proclaimed to be speaking up for. Spoiled little brats trying to destroy the very land that allowed them to be spoiled. Being played by the wizard of Oz. The way information is relayed in this country. It keeps us versus them. In the midst of chaos and so much destruction. Our so called leaders in the media and politics still keep operating from the same play book. The root of it all is a piss poor education system that tells people what to think, instead of how to think.

Sadly, so many innocent people are going to suffer. So many more poor people will suffer. As the businesses looted and burned. The wealthy own the stores, the poor work at them. Now they will be without a job. Others that own a small café or small business that gets burned. Insurance does not cover riot damage! It is heart breaking. There was a moment when everyone was talking about the same thing. The way the police killed a man. People seen, ALL people seen. People that never suffered at the hands of police, they seen and was finally talking about police brutality.

Then the moment was dwarfed by those who wish to destroy. Who drive into states and areas not of their own and steal, burn, same and leave the pain of loss behind. Many areas will never be the same, most will take 5-10 years to recover if ever. One can only pray that the rest of us, can stop the worst of us, from destroying the best of us. I am glad that people that never suffered from the criminal injustice system are seeing how it can be stacked. Poor people, mentally ill, minorities. Worse if a mix of all three. However if the demons that seek to rip the fabric of America apart, keep us from focusing on the loose threads of our society. Then there will never be a chance at being whole. It is easy to blame Trump and the twit-lit on twitter. It is the entire political and media establishment in this country. The guys that started Black mask comics, he started the Occupy movement. The occupy Wall street movement that got lots of attention when them and 99%ers was doing protests some years back. He wrote a wonderful comic as one of his first issues. It was about the Tea Party and occupy Wall street movement. How he seen them to be rivals. He thought of the tea party to be his enemy. That is until he went to a tea party rally and seen they had the exact same signs he had. They was mad at the same issues he was mad at.

He then illustrated the media coverage and how it was clear this idea of the tea party and occupy movement being bitter rivals and natural enemies. It was a false media construct. The puppeteers of America have gotten what they want. A society in flames. No form of democracy has ever lasted for over 250 years. The US is almost to that point. Questions. What creates stereotypes? How does a person think someone else is a certain way, if they themselves never been around 'those' people? What sources in the 80s, 90s and etcetera would give people a visual of others???

What convinced society we needed our police to be like militaries? What caused people to support 'tough on crime' bills? Why do people feel they NEED the death penalty? What conveys this information? Long sigh. Fear its good for business. May we see through the smoke and be able to reach a better future, less the flames burn us all up.

Take care, smile if can and strive for all that you desire.

Veni Vidi Vici

In solidarity

I remain,

Clinton Lee Young #999447

saveaninnocentlife.com

facebook.com/clintonyoungfoundation

Loud & Clear, June 7, 2020

Topic: Pfff, where to start?

In case people couldn't notice. I have been really aggravated as of lately. Part of the reason is that with the Covid-19 lockdown. I knew the US was going to turn into a powder keg waiting to explode. I naturally stress over everything. Sitting in a cell is hell for me. As it makes me helpless. Everything starts to add up for me. I kind of lashed out in a previous blog. That was not fair of me. I am trying to get various projects going. Not getting word from people on stuff slows me down. Then having. Was having to, to fight to get my jpays. I didn't get the jpays send to me from April 19th to April 27th. (I was missing 11 from that period. Only had gotten one or two.) I did not get them until June 4th! As of lately the mailroom is doing something different with jpays, so it seems to be working and appears that I am not missing any. I know the last 2 weeks of May I was not missing any. That is good! Hopefully it stays on that trend. Then waiting on my hearing, stressing over my next appeal filing being right, trying to get projects going, not hearing from certain people, since I was sick in February I have had a slight headache that frustrates me, not being able to get visits. Then my country going up in flames. It all adds up. I have to worry about Merel. Last thing I need is her getting caught up in the chaos that is the US. Anyways.

Ya know, people never seem to fail to amaze me. Just like I had suspected though. I ended up getting some pictures of who first started breaking windows at the AutoZone in Minneapolis. There was a chain reaction. The amount of looting and fires around the US is truly sad. People hijacked a legit protest to rob, rape and kill. Even worse was the people that acted like it was okay. Of course, it wasn't their homes and business being destroyed. Like the guy who is a sports commentator type of person, Chris Palmer. He was posting about 'burn it down' when it was a low-income housing complex going up in flames. Though when the rioters reached his area, he all of a sudden wants to call the police. Amazing how that works huh? Police brutality is a problem in the country that extends from the streets into the county jails and prisons.

I have often blogged about the woes of the police state. One of the biggest problems that allows the abuse of power. It is that police have immunity. Prosecutors do not hold them accountable either. Also, when police and prosecutor mess someone over in a criminal case. The appeals courts do not hold them accountable. The way a court can punish a prosecutor is by reversing the conviction. However, it has gotten to be that as long is there is some sliver of evidence against a defendant. A prosecutor and police can do whatever they want. I have begged to get media attention on a series of cases to highlight this. The only mainstream reporter that seemed to actually focus on flaws of the prison system was Keri Blakinger. Though she has been in prison! Why does it always require some crazy ass event like a cop killing a guy before people get upset? Everyone is speaking about reforms. Okay the most sure-fire way to get reforms is to remove the qualified immunity given to prosecutors and police. Make it so that they can be sued individually. Highlight the way Court of criminal appeals, circuit courts and US Supreme court have allowed police and prosecutors to get away with so much. There is no case worse than mine in Texas when it comes to prosecutor misconduct. Hell, the police didn't even investigate two of the crime scenes that was pivotal in my conviction. One of the DA's committed perjury and had witness lie under oath. The courts have acknowledged this, yet rejected my previous appeals.

The people given the power ignore the problem. The people that are supposed to be the checks and balance to this abuse. They help cover it up by rejecting appeals. Those that then suffer at the hands of this abuse have no recourse. The state is executing people! Yet an uproar doesn't happen until it gets close to the execution date. It's often too late then. We want the police to reform. Great. What about prosecutors, courts, jails and prisons? Unarmed people get killed in jails and prisons all over the USA. The cop that killed George Floyd. We recognize his evil.

Many have rightly called for his prosecution. Also, they have called for the prosecution of the other cops. I want people to calm down and think. One of the cops never touched George Floyd. He even asked that he be rolled over. He had only been a cop for 4 days. Yet people are calling for his head. It is better to call for him to get his job back and allow him to speak out against the brutality he witnessed. We can not be for the law of parties when we want to be and against it when we do not. As the cop was only for the job for 4 days and twice spoke up. He could not legally force that evil pig to do anything. The law gives so much power to police! To those that read this and say "No, he needs to be prosecuted!" I have two words for you. Randy Halprin.

People should not be punished for the conduct of another. More so when they did not directly help the crime take place. They charged them cops that way to satisfy the prosecutors. No one that knows the law will honesty say that the other cops will all be convicted of that crime. No way! There is too many laws on the books that protect the police! Calmer heads should prevail. This cop who had only been on the job for 4 days. He thought enough to speak up against his mentor. That shows the guys heart was in the right place. He just didn't know what to do. He was only on the job for 4 days and his mentor for 19 years! I am not one to generally support the police. Though I am one to denounce the law of parties in all its forms. I am one to speak up for what is right and just. No matter who benefits. Just as it was evil for that pig to kill George Floyd. It was evil also of those that used that as an excuse to harm innocent people. Amazing at the way people stood by and filmed the deaths of other human beings. Like what happened with

David Doren, the older black dude that was a retired cop in St. Louis. His murder was recorded on Facetime live. Other people beaten, robbed, raped and killed. All while a collection of other human beings stood by and watched. Some filming it to be posted on YouTube. Even worse is those that seem to justify and act as if this is okay. I don't care what your breed or creed is. I don't care what your complaint is. At no point is it okay to hurt innocent people. It is sad. Truly sad. At one point everyone in the USA seen evil and truly 99% called it for the evil it was. People were united in the need for change against police brutality. Then some decided it was an excuse to destroy the livelihood of others. Ya know, we never have honest discussions in the US. We partition off specific claims for the day. We point and scream at what has our emotions going. In the US there was over 17.000 murders in 2019. The statistics are on the FNI website. Just go see crime statistics. Also, a Washington Post refers on police shootings. People were talking on the radio about the police shootings. 1004 people was killed by the police. 41 of them was unarmed. Though some of those unarmed was like one guy beating a female cop up and she shot him. That would be legally justified by the law. Though in the discussion of these numbers. They said 10 million people was arrested last year. Why in the hell is there 10 MILLION ARRESTS?!

That makes no sense. When I heard these numbers, I went digging in my 2020 Almanac. I look at the population of places like The Netherlands, UK, Germany, etc. The Netherlands has more than 17 million people. Last year they had what, 70 murders in the whole country? Baltimore. One US city had over 350 murders in one year. That is ONE city with less than 600.000 people in it.

Can take Chicago, Baltimore, and Washington D.C. combined. There is more murders then Netherlands, Germany, Belgium and Spain together! It is not a gun problem. A gun is an object. Yes, makes it easier. Though why do so many people in a country that so much of the world wants to come to. Why are so many so willing to take another human beings life? 17.000 murders. That doesn't count in missing persons who are not yet determined dead and etc. On a Saturday I listened to the radio as the rocket launched US astronauts to space for the first time in 10 years, from US Soil. Go watch that space launch. After watching that, go look at the videos of people destroying cities. How can this country have such a spectrum? In the newspaper that shows the article about the space ship docking with the International Space Station. There was a picture of Johanna Alarlan as she looked around her destroyed store named Honey Girl in Tennessee. Not even in Minneapolis! I understand burning police cars. Not saying should happen. Though the police car is owned by the government. The people can protest and rise up against the government. That is American as an Apple pie. Though Johanna Alarlan wasn't the police. Hell, she isn't even white. It's just heartbreaking at how easy it seems that people can turn a blind eye to suffering of another. The police need to be held accountable. Prosecutors need to be taken to task. The Courts need to be made to be the checks and balance they should be. Though, we should also bring justice to the 100s of people like the owner of Honey Girl.

Johanna Alarlan didn't kill George Floyd. We need to also stop and breathe. Then try to figure out how a country that can put 2 men into space on a damn drone rocket. How can this country be so angry? How can it be so divided? Don't blame Trump! We was divided before him and will be after him. Biden isn't going to bring people together either. The pendulum will jut swing the other way. I have long wrote about how it seems to be so easy in the US to just throw people away. So many with life sentences in prison. We can't just blame the police. It can not be just racism or income inequality. Other countries in this world do not destroy the lives of other humans so easily. I listened to that space launch. Then at night I listened to the news reports of the cities going up in flames. It breaks the heart. Even on death row, I still have love for Texas and the USA. Not the system that is abused by people entrusted to operate it. The spirit of Texas. The US is a blessed place to live. So many around the world go through hell to get there. I value people from all walks of life. I genuinely enjoy people. There are so many, no matter the breed or creed, that I share company with. I just don't understand how in a country of such greatness. Neighbors harbor so much hate for each other. We don't all have to think alike. God, it would be boring if we did. There is nothing wrong with a free-flowing exchange of ideas. It does not hurt one to be challenged on a belief. The ideals of one is not a threat to another. We can not even agree to disagree anymore. Jails, foster homes and morgues. All full of people thrown away.

Long sigh. The world turns.

In solidarity

I remain.

Clinton Young #999447

Loud & Clear, June 28, 2020

Topic: Tired of this sh*t

It seemed that the DA was trying more b/s. Not sure if they will or not try to delay more. Is surely no reason to. No matter though other things are still being worked on by my team. As stated, when filed will post it. They still have not decided as to when will start back up visits. I spoke to a rank and discussed a viable plan to make it work. Couple weeks ago had the idea posted about putting the testing machine in at the unit to test guards and visitors. I know it is a stretch that it would happen, though it wouldn't be me if I didn't try something! Also they decided to be sadistic in the era where the world is screaming for criminal justice reform and better treatment. They stopped allowing phone calls for those that can't access the offender telephone system. Ie G5 closed custody, ad-seg, death row, and such. Got little youngsters from the suburbs getting shot up with rubber bullets and tear gas. Maybe TDCJ wants that to go on inside the system. This sh*t is getting old real fast. We don't even get contact visits, so the covid 19 is not even an issue. Now they have seriously been trying to sort out a plan. Though my position is that based on the, ya know, LAW they should have never halted death row visits. People didn't know about code of criminal procedure 43.17 until I started ranting about it. Now could TDCJ have modified visit for safety reason? Yes, of course they could. That means masks, hand sanitizer, and less traffic. Though the blanket ban was wrong. More so that now they are going forward with executions. Plus really to be honest. This unit has been doing good at containing the spread. Other units are on fire with corona. Though here has only been a couple cases for men in prison and 8 guards I think. They need to step up spraying bleach on door handles and such as been slacking some back here with that. Plus they need to put a TDCJ bottle of hand sanitizer in each areas control picket. When they came through and tested everyone for corona virus. They squirted hand sanitizer on my hands. When I was rubbing my hand together I could small how strong it was. I bet it is way better than what the officers bring from home.

So that needs to be in the kitchens, control pickets, and other high traffic areas. The guards are having to wear more effective KN95 masks. Add in the TDCJ hand sanitizer, up spraying of bleach, and they need to stop allowing guards to wear gloves they bring from home. As they don't throw those away. They touch multiple things and put in their pocket, only to pull out and reuse later. TDCJ provides plastic gloves and latex. Strong hand sanitizer and those gloves would work to help reduce spread. Now for you all that been reading my blogs for a while. Who has constantly been ranting about how little TDCJ focuses on proper cleaning? Who said repeatedly! a virus was going to hit, bouncing around and impact guards more who then would take it home?? Ah, I do believe yours truly has repeatedly blogged on such a matter! But hey, what do I know. Also they are supposed to start in August making it so that if a person is not on someone's list and call list, they can not transfer money to the Inmate Trust Fund account. Death row doesn't get the 20 person phone list, so we are limited and can only change visit list every 6 months. I am discussing various ideas to see how they can do something to not punish death row further, for the simple fact we are stuck in this environment due to their refusal to give us what we should have. Lately they been short of staff, so haven't been able to operate recreations. At least we are getting showers. Then to the damn cake I got a disciplinary case! I got wrote up and punished for something that I have no control over. See we are not able to get access to the barber due to social distance stuff. (Hey, this lady pointed out to me how in the films there is all these different hair styles I got going on ☺ ha. Tryin to get the most out of it as I am losing it!)

Anyways, back to this bullsh*t disciplinary case. Okay so I had cut my long hair all the way off. As a few months ago I was going to start getting Use Of Forces if some stuff went south for me. I cut my hair all the way off, so the officers couldn't grab it to wrestle me down or bang my head off the floor. Things worked out so that plan was scrapped. I thought I was going to get messed on something I didn't do, but the truth prevailed! Anyways, so with no access to the barber. My hair was growing back out. Plus my beard was getting a bit unruly. So I take a razor and knock it down real low. Cleaned it up real good. My goatee area is just a width of a small travel comb longer than the rest of it. Then I shaved half my head and faded the top part in. The top of my head hair is as long as the comb is thick, so real low. It had been a while since I gave myself a fade. I did bad ass. Well I get all cleaned up. Next day here an officer comes with a damn disciplinary case! Get a knock on the door with a "Young, got a disciplinary case on you."

So I jump off the bunk, "What the F**K I do!?" Told me I had a case because it was against the rules to be this damn handsome! ☺ haha. Guilty! I pled, for the first time in my life. Haha

I know, I am so witty and clever! Look, be honest with my blogs you laugh, cry, get mad – be it at other or at me. You can feel what I feel when you read my words. I know some of my recent blogs haven't been the best. Though the country has been in turmoil. Plus when I seen the US go on lockdown, I knew chaos would eventually take place. I wrote to Merel, my mom, and sister about it. Even wanted Merel to leave the Austin area and go stay with my mom or sister. I knew the US would be a powder keg waiting to explode, just needed something to ignite it. Which is why I was stressing so much listening to the news. As I know how fast rumors spread and outlets twist stuff. Which then would cause people to lash out more. The George Floyd murder became that spark. Thankfully the Austin area was not that bad w/ riots and such. They mainly focused on the police. The police are supposed to be trained and sign up to deal with chaos. I hate to see innocent people caught in the middle of anything. Be it the baby killed in the car seat in Chicago. He was caught in the crossfire of gang violence. To the woman who called 911 in Fairfax Virginia and the 911 operator actually told her the police would not be responding, as she pleaded for help and her child cried. This is the United States of America! It should never be that way. Babies should not be shot and civilians should never feel helpless and abandoned by the system. The system has long came up short for us that have fallen into it. The way prosecutors have been given free reign, judges favoring one side over the other, police and correction officers acting like a gang at times. The system gets stacked. Us outlaw, gangsters, and the sort. We expect the system to work against us. Though the police are supposed to be that thin blue line between chaos and order. Some of the hardest gangsters here I have spoken to. Not the types that was out raping, robbin', and killin' for drug money. But those that spent their life in gangs, been in the wars, and such. When this 'defund the police' talk came up. Hands down all said "That's the stupidest shit I ever heard!" Reform the police? Hell yes! Better mental health and drug treatment? All day long! Better training and regulation for police and correction staff? Long over due! One guy I kick it with. After he said it made no sense. He said 'you know why?' I knew why but for sake of conversation said 'Why?'. He said 'Because without the police people like us will take over'. I just do not understand people that say 100% get rid of the police. Do they not understand how many street gang, prison gangs, motorcycle gangs, various mafias, drug cartels, and various kind of wanna-be terrorists are in this country? Not to mention the over 400 million guns! Which includes millions and millions of ghost guns. That guy that killed the cops in California recently. He was throwing bombs at the police! There are tyrants in this land. We need the police. Though we need professionals that follow the letter of the law. Not try to dance around based on the 'spirit' of the law. As that is when they blur that line and they become no better than the criminals they prosecute. I also agree that people in their community need to step up and be better custodians of their environment. Neighbors should know each other and support each other. Doesn't mean that all have to agree and see eye to eye with each other. This is the USA, there should be a free flowing exchange of ideas. Each person should be able to have their voice. Though not try to shout down the next person. That when sharing a common space, they work together for the advancement of that space. We shouldn't be calling the police on our neighbor because their dog is barking at night. The police being called, because the people can't speak. As the neighbors do not even know each other. There is a lot of problems that plague our society that are very simple to resolve. I have noticed a big difference in other countries and many parts of the US. From the Netherlands I have had people write so often whose parents have been married for 20-30-50 years, or a couple married that long will write me. That is so much rarer in the US these days. Plus, are more sociable in the Netherlands. Texas for the most part is known for being a place with friendly people and such. People are always surprised when they move here. My point is, if as a society we treated each other better. If people would be more considerate of others and treat the individual with fairness. Then would not need the police as much. I don't have all the answers. There needs to be changes. Starting with the culture of police, feeling like they are warriors going into battle each day. When you step onto the streets with that attitude, it makes it easier to see each person as an enemy combatant. No, each person should be seen as a civilian who is protected by the US Constitution. Force should only be applied to the point to gain compliance. Really if we stop using jails to warehouse the mentally ill and create more community treatment facilities. Then the police would not need to be called as much. It would free up 25% of their workload! Prison units could be shut down due to less being sent here. Hell, there is like 4-5 guys on death row that stay at Jester 4. The TDCJ psych hospital. Another 4 or 5 here that could there! So is about 10 guys on death that the state will never kill. Not in this day in time.

The last crazy guy to be killed was Kelsey Patterson. His execution shocked people. The parole board for clemency but Rick Perry rejected it because Texas didn't have life without parole at the time. The catch was we didn't have LWOP because Perry had JUST rejected the LWOP bill from becoming law. So it was his fault, at that time, Texas didn't have it. The next session that came in LWOP passed and Perry signed it into law. Texas has these guys just sitting here taking up space. Stuck in a cell. Like the guy from Bangladesh. I don't know how to spell his name. He spent over 10 years straight at the psych ward. They brought him back over here. He was on the section I was in. All he would do is sit there and shake with his head tilted to the side and randomly yell out incoherent stuff. Back to Jester 4 he went. Never sees a lawyer, no action happens on his case. They just got him sitting here locked in a box with no real treatment. Matter of fact, we need to figure out who he is and get some attention to it. As whoever has his case and the prosecutors. They need to be shamed! Rabbi Randy knows his name, so I need to get it. The lawyers and DA can go to parole board and file for clemency so he can get commuted to life. The death sentence makes it harder for TDCJ to treat him. If criminal justice reform is being had in this country. Then it damn sure should include not killing severely mentally ill people who stay in a permanent state of psychosis. Last time he was on the section with me. The mental health lady was doing the usual bullsh*t checks they do each week for certain people. He was having an episode. Yelling random sh*t. "Grah! Yayaa!" and sounds like that. This b/s psych lady didn't even go over there until me and another guy started gettin' on her, about not going over there. She walked down there to his cell. She goes "you okay?" he yells out "aah, gnaha." She said "Okay, I'll see you next week" and walked off. I don't, by personal philosophy, call a woman a bitch. Though that day, she got called everything but a child of god! Next time I seen her, she walked by while I was standing at the door. She asked "how you doing?" I responded with "Shut the fu*k up talking to me." Every time she walks by I just stare at her. The other day as was walking by, she told the officer, "every time I walk by, he is standing at the door just staring at me." She is clueless! and doesn't even remember. I truly DESPISE people that are in positions where they are supposed to help someone and they do nothing for the helpless. People act surprised I help others. I am strong enough to do so. She doesn't get it that I am taking note of who she talks to, her reaction, and what officers are with her.

As I know damn well she is doing what many have done and that is falsify the records. Life is a battlefield. Anyways, this has gone on long enough. Way longer than I expected. I used to do song of the week. Going to start back with that. A good fit is a song by Five Finger Death Punch- Little Bit Off. I heard it for the first time on Friday. It isn't like their normal stuff, though I really like it.

I haven't been in best mood lately. So it is a fitting song.

Alrighty then. Take care, smile, and strive for all that you desire.

Veni, Vidi, Vici

In solidarity,

I remain,

Clinton Lee YOUNG #999447

www.saveaninnocentlife.com

facebook.com/clintonyoungfoundation

Loud & Clear, September 7, 2020

Topic: Almost there

To begin with: I haven't written much as of lately. I have been frustrated about many things. Not getting visits, with no change in sight of that. Can not even get rec like supposed to. I have only been out of this cell 3 or 4 times in 2 months. Federal prisons are going to allow visits in October, though i don't know if TDCj will. There is no reason for them not to. Though people just aren't raising enough hell. All the prison systems has already been infected with Covid-19. Is no harm in opening back up. Jpays was moving good, but seems last week they went back to shit for me at least. I talked to other guys and they have had problems. The talk of tablets. It seems those will be only for video visits. There seems to be a great deal of confusion with all of that. I asked someone to email TDCj to find out officially with everything. Hey also, if you order pictures from Shutterfly or Snapfish.com, be sure to select the FedEx or UPS option. As we have to sign for those, versus if it is just regular postal service USPS. UPS and FedEx are private companies, so anything delivered via them, we have to actually sign for it. It just helps to make sure a person gets it. An extra step, if ya will. It seems that there is a small chance i will not be going back to Midland in October. Not exactly sure as i write this blog. One day it will be that i will never have to worry about this stuff anymore. I am almost there! How can I almost be there if I am going to maybe not be going back to Midland in October? Well it is simple. The prosecutors agreed I deserve a new trial. This is about the Judge paying the prosecutor for work and such. It seems that was just too much. The false affidavits, hidden plea deals, false testimony, failure to investigate crime scenes, all forensics clearing me, co-defendants bragging about getting away with murder, no fingerprints or DNA of mine at the crime scenes, and all the rest of the stuff. None of that was enough. FINALLY, something was enough. It took the breakdown of the system that our country is built upon to finally be enough. The ole straw that broke the camel's back. Ya know, I might get me a pet camel. Name it Humpty Hump. I do not know if you all noticed or not, though I don't put much effort into pet names. ☺

As for the agreement of new trial. I have known for a couple of weeks now. Just didn't publicly post anything, as wanted to give the prosecutor time to notify the victim's family. See the real evil in all that the prosecutors in Midland done. They lied to the victim's families. One DA was so obsessed with getting a death penalty conviction. He really sold his soul to do it. Like i wrote them when i first got here. I was never going to come down here and accept this bullshit. As i said many times. They are not going to get to watch Clinton Young die on his back. One of the driving forces for me, was to make sure that it never came that i be strapped to a gurney. Then have to look up and see that piece of shit DA looking down at me with his ole bullshit ass grin. Part of the reason I put so much online about my case. Beyond wanting to get people to help. I wanted the families to know i didn't do it. The DA that was over my trial. He tossed out all the rules, ethics, law, and etc. to take my life. All because he wanted to obtain a death sentence. He had tried 7 times before and all 7 times the juries gave life. So he went all out with my case. In doing so he gave a false sense of justice to the families. The fight isn't over with yet. Now i have to switch to raising funds so that i can have a top-of-the-line defense for a new trial. The fight goes on. In August my mind was so consumed with the appeals and such, i was not very productive. It came to be that i allowed books to distract me. I read the first 5 books in the Game of Thrones series, first 3 books from the Norseman saga, then parts of several other books. Finally got my book finished. Just need to go over it one more time to make sure all is in order. While i haven't been blogging. I have had postings put on the social medias for my foundation. facebook.com/clintonyoungfoundation or Instagram page. By following those can keep up with faster updates. I am writing more, so have some overdue letters to get done. When i have a more precise understanding of all that is going on. Will have it posted about. Thats all for now.

Veni, Vini, Vici.

In solidarity,

Clinton Lee YOUNG #999447

http://facebook.com/clintonyoungfoundation

Loud & Clear, September 10, 2020

Topic: My new appeal

I received, via JPay, the article the Midland newspaper did on my new appeal. It is dated Sept. 7th 2020, the article that is. Everyone reading this can go to Midland Reporter Telegram site or mywesttexas.com. Which is the news site for the newspaper and TV station. The article in question can be read. In it the county attorney seemingly defends his opinion that was given to the Judge.

First off. Words matter.

#1. Ralph Patty was NOT a county attorney as Mr. Malm described him. Mr. Malm is a county attorney. Ralh Petty was a district attorney. They are not the same. The opinion Mr. Malm gave to Judge Hyde back in 2002 was in itself flawed. As is the way he details the matter to the newspaper. Here is the simple basic facts. Ralph Petty, who was working as a ADA, cannot work as a law clerk in any form. Doesn't matter if it is after hours, or on Sundays. The Texas code of criminal procedure article 2.08 reads as follows – (a) District and county attorneys shall not be of counsel adversely to the state in any case, in any court, nor shall day after cease to be such officers, be of counsel adversely to the state in any case in which they have been of counsel for the state. The law clearly states that a prosecutor, cannot, put himself in a situation, where he can act adversely to the state. If someone is a law clerk assisting and advising a judge. It is presumed that they have to act fairly and objectively. They can't favor either side. As is expected from a judge. If a person holds a position associated with an office. That person is held to the same standards. I.e.: a law clerk is to operate with the same ethics as a judge. Plus, a judge cannot sit on a case, where he is directly connected by employment or such to another party in the case. A law clerk works directly for the judge. The judge cannot then preside over a case where that, just say former law clerk, is now acting as a prosecutor. Given that Ralph Petty was an ADA, he could not then also be a fair law clerk. As if he followed the law, then he would never advise the judge against the states interest. Therefore, as a DA he could not be a law clerk. As a law clerk he could not be a DA. Plus law clerk would fall under Judicial Branch, as working for the judge. The attorneys are part of the executive branch of government. Every child in school is taught the basic format of the United States government. There are three coequal branches that act as checks and balance. Executive, judicial, and legislature. They must operate separately of each other. As a result, it really is elementary. Someone working for executive branch cannot then work for judicial branch. As that creates a breakdown of the basic foundation of our style of government. So by 3 ways Mr. Malm was wrong. His advice to Judge Hyde back then should have been "the executive branch can not be employed by the judicial branch." Though I appreciate the error in his 2002 opinion. If a judge was a lawyer for a law firm, say some big international firm. If that judge left the firm and got on the bench. Then at a later date that law firm has lawyers working on a case in that court. The judge would have to recuse himself. As it is important that no question of favoritism or such into the court. Our adversarial system that is how we do criminal cases.

The integrity of it is maintained by the judge, who is supposed to be the fair observer that makes sure the law is followed and disputes settled without bias. So, there is the fourth reason why Mr. Malm got it wrong. Now my appeal is not about him. He is not under attack by my lawyers. His letter is just an exhibit to show how far back the problem went. Plus to show that while he did at least inform the judge that the ADA Petty cannot work on the same cases. The judge and ADA Petty did not follow that advice. Yes, the other people refused to talk to the media, so they had to go ask Mr. Malm who is the county attorney. He had no role in my trial. He done nothing to harm me. The judge and ADA Petty and DA Schorre knew what they were doing was wrong.

The media attention to my appeal has me frustrated, and highlights away a lawyer dropped the ball. As my appeal could have been so much more. There was a great deal more information that could have been included in the rent. As shocking as that appeal is, it is nothing compared to what it should have been. Which would have brought me way more media attention. One of my lawyers prevented me from being able to fight my fight. I still haven't gotten a clear answer as to why what I wanted done, was not done. I really hate having to depend on other people. There's all kinds of new developments where a DA investigator had someone sign a false affidavit and another guy, he added a paragraph to the statement which was false and did not reflect the persons words. Then he had the statement notarized by someone who did not even witness the signing. Which that also is illegal. One of the codefendants before my trial gave the DA a different version of the crime. The wind they started talking, another DA that was in the room got up and walked out. She is the one that didn't question the codefendant on the stand in my trial.

This way she was not directly aware of what all he said supposedly. Allowing her to operate on the so-called belief that his testimony did not conflict with his prior statements. She could also question Page about his gloves and allow him to say they was work gloves. Which forensics show that was a lie and he admitted he lied about the gloves. Also, the DPS lab expert. When they first got the evidence from the crimes. He looked at the gloves and then called the head DA and told him 'hey just so you know, these gloves are brand new.' He wanted to convey that info, as DNA testing was required and they were going to have to cut on them gloves. Because of this stuff, the head DA had the assistant DA question Page on the stand. This way she can have deniability when it came to false testimony. The comments about the gloves were never included in the DPS labs official reports. Plus, the DA never informed my lawyers before or during my trial. ADA Ralph

Petty also later tried to get the Texas DPS lab expert to sign an affidavit about GSR, based on facts that Petty outlined was not supported. By the trial record. Basically, ADA Petty attempted to get a Department of Public Safety lab expert, to sign a false affidavit. The DPS guy refused to even answer Petty's email. At least someone has integrity. This affidavit attempt was in 2017 when my lawyers was fighting my execution. So not only did the new Midland DA withhold the admissions by Page until after my stay of execution. The other ADA tried to get a false statement to counter my Gun Shot Residue testing reports. Then add in ADA Petty was also working for the Judge that was dealing with my proceedings pertaining to the execution date.

So Nodolf withheld Page's new confessions. Petty sought a false statement and was working as DA and judge clerk. All of that around my execution date. They was trying to murder me. Plain and simple. I noticed the Midland Newspaper never mentioned anything about the current DA withholding critical information as I waited to be executed. These people were doing all of this shit. From start to finish, it was all done to accomplish ONE goal. Every false statement, false testimony, hidden plea bargains, intimidation of witnesses. ADA Petty working for Judge and giving secret information my lawyers filed to the DA. Withholding evidence, on and on. From before trial through my trial up until I had an execution date. It was all done by no less than 6 members of the prosecution office. There was but ONE single objective to accomplish. That singular goal was that I be murdered by the state. That was the driving force behind all they done. THAT is what the media should be pointing out. It all was not to keep me in prison. No, it was all to KILL me. Midland County plain and simple was trying to murder me. When you follow the law and secure a death sentence. It is an execution. When you break the law, so as to secure a death sentence and bring about the execution of a person. It is an illegal act. Thus, it would be murder. 5 prosecutors and a DA investigator tossed out their oath of office, ethics, and the law. Just so that they could accomplish an execution. This is not about one rogue prosecutor. It was systematic throughout that office. Prosecutors are always quick to get some quack on the witness stand to call a defendant a sociopath. Their actions make it clear that we don't need any DSM 5 to diagnose them. If I would have been, say, mentally retarded or close to it, so that I couldn't learn and fight for myself. They would have killed me. More so with the lawyers I had on my first state appeals. We can't forget the crack smoking investigators that falsified statements, which my first State writ of Habeas Corpus was built upon. Thus, denying me one of my initial state appeals. There is two. Direct appeal and state writ of habeas corpus. One deals with matters contained within the trial record. The other deals with matters outside of the record, such as what should have been a part of the trial but wasn't. Not only did these Das do all this stuff. Because Petty and the judge had this relationship also during my appeal proceedings. I was denied any fair appeals. As the same DA that handled my appeals was one working for judges. The evil bastards tried to murder me by all the misconduct at trial. Then to cheat and stack the odds against me. The DA and judge continued their coalition throughout my appeals.

All the felonies the prosecutors committed in my case. None was charged for any crime, nor will they be. You know the real insult to injury on all this? Oh it can get worse! Them rotten scoundrels added up the total cost of my trial and state level appeals to over $293,000. They then place that bill on my inmate trust fund account for TDCJ (my commissary account). Where they garnish a percentage of the funds anyone sends me. Basically, making my loved ones pay for my injustice. As I can't work, so have to depend on people helping me. So not only did they do all their misdeeds. They are making me pay for it. Literally! Till next time. Take care & strive for all you desire.

Veni, Vidi, Vici

In solidarity, I remain,

Clinton Lee YOUNG #999447

Facebook.com/clintonyoungfoundation

Instagram.com/clintonyoungfoundation

Loud & Clear, September 16, 2020

Topic: The world turns

Things about the same around here. The word is that group rec has been approved. Supposedly want to wait until after Covid. This makes no sense as in general population, 30 to 50 people can be in a rec area. Which is okay. Though they are saying three can't back here? Half the time cannot get rec. It's done at least two-person group rec to start, it would help greatly. All they would have to do is cut costs slot into section gate. This way after brought out cell, officer can close gate, remove cuffs and then the guy walks to the room, open door and enter, then close the door. Go get the next guy and repeat steps. Start at with two during Covid for social distancing and also allows officers to get accustomed to it. Then can bump up to three people later. Also just put a cuff slot on the outside rec door. Each pod could be fixed up in a day. On a previous blog, I kind of jumped ahead a bit. I shouldn't have posted that he agreed yet. When I learned that he had filed with appeals court. I wasn't given complete picture. The DA filed that the claim should be authorized. Which means returned to lower court. I didn't want to get ahead of him talking to families. Though all know what end result will be. Anywho. Is some rumor that will be back to letting us make a call here and there. I don't plan to hold my breath and wait on it. Just do not understand why TDCj will not get tablets, namely GTL as it allows video visit on it. But JPay 5 would work. Also supposedly the Covid quick tests are about to be made easier to obtain. TDCj could just invest in some. When cannot see past oppression, hard to develop. My heart goes out to all that have dealt with fire, floods, and explosions in recent weeks. Let your worst day be yesterday, so that your best day can be tomorrow.

Take care, smile, & strive for all you desire.

Veni, Vidi, Vici

In solidarity, I remain,

Clinton Lee YOUNG #999447

Loud & Clear, September 24, 2020

Topic: Broken foot & shower quotas

Before I start in on the subject matter. I want to highlight the law. You know, the thing all people are supposed to follow. First statutory law. Texas Penal Code § 39.04 Violations Of The Civil Rights Of Person In Custody; (it also list sexual misconduct w/such. But that is not relevant to subject of blog) (a) An official of a correctional facility... an employee of a correctional facility... a person other than an employee who works for compensation at a correctional facility... a volunteer at a correctional facility... or a peace officer commits an offense if the person intentionally: (1) denies or impedes a person in custody in the exercise or enjoyment of any right, privilege, or immunity knowing his conduct is unlawful. [(I omitted juvenile facility language as not relevant. (2) pertains to sexual misconduct. Against not relevant.) (b) An offense under Subsection (a)(1) is a Class A misdemeanor. Okay (a)(1) is what I cited above. Misdemeanor is defined as Texas Penal Code § 1.07 (a)(31) "Misdemeanor" means in a sense so designated by law or punishable by fine, by confinement in jail, or by both fine and confinement.

Texas Penal Code § 12.21. Class A Misdemeanor is as follows. An individual adjudged guilty of a Class A misdemeanor shall be punished by (1) a fine not to exceed $4,000; (2) confinement in jail for a term not to exceed one year; or (3) both such fine and confinement. Note: the use of jail and prison are not equal. Jail refers to local county jail. Unless stated as state jail. Which is a department of the TDCj. Texas Code of Criminal Procedure. Art. 1.04. Due Course of Law.

No citizen of the state shall be deprived of life, liberty, property privileges or immunities, or in any manner disfranchised, except by the due course of the law of the land. (Tell that to Midland County!) TX C.C.P. Art.43.24 Treatment of the Condemned. Torture, or ill treatment, or unnecessary pain, shall be inflicted upon a prisoner to be executed under the sentence of the law. Note: this standard actually goes farther than the 8th amendment of the US Constitution. Which states "no cruel and unusual usual punishment." The US Supreme Court has further broken it down that it can be cruel and OR unusual punishment when dealing with prison or treatment.

The Texas law mentions no... ill treatment. It does not say these things shall not be to execute a prisoner. Words matter. It doesn't say no ill treatment during execution or the execution shall not be in a manner that involves ill treatment. Art. 43.14 which deals with execution. It outlines how it is to take place. Okay Art.43.24 states clearly no torture or ill treatment, ... shall be inflicted upon a prison TO BE executed... When a jury sentences person to death. The judge announces that person is to be executed and how. Then the judge stays the execution pending direct appeal to Court of Criminal appeals. So it is halted until appeal court confirms conviction. Once that is done, can be executed unless appeal further. Even if a person drops appeal. Can not be executed until CCA affirms conviction and sentence. Until execution, person is to be held at the TDCj.

Okay a death row prisoner is not under penal servitude. We are a unique class. The very reason why law Art.43.17 allows condemned person 'until the time for his execution arrives.' To have visits w/friends/family/clergy/lawyer/physician. The words "until the" can be matched with "to be". The law clearly outlines that a condemned person is guaranteed more than a regular prisoner under penal servitude. The US Supreme Court has made it clear, a person can not be executed in a case with constitutional violations. Ill treatment applies from the moment of sentencing until the execution. If you abuse me, starve me, and such between sentence and execution. It factors into the punishment. So, it can not be said that only what happens on the gurney matters. Okay. Bare with me here. I want to make it clear that these laws clearly states the condemned are unique and have rights. The Texas government code outlines various laws that require death row plan. A unique plan of managing death row that further shows certain things have to be done. The death row plan, being back by law, indicates we are to have recreation and showers. TDCj policy, state law, and US Supreme Court has that a person cannot be deprived of these rights absent due process. Remember reading about due course of law. Example: I am supposed to get rec five days a week for two hours a day. If I receive a disciplinary case for a rule in fraction. I then will be subjected to a process that informs me of the allegations, allows me chance to give my version of events. Then if case proceeds I can be taken to a disciplinary hearing conducted by a neutral ranking officer and depending on level of case will have a counsel substitute to help investigate and defend me. A kind of prison lawyer. All of this is to ensure I have Due Process. If the disciplinary officer finds me guilty. Only then can he subject me to a period of punishment such as 15 days rec restriction. Even then, because of known effects segregation cells have on people. A prisoner will still be able to get outside rec for one hour each week. This is to receive direct sunlight. This is federally mandated of states. TDCj policy makes clear an officer cannot deprive a prisoner of any rights. There can be no quotas. So you now understand that if an officer is violating the rights of a prisoner, with no due process/due course of law. That this is a Class A misdemeanor punishable up to $4000 fine and one year in jail. Furthermore, the condemned shall not receive ill treatment, as they await execution. Keep that in mind. Next, the US Supreme Court has held that prisoners are entitled to basic health care. No we do not have great free healthcare. That is a myth! The court has further held that prison/medical staff violate eighth amendment "cruel and or unusual" if there is "deliberate indifference".

Estelle v. Gamble 429 U.S. 97 (1976) – only deliberate indifference and not accidents or inadvertent failure to provide medical care violates 8th Amendment.

Zaya v. Sood 836 F.3d 73 (7th Cir. 2016) – deliberate indifference claim stated when prisoner suffered broken wrist and Dr. waited seven weeks to schedule follow up. –

Perry v. Roy 782 F.3d 73 (1st Cir. 2016) – claim stated when nurse failed to provide prisoner with broken jaw constitutionally adequate standard of care.

Coleman v Sweetin 745 F.3d 756 (5th Cir. 2014) – ignored broken hip.

You all also recall no ill treatment/unnecessary pain of condemned?! Now we all know law of the land. 1st – to the medical neglect. The guy in the cell next to me Paul. He is over 50 years of age. Suffers from long-term severe mental illness. Has a broken back, that has healed horribly, from a motorcycle wreck. His back is twisted in a way that completely alters the way he walks. Lives in pain. Refuses to get that surgery due to risk of paralysis. I tell him he is crazy, but not that crazy! ☺ as not going to allow medical students and interns to get their experience in by working on his back. The hospital that serves this half of Texas prisons is UTMB. University of Texas medical branch in Galveston Texas. Most of the complex is for average citizens. One portion of it is a prison hospital. Note the term "University". Students can hone in skills on prisoners, with help in guidance of doctors. Okay Paul has couple had hernias also. I tell him all the time that cell is kickin his ass! He went for hernia surgery. They notice a lump of some sort below hernia. They cancel and say he has to get a CT scan so can see what lump is. Now mind you, he already had surgery once. Though he got what he paid for. The work quickly came undone and hernia popped out worse than before. Months of going through hoops and loops required to get treatment is then repeated. Gets the Okay. Heads down there to the hospital in Galveston Texas. Which requires transport van and three officers. Gets there, they notice lump under hernia. Say he needs CT scan. Okay, he is IN THE HOSPITAL. So they natural wheel. Him over to other area and do CT scan right? Wrong! They say, has to be scheduled. They send him back to Polunsky Unit. He then waits couple months more. They just yesterday get him back down there. Again 3 officers have to leave unit, reducing staff at unit. He goes down to hospital unit. They do CT scan. Do they then look at CT and then wheel into surgery? No. They send him back to Polunsky. Until whoever can look at CT, decide what is what, and then schedule the hernia surgery. Which will be another 2-3 painful months of waiting. That is not even the worse of it. Today is sept. 24th, a Thursday. Last Thursday he broke his foot. Can see the bone is clearly broke and bulging the skin out. Not cracked, broke! That night nurse shows up and sees it. No doubts. They say will schedule you to see provider. Which is a nurse practitioner or general practitioner (whatever he is, we call him Dr. as that is medical role he plays.) Later on, find out he isn't set up until Wednesday! 6 days later. His foot is broke! That day comes and goes. No provider visit. We speak out and get RN back up to see him. He repeats 'will make sure provider see you tomorrow.' Tomorrow morning comes. They tell him he is going to Galveston. So off he goes to get the CT scan. The van has a cage in the back to contain us. It is diamond-shaped steel. The same kind seen on the doors in some of the visitation booths. A steel mesh that criss crosses forming diamond patterns. No seat belts, just sit on a bench chained up with leg irons, hand cuffs and a restraint box that locks over handcuffs. You cannot rotate cuffs. Plus, it is done in a way that does not allow for hands to be in normal way one would be when cuffed in front. No the thing is rotated and it makes it where one hand and arm is above the other. Thus, reducing ones mobility. It is very uncomfortable. Then is chain from box to leg iron chain. In that cage, sitting on metal bench with no seat belt. There is no way to brace if suddenly stops. One can ping pong around inside the cage. During the trip to the hospital, with his hernias, and broke foot, and back injury. The officer had to brake suddenly. Not with malice intent, as some have done before. Hits the brakes and there goes Paul head first into the metal cage. Busts his head open. Lets out a curse. Though knows the van is not stopping until it gets to unloading area of hospital. The back door and cage do not open unless within confines of unit gates. So there he rides with blood down his face.

They get to hospital. Open back door and ask, "What happened to your head?" he makes a joke about driving skills. The hospital unit prison staff. (The prison wing of hospital is called John Seally) he sees his foot. "What happened to your foot?!" Explains it is broke, happened in cell.

Okay he is at the hospital. He gets wheeled in. We always have to be escorted there by wheelchair. Is faster and more secure. They wheel him up to the area for CT scan. Medical staff sees head wound. One is tending to that. While the other is inserting needle to inject the dye for CT scan. They move fast with us to get in and out. His broken foot is pointed out to medical staff. They see it and say, "nothing we can do, he has to see the provider." Paul says, 'okay get me the provider!" they say, "No, has to be one on your assigned unit." The transporting officers express dismay at this and state the obvious. "But he's here now, in the hospital!" The medical staff repeats, nothing can do. Has to go through the process. They at least were kind enough to stop his head from bleeding. But that is the bare minimum. They have to stop bleeding and address life threatening needs. He could have had broken arm/leg. They wouldn't address it then. He does the CT scan and heads on back to Polunsky. Unit medical looked at him again when he got back. Again said would see provider for foot. So it has been a week and a trip to the hospital and still no action for him. Just 800 mg ibuprofen. Once he sees provider. Will then take another trip back to the same hospital, he just left, to then get foot fixed. Again 3 officers used. Then will come back and later on again go again to address hernia. All this spans into 4-5 trips to the hospital spread over months time. With only 600 or 800 mg ibuprofen. Wonder how many trips will require to address ibuprofen messing up his stomach? That is prison health care. Be very afraid of state ran health care! Oh Paul also has a law suit going on, as he has no teeth and they will not provide him with dentures. He had them when he came to TDCj, but they made him take them out as they had metal in it. Keri Blankinger has covered that problem before. TDCj has a 3D printer, yet won't give him dentures. Now Keri has also before covered stories about case quotas within TDCj. There was a scandal at another unit. Guys was being set up with fake contraband cases. The Warden at that unit one Virgil McMullen. He had lower ranks pushing for 2 cases a day and such. These cases would interfere with a prisoner's ability to get parole. The word got out. Investigation was held. Lower ranks was charged with crimes. Got probation and such fines.

McMullen slipped by as couldn't directly link him with it. Lots of cases was dismissed. Some politicians made some noise. TDCj issued new policy. Then couple other units had cases dismissed. The story faded. Now neat twist. McMullen once was the Major on this building.

He had the two case quota thing going here also. But beyond that. He had told an officer one day to write a guy up. Later on he seen her in the hallway and asked her if she did. She replied 'No sir. I took his shower.' They have to escort us to the shower. So this is considered work load. Taking his shower reduces workload and makes everything look good and done. He thinks about what she says and nods okay and walks off. Thus began the shower quotas. If an officer seen a guy doing something wrong. Like passing a magazine to someone. Would take a guys showers.

It got so out of hand, it helped kick off protests. Which brought attention of other ranking officers who expressed that, officers cannot do that. Little bit of time goes by they start back on it. Not everyone done it every time. Some officers were quick draw with it. Others might give warning first. Many just did not do it. Okay during this time period, up pops the story all over the news about the case quotas on that unit and by then Warden McMullen. He had left, but his legacy remained here. Light bulb goes off in my head about showers. I am not one to just set out to get someone in trouble. I barely ever had it happen to me. Though, I do get ideas and I do develop plans. Here comes a warden who was hell bent on harassing death row. A lot of things was happening. Trying to take legal material for to much property. Putting people on disciplinary level for all kinds of petty stuff. Many times causing a guy to lose a special visit that had been scheduled. A guy's friend spends thousands to fly from UK to Texas to see him. Only to get here and be told can only see him for 2 hours, instead of 2 days for 4 hours each. On disciplinary level, visits are restricted. So not only messing over guy here, but his people also. The taking of showers to reduce workload is going on. I tell people here and there. 'Hey, say something to the officer. That cannot take your shower as punishment. No TDCj policy allows such a punishment. If I broke a rule, write me a case.' Officer states not writing a case. Again, the whole thing is to reduce work load. As they have to have a set number of recs and showers done at the end of the shift. Others use threat of case or loss of shower. I then tell him to write the grievance. That officer is extorting for your shower. Others word it as officers took shower as form of punishment. This is not approved form of punishment by TDCj policy. Create the paper trail. Of course get nothing from grievance, as officer just lies and says refused shower. I found out that a couple other guys on other pods were automatically writing it up each time. Nothing changes. Then it gets so out of control that if cell was not in some proper perfect compliance. Would take shower and started to take recs. For like a week there it got bad. Didn't happen to me, as I never put anything in my light or window or cell door and such. Though I tell people to write it up.

I talk to a couple officers that are quitting about what a certain rank said about showers and, etc. Ask that they remember those conversations. I get ready to go forward with plan to expose shower quotas and such. New warden shows up. I figure, okay, will wait and see what's up with this guy. Well this on day they took like 60 showers and all kinds of recs from just A-pod. Several got pissed off, end up on disciplinary level. The new warden walks on pod, just to check things out. Someone asks him if officers are supposed to be doing this with rec and showers.

This is the current Warden Jackson. He looks at the guy like hes crazy and asks him to repeat it. He does. Jackson looks at a lower rank and says "No." everyone on pod got rec and shower back, as that rank told officers ain't happening. At that point they had started using some failure to follow proper procedure or something, as way to cover just refusing it. I see how new guy moves. I decide okay, will hold off on everything. Time goes by. I end up on C pod. While in dayroom, Officer Wendally, I think is how spell her name. I will find out for sure. Well she is in the control picket. She thinks she sees a guy sing his home-made line to pass something. He wasn't, was just at the door. She takes his shower. The guy complains. I tell her 'hey that dude wasn't doing anything.' She looks up there. Shrugs her shoulder like she does care. I stare at her for a bit and think okay and walk off. Now I am getting mad as these guards getting to bold and out of control. See by this point most of death row had calmed down greatly. Now this guy was known as a quiet and passive person. I seen it as her on a bully move. I tell him to write up and how. Time goes by, couple more things happen. We can't get any positive change around this place. I start formulating plan again, after hearing Keri on KPFT the prison show. I'm trying to figure way to minimize fall out while maximize the exposure to the problem. I wasn't sitting around plotting on how to get as many officers in trouble as I could. I wouldn't do that for any group of people. Then here comes a new building captain. It's Carter, who had been ranking officer on this building before and in general population. She is a rank that is respected by officers and prisoners. Back in the day from protesting and such. When doing stuff like that. It exposes a person to the ranking officers more. You get a better idea of who is who. In middle of this time period is a couple different times I speak with Jackson. He doesn't stand there and lie to us with a bunch of bullshit. If it is a legit issue, he will check into it. For what one can really expect from a warden. He is a good warden. Seemingly is a decent person in general, from my reading of him, while talking. So here we are with these ranks. In comes a new head warden, who had been here before also. We have as good of an administration as can reasonably expect for a prison. The bullshit with showers and such had stopped. Then covid 19 hits and all goes to hell with lock downs and etc. Now having to deal with staff shortages. As a result cannot get rec every day, though they was doing a couple sections a day here and there when could. Then got to do whole pod every other day if can. So half the building, 3 pods, go to rec every other day.

Its not the normal rec schedule but it is something. Working with what they got. Not because of all the lock downs and such. Many new officers aren't used to all the work. Other had gotten used to not really having to do anything. They have to escort us back and forth to rec and shower. Up and down stairs and all this. Really is just a bunch of walking for 12 hours. Okay. On Tuesday sept. 22nd I am woke up by officer Wilson, who is a young guy and fairly new. He asks if I am going to rec. I say yeah. He says 4th round outside. Okay. After second round I notice they do not put anyone else in the dayroom. Jeff Woods yells out "what's up with rec?" Officer holds up hand like hold up. Okay they then come around showering people who had already had rec. I ask Officer Wendally "what's up with rec.?" She tells me, someone is supposed to be coming around cleaning dayrooms. Part of covid stuff. I thought that off, as they had just sprayed the day before. Plus got a SSI on the pod. I also know there is my whole row to get rec and some. It never dawns on me one would be so stupid to do what they ended up doing. Time passes by, another asks about rec. They give another excuse about rank said showers are done for people already been to rec. We take it as they are just trying to move slow, so as to put off the work for second shift to do. Second shift comes on. Joubert yells out to officer about get recs out. She says 'They said we didn't have any work load.' So now i'm at the door. One guy hollers at other section and finds out 80 cell still has rec. Woods, Joubert, me, and guy next to me on other side. We all supposed to have rec and shower. Joubert and I make an issue of it all. The night shift ranks walk around. He is talking to one of them. Officer brings paperwork. He looks at it and noticed that all of us was set up for rec. But they came back and wrote VR for Verbally Refuse over that, for rec and shower. He knew that made no sense, more so for so many people. When I talk to him, as he made it down towards the cell I am in. I told him "person matters." He looked at me. I said the 'person complaining matters.' I then went on to say I don't never even talk to lower ranks or complain about little stuff, as when I bring something, I want it taken seriously. He agrees with me and said we will get our rec. Okay during this an escort team came to get a guy for something. I make mention of situation. He asks, 'who was working over here this morning?' I said, "Wilson and Wendally". He shook his head and said "this aint the only pod that's happened on. He done that shit several times." I go to rec. A guy in A-section yells at me about officers forget to put him out. I explain what happened. Officers come get him. He didn't know what had happened.

These two officers had taken it upon themselves to refuse us rec and shower. B-pod-80 cell, 70, 69, 66, 65, and 11 that I know of. On Sept. 22, 2020. I never had that happen before. Never been treated that way. They just flat out said fck everyone that still had rec and shower. They didn't want to do any work, so deprived us of our rights. In prison, usually a violent response gets the best reaction. I am no longer a violent person. Nor do I want to hurt people. I got to thinking. It's my fault. I have neglected my environment. I didn't properly push the issue sooner, in various ways to make sure this officer did not feel that it's cool to do whatever she wats. I am strong enough to be able to do so. I should have refused to leave the dayroom and got rank to the pod and had it addressed. As the guy she messed over back then. He would never take a stand like that. I made excuses in not standing up for what I knew was right. The result of that was, it then happened to me and many others later on. That is bold to just flat out fck over so many guys. Some of these guys have some colorful history here.

The grievances will be written. That's been discussed. I am writing this to make sure proper action is taken with them two. More so her, as she has a history of messing people over. I have never written a grievance on an individual officer before. I used to always say, 'I never try to mess with their bread and butter. Always another way to address it.' Meaning, I'm not going to try to get someone fired just to do it. As problems can be addressed in other ways. A wrong can be corrected with conversation between two adults, instead of running to rank and all that.

If I have a problem, after a bit of time and things calm down. I have usually always been able to talk to a person. Get the problem sorted and everyone go on to a better day. Though this action taken did not stem from a conflict or some perceived slight or such. They lied to us repeatedly and just took our rec and showers so as to zero out the work load. Making it seem as if they done everything. I am not letting this go. As it has become a pattern for them. Plus, if they will feel so bold as to do that. What will they do to some mentally ill prisoner or one afraid to speak up? What could happen to them, who can't speak for themselves? A guy named Greene in Ad seg died last year, because he just started to get insulin injections. He had no food in his cell due to being on level. His blood sugar dropped. Medical just bullshitted around. Told him to relax and drink water. By 8pm he was dead. I don't know the guy. Just that he was an old black guy whose life depended on medical staff doing their job. They didn't and he died. In that situation the officers had actually done what they could, as other guys were pushing the issue. But they can't make medical care. I have someone trying to find his family, so they can get the truth.

With all that has happened this summer. The focus on criminal justice reform. The platform I have. I cannot remain silent. Now I am not about to go on about every single thing.

Just is not my nature in how I deal with things. There is always a way to resolve a problem. However, it has got to the point with Wendally and I guess now this guy Wilson. They are so out of control. That it risks the safety of other officers and prisoners. How would they conduct themselves in a Use of Force? The activity log is a state document. They had no problem falsifying it repeatedly! Keri Blankinger, you can reach out to all the guys on death row you know and mention names and shower extortion/theft! You will see it validated. We can't get visits. Can't make calls. Now when barely able to even have chance at rec. Gonna subject us to this ill treatment and deprive us of what we are supposed to have? Cannot get group rec, cannot get work program. Which supposed to have. Cannot properly get JPays half the time. Some people have had more problems with JPay than others. I only had problem for couple days a couple weeks ago and then, well, today I didn't get anything at all. So instead of answering mail. I had plenty of time to write this blog. There is some other stuff I might have time to think about and write about. As I wrap this up. See I bet they didn't even know they was committing a crime. As when ya got a 'f*ck a prisoner' mindset. You then start to believe that rules and laws are not in place to benefit or protect prisoners. That or you become so callous and indifferent that you no longer care. They might not know specific offense. They do know it is unlawful. As TDCj trains staff on such. Since I got here I have fought to make death row have better conditions. Nothing crazy, just give us what death row plan fully allows and what other people held in prison get.

We get treated just like ad seg and they are in the building for disciplinary reasons. We are here just for our sentence. Already killing us, why all the ill treatment?

Take care, smile, and strive for all you desire.

Veni, Vidi, Vici

In solidarity, I remain,

Clinton Lee YOUNG #999447

http://Facebook.com/clintonyoungfoundation

http://Instagram.com/clintonyoungfoundation

Loud & Clear, September 12 – October 4, 2020

Topic: FB trying to hold me down

I have recently encountered some complications by Facebook, due to new regulations pertaining to political ads. A day after being notified of this. I get a Wall Street Journal Newspaper. In it there was an opinion article about Facebook and the action taken in a recent high-profile case. Before I read the article, just by the headline. I knew I had to write a blog about it. My complication is because the words Clinton and Foundation are in my social media name. Facebook flagged and prevented an ad. Indicating it is political and Facebook is preventing any political ads before election time. Extreme policies result in unintended consequences always. Facebook also has seemingly blocked out any praise or support for a 17-year-old by the name of Kyle R*tt*nhous*. He was arrested for 2 murders in a high-profile case and politics have gotten involved. One side says murder. Another says self-defense. It doesn't matter what he did or didn't do. He has not been convicted. To keep it simple. He is charged with crimes. As a citizen he has the right in court to defend himself. Facebook's claims is he fits the mass murderer category. Okay, words matter. We use the term mass murderer for a specific type of killer. Like we do with serial killers. A person walks into a bar and starts shooting. The intent is to kill several people. That person would then be a mass murderer. The law allows for self-defense. This guy seeming did not set out with intent to murder people. The store he was in front of. The owner said he requested for him to come down there to help protect the property. A possession of a firearm is not within its self-intent for any crime. Unless the very possession of it is illegal. Then the intent is limited to that possession. And no, having a gun does not indicate expected could murder someone. It can indicate a plan to defend self or others. All murders are illegal. All "homicides" are not. When someone invites you to a location. That is different than jumping up one night and saying, "I'm headed to town to guard some random place." Given that self defense is legal in this country. (Some states the laws are stricter than others.) he has a viable defense to the charges. Charges which he has not been indicted for. The problem is this. The way our world operates. Social media has become basically a pillar of many people's lives. It is like the local park, town square, or such places. It has become such an essential element that the danger comes in how one or two people can pick winners and losers. More so when that pick derives from mob passion or politics, and someone liberty or livelihood is at stake. This case provides an example. This guy's lawyer says that the two that died attacked him. If that is true, then those two would have engaged in a criminal act. under the law they then would hold more criminal responsibility than the kid. As the kid would, based on self defense laws, not be criminally liable. This is a legal and plausible defense. Given that there is this possibility. Facebooks restrictions are preventing him from informing the public as to any injustice he might have suffered or will suffer by the state. It limits his ability to defend himself 'to the people'. Newspapers was once the main way government corruption/ oppression could be spotlighted. Now it is social media platforms mostly. Facebook does not have to give free speech or due process. It is a private company. People in the US seem to think, the amendments of the constitution they favor most, applies to all areas of life. The 2nd amendment doesn't give you the right to carry a gun anywhere and everywhere. The 1st amendment does not give you free speech at work or within someone's business. The constitution is about what rights the Government can not take from the people. People seem to think they have some absolute right. The public education system is to blame for that. Most Americans are sadly, grossly, uneducated when it comes to anything about the government. So, I will not say that Facebook CAN'T put forth the policy it wants. Mark Zuckerberg leads the company, he created. (If I come to your house, you have the right to tell me I have to take my shoes off before walking on your carpet. It's your carpet.) Now SHOULD such a policy be in place? Now as it does not serve the greater good of due process and free speech by informing the public. The people matter. They also have an interest in knowing. Preventing images of child rape is a good policy. Facebook should prevent obscene illegal images. Just as you should make a person take off their shoes. When a person enters your home though, they do not lost all protections afforded by law. You cannot force your hand over their mouth to silence them. Given the nature of social media. It should be expected that a persons rights will be honored. While illegal images and direct threats, which are criminal, are prohibited. Social media has helped to free people wrongfully convicted. Some even from death row. It has empowered the person to be able to have a louder voice. If the people hear that persons proclamations and accept it. They then stand I support of that persons cause. That's how a democracy works. Imagine if Socrates could not speak to the crowd? Just because there is people with a desire to use this kids situation as a political ping pong ball. (Mainly as a way to distract from other things.) It should not then be, that he cannot speak to the people.

More so once politicians began using the case to further their agendas. Being that these 'government' officials have gotten involved. It makes all the more need for the case to be spotlighted. This way the 'people' will be able to check the governments words and deeds.

When a company which literally can only exist by the people's willing participation. Yet, in some ways forces a person to, due to being a significant infrastructure of society. When it then takes actions that are beneficial to one side of politics. It then can become oppressive to the other side, which sacrificing the individual. Being that prosecutors are elected officials. They are swayed by public perception. It impacts how a prosecutor will resolve the case. (Which really should not be like that) Like how local media can make a guy charged with a crime look like a monster.

The corrupt Das and judge then send the guy to death row. The local media never highlighting the criminal acts and misconduct by Das. Stuff like that happens. Which then makes Das feel more comfortable doing misconduct. As no one will expose them to the people that vote. I thought we had protests, riots, and a social awakening, so in part, criminal justice would be under a microscope? As I mentioned in a previous blog. Midland newspaper said nothing about current DA withholding favorable evidence as I awaited execution. Which was mentioned through out the appeal that was the basis for the story. How then are the people of Midland able to find out what their "government" officials have been doing? Social media! A newspaper is owned by a specific company or person that can control what news is covered. Same as TV stations. The people would be at the mercy of the decided coverage. Facebook is supposed to empower the individual. As I mentioned it survives solely based on willing participation. (While profiting greatly from their presence. Which is okay, as they get a free service.) When it then silences a person so completely. It offends the democracy our republic is built upon. As it blocks the person from speaking "&" the people from hearing. I wonder what ever happened to ole Socrates.

When it comes to political ads. It seems because of the words Clinton and foundation are in the page. It is getting flagged based on Hillary Clinton's foundation. Which is The Clinton Foundation. My page is clearly established for what it is, along with a website. It also has my last name, making it obvious that it is pertaining to a different individual. Beyond all that. Hillary Clinton is not running for office and her foundation is a nonprofit, not a political action committee. Really should not be any blocking of her and that. When it comes to political ads in general. Yes, Facebook has the right to limit such. Though what if a news story is readily available and shared on Facebook about a particular candidate. Say that news story is false and the result of that candidates more powerful opponent. Who has in some form able to create a false or misleading story, that is then shared in the news. This news story would then be a type of hit piece that serves a political end, beneficial to a politician. It can act as an ad against the other candidate. If that other candidate can not get that media outlet to correct their story with the same energy they broke the false story or if they refuse to even correct or take down the story. That person's best option to counter that false story would be to take out an ad. Facebooks ban on political ads thus harms those running for office who are less connected and poorer. In their attempt to counter, I guess, stuff like what Russia done in 2016 and so forth. The problem with the Russians, was not so much political ads as it was pages professing to be for certain groups. Then using those followers to share and repeat false information. Like the one guy that operated two pages. One for black militant types and the other for tea party or some type group that is majority white. He then stirred up conflict in Houston. That kind of stuff was the problem more than ads. False ads are a problem for people that see what they want to see. Facebook ban on ads while I guess was based on good intentions. It only serves to benefit the candidate that has the most money and can take out the more expensive TV and newspaper ads which tends to reach the older population more. The older population votes at a higher percentage than the youth. The youth use social media more. End result: Wealthy and powerful candidate can reach a higher percentage of actual voters. With a then limited counter by the opponent. If people dislike the Supreme Court ruling Citizens United, which allowed for more money in political campaigning.

Facebooks ban on ads then becomes a prop for those that benefit from being able to raise more money. More so since all but one election is local. Only the ones running for president and their supporters have a need for nation and regional wide ads. The poor lady in Small Town, USA running against some crony mayor. She needs to reach her city only. Another element is that Newspapers will endorse political candidates. Which is a direct act against the opposing candidate. If poor lady in Small Town, USA has a local newspaper that endorses crony connected mayor. Older people read printed newspapers. Poor lady, due to ban, cannot then use Facebook to get adds before younger voters to attempt to energize them to vote for her. So she can get elected and fight the coal plant storing waste next to the elementary school/chemical plan polluting waterways or such stereotypical corporate misdeeds a crony mayor would cover for. The ban does not then sync up with Facebook's professed belief in progressive causes. When seen in such a way. As I said: extreme policies result in unintended consequences. What it really is, is this. Facebook is such a powerful entity in the world. Where as in the past the real power was held within the hands of a few. Who then played the role of puppet master. Here comes along Mark Zuckerberg who changed the game. Whole countries political foundation was upended based on social media posts by the common folk. That used to be reserved for the CIA, KGB and a few select old people who inherited the game from some other old money. So now they got to use this scandal or that to try to force Zuckerberg towards some specific end. As no one person can have an impact on more people than him. Many crave that kind of power. Some say that government should take it over. Though that's because they know government officials can be bought and controlled. If they cant directly get him to do what they want. They got to take the ole catspaw approach. That or rant about "regulating Facebook!" based on some outrage. "Why is Zuckerberg not controlling the people?!" "Why are these people acting all free?!" "Get the subjects in order!" I keep up with the news and politics much more than average person. I have heard and read many stories on him over the years. He was basically a kid that became one of the richest people in the world and with the power, almost overnight, that religions, governments and the sort have spent centuries worth of gold and blood trying to obtain.

He didn't come up in the street. He didn't spend decades rubbing elbows with Wall Street CEOS, lawyers, military, and government officials learning how the game goes. How to effectively wield power. He seemingly has good intentions, but he keeps allowing this or that to pull him here or there. (I don't see Exxon or GE getting pulled this way or that. Politicians aren't demanding school leaders to testify and explain failing grades and illiterate teenagers.) Like when Facebook was assisting states with actions pertaining to social media accounts linked with people in prison. Prison and state officials was complaining about prisoners having social media accounts. He then agreed to shut some down and assist officials who was investigating the pages. Those officials then used that info to justify banning loved ones and giving draconian punishments to prisoners. There was an outcry about that due to South Carolina prison systems oppressive tactics. So, he agreed to stop helping in that way. Governments complain in other ways and he said if a prison system has an actual policy on paper and the page violated the policy, he would deactivate the page. What he should have said was, "It's your job to control your prisons. My company isn't part of any sentencing guidelines. And since you are so outraged by prisoners having some kind of voice. Im going to create more platforms that allow for exposure of excessive use of forces and other misconduct by guards and medical staff." Had he said that those same prison officials would have turned around and went back to where they came from. As it was the systems with typically the most abuses that complain the loudest. Instead of telling adults what content they can have access to, as if everyone is children in need of parental controls. I would focus on educating and encouraging people to be able to research what they are exposed to. As educating a person empowers them. Instead of banning the political ads. I would have created some option where people exposed to the ad could pull up who exactly paid for it, what region that person is from so can know if out of state or another country. If any specific topics of the ad pertain to news stories or actions by another. The person could pull up related media stories or actions by another. The person could pull up related media stories from multiple sources so can read the various versions of what happened. Doing this would enable the person to know if the ad is sponsored by someone or some group based out of state, who are just trying to influence a ballot initiative for example or attack a certain candidate that is a threat to some corporate, social, or government interest. That person could then disregard that ad and ignore it. If the ad is by a local politician. The ad then lies on an opponent. The person could see who paid for ad and check related stories from various sources. This would help a person know if the candidate is being dishonest in his/her ad. If seen as being dishonest, then people wouldn't vote for that candidate. Doing that would empower the people being exposed to ads and would reduce the effectiveness of misleading ads. It would be a checks and balance for the people to help keep politicians a tad bit more honest. People would go to Facebook to see ads, as know can fact check unlike TV and newspapers. That a pretty good idea I came up with there. I came up with that all while writing this blog. I don't rough draft. I just sit down and go with it. (Though I did add more to this one. So to make my opinion and law clear.) Everything comes to me as I write. I was frustrated as Facebook kept my foundation from posting ads about the new appeal. Where the judge was paying the DA to help. Hillary Clinton's foundation does need ads. She famous and powerful. I have the state trying to kill me for a crime I did not commit. I am poor and oppressed by corrupt prosecutors and judges. Huh, I am surprised I didn't think of that angle first. It's a good way to end the blog though. I know this blog is long. I wanted to get people to think. You should always question any restriction applied to the free flow of information.

No matter who is doing the restricting. Just because you agree with the specifics today. It does not mean it will go your way the next time. If any restriction is applied. Ask why and inquire as to why alternatives could not be utilized. When you allow someone to decide what is best for you. You then cease to be the master of self. Don't teach me what you want me to know. Educate me so that I know how to learn. Allow me all the information so that I can come to an informed conclusion that reflects my individual perspective. That is how schools should operate.

Alrighty then. Take care, smile, & strive for all that you desire.

Veni, Vidi, Vici

In solidarity, I remain,

Clinton Lee YOUNG #999447

Facebook.com/clintonyoungfoundation

Instagram.com/clintonyoungfoundation

Loud & Clear, October 11, 2020

Topic: People lie and TDCj remains TDCj. I was going over some legal stuff recently. It just amazes me at how people lie just to be lying. There are some psychological effects caused by being exposed to a prosecutor or police. Many people start saying stuff just to say something. This person connected to co-defendants gave some telephone testimony many years ago. I was reading over it. Meth and pain pills surely had twisted her brain, as she acts like was around me during a time period was not even possible. Plus talked about events she wasn't even around during. So tired of being help to the mercy of dophines. Just like with Page, he lied about the dumbest shit that indirectly hurt him. He could have blamed me for murders and robbery, for example, but told the truth about everything else. He would have got less prison time.

Anyways. As for TDCj it seems is no end in sight for visits. People can go to bars and everything else, but we can't have a visit behind glass? The way things are looking, I am starting to doubt if the so-called changes that was expected to take place here are going to. When it comes to the matters I previously wrote about. Several of us wrote grievances, so shall see how that goes. TDCj officials at Polunsky unit have the ability to properly resolve complaints. As for Paul. Nineteen days after his foot was hurt, he finally got to see the provider. I thought it was going to be on day 15, but no turned into day 19. The X-ray tech, upon seeing the X-ray, said his foot was broken in two places. Now, her only job is doing X-rays! Though apparently, she was wrong. Supposedly, according to the provider, Paul damaged his cartilage, and the X-ray lady misread the X-ray. Who knows. X-ray lady thought it was broke, Paul thought it broke, an officer then seen how his foot looked said the same thing happened to him and said it was broken. Other medical staff said the foot looked broke. If it was broke or not, doesn't matter. It could have been broke and damn sure should not have taken that long to be seen by the provider and get a X-ray. I am not accepting that it is not broken. Though Paul will find out soon enough from someone not associated with this place. The good ole second opinion. Still on the security lockdown. Not sure how much longer it will last. I am so damn tired of being in this cell. When it comes to this visit stuff. As a collective we are going to have to come together and work towards something. There is 130,000 people in prison. Y'all mean to tell me that 10,000 plus families and friends can't work together to protest? I mean people in the free who are being denied access to their family who is incarcerated. More so those connected to people on death row. Bars have 50% capacity. Okay great! I think it should be 100% capacity. Though we cannot have visits? We are behind glass! Visitors can wear N95 or KN95 masks. TDCj makes hand sanitizer. Sitting around hopeful that people will stop abusing their power is what can call a failed venture. I do not really understand why Greg Abbott is taking this approach to prisons. Federal prison and states have opened up. Though all you people focused on criminal justice reform. The current oppressive tactics are being imposed upon prisoners and their families. This is an extension of the failure for the government to take serious the cost of mass incarceration and punitive policy that serves no social interest. The COVID test kits are cheaper than was when I first kicked up the idea about getting testing machines in TDCj there are many ways to go about allowing visits. These people will not even allow people in restrictive housing and death row to have the calls. There is ways beyond oppression. People in power will never understand your pain unless they feel your pain. The only way to effectively do that is by organized protest, so as to properly express yourself. This is what I know. Them white folks don't give a damn, unless you make them have to give a damn. I told people when I was going to trial about them white folks. They all looked at me like I was crazy and said "You're white!" I said, "Yeah, but not they kind of white!"

I been stung by them WASPs ☺ Haha. Let me wrap this up for now. I get more worked up. I been reading on the next 3 books in the Norseman saga. Got me in the cell thinking about Shield Walls and Glory in Vahalla. Haha. Take care, smile, & fight for your right.

UPDATE: The officer's name was actually Wendling, not Wendally. Also, the X Ray technician visited Paul and said his foot was broken in two places. Provider says it isn't, the cartilage is fractured. Pfft. We shall see.

Veni, Vidi, Vici

In solidarity I remain,

Clinton Lee YOUNG #999447

Facebook.com/clintonyoungfoundation

Instagram.com/clintonyoungfoundation

Loud & Clear, November 5, 2020

Topic: Never ask what's next

2020 being as it is. It is only fitting the election be total chaos. My hearing was moved out of 2020. As it stands now, it will be January 2021. The delays have caused me harm as a couple of people have passed away recently. The judge is aware due to my filing to represent myself. I was frustrated over the delays and felt a lawyer was not clearly expressing to the DA my idea of how to compromise. After reaching an agreement with my lead counsel, I withdrew my request to rep myself. I am tired of all the delays. Most guys on death row want to delay and drag things out. There is a saying about innocent versus guilty. They say the guilty lay down to sleep, the innocent crawl the walls with stress. It is not absolute, but I fight like I am what I am. Innocent of this crime. The fight goes on. As does lockdown. ☹ The good news is that Merel passed the bar. I am very proud of her and knew she could do it. For a foreigner to be able to pass the Texas bar exam on the first try. That is a rarity. I think in one class was only one person who passed it last year or so. People go to law school in Texas for 4 years to be able to pass the bar. There is a language factor, plus being raised in a different type of system. She overcame astronomical odds to pass. As also reported, the US foundation has also been established in Texas. So, some good things are happening.

Alrighty then.

Take care, smile & strive for all you desire

I remain, in solidarity.

Veni Vidi Vici,

Clinton Lee YOUNG #999447

Facebook.com/clintonyoungfoundation

Instagram.com/clintonyoungfoundation

Loud & Clear, January 12, 2021

Topic: 2021 starts with a bang! I know that I have been silent. My thoughts have mainly been on the case. The good news is that things are moving much faster. You all should be up to date on all that. I was not writing much at all. Beyond some frustrations getting to me. Namely being here. The whole no visits for going on a year with no end in sight. It is mainly more upsetting due to how little people fight. It is why Texas prison system is so bad. Anyways, I wanted to address both of my appeals. As I have two different ones pending. Though decided to go with the one that would allow everything to move the fasted. Plus is the one that the judge wanted to focus on, as did the prosecutor. Shall see how things unfold in the coming months. 2021 seems to be starting off where 2020 left off. This country is going off the rails. I was also limited in writing as for a while they were only letting us get commissary (stamps) once a month. Though that has faded and we are back on regular schedule. Then they were not selling international stamps.

Again, though, that has been resolved. I am going to try to do some writing this weekend. More so since mail is finally getting back to normal. Tonight I got letters from here in the US that was dated Dec. 10th! Oh, back to the hearing. The one on the 25th of January will not be the only hearing. Just the first and will deal with the appeal about the DA being paid by the judge.

I will be back soon. Thank you for all the support.

Until next time. Take care, smile & keep on keepin' on.

Veni. Vidi. Vici.

Clinton Lee YOUNG #999447

http://facebook.com/clintonyoungfoundation

https://www.instagram.com/clintonyoungfoundation

Loud & Clear, January 27, 2021

Topic: Recent hearing and people

I am getting back into writing. I could barely sit still for a while. I was spending hours pacing the cell floor thinking about the case and all that needs to be done. One starts to worry about everything. Being stuck in a box, that's not a good combination. The hearing went better than expected in some way and in other ways, I would liked to have been able to dig into some harder.

The way the set up on Zoom was, there was no way for me to just lean over and tell my lawyer to ask certain questions. That irked me to no end ☺ ha. Then they were stripping and re-waxing the floor outside the room I was in for the hearing. I could not hear that good as a result. They were using floor buffers, industrial fans and etc. The officer had to keep telling them to turn stuff off, stay away from the door and be quit. Though, as long as the court reporter could hear, that's all that matters! Mass majority of you know nothing about the law. Some seem to think they know about it. ☺ There is a reason law school takes so long as it is complex. Anywho, those that have followed the death penalty will at least know how fast everything is moving. It is lightning fast. My appeal was filed in August. The court authorized the claim Dec. 16th. My hearing was held Jan. 25th. The final filings will be done by the first week of March. That is unheard of in appeal proceedings, much less so death penalty litigation. While on the law. I noticed every so often random people make this future conviction law of parties comment. What the hell are you talking about? You all understand Page is in prison for 30 years for kidnapping? You understand that right? You understand that the prosecutor over my case has 100% nothing to do with Page and Midland has jurisdiction over Page. Midland, due to all the misconduct, are not allowed to be involved with my case. I just do not understand how some of you come to these conclusions.

Beyond the simple fact of not knowing the law. The law of parties is not some all-encompassing trap. People have this idea of 'if you were there'. No the law says presence alone does not warrant a conviction. Each state in the US has its own version of laws. What you see on TV is not an adequate reflection of the law. More so for Texas. Also there is what is called a structural error. Guilt, law of parties, or any other convoluted legal theory does not matter. David Page is not relevant to my appeal that is being processed right now. It seems like some people just want to hate on me. Recently someone made comments about the people that run my foundation.

About all being attractive or something. What people do not know is I did not pick all those people. Most that are part of my foundation I have only exchanged like one or two letters with if that. They are a part of the foundation because of their personal belief in justice. They want to act on that belief. They all work in the legal community. Plus, the foundation is getting build to be so much bigger than my case. Most likely soon the US chapter will have hired staff. There will be other cases that are taken on. It is not going to be 'my' foundation. It just started in my name, Merel is already working on a guy's case that is serving life in TDCj. More about him will be posted soon. So again, people do not know what they are talking about. I am building something to help people, from a jail cell. Don't try to hate on me, be a part of the solution, not the problem.

This takes me to the comments people made on the YouTube channel the hearing was on. Normally the comment section would have been shut off. For some reason it wasn't. Though what I didn't expect from people was comments that would be made. After the hearing was over and the YouTube link was shut off, there was a discussion about the YouTube between the judge and another on the Zoom. It doesn't 'hurt' me. Though it does make me a bit sad. As I expected people to treat it with the severity that it is. Also, with so much media watching it. I, along with those in my foundation. They work hard to dispel the stereotypes that are put on women in this struggle. I want media to see the foundation as I want the legal society to. The judge over my case is one of the most respected judges in the state of Texas. There is a chance in the future that Merel or other future staff lawyers from the foundation will have to stand before him to represent clients the foundation takes on. I want him and other judges to see these people for their intelligence, integrity and dedication to justice and the rule of law which motivates them. So for those that do not understand. The foundation started off for me though it is growing to be so much more. It will be an aggressive organization that takes on more complex cases the other innocent network organizations do not take. As their requirements are often focused on DNA. Not all cases hang on DNA. DNA is really not relevant to my case at all, for example. There will also be scholarships and internships for girls from countries where women are disenfranchised, and also poverty-stricken people from the US and etcetera. This is why I want the focus to be on justice and the law. Not on my appearance during a viewing of a hearing for a capital murder case. I am not mad at anyone. I should have took additional steps to explain that YouTube was not the place for discussions. As for life around here. Covid seems to be on the rise again. It seems the lack of visits are having zero impact on covid here. As it keeps circulating. Plus, in the free, people can go to the mall, bars and etc. Go to a strip club. Yes. See a lawyer while facing the death penalty. No. Someone surely has their priorities straight. Of course they do. As the no lawyer thing is by design to reduce the effectiveness of representation. I guess it can not be to shocking that Texas lawyers are not uniting to raise hell about this. Visits are non contact, so the blanket ban is unreasonable. Some restriction can be applied. But a blanket ban is totally uncalled for in other matters. I heard about Lisa

Montgomery's execution also after getting the printouts from the social media pages from last month. I read what people wrote about her execution. Yeah, she had a horrible case. Most capital cases are. Though I can understand how certain cases strike women harder than others. The question is: did she have to be executed?

You might feel a desire for revenge or such. The death penalty in the US is supposed to be used for the worse of the worse that are so bad they have to be put down. It is not revenge. The law is supposed to be void of emotion. She would have spent life in prison. If death is some blank void. Then when her switch was flipped, she has no pain or suffering. Absent the moments leading up to her execution. There is no stress, fear or anything. If there is an afterlife and the bible is true for example. If she became born again and saved, then she will not go to hell. If Judaism is right, there is no hell. So forth and so on. Everyone that wanted her to die and others. They can not force a person into the gates of hell. Your emotions and desire for that is more your problem than others. As it is a pointless wish of destruction. Something us humans are pretty good at. I am not trying to get into theology or right and wrong of the death penalty. My position is much simpler. What is the point? Other women done what she did before she done it and have done it after she was sentenced to death. Sadly, it will happen some other time. As no matter what, people are good about messing things up. Though I believe that most people are decent. I know this is though. Prison sucks! And this no visit stuff ain't no kind of decent. Ole Blaine got a stay. That was good. He told me the prosecutor in his case made a comment to his lawyer supposedly. That he wanted to respect the jury's verdict. Many prosecutors say this. That becomes their justification to keep pushing for execution, when other facts develop. Okay, how can one respect the jury's verdict. When the jury gets so disrespected by a prosecutor that withholds information from them, has a witness lie. Doesn't properly explain all facts in accordance with the law.

Not saying all that happened in Blaine's case. It happens in most cases. So I am sure that I did.

Respecting a misinformed jury verdict is more about getting what that prosecutor personally wants. Alrighty then, my fight is not over with yet. Still much to do. I thank everyone for the love and support. Now that I am back writing, I will be posting more. I got stamps, so getting caught up.

Take care, smile & strive for all that you desire.

Veni Vidi Vici

In solidarity, I remain.

Clinton Lee YOUNG #999447

D.R– Polunsky Unit

3872 FM 350 South

Livingston, TX 77351

USA

STATEMENT Clinton Young Foundation

We want to thank everyone for their love and support, but also would like to kindly remind everyone that posting comments on a YouTube channel during a hearing in a death penalty case is inappropriate.

We ask everyone to please be mindful and considerate of that. You can post all the comments you want on our Facebook page, but not the YouTube channel.

facebook.com/clintonyoungfoundation

instagram.com/clintonyoungfoundation

Loud & clear, February 11, 2021

Topic: USA Today article

The article posted by USA Today newspaper was well written. I liked how it covered the problems in my case and she tied it into the bigger problem of poor people not getting lawyers. Which is an angle the foundation is growing to help address. More so for those serving heavy time, such as life. This no automatic lawyers really takes a worse turn in the fact that it also applies to juveniles. If a 13-year-old kid gets scared into pleading to a crime he didn't do or wrongly convicted, he is not provided a writ of habeas corpus lawyer. Okay how the hell is he supposed to pay for one? A 13-year-old can not even technically work for a paycheck. If he comes from a single home, siblings and a mother on financial assistance. How could he get a lawyer? The juveniles are often overlooked. Take Robert Pruett, he was given 99 years for a crime his father done when he was 15. His direct appeal was filed and court appointed counsel covered that. Though the direct appeal only deals with the actual trial record. Not any new evidence and such. To the main subject though. The interesting thing is how people respond to what Petty has done. The Midland DA was 'furious' because she didn't know what was going on. Okay, so she was not furious about people's constitutional rights being violated? She said she was upset at the hearing, because Midland would have to get off my case. That they had spent so much time and money on the case. Meaning, invested so much in killing me. She was not upset information that would have guaranteed me a stay of execution was withheld? No, she wasn't. It is amazing at times people clearly tell you who they are. At the hearing she had the nerve to say her office was the most ethical in Texas. Petty in the article said he worked for the state, not the judges But then turns around and says the judges insisted on paying him for the work he done for them. He also said they wanted him to respond to the writs because no one else in the office was.

My wonderful readers. Please give me your full attention here. If someone PAYS you for something. You done what? For them? They call that work, right? Also, when a defendant files an appeal, the judge is not supposed to 'respond' to the appeal. That is 100% the DA's job.

Laura Noldolf at the hearing even said: "Petty was late and missed the deadline to respond to the writ." Writ is short for writ of habeas corpus. A type of appeal. Okay, so it was clearly the PROSECUTOR'S job to respond. There is no way there would not be someone in the DA's office that would not respond to an appeal. If they didn't then every defendant would win their appeals! The judge is supposed to decide which side wins. Not fight for one side over the other. That makes no damn sense what he said. One of the people that testified at my recent hearing. His job is mainly focused on the appeal division. IE: To respond to appeals! Then all these Midland lawyers say he is so honorable. Okay, question to all you fuckin defense lawyers in Midland. HOW MANY TIMES. I ask again HOW MANY TIMES did Ralph Petty sign off on an appeal for the judge to where the defendant won? If he is so honorable. So noble. Then why did he provide ex parte filed documents that was filed under seal by defense lawyers, to the head DA? He used his job to the advantage of the DA's office. I am so glad to read some of the lawyers quoted in the article, As one lawyer is well known and kind of famous for being one of the best out there. Was glad to read his bullshit quote. As I had actually considered him to be one of the lawyers to hire at a new trial. Won't be doing that! Petty has been screwing these defense lawyers over for decades. Or has he? Also, there is no 'at home' I done this. 'At work' I done that.

Hey everyone, Donald Trump never tweeted anything crazy at work. No, he only done it at home! A DA doesn't get paid by the hour. They get a base salary for a specific time period. They are a DA 24/7. The Texas Code of Criminal Proceedings is very clear about the role of a DA. It is clearly defined by Article 2.08. (a) district attorneys SHALL not be of counsel adversely to the state in any case, in any court… Shall is a force word. It means a person Must do something.

The law gives clear meaning to words and terms. So it doesn't say a person MAY not or may be of counsel adversely, which would allow for some personal discretion there. It says 'shall not'… The judges do not hire lawyers to respond to appeals. That is 100% the sole responsibility of the District Attorney. The judge can hire someone to help him write orders and such. That is called a law clerk, but the law clerk has to be fair and impartial. Meaning at times be adverse to the state.

What does 2.08 say? A DA can't be adverse. Y'all notice that ONLY lawyers in Midland acted like all was peachy? Yeah I think there is a bit more to it all. Oh, let us not forget article 2.03 Neglect of duty. The Code of criminal procedure clearly says. 2.03 (b) It is the duty of trial court, attorney representing the state, attorney representing the accused and all the peace officers to conduct themselves as to insure a fair trial for both the state and the defendant, not impair the presumption of innocence. A DA working for judge and prosecutors. How is that fair to me? He told the prosecutor over my case what my lawyer was up to. Did he come tell is what the prosecutor was up to? Hell no he didn't. So how is that fair or noble? Just because someone has been doing something for so long and he can discuss the law with people who ask. That doesn't mean his actions are all noble right. Even judges in Midland know they fucked up. Most of the other cases. Petty only worked on appeal issues. He didn't take the role with them as he did in my case. Though in my case he wanted to make sure the DA's office did everything right so I wouldn't win an appeal. Then he deals with my appeals and writes the orders for the judges.

Yeah, what a great guy. Oh, haha! I get it! These defense lawyers in Midland. They represented clients who later might have filed appeals saying their lawyer was ineffective and did poorly. Ralph Petty comes along and writes up an order for the judge to sign, saying:

'No the trial lawyer did a great job and no error was found.' Ah, okay I see it more clearly now. If lawyers was being found to be ineffective, it could hurt how much people would retain the for in the future. Petty's role was never adverse to any of these lawyers, so naturally they will say he did no wrong. They are right. He done no wrong BY THEM. Petty wasn't a trial prosecutor, so he didn't fight them at trial. Only in my case did he take on a role in the trial that I know of. But maybe he does the same in these other guys mentioned. Anywho. Life goes on. Oh, for those that seen the USA Today story online. There is a, from what I gather a video clip is what it seems to be according to print out I got. The reason I was looking down and talking like that. I was looking at the iPhone laying on the table that the other visit booth phone was laid up against. No visitors are allowed in, so they say. As a result, the media visit had to be done with a TDCj media spokesman's phone on speaker phone and the visit phone laid beside it. There was a camera operated by a TDCj person, recording it all. They put another phone just to record above the cage I was in. Then I guess they spliced the audio and video together like that. I needed a haircut, hadn't had any sunlight in like 8 months due to Covid lockdowns over summer and cell I am in. I get rec first in the morning or later in the evening when go outside. Merel sent me the printout of the article. I seen that picture and said 'damn that's a bad picture of me. Plus me talking and looking down like that, had to look crazy. It is crazy how I look so different with different hairstyles. That makes it like 10 different hair style I had in images. Ha. I was actually going to cut it all off, but I decided against it because my hair was a bit different than other pics. The way I looked different throughout the film, became a kind of talking point with some so I wanted to play into that. Though just from knocking my beard down and cutting my hair low into a fade. I looked 5 years younger. I need to go to Hollywood. I am just made to be able to play different roles. "Alright, Alright, Alright." ☺ Haha Alrighty then. Thanks to all who have followed my case, supported my efforts and is helping to make a difference.

Until next time. Take care, smile & strive for all that you desire.

I remain,

In Solidarity

Veni, Vidi, Vici

Clinton Lee YOUNG #999447

http://clintonyoungfoundation.com

http://saveaninnocentlife.com

Loud & Clear, February 8, 2021

Topic: Court hearings and next step

I had previously written a message for the Clinton Young Foundation social media platforms.

My hint was that I was moving back some. As when I heard that was only around 1.200 people that watched the live stream of the hearing. To be honest: that really depressed me. There is over 5.000 people on the Facebook page alone. My thinking was that if I can not do better than that, I need to just hang it up and give up on all that. I was also missing many Jpays. Which will get to that later. I did not get a Jpay really outlining everything until Feb. 4th. It was sent to me on the 25th of Jan. I had sent a message for the hearing to be made available for everyone to see. Though, it appears my message was lost in transition. As instead of reaching out to law professors at universities all over the US, UK, Netherlands so that law students all over could watch this once in a life chance of being able to see an adversarial proceedings during a death penalty case. I thought that various media outlets, bloggers, key groups, and figures in the anti- death penalty movement would have been informed. This way, they could help spread the word. So I was expecting a minimum of say 50.000 people watching from all over the world. Which in doing so,

they would have posted about it and tweeted about it as it happened. Thus drawing more attention. It would have kept the conversation going until the USA Today article came out. So, as the conversation kept going, more would have checked out the films and foundation. That would have expanded into the area of 100-200.000 people made aware. More so with some of the law related blogs and people that have posted before about my case. This would have been the bare minimum of people learning about the hearing/ case. In the week up to the USA Today article coming out, everything could have been circulating. Then the article and it would have been a mega boost into the millions. As a result, the foundation could have grew by leaps and bounds. Though because my message was lost in transition, this once in a lifetime chance was instead limited to the 1.200+ people, already on my social media platforms. I am grateful that you, all you watched it, did so. I have another proceeding this month or so. It will be the closing arguments for the hearing. Will not be very long. Just wraps everything up. I am sure that many more people will be watching it. This time though, if the judge doesn't shut off the comment section. Would people please refrain from posting comments for me. As it is not my YouTube channel and I cannot even see all that as it happens. Yes that 'please refrain' also extends to not posting little hearts and or act as if you are a scholar of Texas law. I finally received the printout of screen shot of comments. The guy posting about law of parties. Look, first this is not a me and you issue. Please do not feel as if I am attacking you. I don't know you. I am frustrated. Not at you, but at the way myths germinate society. This results in a confusion of the law. Which can then be harmful to a person who encounters a dishonest cop. When it comes to the law. There are different degrees of responsibility. Follow with me here. My goal is to educate. The law prescribes Culpability. You can look up Texas Penal Code Chapter 6. It covers these degrees. Texas penal code article 6.02 and 6.03 are key for determining the criminal response of an individual. 6.04 is the part of law that is where, say you take a hostage and during the standoff the police move in. A cop then accidently kills a hostage while trying to get you. You are guilty of that death. The cop has the legal author to use force. You have no legal authority to take hostage and then escape. Had you obeyed the command to release the hostage, the cop would not have had to move in with force. Now if people partake in a crime. Under 7.02 a person can be responsible for another's actions. But this is not a blanket all-encompassing trap of law. There is what's known as Mens rea that still applies. Also, each element of the offense. Here is an example. Say you are in college and y'all have a party bus. Everyone is out of beer. Someone gets the bright idea to do a beer run on a store. To grab some beer and run out with it. All are in agreement that you will just grab a couple cases of beer and run for it. When everything begins to unfold, One guy pulls out a weapon and decided to rob the place, then shoot the store clerk.

You all are not responsible for his actions. You can refuse to speak to the police and remain silent. The burden is on the state to prove the case. Just because you all was there means nothing. More so if the guy told everyone he was specifically not going to do anything crazy. Then you are not responsible. More so, if you did not encourage anything, say some girl named Rachel was sitting at the back of the bus. She did not even comment on the grab and dash of the beer. She was just riding along. She is not guilty of anything related to the shooting. Even if she drank some of the beer that night and refused to tell on anyone, now they could get her with possessing stolen property as she drank the beer. If she threw away the beer cans in a way making them hard to locate, they could get her with tampering with evidence. As technically the beer can be evidence of the offense. An unethical cop is going to tell her: "You can face the death penalty." An honest cop would tell her: "You are facing a few months in jail and maybe some probation."

Texas does not have 'accessory after the fact.' Some states do. Texas, beyond popular belief.

It does not have the harshest laws in the U.S. California has some laws that are just crazy when it comes to this type of stuff. The law is very complex. There is the statutory law as written by the legislature. Then there is the interpretation of the statutes by the judicial branch. That is, judgements that become judicial precedents. Then there comes into play rules of evidence. Not just anything can be used against someone. The law is not designed to deprive innocent citizens of their liberty or life. Along the way, some bullshit ass politicians have damn sure tried to destroy the Constitution and feed the mass incarceration machine. This is how we ended up with Jim Crow laws, the war on drugs and, et cetera. The people being uneducated in law and the political process. They was not able to understand what the special interest groups was pushing politicians to do. Hell, most politicians didn't understand the full effect of their votes just because a politician is in office and has a fancy degree. When he speaks of the death penalty and such. It doesn't mean he knows what he is talking about. Someone else along the way told him something needs to be done and he done it for the vote and or for financial backing. It is clear there are some politicians in the US that are envious of the Ayatolla of Iran. As they want to turn the US into a theocracy or dictatorship. They pass draconian laws related to say sexting. These laws then trap teenagers. Say a 15-year-old boy and girl are dating and share nudes with each other. No one else sees it. A teacher later hears about it and calls the police. Now both kids are charged with child porn. Labeled for life. There is just dumb ass shit like that, that happens.

More so when you have prosecutor discretion. Which is often the problem. As then his own personal bias come into play. This is how people get trapped by the system. While can look back in history and find some fault with the founders of this country. Though when looking at the bill of rights and the intended design of our government. They was both genius and radical. Some of these tough on crime types. They generally are the ones that, during political times, yell the loudest about the constitution. Okay, they seem to overlook in the bill of rights, the first ten amendments. Four out of ten pertain to protecting people charged with crimes. The last line of the 1st says: to petition the government overreach in criminal prosecutions. The social order can be maintained without legal traps. The people just need to be educated. It really is a travesty of justice though on one thing. In Texas a 14-year-old can be certified as an adult and given 99 years in prison. Yet the government does not mandate schools teach criminal justice classes. The government will deprive you of your liberty, when it will not previously have made effort to educate you on what can cause this deprivation. Then someone goes to prison and get labeled as a horrible person who is to remain a 2nd class citizen for life. Sure, there are horrible people in prison. Though how did for example Texas prisons go from 40.000 people in prison before 1985 to 120.000 after 1995? Did 80.000 horrible people suddenly get born or move to Texas?

Or did politicians go against the spirit of the constitution and trap more people? While Texas is not the worst state in the union when it comes to laws on the books, It does have one of the worse courts when it comes to interpreting the laws. The Texas Court of Criminal appeals raises the bar to the highest level possible. They rarely hold prosecutors accountable. Which is what leads to stuff like what has happened in my case. Prosecutors have forgotten that the sword lady justice holds is double edged. It is meant to cut both ways. To the Clinton Young foundation matters. There are advancements being made. A great team is being formed. Renate, who helped get it all started, has recently stepped down. Renate helped to encourage Jessica Villerius to take an interest in the death penalty and my case. The first film was received so positively, that a film just on my case was done. This has helped people to think about the death penalty more. More got involved with helping. Now here we are, on the way to having three chapters of the foundation in three different countries. This growth and various projects has caused a problem. A good one to have. Though one none the less. Got too much going on. I have a habit of piling things on people, that I believe in. At times i expect too much from people. Thankful I have ready available talent to be the solution. There will be someone else coming on board, so as to better help navigate everything and make sure that no person gets overwhelmed. As not only is there multiple countries involved. There is also my desire to create a scholarship program. To help young girls in countries where being born a girl is a strike against her. In the West, the focus will be on those with the talent but being held back by poverty. There is also effort to be made for educating the youth on the law. The main goal is legal team for a new trial. Yes, I have a chance for a new trial. Though there is also chance of farther litigation. No one can say with certainty as to how the next few months will unfold. It does look good for the home team. However, I try to stay grounded. I have been on death row for 17 years and seen many times where the courts have defied logic. Watch the films about Todd Willinghams execution. Had it been up to the appeals court of Texas? Anthony Graves would have been executed. The execution of Robert Pruett. There can be many other examples. We just got to keep fighting forward. Anne-Sophie has taken a greater role with the foundation. This is, as has been, positive growth.

Farther advancements should be detailed by next month. Oh, many that are part of the foundation. I did not pick them. I think this is part of the reason why it has been able to grow. Sure, I have had input here and there. One day, I got some of the social media messages in the mail. They get printed for me. I have seen this guy smiling and a post about new member. I was thinking: who the hell is this dude? I had forgot that Merel had told me that they was bringing someone else on board. I was too busy stressing over my case and hearings. Anywho. So good things are happening. I have not yet read the USA Today article, as I do not get any newspapers. Another guy around me does get it. Sadly, it takes over a week to get the newspaper, that is meant to be delivered daily. Jpays are supposed to be passed out daily. Since my hearing and the positive developments. All of a sudden, mine is taking 5-9 days. I am missing many days worth. Other people here have had other guys Jpays stapled to his 3 days in a row. My neighbor Paul, who still has no treatment for his broken foot! He just discovered he is missing 2 or 3. The missing Jpays are not unique to me. The 5-9 days timeline is. I just do not understand why they do not sell us the tablets like other states. They could use half the money to fund grants for small police forces to get training in mental health related matters. This way cops can be better trained in MHMR and not kill so many unarmed and or crazy people. As the state would make millions off of the people in prison. So grants to small police forces would be helpful to provide farther training in MHMR tactics. Could train two officers who worked different shifts for example. The tablets would help increase interaction between people in prison and family and friends. State could raise funds to address a problem needed in criminal justice/police reform. While not having to raise any taxes. A win-win for everyone. But hey, what do I know.

Alrighty, will be back soon. Take care, smile & strive for all that you desire.

Veni Vini Vici

In solidarity I remain

Clinton Lee YOUNG #999447

http://facebook.com/clintonyoungfoundation

http://instagram.com/clintonyoungfoundation

http://clintonyoungfoundation.com/

Loud & Clear, March 7, 2021

Topic: Next step

It seems that visitation will open soon in a limited form. I heard they have some quick test machines to do Covid tests on visitors. Huh. That is really neat. I wonder who was pushing for that before and having all kinds of people email the Governor, Executive Director of TDCj, and even the company that makes the machines. I wonder who that was. My dear ole pal Rabbi Randy here told me that TDCj would not get these here machines for visitors. Huh. I surely do thank TDCj for taking step to open visit. Sadly, Covid cases are spiking on the unit again. Until they get the vaccines in here it will keep on. This is why prisons are supposed to be at the front of the line, it is a public safety thing. The next step in the appeal should be soon. There will be a filing about the elements of the current claim. This is about the various fact points and the law that applies. The Judge can sign off on it, add to it, or just write his own. Though there is also a closing argument hearing that will take place soon. Bottom line is that everything on the local level will soon be wrapped up. Then it will go to the CCA. They are supposed to decide death penalty cases quickly per 11.071 sec.11. Though they tend to rush us, and then take their sweet time. Though because the DA asked to speed things up, I think they will move faster than normal. I am getting the lawyers sorted that I will want for a new trial on that topic. I thank everyone that has donated the last couple of months. I fully understand how difficult these times are. Thankfully the vaccine numbers are going up and states are being opened up fully in the US and other countries will be soon to follow. The foundation will be expanding soon. More people are coming on board. When it comes to donating, it seems the ideal way would be for people to set it up to donate something each month. A sustainer or whatever it is called. Right now we are trying to get as much of a lump sum as can. This way can get the fund raiser tools, promotional items and to get the sites developed as needed properly serve the goals of the foundation.

Plus be in a position to get the legal team I need signed up. So right now just trying to get all that can. Beginning in May. The idea will be to get as many people to commit to donating each month with automatic deposits and such. Say a person is willing to donate, for example $100 every three months. It would be better, starting in May, to get it set up where there is an automatic donation to the foundation each month for $30. Yes, the 100 every 3 months would be more in total. Though it would not be seen as consistent. Stability is the key for encouraging people to invest greater in the future. Plus by May/June can have more to show for what has been done thus far. I have been blessed in the people I have available to me to work for free right now. Though to keep on that way is not feasible. The foundation will be unique and unlike any other. Unique in a better way. By September the goal is to have paid staff. I thank everyone for the help. Please keep encouraging others to follow the foundations social media pages. Hopefully can double the number of followers for each format by September also. Right now, I am still the main focus. It is fully understood why everyone that follows the foundation right now, does so. No one is losing sight of that. Just want to be strong enough to do more. Now, I rarely ask people to step up and help out. I do not want people to get exhausted by being asked to do something over and over all the time. Now I need people. I need people to donate and get others to follow the foundation's social media pages. In a few days I will outline some of the future plans on the social media pages. Hopefully there are people that can help specifically in the different fields of interest that I will outline.

To other topics. I am glad it is warming up. More so after this crazy ass winter. While the water going out was a discomfort. We still had heat here. Many didn't around the state and some other units didn't have water or heat. Prisons puts people in a childlike state of dependence. That's never been more evident than when the unit is shut down due to bad weather. We have to depend on guards for everything. Then when someone complains they get called a crybaby. I have heard officers before make comments when someone complains about something. I am a man. I expect what I am supposed to have. I believe people are supposed to speak up for what they are due by right, policy or need. Now sure, some people in prison will just complain about anything. There is always that one! I personally try to put things in perspective, plus try to need as little from others as possible. Like with the water. I had water bottles saved up and juice. I was good and was able to give someone a bottle of water. Though I know there was many locked in cells. More so in Ad-seg, that have nothing. Say a mentally ill older person with no support. Not having access to water, beyond a cup, for 24 hours is a bad go. Someone free could always go out and do something. In prison, more so in lock up, one is at the mercy of the staff. No one in Texas is really expected a winter storm like that. Hopefully being that there is hurricanes and freak winter storms. That TDCj can stock a region warehouse and on unit, cases of water and such. Be ready for these kind of situations. I will not blame TDCj for a freak winter storm. Though they can be blamed if next time they are not better prepared. Hurricane season is coming up. I am sure TDCj could start building up an reserve of MRE's and cases of water from FEMA and such. (MRE is Meal Ready to Eat. It is what the military eats.) Being that people in prison are getting these stimulus checks from the federal government. Hopefully they take the responsible steps to stock up on water and et etcetera. TDCj has property restrictions. Though I am sure being that summer is coming up and we have these freak storms and such. That going forward, TDCj will allow a property exception for 24 bottles of water, 30 electrolytes and a square foot of food items. The property limit is 2 square feet. The idea is about flammable material. Okay, water by its nature, yeah no need to explain that one. Though TDCj saying that we can have this as not counting against out property. It would encourage people to keep water bottles for emergency times. Most dudes if it came between keeping commissary food and legal papers. they would throw out the legal! It is really just disgusting at times how dudes act towards commissary. People have shown that they will not make the best choices. The very fact they are in prison makes that clear. I feel that TDCj easing property limitations like this. More will set aside a case of water and such. Get more water to the units and encourage the purchase of some to have set aside. Believe me, I am sure even if TDCj done that, some would still not do it and blame others when stuck out. Then when the shit hits the fan, they will complain they are stuck out. Some will say it is not their responsibility.

Well, we all have personal responsibility towards taking care of our own needs first, before depending on another. The first step towards freedom is independence. We often say we dislike the system. We say the system hates us. Okay, then why would one accept being so dependent on the people that dislike you?! If you have someone in prison that complains about these things. Gently encourage them to be more responsible and make sure they have what they need for times of need. From the perspective of death row. Most of the complaints this unit gets is about Jpays. It is crazy. 90% of the complaints is about that single issue. I get pissed and go on and on about it because people pay for a service they expect to be rendered. TDCj makes money from this service. TDCj is a government agency. Their obligation is purely to the people confined and connected to such persons. The core principle of government is to insure the people have what they are supposed to have. Period! Sell us Tablets and we wouldn't need staff for Jpay printouts.

Alrighty then. Gonna wrap this one.

Take care, smile & strive for all that you desire.

Veni Vidi Vici

In solidarity, I remain,

Clinton Lee YOUNG #999447

http://clintonyoungfoundation.com/

http://facebook.com/clintonyoungfoundation

http://instagram.com/clintonyoungfoundation

www.saveaninnocentlife.com

Loud & Clear, May 2, 2021

Topic: Lockdown & shitty situations

It seems will be on lock down for two more week. We already had to endure COVID lock downs and then staff shortages, so the past two months only been able to get rec a few times. So tired of being stuck in this damn cell. The staff shortages cost us about two week's worth of recs.

These people refuse to adapt and change with the times. They just torture us with being stuck in cell. Plus this pod AGAIN got lockdown right before commissary. It is not enough we can not see family like should be or make calls and such. They do not want us to have writing materials either. They could make a change such as single man escort to visit for death row level ones, with no designators. That alone would make a world of difference in staff problems. They do it for closed custody which is the worst group of population. It just amazes me at how every damn time we got locked down. It happened between 3-1 days before we was due to get commissary on "this" pod. Now because of how short of staff they are. It will drag on. Nevermind peoples mental health and such from being locks in a cell so much. Plus they will not allow death row to have Saturday visits, as we are supposed to. Yet people not on death row can. (I mentioned this in a social media msg.) Ya know so I guess our people don't have to work on weekdays or such. I guess only people who are not on death row, their people are only ones that have weekend off. We are only class of prisoner by law allowed visit. As I said before – code of criminal procedure 43.17. if we got our Saturday visit slots like supposed to. Then they could make visits 2 hours. Everyone's tested that comes in and has to test negative for COVID. So why they have to sit so far apart makes no sense when rest of Texas is opened up. If they would go to 3 feet space here, could have enough room for everyone to have two-hour visits and since people coming would travel together. It should be that we can see two people. After all, they did drive in the car together. It should not be one hour one person and one hour the next person. Makes no sense. They will have driven to the unit in the same damn car! Both would have tested negative to get in here! Damn it just amazes me at how little these people give a fuck about how things effect people. Dudes can't even see their children under 13. The shit they do here does not match the science! Just oppress to oppress. Now to expand on mental health. There is a guy in the section next to me. His name is Rockwell, he is crazy! One of those people that this place made crazier to the point he cannot be executed. Well he will not flush his toilet. Dude lets feces backup for days and days! I have asked officers, who ALL complain about horrible smell. To make him come out cell and flush the toilet. Last time it built up for 10 days! Lower ranks walk day every day and do NOTHING! There was only one officer who forced him to come out and had the service inmates go in and clean his cell. They had to dig out the feces, it had stacked up so high in his toilet. They could not flush it without it flooding. Food and trash is also all over the cell with piss. Again, no one does anything. Officers told me they wrote him a disciplinary. Uh, DUH you dumbasses he is crazy. What the fuck does writing him up a case going to do?! Think a mofo that shits in the same toilet for 10 days gives a damn about a write up?! The very sad thing is Raymond Riles, an old man that has been on death row for 40+ years and is in bad health. He is in the cell right next to Rockwell, so he has to smell this all day every day. I am way over here at the end of another section, so it doesn't effect me/us same. Though I like Raymond and known him since I got here. He is also VERY mentally ill. Recently he was thankfully able to get a new punishment phase which he will get life sentence and be able to get parole soon like Bobby Moore did. He should have never come to death row! 30 years ago on Ellis Unit when death row was over there. He built a big fire and sat in it to be cleansed by the flames. He did not scream one time! Yeah, he should not have been here. Anyways, now he is forced to have to suffer breathing feces particles every day because no one will do their job. Mental health never does anything about it. Medical does nothing about it. The only person I seen do anything about it was last time when the Captain for 12 building walked through and made them clean it up. Then another officer 10 days later did. All they have to do it make him exit the cell and get support service inmates to clean it up. Yet they do nothing. Not a fucking thing! These fuckin people. I tell you what. I got a chance to beat this case and get out of here. These fuckin people have tortured me for 18 years now, as of last month. Once a year they lie to us about group rec coming and such. Always getting locked down. Now my baby sister comes to see me. She passes a covid test, is behind glass, no one is near her and yet she has to wear a mask and can only visit for 1 hour. After a 3.5 hour drive down here. Again passes test, behind glass! And I can't even see my sister's face. Then got this old, sick, mentally ill man having to live next to this dude and breath in his feces all day every day. We can't get rec or writing supplies. You fuckin worthless piece of shit fuckin snakes. The latest new is will not allow death row to get video visits. It's okay for yall to torture people in these cages. Jump through hoops to kill people. Yet can't even see our family? Long sigh. I am going to write out some course of action for people to follow up on. We got to stick together and do something. Take care.

Veni, Vidi, Vici

In solidarity,

I remain,

Clinton Lee YOUNG #999447

www.saveaninnocentlife.com

facebook.com/clintonyoungfoundation

Loud & Clear, May 3, 2021

Topic: Fixes and Lies

Yesterday sent a blog to be posted about shitty situations and etc. That was written on the 2nd and sent out on the 3rd. This was written on the 3rd and sent out on the 4th. This morning, they came to get Rockwell to, I assume address the cell or move him. He displayed some behavior that resulted in chemical agents (pepper spray) being used on him. Hate to see such take place. The silver lining is that the cell will be cleaned, and Mr. Riles will not have to breathe in feces all day. Then, this evening the commissary staff came on the pod announcing we would get to buy hygiene, writing material, and such. Not food, etc, as we are on lockdown. Hopefully after lockdown, this pod will be first in line to go for a regular spend. As a rule, I do not complain about the food items/snacks sold on the commissary. As that is their control tool, and sadly, many dudes here care more about commissary than they do their case and etc. I personally am glad to get stamps. Next up. There has been an issue with jpays and MSCP. The MSCP oversees the mailrooms for the TDCj. Before if jpays came up missing, we could write the mailroom for print out of all jpays received to identify ones missing. That or ask for reprint of a specific one. Some dudes would ask for whole months and all this crap and that is a waste of time and bad go for doing a reprint. But most of us did not do that. Okay, MSCP came over here and told two wardens, a major, and the mailroom staff that the mailroom is not to reprint jpays or summaries. Mailroom told us we have to write the MSCP about missing jpays. Okay, MSCP started to get so many calls and such they changed their tone. At first, they lied and told Merel and Emily that they would tell the mailroom to reprint specific days for me. As I could show that I did not receive them due to us having to sign for jpays. I could show I was legit in my complaint. Okay I write mailroom on the days the missing mailroom writes back and says MSCP says no reprints. So I ask two different supervisors about it. Both say no one from MSCP called or emailed them anything about reprints. So more calls was made. Then MSCP changed their tune and said "well actually we do not have any control over that. It is up to the unit mailroom." So the people OVER the mailroom orders the mailroom to not do an act. Then turn around and say they have no say over the very act needed to be done by the mailroom that the MSCP is over! These fuckin people! So

Here is the plan. If you write to someone and jpays come up missing. Spend the next 60 days keeping track of them. If you write often, number your jpays so a person will know if he is missing one. For example, if he get #5 and #7, he will know he is missing #6. Keep track of them. And have him write a complaint to the unit mailroom is any are missing. You email ombudsman and write and mail a letter to the MSCP and TDCj director. The name and address for these can be found on the tdcj.gov website. Make sure it is the TDCj-ID director. That specific title. Send letter to both MSCP and TDCj director. Indicate missing jpays and request refund as the contract indicates that the service will be provided in a specific time period. After 3-4 months from now, which provides time for response from the 60-day-period of missing jpays. If the problem does not remedy itself, then we need to work together on a class action lawsuit in Austin by people in the free world. It can be filed in state court by you all. Also complain to jpay about undelivered jpays. Keep a record of everything. The prison system makes money from jpay. They use that money to oppress us. There has been no benefits for death row or the rest of the prison population. Video visits have nothing to do with jpay. Aren't they going to charge for those also? The only way you can make changes is by uniting and addressing the problem. Texas charges more than any other state for each jpay. They exploit you and us when they do not guarantee the service is provided. It doesn't matter if it is a CO or mailroom. They all work for TDCj. I am already due to have some discussion with a group of lawyers that focuses on government over reach and abuses. It damn sure should not be that the MSCP is playing this game, putting it off on the mailroom. The mailroom has no choice but to follow the MSCP. That is their boss. Multiple people called the MSCP, so they can not backtrack. They can fix the problem. If the TDCj would get with the modern times like other prisons. Would not have these problems. Though again, they want to operate a prison system like it's 1970, with 2021 minded officers. It aint gonna work. What they are doing is not working. They need to adapt and make changes. I do not want to fight with the TDCj. I want what I am supposed to have and for the TDCj to do better and make changes that help people in prison with emotional and mental health. As well as improve social skills and make it easier for people to be productive citizens when released. Also, so that people locked in these cages for 10-15-20 years do not end up spun off the edge like Rockwell. Damn hold up, I think I forgot to flush the toilet!

Take care, smile, and strive for all that you desire.

Veni, Vidi, Vici

In solidarity,

I remain,

Clinton Lee YOUNG #999447

www.saveaninnocentlife.com

facebook.com/clintonyoungfoundation

Loud & Clear, May 31, 2021

Topic: No rec. forever

There has seemingly been one thing after another lately since January 1 I have been locked in the cell over 122 days. Of the available rec days which is five a week I have missed 82 due to lockdowns in short of staff. On Thursday, May 27 they had wreck, though due to officers in ability to properly operate the pod schedule. They only had two rounds of rec on the side of the pod I am on. Second shift was short of staff. Instead of doing rec day was to finish up showers. By the time was to get to me for a shower, it was already 9 PM. Which is the time the overtime officer had to leave. As a result, I did not get rec or shower on the 27th. This after not being able to wreck or shower at the 25th and 26th. Since April 21 I have been able to leave the cell for rec only two days. TDCj refuses to do anything to mitigate the staff shortage problems. These problems will not end. This unit gets more money than any other unit in Texas. CTDCJ gets over $20 more per person on death row. Yet they have not brought in any substitute to wreck, solved the staffing problems, or do anything to mitigate the problem. Today there was three officers working hard. We could have gotten wet, but they chose to not do recreation. An officer said staff shortage and then said because of it being a holiday. I am not sure if that was a joke or not I know at times they do not run wreck on Christmas and such. From now on I will file on that also, as nothing in the recreation plan says no wreck on holidays. Another interesting thing, since talking about stuff and money here. The TDCJ Counts the number of people on death row as being higher than it is. They still count men who are in the county jail for new punishment phases, as they have not officially been given a different number by TDCJ. A pod and the pod hold 84 people. C pod has two sections for death row. $84 \times 2 = 168$. Two sections is 28 cells total. $168+28 = 196$. OK not every cell is full. A pod a section which is deathwatch, only has seven people eight at most. There are a few other empty cells. So on Polunsky there is maybe 186 people. 2 are housed in ten building medical. Estelle unit has one or two in medical housing. Jester 4 has maybe 4 who are so crazy they are housed at the psych unit. All those are less than TDCj's stated men on death row population. A couple guys currently on B pod have been given new punishment phases and one has a life sentence. Why he is still housed on death row is beyond me. The math does not add up to what the TDCj lists as men on death row. Why are they getting 80 something dollars a day for men who are not even in custody of TDCj and who are not even under death sentence? Those guys are sitting in the county jail. TDCj gets money for people not even here, so is really free money by the thousands each month. Yet we cannot even get rec.? The unit administration has no control over policy. The directors of the TDCj refuse to allow any changes. Just like video visit. We are not G5, we are a unique class of prisoner. Thus, there is no reason to exclude us. There is no reason for us to not have group rec and etc. Guys with capital life do not get restricted the same way. There are surely guys serving life with worse cases then most of us on death row. What guys are going to have to start doing is file in appeals about the 15+ years on death row in these conditions. As it has surely risen to the level of ill treatment which would violate article 43.24 of the Texas Code of Criminal procedure. State law prohibits ill treatment for those 'to be executed'. This is a lower bar than cruel and unusual punishment. Which courts more and more are finding long term segregation is such a violation. Once guys start getting traction on appeals, then these people would surely change up their ways. See, they thought with Trump appointing justices, they would have a court their way. The powers that be in this here state that is. Well, the fact the United States Supreme Court ruled against TDCj twice recently over lawsuits by prisoners. the Taylor and McCoy case. Then plus the way the USSC ruled in the Chaplain/spiritual advisor during executions. It is NOT the court they hoped it would be. Trump didn't know a damn thing about the supreme court. Someone just told him who to pick. They damn sure did not pick justices like Bush did. Now due to the rulings in the Taylor and McCoy case it will be easier for guys in prison to sue. The door will only continue to crack open wider. It's a slow march but eventually we will get there. I had to take a few weeks off. As I had been holding everything in for years. Letting my frustrations pile up while fighting my case. When I had the good recommendation it was as if the flood gates blew open. All that anger that had piled up came rushing forward. I was not any good to anyone in such a state. It had been 15 years since I took a break to relax and reflect. That is a long time of go, go, go. We all need a vacation. Even when I was not writing blogs, I was still writing letters, or working on my case, focused on problems around here. Recently for a couple weeks I done nothing but write a couple legal letters. I didn't focus on much of anything. Just sorted through my thoughts. I reached a peak after about 10 days where I was consumed with rage. Then the clouds started to break and sunshine through. I am in a much better place mentally and emotionally now. This allows me to see things in a clearer fashion. Which will allow me to be more effective. I do thank everyone that has continued to write and support my efforts. The fight is not over, but is one step closer. Not sure if missing any Jpays from last week. They had started to get to me on time and without any problems. Then last 3 days of last week I did not get any. But I did go without writing for weeks myself, so is a factor. Regular mail did seem to pick up a step. The problem is that it is not only security staff that are short, it's the mailroom staff also. Then add in US postal service problems. As I stated I was not writing for a spell. Though I am back at it. I am sure that people was able to pick up on my frustrations in my letters, blogs, and messages I posted on the foundation social media pages. Long sigh. The road goes on.

I will be back soon. Until next time. Take care, smile, and strive for all that you desire.

Veni, Vidi, Vici

In solidarity,

I remain,

Clinton Lee YOUNG #999447

Loud & Clear, June 27, 2021

Topic: The b/s never ends

As heat rises, so does staff shortages. Now, there has been a couple days that we missed rec and shower. While I had hope some emotional/mental relief would be on the way by the normal visit schedule. The TDCj never fails to prove that Nietzsche's declaration was prophetic. "Hope is but a waking dream, for it prolongs the torment of man." While the rest of the state of Texas is wide open. The Executive Dictator of the TDCj waved his fascio and decreed that I can not see my mother for 2 hours behind glass. The only way I can see her for longer than 1 hour, after her 3.5 hour drive to get here, is if 70% of the staff and prisoner population are vaccinated. Never mind that I have been fully vaccinated. My mother has to travel a combined 7 hours and sit at the unit for 1-1.5 hours just to see me for 1 hour instead of two hours. All because at least 20% more of the prison population at this unit does not want to get vaccinated. Never mind that these other people in prison will not be sitting in the booth with me. Death row is the only portion by law allowed to visit. We are at 70%. Though must be held to the mercy of guys who are allowed to use the phone all day every day and get video visits. Their family doesn't have to drive 7+ hours. They can have video visits. Yet, we must be held to the mercy of others who enjoy privileges we are denied. There is only one as of June 25^{th,} 2021. 4 units at over 70% vaccinated. Those units are all small units with older people held there. None of the large maximum-security units was listed. Word is this unit is at 45-50%. While frustrated and voicing such. I understand the TDCj's desire to have as many people vaccinated as possible. Look, I get it 100%. I do not disagree with that goal. The problem is that people in prison are by nature distrustful of the people holding them captive. Some black guys, for example, are put off from getting the vaccine because of the historical record of the government's abuse towards minorities w/medical experiments. Add how in the past, people in prison were used to test out medications for pharma companies. I am shocked ANY unit is at 70%. I did not want to get it. Initially, I was only going to take the 1st shot and refuse the second. Hey, I don't trust these white folks either! ☺ Though I decided at the last moment to go ahead and get it. Only because I wanted to be able to voice my complaints in just this kind of situation. The better metric for TDCj would be the number of positive cases on a unit. That or the % of people fully vaccinated and % with at least one shot. For example, 50% are fully vaccinated with additional 10-20% having at least one shot. That would be a more plausible goal to reach. As some guys would maybe take at least one shot. If they knew that would not be forced to take the second. (They have been using Pfizer and Moderna.) I have not seen medical staff come around and ask anyone that had initially refused, if they want the shot yet. Look, recently there was an advertisement in the USA Today. It was a cover sheet made to look like a real front page of the paper. It was advertising the show Sweet Tooth about the hybrid kids. On the cover was an image of a nursery with a baby with bat wings. Guys in here thought that was a real picture! Being that COVID-19 came from bats, supposedly. The thought was that the vaccine was causing hybrid bat babies! Now just how in hell are you going to get someone that believes such a thing to get a vaccine!? There was several someone's who believed that ad was real life! Maybe if the TDCj offers the Johnson and Johnson and explains was no adverse cause of effects on any men. Now, people are hearing on the news that Pfizer can cause heart inflammation in young men. TDCj is setting impossible goals. While talking sh*t, I do get the Directors concerns. They just got to alter their goals some to reach a plausible milestone. (Plus I had to exhibit my famous wit + sarcasm. ☺) Given that this unit for example has such a high staff turnover rate. Plus prison by its very nature has a fluid population. People come and go. Some go home, some to other units. New people come in. How is 70% going to be measure effectively when there is such a fluid populace? A TDCj officer can refuse a vaccine, leave work and go to a strip club in Texas with no mask on. Yet ,I can not see my mother for 2 hours after having to drive 3.5 hours for a NON contact visit? This sh*t gotta make sense somehow.

Veni Vidi Vici

In solidarity,

I remain,

Clinton Lee YOUNG #999447

D.R- Polunsky Unit

3872 FM 350 South

Livingston, TX 77351

U.S.A.

www.saveaninnocentlife.com

facebook.com/clintonyoungfoundation

Loud & Clear, June 30, 2021

Topic: Another thought

I heard DR will get two Zoom visits. If so, good deal! I was thinking, as I tend to do when something comes to mind. That usually happens when you think! The TDCj has come up with the 70% number for visits to get back to normal. The whole vaccine goal. 70% of the prison system does not even get visits each week. I would say that only 25% gets visits. Before the stimulus checks was given to people in prison. 60% of the prison population was indigent. (this number doesn't match with death row as DR gets way more support than other classes of prisoners.) Okay, so with 60% indigent we can assume that an easy 70% doesn't get visits. More so since there is video visit and phones now. How in the hell is TDCj going to use visit to push people to get a vaccine. 65-75% of the prison doesn't give a damn about a visit they can not have.

There are dudes that in general population that think that the vaccine has microchip nano bits in it. I heard officers say this even. The mofo's are smoking crack and eating dog food! If you are in the free and send someone in prison K2, please stop! The secondhand smoke is making everyone lose their rapid ass minds! What is amazing is there are guys that will smoke K2, shoot up meth and have unprotected sex with prison punks. Yet they are scared of a vaccine. Really!? That's what puts the brakes on ya?! Look, the TDCj will have to come up with a plan B. Y'all gonna have to play to greed or need. Offer a month of free calls, extra visits like get 2 a week for a month or 4-hour visits for family members that would not normally qualify. Tell dudes on G5 of level 2 or 3 they can move up to G4/G3 if they get the vaccine or back to level one if they get at least one shot. If a dude is G5 and he got those stimulus checks. He has months of commissary restriction. He can not spend it. He will be stuck out for 1-2-3 months at times. If TDCj goes to a G5 with lots of restriction or such and says: "Look, get the shot. We will remove all restriction and put you on G4/G3." That would push you guys to get it. That is a major carrot to hang in front of a person. To those not hip. G5 is closed custody. When not in restriction, they can only spend $25 every two weeks. So to remove the restriction and put them on G4. They then can spend up to $60 and I think have access to the offender telephone system. (DR and Ad seg doesn't have access to it.) G5, G4 up to G1 is a custody level. Being these dudes have money whereas the before didn't. Once they get off G5 and able to use the phone and talk to people. They might chill and break the cycle of messing up and rioting with their homeboys. For others the extra video visit time or free phone time and such. Might be a carrot for them. The G5 idea would impact maybe 20-30 people per unit at least that would go for it. Maybe more depending on who all got the stimulus checks. Some of these dudes with money now, could get up a custody and then get into the craft shop now and be able to order the supplies for leather work and etc. I would say if the TDCj said get at least one shot. Many would go for some reward and privileges gained. As everyone is scared of the second shot it seems. I didn't want to get that sick feeling again, more so since I had anti bodies as I had covid already. I am glad I took the second shot though as it now gives me room to raise hell about all this. :) Anyways. Maybe someone will think something based off my idea. The G5 idea would serve multiple goals. Dudes would see it as a clean slate on G4 and a chance to get to G3 quicker. Maybe times when dudes get knocked down the custody levels. They just get trapped. The removal of commissary and other restrictions doesn't hurt TDCj any. As chances are they will have a chance in the near future to put many back on it. I figure it would be better if guys are 35% covered by the vaccine then 0%. So even if they only take one shot. It is better than nothing. Just my thoughts. On the tablets. TDCj has approved the JPay tablets. Curious to see who all gets them. Ad seg level one and DR get radios, like the rest of prison. TDCj has never sold TV on commissary which really makes NO sense. If radio was just invented today, would TDCj not allow DR and Ad seg level one to have them? Death row has its own operational plan. No where in it even with the work program suspended does it say DR cant have TV. TDCj just doesn't give it to us based on how Ad seg is treated. Though, Ad seg restrictive housing as it is now known. They are there for punishment, regardless of what TDCj calls it. They have a way top work out of that housing, we do not. We are not supposed to be excluded from things as we get 95$ spend for commissary just as G1 gets. We are only 'housed' in this manner for so called dangerousness. Okay, that doesn't mean to be deprived of privileges. It is supposed to be about containment, not punishment. The TDCj should allow DR and restrictive housing level ones to have the tables. More so since there is such staff shortages and many places can not get rec. Shall see how it all goes. Anywho. There is my ideas for the vaccine and such. At the least DR should go back to visit as normal as we are over 70% and can not have contact visits. At the least allow those that are fully vaccinated to have visits. Prison by its nature is supposed to be a reward and punish facility. There has to be a reward for a desired outcome. I do not advocate punishment for not taking a vaccine. As we are all set at a level due to pandemic. Offer more for those that do what is desired by the system. I'm just saying. But hey! What do I know.

Take care,

Smile & strive for all that you desire.

Veni Vidi Vici

In solidarity

I remain,

Clinton Lee Young #999447

Loud & Clear, August 16, 2021

Topic: Caged in forever

This month of August alone, I have been denied access to shower a total of 7 days. August 3rd, 4th, 5th, 11th, 12th, 13th and 16th. Can wash it off in the sink, but it is not the same as a hot high-pressure shower. Been denied recreation for weeks. Since august 1st, only been to rec 2 days. That is it! They started a new guard work schedule and that worked for about a day or two. If rec days are missed, they can do make up rec on Sundays. There was a Sunday with enough staff, but they done no make up rec. These people will not do anything or change anything. All it would take is to ask the board to modify policy. It is not just death row, it is to ad-seg prisoners also. Other units have the problems. This is to such a degree that it is a public safety matter. The staff shortages are so bad there is no way to maintain proper security across state prisons. Even if you do not care about prisoners being able to have recreation and, etc. You do want guards and people to be safe. TDCj refuses to adapt. They are wasting millions of dollars on bonusses for new officers, who only stay for a couple of months. Now they ban us from having bikini pictures and such. So, that is their big focus? Guys risk getting People, US weekly and such magazines denied if it has a celeb in a bikini. Yet they do nothing about the countless suicides throughout TDCj? The drug overdoses? The murders and rapes? The assaults and excessive use of force? So do nothing to address these things, but you can pass a rule that bans an image that any 12-year-old could look at in the free world?! Way to have your priorities straight, TDCj. Also, they ban sex offenders from being on pen pal sites. I personally do not care about such people. But now is a bigger class of prisoners who will be unable to gain support from pen pals and such. This means more theft, extortion and prostitution in prison. Way to make things better and safer. But hey! You people went to school for all this shit, huh?! I forget they are the ones with the college degree. How about making prison a safer place to where people can be rehabilitated? What will it take before the powers wake up and do something? Need more teachers raped, guards killed, mass escape? I mean, when is enough enough? If TDCj would just change seg policy and reinstate death row plan for men's death row. This would drastically impact staffing. As there would be less in seg. The question is: are people willing to speak up? Do you care about millions of tax dollars wasted, criminals coming home more dangerous than when they entered, nurses/teachers/guards being at risk and so forth? I do not want prisons totally closed down. Could close a few more! But society needs prisons to some degree. No matter if Texas has one or 100. Changes need to be made to better adjust to the reality of the job markets impact on staffing. Leaving people stuck in cells for 10- 20- 30 years purely for their sentence like us on the row. This needs to change. It is getting to the point that lawyers can start using 20+ years stuck in seg., more so with the no rec and shower. Well, can start raising this in appeals that they can no longer be executed due to the ill treatment and would even say cruel and unusual treatment should negate the execution. As TDCj has violated state law and the constitution. All it will take is just one judge to give it a chance to be heard. Add in a liberal DA that agrees. Once having a hearing on it all, it can stand the test to reach the US Supreme Court. The question needs to be asked. Is TDCj going to make changes or what? Will be back soon.

In solidarity,

I remain

Clinton Lee Young #999447

D.R- Polunsky Unit

3872 FM 350 South

Livingston, TX 77351

USA

Loud & Clear, September 19, 2021

Topic: These people

Greetings! Hope all is good out there. In here I have been getting a little bit of rec each week. With the governor of Texas taking $250 million from the already struggling TDCj, I think will be even more struggles going forward. Greg Abbott wants to use the funds for border security. I read it is for 10 miles of fence. Texas has a southern border of like 1200 miles. Not sure what 10 miles of fence will do. Though I am sure I know what prison will be like with 250 million less dollars. It damn sure will not be a safer place for prisoners, guards and society that depend on prison security to keep people from escaping or hurting people inside the prison. Last prison security more border security. Huh. A while back I wrote about what all the overtime guards had to do. I mentioned that one day a guard will fall asleep at the wheel and get someone killed. A month or so ago it happened. Guard was killed, as was people in the other car he hit, when he fell asleep after working 15 to 16 hours straight. From 1980 to 1999 I do not think one guard was killed. Might have been one. From the last 20 years, four have been killed. I wonder how many staff was attacked from 1980 to 2000 and how many has been attacked, raped etc. in the last 20 years? The case Robert was blamed for I think happened in 1999 maybe, I forgot. So, might have been one in previous timeline and three in current. I wonder how many prisoners were pronounced dead at the hospital, but were labeled 'unresponsive' when the ambulance picked them up. Which means they were dead at the unit but were not pronounced officially until they got to the hospital. I think that would be a great project for the media. Maybe it will take another mass escape and murders to get the powers that be to re-evaluate the broken way they operate the system. I want TDCj to be able to have an environment where people can change and become better people that cannot happen with the band-aids being applied and the way they operate on the edge of disaster. If TDCj had not become such masters at controlling the media in Texas, there would be more scandals. How most of that have been in the media is due to Kerri. Though it took an ex-con from New York to shine a light and make some changes. Thankfully on this unit is a warden that actually gives a damn about trying to help men change their lives. He has instituted more faith-based programs. I am not the most religious guy, but I support it as I know it will help people. It is helping, as some that were trapped in a cycle of negativity are breaking that cycle. He gave them a chance and treated them like a normal human being. It is amazing that they then started to act like human beings should. Most on other units though do not give a damn, because the system does not give a damn and the state does not give a damn. Most are also too cowardly to attempt to do something more. Most feel if they just stick to the outdated way of doing things, then if something happens, it's not on them. Blame visitors for contraband. Place new rules on pictures and magazines.

Yeah, I don't think that is helping anything. Things would change if more knew how bad it really was.

There are 1,000 people in Harris County waiting on trial that are charged with capital murder. Meaning they face death or life. This is one county in Texas, out of over 200 counties. So it is possible there is 2 to 3000 all over Texas waiting to be sentenced under capital murder. Think about that. Look up statistics of those already locked up serving life. In 10 years it will be that damn near 30% of TDCj will be serving life. How is that sustainable? How can they justify keeping so many locked in seg, which requires so much more staff? People on death row are in seg for up to 21 years already. Many going crazy, so crazy they will not be able to be executed. One dude that was cool, he is punching himself now. Another who was liked by all is talking about people trying to watch him and mock him in private moments. Are couple others that went crazy some years ago. A guy just recently threw water at me, that supposedly hit an officer. He told everyone he done it, because I was trying to rape him! I'm locked in a cell! Now he was already crazy, but fact is being here in this cell made him much worse over the last five years or so. I have had guys I am friends with tell me in secret, that this place is starting to get to them. No one wants to appear weak, so they hold it in. I have not been writing much because this place is really fuckin with me also. It is aggravated by people I should be able to depend on, not properly helping me or bullshitting and etc. I have a chance to leave here, better than most. Though this place due to being locked in this bitch ass box so much. I don't want to begin to write about what's gone through my mind. I truly believe in security housing unit syndrome now. Thankfully I'm smart enough that I can recognize this problem period, not everyone can though. Now if it isn't bad enough, word is TDCj will be changing the visitation plan to make death row visits stay only on Tuesday and Thursday and Saturday night. (look, if it wasn't for me talking to the ranks here and pointing some things out, we would not have had Saturday visits recently. At least until COVID restrictions were lifted, not sure how they would have done it once lifted. But at first we wasn't getting them.) They are trying to go by COVID visits, where many people were not even getting visits due to how it was only one hour. To judge traffic based on that is flawed. Plus people are not getting special visits and etc. right now. Now if it stays at Tuesday and Thursday. OK special visits are supposed to be back-to-back. So, they gonna take away special visits? They refused to allow death row and seg to get video visits. D.R cannot have access to the offender telephone system. (Which actually policy only says no security detention. We are not that. That is restrictive housing and such.) You know, a guy can rape three little girls repeatedly and get Jessica's Law life without parole. Or a guy can burn down a daycare full of little kids and get eight life without parole sentences. A liberal DA gives him life instead of death. Those two kinds of people will enter the system and be classified as G3 and get video visits, contact visits, telephone daily, group rec, religious services and etc. Yet people come to death row due to the law of parties and get stuck in a box for 20 plus years. That makes no damn sense. Back to visit issue. Now if someone on D.R, just because they are on death row. Their family our friend if they want to have a special visit will have to pay for an extra motel room and daily rental car fees. As well have to stay from Tuesday till Thursday. Three days and two nights versus two days and one night. Plus is no way can do all the death row visits in just two week days with regular schedule. They don't have staff as it is. I understand they want to expand visit for general population due to video visits and such. They got to use phone every day and could video visit in other areas of the prison. More so since they only do three to five video visits at a time. They also have better access to more space to visit, have contact visits and also get Sunday visits. Many guys down here have family members that work Monday to Saturday. The death row plan says we get visits on certain days. So will they change the death row plan? Texas law says we get visit. TDCj is not using a reasonable standard, as they are placing a greater burden on our family and friends. That is not the least restrictive manner. Also being that executions are during weekdays. I guess the administration wants to make a circus of all that. I guess they want all those general population visits seeing our family cry as they are leaving etc. There is a reason why the visit schedule has always been the way it is during weekdays for death row. Saturday night was put in place because most people work weekdays and all other prisoners can have a weekend visit. Anyways. These fuckin people, they want to sit up in their fake ass ivory tower and not give a fuck. Bobbi Lumpkin. Bryan Callier. Patrick O'Daniel. They don't give a fuck who loses their minds. They don't care what burden they place on people's family. To all the future murderers out there. Do your murdering and raping in liberal counties, because if you're murdering and raping in conservative counties then TDCj will put you on rec restriction! These fuckin people.

I'm gone.

Clinton.

P.S Oh, I forgot. Also, to you rapists and murderers, if you do your raping and murdering in a conservative county, that means you are so much more dangerous than the raper/murderer from the liberal county. So TDCj will also put you on TV restriction! So if you want to watch yourself on Dateline, you better do your mass raping and murdering in liberal counties! That comes officially from Bryan Callier, Bobby Lumpkin, and Patrick O'Daniels. Hey, I don't make the policy. I just quote it.

Will be back soon.

In solidarity,

I remain

Clinton Lee Young #999447

Loud & Clear, September 27, 2021

Topic: One step closer

Greetings!

One step closer. The fight for me is not over with yet. I will have a better idea of how everything will sort in the short term within a week or so. I thank all for the support. To anyone from Midland wondering how the ruling will impact other cases. The CCA wrote up that opinion in a crazy ass way by not making it clear which exact point of my 3 claims I won on. Which is NOT how opinions are written. Also, they do not publish on it. This goes back to the old days when controlling cases was published. Basically, what it means is that no one will ever be able to cite the ruling in my case to help their case. It is a ruling for me and only me.

Thus, the CCA is going to address any other cases out of Midland on a one-on-one basis. My sister wanted to come visit me here on Saturday. They said visit is set up for all of September. I guess going forward half of death row will not be able to get visits?! Visit was not full as two people canceled. Plus could have had others set up. Always something. Alright then. The next chapter begins. You all will be updated as soon as we know something.

Veni Vidi Vici,

Take care, smile, strive for all that you desire.

I remain.

With love,

Clinton

Loud & Clear, November 25, 2021

Topic: Another battle won

As I reach the 20th year on this case. I have won some battles, though this little war wages on. Now I sit in a cell, larger than the one I left behind on the Polunsky Unit, though smaller in the sense of what freedoms I am allowed. Not being able to have a radio or a typewriter is a loss. Leaving behind friends whom I had a shared understanding with, it has become all the more noticeable in my dealings with others here. People complaining about months in jail. I do not hold animus towards such persons. Each person's struggle is a matter of perspective. Trying to explain to someone to not stress but just ride it out a few more months, it is simple to say, hard to do. It is easy for me to say, but hard for them to hear. I have done twenty years fighting to live, a day away from free life is too much. The days here are only stressful to me as I am so close. I can hear the trains pass by coming from somewhere, going everywhere. I just want to be anywhere but locked up. More so that I can have a real pencil and not this made for a three-year-old flexi pencil they allow us here. :(To be able to tie a pencil in a knot should defy Newton's 6th law or something. In prison I can have pens, pencils, typewriter, and etc. Needless to say, the fact that I have to use a rubber pencil to write, it has put a damper on my writing. The low life that invented this device from the Spanish Inquisition to torture authors. The miscreant could not even have the decency to put an eraser on it. No, I had to buy one from commissary. Score 1 for crony capitalism.

Anywho. People always ask how I feel. I'm not excited as I am still in jail. Still more battles to fight. I do miss being able to talk to friends I left behind. I feel more anxious about the future than I did when I had my execution date. Maybe I just never fully accepted that they would kill me, who knows what goes on with my brain. I sure don't :) It has been a blessing that people are still supporting me and helping. Many people wait until a person has an execution date before helping. It is usually far too late by then. Maybe the drama of the countdown to die gets better ratings. Consider the amount of people that watch Tiger King. It is clear that people do love the combo of a train wreck and drama. As I wrap this up, I extend a thank you to all. Please continue to help.

Till next time,

Take care, smile, and strive for all that you desire.

Veni, vidi, vici,

In solidarity, I remain

Clinton Young

Loud & Clear, November 18, 2024

Now as I was saying: before being interrupted by freedom, life and more legal drama, the problem with the justice system is... Long sigh. The sage continues. I surely did not expect to be doing this again. Though here I am, like a twisted TV series where the writers do not know when to quit. My re-entry to TDCJ was, once convicted, shockingly fast. No time for the normal adjustment phase that the county jail allows. As I went from free to TDCJ in under 48 hours. After being convicted, I was kept in a holding cell at the county jail. While only for about 36 hours. It was made worse due to the fact I had nothing. No mattress, no blanket, nothing. Just me in jail clothing, locked in a concrete box. I couldn't get a straight answer at first as to how long I would be in there. Eventually, someone told me. They were worried about my mental health, so they had me under observation. I found that ironic. Care about my mental health, but then put me in a box with nothing but my thoughts. Eventually, someone else seen the irony. They let me out, to sit on a metal bench for a bit. My re-entry to TDCJ did not disappoint. I moved units several times before ending up at the Coffield unit. Along the way I enjoyed a stay at the roach infested Byrd Unit. I have never seen so many roaches in my life. Then went to Ferguson Unit and naturally, it went on lockdown the night I get there. Of course it is only fitting that also upon my arrival there, that I get put in a cell that was red tagged. Meaning "don't put anyone in it, because it don't work!" There I am, on the worst housing block. In a cell with no electricity or light, absent a mattress for the first night. As I stood in the middle of the tiny dark cell, listening to the array or noises, that only ad seg level 2 and 3 are able to produce, a smile crossed my face, while taking in my new environment. "Hello old foe," I spoke aloud. There was none of the anger I would have had in the past. The oppressive cell was fitting. Like maybe I would have been disappointed had TDCJ welcomed me back another way. A couple of days later, without my asking, I was moved to another cell. Then off to another unit. Each unit move happened the night before I was to speak with my lawyers. During this, my trial lawyer got off my case. As I wanted to retain a new lawyer. Even though she knew this, she filed to have another lawyer, one that was her mentor/friend. She filed to have him court appointed to my case. The judge, not knowing that I wanted to retain counsel, appointed instead someone from West Texas. This caused more chaos and wasted time. As my first type of appeal was only 30 days from the conviction date. Beyond getting my convicted, she interfered with my obtaining counsel of my choice. Now that I am settled in, it has all been sorted. My retained counsel will be on board this week. At least that is the plan. That everything be stable now. I'm on my assigned unit Coffield, in a cell that works properly. With actually no roaches! A qualified lawyer at the helm. With my being frustrated at Securus. Yeah, seemingly back to the old normal.

Joking aside, the system will never break me. There are some new struggles. Which I cover all that in my next blog. Prison, however, is something I've had plenty experience with in life sadly. The difference this time being I did not enter it a short sighted, angry, and immature teenager with a series of bad choices. This time I had been a productive citizen who followed the law. I matured into a responsible adult that had built a great life for myself. The "all or nothing" that is the extreme design of capital murder laws in Texas. It showed the unforgiving flaw in its sentencing. Life or death is all capital murder allows for. Unlike other crimes with much more diverse and thus understanding or forgiving sentencing options. Murder carries 5 to 99 or life. Same as aggravated sexual assault. Agg. Sexual assault is rape while using a weapon and the possible punishment range can be as low as 5 years probation to as high as 99 years in prison. Same as murder, aggravated robbery, etc. Yet with capital murder, even if not the actual killer, but found guilty of conspiracy as a party to the offense, the only option is life or death. Like Randy Halprin, who the state admits never killed anyone. He until recently had a death sentence. But for a crazy, racist judge being over his trial, he would have been executed already. The State offered nothing at all that showed I even threatened anyone, much less killed a person. (David Page is no longer a witness in the case) The State read the flawed testimony from my first trial of people who had since died. Again I suffered, due to errors made by lawyers and corrupt investigators during my 2003 trial. All aggravated by my new lawyer's errors. Once convicted, an automatic life sentence. The law allowing no understanding or consideration for lies, misconduct by the State, or the man I had become.

Until next time. The struggle is never ending.

Take care, smile, and strive for all that you desire.

Veni, vidi, vici,

In solidarity, I remain

Clinton Young

Afterword

Reading over the years of my writing, it shows the emotional rollercoaster that is death row. With each experience being magnified due to being in solitary confinement. One thing that became clear to me: it was the level of desperation that the circumstances created. Desperate to get the help required to win. Desperate to define my own legacy. Desperate to maintain control of my mental, emotional, physical, and even social vitality. To be more than a 'death row inmate'. Instead, to have the world to see me as a 'man on death row'. Going back and changing parts, would entail altering the reality of the moment I existed in. Having survived death row, then living in the free world. Being able to just be an actual adult. It allowed me to grow and mature in a more complete way.

This adds a new element to the struggle I now endure. No longer am I fighting for myself. Now I am fighting for my family. To regain my freedom, so that I can be the protector and provider for my wife and son.

This book is dedicated to my son. I want him to learn about the struggles, failures, and fears that I had. This way he can know the success, rewards, and happiness that I pray and fight for him to have. To be so much more than I ever could. Prison defined so much the man that I am. It will not define the father I am.

With love,

Clinton

To read Clinton's newest blogs,

please consider subscribing to his Patreon account.

Printed in Great Britain
by Amazon